Bombing the European Axis Powers

A Historical Digest of the Combined Bomber Offensive 1939–1945

RICHARD G. DAVIS

Air University Press
Maxwell Air Force Base, Alabama

April 2006

Air University Library Cataloging Data

Davis, Richard G.
    Bombing the European Axis powers : a historical digest of the combined bomber offensive, 1939-1945 / Richard G. Davis.
        p. ; cm.
    Includes bibliographical references and index.
    ISBN 1-58566-148-1
    1. World War, 1939-1945—Aerial operations. 2. World War, 1939-1945—Aerial operations—Statistics. 3. United States. Army Air Forces—History—World War, 1939-1945. 4. Great Britain. Royal Air Force—History—World War, 1939-1945. 5. Bombing, Aerial—Europe—History. I. Title.

    940.544—dc22

Disclaimer

Air University Press
131 West Shumacher Avenue
Maxwell AFB AL 36112-6615
http://aupress.maxwell.af.mil

Contents

Part III
1943

Page

Part IV
1944

Appendix

1   Bomber Command Losses and Tonnage by
Month, September 1939–May 1941 (located on
CD-ROM disk, Worksheet 1, BC 1939–41, file
name: 1939–41.xls)

2   Bomber Command Operations by Month,
15 May 1940–31 May 1941 (located on
CD-ROM disk, Worksheet 2, BC 1940–41,
file name: 1939–41.xls)

About the Author

Dr. Richard G. Davis is a member of the historical staff at the Army's Center of Military History. He was previously historian for the United Nations Command, Combined Forces Command, and US Forces Korea Command. He began his assignment in Korea in May 2001. Before that he served as a senior historian with the USAF Historical Support Office, Bolling Air Force Base, Washington, DC. He received his BA in history from the University of Virginia at Charlottesville, his MA in European history from the University of North Carolina at Chapel Hill, and his PhD in military history from George Washington University, Washington, DC. He spent eight years as an archivist in the National Archives where he participated in the declassification of major military, intelligence, and diplomatic records of the US government concerning World War II and Korea. The author joined the USAF History Program in 1980.

In addition to several articles in scholarly journals, he authored *Carl A. Spaatz and the Air War in Europe 1940–1945,* a study of the combined US-UK strategic combined bomber offensive against Germany and of US Army Air Forces (AAF) doctrine and operations in North Africa, the Mediterranean, and northwest Europe. The Historical Support Office and the Smithsonian Institution Press copublished this work. In 2002 the USAF History and Museums Programs published his second book, *On Target: Organizing and Executing the Strategic Air Campaign against Iraq.* Dr. Davis has published several monographs, including a work on US Army and US Air Force cooperation, *The 31 Initiatives.* That work has served as a text on "jointness" at all three services' professional military education establishments. He also edited "The USAF Desert Shield/Storm Oral History Project," a series of security-classified oral histories with key USAF personnel. Finally, although he points out that the director ignored virtually all his advice, Dr. Davis served as the official USAF historical advisor for the movie *Pearl Harbor.*

Preface

This undertaking is a work of unusual form and format that includes a compact disk that has tables, maps, photos, and drawings. At its core this work is a database covering Anglo-American strategic bomber operations against Germany, Italy, and Axis associated or occupied Europe. As such it allows swift and easy listing of day-by-day bombing, bombing of strategic target systems by location and tonnage, bombing of specific countries, comparisons of US and British targeting and operations, and much more. The work details strategic operations only—B-17 and B-24 bomber sorties by the four US numbered air forces in the European and Mediterranean theaters (Eighth, Ninth, Twelfth, and Fifteenth) and all bombing sorties for aircraft assigned to the Royal Air Force (RAF) Bomber Command and RAF 205 Group. This definition excludes US twin-engine medium bomb groups, which often hit the same aiming points as their four-engine compatriots, but includes twin-engine British Wellington medium bombers and twin-engine British Mosquito, Boston, and Ventura light bombers. Although the US heavy and medium bombers had instances of overlapping, targeting those instances usually fell into areas of what US doctrine defined as tactical rather than strategic bombing, such as frontline troops, transportation facilities feeding the front line, and airfields. US medium bombers did not fly deep into enemy country to attack industrial and strategic targets. The case differed for the RAF. Wellingtons and other medium bombers formed the backbone of the main bombing force from 1940 through late 1942 and throughout 1943 for 205 Group. Bomber Command's short-ranged Bostons and Venturas of No. 2 Group raided French ports, power plants, and industrial targets until transferring to Tactical Bomber Force in May 1943. Likewise, Mosquitoes conducted numerous hit-and-run daylight raids until May of 1943 and then switched to night harassing attacks on German population centers, particularly Berlin, until the war's end. Such bombing furthered Bomber Command's campaign against the morale of the German labor force.

This study, of course, rests on a foundation of assumptions that the reader should understand, if not necessarily agree with, so as to not form unsupported conclusions or extrapolations. The study does not attempt to assess actual damage inflicted on a specific target by a specific raid. Nor does it uniformly attempt to identify the extent of damage assessed by Anglo-American intelligence to a target at a particular time. Such effort would not only be voluminous but lead to fruitless quibbling as experts disputed the significance of the data. To this study it matters less if the target actually required attack than that the Allied bomber commanders judged that it did. Furthermore, an entry stating a force of 400 bombers attacked Ludwigshafen through complete cloud cover may not indicate the damage to the target. The formation may have hit Mannheim or missed completely and struck surrounding open country. Conclusions based on the database will become increasingly accurate when based on an aggregate of raids.

The number of aircraft attacking a target indicates the effort and tonnage reaching the target. The number of aircraft dispatched on a mission does neither and raises questions as to abort rates and weather. For that reason this work excludes aircraft dispatched as a possible data category. However, if a large discrepancy existed between aircraft sent out and planes attacking, a note of the fact appears in the data entry. If a great many aircraft failed to attack a target on one day, the bomber commanders would usually attack it again on the next suitable day.

The study further contains extensive annotations and entries on operations methods, sighting methods, special operations, and mining, the implications of which become more far reaching as the readers expand their knowledge of the subject area. The relatively effortless manipulation of the numbers should allow the reader to reach a new understanding of the combined bomber offensive. The purpose of this work is not so much to present my ideas concerning the strategic bombing of Germany as to enable readers to form their own judgments.

The book and CD-ROM cover bombing sorties, mining, supply missions, and special operations of all two and four-engine bombers of the RAF Bomber Command in Great Britain and the RAF 205 Group in the Mediterranean as well as all four-engine bomber (B-17 and B-24) operations of the US Eighth Air Force in Great Britain and the US Ninth, Twelfth, and Fifteenth Forces in the Mediterranean. The database contains such entries as date, total bomb load and bomb mix, method of sighting, target struck, attacking aircraft, and aircraft lost for virtually every aircraft sortie credited with attacking a strategic target in Europe. The almost unlimited ability to manipulate these statistics via the electronic spreadsheet gives the reader the capability to reach new insights not only into the strategic air operations of World War II but in air warfare in general.

Sources and Methodology

Original documentation supplied all the bombing information gathered for this project. Whenever possible, I used separate data sources to cross-check numerical and other information supplied.

For coverage of Royal Air Force Bomber Command night raids (January 1942 through May 1945), I relied on Bomber Command Night Raid Reports and the Air Ministry War Room monthly operations summaries. Bomber Command weekly operations and intelligence reports and Air Ministry War Room monthly operations summaries furnished information on Bomber Command daylight raids and provided a cross-check of night raids. Primary documentation provided the only, albeit scanty, information on RAF 205 Group. I could not locate details for any RAF 205 Group operations before the end of February 1943, when it became part of the Northwest African Strategic Air Force (NASAF). From that time onwards, NASAF and Northwest African Air Forces (NAAF) daily operations and intelligence reports described 205 Group activities. However, both series seemed based on the same source, and I could find no other independent source with which to cross-check data. The information supplied by Mediterranean Allied Air Forces (MAAF) and Mediterranean Allied Strategic Air Force (MASAF), which succeeded NAAF and NASAF, had the same flaws. All information on 205 Group was particularly deficient in method of sighting.

The US Army Air Forces presented similar difficulties. The sheer weight of Eighth Air Force documentation easily exceeded the bomb lift of at least one of its bombardment aircraft. For this study, I relied on the targets and bomber operations segments of the Eighth Air Force monthly operations reports (January 1944 through April 1945), the Eighth Air Force target summary (25 May 1945) and, most importantly, on the individual mission folders (17 August 1942 through 25 April 1945). The mission folders usually contained the daily Eighth Air Force operations and intelligence report, which gave intended target, target actually bombed, weather, and sighting method. The Bombardment Division bombing sheets detailed strikes down to the individual aircraft level and often further specified the nature of the target and method of sighting. Likewise, the Fifteenth Air Force possessed excellent sources. A machine printout, prepared shortly after the end of the war, of all its bombardment missions vouchsafed all the information required for this study. Nonetheless, the author inspected each Fifteenth Air Force mission folder and located some changes in methods of sighting and targeting. Information on the heavy bomber units of the Ninth and Twelfth Air Forces proved far less voluminous. In addition to Northwest Africa Air Forces, Northwest Africa Strategic Air Force, Mediterranean Allied Air Force, and Mediterranean Allied Strategic Air Force daily operations and intelligence summaries, the author examined bomb group histories and Ninth and Twelfth Air Force operations summaries. Information on Twelfth Air Force heavy bombardment operations between November 1942 and late February 1943 is fragmentary and cannot answer the questions I pose in this study.

For hard data—number of attacking aircraft, number of aircraft lost, and tons and types of bombs dropped—this study tended to employ weekly and monthly reports, where available. Such reports usually reflected data such as a group's issuing tardy reports or aircraft landing on friendly fields and returning later to home base not caught by daily reports. Data collated after the war, at too far a remove from events, has the advantage of wide perspective and possibly greater overall accuracy but is also at the mercy of postwar interpretations and agendas. Witness the "Eighth Air Force Target Summary" of 25 May 1945, which changed all city raids conducted by the Eighth Air Force to other categories. On the other hand, documents more immediate to the event were used to identify actual targets struck and method of sighting. American documents prepared the day of a raid make no bones about hitting city targets. As those reports went up the American chain of command, the tonnage dropped on cities decreased. While it is possible, especially when bombing targets of opportunity, that bombardiers might well mistake one town or village for another, they certainly knew if they aimed at the city's center or factories on the city's outskirts. They also knew if they employed visual or radar sighting.

Acknowledgments

I thank the many people who made this book possible. First, my wife and family whose support gave me the strength and energy to complete the task. Second, I tender a hearty appreciation to my colleagues in the Air Force history program at Bolling Air Force Base, DC. They encouraged the statistical approach to the subject and read the first drafts. In particular, I thank my supervisors, Jacob Neufeld and Herman Wolk, who defended my efforts to research the "ancient history of World War II" as opposed to countervailing demands for history "right from the exhaust pipe." Finally, I thank the Air University Press, especially my editor Carole Arbush, who asked many clarifying questions and forced me into a standardized set of capitalization, and to the AU Press staff, especially, Sherry Terrell, copy editor; Mary Ferguson, page layout and design; Daniel Armstrong, for his magnificent cover art; and Joan Hickey for administrative tasks. Of course, any mistakes in the text or in the CD-ROM are my own responsibility. I have done my best to keep them to a minimum.

PART I
OVERVIEW

Introduction

The theory of strategic air bombardment states that airpower is best used offensively to penetrate an enemy's home territory and disrupt or destroy the economy and means of war production to force the enemy to surrender. Strategic bombing will succeed either because it has fatally compromised the ability to carry on hostilities or because bombing has broken the will of the people and/or leadership to continue the fight. In World War II only multiengine bomber aircraft had the range, payload, and accuracy to accomplish this task.

The strategic bombing theorists posited that destruction of the foe's means of production—by aiming bombs almost entirely at manufacturing, service, and distribution facilities—would quickly lead to the surrender of its armies at the front when, or even before, they exhausted the supplies remaining in their logistics system. This was the ideal result. If, for any number of reasons, that direction of attack proved impractical or insufficient, then strategic bombing theory suggested that an attack on the enemy's will to resist by applying force against the civilian population (i.e., bombing the enemy's principal population centers) might achieve the same end. In this study the author examines the employment of strategic bombers by and the target selection of the British Royal Air Force (RAF) and the US Army Air Forces (AAF) in their campaign against Germany in World War II. In doing so he provides readers with a statistical basis of analysis that will enable them to form their own judgment as to the validity of the theory of strategic bombing and the intentions of the Anglo-Americans in their use of it.

At first it seemed that air bombardment offered a means of avoiding the slaughter of the First World War's trench fighting. However, Japanese bombing of Chinese cities in the Sino-Japanese War of the 1930s and Nationalist bombings of Republican cities in the Spanish Civil War appeared to have transferred the slaughter from both sides' frontline soldiers to the enemy's civilians on the home front, instead of lowering the overall human cost of modern warfare. For example, on 26 April 1937 (a market day), bombers of the German Condor Legion supporting the Spanish Nationalist forces led by Gen

3

Francisco Franco attacked Guernica, a town of 7,000 people—a figure that apparently included refugees and those attending the local market. They dropped 40.5 tons of bombs on the undefended and totally unprepared municipality, killing between 200 and 1,650 people and wounding an additional 889.[1] At the worst, this resulted in a ratio of dead to tons of bombs dropped of more than 40 to 1. Likewise, in March 1938, 42 tons of Italian bombs on the defended and prepared city of Barcelona purportedly resulted in more than 3,000 casualties.

Most observers at the time seemed to overestimate the casualties of these attacks while failing to consider the general steadfastness of the population under bombardment. In the midst of the international furor over the bombing of the town of Guernica during the Spanish civil war, the plans committee of the British joint chiefs of staff predicted the possible effects of the first week of a German air offensive against Britain at 150,000 casualties.[2] These figures were based on analysis of the German bombing of London in World War I.[3] The perceptions of the general public, apparently based on a straight-line extrapolation of the Guernica casualties, rested on what would eventually prove, from later and much larger World War II experience, a statistical freak.

Only three bombing raids during the Second World War exceeded these figures: Tokyo (10 March 1945), Hiroshima (6 August 1945), and Nagasaki (9 August 1945). In fact, by the beginning of World War II, the RAF air staff estimates of civilian deaths reached the astronomical level of 72 per ton of bombs.[4] In supplying this knowingly or unknowingly vastly inflated casualty figure to His Majesty's government, the air staff may well have encouraged those who counseled appeasement. Such seemingly authoritative numbers could only have weighed heavily on the mind of Prime Minister Neville Chamberlain during the Munich crisis of 1938—a supposition confirmed by Winston Churchill when he wrote in October 1941, "Before the war we were greatly misled by the pictures they painted of the destruction that would be wrought by air raids. This is illustrated by the fact that 750,000 beds were actually provided for air raid casualties, never more than 6,000 being required. The picture of destruction was so exaggerated that it depressed the statesmen responsible for the pre-war policy and played a definite part in the desertion of Czecho-Slovakia in August 1938."[5] By the mid-1930s, only two of the world's air forces had committed themselves to the doctrine of strategic bombardment, the RAF and the US Army Air Corps (AAC).

The Royal Air Force
Prewar Experience, 1919–1939

The US and British air forces took much different paths to reach their doctrinal stances. The advantage of being a third and independent service, equal to the British Royal Navy and Army, smoothed the RAF's way. Unlike the AAC, which was a subordinate part of the US Army, the RAF controlled and shaped its official doctrine. Marshal of the RAF Hugh Trenchard, who had served as the chief of staff of the Royal Flying Corps and commanded an independent bombing force in World War I, served as the postwar chief of staff of the RAF for an extraordinarily long term of 10 years in the 1920s and 1930s. He used his tenure to mold the RAF's doctrine after his own concepts of airpower. He believed the strategic objective of the RAF was "the overthrow of the enemy by a bombing offensive without which neither the [Royal] Navy or the [Royal] Army could achieve victory in a continental war." He argued that this goal was "the raison d'être of an independent Air Force and its main claim to a substantial portion of the slender funds devoted to armaments."[6]

Throughout the 1920s and early 1930s, Trenchard and the other British chiefs of staff labored under the "Ten Years Rule"— a planning restriction annually imposed upon the British armed services by the chancellors of the exchequer—that required the services to assume that no war would break out for another 10 years. This restriction was first imposed by none other than Winston Churchill when he served as the government's chief fiscal officer. Ironically, he would bear the full brunt of the consequences of this decision during the Second World War. The Ten Years Rule, not unreasonable considering that the United Kingdom faced no potential great power conflict in the 1920s, allowed the British government to cut military expenditures to the bone.

So fiercely did Trenchard believe in the primacy of the offensive that he resisted air-raid precaution (ARP) programs and production of antiaircraft artillery (a function of the Royal Army). He restricted the size of the Air Defense of Great Britain (later Fighter Command) because he felt it would divert resources from the bomber force. Possibly because of exaggeration of the effects of bombing on the civil morale of London and German cities in World War I, Trenchard recognized that strategic bombardment would cause collateral damage—the killing, wounding, and destruction of civilians and their property—in attacks on legitimate targets. He suggested that bombardment might achieve results far greater than in World War I. Enough bombing of civilians, he stated, might well break the will of the civilian population to resist.[7] He was certain bombing would have a tremendous negative effect on civilian morale and that it would prove easier to undermine the civilian will to resist than to destroy installations.[8] Officers who had long served under Trenchard and who eventually would succeed him adopted his ideas.

The leaders of the RAF clung to their doctrine. However, they faced an increasingly difficult strategic situation. By 1931, Imperial Japan had scrapped its entente with Great Britain and had become a potential threat to British possessions in the Far East. Closer to home, Adolph Hitler and his National Socialist German Workers Party [*Nationalsozialistische Deutsche Arbeiterpartei* (NSDAP), normally shortened to Nazi] had acceded to power by 1934, replacing a weak, rootless, and struggling democracy. The Nazi government under Hitler's leadership was an authoritarian regime bent on revising the peace settlement of World War I. Hitler, with the cooperation of many German industrialists, began a showy program of rearmament and exaggerated its extent with a brilliant propaganda campaign. The new German air force (the Luftwaffe) reaped great benefits from both the buildup and the hoopla.

In actuality, the Nazis feared that if they placed too many restrictions on German consumerism, they would lose popular support. Thus, they did not begin to mobilize their economy and put restrictions on consumption fully until 1942. In Africa the fascist government of dictator Benito Mussolini conquered Abyssinia and Ethiopia, territory adjacent to British colonies. Italy's large fleet and air force had the potential to open a third front that was beyond the capability of the British armed forces to withstand. In the mid-1930s, in spite of the needs of the army and navy, the British government gave priority to the needs of the RAF, especially to the bomber force. Although committed to maintaining parity with the Luftwaffe in frontline aircraft, no amount of new funding could reverse, in a year or two, the effects of the Ten Years Rule.

Likewise, His Majesty's government, partially out of parsimony and partially out of a political philosophy that discouraged subsidy of private business, almost completely neglected the British civil air sector. Unlike European governments, Britain for the most part failed to provide significant direct or indirect funding to civil airline companies. Nor, like the governments (local, state, and federal) in the United States, did the British government provide funding for civil airports and navigation needs. As a result, British civil aviation lagged far behind the world standard, particularly Germany and the United States where large airlines routinely flew night schedules and in inclement weather. The airliners and aircraft used for carrying mail and cargo purchased by these airlines sustained their nation's aircraft industries, particularly so in the production of large multiengine aircraft. The large civil airline companies also provided a potential pool of pilots and ground support staff as well as an enormous body of experience and advanced technical knowledge for their respective air services, none of which accrued in a like manner to the RAF. When Chamberlain flew to Munich, he did so in an American-built passenger aircraft.[9]

In 1935 the Air Ministry informed the British cabinet that it had no satisfactory medium or heavy bombers in production—the Whitley, Hampden, and Wellington bombers, planned in 1932, were not ready for mass production.[10] Not until 1936 did the RAF begin the development of four-engine heavy bombers. In the meantime, the RAF suffered from a constricted production base and the fear of the air staff, gradually overcome, that too rapid an expansion would disorganize the force and strain training facilities.[11] In mid-1937 the government decided to gradually convert Bomber Command (BC) to a force of 1,442 aircraft (all four-engine bombers) by 1943. This plan would give Bomber Command the ability to strike deep and hard into Germany. It also added ancillary costs such as new ground facilities and concrete runways for all bomber bases. Hitler's annexation of Austria on 12 March 1938 solidified the cabinet's decision to instruct the Air Ministry to change its aircraft procurement priorities and increase the number of fighter aircraft. The Munich crisis of September 1938 caused the cabinet to order more fighters. The British had recently developed radar, which allowed reliable tracking of aircraft in the air, stripping attacking bombers of their ability to avoid defenses while increasing the effectiveness of interceptors.

The Munich crisis further demonstrated numerous operational shortcomings in Bomber Command. Of 42 squadrons mobilized, only 10 were heavy bombers; of 2,500 reserve pilots planned, only 200 were ready for immediate operations. Using peacetime standards, only half the force was ready to fight. The bombers lacked self-sealing gas tanks and armor. Most could not even reach Germany unless they flew from the continent.[12] For the RAF as a whole, not a single repair depot existed in the British Isles, and every link of the logistics chain of supply lacked essential spare parts. Moreover, the service had failed to obtain training, bombing practice, and experiment areas. For example, the RAF had no single school or standardized course for the instruction of aerial gunnery. This deficiency left the teaching of that important skill almost entirely in the hands of the frontline units, which were already far overburdened with other tasks resulting from the rapid expansion and consequent dilution of experienced personnel and combat readiness.

Exercises for active duty crews revealed a systemic, servicewide bias against navigation training, little night experience, and, in dead reckoning daylight conditions, an average circular error probable (CEP)* of 50 miles in dropping bombs.[13] The government's delay in introducing conscription until June 1939 postponed the procurement and training of necessary air and ground personnel. In the last year of peace, Bomber Command lost strength as its Blenheims reinforced Fighter Command. Still, the

---

*Circular error probable: the radius of a circle within which half of ordnance delivered by aircraft or a missile's projectiles are expected to fall. It is used as an indicator of the delivery accuracy of a weapon system and as a factor in determining probable damage to a target.

cabinet continued to support its eventual expansion to a force of 80 squadrons of new bombers in 1942.

Bomber Command: Adoption of Night Operations and Area Bombing, 1939–1941

"During the first two years of the war Bomber Command was small, ill equipped and ineffective."[14] In September 1939 fear of a German aerial retaliatory, knockout blow against Britain and the wretched condition of Bomber Command made the launching of a strategic air offensive impracticable. Air Marshal Sir Edgar Ludlow-Hewitt, air officer commanding (AOC), Bomber Command, and the Royal Air Force air staff were fully cognizant of their force's shortcomings. At their insistence, the cabinet refrained from ordering any offensive action against Germany.

The RAF's unwillingness to conduct offensive operations had a basis in strategy, not merely in lack of readiness. Until the Czech crisis in the summer of 1938, the air staff had assumed that the first German blow would fall in the west. If the aerial portion of that initial German offensive fell heavily on England, especially its cities, the RAF would be forced to retaliate in spite of its manifest unreadiness. However, the Czech crisis and the following German threats against Poland made it more likely that the Germans would move east before confronting the Anglo-French allies. In that case, it would be the height of folly for the RAF, in its current condition, to undertake unrestricted offensive operations. Such a course, undertaken at a maximum intensity, might not only provoke an unnecessary and possibly avoidable German riposte, but it also would further expend resources that the RAF desperately needed for expansion and future operations. Therefore, to avert a like German response, Bomber Command could on no account select targets that involved even the slightest risk of civilian casualties. The principles laid down by Prime Minister Neville Chamberlain in the House of Commons on 21 June 1938 guided the service:

- It is against international law to bomb civilians as such and to make deliberate attacks upon civilian population.

- Targets . . . aimed at from the air must be legitimate military objectives and must be capable of identification.

9

- Reasonable care must be taken in attacking these military objectives so that by carelessness a civilian population in the neighborhood is not bombed.[15]

Although these considerations would eventually fall by the wayside in regards to bomber operations against Germany proper, they would form the rubric concerning the bombing of all non-German territory occupied by the Germans for all subsequent RAF directives until the war's end. Thus, a force that had planned for the offensive for 20 years had produced aircraft incapable of surviving in daylight over enemy territory and aircrews unable to find targets at night. Instead of conducting strategic operations, the RAF dropped leaflets by night over Germany and trolled the North Sea for German shipping for eight months.

These missions familiarized some aircrews with night operations and proved convincingly that Bomber Command's aircraft were, indeed, too deficient to survive during the day. In the first six months of the war, 3 September 1939 through 3 March 1940, Bomber Command dropped a grand total of 33 tons of bombs.[16] Some part of this lack of effort stemmed from simple geographic constraints. As long as both sides respected the neutral airspace over Holland and Belgium, Bomber Command could only get at German targets by going directly over the North Sea, a route stoutly defended by the Luftwaffe, or by taking a dogleg over France, a route beyond the range of many of the command's aircraft. The Ruhr, Germany's prime industrial region and the obvious target of any bombing campaign, lay behind the protection of the Low Countries. The neutral skies over those countries offered the same protection to Great Britain. Their loss to the Germans would severely complicate the air defense of the United Kingdom.

On 2 April 1940 Air Marshal Sir Charles A. Portal replaced Ludlow-Hewitt as AOC, Bomber Command. Portal was a colorless officer unlikely to win any popularity contests. Called "Peter" by his close associates, Portal would become the youngest of the combined British and American chiefs of staff. He began his military career in 1914 as a motorcycle dispatch rider. A year later he joined the Royal Flying Corps, earning a Distinguished Flying Cross and shooting down several German aircraft before the end of the war. Between the wars he served as commander, British Forces, Aden; as an instructor at the Imperial Defence College; and as the director of organization on the air staff. Somewhat personally remote and cool, he nonetheless established excellent working relationships with high-ranking Americans. The British chiefs of staff and Churchill respected him for his strategic ability and brilliant intellect. Because he was virtually unflappable, he could weather the storm of Churchill's fanciful military ideas—often hurled with insulting vehemence by the prime minister at the chiefs of staff—and temper those ideas with wisdom. Portal worked exceedingly long and hard hours during the war, leaving behind him a voluminous official correspondence but little of a personal nature.

After the years of gloomy outlook and forecasts offered by his predecessor, the command found him a refreshing change. Later, in April, the command aided Allied forces in Norway by bombing Stavanger airfield and German shipping, doing minimal damage to the latter. It also began to mine enemy waters in hopes of disrupting German supply lines into Norway and shipments of the high-grade iron ore from Narvik to Germany.

During the first phase of the air war, Bomber Command—on the basis of remarkably few operational sorties—drifted into a decision of immense consequences to itself and the strategic offensive against Germany. The command decided to switch the bulk of its operations from daylight to nighttime. Daylight sorties by heavy bombers, particularly two raids on 14 and 18 December 1940 against the German fleet and naval facilities at Wilhelmshafen, proved extremely costly. Bomber Command lost 17 out of 36 Wellingtons dispatched. These raids flew into the teeth of Germany's heaviest air defenses, those specifically designed to protect the fleet and important naval bases from British attack over the North Sea. The defenses employed radar, a fact unknown to the British, and primitive ground-controlled interception.[17] The fate of these missions, which failed to reach German airspace other than Heligoland Island, shook the faith of the leadership of Bomber Command in the ability of their current generation of day bombers to penetrate into Germany, whether or not they flew tight, self-defending formations. Later losses in the battle of France further demonstrated the fate of unescorted

11

daylight attacks. In contrast, the night leaflet missions of the Whitleys of No. 4 Group, Bomber Command's only unit with any night training, seemed positive. They encountered no opposition and their crews reported excellent results. In March 1940, Ludlow-Hewitt ordered Nos. 3 and 5 Groups to join No. 4 Group in leaflet dropping and night reconnaissance missions over the Reich. The hard fact of the day losses compared to the seeming success at night argued for a change of policy, but the command never made a formal pronouncement. Although Bomber Command never totally abandoned the daylight bombing, especially for its light bombers, and arguments for daylight bombing would surface throughout the war, the command did not consistently launch heavy bomber daylight raids from March 1940 until June 1944. Adoption of this policy, which was so greatly at odds with prewar conceptions, apparently incurred little opposition within the service. Virtually no senior officer appears to have gone on record as advocating a continuance of daylight heavy bomber missions. Night bombing introduced not just problems of operation but those of administration.

Many observers gloss over the side effects of such a change in methodology. However, the switch to night bombing entailed far-reaching costs for the entire command, if not the service. The command needed to revamp training programs for beginning to advanced pilots, bomb aimers, gunners, and other crew members. Instructors needed to learn or relearn skills. Experienced crews from operations needed schooling. Aircraft already in service needed modifications such as flame dampeners while aircraft on the drawing board or on the production line also required modifications for night. The RAF had to upgrade airfields to conduct large-scale night operations. Finally, given the primitive state of equipment, night flying placed a deadly surcharge of 300 percent over and above the accident rate for daylight flying. This penalty applied to each and every aircraft taking off on night operations or training flights, even those that failed to drop a single bomb. The switch to night flying was one area in particular where the RAF suffered from the stunted state of British civil aviation. Unlike the Luftwaffe, the RAF could draw on no preexisting base of civilian equipment or experience in night flying.

On the night of 9 May 1940, German parachutists began the German offensive in the West by seizing key points in the Low Countries. In the morning the Germans marched into neutral Holland and Belgium. On the next day Winston Churchill became prime minister of a new British coalition government. He had supported the RAF and its doctrines for more than 20 years and had even served as the secretary of state for air from 1919 to 1921 as well as first lord of the admiralty from 1914 to 1915 and 1939 to 1940. In 1916–17 he had helped to develop the tank to break the gridlock of trench warfare. More than any other contemporary head of state he understood the continuing relationship between science, technology, and modern warfare. He also produced a considerable body of military history, including a multivolume work on World War I, a study of the eastern front in World War I, and a multivolume biography of his ancestor the First Duke of Marlborough. Such analysis, added to his own bitter experiences, confirmed his suspicions about the ready promises of military men and scientists as to the imminent success of their proposals and schemes. His lifelong command of the English language and talent for self-promotion coupled with his natural pugnacity, especially in relation to his predecessor's history of appeasement, made him an inspiring leader to the average Briton. As a war leader, his heavy drinking and verbal harassment of his military chiefs of staff made their lives more difficult and caused one, Gen Sir John Dill, army chief of staff, to resign. Although usually a sound strategic thinker, Churchill sometimes succumbed to unwise impulses, such as the Dardanelles campaign in 1915, the invasion of Norway in 1940 (which helped to trigger the German invasion of that country), and his desire to have the Anglo-Americans invade the Balkans in 1944–45. He was a man of some flaws but also of honor and great character and was totally committed to the destruction of the Nazi state. Such a man would waste little time in striking back at his foe. On 15 May 1940 the day Holland surrendered to the Nazis and the day after the German armored spearheads broke out of Sedan and began their race to the sea, the cabinet authorized Bomber Command to strike oil and railway targets east of the Rhine. The dispatch of 99 bombers that night marked the start of an almost five-year-long offensive against Germany.

For the next month, until the fall of France on 17 June 1940, Bomber Command's bombing of oil targets in Germany and transportation targets in France was ineffectual. After Germany knocked the French out of the war, the Luftwaffe launched the Battle of Britain in an attempt to gain air superiority over the British Isles to enable a German ground invasion from France. Bomber Command, with no more effectiveness, struck at the German air industry and continued to hit oil, "the weakest link in Germany's war economy."[18] Throughout the summer of 1940, the Bomber Command continued to go after its precision night targets and to bomb invasion barges and other preparations. On 24 August two or three German aircraft violated Hitler's express orders and jettisoned their bombs over London. This tiny mistake, like the feather that tips the largest scale, may have changed the course of history. Churchill, who was determined, like many of his countrymen, to give as good as he got, ordered immediate retaliatory air strikes on Berlin, which the RAF flew the next evening.[19] The 80 bombers sent that night hit little, as did those dispatched on the next four nights to Berlin. However, these pinpricks shocked the Berliners; and the attacks humiliated Hitler as well as the number two man in the regime, Hermann Göring, commander of the Luftwaffe. By 30 August, Hitler, demonstrating once again his fatal inability to separate national policy decisions from personal pique, withdrew his order protecting London and encouraged Göring to retaliate. On 5 September Göring publicly promised to do so. At the same time a crisis arrived in the Battle of Britain; the Luftwaffe, in spite of heavy losses, had reduced Fighter Command to a state where British aircraft losses exceeded new production, and overall pilot experience had begun a serious decline. The German targeting change from counterair operations to area bombing of London took the pressure off Fighter Command, whose losses proceeded to drop. German losses rose as their Bf-109 fighters had only enough fuel capacity to remain over London for but 10 minutes after which they had to abandon their escort of Luftwaffe bombers, leaving them to their own fate (oftentimes a disastrous one at the hands of a RAF fighter). Casualties soon forced the Germans to turn to night bombing. Hitler postponed the invasion, probably no more than a bluff in any case, and turned to other projects, but he had left an enemy behind—one whose only means of striking back was strategic airpower.

Churchill appreciated this perfectly. Even before the Battle of Britain ended on 3 September, he submitted a memo on the munitions situation as he saw it:

> The Navy can lose us the war, but only the Air Force can win it. Therefore our supreme effort must be to gain overwhelming mastery of the Air. The Fighters are our salvation, but the bombers alone provide the means of victory. We must therefore develop the power to carry on an ever increasing volume of explosives to Germany so as to pulverize the entire industry and scientific structure on which the war effort and economic life of the enemy depends, while holding him at arms length in our Island. In no other way at present visible can we hope to overcome the immense military power of Germany, and to nullify the further German victories which may be apprehended as the weight of their forces is brought to bear upon African or Oriental theaters. The Air Force and its action on the largest scale must, therefore, subject to what is said later, claim the first place over the Navy or the Army.[20]

At the same time the prime minister made an explicit suggestion to the AOC, Bomber Command, that the bombing offensive should be spread as widely as possible over the cities and small towns of Germany that were within reach. Portal immediately championed the idea, which agreed with the conclusions that the recent experiences of his command had forced upon him. He suggested bombing 20 cities. The air staff demurred. Air Vice-Marshal (AVM) Sir Richard Peirse, vice chief of staff, conceded that the bombing of strategic targets located in populated areas produced a by-product of collateral damage. Such damage, although unfortunate, was legitimate according to the rules of war. What made British bombing more effective than German, in the opinion of the air staff, was its discrimination in choosing specific targets rather than the indiscriminate bombing of city areas. On 21 September 1940 the Air Ministry issued new instructions to Bomber Command. They placed German oil at top priority, followed by communications, the air industry, the U-boat target system, and invasion preparations. As a concession to Portal's views and in recognition of the continued German bombing of London, the Allies could attack Berlin, which contained no strategic targets associated with major plans, with the object of causing "the greatest possible disturbance and dislocation both to the industrial activities and civil population generally in the area." The beast of area bombing had thrust its snout into the tent. The body quickly followed.

On 4 October 1940 Sir Charles Portal became chief of the air staff, a post he would hold until the end of the war; Sir Richard Peirse became AOC, Bomber Command. On 30 October Portal made his previous views official policy—lowering German morale would no longer be the by-product of strategic air attack but the end product. The air staff ordered Bomber Command to concentrate on oil and morale—oil when visibility allowed, morale when it did not. The command would devote limited efforts to U-boats, communications, and airfields. The initial draft of instructions suggested 20 to 30 cities. Peirse reduced the list, which included Berlin, Hamburg, Cologne (Köln), Munich (München), Leipzig, Essen, Dresden, Breslau, Frankfurt,* and Düsseldorf. The final draft left to Peirse the timing of the attacks and urged him to adopt the German technique of opening each raid with a fire-raising attack. The next attack waves should focus their bombing on existing fires to prevent firefighters from containing them and allowing them to spread. The directive erased the fiction that the bombers struck precision military targets and substituted an objective in keeping with the aircraft's limited capability to locate and bomb enemy targets. Yet, Bomber Command and the Air Ministry still refused to commit themselves totally to area bombing. By the end of October 1940, they raised a precision night campaign against German synthetic oil to first priority. On 16 December 1940 Bomber Command attacked Mannheim in its first "city bombing attack" as opposed to an area attack. The attack began with a force of picked crews ordered to drop incendiaries on the center of town and the remainder of the force directed to bomb the fires. The attack had the clear intention of burning out the city center. The War Cabinet had authorized the raid three days earlier in retaliation for the German night raid on Coventry on 14 November 1940. In December 1940, British intelligence reports, which underestimated

---

*Unless otherwise indicated all references to Frankfurt refer to Frankfurt am Main and not to Frankfurt an der Oder, which lies near the boundary between the former East and West Germany.

German oil stocks, encouraged yet another swing in bombing policy. A new directive dated 15 January 1941 enjoined Bomber Command to put all effort into attacks on oil production and storage facilities, but when conditions prohibited oil attacks it was to continue area bombing. Under the January directive, "it became a common practice to designate as the target the 'industrial centre' of a large German town and a number of these attacks on the model of the Mannheim experiment were carried out against such places as Berlin, Düsseldorf, Hannover, Bremen, Cologne, and Hamburg."[21]

The January 1941 bombing policy lasted until 9 March 1941; a national emergency rather than targeting changes forced another shift in focus. At that point the Battle of the Atlantic between German merchant raiders, surface naval units, and submarines (U-boats) that were against the Royal Navy and merchant marine reached a crisis point. Churchill ordered that all resources, including Bomber Command, must devote their efforts to stemming the assault on British shipping. The light bombers of No. 2 Group assisted RAF Coastal Command by flying daylight antishipping and antisubmarine sweeps. Bomber Command's heavy and medium bombers switched from the ineffective "precision" attacks on German oil to attacks on naval targets, when weather permitted.

The naval targets consisted of three types: precision attacks on German surface units, precision attacks against U-boat yards and factories producing the FW-200—the Luftwaffe's long-range, four-engine, antishipping and reconnaissance aircraft—and "Mannheim technique" attacks on ports and naval towns. The precision attacks accomplished little other than to add to the growing realization of Bomber Command's inability to strike small targets. The German battle cruisers *Scharnhorst* and *Gneisenau* sat out numerous attacks in the French port of Brest, suffering no fatal damage from night and day raids. Raids on U-boat yards differed little in their results from area raids, although a raid on 12 March 1941 in perfect conditions on the Focke-Wolf aircraft factory in Bremen, which assembled the FW-200, damaged the plant and led the firm's management to begin to move its plants to the east. The command also found resources to attack Berlin and other towns besides those on the naval list.

As quickly as the naval emergency emerged, it faded, not so much because of British actions but because of those of the enemy. The Germans moved south and east. In the South, Hitler intervened to save his Italian ally. The German Afrika Korps and its air support under the command of soon-to-be renowned Lt Gen Erwin Rommel began arriving in Libya in April 1941. They soon had their bewildered British opponents bundled back to the Egyptian border, with the exception of the Australians in Tobruk.

In the Balkans the Germans stormed through Yugoslavia and smashed the Greeks, who heretofore stymied the Italians. A British expeditionary force, drawn from forces in the Middle East, lost 15,000 men, one-fourth its strength, in a fruitless three-week intervention in Greece. That force suffered further heavy casualties in the loss of Crete. Then, on 22 June 1941, Hitler launched the struggle that decided World War II—the invasion of the USSR.

For the RAF the German sweep into the Soviet Union had two implications. First, it allowed reinforcement of the Middle East. Bomber Command sent two squadrons and personnel for three more to that theater. Second, it created the possible opportunity to extend British air supremacy from the United Kingdom to France and beyond as the Luftwaffe committed the bulk of its fighters to the east. At the very least, aggressive British action would ease the pressure on other fronts by forcing the Germans to keep fighters in the West. The scheme required the participation of Bomber Command—its aircraft would strike daylight targets in France and draw the Germans up to defend those targets. With the bombers acting as bait, Fighter Command's aircraft would engage and destroy the German defenders. Once attrition had sufficiently weakened the Germans, Bomber Command could launch precision daylight raids into Germany. The combined Fighter and Bomber Command operations proved every bit as uselessly bloody as their code name Circus.

The Germans held every advantage. The short range of the RAF Spitfire Vs left them with little time to fight or maneuver during a medium penetration of Luftwaffe airspace; the Germans did not have to oppose a slight penetration. The Luftwaffe's Bf-109Fs had a slight performance edge on their British counterparts. Their early warning system, which improved rapidly with practice, gave the Germans sufficient warning of attack so that they could climb higher than the attackers and their escorts and then strike with the advantages of greater altitude and coming out of the sun. The extensive French airfield system allowed the Luftwaffe fighter groups (*Jagdgeschwader*) to displace themselves into fields less vulnerable to attack. Bomber Command continued to participate in the Circuses until September 1941 when it became obvious that the campaign would not weaken German defenses enough to allow resumption of daylight bombing. Fighter Command, under its opinionated AOC Air Marshal Sir W. Sholto Douglas, continued to commit one-third of its forces to daylight fighter sweeps until August 1942.

Douglas, as had the leadership of Bomber Command in a different instance, fell into the trap of complete acceptance of pilot reports. At that stage in the conflict, British intelligence had developed no means of confirming German aircraft losses from German sources. Fighter Command overestimated Luftwaffe fighter losses and continued Circus operations far past the point of diminishing returns. From June to December 1941 Fighter Command lost 463 pilots, more than it had lost in four months during the Battle of Britain. Fighter Command claimed that it destroyed 731 German aircraft. However, postwar examination of German records revealed a loss of 154 aircraft, 51 of which were damaged in accidents rather than enemy (British) action.[22] So futile was the campaign (Circus) that the Germans never bothered to reinforce their two fighter groups in the West.

In the meantime, British bombing policy went further down the path of unrestricted area bombing. On 9 July 1941 the Air Ministry issued yet another new directive to Bomber Command. Like earlier directives, it rested on a foundation of wishful thinking, unevaluated intelligence, and doubtful assumptions (as does a great deal of planning of all types—Christopher Columbus being, perhaps, the archetype). The new plan called for precision night bombing of nine marshaling yards in the Ruhr (when moon conditions permitted). When the moon provided insufficient illumination (three weeks out of four), Bomber Command would attack cities in the Ruhr to destroy "the morale of the civil population as a whole and of the industrial workers in particular."[23] Whenever conditions ruled out attacks on the primary targets, the directive authorized strikes on Hamburg, Bremen, Hannover, Frankfurt, Mannheim, and Stuttgart. British intelligence had amassed considerable documentation from neutral countries, travelers in Germany, and all types of experts, from Pres. Franklin D. Roosevelt to a member of Parliament's greengrocer, which stated that German civilian morale would collapse with only a push or two. Furthermore, it seemed reasonable that with the invasion of Russia, the German state railway system, the Reichsbahn, must be straining to supply the new front and reorganize the new conquests in the Balkans. This ignored the Reichsbahn's ability to control all the rolling stock of occupied Europe. If Bomber Command could attack the marshaling yards often enough to keep them closed, it should isolate the Ruhr—Germany's most important heavy industrial area—and put greater strain on the entire war economy. Crumpled civilian morale in the Ruhr might soon infect other areas. Rail yards and morale complemented each other strategically and tactically. The rail yards lay "in congested industrial areas and near concentrations of workers' dwellings." Precision bombing of yards would produce collateral damage and disturb workers and factories; area bombing the city should land some bombs on the rail yard.

However, the expansion of the war into the Mediterranean put an increased strain on the British Royal Navy and Army. The Germans and Italians closed the Mediterranean to British convoys, forcing them to go the long way—around the Cape of Good Hope. This detour consumed much shipping, already in extremely short supply, and extended the Battle of the Atlantic into the South Atlantic. The British navy needed more escort ships. In Libya and Egypt the British army suffered setback after setback at the hands of the Germans. The Royal Army needed more tanks, artillery, and close air support as well as heavy bombers for attacks on Axis supply lines. Bomber Command found itself being drained of experienced crews and having to justify its production priorities before an anxious prime minister.

In the meantime, the phenomena of target creep soon confronted Bomber Command. In such a situation the various forces and organizations with input into target selection begin to push for the inclusion of their own pet target into the active list. Peirse, who had produced no outstanding success thus far in his tenure as AOC Bomber Command and lacked strong backing in the Air Ministry, found himself forced to accept several new targets. Because they all were to be accomplished within the objectives of the 9 July directive, he retained the authority to set the tactical priorities. On 30 August 1941 the Air Ministry instructed Bomber Command to expand the bombing of transportation facilities and morale targets to 21 smaller towns. Eleven days later, the air staff requested that he add the town of Schweinfurt, estimated to produce 45–70 percent of Germany's ball bearings, to his target list. Finally, on 27 October 1941 the deputy chief of the RAF air staff ordered him to give high priority to German ports supporting the U-boat industry and warned him that he would face diversions to the U-boat bases in the ports of Brest and Lorient.

As changes in bombing policy hit Bomber Command from one side, German defenses began to challenge it from the other. Luftwaffe night fighters, antiaircraft artillery, and radar had gotten some measure of their opponent. In the first six months of 1941, night bombers missing in action had averaged less than 2 percent. The percentage climbed to 3 percent in July 1941 and 4 percent in August when the command lost 121 aircraft. In September and October, losses declined to 3 percent, but bombers crashing reached a yearly high. The command's losses peaked in November at 5 percent, with almost half of them taken in a single night, 7 November 1941. That night Peirse dispatched the command's largest raid so far—400 aircraft. The bombers ran into severe weather. Of the 169 bombers sent to Berlin, 21 failed to return and only 79 reached their target; of 55 sent to Mannheim, seven failed to return; and of 43 sent to the Ruhr or dispatched on mining missions, nine did not return. Only one raid into Germany, against Cologne, suffered light losses (only one out of 53 aircraft). Three small raids, 56 planes total, on the channel ports of La Pallice, Boulogne, and Ostend, had no losses. Overall the raids sustained more than 9 percent casualties with 37 aircraft missing, twice that of any other night of the war so far.

Churchill reacted immediately. He ordered Bomber and Fighter Commands to begin a policy of conservation to rebuild their forces for the spring. In his report on the mission to the chief of staff, Peirse blamed its failure on the lack of meteorologists' warning and the state of crew training. Air Chief Marshal Portal, the chief of staff, found this unacceptable. Two weeks later he returned Peirse's report noting that his information stated that meteorologists had, indeed, warned of severe icing conditions and that one group commander refused to send his aircraft on a long-range mission and had requested and received permission to attack an alternate target. Portal questioned Peirse's judgment in having sent aircraft so deeply into Germany in known bad conditions. Peirse's second report repeated the assertions of the first, while adding defenses for his actions. Portal appeared inclined to let the matter rest, rather than further undermine Peirse with his command, but the Secretary of State for Air Sir Archibald Sinclair, the civilian head of the service, insisted that Portal lay the matter before the prime minister.

On 4 January 1942 Portal submitted the reports and associated air staff papers before Churchill, then in the United States for the Washington Conference. Churchill transferred Peirse to the thankless post of commander in chief of the Allied Air Forces of the American-British-Dutch-Australian (ABDA) Command in the Far East. Like many an unsuccessful general before him, the departing AOC, Bomber Command, had fought his campaign without the benefit of the added strength and scientific improvements that would enable his replacement to earn the victor's laurels.

Peirse may well have used bad judgment, but he in all likelihood fell afoul of the complexities of a modern armed service in which administrative decisions, in this case training and personnel policies, may have had disproportionate consequences on operations. Bomber Command had the responsibility of supplying advanced flight training for the bulk of the RAF's multiengine bomber crews. It accomplished this training in operational training units (OTU) equipped, insofar as possible, with the same types of aircraft as frontline operational units. In early 1941, OTU training lasted 12 weeks. However, Bomber Command planned to expand its number of squadrons and aircraft by more than 50 percent by January 1942. This expansion would require aircrews over and above replacement of losses. Shortly after the command undertook to address this requirement, it was overtaken by unexpected requirements. Beginning in April 1941, Bomber Command had to provide heavy and repeated personnel drafts. It needed to draft men to establish and maintain a bomber force for operations in the Mediterranean theater (Britain's major active theater against Germany and Italy), supply three squadrons to Coastal Command for antisubmarine work, and provide pilots for the Atlantic ferrying organization, which flew aircraft purchased from America to the United Kingdom. These aircrews and pilots were as lost to Bomber Command as those shot down over Europe. To make matters worse Bomber Command had to send experienced aircrews to meet these obligations, which reduced the combat experience and readiness levels of its own frontline units. The command also had to permanently devote some OTUs to providing continued replacements to the Mediterranean.[24] In 1941, of the 17 new squadrons raised from Bomber Command OTUs, all went to other commands.[25]

Bomber Command's OTUs were hampered in their task of turning out replacement crews [for their own frontline units] not just by the RAF's urgent needs in the Mediterranean but also by a systemic flaw—the RAF had not clearly defined the proper role of each member of the aircrew. As the RAF official history ruefully admitted, "at the outset, there was no clear idea of what a bomber crew was, beyond the general belief that all heavy aircraft required two pilots."[26] The crew of the Wellington bomber, Bomber Command's mainstay into 1942, consisted of two pilots, an observer, a radio operator, and two gunners, "but the precise nature of the duties to be performed by these men and the extent to which they required pre-operational training was obscure."[27] In short, a force plagued by feeble navigational skills and an inability to hit targets was not training aircrew members to become specialists in navigation and aiming of bombs.

Nonetheless, Bomber Command needed more aircrews, whether or not they were correctly trained. The command could not grow aircrews overnight. Increasing the outflow of aircrews from the OTUs could be accomplished only by two means. The command either had to increase the overall personnel flow into the OTUs or cut training time for personnel already in the existing cycle. Both methods or any combination of them had serious drawbacks. If Bomber Command chose to increase the total number of aircrews being trained, it would take anywhere from six months to a year for the increase to work its way through basic training, basic flight training, and the OTUs to operational units. Increases in the training establishment to handle the increased requirement for flyers would also entail additional investment of resources, including airfields, aircraft, and experienced instructors. Expanding personnel would further encounter the Achilles' heel of the entire British effort—manpower.

Throughout the Second World War, the United Kingdom had to balance its very limited manpower carefully as compared to the other great powers against industrial and military requirements. Aircrews required the very highest quality human material—men who were physically, mentally, and technically superior. These individuals were in the shortest supply and the greatest demand. Increasing the numbers of such individuals above the great number already allotted to the RAF would have repercussions throughout the war effort. One fact starkly illustrated the manpower shortage on Bomber Command itself; throughout the entire war the command always had more bomber aircraft available to it than it had aircrews to fly them.[28] Because of the time delay and resource constraints, Bomber Command ruled out training expansion in favor of cutting back OTU training time.

In April 1941 Bomber Command reduced OTU training time to six weeks, the shortest syllabus of the war. The policy remained in effect until the end of the year even though unfavorable flying weather adversely affected training. Although some OTUs continued to take up to 12 weeks to turn out pilots, others sent their half-trained students to the squadrons. The reduced training time—when combined with normal attrition, increasingly effective German defenses, and the constant siphoning off of experienced aircrews to the Mediterranean and elsewhere—had several deleterious effects. The replacement of experienced aircrews by inadequately trained aircrews and pilots quickly diluted the squadrons' ability to perform their mission. They "became incapable of successful or sustained operations."[29] The new pilots had far higher accident rates, especially in bad weather, but also in favorable weather. The loss of aircraft, which could not be quickly replaced, drove down unit capability yet more. To erase the deficiencies of these newbies, active squadrons spent up to 40 percent of their flying time on training.[30] The poor performance of Bomber Command on the night of 7 November reflected these training deficiencies.

In the immediate aftermath of the raid, the active squadrons stopped accepting new crews. This action blocked the flow of crews through the OTUs and the remainder of the training system. It also allowed the OTUs and operational squadrons to devote additional training time to aircrew members on hand. Because of the shortcomings of fresh crews coming out of the OTUs, Bomber Command discontinued the policy of rotating its experienced aircrews to other commands; instead it diverted aircrews that had just graduated from OTU to those units. This move transferred some of the consequences of the training shortfall to the other commands and increased the level of experience in Bomber Command.

In January 1942, Bomber Command increased the training period for both pre-OTU and OTU aircrews. The OTU syllabus expanded from six weeks to eight, 10, or 12 weeks, depending on the time of the year: eight weeks when summer offered the most flying hours to 12 in the harsh winter weather. The new schedule included an additional week of ground training, which eased the requirements for training aircraft and flight instructors.

In February 1942, Peirse's replacement, Air Marshal Arthur T. Harris, accepted a proposal that went far to solve the systemic problem of improper aircrew flight roles. He reduced the standard aircrew from two pilots for each bomber to one. This decision greatly reduced the demand for pilots and meant that the remaining pilots could receive additional and more thorough training. Men who would have made mediocre pilots could be diverted to other aircrew positions. One pilot per aircraft allowed the command to operate a larger number of aircraft at any one time. Without the new pilot policy, Harris could never have mounted his 1,000 bomber raids of May 1942.[31]

Dropping the second pilot also enabled the command to reorganize aircrew training. In March 1942 the command redefined and subdivided the duties of the observer. He became the navigator and a new aircrew member, who replaced the second pilot, became the bombardier. The radio operator would no longer be cross-trained as a gunner and the two gunners were relieved of radio cross training. To assist the pilot in four-engine aircraft, which were just coming on line in 1942, the OTUs added a new position: the flight engineer. "These changes had the effect of allowing each member of the crew to specialize, and it, therefore, permitted him to receive much more thorough training than had previously been the case."[32] These decisions enabled the command to field a larger and more effective force in 1942 and through the end of the war.

In retrospect, Churchill's conservation order seems well timed. It gave Bomber Command a chance to correct its deficiencies. The RAF was also fortunate in that the German engagement on other fronts left the Luftwaffe with no effort to spare to increase the pressure on the United Kingdom. Sustained pressure may have prevented Bomber Command from righting itself from the downward spiral of reduced training time and falling performance.

After more than two years of war, Britain's strategic bombing force had proved itself as little more than an annoyance to its enemy. From September 1939 through December 1941, the command succeeded in dropping only 50,142 tons of bombs of all types on all targets. This represented only 5 percent of the command's overall tonnage dropped during the war. The delivery of that ordnance cost the command 1,547 aircraft, almost 20 percent of the command's entire wartime loss. This averaged out to a cost in dead, captured, missing, and wounded of one member of Bomber Command lost for each 10 tons of bombs released and one aircraft for every 32 tons of bombs dropped. Bomber Command's decision to switch to night bombing, while conserving the force, probably resulted in the least accurate bombing campaign in air history.

German countermeasures consumed only a tiny fraction of their strength, and Bomber Command's inability to strike precision targets in Germany day or night left the enemy's strategic target systems intact. New developments would dramatically alter Bomber Command's effectiveness. A massive building program to improve the command's base infrastructure neared completion. All fields would soon have three concrete runways, concrete hard stands, and blind-flying instrumentation. On 14 February 1942 area bombing became its number one priority. Not only were cities the easiest targets to locate, but new electronic navigational aids, such as Gee [see the appendix on electronic and radar bombing], would make them easier to locate and concentrate against. No longer would bombs strike targets as much by sheer luck as by intent. Heavy bomber production continued to retain high priority in the British economy, in spite of the pleas of the Royal Army and Navy, both heavily involved in the war against Japan. Given the long lead times in the production of major new items of equipment, the reversal of the bombers' production priority would have led to chaos in war production and would have done little for the other services for several years. With bomber production virtually locked in, Bomber Command could count on a growing force of first-line, modern four-engine aircraft with hefty bomb lift capacity and long range. The Germans would face a far more effective and deadly force. Whether she willed it or not, Britain had committed herself to a strategic bomber offensive.

The Night Bombing Problem

Successful night bombing presents the attacking force with four problems: weather, navigation, lighting the target, and enemy defenses. Bomber Command's most implacable foe, weather, favored the Germans. Central European weather conditions predominated during the day—days of significant cloud cover greatly outnumbered clear days—a factor only slightly alleviated by the standard meteorological phenomenon of limited dispersion of clouds at night. Even though clouds dissipated to some extent at night, a bomber or other aircraft in proximity to a target would still need to see through the overcast with electronic devices or fly under the clouds—and avoid excessive exposure to antiaircraft artillery—to identify the target. If not, the bombers would have to bomb on dead reckoning—a wastefully inaccurate method that will usually land bomb loads miles from the aiming point. In cloudless skies—provided the experienced bomb aimer could identify the target—accuracy might improve to a CEP of 600 yards as opposed to a CEP of several miles.

Of course, one Bomber Command report admitted that even in the best conditions 50 percent of inexperienced crews would fail to locate the target.[33] An unpredicted storm or other weather conditions—such as high humidity, extreme cold, unexpected high-altitude clouds, severe winds, or rapidly moving weather fronts—might scatter an attacking force, cause icing, or produce other unsafe conditions. The bomber, an aircraft not designed for night flying, reacted badly to cold conditions. Oxygen systems froze, as did condensation in the unheated cabins. The seasons of the year also worked against Bomber Command. Summer, with the clearest weather, had the shortest nights, which limited how far missions could penetrate into Germany during darkness. The long winter nights hampered operations with the bitterest weather of the year. The monthly orbit of the moon greatly affected bombing. For one-fourth of the lunar cycle, light reflecting off rivers and lakes under the full moon helped the bombers find their targets or even showed the targets, but that same moonlight illuminated the bombers for the German night fighters. The new and quarter moon periods (the other three-quarters of the month) produced so little light as to make identification of night targets such as oil plants, marshaling yards, and individual factories tactically invisible without electronic aids. Low-light periods meant that Bomber Command could identify only the absolute largest of targets—cities located near rivers or the coast—with much hope of landing bombs on them. Throughout the war, weather remained a constant foe, but, as in other matters, increased crew experience and improved aircraft design and performance mitigated some of its worst effects. Like all the air forces in the conflict, Bomber Command never defeated the elements but it learned to cope with them.

Navigation—the ability to set and follow a correct course to the target area—was a blind spot for Bomber Command. In some cases, aircrews still relied on the World War I–era "map and a flashlight" navigation techniques. In addition, numerous prewar exercises and prewar flights highlighted the fact that an alarming number of pilots and aircrews simply did not know where they were—a circumstance that caused a few prescient debriefing officers to wonder how all the incoming crews could have hit their targets when they could not even find their home base. Yet, Bomber Command not only ignored the problem, it acted as if it did not even have one. This was a clear case of wishful thinking.

For the first 13 months of the war, the command exacerbated problems by its unquestioning reliance on two extremely poor methods of gathering bomb damage assessment (BDA) intelligence—uncorroborated reports from returning aircrews and business sources from neutral countries. The command accepted the returning crew reports without question—a foolhardy practice given the systemic overoptimism from this source. Such information demands backup verification by independent reconnaissance and gun-sight or other cameras, for example. However, the few bomb cameras employed were not used properly or their pictures were discounted. The command gave much credence to businessmen from neutral countries who had recently visited Germany. They reported that German resentment toward the Nazis grew with each raid. These individuals, who, of course, were not professional military observers, provided overly optimistic reports as well that could not be confirmed independently. Since both sources indicated success, Bomber Command accepted them positively. Not until mid-November 1940 did the RAF activate Spitfire (fighter) photographic reconnaissance flights from England. The first mission raised doubts as to Bomber Command's actual effectiveness. It photographed Mannheim on 17 December 1940, the day after Bomber Command's first designated city raid; the photographs revealed poor results. This reconnaissance indicated failure and thus found little favor at Bomber Command headquarters, which continued to live in a dream world of denial and unquestioning belief in more palatable intelligence. Faith in Bomber Command's ability to locate targets declined, except within the command itself.

This unhappy state of affairs lasted until the Butt Report was issued in mid-August 1941. The report, a product of civilian loss of faith in Bomber Command's effectiveness, rubbed the command's nose in its errors. At that time, after examining over 600 bombing photos taken in June and July, D. M. Butt, an assistant to Churchill's influential personal scientific advisor Lord Cherwell (Frederick Alexander Lindemann), determined that overall only one bomber in five dropped its bombs within five miles of the target. In the Ruhr, Germany's main industrial area, only one bomber in 14 dropped within five miles (25 square miles) of its target. Postwar studies showed that 49 percent of the command's bombs dropped between May 1940 and May 1941 fell in open country, confirming Butt's gloomy assessment.[34]

Clearly, drastic measures were required. Bomber Command, which had heretofore worked only reluctantly with scientists, now became alive to new possibilities. The crews could learn a new electrical gizmo far more quickly than traditional celestial navigation. By spring 1942 the command hoped to field its first electronic navigation aid, Gee, whose advent would solve some navigational problems. A follow-on navigational system, Oboe, stayed in use until the end of the conflict. In experienced hands, Oboe could produce bombing with aiming errors of 600 yards to one mile—a scale of accuracy sufficient for area attack but not precision operations.[35] With these devices and others, both the command and the German night fighter force began the first of a series of electromagnetic battles.

Lighting the target presented another technical challenge. Once the bombers defeated the elements and plotted themselves to a position near the target area, they required a visible aiming point to strike effectively. In good weather and moon conditions, experienced aircrews might locate the target by eyeball—a combination of events occurring all too seldom in the first two years of the war. Otherwise the attacker had to illuminate the aiming point with either electronics or pyrotechnics or a combination of the two. Flares existing at the start of the war proved pitifully inadequate—if for no other reason than financial exigencies had prevented any exercises with them. Developing long-burning flares and marker bombs with a minimum of drift and accurate ballistics took time and competed with other high-priority programs. Not until August

1942, after experiments by individual bomb groups, did the command establish a dedicated Pathfinder force (PFF) to mark and illuminate targets just before and during the assaults of the main force. As the war continued, the abilities of the pathfinders and their specialized techniques would produce remarkable accuracy. As for electronic identification of the exact target and aim point, as opposed to pure navigation, the British reworked their air-to-surface vessel (ASV) radar for aerial use. This variant, the H2S, could distinguish distinctive landmarks and locate cities but was limited in its ability to find smaller targets. H2S served as a useful blind bombing system as well as a further aid to the pathfinders.

Concentration of the bombers over the target was a subsidiary problem in lighting the target. If the force came over in dribs and drabs, then marker aircraft would have to stay over the target longer, giving enemy fighters, now that the target was identified, more time to find them and others. In addition, a slow-developing raid would lose much of its force; incendiary bombs, in particular, require a quick, mass drop for greatest effectiveness. The navigation aids, precise scheduling, practice, and experience gave Bomber Command remarkable skill at this difficult task.

Until late in the war, when they ran out of aviation gasoline and real estate, the German night defenses stubbornly contested Bomber Command's operations into Germany. In the prewar period, the Luftwaffe had made little provision for night air defense. Thus, initial Bomber Command night operations dropping leaflets and bombs met no effective opposition, which encouraged Bomber Command to engage in yet more night operations, albeit ineffective ones. Night operations, given the equipment of the time, forbade formation flying as too dangerous.

Consequently, the RAF adopted the tactic known as the bomber stream. Aircraft would take off, climb to altitude, proceed along a common course to the target, and return. Each aircraft had as much chance of survival as any other. Radar-directed antiaircraft artillery, usually near the target, downed its share of aircraft, but conflict in the air was more deadly. Weather affected the night fighter as it did the night bomber. However, the night fighter, unless acting completely independent, had an easier navigation problem. Powerful early warning radars could locate the bomber stream and ground controllers could then infiltrate fighters into it, provided the stream's flow could be determined. Radar in France and the Low Countries could provide warning of a large-scale attack. Once fighters entered the bomber stream, they still had to locate and engage individual bombers. Sometimes the atmosphere betrayed the bombers by producing highly visible contrails streaming from their wings or bright moonlight revealed their presence. Increasingly, as the war continued, the individual night fighter carried its own radar for the final stage of the hunt. For its part Bomber Command set up a special radio countermeasures group that confused the Germans by using fake ground controllers to send false voice messages, jamming their radar, and making extensive use of electronics to fly spoof missions. At times the command also bombed night fighter airfields and employed escort night fighters. The liberation of France and Belgium further eased the night bombers' problems because the Luftwaffe lost much of its early warning network. Bomber Command may not have defeated the German defenses, but it kept casualties within a low enough range to conduct continuing operations.

The American Experience

Whatever the basic soundness of a doctrine's thesis, it succeeds or fails on the basis of its actual employment in wartime. The integration of the force structure with the new elements required by new military doctrine and their combined application in appropriate circumstances constitutes the practical component of doctrine. However, by its very nature, doctrine can be a hothouse plant that often requires pruning when exposed to the outside world. Such was the case of the United States Army Air Forces (USAAF), which began World War II committed to a doctrine based on the theory of strategic bombardment and the practical technology of the four-engine heavy bomber and stabilized visual bombsight.

The US theory of strategic bombardment held that a modest number of modern bomber aircraft could accurately attack key sections (bottlenecks) of an enemy's war industry, bring manufacture to a halt, and/or panic the civilian population into surrender. Unlike World War I this strategy would be inexpensive in lives, cheap in resources, and speedy. The doctrine profoundly affected every aspect of the USAAF, which was created in June 1941. National strategy, air training programs, aircraft procurement, national industrial priorities, logistics and shipping, and weapons and technical research and development all geared their efforts toward the production of a strategic air armada. The United States committed 40 percent of its war production to aircraft and limited its ground forces to 100 divisions to provide high-quality personnel to the USAAF and to production lines. Conversion of the personnel and resources devoted to the $81\frac{1}{2}$ heavy bomber groups raised by the USAAF might have produced 25 armored divisions and an adequate supply of infantry replacements. Had US strategic bombing failed, that failure would have had serious repercussions for any USAAF hopes of postwar independence and, more importantly, for the eventual victory of the Anglo-American alliance.

The US theory of strategic bombardment, derived in part from airpower thinkers and bombardment exponents such as William "Billy" Mitchell, Hugh Trenchard, and Giulio Douhet, was developed and refined by the faculty of the Air Corps Tactical School (ACTS) from 1926 to 1940. Although the instruction of ACTS influenced several generations of airpower advocates, it lacked the official approval of the War Department. This renegade status limited the spread of its theories beyond the school and kept funding and personnel to a minimum. Limiting the theory to a small group of ACTS instructors had the advantage of maintaining it as "pure" airpower thought, but doing so had the concomitant disadvantage of reinforcing groupthink and blind spots in interpretation. Given the military's constant churning of personnel, ACTS had one advantage: continuous tenure, not of individuals, but of ideology.

The ACTS theory of strategic bombing consisted of the following tenets:

1. The national objective in war is to break the enemy's will to resist and force the enemy to submit to our will.

2. The accomplishment of the first goal requires offensive warfare.

3. Military missions are best carried through by cooperation between air, ground, and naval forces although only air can contribute to all missions.

4. The special mission of air is the attack of the entire enemy national structure to dislocate its military, political, economic, and social activities.

5. Modern warfare places such a premium on material factors that a nation's war effort may be defeated by the interruption of its industrial network, which is vulnerable only to the air arm. The disruption of the enemy's industrial network is the real target, because such a disruption might produce a collapse in morale sufficient to induce surrender.

6. Future wars will begin by air action. We must have an adequate standing air force to ensure defense and to begin immediate offensive operations. We must begin bombardment of the enemy as soon as possible.[36]

In 1935 the Air Corps acquired the weapons system, albeit in extremely small numbers, that enabled it to carry out its musings—the four-engine B-17 heavy bomber. (By 1941 the other mainstay of the American heavy bomber fleet, the B-24, had also entered full-scale production.) Relatively fast for the day and designed to fly in a self-protecting formation, B-17s carried up to 12 .50-caliber machine guns—contemporary pursuit aircraft carried lighter weapons. At standard ranges the bombers carried a payload of 5,000 to 6,000 pounds and were equipped with an excellent visual bombsight designed for daylight use.[37] ACTS theorists assumed that bomber formations would reach their targets undetected or fend off their attackers. They further expected to encounter the enemy only over the target, where he would concentrate his defenses, rather than having to conduct a running battle to and from the objective. Since the bomber would always get through to the target, it would not require escort aircraft. Escort aircraft would have to carry fuel and weapons to the target and back and still retain the ability to dogfight with smaller, faster, more agile interceptors or withstand their repeated attacks as they defended the bombers. Such a design seemed impractical to most, who deemed it unlikely that the Air Corps would have sufficient funds to build both a fleet of bombers and escorts.

Nor, until the defense could track bomber formations in-flight, was it necessary.

In good weather conditions, such as those found in the southwestern United States, an experienced bombardier in the B-17, thoroughly familiar with his bombsight, could, from 12,000 feet, put bombs 250 pounds or less on target with remarkable bombing accuracy. These results encouraged Air Corps officers to overestimate the efficiency of bombs and bombing. Since they had few bombers and little money to develop or test ordnance, they were quick to jump to such a conclusion. Moreover, they did not study European weather patterns or ask others for this information. Had they done so, these officers might have realized that, on average, weather in Europe changed six times faster than in the continental United States and that for extended periods of the year clouds covered the major cities of central Europe.

A common truism is "you don't know what you don't know." The US Army and its Air Corps suffered from the lack of an overseas intelligence service. They relied on the military attaché system, which did not operate covertly and concentrated on foreign ground forces. Consequently, the Air Corps had inadequate target folders for foreign targets. ACTS instructors developed their concepts of industrial choke points and key facilities from a study of the US economy.[38] The Air Corps remained uninformed of many foreign aeronautical developments in the field of engine technology and items such as self-sealing gas tanks.[39]

ACTS instructors were unaware of the development of radar, which took place far from Maxwell Field and in the strictest secrecy. The US Army Signal Corps first demonstrated a prototype set in March 1938, but only to the highest Army officials. American air planners knew nothing of British or German radar developments until August 1940 when the British, the most advanced in the field, revealed their resources to US military observers. As Maj Haywood S. Hansell, an ACTS instructor and World War II bomber leader, acknowledged, "our ignorance of radar development was probably a fortunate ignorance. Had this development been well known it is probable that the theorists would also have reasoned that, through the aid of radar, defensive forces would be massed against incoming bomber attacks in a degree that would have been too expensive for the offensive. As it ultimately developed the school's basic concept that the offensive enjoyed a particular advantage in air warfare did later turn out to be substantially correct."[40] Throughout the 1930s and before the United States' entry in World War II, the US Army Air Corps continued to emphasize precision daylight bombardment and intended to conduct it once it entered the hostilities.

US rearmament can be said to have begun on 14 November 1938 when Maj Gen Henry H. Arnold, commanding general of the Army Air Corps, attended a special and highly confidential meeting with President Roosevelt at the White House. Also present were Harry Hopkins, head of the Works Progress Administration and one of Roosevelt's chief advisers; Robert H. Jackson, solicitor general of the United States; Louis Johnson, assistant secretary of war; Herman Oliphant, general counsel of the treasury; Gen Malin Craig, Army chief of staff; and his deputy, Brig Gen George C. Marshall. The president called the meeting in response to a series of disturbing European events. In late September, the Munich crisis, which resulted in the German occupation of the Czech Sudetenland (and Czechoslovakia's modern border fortifications), had unmistakably revealed the unrelenting nature of Hitler's territorial demands. A meeting on 13 October with the US ambassador to France, William C. Bullitt, confirmed for Roosevelt the dangerous state of European politics.

The increasingly barbaric behavior of the Nazis toward the German Jews, displayed in such incidents as "Crystal Night" on 8 November 1938, amply illuminated the vicious nature of the German state's internal politics. These events—the culmination of years of Hitler's foreign and domestic policies—conclusively demonstrated the rogue nature of the regime. When the congressional elections of 7 November 1938 returned reduced (but still overwhelmingly large) Democratic majorities, the president felt secure enough to take the first steps toward rearmament. A whiff of such intentions before the elections, given the public's predominant antiwar sentiment, might have cost the Democrats many seats. In one of his first public moves, the president recalled the US ambassador to Germany on 13 November 1938.

At the meeting on 14 November, the president did most of the talking. He noted the weak state of US defenses and pointed out that Germany had a reported air strength almost double the combined Anglo-French total. He pointed out that the United States needed to enlarge its airplane production capacity greatly to counter the mounting security threat to the United States posed by the Germans. Roosevelt intended these planes not only for the Air Corps but for the French and British as well. The president hoped that making an increased US manufacturing capacity available to the French and British would enable them to procure enough aircraft either to forestall an attack by Hitler or to help them defeat him if war came.[41] The president sought an AAC of 20,000 planes with a production capacity of 2,000 planes a month. He knew, however, that such a program would not pass Congress. Therefore, he asked the War Department to develop a plan for building 10,000 aircraft and for constructing new plant capacity for an additional 10,000 aircraft a year.

Although his meeting concentrated on airplanes, it supplied the spark for all subsequent Army and Air Corps prewar matériel and manpower expansion—the War Department sought not only new planes but funds to provide a balanced, combat-ready Army.[42] This plan served as the blueprint for further expansion of an Air Corps that, in the autumn of 1938, had only 1,600 aircraft on hand. Plants working on aircraft contracts for the Air Corps could produce only 88.2 planes a month.[43] Even six months later, June 1939, the AAC still had only 13 operational B-17s and 22,287 personnel—only twice the strength of the Cavalry.[44]

Roosevelt rejected the initial expansion plan presented to him by the Army and the Air Corps. He had asked for $500 million in Air Corps planes, but the Army and the Air Corps had requested an additional $200 million for Army matériel and $100 million for Navy aircraft plus unstated amounts for air bases and air training. The president, who was not at all sure Congress would approve the additional $500 million in the first place, redistributed the funds, giving $200 million of the $500 million to the Army matériel branches, earmarking $120 million for air bases and other nonaircraft items, and leaving $180 million for procurement of 3,000 combat aircraft.

He promised to find the Navy's money elsewhere. Congress passed the expansion bill in April 1939, authorizing an Air Corps ceiling of 5,500 aircraft.[45]

The problem of providing aircraft for the French and British, which denied those aircraft to the Air Corps, proved vexing from the beginning. On 23 January 1939 an advanced model of the US Army dive-bomber crashed during a flight test, killing the US copilot and injuring the French pilot and 10 others. This accident gave ammunition to members of Congress and others who wished to build up US forces before aiding Britain and France or who sought to avoid sending aid to any belligerent in the hope of avoiding entanglement in the coming war.

The accident also established a precedent permitting a policy of more liberal release of advanced aircraft. Within weeks the British purchased 650 aircraft worth $25 million while the French added another 615 planes worth $60 million. In the course of the year, Canada, Australia, Belgium, Norway, Sweden, and Iraq placed further orders. Although the American aircraft industry accepted the orders, it feared that the US neutrality laws might prevent delivery in the event of war and was reluctant to expand production facilities. In the face of this reluctance, the French agreed to underwrite the cost of expansion for huge engine orders from Pratt and Whitney and airplanes from Wright Aeronautical. By November 1939 the British and French had invested more than $84 million in engine plants alone.[46] These large orders ran head-on into the Air Corps' own 5,500-plane program. In July and August 1939, the Air Corps let contracts of $105 million, more than the entire business of the industry in any prior peacetime year. Moreover, Congress spent an additional $57 million to buy new manufacturing equipment for the aircraft industry. By the end of 1939, the industry had a backlog of orders worth $630 million, $400 million of which was attributable to foreign purchases.[47]

The outbreak of war on 1 September 1939—the same day that Gen George C. Marshall officially became chief of the War Department General Staff—increased the pressure from the Western Allies for aid. On 25 March 1940 the Allies received permission to purchase all but the most advanced models of US combat and trainer types. Aircraft available to the Allies included the B-17, B-24, B-25, B-26, A-20, and P-40—all front-line aircraft in the Air Corps inventory. After the fall of France, the British took over all French contracts and added more of their own. Their orders soon reached 14,000 planes, and, after Dunkirk, the administration continued its policy of filling Britain's immediate combat needs over the requirements of Air Corps expansion.[48] As a result, the Air Corps was short of air-craft for training and equpping its new and existing units. In March 1941, Brig Gen Carl A. Spaatz, the chief of the Air Corps Plans Division, complained to Arnold: "It might be diffi-cult to explain in the case of the collapse of England and the development of a threat against the Western Hemisphere or our possessions how we can agree that any airplanes can be diverted at a time when we have only sufficient modern air-planes to equip a paltry few squadrons."[49] Spaatz would one day direct the US strategic bomber offensive.

In the spring of 1939, the Air Corps adopted a planning goal of raising a total of 24 combat-ready groups—units fully equipped, completely trained, and capable of fulfilling their assigned missions—by 30 June 1941. The 16 May 1940 ex-pansion program raised these goals to 7,000 pilots a year and 41 groups. A bare two months later, on 8 August, newer plans called for 12,000 pilots and 54 combat-ready groups. The 8 August plans also called for 21,470 planes and a total of 119,000 personnel, almost six times the personnel envisaged in summer 1939. On 17 December 1940 a new program called for 30,000 pilots a year.[50]

This huge influx of resources had a negative effect on readi-ness. Existing units lost most of their experienced personnel to training programs and as a cadre for new formations. Newly created groups consisted of a few experienced men and a large majority of half-trained pilots and aircrews with too few as-signed modern combat aircraft available to these pilots and crews to allow sufficient flight time to maintain skills. Unique support services, such as air intelligence, air logistics, air sur-geon, and inspector general offices, either needed drastic up-grading or had to be created out of whole cloth. Absorbing these changes would take longer than the Japanese and the Germans would give. Without these two years of lead time, the

39

United States would have found itself in far worse shape to fight a major war on two fronts.

The Air Corps reorganized as its strength ballooned. In October 1940, General Marshall began a new study of Air Corps needs, which resulted in the unsuccessful reorganization of 19 November 1940 under which Arnold became acting deputy chief of staff for air. However, the General Headquarters (GHQ) Air Force was removed from his authority and placed under the authority of the Army chief of staff in peacetime and under the control of the headquarters of the commanding general of the Army in wartime.[51] This scheme, which separated the Air Corps combat function from its supply and training function, did not survive long. By the end of March 1941, Marshall initiated new studies that resulted in the final prewar air organization.[52]

On 20 June 1941 the War Department issued a revised edition of Army Regulation 95–5, which governed the status, function, and organization of the air arm. It created the Army Air Forces (AAF), headed by a chief who also became the deputy chief of staff for air and had the authority to supervise and coordinate the work of the Office of the Chief of the Air Corps, the GHQ Air Force (redesignated as the Air Force Combat Command), and all other air elements. The regulation further created an air staff to assist the new deputy chief, which freed the air arm from much of the dominance formerly exercised over it by the ground officers who controlled the War Department General Staff. At General Arnold's behest, Spaatz became the first chief of the air staff at the end of June 1941. This organization sufficed until 9 March 1942 when a final rearrangement of positions gave the AAF equality with the Army Ground Forces and greatly reduced the power of the General Staff.[53] In another War Department organizational move in December 1940, Robert A. Lovett became special assistant to the secretary of war on all air matters. The following spring Lovett advanced to the post of assistant secretary of war for air, a position left vacant by the Roosevelt administration since 1933. Lovett would prove a powerful, friendly, and effective civilian advocate for the AAF.

Strategic planning and negotiations with the British kept pace with air expansion and reorganization. On 29 January 1941 committees from the US and British armed forces began secret meetings "to determine the best means whereby the United States and the British Commonwealth might defeat Germany and her allies should the United States be compelled to resort to war."[54] President Roosevelt had personally read, edited, and approved the US delegation's initial statement of views presented to the British at the conference's first session.[55] The final report, *American British Staff Conversations No. 1 (ABC 1)*, submitted on 27 March 1941, stated, "the Atlantic and European area is considered to be the decisive theatre." Both parties agreed to the principle of defeating Germany first and, if necessary, Japan second. *ABC 1* also provided for a joint planning staff, joint transport service, unity of command within each theater, and integrity of national forces, and called for the prompt exchange of military intelligence and for "US Army air bombardment units [to] operate offensively in collaboration with the Royal Air Force, primarily against German Military Power at its source."[56]

A second report on these staff conversations (*ABC 2*) dealt with air matters. The United States agreed that until it entered the war, all aircraft production from newly constructed manufacturing capacity would go to the British. This decision delayed the Air Corps' 54-group program. It was also agreed that if the United States entered the war, new manufacturing capacity would be split equally (50/50).[57] The chief of the Air Corps Plans Division vigorously objected to the agreement because of its open-ended commitment to supply aircraft to the British at the expense of reinforcement of the US overseas possessions and reduction of the aircraft available for hemispheric defense.[58] Arnold agreed and protested that the shortage of aircraft reduced "to the vanishing point the present low combat strength of this force." Nonetheless, he reluctantly agreed to defer full implementation of the 54-group program.[59]

On 9 July 1941 President Roosevelt requested the Joint Board of the Army and Navy—the predecessor of the current US Joint Chiefs of Staff—to prepare an estimate of the "over-all production requirements required to defeat our potential enemies."[60] When the president's request descended on the War Department General Staff, the War Plans Division was already swamped. Arnold feared that the Army ground officers who dominated the War Department staff would base their estimates on tactical close air support needs while shortchanging strategic air war needs. He suggested that the Air War Plans Division (AWPD), a section of the brand new AAF Air Staff, help draw up the air requirements. The War Department staff agreed.

Col Harold George and three other air officers—Lt Col Kenneth H. Walker, Maj Laurence S. Kuter, and Maj Haywood S. Hansell, all ACTS activists—prepared the air annex in one week, 4–11 August 1941. Because of its clear definition of the AAF's strategic aims and its call for a gigantic air arm to accomplish those aims, the Army Air Forces Annex, AWPD 1, "Munitions Requirements of the AAF for the Defeat of Our Potential Enemies," was a key document in the AAF's preparation for the war. It defined three AAF tasks in order of importance: "Wage a sustained air offensive against Germany," conduct strategically defensive operations in the Orient, and provide air actions essential to the defense of the continental United States and Western Hemisphere. The air offensive against Germany had four goals: reduce Axis naval operations; restrict Axis air operations; undermine "German combat effectiveness by deprivation of essential supplies, production, and communications facilities" (a strategic bombing campaign); and support a final land invasion of Germany.[61] To accomplish its mission, AWPD 1 called for 2,164,916 men and 63,467 aircraft, of which 4,300 combat aircraft (3,000 bombers and 1,300 fighters) were slated for Britain.

AWPD 1 listed four lines of action that would fulfill the US air mission in Europe, including "undermining of German morale by air attack of civil concentrations." In discussing that action, AWPD 1 stated,

> Timeliness of attack is most important in the conduct of air operations directly against civil morale. If the morale of the people is already low because of sustained suffering and deprivation and because the people are losing faith in the ability of the armed forces to win a favorable decision, then heavy and sustained bombing of cities may crash that morale entirely. However, if these conditions do not exist, then area bombing of cities may actually stiffen the resistance of the population, especially if the attacks are weak and sporadic. . . . It is believed the entire bombing effort might be applied to this purpose when it becomes apparent that the proper psychological conditions exist.[62]

Even before US entry into World War II, the AAF had clearly not ruled out area bombing for morale purposes, albeit if only for kicking the enemy when he was down.

In mid-August, the War Department staff reviewed and accepted AWPD 1. General Marshall followed suit on 30 August, as did Secretary of War Henry L. Stimson on 11 September. AWPD 1 reached the president's desk a few days later. Along with the Army and Navy requirements, it formed the beginning of the Victory Program on which the government based its initial industrial mobilization. Stimson and Marshall's agreement with the plan meant that the War Department's top civilian and military officials approved the AAF's ambitious wartime expansion.

The Japanese attack on Pearl Harbor on 7 December 1941 and Hitler's fortuitous declaration of war on the United States four days later caught the US military with its plans down. AWPD 1, Joint War Plan Rainbow No. 5, and all the production training schemes either no longer fit the circumstances or were only half complete. It took the AAF two years to train a bomber crew and mate it with an aircraft. As the RAF experience had shown, reductions in course length merely resulted in greater inefficiency and casualties in the field. The war in the Pacific consumed assets more quickly than anticipated. Before the war the Philippines had become the focus of overseas deployment. Once hostilities commenced, Australia received all equipment destined for the Philippines and more. The AAF had to set up a ferry service (airfields, beacons, etc.) to the United Kingdom for US aircraft. Even when the Eighth Air Force—the AAF numbered air force designated to conduct air operations from the British Isles—began to move to England in late May 1942, General Marshall directed its combat units to the west coast to await developments in the Battle of Midway. The Navy victory there freed the Eighth to move east. The first US heavy bomber arrived in England on 2 July 1942, almost seven months after US entry into the war. The Eighth flew its first heavy bomber mission on 17 August 1942 when it dispatched 12 B-17s against the Rouen-Sotteville marshaling yards in France.

The start of the US heavy bomber missions against the European Axis in August of 1942 marked the opening of the combined Anglo-American bomber offensive. The only two air forces in the world that had espoused the doctrine of strategic bombing before 1939 would now jointly employ it against a modern industrial power. Bomber Command had worked through many of its teething problems, and British technology and industry had begun to supply superior pyrotechnics, ordnance, and electronic devices and a growing stream of heavy four-engine bombers. It would generously share many of its solutions and devices with its American ally, the US Army Air Forces. For its part the AAF, the beneficiary of the production capacity of the world's greatest industrial power, would quickly grow until it equaled the efficiency and bomb lift capacity of Bomber Command. From January 1942 through May 1945 both air forces would suffer many losses and overcome many obstacles, not the least of which was the stout defense of a resourceful and ruthless foe. Yet, in the end they triumphed. The remainder of this work chronicles the tale of their joint efforts and accomplishments and their considerations of targeting and bombing techniques in the last 41 months of World War II in Europe.

Notes

(For full citations, see bibliography.)

1. Thomas, *Spanish Civil War*, 806–7. Thomas cites the upper limit number of deaths—1,654. The Germans and the Nationalists, who occupied the town soon after the attack, claimed that as few as 200 died. Given that reports of civilian casualties inflicted by bombing have more often than not proved greatly exaggerated, the actual number of dead in Guernica may have been closer to the lower figure. The international perception of many hundreds dead had a life and influence of its own.

2. Webster and Frankland, *Strategic Air Offensive*, 1:89.

3. Neville Jones, *Beginnings of Strategic Air Power*, 35, cites air staff note, 13 October 1941, PRO AIR 8, no. 258.

4. Parks, "Air War and Law of War," 48.

5. Jones, 34–35. Cites minutes, Churchill to chief of the air staff, Sir Charles A. Portal, 7 October 1941, PRO AIR 8/258.

6. Webster and Frankland, 1:62.

7. Ibid., 1:64.

8. Ibid., 1:86.

9. For a broader discussion of the British treatment of civil aviation and its consequences for the RAF, see Jones, 22–26.

10. Webster and Frankland, 1:68.

11. See, Kirkland, "French Air Strength in May 1940," 22–34. In this article Kirkland demonstrates that the personnel policies of the French air staff, which successfully resisted the requirement to greatly expand its training basis before the war, resulted in a catastrophic shortage of trained aircrews in May 1940. He further argues that it was this shortage of French aircrews not a paucity of French aircraft that accounted for the Allies' inability to successfully contest German air superiority during the fall of France.

12. Webster and Frankland, 1:79.

13. Ibid., 1:112–13.

14. Ibid., 1:129.

15. Jones (141) cites Feiling, *Neville Chamberlain*, 403.

16. Webster and Frankland, appendix 44, 4:455.

17. Murray, *German Military Effectiveness*, 71–72. The radar on the German island of Heligoland, 40 miles out into the North Sea, gave the Luftwaffe at least 10 extra minutes' warning of these and other missions approaching over the North Sea.

18. Webster and Frankland, 1:151.

19. Richards, *Hardest Victory*, 63.

20. In AHB, *Bomber Command Narrative History*, vol. 2, *Restricted Bombing, September 1939–May 1941*, 118, PRO AIR 41, document no. 40.

21. Webster and Frankland, 1:230.

22. Hinsley, *British Intelligence in the Second World War*, vol. 2, *Its Influence on Strategy and Operations*, 2, 269.

23. Webster and Frankland, appendix 8, table 16, 4:135–40. This is a complete copy of the 9 July 1941 directive.

24. AHB, 2:14–15.

25. Richards, 138.

26. Webster and Frankland, annex 3, "Operational Training," 4:26.

27. Ibid.

28. Ibid., appendix 39, "Average Daily Availability in Bomber Command of Aircraft and Aircraft with Crews at Selected Dates, 1939–1945," 4:428.

29. AHB, 2:25.

30. Richards, 138.

31. AHB, 2:26–27.

32. Webster and Frankland, annex 3, 4:27.

33. Ibid., 1:211.

34. Richards, *Royal Air Force, 1939–1945*, vol. 1, *At Odds*, 239.

35. Webster and Frankland, 2:135.

36. This list roughly paraphrases a more detailed list found in Craven and Cate, *Plans and Early Operations*, 1:51–52.

37. AAF security policy tightly restricted access to the Norden visual bombsight. Many bombardiers had never had the opportunity to train or practice on it. In December 1941, in at least one instance, only one bombardier in an entire group had a working knowledge of the sight. Inadequate

wartime training of bombardiers would bring into question the "precision" portion of "precision daylight bombardment."

38. This situation significantly improved in July 1941 when RAF intelligence handed over more than a ton of target folders to the USAAF.

39. After the fall of France in June 1940, the British, who had heretofore withheld intelligence and technical information, became more forthcoming. The RAF gave the Air Corps a complete set of its European target folders and, after December 1941, the British shared the Ultra secret of breaking German codes. Since the Luftwaffe had the weakest signal security of the German armed forces, the RAF and the AAF were always particularly well informed of the Luftwaffe's status and intentions.

40. Haywood S. Hansell, "Pre–World War II Evaluation of the Air Weapon," cited in Futrell, *Ideas, Concepts, Doctrine*, 1:100.

41. Watson, *Pre-War Plans and Preparations*, 132–36.

42. Ibid., 136–43.

43. Ibid., 127.

44. Ibid., 279.

45. Ibid., 142–43.

46. Holley, *Buying Aircraft*, 200–201.

47. Ibid., 180, 202.

48. Craven and Cate, 1:128–29.

49. Memo for chief of the Air Corps from chief, Plans Division, 4 March 1941, Spaatz Papers, Manuscript Division, Library of Congress, Washington, DC, Diary File.

50. Craven and Cate, 1:278–79.

51. Watson, 289.

52. Ibid., 289–90.

53. Ibid., 291–93.

54. Craven and Cate, 1:136–37.

55. Watson, 371–73.

56. Ibid., 138.

57. Ibid., 379–82.

58. Memo, Spaatz to Arnold, 4 March 1941, in Spaatz Papers, Diary.

59. Watson, 382–83.

60. Joint Board Document No. 355 (serial 707), subject: Joint Board Estimate of United States Overall Production Requirements, 1–2, AFHRA 145.81–23, Air Force Historical Research Agency, Maxwell AFB, Ala.

61. AWPD/1, Spaatz Papers, Subject File 1929–1945.

62. Ibid.

PART II
1942

January

4 January: Bomber Command—Air Marshal Sir Richard Peirse relieved as air officer commanding.

20 January: Wannsee Conference, Berlin—high-ranking Nazis agree on the "final solution" for the Jewish problem—extermination.

21 January: Field Marshal Erwin Rommel launches Axis counter-offensive in Tripolitania and retakes Benghazi from whose airfields he can keep Malta suppressed. British stage hasty retreat.

28 January: Eighth Air Force—headquarters activated in Savannah, Georgia. Originally intended to command air support force for invasion of French North Africa but invasion cancelled.

In January 1942, as it had for the previous 28 months, RAF Bomber Command conducted the strategic bombing of Germany, its allies, and Occupied Europe alone. On 4 January 1942 the Air Ministry reassigned the command's air officer commanding (AOC) Air Marshal Sir Richard Peirse to the thankless post of commander in chief of the Allied air forces in the American-British-Dutch-Australian (ABDA) Command, where the forces of Imperial Japan seemingly advanced at will. Under the policy of conservation decreed by Prime Minister Winston Churchill, Bomber Command made no deep penetrations into Germany. It continued its assistance to the Battle of the Atlantic by flying 12 relatively large missions against the German battle cruisers in Brest, France; 16 raids against French ports; and several raids on the German cities and ports of Emden (nearest port to Britain), Hamburg, Wilhelmshafen, and Bremen centers of U-boat construction.

The missions against the German surface fleet proved immensely frustrating to the aircrews. Although they lost only seven aircraft against them, the German early warning network always gave enough notice of attack for the defenders to produce a thick smoke screen to cover the port. This tactic, in the era before any electronic bombing aids, deprived the bomb aimers of any visual references, forcing them to drop blindly into the smoke. Bomber Command had attacked two of the ships for more than a year, and, through the law of averages, if nothing else, it had at one time or another inflicted damaging hits on all the German ships. Of the first 1,655 tons directed at the capital ships by the command, only four bombs hit their mark, not enough to put them permanently out of action.[1] Moreover, the ships had stationed themselves in the finest naval yard in France and had access to repair facilities and dry docks more than able to repair the random damage inflicted by Bomber Command. The presence of these ships represented a great threat. They forced the Royal Navy to keep substantial forces close by to watch them. Should they break out and avoid the British covering force they might overwhelm a convoy escort or draw it off in pursuit, which would allow U-boats to attack the undefended (and perhaps, scattered) convoy.

Note

1. Richards, *Fight at Odds*, 1:236.

February

8 February: Hitler appoints Albert Speer as minister of armaments and production to replace Dr. Fritz Todt, who was killed in an airplane crash earlier the same day. Initially Speer has authority over only army procurement.

12 February: German warships *Scharnhorst, Gneisenau,* and *Prinz Eugen* leave Brest and pass through the Strait of Dover to Germany. Bomber Command's first use of Boston light attack bombers. Maj Gen Henry H. Arnold announces that the AAF will send 12 heavy bomber groups, three pursuit groups, and photographic reconnaissance squadrons to Great Britain in 1942.

14 February: New bombing policy directive issued to Bomber Command. It ends conservation policy and makes the primary target of Bomber Command, "the morale of the enemy civil population and in particular, of the industrial workers."

15 February: Japanese take Singapore.

22 February: Air Marshal Sir Arthur T. Harris assumes command of RAF Bomber Command.

23 February: AAF—Brig Gen Ira C. Eaker establishes Headquarters Eighth Air Force Bomber Command (VIII Bomber Command headquarters) in England.

Bomber Command operations repeated those of the month before with attacks on the German fleet and French and German ports. Numerous small missions of one to five aircraft attacked Luftwaffe night fighter fields and German cities with the intention of forcing the German authorities to invoke air-raid precaution (ARP) procedures. A night in an air-raid shelter with screaming children and frightened adults would presumedly have some negative effect on the next day's productivity. Official discussion of this tactic had occurred before war, at least as early as March 1938, when Ludlow Hewitt suggested that in addition to high-level, low-level, and dive-bombing forms of attack, a fourth technique existed, namely, "harassing bombing," which would damage the enemy by causing air-raid alarms, forcing them to sound warning sirens and close factories. The prewar air staff rejected this proposal as "indiscriminate" bombing, but the wartime conditions of 1940–41 and the switch to area bombing for the main force had caused the tactic to become part of Bomber Command's repertoire.[1] The apparent success of this bombing, and the manifest suitability of the new fast two-engine Mosquito light bomber for carrying it out, meant that over the course of the war the command would steadily increase its effort devoted to this type of bombing.

On 12 February 1942 the German fleet left Brest and sailed through the Strait of Dover to Germany. It was a low point for the British military, especially the RAF, which apparently allowed them to make the voyage unharmed. Bomber Command sent out 242 aircraft; only 37 made contact and 16 of those were lost. Coupled with the reverses in the Western Desert and the fall of Singapore, the channel dash brought the Churchill government to its nadir of popular esteem.

Air Marshal Arthur T. Harris's assumption of command brought a new spirit to a frustrated force. Upon taking charge, he found a total operational force of only 374 medium and heavy bombers, of which only 44 were four-engine Lancaster heavies—the future mainstay of the British night bomber campaign.[2] He also found the directive of 14 February 1942, which authorized him to employ his effort "without further restriction" in a campaign whose primary objective "focused on the morale of the enemy civil population and in particular, of the industrial workers." The Air Ministry had issued the February directive to take advantage of a newly developed radio navigational aid, Gee, which promised greater accuracy in night bombing of targets within its range, 350 miles from Mildenhall. The accuracy of the system varied from 0.5 to 5.0 miles. Targets within range included Germany's chief industrial area (the Ruhr) and the coastal ports of Bremen, Wilhelmshafen, and Emden.[3] In an explanatory note Portal added, "the aiming points are to be the built-up areas, *not* [*sic*], for instance, the dockyards or aircraft factories. . . . This must be made quite clear if it is not already understood."[4]

The bombing of Germany to reduce the morale of its civilian population, especially the workforce, emphasized the targeting of city centers rather than precision targets and the use of large numbers of incendiary bombs. This strategy became an idée fixe with Harris. He had observed how the RAF had scattered its effort in vain attempts to bomb the Germans' transportation system, synthetic oil industry, and capital ships at Brest. From these failures he drew firm conclusions that Bomber Command lacked the accuracy to destroy precision targets and that any attempt to divert his forces to such targets should be resisted at all costs. Harris dubbed those plans that promised to end the war by knocking out a single system of key targets, "panaceas," and those who advocated them, "panacea mongers."

Like the majority of high-ranking British and American airmen, Harris had spent his adult life in the service. In 1914 he joined the Rhodesia Regiment and fought as a mounted infantryman during the conquest of German Southwest Africa. Forswearing the infantry, he trekked to England where he joined the Royal Flying Corps and finished the war as a major. For the next 15 years Harris commanded various bomber formations throughout the British Empire. He served on the air staff for five years before going to the United States in 1938 to head a British purchasing commission. At the start of the war he commanded the crack No. 5 Group, where he displayed his talent as a hard-driving director of bombing operations. Harris had a forceful personality and was prone to wild overstatement of his views. For example, in support of his opinion that the British army would never understand airpower, he was said to have remarked, "In order to get on in the Army, you have to look like a horse, think like a horse and smell like a horse."[5] In an even more pungent utterance Harris was supposed to have said, "the Army will never appreciate planes until they can drink water, eat hay, and sh__!" When stopped for speeding on a road between High Wycombe and London, he replied to the constable's admonition that he might kill someone: "Young man, I kill thousands of people every night!"[6]

Harris also enjoyed a special relationship with Winston Churchill, which, if not personally close, was at least founded on a mutual interest in advancing the Bomber Command. Churchill needed a means to strike at Germany proper before the cross-channel invasion into France, and Harris wanted as large a force as possible to bomb Germany into surrender by air alone. Harris had "direct contact" with the prime minister.[7] The proximity of High Wycombe (Headquarters, Bomber Command) and Chequers (Churchill's country residence) facilitated frequent and frank exchanges of view between the two men. This easy availability for face-to-face discussions often allowed Harris to gain Churchill's support and strengthened him in his dealings with the Air Ministry.

During February 1942, the German navy introduced a new signal encryption method. Its submarine fleet began to use an Enigma code machine, the standard German high-grade signals encoder that added a fourth wheel or rotor.[8] This revision to Enigma stifled the ability of the Anglo-American code breakers and their navies to break and read high-grade message traffic between the U-boats and the German admiralty. Losses of merchant shipping to U-boats increased alarmingly, prompting pressure from the Royal Navy on Bomber Command to assist in the Battle of the Atlantic. Harris resisted the pressure to some extent, but the constant attention his command would pay to German ports and their U-boat facilities for the remainder of the year would testify both to the need of the fleet for assistance and to Harris's conviction that area-bombing the ports would do more good than turning his force over to Coastal Command.

Notes

1. Webster and Frankland, *Strategic Air Offensive*, 1:118.
2. AHB, *Area Bombing*, vol. 3, appendix C, "Average Availability of Aircraft, Crews, and Aircraft with Crews in Operational Groups, June 1941–February 1942," PRO AIR.
3. Webster and Frankland, 4:4–6, 135–40, 143–47.
4. Ibid., 1:324.

5. Terraine, *Time for Courage*, 468. For a negative judgment of Harris, see Messenger, *"Bomber" Harris*.

6. Hastings, *Bomber Command*, 135.

7. Webster and Frankland, 1:340, 464.

8. See the concluding essay in Putney, *ULTRA and the Army Air Forces in World War II*, 65–104, for an excellent brief discussion of the physical workings of the Enigma machine and US-UK exploitation of it. The addition of an extra code wheel to the standard three-wheel Enigma machine greatly increased the possible number of code settings, which in turn greatly increased the difficulty of reading its transmissions.

March

March: Belzec death camp established in occupied Poland.

3–4 March: Bomber Command—first operation by Lancasters, sea mining.

8–9 March: Bomber Command—first operational use of Gee.

10–11 March: Bomber Command—first bomb raid by Lancasters, on Essen.

In March 1942 Bomber Command began to offer proof of its capability to damage the German war effort. The previous month the War Cabinet had approved raids on French industries working for the enemy. Air Marshal Arthur Harris selected as his first target the Renault plant at Billancourt, near Paris, which reputedly produced 18,000 trucks a year for the Germans. He also used the mission against the lightly defended target to test recently formulated illuminating, marking, and concentration tactics. The crews, who attacked in the full moon, had no trouble identifying the target, while the light defenses allowed for low-level delivery. Photographs revealed significant damage. The attack cost the plant an estimated production of 2,200 trucks, but, unknown to British intelligence, within four months its output exceeded the preraid level.[1] Some bombs fell in workers' housing, killing 367 Frenchmen—twice as many souls as Bomber Command had as yet killed in a raid on Germany.[2]

At the end of the month, on the night of 28 March, the command area-bombed the lightly defended and heretofore untouched port of Lübeck on the Baltic Sea. Harris described it as "built more like a fire lighter than a human habitation."[3] The heart of the town consisted of the old medieval city—bone-dry wood (that sparked easily) and narrow twisting streets (that provided no natural firebreaks). Using Gee to help navigate to the target area (out of range for Gee bombing), the crews of the 204 attacking aircraft easily identified the port. Carrying almost equal weights of incendiary and high explosive bombs, they dropped 340 tons, smashing the old town and destroying or heavily damaging 3,400 houses. The raid sent a shock through Germany, while British Intelligence, based on similar raids on British cities, estimated a period of at least six to seven weeks for total recovery. Once again postwar study revealed the difficulty of assessing results. Lübeck suffered a total production loss of less than one-tenth of one percent (.01 percent) and production recovered to 80 to 90 percent of normal in one week.[4]

The mass destruction inflicted on the city and the failure of government relief agencies to respond efficiently to the catastrophe led Hitler to place bombing relief efforts under the direct control of the Nazi Party. On the whole the party seems to have carried out the task efficiently, which contributed to the steadfastness of the German people under the Allied bombing campaign.

Bomber Command's first significant stings had a far-reaching result—they revived Hitler's interest in the long-range bombing of Great Britain. In particular these raids salvaged the V-1 and V-2 retaliation weapon projects. In the halcyon days of the summer of 1940 and early 1941, the Germans had cut the funding of these expensive and exotic programs as part of Hitler's general cutback of arms production. However, the Baltic raids raised the prospect of large-scale damage and, perhaps more importantly, loss of faith in the Nazi regime. As a result Hitler's interest in the programs reawakened.[5]

By temperament Hitler and the Nazis, who had come to power by using tactics of intimidation, had little use for solutions based on passive defense. Therefore, the idea of revenge weapons had a much greater emotional appeal to Hitler than schemes resting on the creation of a defensive fighter force. When the Germans did think of air defense, they drew from their experiences in the Spanish civil war where bombers had attacked at relatively low altitudes and relied more heavily on antiaircraft artillery than the British.[6] In any case, from March 1942 onwards the emotional and financial investment in revenge weapons spiraled upwards at the direct cost of interceptor production. If the vast amount of labor, resources, and brainpower expended on the V-weapons had instead been turned to the creation of a powerful air defense force, the later operations of the Allied strategic air forces might have been stopped in their tracks. Given the long industrial lead times to build and deploy air defense or revenge weapons, Hitler's decision of March 1942 would have long-term and fateful consequences.

Harris also launched five major attacks against Essen, the headquarters of the famous German armaments and steel firm of Krupps. The attacks employed Gee-equipped aircraft as illuminators and fire raisers; bombers—which were, for the most part, not equipped with Gee—bombed on the fires started by the lead aircraft. Essen, perhaps the most difficult target in the Ruhr, presented a challenging problem, one insoluble to Bomber Command at this stage in the war. Its heavy defenses kept the bombers at higher altitudes. Moreover, the dense ground haze resulting from the air pollution emitted by the Krupps industrial complex and the many other heavy industrial firms in the region totally obscured all aiming and reference points.

While the heavies penetrated into Germany at night, light aircraft of No. 2 Group attacked targets in occupied Europe. These included motor transport plants, ports, marshaling yards, night fighter airfields, and power plants in France and Belgium. Other single aircraft continued their nuisance night raids over German cities.

Notes

1. *USSBS*, Motor Vehicles and Tank Branch, *Renault Motor Vehicles Plant, Billancourt* (Washington: GPO, January 1947), 80.
2. Richards, *Hardest Victory*, 118.
3. Webster and Frankland, *Strategic Air Offensive*, 1:393.
4. USSBS, *Detailed Study of the Effects of Area Bombing*, vol. 38.
5. Irving, *Mare's Nest*, 19.
6. Murray, *German Military Effectiveness*, 78.

A Note on Electronic and Radar Bombing

During the course of the war, the RAF and the AAF came to depend on electronic devices—Gee, Oboe, Gee-H (GH), H2S, and H2X—to direct them to targets at night and in overcast conditions. These devices, all based on British research and development, used two different methods. One involved coordination between ground stations and aircraft in flight and the other independent radar carried on individual aircraft. Gee, Oboe, and GH involved ground and air coordination.

Gee used a series of broadcasters sending out precisely timed signals to an aircraft using a Gee receiver. If the signals from two stations arrived at the same time, the aircraft must be an equal distance from both, allowing the navigator to draw a line on a map of all the positions at that distance from both stations. Gee entered service in March 1942 and was accurate to about 165 yards at short ranges and up to a mile at longer ranges over Germany. At its extreme range, which was about 400 miles, it had an accuracy of two miles. Because Gee pulses were not directional, even if they were detected, they would not reveal the likely destinations of the bombers. Since the system was passive, there were no return signals that would give away the bomber's positions to night fighters. However, the system was open to jamming, which became a routine problem about five months after Gee came into widespread use. Because jamming was effective only over Europe, aircraft still used Gee for navigation near their bases.[1]

The RAF put Oboe into operational use in December 1942; the AAF did not use it until October 1943. Oboe was a radio ranging device that used an onboard transponder to send signals to two ground stations in the United Kingdom. Each of the ground stations used radio ranging to define a circle with a specific radius and track distance to the aircraft. The aircraft would fly a course along the circumference of one of the two circles. The target would lay at the intersection of the two circles. Oboe was extremely accurate with an error radius of about 120 yards at a range of 250 miles, but it was limited by the fact that it was a line-of-sight-based system that could track aircraft to targets in the Ruhr Valley but not deep into German territory. Ground stations were located throughout southern England and could guide multiple missions.

The range of Oboe depended on the altitude of the aircraft. Mosquitoes, which had the highest ceiling in Bomber Command—28,000 feet (a figure that increased as the war progressed)—led the raids. The speed and altitude of the Mosquito made it more invulnerable to German fighters and flak—an important factor in keeping the crews concentrated on marking targets. They dropped their marker bombs on signal of the Oboe equipment not on visual sighting. The Pathfinder force Halifaxes and Stirlings, which carried H2S, flew well within the range of German defensive measures, which unnerved the aircrews and may account for some of the loss of accuracy in H2S marking.

The Germans tried to jam Oboe signals, though by the time they did so the British had moved on to Mark III Oboe and used the old transmissions as a ruse to divert German attention. Along with the range restriction, Oboe had another limitation: it could be used by only one aircraft at a time.[2]

Consequently the British rethought Oboe, and came up with a new scheme named Gee-H (also known as GH) based on exactly the same logic, differing only in that the aircraft carried the transmitter and the ground stations were fitted with the transponder. Multiple aircraft could use the two stations in parallel because random noise was inserted into the timing of each aircraft's pulse output. The receiving gear on the aircraft could match up its own unique pulse pattern with that sent back by the transponder. The practical limit was about 80 aircraft at once. Gee-H had the same range limitations as Oboe.[3] The RAF first used GH in October 1943, and the Americans began to use it in February 1944.

The British first used H2S air-to-ground radar on 30 January 1943. The Americans began using it on 27 Sepember 1943 and began to use their H2X variant on 30 November 1943. The Germans could track both systems with airborne fighters and sea or ground antiaircraft receivers. Since the radar was independent of ground stations it could be used at any range to which an aircraft could carry it.

Finally, the Allies began large-scale use of a combination Gee and an H2X system known as Micro-H or MH in November 1944. This highly accurate system used Gee to give the bombers a straight course to within 35 miles of their targets and then the bombers' H2X devices would pick up special pulses from two ground stations located in France and Belgium and proceed to their targets. MH bombing became a specialty of the B-17s of the Eighth Air Force's Third Air Division.[4]

Notes

1. See http://en.wikipedia.org/wiki/GEE.
2. See http://en.wikipedia.org/wiki/Oboe_(navigation).
3. Ibid.
4. Craven and Cate, *Argument to V-E Day*, 3:667.

April

April: Auschwitz concentration and labor camp becomes death camp for Jews.

7 April: US War Department designates the Eighth Air Force to serve as the intermediate command between the overall US headquarters in Great Britain and the subordinate Air Force commands.

9 April: US-Filipino forces in the Bataan Peninsula surrender to the Japanese.

10–11 April: Bomber Command drops its first 8,000-pound bomb, on Essen.

14 April: Anglo-American Combined Chiefs of Staff (CCS)—Agree to the "Marshall Memorandum," setting 1 April 1943 as the date of the cross-channel invasion from Britain to France.

17 April: Bomber Command Lancasters conduct day attack on Augsburg.

29–30 April: Bomber Command—Whitleys fly last combat operations. Whitleys remain in service in operational training units.

In April 1942 Bomber Command heavy bombers made two night attacks over France: the Ford Motor plant at Poissy and the Gnome aircraft engine plant at Gennevilliers, both near Paris. The latter raid produced little damage. The command made several attacks on the German port of Hamburg and the cities of Dortmund and Cologne, most foiled by unanticipated bad weather. Three raids on Essen also produced little damage. On 12 April Harris sent 12 aircraft to attack Turin, Genoa, and the

Fiat Motor transport plant in Genoa. These psychological strikes reminded the Italians that they still had air defense and ARP responsibilities and hinted that worse might come. On 17 April Harris sent out a daring daylight raid against the U-boat diesel engine plant in Augsburg, 600 miles from their base. The Lancaster crews made a gallant effort. Of the 12 aircraft dispatched, German defenses downed four before they reached the plant. Intense light flak at the target destroyed three more aircraft as they attacked it from altitudes ranging between 50 and 400 feet. At best the effort delayed work; it had no significant effect on engine production. At the end of the month the command even found itself back at the hated task of attacking the German fleet—the *Tirpitz* in Trondheim Fjord.

However, on four consecutive nights, 23 through 26 April, Harris sent his force against the port of Rostock and an associated Heinkel aircraft plant. In all, more than 500 aircraft attacked the lightly defended and easily identifiable port city. They dropped over 800 tons of bombs, 40 percent of them incendiaries, on the town and factory. The raids burnt 70 percent of the center of Rostock, a medieval city similar to Lübeck, and caused tens of thousands to flee in panic. But within four days the major war plants in the town returned to full production, and the heavily hit Heinkel plant staged a "brilliant" recovery.[1] The raids on Lübeck and Rostock showed that the command could damage minor towns, but it had yet to show such skill when bombing a major city. Bomber Command's light forces continued their daylight, low-level attack on French and Belgian marshaling yards, ports, and power plants.

Note

1. Webster and Frankland, *Strategic Air Offensive*, 1:485.

May

May: Sobibor death camp established in occupied Poland.

4–8 May: Battle of the Coral Sea—US aircraft carrier task forces check Japanese southward advance toward Australia and damage two fleet carriers.

5 May: Maj Gen Carl A. Spaatz assumes command of the Eighth Air Force at Bolling Field.

6 May: US forces on Corregidor, Manila Bay, the Philippines surrender to the Japanese.

30 May: USAAF—General Arnold promises Air Chief Marshal Sir Charles A. Portal, chief of the RAF air staff, to have 66 combat groups in Great Britain by March 1943.

30–31 May: Bomber Command—first raid of over 1,000 heavy bombers, Cologne. Operational training units (OTU) first employed in a bomb raid over Germany, Cologne.

31 May: Bomber Command—first operation by Mosquitoes; attack on Cologne.

In the first four weeks of May 1942, Bomber Command dispatched only two raids of more than 100 heavy bombers. One of 167 aircraft attacked Warnemünde and its associated Arado aircraft plant on 8–9 May, the other—also of 167 attackers—against Mannheim on 19–20 May. In an experiment Harris did not repeat, an additional 25 bombers assisted the Warnemünde raid by making low-level attacks on the town's searchlight and anti-aircraft defenses. The force lost seven aircraft, almost 30 percent of its strength, thus belying the notion that the bomber force might support itself in such a fashion. Three bombers struck the

Skoda arms production complex at Pilsen, Czechoslovakia. Meanwhile the command continued its mining of German coastal sea routes and the dropping of leaflets, mostly on France. During the day, No. 2 Group continued its harassment raids on marshaling yards, shipyards, power stations, and coking plants in occupied territory.

At the end of the month, on the night of 30 May, Bomber Command made the first of three 1,000-plane raids (Operation Millenium), dispatching 1,046 bombers. Nine hundred forty aircraft, using fire-raising tactics, attacked Cologne, dropping 1,698 tons of bombs—two-thirds of them incendiaries—with a loss of 42 bombers. Air Chief Marshal Sir Arthur Harris, commander of Bomber Command, employed every expedient to field this unprecedentedly large force. All operational squadrons put every available aircraft, including reserves, in the air. He stripped the heavy conversion units (HCU), which converted crews flying two-engine bombers to crews for four-engine bombers, and OTUs of suitable aircraft and instructor crews and he assembled scratch crews from excess squadron personnel. At the last minute, the Admiralty forced Coastal Command to withdraw 250 of its bombers from these missions— an action that forced Harris to press into combat service the most advanced of the OTU students. If the raid suffered heavy casualties (he predicted no more than 5 percent to Churchill) or if the OTU crews suffered excessive losses, he would have literally sacrificed the seed corn of his training program. The command would have suffered tremendous disruption, which would have placed the idea of strategic bombing into even more question.

At first blush, Operation Millennium appeared spectacularly successful. German records documented that the raid inflicted more damage than all the previous 2,000 sorties and 2,200 tons of bombs directed toward the city. It killed 474 people, seriously injured 565 more, destroyed 3,330 houses, damaged another 9,510 dwellings, and rendered 45,152 homeless. The British Ministry of Economic Warfare (MEW)—whose functions included assessing the German economy, collecting intelligence on the German economy, and supplying targeting recommendations to the armed services—evaluated the physical damage accurately but misinterpreted its effect. MEW estimated a loss of two months' production in the city. However, a month later reports noted that the city had returned almost to normal in two weeks. In any case the raid had done little damage to the main war factories located on the outskirts of the city.[1]

Whatever its damage to the Germans, the raid did much for the Allies—American, British, and Russian propaganda could point to the blitz of a major enemy city. Bomber Command had demonstrated that it could launch damaging raids on large cities. Tactically, it learned much about the handling and controlling of large forces during night takeoffs and landings. It had shown that it could mass its aircraft and get them over the target in a minimum of time and deliver a concentrated attack. Any equation involving conventional strategic bombing must include concentration of bombs and massing of effort to produce effective bombing. Of course, bombing accuracy multiplies both mass and concentration, but, if accuracy is low, then mass and concentration may, to some extent, substitute for it.

Note

1. Webster and Frankland, *Strategic Air Offensive*, 1:485–86.

June

June: Germans lower draft age from 18 to 17½.

1–2 June: Bomber Command—second 1,000-plane raid; target Essen.

4 June: US Navy wins decisive defensive victory at Midway. Japanese carrier air arm fatally damaged by loss of four fleet carriers and pilots.

Eighth Air Force—US victory at Midway frees Eighth Air Force to resume its move to Britain.

12 June: HALPRO—(Provisional Bombardment Detachment commanded by Col Harry A. Halverson) sends 13 B-24s to bomb oil targets at Ploesti, Rumania. First US bomb raid in the European, African, and Middle Eastern theaters of war.

18 June: Eighth Air Force—Eighth Air Force Commander General Spaatz arrives in Great Britain.

20 June: Maj Gen Dwight D. Eisenhower assumes command of the European theater of operations, including the US Army and Eighth Air Force.

21 June: Tobruk falls to Axis.

25–26 June: Bomber Command—third 1,000-plane raid; target Bremen. Last operation by Bomber Command's Manchesters.

28 June: US Army Middle Eastern Air Forces (USAMEAF)—assumes command of HALPRO and other AAF forces in the Middle East. Germans begin summer offensive in USSR.

30 June: British 8th Army finishes withdrawal to El Alamein, last defensible position in front of metropolitan Egypt (75 miles from Cairo).

In June 1942 Bomber Command launched two more 1,000-plane raids and concentrated on three German cities: Essen—a primary manufacturing center and the nearest port to the British Isles; Emden; and the port of Bremen—a center of U-boat construction and aircraft assembly, which, at that time, was the favorite target of the prime minister. Two days after the 30 May raid on Cologne and the last day of sufficient moonlight, Harris unleashed 956 aircraft on Essen—a curious choice given the difficulty of locating the target and the poor results of previous raids. Seven hundred ninety-seven aircraft attacked—34 went missing. This bombing force scattered 1,500 tons of bombs (two-thirds of them incendiaries) throughout the Ruhr. Most of the aircrews failed to identify their targets and dropped their ordnance on other cities in the region. Besides Essen, which suffered eight dead and never even realized it was under heavy attack, 11 other cities in the region reported casualties. Unfazed, Harris sent three more attacks of more than 100 heavy bombers against Essen in the next week with no more success. He sent four raids totaling 680 sorties and 1,550 tons of bombs against Emden with no outstanding success. Finally, he dispatched three missions of 100 aircraft to Bremen (479 sorties, 950 tons of bombs, and the third and last 1,000-plane raid) on 25–26 June. Using 102 bombers from Coastal Command, Harris sent out 1,004 aircraft. Bombers from No. 5 Group would attack the Focke-Wolf plant, Coastal Command would attack the Deschimag U-boat works, and 20 Blenheims of No. 2 Group would attack the A. G. Weser shipyard. The remainder of the force would attack the town and dockyards. Only 661 aircraft claimed to have attacked; the command lost an additional 44 planes. They dropped almost 1,300 tons of bombs. The raid inflicted little damage other than to the aircraft plant. In this case the weather had deteriorated unexpectedly. Once the force had become airborne, the wind shifted. Instead of clearing the port, clouds concealed not only the port but also the route to it. Of the three 1,000-plane raids,

OTU student pilots, for the first time, suffered disproportionate losses, probably because the difficult weather conditions proved too much for their limited navigational skills. Although Bomber Command used OTU aircrew in several other combat missions, it ceased the practice in mid-September 1942. The cost of disruption and personnel losses to the training organization had become too severe; it was the last 1,000-plane raid. Harris warned Churchill not to expect such efforts again. Harris noted that his force had fallen to 35 squadrons. Since the first of the year, of the 19 squadrons raised from Bomber Command OTUs, 16 had gone to other theaters.

July

July: Treblinka death camp established—occupied Poland.

2 July: Eighth Air Force—first B-17 lands in the United Kingdom.

4 July: Eighth Air Force—fulfills General Arnold's promise to Churchill to have US aircrews from the British Isles in combat by 4 July. Six American crews flying in formation with British crews, in borrowed British Bostons, attack Dutch airfields. Two crews lost.

5 July: British War Cabinet gives permission to use magnetron valve in H2S.

24 July: US Joint Chiefs of Staff (JCS) withdraws aircraft intended for the Eighth Air Force and assigns them to upcoming invasion of French North Africa and to the Pacific.

In July 1942 Bomber Command expended its greatest effort—four missions, totaling 864 attacking aircraft and 2,067 tons of bombs with 36 aircraft missing—on the city of Duisburg in the Ruhr, a target almost as difficult as Essen. Other large raids struck the ports of Bremen, Hamburg, and Wilhelmshafen. The largest raid of the month employed OTU crews and hit Düsseldorf on 31 July. The Düsseldorf raid consisted of 486 attacking aircraft dropping 1,031 tons of bombs; 29 aircraft were reported missing. None of the raids appeared to have inflicted significant damage on the German war economy or caused more than a week or two of lost production.

In July the US Army Air Forces, based in Great Britain, flew their first combat missions against the Axis. The US Eighth Air Force's mission on 4 July 1942 was a propaganda stunt, pure and simple. Six inadequately trained crews in borrowed aircraft made low-level daylight attacks on targets defended by light flak.

As a bonus a legitimate war hero emerged from this mission. Maj Charles C. Kegelman, who brought his heavily damaged plane back, earned a Distinguished Flying Cross. While the mission may have had some slight effect on US and British public opinion, its practical value was nil. The Anglo-American decision to invade French North Africa, reached in July 1942 and forced upon the US Joint Chiefs of Staff by the president and the British, had a much greater impact on the Eighth. The invasion forces, supported by the newly formed Twelfth Air Force, had first call on bomber groups assigned to the Eighth because the US Army Air Forces regarded the Eighth's units as the best trained (albeit still insufficiently trained) in the service. Moreover, the Eighth would have to supply the Twelfth with spare parts, specialized personnel, and most logistical items for several months after the invasion. Nonetheless, the raid was a harbinger of things to come. From Independence Day 1942 onwards, Bomber Command would no longer fight alone. It would be joined by ever-increasing numbers of US strategic bombers.

August

7 August: US Marines invade Guadalcanal Island in the South Pacific and seize Japanese airfield, which they rename Henderson Field. Americans gain strategic initiative against Japan.

17 August: Eighth Air Force—General Eaker leads 12 B-17s against rail marshaling yards at Rouen-Sotteville, France, in the first heavy bomber raid into western Europe by the United States from the United Kingdom.

17–18 August: Bomber Command—last operation by Blenheims.

18–19 August: Bomber Command—Pathfinder force (PFF) takes part in its first bomb raid.

19 August: Bomber Command—bombers employed in combined operations at Dieppe.

20 August: Twelfth Air Force (US)—activated at Bolling Field with the mission of supporting American forces participating in the North African invasion. Brig Gen James H. Doolittle appointed commander.

During August 1942 the pattern of Bomber Command's operations changed little. The increasing availability of the extremely fast, long-range Mosquito light bomber enabled the command to extend its annoyance raids into Germany. Single aircraft attacked chemical plants at Mainz and Wiesbaden. Other Mosquitoes struck at German power plants. The command's heavies mounted area raids on Duisburg, Osnabrück, and Mainz. The command also introduced an innovation—the PFF. Although the PFF would have little immediate effect on operations, it was of great long-term significance. The pathfinders consisted of crews highly trained in navigation and the use of the latest electronic aids (often before these devices were introduced into the main force). The PFF preceded the bombing force, located the target, and marked it accurately throughout the attack. Since the skills and techniques involved in this task were in their infancy, the pathfinders had to develop them in combat, a process that took several months.

Although the idea of specialized crews to lead the bomber stream seemed both logical and self-evident, given the gross bombing errors consistently produced by average crews, Harris and his group commanders stoutly resisted the idea since its proposal in November 1941. Their chief objection stemmed from the fear of establishing a corps d'elite within the command—a practice contrary to service mores. Fighter Command, for instance, did not widely publicize its aces.

Formations composed of picked crews could adversely affect the manpower situation of the entire command in two ways. First, losses suffered by the PFF reduced the number of experienced crews. The PFF would lose only experienced crews and not a mixture of experienced crew members and replacements that formed the crews in frontline bomber units. Because the PFFs would stay over the target for the entire attack, their losses to enemy defenses would likely exceed those of regular formations. Second, and more importantly, the creation of an elite force out of the established units would skim off the leadership cadre of the frontline squadrons and groups. Thus, those units would be stripped of a significant percentage of their experience and their junior leadership. The personnel imbalance of 1941 had left the command with no taste to repeat it. The RAF chief of the air staff, Air Chief Marshal Sir Charles Portal, overruled Harris and ordered the creation of the PFF. Even then not all groups sent their best crews to it, and one group went into direct competition with it.[1]

At long last, more than nine months after Pearl Harbor, US heavy bombers began to fly combat missions from the United Kingdom. On 17 August 1942 12 B-17s of the 97th Bomb Group (already scheduled for transfer to North Africa) attacked the Rouen-Sotteville marshaling yard. In the next two weeks, the Eighth made six more raids, hitting airfields, shipyards, and more marshaling yards in France and the Netherlands. All the raids flew with heavy RAF escort and covering forces. US fighters, except the 31st Fighter Group equipped with Spitfires, lacked radio and identification, friend or foe (IFF) equipment that would enable them to fly combat. In effect the Eighth began its career flying Circuses for Fighter Command. (see "Overview," p. 19.) These initial raids greatly encouraged the AAF leadership, producing unreasonably buoyant expectations that concomitantly made the disappointment even more frustrating when events punctured their balloons. The Eighth lost no bombers in combat in August; this fact heightened its determination to prove the efficacy of daylight precision bombing.

On 19 August 1942 both Bomber Command and the Eighth sent out missions in support of land operations—the disastrous Anglo-Canadian expedition against Dieppe. In its first such support mission, its second mission overall, the Eighth attacked the Drucat airfield at Abbeville with its 22 operational B-17s. Bomber Command, for the first time since the fall of France, sent 85 aircraft (five missing) in daylight to bomb German gun positions. Harris and Maj Gen Carl A. Spaatz, the commanding general, Eighth Air Force, had demonstrated a willingness to support the ground forces when required.

Note

1. Webster and Frankland, *Strategic Air Offensive*, 1:432–33.

September

6 September: Eighth Air Force—suffers first lost heavy bombers; two B-17s over Meaulte aircraft plant.

14–15 September: Bomber Command—last operation by Hampdens.

19 September: Bomber Command—first daylight raid (by Mosquitoes) on Berlin; only Allied air raid on Berlin in 1942.

25 September: Bomber Command—daylight Mosquito raid on Gestapo headquarters in Oslo, Norway.

In September 1942 Bomber Command struck the untouched city of Karlsruhe with a raid of 177 attackers (eight missing) that dropped 434 tons. Other large area raids struck Duisburg and Essen in the Ruhr, Düsseldorf, Frankfurt, and the ports of Bremen and Wilhelmshafen. On 25 September in one of its most spectacular missions, the command sent four Mosquitoes (one missing) to Oslo, Norway, where they attacked German secret state police (*Geheime Staatspolizei* [Gestapo]) headquarters. Although the raiders dropped most of their weapons on the house across the street from Gestapo headquarters, the effort purportedly raised Norwegian morale. As for the Eighth, it flew three missions against French airfields and marshaling yards in the first half of the month and no completed missions in the second half of the month.

The Eighth's growing presence in Britain and its projected vast increase required its cooperation with and integration into RAF air control and air defense procedures. Fighter Command wanted US fighters to assume complete responsibility for one sector of the British air defense network, perhaps the one covering US bomber bases. The Americans insisted that their fighters had only one function, fighter escort for US bombers. In August 1942 Maj Gen Carl Spaatz agreed to have his fighter groups attach one squadron to British groups for acclimatization and final training. He even promised to take over a defensive sector eventually. In the meantime he gained full access to the finest air control network in the world. On 8 September the Eighth and the RAF promulgated the "Joint American–British Directif [*sic*] on Day Bomber Operations Involving Fighter Cooperation." The directive divided future operations into three phases and provided command procedures for implementing each. In phase one, US bombers would fly with combined AAF and RAF cover. In phase two, American fighters would escort the bombers while the British would conduct diversions and supply withdrawal cover. In phase three, the AAF would operate independently in cooperation with the RAF, a phrase ambiguous enough to allow the AAF complete control over its own operations.[1] The transfer of all the Eighth's active fighter squadrons to North Africa, except the Eagle Squadrons, delayed implementation of the agreement. The Eagle Squadrons—American citizens who had joined, trained, and fought with the RAF—transferred back to the AAF, with their Spitfires. They were activated as the 4th Fighter Group on 12 September 1942. They, of course, knew British procedures as well as the British themselves.

Note

1. Davis, *Spaatz*, 88.

October

October: Germans raise draft age from 49 to 60.

9 October: Eighth Air Force—dispatches more than 100 bombers for the first time.

21 October: Eighth Air Force—flies first mission against U-boat targets.

22–23 October: Bomber Command—begins a series of attacks on northern Italy with a raid by 100 bombers on Genoa to aid invasion of North Africa and operations in Egypt.

23 October: British 8th Army—begins counteroffensive at El Alamein, Egypt.

24 October: Lancasters attack Milan.

Continuing pressure from the Allied navies for assistance in the Battle of the Atlantic resulted in both Bomber Command and the Eighth taking on additional tasks. Antisubmarine activities led Bomber Command's No. 2 Group to search out new targets such as U-boat yards in Flensburg and the Stork U-boat diesel engine works at Hengelo in the Netherlands, which it attacked four times. The command, on the 13th of the month, also sent 246 heavies to attack the city area of Kiel, a port that contained a major German naval base. On 17 October Bomber Command sent out 94 Lancasters in a daylight raid to demolish one of the largest armaments factories in France, Le Creusot–Schneider and its associated transformer—power plant at Montchanin. Their round-trip amounted to almost 1,700 miles, the longest mission yet flown by the command. Flying from the tip of the Cornish Peninsula, they made a wide loop around the Breton Peninsula and entered France from the Bay of Biscay. The circuitous route, their low altitude, and good luck let them avoid

German early warning radar. They found the targets lightly defended and reported good results. The 81 Lancasters that struck the factory flew at heights of 2,500 to 7,500 feet. They suffered no losses. Five aircraft attacked the power plant, approaching the target at 150 to 800 feet; they lost one of their number. Although the mission hit both targets and the crews, as usual, reported fine results, postraid photography showed that the greater part of the arms plant still stood and that at least half the bombs had overshot the plant and landed in a nearby suburb. Intelligence reported that the mission killed 60 French workers in the manufacturing facility.[1] When considered in conjunction with the Augsburg raid of April 1942, this raid made sustained daylight operations by the command less likely—very low-level attacks involved unacceptable casualties. Likewise daylight attacks made at higher altitudes appeared little more accurate than those flown at night.

Events further compelled Air Marshal Harris of Bomber Command to launch a series of raids on northern Italy. In the Western Desert, the British Eighth Army planned to begin a major counteroffensive against the Axis on the morning of 23 October and the Anglo-Americans had scheduled their invasion of French North Africa for 8 November. Many of the convoys had already sailed. On the night of 22 October, Harris area bombed Genoa with 100 heavy bombers. The next night 107 bombers attacked targets in Italy, with Genoa receiving the bulk of it. On 24 October 77 bombers made a daylight attack on Milan and 43 more followed it up with a night attack. The attacks dampened the already shaky morale of the Italian people and may have forced the Italians to keep aircraft and antiaircraft guns meant for Egypt or Libya in Northern Italy.

The Eighth took on the assignment of bombing U-boat pens in the French ports of Brest, La Pallice, St. Nazaire, and Lorient. Its first raid on U-boats hit Lorient on 21 October. The Eighth would continue to focus on that target system as its primary objective until June 1943. These targets would prove tactically limiting for the Eighth. It had no bombs capable of penetrating the hardened concrete roofs of the pens, which served as shelters, maintenance, and repair facilities for the submarines. While the attacks accomplished little of military value, they flattened the French cities surrounding the targets, thus depriving the Germans in the pens of the opportunity to dine out while causing ill will among the French populace. The limited number of targets allowed the Luftwaffe to concentrate its aircraft and flak defenses. The German fighter aircraft could pick their opportunities for engagement; the flak batteries quickly learned US operating procedures. The situation produced high losses and low morale among the Americans, forcing them to study their methods in a school of hard knocks. It also brought tough-minded men, such as Curtis LeMay, commander of the 305th Bombardment Group, to the fore. LeMay did much to develop American tactics in defensive formation flying.

Besides the raid on Lorient, the Eighth carried out two other raids during the month: 2 October against an aircraft plant in Meaulte and 9 October against locomotive manufacturing and repair plants and other rail facilities in Lille. These three raids, together with the previous 12 raids, all over France, brought a continuing problem into focus for the first time: the accidental killing and wounding of friendly civilians in German occupied territory. For example, the Eighth's raid of 5 September 1942 on the Rouen-Sotteville marshaling yard purportedly killed 140 and wounded 200 French civilians. A dud bomb hit the city hospital during the same raid. The 9 October 1942 raid on Lille killed 40 and wounded 90 civilians.[2] General Ballin, chief of the Free French Air Force, forcibly brought this problem to General Spaatz's attention when the two dined together on the evening of 5 October. Ballin urged the Americans to contact the French people by radio to advise them that:

> American bombing was aimed only at the Nazis and towards activities in France and occupied countries that contributed to the German war effort. Therefore, all people of France living within two kilometers of recognized German war effort factories are advised to vacate such residences.

> The United States of America has only the kindliest of feelings toward the French people. This advice is aimed at assisting the French people to safeguard their families.

> Bombing at great altitudes on small targets may result in some bombs falling over and short of the target. Hence, the warning to all people of France living within the two-kilometer zone.

> Recognized targets in France are factories manufacturing aircraft, tanks, vehicles, locomotives, firearms, chemicals, etc., as well as main marshaling yards, ship yards, submarine pens, airdromes, and German troop concentrations.[3]

Spaatz agreed with Ballin's advice and requested that the British, who at that point controlled Allied propaganda efforts directed towards Europe, prepare radio broadcasts and leaflets.[4] By 9 October the British Broadcasting Corporation (BBC) had broadcasted the message to occupied Europe five times in both French and English.[5]

At the end of October, either in response to the American initiative or as part of an effort to clarify its own and Allied policy, the RAF issued new instructions on bombardment policy to all its commands. The letter drew a sharp distinction between the bombing of German occupied territory and Germany itself. In occupied countries, bombing was confined to "military objectives" only; the following rules applied:

1. Bombing of civilian populations, as such, forbidden,

2. The objective must be identified,

3. The attack must be made with reasonable care to avoid undue loss of civilian life and if any doubt exists as to accuracy or an error would involve the risk of serious loss to a populated area, make no attack, and

4. Observe the provisions of the Red Cross conventions.[6]

The letter supplied an extensive listing of military objectives in occupied countries authorized for attack: enemy naval, air, and ground units; bases; depots; camps; dockyards and billets; war factories and associated power plants; and military fortifications and works. The definition specifically excluded lighthouses and the power stations feeding the electrical pumps that kept the Netherlands from flooding. As for transportation lines in occupied countries, the letter limited day attacks to locomotives and goods trains but forbade attacks on passenger trains and attached locomotives. At night all trains were subject to attack. However, the instructions included a blanket clause subject to the provisions of avoiding loss of civilian life that allowed the attack on any other objective: "the destruction of which is an immediate military necessity."[7] The letter further addressed a problem affecting the British but not the Americans, namely, British territory occupied by the Germans—the Channel Islands. The letter limited attacks to those "necessitated by operational considerations of real importance" and confined those attacks only to the objectives against which attacks were specifically ordered. The letter added a last restriction: "owing to the difficulty of discriminating between troops and civilians, machine-gun attacks on personnel are not to be made."[8]

The concern for their own and for the people of their subjugated allies did not extend to the enemy. In two pithy sentences Air Vice-Marshal John C. Slessor, assistant chief of staff (policy), who issued the instructions, wrote, "consequent upon the enemy's adoption of a campaign of unrestricted air warfare, the Cabinet have [sic] authorized a bombing policy which includes the attack of enemy morale. The foregoing rules governing the policy to be observed in enemy occupied countries do not, therefore, apply in our conduct of air warfare against German, Italian, and Japanese territory, except that the provisions of the Red Cross Conventions are to be continued to be observed."[9] For the RAF, this policy directive remained in effect until the end of the war. On 6 November 1942 Spaatz ordered the Eighth Air Force to "conduct its operations in accordance with the rules as set forth" in the RAF memo.[10]

Although Spaatz's action gave the AAF and the RAF the exact same policy in theory, it did not have the same effect in practice. In this instance, the first of many throughout the war, the differing circumstances and operating techniques of the two air forces led each to employ the policy in differing manners. At this stage in the war, Bomber Command's No. 2 Group of light bombers was conducting regular, mostly small-scale daylight raids into occupied Europe. These raids were far more accurate than the Eighth's high-level bombardments. In addition Bomber Command devoted its main effort to bombing targets in Germany, where none of the restrictions applied. As a consequence, strict compliance with the new bombardment policy made little difference in the planning and conduct of Bomber Command's operations. Such was not the case with the Eighth Air Force, which operated exclusively over occupied

Europe and with high-altitude precision techniques that could hardly avoid collateral damage. Strict compliance with the directive would have halted American heavy bomber operations. The Eighth would appear to have made no changes to bring its day-to-day operations into compliance with the new policy.

As the broadcasts ordered by Spaatz indicated, the Americans did not purposely intend to injure civilians, whatever the limitations of their technique. Throughout the strategic bombing campaign against Europe, American bombing policy would oscillate, sometimes at virtually the same instant, between the very genuine American desire to avoid harming civilians, a feeling shared by all top American air commanders, and the realities of weather and bombing accuracy. Even when American bombing operated at its greatest severity towards civilians, in July 1944 and February 1945, one or more American officers would go on record as questioning the actions of his own forces.

On 30 October in the Mediterranean theater, where the British, Germans, and Italians were locked together in the ongoing and eventually decisive Battle of El Alamein, the US Middle Eastern Air Force used its heavy bombers, all 13 of them carrying a total of 30 tons, to attack Maleme airfield on the island of Crete. The base served as a major German air supply and antishipping point.

Notes

1. Royal Air Force Report, 22 October 1942, Spaatz Papers, Subject File 1928–1945, Library of Congress, Manuscript Division, Papers of Carl A. Spaatz.

2. Craven and Cate, *Torch to Pointblank*, 2:218, 220–21.

3. Memo, Col George C. McDonald, Headquarters Eighth Air Force, assistant chief of staff A-2, to AVM Charles Medhurst, 6 October 1942, Spaatz Papers, Subject File (Targets), 1928–1945.

4. Craven and Cate, 2:218, 220–21.

5. Letter, Air Commodore P. R. C. Groves, Political Intelligence Department of the Foreign Office, to Lowell Weicker, Eighth Air Force, Intelligence Section, Spaatz Papers, Subject File (Targets), 1928–1945.

6. Letter, Air Ministry, CS15803–ASP1, to all air officers commanding (AOC), "Bombardment Policy," signed AVM J. C. Slessor, ACAS (Policy), 29 October 1942, enclosure to letter to MP–6496–D. B. Ops, Air Commodore Bufton to Spaatz, subject: [USSTAF] Bombardment Policy in Regard to

Enemy Occupied Territories, 22 January 1945, AFHRA, microfilm reel A5616, frs. 16 and 17.

7. Ibid.

8. Ibid.

9. Ibid. Bufton states that the Slessor letter remained in force up until the date of his letter. There is no reason to suppose it was withdrawn before the end of hostilities.

10. Memo, CG, Eighth Air Force to CG, VIII Bomber Command, VIII Fighter Command, etc., 6 November 1942, subject: Bombardment Policy, Spaatz Papers, Subject File (Bombing Policy), 1928–1945.

November

3 November: Bomber Command—first operation by Ventura light attack bombers, Hengelo.

3–4 November: British 8th Army breaks through Axis lines, begins pursuit.

8 November: Anglo-American invasion of French North Africa begins.

11 November: Germans enter unoccupied France.

12 November: Ninth Air Force replaces US Army Middle East Air Forces.

13 November: British retake Tobruk.

20 November: Benghazi falls to British 8th Army.

22 November: Red Army begins counteroffensive at Stalingrad.

27 November: French fleet scuttled at Toulon.

The bombing pattern of the previous month continued during November 1942. Of the Eighth's nine missions for the month, eight were on submarine pens. In addition to a large raid on the port of Hamburg on 6–7 November, Bomber Command sent 67 of its heavies to pummel Genoa; the next night 147 planes hit the same target. Two additional raids struck Genoa on the nights of 13 and 15 November. Harris then switched to Turin, attacking it with 71 heavies on 18 November and with large raids of 200 bombers on the night of 20 November and 195 bombers on 28 November. Twenty heavy bombers attacked the Fiat vehicle plant in Turin the next night.

Bomber Command Minelaying Operations

November 1942 marked the mid-point of Bomber Command's wartime mining operations against the European Axis. From April 1940, with initial operations off the Norwegian coast, through April 1945, with the mining of U-boat training areas in the Baltic Sea, the command devoted approximately 4 percent of its entire effort (and suffered almost 3 percent of its total losses) in a continuing campaign to mine routes and areas used by Axis merchant shipping, naval surface units, and U-boats.

Bomber Command's mining operations began on a small scale, off the coast of Denmark, during the Norwegian campaign of April 1940. They continued after the fall of France and spread to the French Atlantic coast, the waters off Holland and the Frisian Islands, and Kiel bay and the Elbe estuary. Initially, only No. 5 Group's Hampden bombers possessed the ability to deliver mines—one 1,500-pound mine per aircraft per sortie. The mines had to be laid from no more than 600 feet, otherwise they would break up on impact. Throughout 1940 Bomber and Coastal Commands averaged a combined 100 mines a month, delivered by five or six aircraft per mission. Because these flights did not normally encounter German night fighters or other antiaircraft defenses, Bomber Command used mining as a method of giving new aircrews operational experience at less cost and risk than other combat missions. By the end of 1940 the Germans reported the loss of 82 merchant vessels (small coastal types averaging 1,000 tons each) and damage to 55 others. The RAF loss rate averaged 2 percent.[1]

Mining operations continued on a lesser scale in 1941 and resulted in a loss of only 45 vessels (51,000 tons). However, the British Admiralty, pressed hard by German U-boat operations, pushed for a greater effort. When he assumed command in February 1942, Harris supported this request. He had led No. 5 Group and "was always keen on minelaying as long as it did not interfere with the bombing of Germany."[2] He stipulated only that mining would take place when weather prevented attacks on Germany and that experienced crews would also participate. By July 1942, Harris committed the command to dropping 1,000 mines a month. By the end of the year, the command had given all its bombers a mine-laying capacity—the newly on-line Lancasters could carry six per sortie. Also, by the end of the year the command began to lay a new acoustic mine to supplement its standard magnetic mine. In 1942 the Germans lost 163 vessels (almost 174,000 tons) as a result of the command's delivery of 9,500 mines. Although it could now deliver mines from 2,000 to 3,000 feet, the command's loss rate climbed to 3.3 percent—a testimony to the difficulties of night operations, even with minimal enemy opposition.[3]

From January to July 1943 the command averaged more than 1,100 mines per month. In April it laid 1,809 mines to take maximum advantage from surprising the Germans with the deployment of a mine with a freshly developed firing package that combined magnetic and acoustic fuses.[4] At the end of April, Harris launched his two largest mining raids of the war. On the night of 27 April, 128 aircraft dropped 458 mines at nine points off the French coast and the Frisian Islands. Only one bomber failed to return. The next night 179 aircraft mined 28 points in the Baltic Sea with 593 mines, the largest nightly total of the war. However, they suffered a loss of 22 aircraft, the highest of any wartime mining mission. The depth of the penetrations and the large number of drop points and aircraft, which may have put the defenders on high alert and given them time to react, all possibly contributed to the casualty total. For the entire year of 1943 the command's mines sank 133 ships (96,000 tons) and damaged 92 at a cost of slightly less than 3 percent. From June onwards the casualty rate dropped as the command developed methods for effectively dropping mines from 6,000 feet.[5]

For the first six months of 1944, the RAF averaged over 1,600 mines and 535 sorties a month. In late May Bomber Command sowed minefields on both flanks of the invasion routes to the Normandy beaches to disrupt or prevent attacks by German E-boats (motor torpedo and gunboats) on the tightly packed invasion armada. In the second half of 1944 the command reduced its operations to approximately 1,300 mines and 315 sorties. As the Allied armies freed the French coast and advanced into the Netherlands, the mines increasingly fell in the Baltic. In the course of 1944 air-dropped mines sank 204 enemy-controlled ships (136,000 tons) and damaged 81 others. The loss rate for the year amounted to 1.6 percent. From January to May 1945 the command released almost 1,150 mines and flew 250 sorties each month. That effort sank 86 enemy ships (164,300 tons) at the cost of 22 aircraft (a 2.3 percent loss rate).[6] More importantly, in the last 11 months of the war the command mined the U-boat training areas in the Baltic. Although their mines (now armed with even more sophisticated fuses) sank only one submarine, they forced the Germans to close the training areas. This effort forestalled the enemy effort to field his advanced type XXI and XXIII submarines. Out of 182 such boats delivered to the German navy, only seven were fully operational at the end of the war. If large numbers of these had been able to attack Allied shipping in the Atlantic, they may have produced a serious crisis. Indeed, the British official history of the strategic bombing effort claimed that the stoppage of the advanced submarines was the naval equivalent of the decisive strategic air attack on oil production, which fatally hampered German land and air operations. The same source also notes that mining led the Swedes to withdraw their shipping from the German trade and delayed the deployment of U-boats from French ports against the convoys sent to North Africa in late 1942.[7]

All in all Bomber Command's strategic mining campaign played a significant role in increasing the overall attrition of German economic resources. In particular, diversion of freight from the sea, the cheapest method of shipment, to rail constituted an added burden to the German state rail system and contributed to its eventual collapse. Likewise, the diversion of effort to minesweeping and other defensive countermine measures consumed resources needed elsewhere. Given its price to the command, mining proved an effective and cost-efficient method of warfare. Even in the world of twenty-first-century warfare (especially one wedded to on-time manufacturing and logistics), the ability of an enemy to undertake sea or aerial mining of sea lanes and of ports of embarkation and debarkation might prove extremely damaging or impose unacceptable delays on a deploying force. Personnel can be flown in, but the bulk of the heavy equipment and logistics mass must still come by sea.

Notes

1. Richards, *Hardest Victory*, 180.
2. Ibid., 181.
3. Ibid.
4. Ibid., 182.
5. Ibid.
6. Webster and Frankland, *Strategic Air Offensive*, 3:278, n. 1. See note 1 for figures.
7. Ibid., 278.

December

1 December: Eighth Air Force—Maj Gen Ira C. Eaker assumes command from General Spaatz, who moves to North Africa to command Anglo-American air forces for General Eisenhower.

12 December: Ninth Air Force—first American heavy bomber raid on Italy; Naples, in southern Italy.

20–21 December: Bomber Command—first use of Oboe, in bomb raid on Lutterade power station.

24 December: Eighth Air Force—receives its first P-47s. Because of technical problems they do not enter combat until April 1943.

In December 1942 experts of the British Government Code and Cipher School (GC and CS) assisted by their US associates cracked the code of the four-rotor Enigma cipher machine U-boat used by the German navy. The ill-considered signal security practices of the German navy in using the system facilitated this intelligence breakthrough. However, delays in reading messages and breaking internal message codes to determine a submarine's exact location often hampered the operational use of information. Nonetheless, it facilitated the rerouting of convoys and mass attacks on wolfpacks. A harsh winter, improved Allied radar, and increased numbers of Allied airborne antisubmarine patrols increased the Germans' difficulties. From an all-time high in sinkings of Allied shipping in November 1942, the German total entered a steady decline. By May 1943 the Germans had withdrawn their submarines from the Atlantic. The urgings of the Anglo-American navies that Bomber Command and the Eighth spend ever more effort on U-boat targets also began to ratchet downward slowly.[1]

During December 1942 Bomber Command sent heavy raids against Mannheim, Duisburg, and Bremen, Germany, and conducted two raids against Turin, Italy. In a daring daylight mission, No. 2 Group flung 93 of its Bostons, Venturas, and Mosquitoes at the Philips Radio Plant in Eindhoven, Holland. The plant, situated in a sparsely populated area, supposedly produced one-third of Germany's radio components. Flying at an extremely low level, 84 aircraft reached the target and inflicted heavy damage. They lost 14 bombers, many to collisions with trees and buildings obscured by smoke; 53 of the returning bombers were damaged, seven seriously. Many of the damaged bombers suffered from encounters of the avian kind. Sadly, the raid killed 148 Dutch civilians.[2] This experience against a fringe target, and which barely pierced German defenses, did nothing to convince Harris or the air staff of the feasibility of daylight precision bombing against the Reich. On 20 December the initial use of Oboe marked a significant step forward in Bomber Command's ability to place a higher percentage of its bombs on an area target. Only its restricted range, not much beyond the Ruhr, and its ability to handle only a few aircraft at a time limited its usefulness.

Notes

1. Hinsley, *British Intelligence in the Second World War*, 2:547–55.
2. Richards, *Hardest Victory*, 148.

PART III
1943

January

11 January: Bomber Command—War Cabinet authorizes area bombing of U-boat bases along Bay of Biscay coastline.

16–17 January: Bomber Command—major strike on Berlin for the first time since 7 November 1941; also drops first 250-pound target indicator bombs.

21 January: Combined Chiefs of Staff issues a directive establishing a Combined Bomber Offensive (CBO) from the United Kingdom. Sets target priorities as follows: U-boat construction, the aircraft industry, transportation, and oil plants.

22 January: Bomber Command—first operation by Mitchell medium bombers—raid on Ghent Terneuzen Canal.

23 January: British 8th Army takes Tripoli.

24 January: AAF—Spaatz and Arnold agree to send all P-38s to North Africa and to equip the Eighth only with P-47s.

25 January: Bomber Command—No. 8 Group reformed to take over Pathfinder forces (PFF).

27 January: Eighth Air Force—attacks targets in Germany for first time as 55 bombers strike the port areas of Wilhelmshafen and Emden.

30 January: Bomber Command—daylight Mosquito raid on Berlin on occasion of Nazi Party's 10th anniversary in power.

Ninth Air Force—bombs ferry facilities in Messina, Sicily.

30–31 January: Bomber Command—first use of H2S in bomb raid—against Hamburg.

The Battle of the Atlantic still received first call on the efforts of the US and British strategic air forces in January 1943. On 11 January the War Cabinet approved a policy of area bombing against the U-boat bases on the west coast of France at Lorient, St. Nazaire, Brest, and La Pallice. Three days later a directive to Air Marshal Sir Arthur Harris specified the cities mentioned above and ordered him to level Lorient first. Once Bomber Command had finished with Lorient, a review of photographic and other evidence would decide further bombing policy. The air staff added that bombing the ports should not interfere with the bombing of Berlin or other parts of Germany and Italy.[1]

The new directive reversed the long-standing British policy of avoiding attacks on the civil population of occupied countries. France, in particular, represented a sensitive case; the British attack on the French Fleet in July 1940 had engendered much hard feeling. Only the sovereign need to keep the oceanic lifelines to Britain open could have justified this policy. The change infuriated Harris. He had suggested targeting the pens a year earlier, before their completion; he regarded the attacks now as "completely wasteful."[2] Bomber Command did not have the ordnance to penetrate the pens. Its 4,000-pound bombs had light steel walls designed for blast effect not burrowing through concrete. Harris, nevertheless, sent five raids (four of more than 100 bombers) against Lorient. In February 1,636 sorties attacked Lorient and St. Nazaire five times. As Harris had predicted they left nothing standing save the pens. Grand Admiral Karl Dönitz, commander in chief of the German submarine fleet, noted, "the towns of St. Nazaire and Lorient have been eliminated as main U-boat bases. No dog or cat is left in these towns. Nothing remains but the U-boat Pens in which the U-boats are repaired."[3] Bombing had not rendered the bases useless, but, by eliminating much of their ability to live off the local economy, the bombing had reduced the efficiency of these U-boat bases.

During the month Bomber Command introduced three operational techniques and devices that promised great improvements in future performance: first use of 250-pound target-indicator bombs, reorganization of the PFF, and the first use of H2S radar. The initial use of the target-indicator bomb began a stream of continually improved pyrotechnics for the PFF and other marking units. The availability of special bombs enabled greater training and practice, while their more frequent use spawned enhanced experience and new tactics in combat. The reorganization of the PFF into a new Bomber Command unit, No. 8 Group, regularized the existence of that force and fostered a unit spirit that contributed to innovation.

The introduction of the airborne H2S radar opened a vast operational potential. Since the aircraft carried the device onboard, they could no longer outrun sighting aids such as Gee or Oboe that had ground-based components. The H2S sets, more or less hand built, suffered many teething problems. With target-indicator bombs, PFF, Oboe, and H2S, Bomber Command at last had the ingredients on hand needed to mount a devastating area bombing campaign. However, the command still lacked the necessary mix of components and techniques that separate success from failure. It would develop that recipe in the coming months.

The Combined Bomber Offensive gained its first overt official sanction on 21 January 1943. On that date the Combined Chiefs of Staff (CCS), in conference with their heads of government, Pres. Franklin Roosevelt and Prime Minister Winston Churchill, issued a CCS directive for the Bomber Offensive from the United Kingdom. It defined the goal of the Bomber Offensive in the broadest terms, stating "your primary object will be the progressive destruction and dislocation of the German military, industrial and economic system, and the undermining of the morale of the German people to a point where their capacity for armed resistance is fatally weakened." Next, it specified four specific target sets: submarine construction yards, the German aircraft industry, transportation, and oil plants. It further suggested "other objectives of great importance from the political or military point of view," such as Berlin and the Biscay U-boat ports.[4] The directive allowed Bomber Command and the Eighth Air Force wide latitude in accomplishing their joint mission. As part of the discussions concerning the directive, but not part of it, the Combined Chiefs, at Gen George C. Marshall's suggestion, placed Air Chief Marshal Charles Portal in command of both strategic air forces. The Eighth's commander, Maj Gen Ira C. Eaker, retained the autonomy to decide the technique and method he would employ.[5] Thus, while Portal, in theory, controlled targeting and coordination of the effort, the RAF could not force Eaker to switch from daylight to night bombing. At the Casablanca Conference, Churchill's possible opposition to daylight bombing naturally alarmed the AAF. The prime minister, although enthusiastic about strategic airpower, did not subscribe to the claims of strategic airpower extremists, such as Harris, who believed it could win the war alone. At best he saw the strategic air offensive as a partial means, in parallel with huge Anglo-American ground operations, of defeating the enemy. Nor, as a practical politician experienced in technological development, did he believe in cut-and-dried formulas. In fact he tended to view them with skepticism.[6]

On 27 January the Ninth Air Force inaugurated a heavy bomber campaign against the Sicily-to-mainland-Italy ferry and its support facilities at the Strait of Messina. The campaign lasted until early August 1943 and ended only when the Axis completed their evacuation from the island. In the following six months numerous missions from the Ninth and Twelfth Air Forces would strike the Sicilian terminus (Messina) or the Italian one (San Giovanni).

Three days earlier Arnold, on his return from Casablanca, visited Spaatz. The two made a key decision. The service would allocate all twin-engine P-38s (except those bound for the Pacific) to Northwest Africa. The great distances flown in the Mediterranean required the AAF's fighter with the longest potential range. Limiting the Eighth to a single type of fighter aircraft, the P-47, would simplify its logistical tail, not to mention saving shipping and reducing training problems. Likewise, basing all P-38s in a single theater would have a similar effect, save that the Twelfth still had P-39s and P-40s. The implications of this arrangement are important. The leadership of the AAF in the persons of its commander in chief and of the former commander of the Eighth saw no convincing reason to supply the

Eighth with the longest ranged fighter in the AAF's current inventory. After 14 months of war and five months of bomber operations in Europe, the AAF had not retreated one step from its original stance: unescorted bombing deep into Germany was feasible at an acceptable casualty rate. Sinclair and Portal had read the Americans to a nicety. Furthermore, allotting short-ranged early model P-47s to the Eighth likely resulted in the loss of many aircrews that the P-38s might have saved. This decision delayed the introduction of the P-38 into the Eighth until October 1943, after the Eighth had temporarily lost its fight for air superiority against the Luftwaffe.

Notes

1. Webster and Frankland, *Strategic Air Offensive*, table 27, 4:152–153.
2. Harris, *Bomber Offensive*, 137.
3. Webster and Frankland, 2:97.
4. Ibid., 4:153–54. For the text of this directive see table 28.
5. *FRUS, The Conferences at Washington, 1941–1942*, and *Casablanca, 1943*, 671–72.
6. Webster and Frankland, 4:161, 343–44.

Churchill and US Daylight Bombing

At the Casablanca Conference Churchill's possible opposition to daylight bombing naturally alarmed the AAF. The prime minister, although enthusiastic about strategic airpower, did not subscribe to the claims of those, such as Harris, who believed strategic airpower alone could win the war. At best, Churchill asserted that the strategic air offensive was a partial means to victory to be used in parallel with massive Anglo-American ground operations. Also, as a practical politician experienced in technological development, Churchill did not believe in cut-and-dried formulas. In fact, he tended to view them with skepticism.[1]

At Casablanca the prime minister's doubts concerning the effectiveness of American daylight bombing was a matter of importance. That the AAF had failed to mount a single bombing raid on the German homeland in the 13 months since the United States had entered the war heightened Churchill's misgivings. As late as mid-September 1942, Churchill had expressed unreserved support of General Spaatz and US daylight heavy bombing.[2] Within a month, however, the prime minister took the opposite tack. Portal, too, expressed skepticism. "It is rash to prophesy," he told Churchill, "but my own view is that only very large numbers (say 400 to 500) going out at one time will enable the Americans to bomb the Ruhr by daylight with less than 10% casualties and I doubt even then the bombing will be very accurate."[3]

However, Air Vice-Marshal John Slessor (the assistant chief of the air staff [policy]) and Sir Archibald S. M. Sinclair (secretary of state for air [the civilian head of the RAF]) warned of the dangers of appearing to thwart US designs. Slessor, the RAF senior officer, had, perhaps, the clearest understanding of the US determination to carry through with daylight precision bombing. He spoke of the professionalism and determination of the US aircrews to succeed, concluding, "I have a feeling they will do it."[4]

On 16 October Churchill sent a message to Harry Hopkins, FDR's alter ego, that the AAF's achievement to date, "does not give our experts the same confidence as yours in the power of the day bomber to operate far into Germany." Churchill asked Hopkins to look into the matter "while time remains and before large mass production [of day bombers] is finally fixed."[5] The prime minister expressed himself more bluntly within his own government. He suggested diverting the Americans to anti-submarine patrols and night bombing and urged that the Americans produce night bombers on a large scale.[6]

Sinclair immediately took up the challenge. He argued that the Americans had come to a critical point in allocating their air priorities. If the prime minister pressed the United States to convert to night bombing, he would set himself against their cherished policy of daylight penetration. In doing so, he would confound those in the US military who wished to effect a major buildup of bomber forces in England during 1943 and 1944. The prime minister replied that Sinclair's impassioned plea had neither convinced him of the "merits" of daylight bombing nor the tactics to pursue toward the Americans.[7]

A few days later Sinclair, speaking for Portal and himself, reiterated his arguments, "We feel bound to warn you most seriously against decrying the American plan for daylight attack of

[Germany]. We are convinced that it would be fatal to suggest to them at this of all times that the great bomber force they are planning to build up is no good except for coastal work and perhaps ultimately night bombing." In November Portal advised the prime minister against premature scuttling of the US effort, "I do not think we can decide what to do until we have balanced the probability of success, which may not be very high but is not negligible against the results of success if achieved." Success would have tremendous consequences in wastage for the Luftwaffe fighter forces and destruction of German industry, "It is solely because of the great prizes that would be gained by success that I am so keen to give the Americans every possible chance to achieve it." Sinclair pointed out the difficulties Spaatz had encountered in training and keeping an adequate force and spoke of his determination not to fly over Germany with inadequate numbers and half-trained gunners.[8]

Portal suggested that the Americans be encouraged to press on with night adaptations and alternative day methods in case daylight precision bombing failed. He feared that premature opposition to daylight bombing would lead to commitment of US resources to other theaters.[9] On 21 November Portal took the additional step of asking the RAF delegation in Washington to press Arnold for an attack on Germany "at the earliest possible moment without waiting for the build-up of a very large force." The inability of the AAF to bomb the Reich weakened Portal's defense of the shipping priorities for aviation fuel, personnel, and supply requirements of the Eighth Air Force as well as US bombing policy in general.[10]

Churchill remained unconvinced. In mid-December he noted that the effect of the US bombing effort judged by the numbers of sorties, bombs dropped, and results obtained against the enormous quantities of men and matériel involved "has been very small indeed." During the previous two months he had "become increasingly doubtful of the daylight bombing of Germany by the American method," noting that if his ally's plan failed, "the consequences [would] be grievous." The collapse of daylight bombing would stun US public opinion, disrupt an industrial effort increasingly committed to production of bombers unsuitable for night work, and render useless the tens of thousands of

American air personnel and their airfields in Britain.[11] Perhaps for domestic political reasons the large, seemingly useless mass of AAF personnel in Britain (which would eventually be dwarfed by the million Americans in Britain before the Normandy invasion) particularly raised the prime minister's ire. He returned to it time and again in the course of the debate. Nonetheless, Churchill had fixed his policy: "We should, of course, continue to give the Americans every encouragement and help in the experiment which they ardently and obstinately wish to make, but we ought to try to persuade them to give as much aid as possible (a) to sea work and (b) to night bombing, and to revise their production, including instruments and training for the sake of these objects."[12]

Churchill's persistence in advocating antisubmarine work by the US air forces reflected the uncertain status of the Battle of the Atlantic in late 1942. The British were losing merchant shipping faster than they could replace it. British import tonnage, the lifeblood of an economy not blessed with abundant native supplies of raw materials and agricultural resources, had fallen from a prewar annual average of 50 million tons to 23 million tons in 1942. Even the most stringent shipping measures could not close the gap between imports and domestic requirements, which forced the British to consume internal stocks, reducing them to the minimum needed to support the British war effort. In early November, the British came hat in hand to Washington to plead for an additional 7 million tons of US-built shipping, a request Roosevelt granted without even consulting the military.[13] However, it would take months for the American yards to deliver the ships; Churchill felt that in the meantime a diversion of the US bombing effort to sea work would pay greater dividends. The aircraft assigned to this mission would more than likely have been based in America than in the United Kingdom, thus reducing the number of US forces stationed there. Those forces would not have to be resupplied by ship nor would they siphon away crucial supplies from the British economy. Reducing the number of US forces stationed in Britain would increase the supplies desperately needed by the British populace.

Sinclair continued to resist what he considered a dubious policy. He admitted that the RAF might be wrong in its perception that the Americans would pick up their toys and go to the Pacific if threatened, but his officers were convinced that "any attempt to divert the American Air Forces from the function for which they have been trained to a subsidiary role over the sea or in secondary theaters would be fiercely resented and vigorously resisted." If daylight bombing proved unsuccessful, the Americans themselves would abandon it and turn to night action. "They will not turn aside from day bombing," estimated Sinclair, "'till they are convinced it has failed; they will not be convinced except by their own experience."[14] Writing just a few days before the Casablanca conference, Sinclair counseled patience, advising that at the present stage it would be wrong to discourage the Americans from what might still be a successful experiment.[15]

All this drew an exasperated retort from Churchill. The Americans had not even begun their experiment; when they did, it could take four or five months to convince them one way or the other. The prime minister asserted, "I have never suggested that they should be 'discouraged' by us, that is to say we should argue against their policy, but only that they should not be encouraged to persist obstinately and also that they should be actively urged to become capable of night bombing. What I am going to discourage actively, is the sending over of large quantities of these daylight bombers and their enormous ground staffs until the matter is settled one way or the other."[16]

Churchill had not rejected daylight precision bombing, but the time was obviously fast approaching when it must begin to justify itself by deed rather than potential. Without results the prime minister could no longer accept the expenditure of resources devoted to the project. However, his threat to halt the buildup of US heavy bomber groups could in the end jeopardize the entire experiment. The precision-bombing concept, whatever its emphasis on bombing accuracy, included a large measure of attrition, for both friend and foe, in its formula for success. Without sufficient logistical backup, including large numbers of aircrews and bombers, the US effort could not succeed.

Once Arnold learned of Churchill's questioning of US bombing, he marshaled some of his biggest guns—Spaatz, Frank Andrews, and Eaker—to help persuade "Big Boy" (Churchill's code name in the preconference planning) to change his mind.

The night before the conference opened, 13 January, Arnold ordered Eaker to Casablanca. Once there, Eaker worked frantically to prepare a brief to present to the prime minister, who had consented to see him.[17] On 20 January, Spaatz, Andrews, and Eaker all met Churchill.

Eaker proved by far the most convincing. Churchill, writing his memoirs eight years after the event, admitted his frustration with US bombing. "It was certainly a terrible thing that in the whole of the last six months of 1942 nothing had come of this immense deployment and effort, absolutely nothing, not a single bomb had been dropped on Germany." Eaker's defense included a promise to attack Germany proper with 100 bombers a minimum of two or three times before 1 February and frequently thereafter. He pointed out the advantages of round-the-clock bombing of Germany. The intensity of Eaker's arguments changed the prime minister's mind.[18] "Considering how much had been staked on this venture by the United States and all they felt about it," stated Churchill, "I decided to back Eaker and his theme, and I turned around completely and withdrew all my opposition to the daylight bombing by the Fortresses."[19] Eaker recalled that Churchill merely agreed to allow the AAF more time to prove its case.[20]

Eaker's recollection seemed the more probable. As Churchill had said 10 days before the conference, he was not opposed to daylight bombing; he simply wished to encourage nighttime bombing as a reasonable alternative. Spaatz, Andrews, and Eaker confirmed that the RAF staff and the secretary of state for air had advised the prime minister that the Americans would not abandon daylight bombing until they were convinced it had failed, and that they were willing to devote vast amounts of human and material resources to ensure its success. In addition, an attack on daylight bombing could not help but alienate the AAF, jeopardizing British aircraft allocations and slowing the bomber buildup in Britain. The Americans had bet enormous stakes on daylight bombing and the prime minister, who always felt that night bombing would offer a quicker payoff, realized that they could not be asked to hedge their bet at this particular time. Having won the main point of the conference by keeping the Mediterranean front open (discomforting the US Army and its chief of staff in the process), the British knew it would be folly to risk the goodwill of the AAF and further harden feelings over a matter that would prove itself one way or the other in a few months. On 27 January, Eaker partially kept his promise to the prime minister; 55 B-17s struck Wilhelmshafen and Emden in the first American heavy bomber raid over Germany; more small raids followed in February.

Notes

1. Webster and Frankland, *Strategic Air Offensive*, 1:161, 343–44.
2. Message C-150, Churchill to Roosevelt, 16 September 1942, in Kimball, *Churchill and Roosevelt*, 1:597–98.
3. Minute, Portal to Churchill, 13 October 1942, PRO AIR 8/711.
4. Minute, Slessor to Portal, 26 September 1942, PRO AIR 8/711.
5. Message T.1345/2, Churchill to Hopkins, 16 October 1942, PRO AIR 8/711.
6. Note on Air Policy, W. S. Churchill, 22 October 1942, PRO AIR 8/711.
7. Minute, Churchill to Portal and Sinclair, 26 October 1942, PRO AIR 8/711.
8. Minute, Sinclair to Churchill, 28 October 1942, PRO AIR 8/711.
9. Minute, Portal to Churchill, 7 November 1942, PRO AIR 8/711.
10. Message 408, Air Ministry [Portal] to RAF Delegation [Slessor], 21 November 1942, PRO AIR 8/711.
11. W.P. (42) 580, Note by the Prime Minister and Minister of Defense, subject: Air Policy, 16 December 1942, PRO PREM 3/452/1.
12. Ibid.
13. Leighton and Coakley, *Global Logistics*, 1:677–79.
14. W.P. (42) 616, note by the secretary of state for air, subject: Air Policy, 29 December 1942, PRO PREM 3/452/1.
15. Note by the secretary of state for air, subject: The Bombing Policy of the U.S.A.A.F., n.d. [9 January 1943], PRO AIR 8/711.
16. Minute 26/3, Churchill to Sinclair, 10 January 1943, PRO PREM 3/452/1.
17. Parton, *Air Force Spoken Here*, 217–20.
18. Papers given to Prime Minister Churchill by General Eaker (20 January 1943), PRO PREM 3/452/1.
19. Winston S. Churchill, *The Second World War*, vol. 4, *The Hinge of Fate*, 679.
20. Parton, 221–22.

February

February: Belzec death camp in occupied Poland closed.

2 February: German Sixth Army surrenders, ending resistance in Stalingrad. Luftwaffe suffers heavy losses in experienced bomber and air transport crews (including instructor pilots) in a failed attempt to keep the pocket supplied during the campaign.

4 February: Eighth Air Force—raid on Emden opposed by German twin-engine fighters for first time.

Bomber Command—directed to make U-boat bases "top priority."

14 February: Soviet winter offensive retakes Rostov.

On 2 February 1943 the Eighth Air Force's strength had risen to six operational heavy bomber groups with an authorized strength of 210 heavy bombers plus reserves—35 frontline and 18 spare aircraft per group.[1] Eaker would have happily accepted that total—none of his bomb groups came close to their paper strength. The records showed that the Eighth had a total of only 182 heavies actually in-theater (including those en route and under repair). Of those bombers only 98 were ready for combat. The Eighth had fallen to its lowest combat-ready strength of the year. Eaker's available forces were further marginalized by weather conditions, which permitted daylight operations on only a handful of days. For the month he launched but seven missions, two of which failed to reach their targets; none exceeded 93 bombers. They struck at the U-boat pens in Brest and St. Nazaire, submarine yards in Emden and Wilhelmshafen, and an armed German merchant raider in Dunkirk—all targets contributing to the Allied victory in the Atlantic.

During the month Bomber Command conducted four missions against Lorient; a total of 1,223 aircraft dropped 3,533 tons of bombs including 2,002 tons of incendiaries. On 28

February another mission of 413 attacking aircraft smashed St. Nazaire with 1,264 tons of ordnance. As Harris had predicted, the raids pulverized the French towns surrounding the pens, but failed to damage the submarine pens themselves, which continued to spew submarines into the Atlantic. Bomber Command also struck U-boat construction centers in Germany: Hamburg once, Bremen once, and Wilhelmshafen three times. At the prime minister's urgings, Harris sent two large raids—Turin and Milan—into northern Italy. In addition small RAF daylight raids disrupted operations at the Hengelo Diesel Works and the Den Helder torpedo factory. Finally, Harris sent several radar-directed, single aircraft night raids against Essen to harass it and other cities. This demonstrated to the German populace that their cities still lay vulnerable to attack. Other than demonstrating the limitations of their new equipment and providing on-the-job training to the crews, these harassment raids had little practical effect.

In the Mediterranean, the Ninth and Twelfth Air Forces, which between them had six heavy bomber groups, pounded away at Axis airfields and carried out interdiction missions against Axis ports and lines of communication. They struck the ports of Palermo and Messina on Sicily, Cagliari on Sardinia, and Naples on the Italian mainland. The Ninth and the Twelfth also struck ports and airfields in Tunisia and flew one mission to bomb Rommel's soldiers as they retreated from the Kasserine Pass.

In mid-February the Allies instituted new command arrangements in North Africa. Under Eisenhower's overall command the Allies formed all land forces in Tunisia under British general Sir Harold Alexander and all Allied airpower in the Mediterranean under RAF Air Chief Marshal Sir Arthur Tedder as head of the Mediterranean Air Command (MAC). Tedder was one of the premier airmen of the RAF. In May 1941, at the age of 51, Tedder had become air officer commanding, Middle East. He found himself in the midst of crises on several fronts. Rommel swept all before him in the Western Desert; the Italians still held out in Abyssinia; dissident Arabs attacked RAF airfields in Iraq; the Italians and Germans made daily air raids on Malta; and the final stage of the retreat of commonwealth armed forces from Greece to Crete had begun. The disastrous battle of Crete and stern fighting in the Western Desert lay ahead. By February 1943, Tedder had already served more than two years fighting the Axis in the Mediterranean. He had learned the bitter lessons of British defeats at Crete, Tobruk, and El Alamein, and during the Axis retreat to Tripoli gave Rommel a few lessons of his own. No American air commander at that stage of the war matched Tedder's combat experience and practical knowledge in conducting air operations in the face of the German and Italian air forces. Under his leadership and that of his subordinates, particularly Air Vice-Marshal Arthur Coningham, the RAF in the Middle East had become the Allies' most effective ground-support air force.

Before joining the British army in 1914, Tedder had taken a degree in history from Cambridge University and won the Prince Consort Prize for an essay on the Royal Navy during the 1660s. In 1916 he transferred to the Royal Flying Corps. After World War I, he served as an instructor at the RAF Staff College. In 1934 he served on the air staff as director of training and in charge of the Armaments Branch. In 1936 he had commanded the Far Eastern Air Force in Singapore, where he observed firsthand the interservice disputes that presaged the mismanaged defense of Malaya in 1941–42.

In 1938 he became director general of research and development and virtual deputy to Air Marshal Wilfred Freeman, the man in charge of all RAF aircraft production until 1940. Upon leaving the Ministry of Aircraft Production, Tedder joined Air Marshal Arthur Longmore as deputy air commander in chief, Middle East. For the next five months he assisted in the operations and administration throughout the vast theater under Longmore's purview. From December 1940 through January 1941, Tedder had direct command of the air forces assisting Lt Gen Richard O'Conner's Western Desert Force in its destruction of the Italian Tenth Army and the conquest of Libya. When Churchill and Portal lost patience with Longmore's inability to do the impossible, they relieved him and appointed Tedder.[2]

Unlike Harris or Spaatz, Tedder was not identified with a particular type of aviation. Instead, during his wartime service in the Mediterranean, Tedder spent more than two years in the pit of joint army-navy-air action. He learned how to balance the conflicting demands of the services while maintaining his own and his service's integrity. He became, out of self-defense, an expert in unified command, acquiring a deep-seated belief in the necessity of joint service operational planning and unity of command for airpower under air leaders. After the war he said simply, "each of us—Land, Sea, and Air commanders—had our [sic] own special war to fight, each of us had his own separate problems; but those separate problems were closely interlocked, and each of us had responsibilities one to the other. Given mutual understanding of that, you get mutual faith; and only with mutual faith will you get the three arms working together as one great war machine."[3]

Under Tedder, Spaatz commanded the Northwest African Air Forces (NAAF), composed of three component air forces, each with British and American air units:

1. Northwest African Strategic Air Force, under the command of Maj Gen James H. Doolittle, which included four groups of B-17s assigned to the Twelfth, and the Wellingtons of RAF No. 205 Group;

2. Northwest African Tactical Air Force, under the command of Air Vice-Marshal Arthur Coningham; and

3. Northwest African Coastal Air Force.

The Ninth and its two groups of B-24s, under the leadership of Maj Gen Lewis H. Brereton, fell under a different command structure—the Middle East Command, headed by Air Chief Marshal Sir W. Sholto Douglas. Tedder also controlled the Middle East Command.

Notes

1. By 1 June 1943, if not earlier, this ratio had changed to 48 frontline and five spares. See Craven and Cate, *Torch to Pointblank*, 2:417.
2. See Tedder's autobiography, *With Prejudice*, for his early career.
3. Tedder, "Air, Land and Sea Warfare," 64.

March

5–6 March: Bomber Command—begins "Battle of the Ruhr," a series of heavy attacks on the Ruhr region of Germany until 30–31 July 1943.

28 March: Eighth Air Force—first American photoreconnaissance flight.

31 March: Speer gains control of German navy arms procurement in effort to increase U-boat production.

In March 1943 the Eighth's fortunes began to improve. Its number of heavy bombers ready for combat climbed to a monthly average of 129 per day and the number of aircraft flying missions more than doubled. The number of effective sorties (individual aircraft actually releasing bombs on a target) in the month climbed from 249 to 527. It launched 10 numbered missions and recalled one, because of weather conditions.[1] Five of the missions—two against U-boat yards in Germany, two against shipyards in Rotterdam, and one against the submarine pens in Brest and Lorient—struck high-priority targets, all beyond the range of RAF fighter escort. The Eighth aided the RAF with four missions that flew Circuses over French marshaling yards: one against the yards at Rennes and Rouen, one over Amiens, and two over Rouen alone. Rouen and Amiens, two targets that the Eighth had attacked during two of its first three missions in August 1942 and had revisited since, still functioned effectively. At this stage in the war the Eighth still lacked the numbers of heavy bombers it required to deliver enough tonnage over a target to knock it out for a considerable period. The Eighth could not deliver enough bombs in one raid or return soon enough with another raid to suppress these yards or other important targets.

The attack on Rennes may have been counterproductive. Inaccurate bombing caused 300 French civilian casualties. More accurate attacks on other marshaling yards, also (and usually) located near or in a populated area, inflicted fewer casualties. The French could understand and, to some extent, forgive attacks on the ports and U-boat pens, which directly supported German military operations and which, in any case, they had evacuated. They were not so understanding in the case of marshaling yards, which were far more numerous than ports and seemingly only provided indirect support to the Germans while serving as essential parts of the transportation system that maintained the French civilian economy. The sheer number of marshaling yards (one for every major town in France) precluded wholesale evacuation of their environs, which would have caused great dislocation of economic activity had it been permitted by the Germans. In the eyes of the French, the raids on the rail yards spilled too much French blood for *un si court delai et ralentissement du traffic* (so little delay and disruption of traffic). In contrast to their disdain of the Eighth's mass attacks, the French considered the frequent low-level raids of one or two of Bomber Command's No. 2 Group aircraft as "amazingly accurate."[2] As noted earlier, the Allies gave the populations of occupied nations general warnings of the danger of living near or working in bombing targets, but operational security considerations prevented these warnings from becoming too specific as to time and place.

Seven months after its first mission the Eighth bombed the same targets and flew under RAF escort. The demands of North Africa, the Battle of the Atlantic, and reduced shipping priorities eviscerated the Eighth's strategic capability. Still, however slightly, the raids furthered one Allied goal, the establishment of air superiority over as much of France as possible. Air superiority over Europe was an essential ingredient before the Allies could undertake a cross-channel invasion into France. The Ninth and Twelfth Air Forces in North Africa remained chained to their missions of interdiction and counterair. They focused on the Axis forces in Tunisia but bombed ports and airfields as far afield as southern Italy, Sicily, and Sardinia.

On the night of 5 March, Bomber Command began the battle of the Ruhr with an attack on Essen. Of the 442 bombers dispatched, 366 claimed to have bombed the target. Photographic evidence indicated that only 153 actually bombed within three miles of the aiming point. However, this attack proved more than enough to deliver the first punishing attack on a target that had theretofore withstood the command's efforts. The new techniques paid their first dividend as Oboe-equipped Mosquitoes led the PFF marking aircraft to the target.[3] Photographic reconnaissance revealed 160 acres in the middle of the city burnt and showed heavy damage to the Krupps plant.[4] The new techniques (use of Oboe and PFF planes) had paid their first dividend. Essen was unique among German towns in that its major war industry occupied the center of the town instead of the outskirts. The city was a relatively new city, a company town, built around its major employer.

In perusing the list of targets (see below) struck by the command in the next few months, one will quickly realize that the term *battle* used to describe Harris's campaign against the Ruhr was something of a misnomer. It probably harkened back to World War I where a monthlong struggle over a single section of the front was labeled a battle, hence, the Battle of Verdun, the Battle of the Somme, or some other protracted major campaign. By its very nature, a strategic air offensive does not fasten on a single target or region to the exclusion of all else. Weather conditions, conflicting priorities, and tactical considerations often dictate attacks on distant, seemingly unrelated targets. Therefore, the reader might do well to conceive of Bomber Command's great battles in 1943—the Ruhr, Hamburg, and Berlin—as extended campaigns loosely focused on the named objective with a wide range of actions extending over a large geographical area. Within each campaign, the large raids directed at individual targets would become subsidiary battles. Such was the case in March 1943 when the command bombed Berlin and Turin, southern Germany, and French and German ports.

Targets

Bochum	Gelsenkirchen	Oberhausen
Bottrop	Huls	Rechlinghaus
Dorsten	Krefeld	Remsheid
Dortmund	Leverkusen	Soligen
Duisburg	Mulheim	Witten
Düsseldorf	Munich-Gladbach	Wupperthal
Essen		

No. 2 Group, as always, attempted to keep the Germans on edge with its harassing low-level daylight attacks on rail facilities and small, but important, items such as diesel engine plants and electronics manufacturers. One such raid occurred on 3 March 1943 when 10 Mosquitoes attacked a molybdenum mine at Knaben, Norway.* The raid put the mine out of commission for a considerable period, but the Germans, as they almost always did when pressed, found new methods to work around its loss.[5]

Notes

1. The Eighth assigned a specific mission number to each day's operations. Leaflet and supply operations also received mission numbers, in the same sequence of overall mission numbers. For example, Eighth Air Force Mission No. 1 was the Rouen marshaling yard attack of 17 August 1942. The Eighth flew 10 missions in March 1943 (nos. 39–48). Number 44 was recalled because of worsening weather conditions before any of aircraft entered into combat. A mission could be a single aircraft dropping leaflets at night over Europe or 1,000 bombers hitting a dozen or more targets during the day. In all the Eighth conducted 986 missions from 17 August 1942 through 8 May 1945. As it did with many of its reporting procedures, the Eighth apparently copied this system from RAF Bomber Command, which also assigned overall mission numbers to its daily and nightly operations.
2. Craven and Cate, *Torch to Pointblank*, 2:320.
3. See the appendix on electronic bombing and radar for a fuller discussion of Oboe and the other methods of bombing sighting and navigation employed in WWII.
4. Webster and Frankland, *Strategic Bombing Offensive*, 2:118.
5. Ibid., 2:292.

---

*Molybdenum, a rare metal, served as a hardening agent for specialty hard steels crucially important to the German war effort.

April

5 April: Eighth Air Force—Belgian ambassador to the US protests collateral damage inflicted on Antwerp.

Eighth Air Force—first crew members in Eighth Air Force complete their 25-mission combat rotation.

8 April: Eighth Air Force—P-47 fighters begin operations.

In April 1943 the four active bombardment groups of the Eighth Air Force flew 351 effective heavy bomber sorties. This total was one-third less than in the previous month and, even worse, the Eighth's total was only 20 more sorties than that of the ninth, which had only two heavy bombardment groups. Weather, which prevented operations by the Eighth in the last two weeks of the month, and far stronger opposition accounted for much of the difference. Lt Gen Frank M. Andrews, the American theater commander and an AAF officer of great experience and ability who had a career-long advocacy of strategic bombing, wrote to his son at the end of the month. "Our buildup is coming along nicely now but we continue to have a tough time with our daylight bombing. It is quite evident that we have not yet found just exactly the right combination. We should grow better at a faster clip, I am looking for the answers, our losses are running too high. Leadership and experience are two of the troubles. We will work it out."[1]

Five days later Andrews died in a tragic air accident. His doubts and dissatisfaction demonstrated the growing realization within the AAF leadership that all was not well with some of the assumptions upon which US air doctrine rested, especially sole reliance on visual bombing techniques, which required clear weather, and the ability of the unescorted bomber to penetrate, with acceptable losses, deep into enemy defended territory.

The Eighth sent out only four missions in April 1942: one to the Renault Works at Billancourt, near Paris; one to the Erla aircraft repair works near Antwerp; one against the U-boat pens in Lorient and Brest; and the last to the Focke-Wolf assembly plant in Bremen. The last mission, mission number 52, on 17 April, met heavy German resistance. The German fighters had learned to wait until the Allied escort fighters had run low on fuel and were forced to return to base. Without fear of interference they swarmed over the American bombers. Sixteen of the 107 bombers attacking went down—double the Eighth's previous highest loss. The attackers suffered a further 39 bombers damaged. Of the two wings involved, the one flying the looser formation suffered all the losses, a circumstance that further convinced the Eighth's leadership to stress the defensive advantages of tight formations over the superior bomb patterns and easier maneuvering of looser formations. The Eighth did not go back to Germany until 14 May 1943.

The month's second raid on 5 April against the Erla plant at Antwerp drew a sharp protest from the Belgian government. The mission had resulted in 1,200 civilian casualties, the majority women and children. The British War Cabinet reexamined the policy of bombing occupied Europe and ruled that it would permit such bombing only if it could be accomplished without excessive risk of collateral damage. A strict interpretation would have forced the Eighth to close up shop. The AAF protested. The matter came before the Combined Chiefs of Staff (CCS) in June 1943. The CCS, with their governments' consent, stated that targets of inherent military importance, such as oil refineries and armaments plants, could be subjected to precision bombardment under suitable conditions.

In the Mediterranean NASAF and the Ninth went about their interdiction and counterair missions. On 10 April NASAF B-17s sank an Italian cruiser in harbor. In mid-month the air forces began intensive bombing of Axis airfields. They sought not to destroy Axis combat aircraft but to help annihilate the enemies' air transport fleet. As the Axis supply situation in Tunisia deteriorated, because of loss of shipping to the Allied coastal air forces, they pressed their air transport fleet into the gap. The Axis transports carried fuel as their number one cargo. The NASAF attacks, together with fighter interceptions, choked off this last line of supply. Only a small fraction of the transports survived. This catastrophe, combined with the losses suffered at Stalingrad, virtually destroyed German air transport capability for the remainder of the war.

The Battle of the Ruhr absorbed Bomber Command's attention with large raids on Essen and Duisburg. Other raids smashed the Baltic ports of Kiel, Rostock, and Stettin. In Central Germany the command swiped at Frankfurt and Mannheim. In the south Bomber Command gave Stuttgart a rap. The raids on the Ruhr, which were within Oboe's range, proved far more damaging than raids in which PFF Halifaxes and Stirlings used H2S to mark targets. However, H2S supplied a good contrast between water and land allowing for excellent results on Stettin. After 20 April, the lengthening hours of sunlight cut into the command's range, encouraging more concentration on the Ruhr. Shorter range also meant heavier bomb loads because less fuel was required. Harris fulfilled other commitments by sending two large raids to La Spezia in northern Italy.

Not every mission succeeds; some go completely awry. One such mission occurred on the night of 16 April. Harris sent out more than 300 Lancasters to make the long flight to Pilsen, Czechoslovakia, where they would bomb one of the largest armaments complexes in Europe, the Skoda Works. Since the target was far beyond the range of Oboe, the attack used H2S. The H2S operators mistook the town of Dobrany for Pilsen (a 12-mile error) and a large mental hospital for the Skoda Works. Two hundred eighty-five bombers proceeded to deluge the area with 691 tons of bombs—a nightmarish absurdity that even Franz Kafka would have found difficult to express. The attacking force suffered grievously too. It lost 36 aircraft, more than 12 percent of the attacking force.

Note

1. Letter, Frank M. Andrews to Allen Andrews, 28 April 1943, cited in Dewitt S. Copp, "Frank M. Andrews: Marshall's Airman," in Frisbee, *Makers of the United States Air Force*, 70.

May

3 May: AAF: General Andrews dies in air crash in Iceland en route to the United States. Allies launch final ground assault in Tunisia.

14 May: Axis forces in Tunisia surrender. Eighth Air Force— sends out its largest heavy bomber raid to date, 198 aircraft against Kiel and other targets.

16–17 May: Bomber Command—attacks the Mohne, Eder, Sorpe, and Schwelm dams with Lancasters of 617 Squadron.

17 May: Eighth Air Force—After a mission against the submarine pens at Lorient, France, the crew of the *Memphis Belle*, a B-17, become the first members of the Eighth Air Force to complete their 25-mission combat tour of duty. The crew returned to the United States to conduct a war bond drive.

18 May: CCS—approves a new plan for an Anglo-American Combined Bomber Offensive. The plan made the destruction of the German fighter force the first objective and gave, in order, priority to the following targets: submarine yards and bases, the aircraft industry, ball bearings, and oil. Approves Operation Tidalwave, which temporarily sent two B-24 groups already flying with the Eighth AF, and one destined for it, to the Ninth AF to conduct a special one-time raid on Ploesti.

31 May: Bomber Command—last operation by No 2. Group under BC, transferred to Tactical Air Force. Last operation by Bostons, Venturas, and Mitchells of No. 2 Group under BC.

In May 1943 seven of RAF Bomber Command's eight raids of 100 or more heavy bombers assailed the Ruhr. On the nights of 4 and 23 May, the command hit Dortmund: first with 1,759 tons of ordnance (including 816 tons of incendiaries) and then with

764 bombers that dropped 2,518 tons (including 1,211 tons of incendiaries). On the night of 25–26 May, the command pummeled Düsseldorf with almost 2,330 tons of bombs (1,070 tons of incendiaries) and, on 29 May, 644 heavy bombers rained 2,123 tons (1,116 incendiaries) on the Barmen area of Wuppertal. In that one night units of Bomber Command destroyed 90 percent of the built-up area of Barmen.* The bombing also inflicted tremendous damage on Dortmund. The command's bombing proved so effective that by the end of May the industrial haze shielding the Ruhr almost disappeared, revealing the extent of damage and the location of as yet undamaged targets. In the remaining large raid of the month, Harris tried again for Pilsen. This time 150 bombers correctly identified the target, but landed almost all their bombs in a field outside the plant. The Skoda Works led a charmed life throughout the war.[1]

Before No. 2 Group transferred from Bomber Command to the newly created British 2d Tactical Air Force, also stationed in England, it continued low-level daylight raids against power stations and rail facilities in northern Europe. On 27 May it conducted one of its most interesting raids on the optics manufacturing center of Jena in eastern Germany. Three aircraft struck the Zeiss Optics Company (at that time the manufacturer of some of the world's finest and most advanced optical equipment), two hit the city, and three went after the Schott Glass Company (maker of naval optics, which had much earlier, given its name to a certain type of barware). The raid cost two aircraft. Although no damage assessment was possible, the raid may have delayed some production or thrown highly sensitive equipment out of kilter. On the other hand the raid may have inflicted no useful damage whatsoever other than putting the town and its specialized workforce on edge and on notice that the war had reached them.

In May 1943 the Eighth's strength—bombers in-theater—increased from 379 to 605 while combat-ready aircraft ex-

---

*The "built-up area" refers to the portions of the city in which the majority of the ground is covered with buildings. Such buildings may be of any type, from industrial structures to shops and residential areas. In its usage by RAF Bomber Command, the term is a euphemism for city area.

panded from 161 to 209. The Eighth doubled the number of days it sent out missions from four (the number flown in April) to eight. Targets included U-boat pens and airfields in France, U-boat construction yards in Germany, and an aircraft plant in Antwerp. On 29 May the Eighth began experimenting with the YB-40, a long-range escort aircraft. The YB-40 was a variant of the B-17, designed as a convoy escort, not a fighter. The AAF and the Eighth had no clearly thought-out doctrine of tactical use, one reason the Eighth needed to experiment with it. Those who conceived it and pushed for its introduction—Eaker begged for the plane—seemed to have envisioned it as a heavy gun platform stationed at the weak spots in bomber formations. The aircraft was armed with several more .50-caliber machine guns than a regular bomber, including two power-operated upper turrets; it had substantial armor plating and extra ammunition for the gunners. So armed, it weighed more than a B-17 with a full bomb load. With its excess weight the YB-40 could not climb as fast as or keep station with a regular B-17 loaded with bombs, let alone keep up with a much lighter B-17 returning home after releasing its bombs. In short the YB-40 attenuated the formation it was supposed to defend. Nor could it protect stragglers and its armor could not withstand direct hits from the large caliber (23 mm or 30 mm) German cannon shells.[2] After a few flights, the Eighth abandoned the YB-40.

Following the Axis surrender in Tunisia, the Allied air forces shifted to new target priorities. NASAF and the Ninth Air Force worked over ports and airfields in Sardinia and Italy. They saved their heaviest blows for Sicily—the Allies had already agreed that it would be the site of their next major ground operation. Allied bombers struck both ends of the ferry crossing the Strait of Messina. On 11 May 100 B-17s attacked the city of Marsala on Sicily but not its port, which served as a transshipment point for Tunisia. Two days later 102 B-17s struck the Sardinian city of Cagliari. No. 205 Group followed up the raid that evening with 23 more bombers directed at the city. Both raids were seemingly intended to weaken the morale of the Italian people as well as to keep the Axis powers in doubt as to the next Allied goal in the Mediterranean—Sardinia or Sicily.

Notes

1. The Pilsen complex remained so intact that at the end of the war it still had its complete set of jigs, gauges, and related equipment for production of the Me-109 fighter. These Czech-built fighters were the first combat aircraft of the Israeli air force.

2. Craven and Cate, *Torch to Pointblank*, 2:680.

Pointblank

In mid-May 1943 Roosevelt, Churchill, and their chiefs of staff met in Washington for the Trident Conference. Their agenda included the so-called Eaker Plan. The plan, prepared by the Eighth Air Force, had Portal's full support and the co-operation of British intelligence and economic agencies. Based on the questionable assumption that the Eighth had proved its case that daylight bombing deep into Germany could succeed, the plan did not claim that strategic bombing would win the war. Rather it posited that a cross-channel invasion would not succeed without extensive strategic air operations beforehand. The plan proposed a buildup of the Eighth to 1,750 heavy bombers by January 1944 and 2,700 by April 1944. As originally written, the plan had advocated coordinated operations by Bomber Command and the Eighth Air Force. The Eighth was to conduct precision daylight bombing missions and Bomber Command would follow with area attacks at night. Harris, however, refused to be bound by plans other than his own. He managed to water down the plan thoroughly before it reached Washington so that he retained the autonomy to direct Bomber Command operations as he saw fit.

The American plan listed four primary and two secondary target systems consisting of a total of 76 targets. As proposed, the bombing campaigns would destroy at least 50 percent of each target system. The major target systems included submarine construction yards, the aircraft industry, the ball bearing industry, and oil production. To succeed, the bombers would have to knock out Ploesti, Rumania, the major source of Germany's natural petroleum. The secondary systems included production of synthetic rubber and military transport vehicles.

The planners could not ignore the increasing opposition of the German day and night fighter forces. Consequently, they made the destruction of those forces an overarching consideration. Before the Allies could successfully attack the other targets, they would have to greatly weaken the Luftwaffe's defenses. The Allies planned to accomplish this task with a systematic bombing campaign directed against fighter assembly and engine factories, including those deep in Germany.[1] The requirement for daylight deep penetration attacks beyond the range of friendly fighter escorts was the Achilles' heel of the plan. If the Americans could not conduct deep precision missions against these plants, with acceptable losses, then the entire plan would unravel. It would take nine long, bloody months before the AAF significantly crippled the German day fighter force, not only with strikes on the aircraft industry but with attritional air-to-air combat between fighter aircraft. The deployment of large numbers of long-range escort fighters, a doctrinal development not anticipated by this plan, would prove decisive in turning the tide. On 10 June Portal issued a directive reflecting the CCS's approval of the plan (including Harris's revisions) to Eaker and Harris. The CCS officially designated the American portion of the plan Operation Pointblank.

At the Trident Conference the CCS also approved Operation Tidalwave—a plan for a large, extremely low-level raid on Ploesti that would be launched from airfields near Benghazi in North Africa. The range of flight, almost 1,700 miles round-trip, required B-24s, but the Ninth Air Force had only two B-24 groups: the 98th and 376th. To augment the Ninth, the CCS detached two B-24 groups (the 44th and 93d) already in service with the Eighth and one group (389th) scheduled to join the Eighth and sent them to North Africa. Once again the Eighth paid the bill for someone else's game.

Note

1. Craven and Cate, *Torch to Pointblank*, 2:367–76.

The Combat Tour
and Aircrew Survival

On 17 May 1943 the men who flew a B-17 named the *Memphis Belle* became the first Eighth Air Force heavy bomber aircrew to complete their initial combat tour (25 missions). The idea of a defined limit to frontline combat flying consisting of either a set number of missions or hours of flight time after which the individual members of an aircrew would be exempt for at least several months from further frontline duty was unique to the Anglo-Americans. In every other air force participating in World War II, an aviator flew until he died or was physically incapable of flying his aircraft. As a result of this practice, fighter pilots like Gunther Rall of Germany and Saburo Saki of Japan amassed astounding totals of enemy planes shot down. Since Axis aviators flew unlimited numbers of missions, the vast majority of them were condemned to die from hostile action or in an accident. For the British or Americans, considerations of the morale of combat crews and the need for individuals with combat experience to serve as aviation instructors dictated a less ruthless personnel policy that allowed aircrew members to hope for survival.

By the end of 1940 the question of aircrew survival in the RAF had become a major issue. All could see that the war in the air was deadly and likely to continue for a considerable period. Just as in 1915 when the British army realized that trench warfare was to be the norm and that it had to develop some policy providing for relief and rehabilitation for the frontline soldiers, so too did the burgeoning loss rates of the air war in WWII dictate some method of providing relief for aviators. Such a standard would, of course, have to provide combat flyers a reasonable chance of survival. The Air Ministry set that chance at a 50 percent aircrew survival rate for a single tour of duty. In January 1941 it recommended guidelines on the length of combat tours based on the special conditions confronting each of the RAF's major commands:

Army Cooperation Command—five months in the face of the enemy or 200 hours' operational flying.

Fighter Command—200 hours' operational flying with latitude both ways.

Bomber Command—after 30 sorties not exceeding 200 hours' flying time.

Coastal Command—unable to assess a limit and wish to deal with each case on its merits.

While these guidelines limited the length of a single tour in the RAF, they did not limit the number of tours an individual might have to serve. Aviators were expected to serve a second tour after spending nine months as an instructor in an operational training unit. The members of each aircrew and their circle of friends, however, with their horizons narrowed to a concentrated focus on their own current tour and on the survival of themselves and that of their closest associates, tended not to look beyond their current tours. In August 1942, when Bomber Command established the Pathfinder force and gave its members a single continuous tour of 45 missions, Harris eliminated consideration of flying hours and set the standard tour at 30 missions for bomber crews. He specified that the squadron commanders verify that each crew had in fact bombed the aiming point before certifying that a crew had completed a mission successfully. On 8 May 1943 the Air Ministry formalized the tour for the entire service (RAF), specifying a first tour of 30 missions and a second tour of not more than 20 missions for Bomber Command. This rule remained in force for the remainder of the war. As John Terraine states in his fine history of the RAF in World War II, "the tour of operations, with its definite promise of relief, was a sheet anchor of morale in Bomber Command. It made the unbelievable endurable."[1]

The AAF in Europe followed a path similar to the RAF. In late December 1942, General Spaatz fixed the policy for combat crew replacement.[2] On 31 December 1942, Headquarters Eighth Air Force issued the following announcement:

1. Combat personnel in the Eighth Air Force will be relieved from combat duty upon the completion of 30 sorties and 200 hours. They may be relieved at the discretion of the Commanding Generals of the Fighter, Bomber, and Air Support Commands, after completion

of 25 missions and 150 hours where circumstances in their opinion warrant.

2. The relief of combat personnel will not be contingent upon the availability of replacements. If necessary, units will be operated at reduced strength until such time as replacement personnel is available.

3. All combat crews will be informed of the contents of this memorandum immediately.[3]

In explaining his reasoning for the tour limits to Arnold, Spaatz noted, "that the British had long ago learned the necessity for setting up an operational yardstick."

He had not set guidelines earlier for the two air forces under his command, the Eighth and Twelfth, only because he had lacked sufficient data as to where to draw the line. He had one heavy bomber unit, the 97th Bombardment Group, that already had completed more than 20 missions, another that had completed 15, and several between 10 and 15 missions. "All of us," Spaatz remarked, "who have visited these units were immediately impressed with their weariness and the first question the crews ask is, What will be the yardstick?" He continued, "We anticipate a decided lift in morale and sustained efficiency as a result. I do not mean to convey the impression that our crews are losing taste for the fight or showing the white feather. Nothing can be farther from the truth. . . . I urge you to have the Air Staff begin immediately planning the combat crew replacement based on this yardstick."[4]

Given the unequivocal wording of the Eighth's memorandum and their own limited horizon, the bomber crews naturally regarded this policy as an ironclad guarantee of relief. Even more than that the crews apparently came to assume that this policy capped their combat service at one tour, after which they would not be sent into combat again. This assumption was contrary to the intentions of the AAF leadership and led to much anger and misunderstanding later in the war as the AAF made provisions to recycle combat veterans back into combat for another stint of action after they had served a tour in the United States. For the Eighth, whose losses continued to mount, the tour soon became capped at the lower limit (25 missions), where it remained until February 1944.

Lower loss rates for AAF heavy bombers in North Africa and the Mediterranean led to modifications. By 1944 the crews of the Fifteenth Air Force had to complete a tour of 50 missions.

In mid-February 1944, before the AAF had gained air superiority over Europe, Arnold notified his field commanders that

> A serious factor which is causing a critical shortage of crews is the institution of local theater policies concerning the return of combat crews to the United States after completion of an arbitrary number of missions.

> When the opposition was much stronger than now it might have been all right to establish local policies such as returning combat personnel after an arbitrary time period, without regard to the adequacy of replacements, the importance of the operation, and above all, the actual capacity of the individuals in question for continued combat. However, conditions will change once the German and Japanese air forces pass their peak. The life expectancy of all our crews will improve with the increase in strength in our Air Forces and the decrease in strength of our enemies.

> If you have made any policies or understandings that combat personnel will be returned to the United States after fulfilling such arbitrary conditions as I have just described those policies will be rescinded at once. Our combat personnel must understand that we plan to use combat crews in accord with war demands.[5]

Doolittle, who had already begun to consider lengthening the tour in January 1944, immediately complied.

To maintain aircrew morale, badly hit by this change in policy, he announced that crews would be "*eligible* [emphasis in original] for relief from further combat duty after 30 sorties." He added, "these figures are only expressions of the lower limits which crews should reach and are only temporary guides to be revised periodically in accordance with existing conditions. Crews will not necessarily be relieved after the completion of that period of combat, but if the command is at a high state of effectiveness, losses are as predicted, and the anticipated flow of replacements is satisfactory, crews may [sic] be removed from active participation in combat operations at the discretion of their commanders."[6]

Spaatz and Doolittle strongly urged the adoption of a policy that crews finishing a combat tour should be returned to the United States for a 30-day leave, exclusive of travel time, and then return to their combat units.[7] Arnold replied that he would do so if possible. In the meantime, to meet the anticipated requirements for aircrew replacements, he had instituted a cut in bombardment crew training from three to two and one-half months and would begin sending out some Training Command instructor pilots as combat replacements.[8] It is perhaps incidental that the imposition of this new combat tour policy coincided with a great increase in the number of American bomber crews interning themselves in Sweden and Switzerland: a problem that would plague the Eighth until the liberation of France in late August 1944. In July 1944 when the Eighth routinely flew two missions a day over France and Germany, Doolittle again raised the tour to 35 missions, where it stayed until war's end. The increase in tour length angered the crews and lowered morale. The evidence does not show that the lengthened tour and the consequent unhappiness of the aircrews caused greater inefficiencies, nor did it condemn a substantially greater number of men to death, wounding, or capture. As Arnold had predicted, somewhat prematurely (the Eighth's loss rate did not show a large decline until May 1944), more aircraft and weakened opposition meant that more missions could be flown before a crew had a less than 50 percent chance of survival.

In its own initial planning, the AAF had anticipated loss rates that exceeded those actually encountered. In its worst month, October 1943, the Eighth suffered a combat loss rate of almost 9 percent. When one factors in the number of aircrews returned to the United States after completing their combat tours and noncombat assignment or leave, the Eighth did exceed its 15 percent replacement rate on some occasions. The AAF based its personnel calculations on a sustained attrition figure—which included losses from all causes—of 15 percent.

Although the Air Staff steadily reduced the planning loss rate, the difference between that figure and reality provided a manpower cushion that eased the strain of expansion and allowed the service to increase the total number of combat aircraft in service with each squadron because it had the crews to fly them.[9] It also allowed the service to plan to provide, although it failed to do so, for double heavy bomber crews for each heavy bomber of the Eighth and Fifteenth in 1944. In fact by the last months of the war, the AAF's requirement for air-crews had dropped to the point that it turned over tens of thousands of its personnel, aviation cadets scheduled for flight training as well as ground crew, to the US Army as replacements for the infantry.

Although bankers and investment counselors speak of the miracle of compound interest—a fascinating subject for one with money to save—the inexorable workings of the aircraft loss rate have a great deal more immediacy and relevance to the aircrews subjected to them. In addition a considerable time lag exists between the actual reduction of the loss and the aircrews' perception of the reduction. The crews continue to react as if the old rates, especially if they were high, are still operative. This circumstance is most visible to the elements in the chain of command closest to combat units. At AAF headquarters in Washington it was all too easy to look at the personnel training, replacement, and loss charts and to speak of loss rates of "only" 2 percent or to applaud the drop in the loss rate from 3 to 2 percent. For a bomb crew in the Fifteenth Air Force's 99th Bombardment Group, a 2 percent loss rate still meant that they had less than a 40 percent chance of completing their required tour of 50 missions without becoming casualties.

Notes

1. Terraine, *Time for Courage*, 527. This discussion of the RAF's decisions regarding combat tours is based entirely on Terraine's groundbreaking study (520–37) of this question and of the ticklish matter of "lack of moral fiber," a term used to describe aircrews that were unable to complete their tours for nonphysical reasons.

2. Notes on a series of conferences between Generals Spaatz, Eaker, and Doolittle on 21 December and subsequent conferences, Generals Spaatz and Eaker, 24–25 December 1942, Spaatz Papers, Diary. See item no. 13.

3. Memorandum No. 75-1, HQ Eighth Air Force, 31 December 1942, AFHSO, microfilm reel A5866, fr. 1137.

4. Letter, Spaatz to Arnold, 27 December 1942, Spaatz Papers, Diary.

5. Letter, Arnold to Nathan Twining, CG Fifteenth Air Force [and all numbered air force commanders], 11 February 1944, Eaker Papers, Manuscript Division, Library of Congress, Washington, DC, Box 22.

6. Memo, Doolittle to Arnold, subject: Policy on Relief of Combat Crews, 4 March 1944, Spaatz Papers, Diary. The policy announced in this letter was publicized to the flight crews on same date.

7. 1st ind., Spaatz, 7 March 1944, to Memo, Doolittle to Arnold, subject: Policy on Relief of Combat Crews, 4 March 1944, Spaatz Papers, Diary.

8. Letter, Arnold to Spaatz, 29 March 1944, Spaatz Papers, Diary.

9. Letter, Arnold to Nathan Twining, CG Fifteenth Air Force [and all numbered air force commanders], 11 February 1944, Eaker Papers, Box 22.

June

10 June: CCS—directive to Portal marks official beginning of the Combined Bomber Offensive. The RAF will conduct city-area attacks at night, while the Americans will strike precise targets by day.

20–21 June: Bomber Command—aircraft attacking German targets from England proceeded to Northwest Africa for first time. First use of the master bomber technique.

26 June: Ninth Air Force—three B-24 Groups on loan from the Eighth finish arriving at airfields near Benghazi.

In June 1943 RAF Bomber Command continued to engage in the battle of the Ruhr. In eight great raids on Düsseldorf, Bochum, Oberhausen (twice), Krefeld, Mulheim, Wuppertal, and Gelsenkirchen, the command dropped 12,354 tons of bombs in 3,617 effective sorties. However, the command did not come away unscathed. It lost 232 bombers in combat, most to night fighters, for a loss rate of almost 6.5 percent of the force engaged. In the long term an air force cannot sustain losses at such a level. At that rate, less than 12 percent of the original aircrews will have survived after 30 missions. Harris had set his sustained acceptable loss rate at 5 percent. Although replacement aircraft and crews may maintain the paper strength of the bomber fleet, the continued high loss of experienced frontline aviators would dilute the overall experience level of the force. As the force becomes less skilled, accident and combat losses increase and can result in a downward spiral of further loss of efficiency of the force. In the air, as well as on the land and sea, the price for experience is blood. Outside the Ruhr, the command flew two large raids against the city of Cologne and two raids against small targets requiring precision or accurate bombing: Le Creusot, France, and Friedrichshafen, Germany. On the night of 19 June, Bomber Command flew 273 effective sorties and dropped 842 tons of bombs in a repeat attack on the Schneider Armaments Works at Le Creusot, France. On the next night 59 Lancasters hit the zeppelin plant at Friedrichshafen on the shores of Lake Constance. The plant manufactured Wurzburg radars employed to control German night fighters. Moonlight and the strong radar return differentiating water and land aided the attackers as did the use of two new techniques, a timed run using offset bombing and the introduction of the "master bomber." The master bomber orbited the target and directed the strike by radio. This technique corrected for faulty placement of markers and other mistakes. Once the raiders finished, they flew on to North Africa—the first Bomber Command aircraft to fly a shuttle mission between the two areas. On the return leg of their journey, they bombed La Spezia, Italy.

The Eighth sent out eight missions during the month but weather forced the recall of one. Four attacked targets in Germany beyond fighter escort range. A mission on 11 June against the Wilhelmshafen U-boat yards lost eight aircraft out of 218 effective sorties. Two other missions suffered much heavier losses. On 13 June the Eighth flew a raid to Kiel and Bremen and lost 26 planes out of 182 effective sorties. Meanwhile, a strike on the synthetic rubber plant at Huls lost 16 out of 183 effective sorties. On 25 June the Eighth attacked a convoy off the German island of Wangerooge, not far from Wilhelmshafen. This mission against ships under way was for the Eighth, unlike other American air forces, almost unique. Out of 167 effective sorties, it lost 18 bombers. Continued losses on such a scale thrust the Eighth into the same manpower problems that also seemed to loom for Bomber Command. For both air forces continuous high losses would not just cause personnel and morale problems, but might do incalculable damage to the fighting spirit of all their aircrews, whose operations already tested them to their limits. In its other missions the Eighth bombed airfields and aircraft plants in France and gates and locks at St. Nazaire. Its aviators completed 333 effective sorties at a cost of 17 bombers. On 22 June three new B-17 Groups—the 100th, the 381st, and the 384th—began operations with the Eighth. Their presence did not increase the Eighth's overall strength because it gained three inexperienced groups while loaning two experienced B-24 groups and one new B-24 group to the Ninth Air Force in the Mediterranean.

In the Mediterranean NASAF began the month by joining the Ninth Air Force in the effort to reduce the island of Pantelleria, which lies between Sicily and Cape Bon, Tunisia, to a surrender. The island posed an obstacle to the upcoming Anglo-American invasion of Sicily. After several days of aerial bombardment, the island's already demoralized garrison, composed entirely of low-quality Italian reservists, surrendered as the invading troops began their run into shore. The AAF touted the surrender as a great victory for airpower, but, as subsequent events in Europe and the Pacific would demonstrate, the quality of the garrison counted for much more than the quantity of the bombs. NASAF and the Ninth continued deception and preinvasion bombing of airfields and ports in Sardinia, Sicily, and Italy. They paid particular attention to both ends of the Messina ferry. As noted above, three groups of B-24s detached from the Eighth joined the Ninth by 26 June. They would participate in a planned attack on the source of 60 percent of Hitler's natural petroleum—Ploesti, Rumania.

July

5–13 July: Battle of Kursk—last major German offensive on eastern front. Halted by Hitler after attack blunted by Soviets to send armored reinforcements to Italy. Soviets gain and hold strategic initiative for remainder of the war in the east.

10 July: Allied ground forces invade Sicily.

19 July: Ninth Air Force and NASAF—attack Rome marshaling yards with 250 heavy bombers.

24 July: Eighth Air Force—first bomber and crew interned in Sweden.

24–25 July: Bomber Command—first use of "Window," in connection with bomb raid on Hamburg. Strike causes firestorm.

25 July: Mussolini falls from power. His successors begin secret peace negotiations with the Allies.

28 July: Eighth Air Force—P-47s first use jettisonable gasoline tanks (drop tanks). War Cabinet approves bombing of Italy to encourage it to surrender.

31 July: A radio broadcast by General Eisenhower warns the Italian government and people of more bombing if Italy does not capitulate.

In July 1943 the Eighth grew to a strength of 15 heavy bomber groups, but, because some units were detached to the Mediterranean, it gained little in operational strength. The number of heavy bombers ready for combat and deployed to units increased from 365 in June to 396 in July. Good weather and long, sunlit days allowed the Eighth to send out 10 missions. The first three, with P-47 escorts, plastered French airfields, aircraft engine and assembly plants, and locks and gates at St. Nazaire. The attackers lost 15 aircraft out of 666 effective sorties. In a fourth raid on 17 July, two new B-17 groups—the 385th and the 388th—attacked the Fokker aircraft plant in Amsterdam on their inaugural mission. Cloud cover hindered their aim, but the crews, who were determined to complete their first mission satisfactorily, missed the aiming point and killed 150 Dutch civilians. On 24 July the Eighth attacked Norway for the first time. It went after two targets. Forty-one bombers flew against U-boat facilities in Trondheim fjord; another 167 bombers struck the hydroelectric facilities at Heroya. Allied intelligence suspected that the Germans were using the power produced to manufacture heavy water, a substance necessary to develop atomic weapons. The missions suffered one loss, a B-17 that crashed in Sweden. Its crew was the first of many American flyers interned in that country. Unlike the Swiss, who imprisoned aircrews in accordance with the strictest definition of the Geneva conventions for the duration of the war, the Swedes treated interned airmen humanely and returned them in 1944 in exchange for Allied equipment and aircraft.

From 25 July to the end of the month, the Eighth sent five raids into Germany. On the 25th, B-17s attacked an airfield in Warnemünde and U-boat yards in Kiel and Hamburg. The next day the Americans dispatched raids against the U-boat yards in Hamburg and rubber plants in Hannover. Weather interfered with operations on 28 July, but several groups struggled through to bomb aircraft plants in Kassel and Oschersleben. The Eighth finished with raids on 29 and 30 July against U-boat yards in Kiel and aircraft plants in Warnemünde and Kassel.

A deciphered German report on damage inflicted at Kassel indicated that production would have to stop at one plant for several days. However, the Eighth Air Force intelligence officer who presented the briefing on damage assessment apparently failed to note a key piece of information in the German message, which stated that "there was here and there serious damage to buildings [but only] slight damage to machinery."[1] Here was a clear indicator that while bombing might damage buildings extensively, it had much less adverse impact on aircraft production machinery and other machine tools, jigs, and gauges. Throughout the war US intelligence failed to appreciate this fact and, as a consequence, consistently overestimated damage inflicted on German industry. A dedicated workforce with its tools can continue production without a roof.

The loss rates of the missions over France and Germany told different tales. Over France, the Eighth lost 21 bombers out of 796 effective sorties, a rate of 2.6 percent. Fighter escorts (from the RAF and P-47s of the USAAF), lightly defended targets, and the Luftwaffe's disinclination to defend fringe targets in France all contributed to low losses. The forces sent into Germany lost 87 bombers out of 839 effective sorties, a rate of 10.4 percent—quadruple the rate over France. Heavier flak, more and more aggressive Luftwaffe fighters, no friendly escorts over long passages of territory, and the increased distance damaged aircraft had to fly to reach friendly territory added up to far more serious casualties during missions over Germany. The overall loss rate of 6.6 percent for all its missions in Europe jeopardized the long-term sustainability of the Eighth's operations.

In the first two weeks of July, NASAF and the Ninth expended their entire effort in supporting the Anglo-American invasion of Sicily. Before the invasion, the heavy bombers concentrated on Axis airfields. However, on 8 July the focus changed as B-24s struck the main telephone exchange on Sicily. The next day a squadron of B-24s hit Luftwaffe headquarters on the island. After the invasion, the heavies divided their attention between airfields and marshaling yards in Sicily and southern Italy.

In early and mid-July RAF Bomber Command concluded the battle of the Ruhr with heavy attacks on two cities—Cologne and Aachen—associated with but not in the Ruhr, and on Gelsenkirchen. Additionally, Bomber Command sent 277 heavy bombers against Turin on the night of 12 July, helping to distract Italian attention from the south, where the Allies had invaded Sicily, and to fix defenses in the north. In a strike on 15 July, 157 Halifaxes, attacking from between 6,000 to 10,000 feet with good illumination from moonlight, struck the Peugeot Works at Montbéliard, France, 20 miles from the Swiss border. However, the marking bombs fell 700 yards from the aiming point, and the bombers missed by another 250 yards. Six hundred bombs landed on the town, but only 30 hit the factory. Production went on unimpeded; 123 civilians died.[2]

In late July Bomber Command embarked on its second large-scale campaign of the year, the battle of Hamburg. It began with heavy attacks on Hamburg (24, 27, and 29 July and 2 August) and Essen (25 July). During the first raid on Hamburg, Bomber Command employed a new weapon for the first time: metal-coated strips of chaff called Window. It did not affect the German Freya search radar, but did disrupt their Wurzburg radar, which helped to control and direct night fighters and provided fire control for flak. Window also affected the airborne radar carried by Luftwaffe night fighters. Many aircrews owed their lives to it. Perhaps many more might have lived, had not the War Cabinet delayed introducing Window for more than a year in fear that German bombers would use it against British defenses.

The Hamburg Firestorm

Bomber Command's four raids on Hamburg leveled the center of the city. The second raid (27 July) sent a wave of shock and fear throughout the Reich. Hamburg presented an almost perfect H2S picture, which enabled the marking aircraft to drop their pyrotechnics close to the aiming point. They hit approximately one mile from the aiming point, well within the built-up portion of the city. The bombers delivered a highly concentrated attack with little "creep back."*

The raid created the first man-made firestorm started by aerial bombardment. Several factors combined to create the phenomenon of a firestorm: favorable weather conditions—dry with low humidity (it had not rained in Hamburg for several days); many large fires started in a short time; and the bomb mix, which included large percentages of incendiaries and high explosives, blanketed the built-up city area. The incendi-

---

*Refers to the tendency of bomb aimers or bombardiers following the formation's lead aircraft to release their weapons a few ticks earlier than the preceding bombs. Thus, the bombs appear to creep back from the aiming point, reducing the bomb concentration and producing an elongated bomb pattern.

ary bombs used included large numbers of small incendiary bomblets designed to penetrate the typical slate roof of a German house. These bomblets, weighing only four pounds each, would lodge in attics where they would start a fire that would be difficult to extinguish. High-explosive bombs with delayed fuses (from a few minutes up to several hours) were used to discourage firefighters from battling blazes or kill them outright. These high-explosive bombs also drove the people and most fireguards into shelters, smashed water main networks, opened gas mains, created roadblocks, shattered windows, opened up buildings, and created holes in roofs.

Unlike an ordinary large fire, which starts at a single point and spreads by easy stages over the course of several hours, a firestorm is a huge blaze that once started spreads with incredible rapidity and explosiveness. Within 20 minutes after the first attack wave struck Hamburg, two out of three buildings in an 8.5-square-mile area were ablaze. This quick build-up to an intense blaze made firefighting impossible. As the flames broke through the roofs, a column of superheated air shot up to a height exceeding 13,000 feet. This column of air sucked in cooler air at its base, creating a street-level updraft measured at 33 miles an hour. (To panicked individuals at ground level this wind blowing directly toward the maelstrom would have seemed even fiercer.) The resultant gale carried burning material and sparks down streets and raised temperatures of all combustibles in the area to the ignition point. Instead of spreading outwardly, the updraft sucked material from the surrounding area into the firestorm, which then imploded as it exhausted the available fuel supply from the perimeter of the fire.

Seventy percent of the deaths in the firestorm came as a result of carbon-monoxide poisoning. The fire consumed the free oxygen in the area and replaced it with the products of combustion, one of which, carbon monoxide, seeped into the basement bomb shelters killing the occupants painlessly and silently. To have avoided death people would have had to leave their shelters before the fire became too intense, brave the fires along the streets, and face the bombs still coming down. This prospect made it difficult for the authorities to convince people of the danger they risked if they stayed too long in the shelters.[3]

The raid killed 45,000 people. Altogether the four raids forced evacuation of the city. In 2,630 effective sorties the Allies dropped 9,657 tons of bombs and lost 87 bombers. Yet, Hamburg survived. Although the city never recovered, its war factories regained 100 percent of their production levels. Large firms lost only 45 to 50 working days. Its small businesses bore the brunt of the loss, many never reopened during the remainder of the war.

Notes

1. Haines, *ULTRA and the History of the United States Strategic Air Force in Europe*, 43. Written as an intelligence report by USSTAF in September 1945. National Security Agency, Special Research History 013 (SRH-013).

2. Richards, *Hardest Victory*, 187.

3. USSBS, *Physical Damage Division, Fire Raids on German Cities*, vol. 193, 1, 35–37, 47.

Strategic Bombing of Italy

The strategic bombing of Italy illustrates the intertwining of the military, psychological, and political aspects of Allied war making. Bombing may well have had a psychological impact on that nation's will to resist that went beyond the physical damage inflicted by the raids. Before the war British and American strategic bombing doctrine stressed that destroying enemy targets by bombing would adversely affect the morale and the will of the enemy's state and people to resist.[1] As Marshal Ferdinand Foch of France (the supreme Allied military commander) suggested in 1918, bombing population centers might induce the people to disarm their government, in which case public opinion would have had a decisive impact on the outcome of the war. Foch and his followers argued that the more fragile the state and the less committed it and its people were to the war effort, the more susceptible it would be to the application of strategic bombing.[2] Italy and the Balkan states formed the weakest links in the Axis and would seem to have been perfect subjects on which to test this theory. Allied conventional strategic airpower as an instrument of military force acting alone had failed to reduce a single member of the Axis to the state of surrender, thus seeming to have disproved the theory.

The expectations of the prewar airpower theorists were altogether too simplistic. Just as the attack on key enemy capabilities, such as oil and ball bearings, proved immensely difficult to mount and follow through on, so too did the attack on the enemy's will to resist. Authoritarian regimes backed by internal security services of varying efficiency held power in each Axis nation. These regimes, whether based on monarchy, dictatorship, oligarchy, class or party, or some combination of governance, sailed a course between Scylla and Charybdis. To continue the fight meant eventual destruction of their regimes by the Anglo-Americans or the Soviets. Of the two, the Anglo-Americans were preferable, being less prone to ruthlessly destroying their opponents and engaging in wholesale expropriation of private property. On the one hand, a popularly based state likely would make significant decisions not in the interests of the current rulers. On the other, abandoning the fight would bring immediate German overthrow of the regime and subject the nation (and its untrustworthy rulers) to the merciless rigors of a Nazi occupation. Given these circumstances, bombing, even to the point of destruction, presented an alternative no worse than that already in the offing.

However, this is not to imply that bombing did not lower morale and productivity. Nor does it indicate that the Allies did not engage in strategic bombing for direct political and diplomatic objectives. The record suggests, more than has been generally recognized, that some individual bombing campaigns and even particular bombing missions had not just purely military objectives but specific political and diplomatic goals as well. Because of its flexibility, long-range strategic airpower could respond quickly to critical situations, and it had a unique capability to strike targets and populations well beyond the front lines. The Anglo-Americans used strategic bombing to emphasize or further political demands or expectations. The Allies directed the bulk of these political raids against the weaker Axis powers—Italy and the minor Axis allies in the Balkans, Hungary, Bulgaria, and Rumania.

Until the end of May 1940, the Anglo-French Allies had sought to keep Italy out of the war. However, when it became obvious that their attempts had failed, one of the Allies' responses was to establish two airfields near Marseilles, in southern France, from which Bomber Command's Wellingtons could attack the north of Italy, the location of the most efficient portion of the enemy's war production. The march of events soon overwhelmed this initiative. On the night of 11 June, No. 71 Group attempted to conduct its first operation with Wellingtons staging from Marseilles and longer range Whitleys staging from the Channel Islands. No sooner had the Wellingtons landed in France than did local authorities issue categorical orders that the group was not to launch a raid on Italy. The French backed up this order by parking trucks athwart the base runways. Of course, by this date it had become quite clear that France had lost the war. From the point of view of the local authorities, allowing the British to launch bombing attacks on Italy seemed a stroke of madness that might well further antagonize the Italians, who presumably would have a seat at some future peace negotiations between France and her Axis enemies. In the meantime the group commander had received explicit instructions from the Air Ministry to continue the operation. As that perplexed officer pondered his options, the chief of staff of the French air force called the senior RAF commander in France, Air Marshal Arthur Barratt, requesting cancellation of the mission. Barratt elevated the matter to the Air Ministry, which, in turn, instructed him to consult the prime minister, who was visiting French Supreme Headquarters. When informed of the matter, Churchill stated that in his opinion the raid should proceed. No sooner had Barratt received this message than he was informed by No. 71 Group of the state of its runways. Barratt went back to Churchill, who obtained an official authorization from the highest echelons of the French government for the raid. By that time, well after midnight, it was too late for the Wellingtons to take off, but 13 of 36 Whitleys reached Turin and Genoa. On the night of 15 June, eight Wellingtons took off from Marseilles, but only one reached Italy. The next night five of nine Wellingtons reached Italy. The following day the French armistice ended what the RAF official history termed, with some understatement, "a singularly unprofitable venture."[3]

The entire operation put 20 tons of bombs somewhere near targets in Italy with no appreciable physical or psychological effect.

From August 1940 through January 1941, Bomber Command continued its pinpricks on targets in Italy. The command flew a combined total of 170 sorties and delivered 104 tons of ordnance, again with little or no effect. The command did not return to Italy until September 1941 when it attacked two major industrial cities in the north: Turin on the night of 10 September (60 bombers, 75 tons of ordnance) and Genoa on the nights of 26 and 28 September (36 bombers, 27 tons of ordnance). Seven months later, on the night of 12 April 1942, 12 planes from Bomber Command struck Genoa and Turin with 19 tons of ordnance. In the first 28 months of Italy's participation in the war, the RAF launched only 336 sorties and delivered but 350 tons of bombs against targets in Italy. The lack of a concerted effort in Italy by the Allied air forces demonstrated the extremely low priority allotted to operations against Italy, and they had no worthwhile or lasting effects.

In late October 1942 the opening of the British counter-offensive in the western desert at El Alamein and the upcoming Anglo-American invasion of French North Africa, scheduled for 8 November 1942, focused more attention on Italy. On 22 October 1942 Bomber Command began a series of much heavier raids on northern Italy, in particular Genoa, Milan, and Turin. The Allies intended the timing of these raids to distract Italian attention and lower morale. Four raids in October, seven in November, three in December, and one in February 1943 amounted to 1,780 sorties and 3,400 tons of ordnance. In December 1942 American attacks on the Italian mainland began with two small Ninth Air Force attacks on the port of Naples.

From January 1943, throughout the Tunisian campaign and until the invasion of Sicily in July 1943, the Ninth and Twelfth Air Forces and RAF No. 205 Group conducted numerous, fairly small-scale operations against Italy. They struck ports—chiefly Naples, a major supply port for Tunisia; Le Spezia, the main Italian fleet base; and Leghorn (Livorno), a major port serving the northern Italian industrial complex. They hammered airfields such as Foggia and Crotone, which supported Axis air forces in the Mediterranean, and they bombarded marshaling yards in and leading into southern Italy. Although these attacks furthered overall Allied strategy and were carried out by heavy and medium bombers, almost none of them contributed to the mission of the Combined Bomber Offensive—the attack on the Axis war economy and civilian morale.

The successful Allied lodgment in Sicily, the consequent weakening of Mussolini's government, and Allied intelligence all indicated a continuing decline in support for the war effort among the Italian people. These developments seemed to offer the opportunity for missions of great psychological impact.[4] On the night of 12 July, two days after the beginning of the Sicilian campaign, Bomber Command conducted its largest operation to date over Italy, hitting the city area of Turin with 900 tons of bombs (a figure that might cause even a German city somewhat habituated to bombing to stagger).

On 19 July 270 heavy bombers of the Ninth and Twelfth Air Forces struck the marshaling yards in Rome while their medium bombers struck nearby airfields. The raid killed 700 and wounded 1,600.[5] This raid was not ordinary. Rome, in addition to its importance as the enemy's chief city and seat of government, had important military targets. It contained factories manufacturing small arms, heavy machine guns, hand grenades, mortar shells, rifles, fuses, and fire-control instruments, such as artillery sights, range finders, and telescopes. Ten airfields lay within a radius of 10 miles of the city's boundaries. In addition, the city was home to five major radio broadcasting stations.[6] Of the four main north-south rail lines of communication in Italy, three double-tracked lines—the only ones in the country—ran through marshaling yards within the industrialized portions of the city (in Italia most roads still led to Roma). The remaining rail line ran down the Adriatic coast, which made it the least useful line for supporting enemy forces opposing Allied operations in Sicily and southern Italy.[7]

Had raids on Rome caused collateral damage to Vatican City or to any of the other priceless antiquities within the city or the Vatican,* the Allied cause likely would have suffered severe political harm. However, as subsequent Allied deliberations revealed, their concern for collateral damage to Rome focused exclusively on the Vatican, not on antiquities elsewhere in the city or on the average Italian in the street. The Allies had planned the attack on Rome for at least six weeks. General Spaatz had championed the raid since late May 1943. Privately he had expressed great faith in the psychological impact of bombing. As recently as 8 May, he had written a personal friend in Washington, DC, stating "we have ample evidence to clearly indicate that they [B-24s and B-17s] can blast their way through any defenses and destroy the will to fight in any nation which may oppose us."[8]

In early June 1943 Churchill and the CCS visited Eisenhower in his headquarters in Algiers, French North Africa. On 3 June Tedder and Spaatz briefed the CCS on the proposal to bomb Rome.[9] They wished to hit the San Lorenzo rail junction and the San Lorenzo and Littorio marshaling yards to prevent or interfere with the movement of the Hermann Göring Panzer Division from northern Italy and France to Sicily. Tedder and Spaatz noted that the city itself was in little danger from this attack. Moreover, since the objectives lay on the opposite side of the Tiber River three miles from the Vatican, the bombings would pose "practically no danger" to the Holy City. Eisenhower supported the plan.[10] The CCS agreed that the city constituted a legitimate military objective. They found "no valid reason for refraining from bombing this target provided that the attacks be made by day and that due care is taken to prevent damage elsewhere." Upon his return to Washington a week later, Marshall proposed an additional proviso that: "the

---

*The Vatican and Vatican City are used interchangeably here. Vatican City is a small enclave of neutral territory near the city center surrounded by the city that serves as the administrative and spirtual center of the Roman Catholic Church. It is the permanent residence of the pope. Any damage accidentally visited upon the Holy City may have caused negative reactions within the United States, especially among its large Roman Catholic minority. Bombing errors undoubtedly would have alienated Roman Catholics in Germany, occupied Europe, and important Roman Catholic countries in South America.

Vatican . . . be informed that all pilots bombing objectives in Italy [Rome] have been individually and personally instructed to take the utmost precaution to avoid the Vatican area." Churchill and Marshall agreed that each would obtain the consent of his government for the implementation of this action when appropriate in support of the invasion of Sicily.[11]

Although only American aircraft would make the daylight attacks, the British recognized and accepted a joint responsibility for the action. Indeed, five months earlier, the foreign minister, Sir Anthony Eden, had stated in the House of Commons: "We have as much right to bomb Rome as the Italians had to bomb London. We shall not hesitate to do so to the best of our ability and as heavily as possible if the course of the war should render such bombing convenient and helpful."[12]

On 10 June Churchill cabled Roosevelt, "On this side we have never agreed that we would not bomb Rome and we are willing to accept retaliation on Cairo. Today my Cabinet without hesitation supports a proposal that Eisenhower should be authorized to take action against these targets at such time as he considers it most advantageous" to Operation Husky, the invasion of Sicily.[13] Roosevelt agreed, but stipulated that pilots should be carefully briefed as to the location of the Vatican and directed not to drop any bombs on Vatican City. He suggested that the Allies inform the pope in advance of the raid and advise him that enemy planes might attack the Holy See "for the purpose of charging us with an attack on the Vatican."[14] The American JCS supported the president, noting that "while the destruction of these objectives would be of material benefit to the Husky Operation, *the psychological effect would be even more important* [emphasis added]."[15] On 15 June the CCS authorized Eisenhower to undertake the operation when he saw fit as long as he issued prior and thorough instructions to the pilots that they "must not permit any bombs to fall in the Vatican City."[16]

Even after the CCS had issued its decision to bomb Rome's marshaling yards, the possible political fallout from collateral damage continued to trouble the Anglo-Americans. On 18 June the British chiefs of staff, on behalf of the Foreign Office, pointed out that three venerable and important basilica belonging to the

Vatican—St. John Lateran, Santa Maria Maggiore, and St. Paolo—rested on the same bank of the Tiber as the marshaling yards. St. John lay only 1,000 yards from the Lorenzo yard, while Santa Maria and St. Paolo lay 1,500 yards and three miles, respectively, from the same target. They requested that the CCS require Eisenhower to ensure that the aircraft crews received briefings to make every effort to avoid these buildings.[17] The CCS dutifully issued the additional directive.[18]

Four days later, on 22 June, the British chiefs raised another issue. In their opinion it was "most important that bombing of military objectives in [the] close vicinity of Rome should be correctly handled in communiqués and correspondent's stories from North Africa. [The] enemy will be quick to sieze the opportunity of asserting that we have attacked the Shrine of Christendom and thus attempt to create misapprehensions which might not be confined to the Catholic world." The British chiefs suggested careful advance preparation of communiqués and guidance to correspondents that both stressed a clear distinction between the bombing of military targets in "the industrial outskirts of Rome" and bombing the city itself and emphasized, as well, the special selection (in actuality none whatsoever), careful training (none of note), and special briefings of the crews chosen for the mission. They further suggested speedy issuance of the news items to preclude any enemy accounts from prevailing.[19]

At this démarche, the American chiefs became restive. Arnold noted that some of the targets were not in the "industrial outskirts" but were well within the city. He commented, "each time you put a restriction on the operative personnel it makes it that much more difficult for them to bomb their target." Adm Ernest King wanted to know if this meant yet more instruction for Eisenhower. Lt Gen Joseph McNarney, Marshall's deputy chief of staff, remarked, "Rome is an enemy city in enemy territory and we should not lose sight of this fact." The JCS deferred action until the regular CCS meeting of 25 June. At that meeting, Arnold, with the aid of a large-scale map, detailed the exact position of the targets relative to the Vatican and other sacred objects. As Arnold noted, since rail lines ran into the heart of Rome and given "the number of churches in the city, it would be almost impossible to insure that none of these were damaged when the marshaling yards were attacked." Arnold further emphasized the importance of the rail lines to north-south communications in Italy.[20] Then Marshall delivered his views. They amounted to a quintessential statement of the American military's philosophy on making war. "The policy of bombing the marshaling yards in Rome was fully agreed . . . these were an essential military objective which should be attacked. The Allies could not afford to fight this war with one hand tied behind their backs. Not only would the destruction of these yards vitally affect the movement of divisions from north to south, but it would have a strong psychological effect in convincing the Italian populace of our intention to prosecute the war with the utmost vigor. It would be a tragedy if St. Peter's were destroyed, but a calamity if we failed to knock out the marshaling yards."[21] To Marshall, in this case, military considerations outweighed political ones. In a nutshell he summed up the American military's conduct of the war-place military objectives before political goals.

When the discussion of the subject concluded, the CCS agreed to instruct Eisenhower to follow the British chiefs' press coverage recommendations. They deleted the reference to the "industrial outskirts," substituting for it the phrase "most essential railroad military objective." The CCS informed Eisenhower that "none of the above is intended in any way to hinder you in attacking this important military objective as soon as you see fit." They added a request that Eisenhower inform them, if possible, 48 hours before execution of the raid so that the "best possible arrangements may be made regarding the readiness of appropriate releases to the press."[22] Finally, the CCS ordered that guidance on handling the coverage of the operations be sent to the US and British propaganda agencies—the Office of War Information in Washington, the Ministry of War Information in London, and, by inference, the British Psychological Warfare Executive (PWE) in London. The PWE directed Allied propaganda towards enemy and occupied territory.

At the end of June Eisenhower, the recipient of this stream of orders, suggestions, and requests, did as he was supposed to do—exercised his own judgment. He informed the CCS that he had examined the timing of the operation and concluded that "this bombing will have little material effect in delaying movement of supplies and reinforcements" to Sicily. Therefore, he had decided not to divert a large air effort from targets directly concerned with the preinvasion air effort. "On the other hand," he stated, "bombing should have great psychological effect particularly if undertaken shortly after [a] successful landing." He thought that an attack three days after the invasion might be most appropriate and assured the CCS of 48 hours' warning.[23] Eisenhower's seeming hesitancy prompted Adm William Leahy to question the whole operation. If the yards were not important militarily and the effect was to be primarily psychological, why risk damage to the Vatican? Marshall scotched this doubt by noting that German troops would probably not begin to move from northern Italy through Rome until after the invasion occurred. Besides which, "he was implacably determined that no outside considerations should be allowed to interfere with the firm prosecution of the war."[24] Eisenhower chose to delay the bombardment until he could spare the air effort, a week after the invasion, on 19 July. The Allies preceded the raid with leaflets warning the populace, a procedure that placed their own aircrews at increased risk from opposition by an alerted enemy.

The next day's photoreconnaissance showed that the mission scored 130 direct hits on railway stock and tracks, with between 50 and 60 railway cars destroyed in the Littorio yard and even greater damage sustained by the San Lorenzo yard. Although neither the Vatican City nor the three churches singled out by the Foreign Office suffered damage, as Arnold had foretold, the twelfth-century façade of the Basilica of St. Lorenzo without the walls (outside Vatican City), another almost equally venerable edifice, was damaged by bomb blasts. The raid had little lasting material effect on the Germans; Axis work crews repaired the main rail lines and put them back into operation within 48 hours.[25]

However, the raid had significant psychological effects. Six days later a coup removed the Mussolini government. King Victor Emmanuel had approved the plotter's plans in part because of the bombing of the capital. The new government, led by Marshal Pietro Bodaglio, assured its German and Japanese partners that it would fight on. In secret, the new regime attempted to initiate surrender negotiations with the Allies.[26]

On 31 July Eisenhower warned the Italians to surrender or face more bombing. He ordered attacks on the yards in Rome for 3 August.[27] The British war cabinet had consented to issuing this threat three days earlier.[28] On 2 August the apostolic delegate in Washington approached the US State Department with a message from Bodaglio's government transmitted through the Papacy. Bodaglio asked the Anglo-Americans to state the conditions for recognizing Rome as an open city, which would make the city off-limits for further military action. The CCS immediately canceled that raid and future operations against Rome until it received instruction from the president and the prime minister.[29]

Marshall could not reach the president, who had left Washington to prepare for the upcoming Anglo-American Conference to be held in Quebec and for a brief vacation at Birch Island, Ontario. No sooner had he advised Eisenhower not to bomb Rome than Marshall received a transatlantic telephone call from Churchill. The king's first minister stated that he and the war cabinet personally thought that it might be a good thing "at this moment to go ahead with the bombing." Although still not able to reach the president, Marshall, acting on his own responsibility, reversed himself and reauthorized the attack. The order reached Eisenhower too late to return to the original plan, but he rescheduled a raid on Rome for 4 August.[30]

The next day the Anglo-American governments, including the president, had had time to reflect upon the full consequences of the Italian offer—they arrived at different conclusions. The question of Rome's status as an open city presented the Allies with a dilemma. An outright rejection of the proposal when publicized would put the Anglo-American governments in an awkward position with neutral and Catholic world opinion. Neither could they prevent, nor did international law forbid, the Italians from making a unilateral declaration of an open city. If the Allies accepted the proposal, then they might have to honor restrictions (i.e., leave the city free of troops, forbid the transit of troops and matériel through the city, and

145

leave it undefended after they had occupied Rome). This appeared to be an unnecessary concession, especially since the fall of Rome, at that time, did not seem far distant.

The then current and applicable international law, Article 25 of the Hague Convention of 1907, stated, "the attack or bombardment, by whatever means, of towns, villages, dwellings, or buildings which are undefended is prohibited." The drafters of the Hague Convention of 1907 had added the phrase "by whatever means" to the *Regulations Respecting the Laws and Customs of War on Land* adopted by the Hague Convention of 1899, for the specific purpose of including attack by airpower.[31] In September 1943, in response to a query from the president and US chiefs on the question of Rome's status as an open city, the US Army adjutant general asserted that "the test was whether . . . the city was defended." The existence of fortifications within an open city's boundaries was not a sufficient test in and of itself to meet the standard of defense of the city. As the adjutant general noted, only two prior instances of a declaration of an open city had occurred in the course of the current war: Paris in June 1940 and Manila in December 1941. In both cases the defending power had evacuated its government and declared that it would not defend the city, which in effect abandoned the city to the control of the enemy.[32] These precedents would not apply to Rome even if the Italians unilaterally declared Rome an open city as long as both the Italians (who had not yet surrendered) and the Germans continued to refuse land access to the city by defending Italy south of Rome. In practice, if the Allies accepted Rome as an open city without land access to it, then they would be giving a promise not to attack the city by air and would have no means of enforcing enemy troop and movement restrictions within the city.

Early on the morning of 3 August (Washington time), the prime minister wired the president: "War Cabinet think[s] that the time for negotiating about Rome being an open city has passed. Surely there would be the utmost danger that any such bargain would encourage the Italians to make a try for the neutralization of Italy itself."[33] Upon seeing this note, the president promptly replied that he would not interfere with

Eisenhower's plans to attack Rome that day. However, he did state that he would direct that no "further raids be undertaken pending the outcome of negotiations concerning the Bodaglio government's offer through the Vatican."[34] This decision sparked a flurry of messages from Churchill, who feared a "serious reaction in British public opinion" at a premature declaration of Rome as an open city.[35] Churchill counseled against open-city status for the following reasons:

> Acceptance of the proposal would compromise the Allies' declaration of unconditional surrender required from the Axis Powers,

> It would give unwarranted prestige and encouragement to the Bodaglio Government, which, according to ULTRA, had assured its partners [the Axis powers] of its continued resistance, and

> Acceptance of Rome as an open city, in the opinion of the British Chiefs of Staff, would make it impossible to use its communications facilities and airfields, paralyzing any northward advance.[36]

He concluded by requesting that the two leaders discuss the matter at the upcoming Quebec conference, suggesting for the present time that operations against the Italian capital continue "in the interest of putting the maximum political and military pressure on the Italian people and Government."

In view of this exchange, the president asked the US joint chiefs for their opinion. They concurred with their opposite numbers on the British joint staff as to the military difficulties of accepting open-city status for Rome. They suggested that the Allies stall the Italians because "the present military situation is subject to decided change in a short time [the successful end of the campaign in Sicily and the invasion of the Italian mainland scheduled for the first half of September]."[37] The president agreed to temporize.[38] Accordingly, the Allies issued no public or other response to the Italian proposal.

Meanwhile, bad weather over central Italy caused Eisenhower to divert the 4 August attack from Rome to Naples. When he informed the CCS of this change, he added that his fighter and bomber crews were becoming increasingly exhausted because of continuing heavy operations. He stated that he would have to husband his air resources and, therefore, would give priority "to the land battle and to the neutralization of enemy air forces."[39]

During this same period, Portal directed Harris "to heat up the fire."[40] Between 7 and 16 August, Harris sent five large raids against Genoa, Turin, and Milan. On the night of 12 August, Harris struck the city area of Milan with 1,400 tons of bombs. In three attacks on Turin, on the nights of 7, 12, and 16 August, bombs damaged the Fiat factory and inflicted heavy damage on the city itself. Forty percent of its fully built-up area was destroyed or damaged, including the firms of Alfa Romeo, Isotto-Fraschini, Breda, and Pirelli.[41] Objects of culture were not immune from these attacks. The La Scala opera house burned, and the refectory of the Church of Santa Maria delle Grazie was left with only one wall standing—the wall on which Leonardo di Vinci had painted the Last Supper.[42] In spite of the continued damage from bombing and other Allied operations, Bodaglio delayed suing for surrender.

In another tap on Bodaglio's shoulder, Eisenhower diverted his bombers from the support of ground operations. On 13 August, Eisenhower sent heavy bombers from the Twelfth Air Force to strike the Lorenzo marshaling yard while medium bombers attacked the Littoro yards in Rome. These raids killed 221 and wounded 565.[43] The next day the Italians unilaterally declared Rome an open city, promising to withdraw their troops, halt arms manufacturing, and cease firing antiaircraft artillery at Allied aircraft. The 13 August mission took the bombers away from another important target—the Axis forces who were evacuating Sicily.

On 16 August a representative of the Italian government arrived in Portugal to begin serious peace negotiations. Unbeknownst to the Allies, he had departed with his instructions a day before the bombing. The sincerity of the offers convinced the Allies to cancel further attacks on northern Italy. Even if the Italian surrender had gone as the Allies anticipated, this diversion of airpower might have made little difference. The Germans had easily occupied the peninsula upon the Italian surrender and had evacuated their heavy equipment and troops from Sicily with relative ease, a fact that would continue to plague the Allies for months to come.

Eisenhower had planned to send the bombers back to the Italian capital on 15 August.[44] However, Italy's unilateral declaration that Rome would be an open city again led the CCS to cancel further attacks until it received clarification from Roosevelt and Churchill.[45] Eisenhower protested, "all our information indicates attacks on Rome have had [a] most profound effect on Italian morale. We believe here that we shall miss another golden opportunity if these operations are restricted before a bilateral declaration is made."[46] Since all the military chiefs, Churchill, and Roosevelt were gathered at Quebec, the Allies consulted and quickly agreed that the two governments would in no way commit themselves to the question of Rome's open-city status. Although the CCS revoked the bombing halt order that had been sent to Eisenhower, the 13 August raids were the last time heavy bombers attacked targets in Rome.[47] From 14 August until the invasion of the Italian mainland and the simultaneous surrender of the Bodaglio government to the Allies, the heavy bombers had concentrated on counterair and communications targets. The German occupation of Italy, little hindered by the enfeebled and confused Italian armed forces, rendered the status of Rome moot. The Bodaglio government and the king abandoned Rome at the end of September to their erstwhile ally (Germany) and fled to the protection of their new allies. Since it no longer controlled Rome and more than half of the country lay under German occupation, the Italian government's practical power to ensure the openness of its former capital was nil. Italy was no longer a member of the Axis; instead Bodaglio's government was now a cobelligerent of the Western allies. As for the Allies, the strategic bombing of Italy the belligerent power under one set of rules ceased, and the bombing of Italy, the occupied country under a different set of guidelines, such as those set for France, began. Raids on the morale of the Italian people no longer served any purpose.

The strategic bombing of an independent Italy had never been a focus of the Combined Bomber Offensive, although the Anglo-Americans used their heavy bombers extensively to provide indirect support for their ground operations and strategy in the Mediterranean theater. Area raids on the north of Italy and precision missions against Rome were flown to affect the morale of the Italian people. The Allies believed that these were effective psychologically. They helped in a significant, but unquantifiable, manner to bring down Mussolini and prod his successors into peace negotiations. Given the small aerial resources devoted to such raids, they more than justified their cost.

By late summer 1943, the Italian state was a house of cards vulnerable to collapse from any puff of wind or the slightest tremor. Bombing may well have supplied the final push. However, one should not conclude that bombing for psychological effect was a panacea or a tactic suitable for all cases. Just as Pantelleria was not Iwo Jima, Italy was not Germany or Japan. By no stretch of the imagination was strategic air a decisive factor in driving Italy from the war. Its hopeless strategic situation—the state of its armed forces (the navy unable to venture beyond its ports, the air force unable to defend its skies, and its army unable or unwilling to defend its home territory), the utter war weariness of its population, and the fecklessness and morally bankrupt positions of its political leadership—minimized Italy's ability to prolong the unequal conflict. Allied airpower in all its aspects had done much to bring Italy to its knees, but strategic airpower alone was not a major contributor to either its material or psychological defeat. Italy, as did others, bowed to the will of its enemies because of a complex combination of economic, political, geographic, and military pressure, not from the coercion of airpower alone.

Notes

1. For the opinion of the Air Corps Tactical School, the fount of US strategic air doctrine, see the memoirs of one of its instructors and theoreticians, Hansell, *Strategic Air War against Germany and Japan*, 7–14. Royal Air Force (RAF) thinking on this subject has been well documented; see the official history in Webster and Frankland, *Strategic Air Offensive*, 1:50–64. Hansell is quite explicit in stating that US doctrine provided for attacks against both the enemy capacity to resist and his will to resist. RAF thinking was somewhat less clear. The chief of the air staff, Air Chief Marshal Sir Hugh Trenchard, advocated bombing military targets but assumed that the concomitant destruction of civilian lives and property would have a telling effect on the will to resist.

2. Webster and Frankland, 1: 64.

3. Richards, *Fight at Odds*, 147. This work (144–47) contains a full account upon which I have based my own description of this frustrating incident.

4. See Hinsley, *British Intelligence*, vol. 3, pt. 1, 100–103 for a discussion of British Joint Intelligence Committee (JIC) estimates on Italian morale. At least as early as 11 April 1943, the JIC had forecasted an Italian collapse as a result of landings in Sicily. On 6 July 1943 it concluded "that the loss of Sicily, combined with heavy and sustained air attack on northern and central Italy and a landing in southern Italy, might well produce a breakdown in civil administration or an Italian request for an armistice."

5. Molony et al., *Mediterranean and the Middle East*, vol. 5, *Campaign in Sicily 1943 and the Campaign in Italy 3rd September 1943 to 31st March 1944*, 172.

6. Memorandum for the president from the US Joint Chiefs of Staff, 5 August 1943, in NARA, RG 218, records of the Combined Chiefs of Staff, Geographic File, Folder CCS 373.11 Rome (6-10-43).

7. See map: Central Italy Principal Rail Lines, Craven and Cate, *Torch to Pointblank*, 2:556.

8. Letter, Carl Spaatz to Lyle G. Wilson, 8 May 1943, Spaatz Papers, Diary.

9. Memorandum for General Marshall, Admiral King, and General Arnold, from JCS secretary Brigadier General Deane, subject: Bombing Objectives, 10 June 1943, NARA, RG 218, records of the Combined Chiefs of Staff, Geographic File, Folder CCS 373.11 Rome (6-10-43).

10. Message, Churchill to Roosevelt, contained in its entirety in Memorandum from Admiral Leahy, the president's chief of staff, to the US Joint Chiefs of Staff, 10 June 1943, NARA, RG 218, Records of the Combined Chiefs of Staff, Geographic File, Folder CCS 373.11 Rome (6-10-43).

11. Memorandum for General Marshall, Admiral King, and General Arnold, from JCS secretary Brigadier General Deane, subject: "Bombing Objectives," 10 June 1943, NARA, RG 218, records of the Combined Chiefs of Staff, Geographic File, Folder CCS 373.11 Rome (6-10-43).

12. Cited in letter, Cordell Hull, secretary of state [Washington] to Leahy, 10 July 1943, NARA, RG 218, records of the Combined Chiefs of Staff, Geographic File, Folder CCS 373.11 Rome (6-10-43).

13. Message, Churchill to Roosevelt, contained in its entirety in Memorandum from Admiral Leahy, the president's chief of staff, to the US Joint Chiefs of Staff, 10 June 1943, NARA, RG 218, records of the Combined Chiefs of Staff, Geographic File, Folder CCS 373.11 Rome (6-10-43).

14. Message, Churchill to Roosevelt, contained in its entirety in memorandum from Admiral Leahy, chief of staff to the commander in chief of the Navy and the Army [the president], to the US Joint Chiefs of Staff, 10 June 1943, NARA, RG 218, records of the Combined Chiefs of Staff, Geographic File, Folder CCS 373.11 Rome (6-10-43).

15. Memorandum for the president, from Admiral Leahy, Subject: Marshaling Yards at Rome, 11 June 1943, NARA, RG 218, records of the Combined Chiefs of Staff, Geographic File, Folder CCS 373.11 Rome (6-10-43).

16. Message, FAN 138 [WDCMC CM-OUT-6169] , CCS to Eisenhower, 15 June 1943, NARA, RG 218, Records of the Combined Chiefs of Staff, Geographic File, Folder CCS 373.11 Rome (6-10-43).

17. Message, 182255Z, British chiefs of staff to British Joint Staff Mission (Washington), 18 June 1943, NARA, RG 218, records of the Combined Chiefs of Staff, Geographic File, Folder CCS 373.11 Rome (6-10-43).

18. Message, FAN 139 (WDCMC CM-OUT-3201), CCS to Eisenhower, 19 June 1943, NARA, RG 218, records of the Combined Chiefs of Staff, Geographic File, Folder CCS 373.11 Rome (6-10-43).

19. CCS 261, British joint chiefs to the CCS, subject: The Bombing of Rome, 22 June 1943, NARA, RG 218, Records of the Combined Chiefs of Staff, Geographic File, Folder CCS 373.11 Rome (6-10-43).

20. Supplemental minutes, JCS 93d Meeting (6-22-43), item 14, The Bombing of Rome (CCS 261), 22 June 1943, NARA, RG 218, records of the Combined Chiefs of Staff, Geographic File, Folder CCS 373.11 Rome (6-10-43).

21. Supplemental minutes, CCS 99th Meeting (6-25-43), item 9: The Bombing of Rome (CCS 261 and 261/1), 25 June 1943.

22. Message, FAN 144 (WDCMC CM-OUT-1021), CCS to Eisenhower, 25 June 1943, and supplemental minutes, 99th CCS Meeting (6-25-43), item 14, both in NARA, RG 218, records of the Combined Chiefs of Staff, Geographic File, Folder CCS 373.11 Rome (6-10-43).

23. Message, NAF 251 (WDCMC CM-IN-81 [1 July 1943]), Eisenhower to CCS, June 30, 1943, NARA, RG 218, Records of the Combined Chiefs of Staff, Geographic File, Folder CCS 373.11 Rome (6-10-43).

24. Supplemental minutes, CCS 100th Meeting (7-2-43), item 14: Bombing of Rome, 2 July 1943, NARA, RG 218, Records of the Combined Chiefs of Staff, Geographic File, Folder CCS 373.11 Rome (6-10-43).

25. Richards and Saunders, *Royal Air Force, 1939–1945*, vol. 2, *The Fight Avails*, 318. Author's note: "The American heavy bombers dropped approximately 1,300 500-pound bombs—10% of them scored direct hits, a percentage somewhat below the average of results for visual bombing with the Norden bombsight in clear weather."

26. Garland, Smyth, and Blumenson, *The United States Army in World War II: The Mediterranean Theater of Operations*, vol. 2, *Sicily and the Surrender of Italy* , 266.

27. Memorandum, Deane, secretary of the JCS, to Commander Freeman, aide to Admiral Leahy, subject: Recognition of Rome as an Open City, 2 August 1943; memorandum, Deane to Arnold and King, subject: Conditions for establishing Rome as an Open City, 2 August 1943, both in NARA, RG 218, Records of the Combined Chiefs of Staff, Geographic File, Folder CCS 373.11 Rome (6-10-43). Both memos note that AFHQ had scheduled a raid on Rome for the next day.

28. Richards, *Hardest Victory*, 195.

29. Memorandum, Deane, secretary of the JCS, to Commander Freeman, aide to Admiral Leahy, subject: Recognition of Rome as an Open City, 2 August 1943, and memorandum Deane to Arnold and King, subject: Conditions for es-

tablishing Rome as an Open City, 2 August 1943, both in NARA, RG 218, records of the Combined Chiefs of Staff, Geographic File, Folder CCS 373.11 Rome (6-10-43). Both memos note that AFHQ had scheduled a raid on Rome for the next day. For the CCS halt order to Eisenhower see message FAN 181, CCS to Eisenhower, also in NARA, RG 218, records of the Combined Chiefs of Staff, Geographic File, Folder CCS 373.11 Rome (6-10-43).

30. Memorandum for the president, from the chief of staff [Marshall], 3 August 1943, NARA, RG 218, records of the Combined Chiefs of Staff, Geographic File, Folder CCS 373.11 Rome (6-10-43).

31. Parks, "Air War and the Law of War," 16–17. Parks points out that the convention only applied to hostilities between powers that had accepted the convention. Since the only two countries to commit themselves to the Hague Convention of 1907 were Great Britain and the United States, it did not cover military operations in either World War I or II. Parks also notes that that the section of the Hague Convention of 1907 concerning "Bombardment by Naval Forces in Time of War" repeated the prohibition against the attack of undefended cities with an exception that allowed naval authorities to engage in the punitive bombardment of undefended city if its requisition of supplies was declined.

32. Memorandum to the Joint Intelligence Committee, Joint Chiefs of Staff, from Maj Gen Myron C. Cramer, The Judge Advocate General, US Army, subject: Recognition of Rome as an Open City, 22 September 1943, NARA, RG 218, records of the Combined Chiefs of Staff, Geographic File, Folder CCS 373.11 Rome (6-10-43). General Cramer also cited Article 25 of the 1907 Hague Convention and stated, "It has long been a settled principle of international law that an undefended town is immune from attack or bombardment." The Army's chief legal officer clearly held his service to the highest standards.

33. Message 398, former naval person Churchill to the president, 3 August 1943, NARA, RG 218, records of the Combined Chiefs of Staff, Geographic File, Folder CCS 373.11 Rome (6-10-43).

34. Memorandum to Brig Gen Deane from Lt Col Chester Hammond, assistant to the military aide to the president, 3 August 1943, NARA, RG 218, Records of the Combined Chiefs of Staff, Geographic File, Folder CCS 373.11 Rome (6-10-43). This memo cites the President's message in full.

35. Message 401, former naval person to the president, 3 August 1943, NARA, RG 218, records of the Combined Chiefs of Staff, Geographic File, Folder, CCS 373.11 Rome (6-10-43).

36. Paraphrase of message 403, former naval person to the president, 3 August 1943, NARA, RG 218, records of the Combined Chiefs of Staff, Geographic File, Folder CCS 373.11 Rome (6-10-43).

37. See memorandum for Admiral King, from Deane, subject: Rome, 5 August 1943, NARA, RG 218, records of the Combined Chiefs of Staff, Geographic File, Folder CCS 373.11 Rome (6-10-43). Attached to this memo is the president's request for information and the joint chiefs' reply.

38. Memorandum for the secretary of state [and Gen Marshall] from Lt Col Hammond, 6 August 1943, NARA, RG 218, records of the Combined Chiefs of Staff, geographic file, folder CCS 373.11 Rome (6-10-43).

39. Message, W-6509 (WDCMC CM-IN-2592), Algiers [Eisenhower] to War [Marshall], 4 August 1943, NARA, RG 218, records of the Combined Chiefs of Staff, Geographic File, Folder CCS 373.11 Rome (6-10-43).

40. AHB Narrative, "Bombing Offensive," vol. 5, p. 93.

41. Ibid., 95–96.

42. Richards, *Hardest Victory*, 196.

43. Molony et al., 172.

44. Message, 1682 (WDCMC-IN-11410), Maj Gen W. B. Smith, chief of staff AFHQ, to Generals Rooks and Whitley, WDGS, 15 August 1943, NARA, RG 218, Records of the Combined Chiefs of Staff, Geographic File, Folder CCS 373.11 Rome (6-10-43).

45. Message, FAN 191, CCS to Eisenhower, 14 August 1943, NARA, RG 218, records of the Combined Chiefs of Staff, Geographic File, Folder CCS 373.11 Rome (6-10-43).

46. Message, 1682 (WDCMC-IN-11410), Maj Gen W. B. Smith, chief of staff, AFHQ, to Generals Rooks and Whitley, WDGS, 15 August 1943, NARA, RG 218, Records of the Combined Chiefs of Staff, Geographic File, Folder CCS 373.11 Rome (6-10-43).

47. Message, FAN 194, CCS [Quebec] to Eisenhower [Algiers], 15 August 1943, NARA, RG 218, records of the Combined Chiefs of Staff, Geographic File, Folder CCS 373.11 Rome (6-10-43).

August

1 August: Ninth Air Force—executes Operation Tidalwave, launching 177 B-24s against Ploesti.

11–17 August: Axis forces stage successful withdrawal from Sicily.

13 August: Ninth Air Force—strikes Messerschmidt, Me-109 assembly plant at Regensburg, first strategic strike on greater Germany from the Mediterranean. B-24 crash-lands in Switzerland. Twelfth Air Force—attacks marshaling yard in Rome.

16–17 August: Bomber Command—last attack on Italy—Turin.

17 August: Eighth Air Force—dispatches 315 heavy bombers on deepest penetration into Germany so far to attack ball bearing plants at Schweinfurt and Bf-109 assembly plants at Regensburg. Although bombing is good, German defenses down 60 bombers. Force attacking Regensburg continues on to North Africa. Two B-17s land in Switzerland.

17–18 August: Bomber Command—attacks Peenemünde research establishment.

27 August: Eighth Air Force—mounts its first attack on a V-weapon (Noball) target.

29 August: Eighth Air Force—Maj Gen William J. Kepner succeeds Maj Gen Frank O. Hunter as commander of VIII Fighter Command.

31 August–1 September: Bomber Command—first use of flares by enemy fighters—Berlin.

In August 1943 Bomber Command carried the battle to other cities with large raids on Mannheim, Nürnberg (twice),

155

Munich-Gladbach, Leverkusen, and Berlin (twice). The second raid on Nürnberg and the Berlin raids, all in the last third of the month, gave indications that German defenses had begun to develop ways to counter Window (chaff). Of 1,758 effective sorties, Bomber Command lost 137 bombers—a loss rate of 7.8 percent. Such a rate boded ill for any sustained attempt at operations deep into Germany. During the month the command also made a series of attacks on northern Italy. However, it conducted its most significant mission of the month against a target on the Baltic—Peenemünde, the German rocket research, development, and experimental station. British intelligence had collected information on the facility as early as November 1939, but not until late 1942 and early 1943 did the British begin to appreciate the true significance of the facility. On 12 June 1943 photoreconnaissance of the complex spotted a V-2 rocket on a transporter. The Germans had already test-fired the weapon and had just completed a production factory for it on the site. Allied intelligence also failed to detect the development area of V-1 jet-propelled, pilotless bombs on one edge of the facility. However, because Peenemünde lay 700 miles from Bomber Command's bases and because of the short nights surrounding the summer solstice, the command had too little darkness to reach the target and return in safety. Mid-August offered 80 percent moon and long enough nights to hit the site.

On the night of 17 August, the command dispatched 596 four-engine bombers; of that number 571 aircraft reached the target. Flying at 8,000 feet, they attacked in three waves. The briefers informed the crews they would hit an experimental radar station, an incentive for accurate bombing that directly related to the crews' future well-being. The crews referred to the mission as *boffin* * bashing*.

The first wave attacked the complex housing the facility's scientists, technicians, and skilled workers. However, due to bad marking many aircraft bombed a nearby slave labor camp instead, killing 500. The master bomber corrected the aim of

---

*Boffin: Royal Air Force slang for *scientist*.

the following aircraft in this wave so that they struck the housing complex. The attack killed 170 out of 4,000 residents—good bomb shelters and advanced warning saved many lives but some important individuals did perish. The second wave targeted the rocket factory, damaging some subsidiary structures but not the production area. The third wave assailed the research and development complex of approximately 70 buildings. The bombers in this third wave destroyed more than one-third of those facilities including the design block. However, this success was offset because the Germans had taken the precaution of duplicating and storing off-site all blueprints, drawings, plans, and similar documents that had changed during the day. The wind tunnel and the telemetry block remained standing. The entire mission cost Bomber Command 40 heavy bombers, most to stiff resistance from night fighters—which had initially been drawn off by feints, but still located the bomber stream in time to down many aircraft.[1] Still the attack delayed production by two months and caused the Germans to disperse the project, sending V-2 research and development to caverns near Salzburg, V-2 production to an underground factory in the Harz Mountains, and testing to Poland.[2]

August proved a harsh month for the Eighth. Although one new group, the 390th, arrived, the number of combat-ready aircraft deployed to units rose less than 10 percent, from 396 to 432. Heavy bombers in the theater actually dropped from 833 to 808. This difference between aircraft fit for combat and the number listed on hand in the theater by AAF headquarters in Washington, DC, was a constant source of friction between Arnold and his combat commanders. Sitting in Washington and looking at the raw numbers of aircraft reported in the theater, Arnold could not always understand why so many fewer aircraft were actually flying combat missions. However, many aircraft had to be withdrawn from daily service to repair combat damage and for modification and maintenance. Arnold himself grumpily reported to the secretary of war in January 1944 that out of 620 aircraft sent to the combat theaters, "on an average mission day" 279 (45 percent) would be out of service. This figure included single-engine fighters as well as multiengine transports and bombers, which, because of their greater complexity, would have an even greater percentage of out-of-service aircraft.[3] In 1943–44 the average heavy bomber in the Eighth Air Force had an average life span of 225 days. It flew combat for 47 days and underwent repair, maintenance, and/or modification for 49 days.[4]

In August 1943 operations consumed heavy bombers faster than they could be replaced. The Eighth sent seven missions into France and Germany. In France the raiders hit airfields, power stations, and newly identified launching stations for V-1s. Out of 916 effective sorties flown in France, the Americans lost 19 bombers—a loss rate of only 2.1 percent. However, the Allies could not win the war by bombing targets only in France.

Towards this end, the Eighth flew two missions into Germany. In the first, on 12 August, the 1st Bombardment Wing (1 BW) attacked steel plants at Bochum in the Ruhr, which had large and experienced flak defenses and radar controllers. The 1 BW lost 23 B-17s out of 133 effective sorties. During the same mission, the 4th Bombardment Wing (4 BW) hit Bonn, relatively untouched and undefended; it lost only two aircraft out of 110 effective sorties. As a whole the attack lost 10 percent of its force.

On the Eighth's second mission into Germany, General Eaker launched 376 B-17s on 17 August—the anniversary of the day the Eighth began operations in Europe. The 1 BW attacked Schweinfurt—the center of German ball bearings manufacture—in central Germany some 85 miles east of the Rhine while the 4 BW struck the Messerschmidt fighter assembly plants at Regensburg—150 miles beyond the Rhine into southern Germany. Both missions went farther into Germany than the Eighth had ever gone before. The ensuing struggle ranks as one the most celebrated battles in American air history. This work can only summarize the bravery and gallant conduct of the American aircrews.

The plan called for both forces to assemble at the same time and proceed to their targets. This tactic would force the German defenders to split their force. Matters went awry at once. Fog covered the bases at launch time. The 4 BW, under the leadership of the charismatic Brig Gen Curtis LeMay, had trained to take off in such conditions. In contrast the 1 BW did not take off until the fog cleared, by which time LeMay had been forced to proceed or face running out of fuel. The large gap in space and time between the two forces contributed greatly to the American defeat. LeMay's force lost 24 of 127 effective sorties and would have lost more if they had not surprised the Germans by continuing on to North Africa instead of running the return gantlet to Britain. Two of LeMay's bombers crash-landed in Switzerland. The 1st Bombardment Wing, which encountered heavy opposition en route to and from Schweinfurt, lost 36 out of 183 effective sorties. The overall loss rate came close to 20 percent—an unsustainable figure. This heavy loss on one raid, added to the month's earlier losses, forced the Eighth to regroup. It did not send another unescorted raid deep into Germany for four months, when it reattacked Schweinfurt. The delay gave the Germans a chance to recover.

The bombing, given the cloudless conditions, was good. Photo intelligence of Schweinfurt showed more than 100 bomb strikes in the three main plants. Allied analysts estimated a 40 percent loss of production.[5] Albert Speer, German minister of armaments and production, not only confirmed the loss of production but stated that within six weeks the Germans had exhausted their reserves and were compelled to survive on a hand-to-mouth basis. He marveled at the Allies' failure to attack the other bearings plant of the Reich.[6] However, the attacks alerted the Germans to their vulnerability, and they took energetic measures to disperse their bearings production and to redesign military equipment and other machines to use far less bearings. As the US Strategic Bombing Survey concluded in September 1945, after examining captured German records:

> The history of the attack upon the anti-friction bearing industry indicates that even in the case of a very concentrated industry very heavy and continuous attack must be made, since otherwise the enemy, if he can survive the initial shock, will be able to take successful countermeasures. At the time of the attacks on Schweinfurt in 1943 the limitations upon the capability of the air force, particularly the lack of a long-range fighter, were such as to make that kind of attack impossible. The Germans were able to survive the initial shock, take successful countermeasures, and thus boast: Es ist kein Greät zurück geblieben weil Wältlager fehlten (No equipment was ever delayed because bearings were lacking).[7]

159

One indication of the intensity of bomber versus fighter combat was the number of fighters claimed by the bomber gunners. On 17 August 1943 the Eighth sent 346 bombers on the Regensburg–Schweinfurt mission (Eighth Air Force mission no. 84). The Eighth lost 60 of its bombers and claimed 288 German fighters destroyed, 37 probably destroyed, and 99 damaged.[8] In fact the Germans lost 34 fighters shot down, 12 damaged beyond repair, and 25 damaged.[9] Although the numbers claimed by the Eighth's aircrews overstated the actual German losses, they accurately indicated the frequency, duration, and ferocity of attack by the Luftwaffe's fighters, at least as they were perceived by bomber gunners and crews.

The matter of actual kills versus claims by AAF bomber gunners was a matter of controversy. The number claimed always exceeded the number actually lost by the Germans by at least eight or nine to one. In part these inflated claims resulted from the inability of any one gunner to be sure that his bullets and not someone else's accounted for a particular kill. The natural confusion of the battle compounded the inability of the participants to assess enemy casualties correctly and accurately. Additionally, the Eighth did not have a remotely foolproof method of debriefing the returning crews to eliminate multiple counting. For morale and propaganda purposes the AAF could not admit that men pointing sticks at the Germans would have been hardly less effective than .50-caliber machine guns in killing German fighters. However, the heavily armed bombers, if not aircraft killers, certainly had enough deterrent firepower to force the Luftwaffe pilots to launch disciplined, coordinated attacks from a respectful distance, which cut down by an unknown, but large, factor, the total number of attacks delivered and losses inflicted during any one raid. Here again the belief in crew reporting, unverified by photography or other means, indicates a state of wishful thinking in higher command levels. Either that or the Eighth's commanders knew or guessed the status of the highly inflated reports but chose to honor them in hopes of their having a positive effect on morale. Reducing claims by 90 percent would surely have the opposite effect.[10]

On 1 August the Ninth Air Force executed Operation Tidalwave—the low-level bombardment of the Ploesti oil refineries by five groups of B-24s from Benghasi, Libya. The first aircraft airborne crashed into the sea, a harbinger of the misfortune to plague this heroic mission. The groups had been withdrawn from service several days before the attack to undergo intensive training in low-level bombing and flight. They practiced intensively against a mock-up of the target and performed flawlessly on the last practice bomb run. Each group had a different refinery complex to strike. As the other bombers took off, they had no way of knowing that the Germans had broken the Ninth's codes and would soon learn enough to alert the Ploesti area defenses, among the heaviest in Europe.[11] The mission's two top navigators went down before reaching the target area, and one group bombed the wrong targets. Another group flew in as the delayed-action bombs of the first group began to explode. All the aircraft used delayed-action bombs to give themselves time to clear the explosions. Two other groups mistakenly flew to Bucharest and returned. The completely aroused defenses forced them to strike alternate targets within the oil complexes. German light flak, useless against high-flying bombers, flayed the B-24s coming in at 500 or even 100 feet. Fighters pursued the bombers out to sea. Of 177 bombers dispatched, the Ninth lost 41 in combat and 13 to other causes. Of their crews, 532 were killed, wounded, or became prisoners of war (POW).[12] The mission's 30 percent loss rate exceeded that of any other major American raid of the war. Four aircrews won Medals of Honor, more than any other single air action of the war.

The courage and determination displayed by the bomber crews did not result in a proportionate amount of damage to Ploesti. The mission destroyed or damaged 40 percent of the area's capacity, and it would take two to six months to repair it. Yet, in spite of the precarious state of Axis petroleum supplies at the time of the bombing, Ploesti used only 60 percent of its capacity. The raid eliminated the excess and had a negligible effect on production. In fact as the repaired capacity came online production increased. Since the Allies planned no follow-up raids, repair proceeded undisturbed. The raid was badly, albeit gallantly, executed, but even so it furnished ample proof that low-level bombing would realize neither of the results touted by its proponents; the low-level bombing of Ploesti failed to reduce casualties and did not produce decisive results.

Notes

1. AHB Narrative, *The Bombing Offensive*, vol. 5, 101–3.
2. Hinsley, *British Intelligence in the Second World War*, 385.
3. Craven and Cate, *Men and Planes*, 6:396.
4. Ibid., 394.
5. Kreis, *Piercing the Fog*, 202.
6. Speer, *Inside the Third Reich*, 284–86.
7. USSBS, *Summary Report (European War)*, 29.
8. Freeman, *Mighty Eighth War Diary*, 89–90.
9. Murray, *Strategy for Defeat*, 182.
10. For an official discussion of this problem, see Craven and Cate, *Torch to Pointblank*, 2: 221–24.
11. *Oxford Companion to World War II*, s.v., 890.
12. Craven and Cate, 2:479–81.

The Evacuation of Sicily

Finally, all our thoughts are concentrated upon the great battle about to be fought by the British 8th and United States 7th Armies against the 65,000 Germans cornered in the eastern Sicilian tip. The destruction of these rascals could not come at a better time to influence events, not only in Italy but throughout the world.

—Winston Churchill to Franklin Roosevelt
29 July 1943

Between the nights of 10 and 16 August, the Germans and Italians, working independently, evacuated more than 100,000 men, 9,800 vehicles, 47 tanks, 150 guns, and 17,000 tons of munitions and stores from Sicily.[1] Three first-class mobile German divisions escaped intact to fight again—a key factor in enabling the Germans to mount a defense of the Italian Peninsula south of Rome. The Allies had made no plans to halt this retrograde movement as they had in the Tunisian campaign. This oversight earned the Allied command structure and each of the three services equal shares of the reproaches from post-war analysts.

The land forces, particularly the British, did not press the Axis forcefully enough to prevent them from disengaging the vast majority of their troops. Unlike Lt Gen George S. Patton (commander of the US Seventh Army), Gen Bernard L. Montgomery (commander of the British Eighth Army), declined to mount significant amphibious landings behind German lines. Adm Andrew Cunningham (commander of the Allied naval forces) would not risk the loss of or damage to his heavy units by bringing them into the confined waters of the Strait of Messina to sink the evacuation ships. Cunningham served in the Gallipoli Campaign as a young officer in World War I. In that engagement, the Anglo-French navies suffered severe casualties in their bombardments of Turkish coastal batteries. He could not overcome this earlier experience nor could he be sure that his ships might not encounter newly laid minefields put down for the express purpose of protecting the strait. Moreover, the presence of his ships in those constricted waters might encourage the Luftwaffe to attack. At that time and place, given the Royal Navy's experiences in the earlier phases of the war, Cunningham could not discount the possibility of effective Axis air intervention.

The Allied command structure not only did not anticipate the evacuation but failed to realize it had begun until very late in its progress. Neither Eisenhower nor his three chief subordinates—Gen Sir Harold Alexander, commander of the Allied ground forces; Cunningham, and Air Chief Marshal Arthur Tedder, commander of the Allied air forces in the Mediterranean—pushed hard enough or coordinated readily enough with their colleagues to mount the combined ground, naval, and air effort necessary to close the strait.[2] The Allies' ability to plan and conduct the type of joint air-land-naval operation needed to choke off the evacuation was inhibited by the fact that Eisenhower allowed Cunningham, Alexander, and Tedder to establish their headquarters several hundred miles from his own and each other. It is conceivable that the Allies may also have misread the strategic and political situation. They had already received peace feelers from the Bodaglio government. If Italy switched sides, the

163

Germans might be forced back to northern Italy or even to the Alps. In early August, before the Germans had greatly reinforced their position in Italy and before the inability of the Italian armed forces to resist their erstwhile ally became all too evident, the escape of a German armored corps from Sicily may not have seemed as important as it subsequently became. Within a month the picture of what would happen on the Italian mainland was much clearer, but by then the opportunity had passed.

The air forces, under Air Marshal Arthur Coningham, commander of the NATAF, made several mistakes. Coningham assumed that the evacuation would take place largely at night, and he anticipated heavy air opposition over the strait. Both reasonable assumptions proved wrong, but he did not abandon them. Although he had the authority to request the assistance of NASAF heavy bombers, medium bombers, and fighters, with 12 hours' advance notice, subject to Doolittle's approval, Coningham apparently never requested the American daylight bombers after 9 August. From 10–16 August, NASAF B-17s and Ninth Air Force B-24s flew no sorties over Sicily or the strait. However, in the same period, No. 205 Group, aided by illumination of the period surrounding the full moon on 15 August, devoted at least 397 effective sorties towards evacuation beaches and related targets on both sides of the strait. Unfortunately, most of the beaches it bombed were the wrong ones. NASAF's American daylight bomber force (the B-17s and medium bombers of the Twelfth Air Force) attacked the Italian mainland distant from the strait in preparation for the upcoming invasion of Italy. On the day the main German withdrawal began, Coningham notified Tedder that, should such a movement develop, "we can handle it with our own resources and naval assistance."[3] However, Coningham overestimated the ability of NATAF to halt the evacuation.

The Axis powers had up to 150 88 mm and 90 mm dual-purpose heavy guns and numerous medium and light antiaircraft guns to defend the crossing.[4] These put up such intense fire that NATAF's light bombers and fighter-bombers could not operate effectively against Axis shipping, which also carried heavy antiaircraft armament.[5] Nor did Coningham press home his attacks, perhaps because he and his superiors sensed no emergency. One must remember that by 15 August the Allies entered into secret peace negotiations with the Italian government. Although he had an available force of 970 aircraft on 16 August, the last full day of the evacuation, Coningham sent only 317 sorties against the strait.[6] After the war, he concluded, "the escape of a large number of the enemy at Messina proved that a density of flak can be provided so lethal that air attack can be held off sufficiently to maintain communications."[7]

The US Army history of the campaign takes Tedder to task for continuing to employ the heavy day bombers of NASAF too far from crucial evacuation ports.[8] Likewise, a recent Air Force study faults Coningham for releasing the B-17s for other duty.[9] Both works give too much credit to the abilities of the bombers and not enough to the 150 heavy antiaircraft artillery pieces defending the strait.[10] At the time of the evacuation the Germans had amassed one of the densest concentrations of antiaircraft artillery in the world around the strait. These defenses would have forced the B-17s and B-24s to fly high, reducing accuracy. Moreover, bombardiers sitting in the Plexiglas nose of the B-17s quickly lost concentration in the face of intense flak, reducing accuracy by another 50 percent. The question of how to approach the beaches would also have presented problems. Flying from east (from the mainland] to west (Sicily) over the strait, the bomb groups may have plastered the beaches (a long narrow target), but, given their usual accuracy, they were just as likely to place bombs short of the beaches into the waters of the strait or long of the target (perhaps into the enemy units awaiting evacuation). However, such an approach would have routed the bombers over the German flak defenses. Moreover, the length of the beaches would have meant that to hit them, the bombers would have to fly in a group-abreast formation, which would put a bomb group or less over each target. Such an attack would have been unlikely to deliver concentrated bomb loads. Placing two or more groups on each target would have meant more than one mission over the strait and increased the loss of bombers and crews. The opposite approach presented the same problems. An approach parallel to the beaches (either north to south or south to north) would have put the bombers into a column 20 or 30 miles long and given the defenders the opportunity to fasten on each group as it approached. NASAF possessed approximately 180 B-17s, while the Ninth added 100 B-24s in mid-August. Flying in formations of long strings over the Strait of Messina would have resulted in heavy bomber casualties and— given the lack of accuracy on occasions when they attacked ground forces—would have produced mixed results. Given that the Anglo-American heavy bomber attacks in the Normandy campaign a year later did not, in most of those instances, materially hinder the Germans indicates that efforts to impair the evacuation of Sicily by bombing would have produced a similar result. Even in Cobra, the 25 July 1944 bombing that resulted in the American breakout near St. Lo, more than 1,500 heavy bombers and several hundred medium bombers attacked an area only 2,500 by 7,000 yards over a period of two hours, a much heavier concentration than would have been possible to mount over the Sicilian beaches.

During the evacuation, both the Ninth and NASAF employed their heavy bombers on strategic missions. On 13 August, the Ninth, whose B-24 groups had been decimated in the Ploesti raid of 1 August, launched the first strategic raid from the Mediterranean into greater Germany. The Ninth returned the heavy bombers it had on loan from the Eighth in a reverse shuttle mission that attacked Wiener Neustadt—a major component manufacturer and assembly point for Me-109s. The bombers achieved complete tactical surprise and inflicted severe damage on hangars, grounded aircraft, and the plants of Wiener-Neustaedter Flugzeugwerke A. G. For much of the remainder of the year, production at the plants slowed noticeably.[11] The raid lost only two out of 65 effective sorties. Originally the raid was to be coordinated with the Eighth's bombing of Regensburg and Schweinfurt (Operation Juggler), but weather in England prevented the launch of the Eighth's bombers.

If Eisenhower or Tedder, or any of the other Allied air leaders, had been determined to halt the evacuation, why did they return three of the 10 heavy bomber groups available to them instead of employing them over Messina? On the same date, 125 of NASAF's heavies hit the Lorenzo marshaling yard in Rome while its medium bombers—168 strong—struck Rome's Littoro marshaling yard. These raids made little sense in conjunction with attempts to derail the Sicilian evacuation. However, if one considers it as part of the strategic air campaign to bring the Bodaglio government to the surrender table, what better target than Rome during the day? As Tedder told Coningham on 1 August, he required NASAF for another purpose, "to punch the Italian people with a view to forcing them to bring pressure to bear upon Bodaglio to sue for peace."[12] On 16 August, the last day of the evacuation, the Ninth sent its entire heavy bomber complement against the Italian airfield complex at Foggia rather than against the Strait of Messina. It would appear that Pointblank, the Italian political situation, and on-going air operations over the Italian mainland bore more heavily on the Allied leadership in the Mediterranean than on stopping the evacuation.

Another factor playing a role in the Allies' failure was the exhaustion of the aircrews.[13] Excellent flying weather in the Mediterranean had permitted Allied airpower to conduct operations at a high tempo. From 1 May to 1 August, Anglo-American aircrews had flown at maximum rates, almost daily, supporting the final operations in Tunisia, conquering Pantelleria, preparing Sicily for invasion, softening up the Italian mainland, flying deception missions over Sardinia, and covering large naval operations. The high operations rate meant that aircrews completed their combat tours more quickly than anticipated and ground crews worked almost without respite. By the time of the evacuation, the depletion of human resources had become severe. On 30 July, Spaatz reported to Arnold that "combat crew fatigue has become the main problem." Two days later Eisenhower sent, at Spaatz's behest, an "eyes only" cable to Marshall in which he pleaded for an immediate increase of the replacement rate from 15 percent a month to 25 percent a month. Eisenhower noted, "it now appears that we must either fail to meet demands or gradually reduce our groups' effectiveness as a result of attrition."[14] Alluding to the surrender negotiations with Italy and the worsening Axis position on Sicily, Eisenhower added, "we have reached a critical position in this area which requires that any favorable development, military or political, be fully and immediately exploited. Air forces, of course, provide our most effective means of rapidly applying pressure where necessary."[15]

On 4 August Eisenhower informed Marshall that because of the increasing state of exhaustion of his aircrews he would have to husband his air resources. He declined to attack Rome so as to give priority "to the land battle and to the neutralization of enemy air forces."[16] Arnold and Marshall, however, could do little to meet these appeals. The vagaries of US military manpower recruitment and procurement, especially in the AAF, had produced a manpower crisis that particularly affected aircrews. The low point in the supply of trained manpower for the AAF occurred in the summer of 1943, leaving Arnold and the AAF unable to meet more than the minimally planned replacement flows.[17] The RAF in the Mediterranean, which rested on a much slimmer manpower pool, undoubtedly was in a similar condition. Tired crews, whatever their motivation, cannot conduct operations with the same efficiency and verve as fresh ones.

Writing with the omniscience of hindsight, the critics of Allied actions are correct when they contend that the Allies could have done much more to impede the evacuation. However, in doing so, they tend to ignore the great differences between the Axis situations in Tunisia and Sicily. First, the analysts must remember that there was no concerted Axis attempt to withdraw from Tunisia, where Hitler, as he did often in the last years of the war, handicapped his soldiers by refusing to permit them to retreat. Although such an operation would have been costly, if it had saved only 20 percent of the Italo-German forces, that would have been 60,000 trained men. Second, the geography of the two theaters favored the Allies in Tunisia, but it worked against them in Sicily. In the final stages in Tunisia, the topography of the land allowed the Allies to maintain contact with Axis forces across almost the entire front and prevented the Axis from detaching large forces to any potential evacuation areas. In Sicily, Mount Etna and the difficult surrounding terrain provided an easily defensible barrier that separated the two Allied armies and shielded much of the Axis front. In addition, the mountainous terrain of northeastern Sicily channeled the attackers onto one or two main roads that were easily defensible by small rear guards and demolition actions. The closest parts of Cape Bon,

Tunisia, and the Island of Sicily were separated by 50 miles of open water; the likely embarkation and debarkation points were even farther apart. Small Axis barges and ferries traveling at 10 knots or less could make no more than one round-trip a day. Allowing time for loading and unloading, they would be exposed to daylight Allied air attacks in open water for some portion of their voyage. Larger ships were constricted to known shipping lanes by extensive mine fields, and their schedules were revealed by Allied code breaking. In contrast, the evacuation route across the Strait of Messina varied from a high of five miles long to only two miles, no broader than some major rivers, most of which were covered throughout their entire length by heavy antiaircraft fire. The evacuation ships could also make several round-trips a night and several more during the day.

Eisenhower, as the theater commander, must shoulder much of the blame for the Allies' failure to press home their operations. There is no evidence to suggest that he appreciated the possible consequences of a successful evacuation or, if he did, that he in any way impressed his subordinate commanders with a sense of urgency and determination. Indeed, his handling of the bombing of Rome, undertaken during the evacuation, suggests as much. Raids against the Eternal City had been considered since early June. On two separate occasions Eisenhower postponed such missions because he gave a higher priority to air operations that assisted the land battle. First, in early July he refused to divert the bombers from preinvasion responsibilities.[18] Second, in early August, he opted to support the battle on Sicily instead of sending bombers against targets in Rome.[19] Given this propensity to support land operations over strategic air operations, why, during the evacuation, did he not only order a strategic strike on Rome and permit the return of the Eighth's three heavy bomb groups on 13 August but also order a second strike, not flown, on Rome for 15 August? This pattern indicates that he was not focused on halting the evacuation at all costs. Eisenhower excelled as a soldier-diplomat in charge of a coalition with a manner suited more to achieving high-level consensus than immediate action. His forte was not field command. In some ways the Sicilian evacuation was a presage of the management style he displayed in the summer of 1944, when he appeared more to ride herd on leaders such as General Montgomery, Lt Gen Omar Bradley, and General Patton rather than actively direct their actions.

It is also of interest to note the lack of recriminations within the Allied high command for the failure to halt the evacuation. For instance, in the campaign in northwest Europe many of the top commanders (for the most part the same men who had led operations in Sicily) chose to air their dirty linen over Montgomery's failure to break out of the beachhead, the mistakes at the Falaise Gap, the Arnheim disaster, and the surprise at the start of the Ardennes counteroffensive. There is no such recriminatory literature among the participants about halting the evacuation. Given the great egos involved and the close infighting over postwar reputation, if one or more commanders dissented or was restrained from doing his utmost, such information would have emerged. The silence in this matter speaks eloquently of the misappreciation of the event throughout the Anglo-American high command.

If the Anglo-Americans had had a joint coordinated anti-evacuation plan in place and if they had been willing to take the necessary air and naval casualties as soon as they confirmed the evacuation had begun, then they probably could have rendered it impossible. The sinking of only 20 or so evacuation craft (Axis records show only one German and four Italian craft lost) would have cut the evacuation capability in half. In using their heavy bombers in their strategic role to pressure the impotent Bodaglio government with psychological bombing, the Allies missed a far more lucrative opportunity to use the heavies in a tactical role to destroy many thousands of German defenders who would be committed to the defense of the Italian peninsula. It is possible in this instance that employment of the heavy and medium bombers as strategic weapons may have prolonged the war rather than shortened it. The entire Anglo-American handling of almost all aspects of the evacuation was not just a mistake but a blunder that would cost the Allies dearly in their plodding advance up the Italian Peninsula. Given the context of events, the Anglo-Americans' decision not to exert maximum force to halt the evacuation was understandable and, perhaps, even reasonable. It was only the last of a series of Allied misjudgments that characterized the Sicilian Campaign from its inception to its conclusion.

Notes

1. Morison, *Sicily-Salerno-Anzio*, 9:215–16.

2. For criticism of the Allied response to the evacuation, see Roskill, *War at Sea*, 3:147–50; and Garland and Smyth, *Sicily and the Surrender of Italy*, 2: 411–12.

3. Roskill, 148. For this account of the evacuation Roskill appears to have examined Coningham's papers.

4. Ammiraglio di Squadra [Rear Admiral] Pietro Barone, *Estratto della Relazione sull'Occupazione della Sicilia*, Italian Navy, Historical Office, 1946, 10, in Morison, 212. Admiral Barone served as the Italian naval commander in Sicily. He organized the Italian evacuation and left the island as Commando Supremo ordered on 10 August 1943. All sources agree that the Axis powers had stationed hundreds of light and medium antiaircraft guns along the sides of the strait. (The best estimate is probably 500 such guns.) The sheer volume of fire from these guns added to the similar guns on Axis shipping made the low-level and dive-bombing tactics of Allied fighter-bombers and medium bombers prohibitively costly. Although the Germans had lost almost their entire inventory of the superior 88 mm Flak 41 guns in Tunisia (Flak is a German short form of Flugobwehrkanone or antiaircraft gun, followed by model number 18,36,41, etc.), they had two independent regiments of flak artillery, each with a standard complement of 24 88 mm Flak 18 or 36 guns plus 88s detached from ground units to protect the strait. These older 88s could place shells up to an altitude of almost 32,000 feet (10,600 meters). The Germans routinely used such guns to defend the homeland against night and day heavy bomber raids. The Italian 90 mm dual-purpose gun was an excellent weapon with comparable performance. At the very least, the 150 heavy guns guarding the strait would have forced the American heavy bombers to attack from high altitude—20,000 feet or above. It is probable that such a concentration of heavy guns would also succeed in inflicting a significant amount of damage against any attacking daylight bomber force.

5. Garland and Smyth, 412.

6. Roskill, 148–49.

7. Coningham, "Development of Tactical Air Forces," 216.

8. Garland and Smyth, 411–12.

9. Mark, *Aerial Interdiction*, 78–79.

10. The Germans naturally feared a nonstop aerial assault on the beaches and the roads leading to and from the embarkation and debarkation points. But as one German source pointed out, the method they feared most was not high-level bombardment, for which there was as yet no prece-

dent in European operations, but "dive-bombing on selected points of the main roads on either bank." Vice Admiral Friedrich Ruge, "The Evacuation of Sicily," 37, cited in Mark, 76.

11. Craven and Cate, *Torch to Pointblank*, 2:483, 684.

12. AHB Narrative, "The Sicilian Campaign, June–August 1943," n.d., 80.

13. Albert Simpson author of "Conquest of Sicily," chapter 14, in Craven and Cate, vol. 2, *Torch to Pointblank*, implies that a possible reason for the lack of substantial daylight heavy bomber activity over the Sicilian strait was that by this stage in the campaign combat weariness in the American heavy bomber crews had reached such a state that operations were curtailed. In contrast to the authors of the US Army history of the campaign, Simpson, writing immediately after the war, does not appear to realize the extent and success of the evacuation. He lauded Northwest African Strategic Air Force's "extensive operations against evacuation ports and shipping" (474) and cited, without question, the Northwest Africa Air Forces' fanciful wartime claims for damage inflicted on evacuation shipping.

14. Letter, Spaatz to Arnold, 30 July 1943, in Spaatz Diary.

15. Message, Eisenhower to Marshall, 1 August 1943, in Spaatz Papers, Diary.

16. Message, W-6509 (WDCMC CM-IN-2592), Algiers (Eisenhower) to War Department (Marshall), 4bAugust 1943, in NARA, RG 218, records of the Combined Chiefs of Staff, Geographic File 1942–1945, folder CCS 373.11 Rome (6-10-43), sec. 1.

17. Craven and Cate, *Men and Planes*, 6:516–22.

18. Message, NAF 251 (WDCMC CM-IN-81), Eisenhower to the CCS, 30 June 1943, NARA, RG 218, geographic file, CCS 373.11 Rome (6-10-43), sec. 1.

19. Message, W-6509 (WDCMC CM-IN-2592), Algiers (Eisenhower) to War Department (Marshall), 4 August 1943, in NARA, RG 218, Geographic File, CCS 373.11 Rome (6-10-43), sec. 1.

September

6 September: Eighth Air Force—dispatches 407 heavy bombers, a new high. No bombers reach primary target (Stuttgart) and only 262 bomb targets of opportunity. Five B-17s land in Switzerland.

7 September: HQ AAF—decides to shut down Ninth Air Force operations in the Mediterranean and reestablish it in the United Kingdom as the American tactical air force supporting the cross-channel invasion. Its assigned units and personnel in the Mediterranean are gradually transferred to the Twelfth Air Force.

8 September: Eighth Air Force—three B-24 groups (44th, 93d, and 389th) loaned to Ninth AF become operational in Eighth Air Force.

8–9 September: Eighth Air Force—first night bombing mission sends five B-17s to join Bomber Command.

9 September: Allies invade Italy at Salerno, south of Naples.

13 September: Eighth Air Force—activates 1st, 2d, and 3d Bomb Divisions.

15–16 September: Bomber Command—617 Squadron drops first 12,000-pound bomb—Dortmund-Ems Canal.

16 September: Eighth Air Force—ordered to return three B-24 groups to the Mediterranean theater to aid Allied operations.

17 September: Eighth Air Force—first AAF P-51 arrives in Britain. Aircraft will not see action until December.

22–23 September: Bomber Command—conducts first "spoof raid"—main target Hannover, spoof target Oldenburg.

23–24 September: Bomber Command—first Oboe marking for main-force raid.

27 September: Eighth Air Force—makes first ordered city-area attack against a cloud-covered target using H2S. Two radar-equipped bombers lead 244 others against the port area of Emden. P-47s, equipped with new belly tanks, provided escort the entire way to the target in Germany for the first time.

In September 1943 Bomber Command dispatched nine major raids—two against French targets and seven area bombing attacks in Germany. On the moonlit night of 15 September, Harris sent 351 effective sorties, at medium altitudes, against the Dunlop Rubber Plant at Montlucon. The next night he sent 295 effective sorties to hit the marshaling yards at Modane on the rail line between France and Italy. Each raid lost three aircraft. Also on the night of 16 September, 19 Lancasters unsuccessfully attacked the Antheor rail viaduct near Cannes. The two rail attacks on French targets represented Harris's cooperation in the Allied effort to halt or delay German reinforcements from reaching Italy. (Rather than retreating when the Italians surrendered, the Germans had quickly seized the country.) In other attacks on 14 September, Harris sent eight Lancasters of 617 Squadron (the "Dambusters") to Greven, Germany, to breach the Dortmund-Ems Canal, which carried a high volume of Germany's riverine transportation. Of the six aircraft that made the attack, only one returned. The canal was undamaged.

Of the seven large raids into Germany, one on Mannheim (4 September) wrought very severe damage. Three others on Berlin (3 September), Munich (6 September), and Hannover (27 September) accomplished little, while attacks on Hannover (22 September), Mannheim (23 September), and Bochum (29 September) also produced only minor damage. Of the above targets only Bochum was in Oboe range. The H2S attacks on the others were hampered by bad weather or clouds, which interfered with the visual marking that followed the initial H2S marking.

The Allied invasion of Italy—south of Naples at Salerno—on 9 September dominated air operations in the Mediterranean.[1] Before the invasion, the heavy bombers concentrated on the marshaling yards in northern Italy before moving their sights gradually south to strike airfields and additional marshaling yards. On invasion day the bombers hit rail bridges and the airfield complex at Foggia. The Allies and the Italian government had timed the Italian surrender to coincide with the invasion. They expected this move to disorganize the German response and, perhaps, force a German withdrawal to northern Italy. However, the Germans were neither disorganized nor in retreat; they had prepared for their erstwhile ally's surrender. They quickly disarmed the Italian army and established civil control over all those regions in Italy not already occupied by the Anglo-Americans. Without local hindrance, the Germans used the Italian transportation system to bring up reinforcements and counterattack the Salerno beachhead. This unforeseen and unwelcome response caught the Allies by surprise; the troops on the beachhead soon found themselves in a precarious position.

Gen Dwight Eisenhower employed all the airpower at his disposal to stem the German onslaught. He even asked Gen George Marshall for the return of the three B-24 groups he had just given back to Eaker. (They resumed operations with the Eighth on 6 September only to depart for the Mediterranean on 14 September.) From 10–13 September, NASAF bombed highway junctions, bridges, and marshaling yards leading to Salerno. For the next 24 hours, the day of greatest threat to the beachhead, NASAF bombed Battapaglia, a key German communications center close to the front. During the following week, NASAF, joined by the Ninth, conducted operations against roads and rail lines in southern Italy. Only at the last of the month did the bombing shift to marshaling yards in Pisa and other cities north of Rome.

The Eighth sent out 10 missions of more than 100 effective sorties in September 1943: eight to France and the Low Countries [Belgium and the Netherlands] and two into Germany. For the first time, the Eighth began small-scale night operations, sending contingents of five B-17s out to join Bomber Command on each of six raids. Although documentation does not confirm or deny the following supposition, the daytime loss rate of the Eighth would suggest that, while the Americans were not abandoning daylight bombing entirely, they had at least decided to investigate the alternative—night bombing. The eight raids into occupied countries focused on airfields, marshaling yards, and ports with side missions against industrial targets near Paris and a V-rocket launch site. The two missions against German targets—Stuttgart and Emden—differed greatly in import.

On 6 September the Eighth dispatched 338 bombers to Stuttgart, 65 miles beyond (to the east of) the Rhine. Clouds covered the primary target; thus, out of the 262 effective sorties, only 46 struck Stuttgart's industrial area. The remainder scattered and bombed targets of opportunity, such as Karlsruhe and Offenburg, both 60 miles west from Stuttgart. The widely separated groups gave the Luftwaffe fighters the chance to rough up several formations. The mission lost 45 bombers in combat, including five interned in Switzerland; an additional 20 bombers of the 1st Bombardment Division ditched in the English Channel or ran out of fuel and crash-landed in England. The B-17s of LeMay's 3d Bombardment Division, equipped with long-range gas tanks, dubbed "Tokyo Tanks" by the aircrews, avoided that fate. As a final blow, one combat wing misidentified the French city of Strasbourg on the wrong bank of the Rhine as a German city and dumped 162 tons of bombs in the center of the town. Stuttgart provided an excellent example of the past problems that had plagued the Eighth while Emden pointed to success in the future. The presence of General Arnold, who had come to England to visit Eaker and the Eighth, may have encouraged the attempt to bomb Stuttgart. Arnold was less than satisfied with the outcome and remarked, "Certain features of the operation never did find their way into reports sent up through channels."[2]

The Eighth Air Force Initiates Area Bombing

In the raid on Emden—the German port nearest to Great Britain—on 27 September, the Eighth first employed H2S; American fighters escorted the bombers all the way to and from a target in Germany. The seacoast target, although cloud covered, gave the newly trained American operator of one of the two H2S sets an excellent return. Of 308 bombers dispatched, 240 bombed targets. One PFF aircraft led 179 bombers to Emden. They suffered the day's only lost aircraft—seven. Eighteen bombers followed the other H2S bomber to Essen, 19 bombers hit Aurich visually, and 31 others struck targets of opportunity in Germany. These raids marked another first—Eighth Air Force headquarters and VIII Bomber Command had ordered the attacking aircraft to aim for the center of the city, not specific industrial or transportation targets.[3]

The conjunction of H2S and area bombing of cities was not a coincidence. Tactical considerations, not strategic ones, dictated the US adoption of area bombing. The Eighth obtained four H2S devices from the British, who had a priority need for it for RAF Bomber Command. A few more H2S devices went to the United States where American scientists reverse engineered and improved them. They began production of a US-manufactured version, the H2X, but it did not reach the Eighth in satisfactory numbers until mid-1944.

In any case the assured scarcity of H2S and H2X meant that one or two PFF aircraft would invariably lead large (100 or more aircraft) formations of bombers. When these large formations dropped on the PFF markers, there was no guarantee of precision, hence the switch to area bombing. Not even Bomber Command used H2S as a precision sight. Like Bomber Command at night, the Eighth could locate city areas, but not necessarily the correct city, through any cloud cover that permitted operations during the day. It could not, however, precisely identify targets within the city.[4] Of course, if weather conditions, such as a break in the clouds, or if the situation demanded, the Americans could fall back on the Norden bombsight and visual bombing. Visually assisted radar bombing was usually more accurate than radar alone. Flying above the clouds over Germany also forced the Luftwaffe day fighters to take off and land in what could be more questionable conditions (as opposed to mostly clear weather) and to spend much of their time climbing and descending through clouds.

Just as any (bomber or fighter) night operations had higher accident rates than daylight so would some daylight operations through cloud cover. Increased operations by the daylight bombers meant increased attrition to the German day fighters operating in less than optimal conditions; attrition almost always worked in the Allies' favor.

Nor was it coincidental that the Eighth Air Force's second area raid on a city—337 heavy bombers (also on Emden) on 2 October 1943—was that air force's first raid to carry in excess of 100 tons of incendiaries (208 tons) and its first major raid of more than 100 aircraft to carry more than 20 percent incendiary bombs (208 of 743) and 28 percent firebombs. By definition an area raid on a city requires a large percentage of incendiaries. On 10 October 1943 the Eighth ordered its first visually sighted area raid when 138 bombers attacked Münster and carried more than 40 percent firebombs. Within two weeks after introducing radar—a mere six sets of radar for the entire force—the Eighth went from never having authorized an area raid to launching more than one such raid a week until the end of the war. It would have been especially ironic four days later if the second Schweinfurt mission had arrived over its target and encountered clouds instead of fair weather. The Eighth ordered it to bomb the city area of Schweinfurt as a secondary target if overcast covered the ball bearings plants. Instead of the gallant Air Force equivalent of Pickett's charge, that famous raid might have gone into the books as something else entirely.

Notes

1. The British Eighth Army invaded the toe of Italy, across the Strait of Messina, on 3 September 1943.

2. Arnold, *Global Mission*, 480.

3. Eighth Bomber Command, Mission of 27 September 1943, 1: AFHRA Microfilm Reel A5940, frame 746.

4. My assessment of the overall accuracy of H2S/H2X-aided bombing is based on perusal of many Eighth Air Force Operations Analysis Section Reports on bomb accuracy and the many after-action reports filed in the Eighth's mission folders. Others have taken a more positive view of the Americans' radar bombing accuracy, which has led some to deny—I believe incorrectly—the extent of actual American area bombing of cities. For the most cogent and well-reasoned expression of this more optimistic view, see Crane, *Bombs, Cities, and Civilians*.

October

October: Sobibor death camp in occupied Poland closed.

1 October: Twelfth Air Force—two B-17s land in Switzerland.

4–5 October: Bomber Command—first operational trials for G-H.

7–8 October: Bomber Command—first Airborne Cigar operations (jamming VHF R/T).

8 October: Eighth Air Force—first use of airborne radar jamming (Carpet) to confuse German defenses. B-24 groups sent to North Africa returned and begin operations with Eighth.

8–9 October: Bomber Command—last raid by Wellingtons under BC. Still employed by 205 Group.

9 October: Eighth Air Force—three crews and aircraft interned in Sweden.

14 October: Eighth Air Force—launches second major raid, also unescorted by fighters, on Schweinfurt antifriction bearing industry. Out of 291 heavy bombers dispatched and 229 attacking the target the Americans lose 60. One B-17 interned in Switzerland.

15 October: Eighth Air Force—first P-38 long-range escort fighter group becomes operational.

16 October: Ninth Air Force—Ninth (Tactical) Air Force Headquarters established in United Kingdom. Under the command of Maj Gen Lewis H. Brereton, this headquarters will oversee the American tactical air force cooperating with American ground forces participating in the cross-channel invasion. Assumes command of all Eighth Air Force medium bomb groups.

22–23 October: Bomber Command—heavy raid on Kassel produces firestorm; first use of CORONA—spoof orders to German night fighters.

Bomber Command dispatched nine large raids in October 1943, all into Germany. Weather foiled the H2S and visual follow-up marking in three missions, producing poor results: Kassel (3 October), Hannover (18 October), and Leipzig (20 October). Three missions devastated their targets: on 4 October the eastern half of Frankfurt was heavily damaged; on 8 October two square miles of the city center of Hannover were destroyed; and, on 22 October, a firestorm ravaged Kassel, killing 9,000 people and leaving 90,000 homeless in a town of only 228,000. The Kassel raid destroyed much of the town's industry (including plants manufacturing V-1s). Raids on Hagen (1 October), Munich (2 October), and Stuttgart (7 October) had no significant results. As the command pursued its battle of attrition with the Reich, one factor constantly grew. As more and more of the aptly named Mosquito light bombers came into Bomber Command, their night buzzing, small irritating bites, and relative invulnerability took an increasing toll on the nerves of the German public and leadership. Oboe-equipped Mosquitoes made increasingly accurate thrusts at select parts of the war economy, such as powerhouses, blast furnaces, and coke ovens. As the war progressed, the swarm grew.

On 1 October the Northwest Africa Strategic Air Force (NASAF) once again ventured into the arena of strategic bombing and learned very roughly what the Eighth already knew: if you intend to conduct unescorted daylight bombing into Greater Germany, you must be prepared to pay the piper. Of 99 effective sorties sent against the Messerschmidt assembly plants at Wiener Neustadt and a tank plant in Steyr, NASAF lost 19 aircraft—a loss rate of almost 20 percent. One group strayed off course and bombed Gundelfingen, becoming the first bombers assigned to the Mediterranean theater to hit Germany. Bad weather over

Germany hindered operations for much of the rest of October. Meanwhile, NASAF flew missions against airfields on Crete and attacked railroad yards and rail bridges in Pisa, Bologna, and Bolzana. The repeated assaults on the Italian transportation system had their roots in the Allied desire to impede the movement of German troops and supplies, which could not move during the day because of ubiquitous Allied fighter-bombers. Slowing supplies from Germany might make a ground breakthrough easier, just as slowing the movement of German reinforcements from one side of the peninsula to the other would have the same purpose. Even though its application in Italy made life miserable for the Germans and restricted their movement in daylight, airpower did not deny them sufficient armaments to defend themselves.

The Eighth dispatched seven major missions in October 1943; all bombed targets in Germany. On 2 October, under orders to area bomb the city, 339 bombers led by two H2S B-17s hit Emden. They lost two bombers. Like all major German ports, Emden had a thick, man-made smoke screen from its local industries; its density varied according to the wind and weather. On 4 October 323 B-17s area bombed the cities of Frankfurt and Wiesbaden. For the first time, the Eighth ordered area bombing in visual conditions—and without H2S aircraft. The lead navigator missed the targets by 100 miles. Consequently, the bombing was widely scattered; 282 aircraft attacked not just the primary targets but also the cities of Saarlautern and Saarbrücken; the mission lost 16 aircraft. Four days later the Eighth sent 399 bombers to Bremen and Vegasack. Approximately half were to bomb the city of Bremen, while the others either hit U-boat yards in Bremen and Vegasack or aircraft plants in Bremen. Once again no Pathfinder force (PFF) aircraft accompanied the raid, and clouds covered the targets. Of the 357 aircraft attacking, 197 bombed Bremen city, 92 attacked the U-boat yards, and 33 hit the fighter components plant; the rest struck targets of opportunity. America lost 37 bombers.

On 9 October the Eighth went after component and assembly plants for the FW-190 at Anklam and Marienburg in Upper Silesia. Of 215 bombers in the Anklam mission, 202 attacked, and 20 planes were lost. The bombing of Marienburg was a particularly fine example of Army Air Forces' (AAF) visual bombing. For once, all the factors came together—attacking from only 13,000 feet—and the bombs obliterated the plant. The Eighth also sent a large force of B-24s and long-range B-17s to Gydnia and Danzig in East Prussia—the farthest penetration yet flown by the Eighth into German airspace. Of the 163 bombers sent to the east, 150 attacked their primary targets, U-boat yards, and port areas. They lost eight bombers. Their course over the North Sea and the Baltic caught the Germans by surprise. The next day the Eighth attacked the city area of Münster without PFF aircraft. Of the 274 aircraft sent out, 236 flew effective sorties. One hundred thirty-eight aircraft hit Münster, losing 30 planes; 68 struck the city of Cösfeld. Twenty-nine bomber crews misidentified the Dutch town of Enschede as German and dropped 86 tons of bombs on it, killing 155 of its inhabitants. None of the attackers, save the Münster force, suffered any losses.

On 14 October 1943 the Luftwaffe day-fighter force and the Eighth Air Force fought the Second Battle of Schweinfurt. The Eighth had reached a nominal strength of 20 groups with none on loan to other theaters. Combat-ready bombers on hand in the units had increased by 30 percent since August (from 396 to 524). Against this force, the Allies estimated the enemy had 800 single-engine (day) fighters inside Germany. Postwar studies showed that the enemy actually had 964 single-engine fighters.[1] As in the first Schweinfurt raid, bad weather at takeoff hurt the attack plan. Of 60 B-24s from the 2d Bombardment Division (2 BD) scheduled for the raid, only 29 made formation. This weakened force made a diversionary sweep rather than a direct attack on the target. The main attack force had just subtracted almost 20 percent of its strength. The 1st and 3d Bombardment Divisions (1 BD and 3 BD) dispatched 291 B-17s. Flying in the lead, the nine groups of the 1 BD ran head-on into the alerted German defenses. German early warning radar on the French coast had tracked the Allied planes from takeoff, through their jockeying for position as they formed up, and along the formation's entire flight path. Dozens of single- and twin-engine (heavy) fighters slashed at the bombers, downing 45 of their number.

This attack put 101 effective sorties over the target and suffered a loss rate of more that 40 percent of the forces engaged. One of its aircraft crashed in Switzerland. As the 3 BD flew to the target, its crews observed the sobering sight of crashed B-17s from the 1st BD marking their path as far as the eye could see. The 3 BD lost 15 bombers out of 128 attacking, a loss rate of "only" 11 percent. Claims by the bomber's gunners attested to the fierceness of the struggle: 186 Germans shot down, 27 probable, and 89 damaged. It was just as well for the survivors' morale that they did not know the actual German losses—31 destroyed, 12 written off, and 34 damaged—a loss of 3.5 percent of total fighter aircraft available.[2]

Weather may have hampered the takeoff on 14 October, but at payoff time the B-17s found the targets clear or barely obscured by smoke. They bombed well, placing numerous bombs on the three main bearings factories. Albert Speer, Hitler's minister of armaments, recalled that this raid had cut production of ball bearings by two-thirds at a time when the Germans had already exhausted their reserves due to production lost in the 17 August raid. He further noted that attempts to buy bearings from Sweden and Switzerland had scant success, in part because of Allied preemptive purchases. Only the substitution of slide bearings whenever possible and the Allied failure to follow up the attack prevented catastrophe for the Luftwaffe.[3] On this point Speer displays a somewhat selective memory. The Allies had negotiated an agreement with the Swedes that limited their sale of bearings to the Germans, but the agreement had a monetary ceiling, not a ceiling on quantity. The Swedes, surrounded by the Germans and Finns, managed to maintain themselves. They simply sold to the Germans exactly the type of bearings they most needed up to the monetary maximum agreed upon with the Allies. A survey of German industry revealed enormous amounts of bearings on hand, well above standard American and British practices— another example of how disorganized German industrial mobilization was.[4] Although in this instance, at least, haphazard inventory controls proved of great benefit.

The Germans had more slack in their economy compared to their enemies. This slack accounted for a large proportion of its resilience to strategic bombing. For much of the war, bombing only knocked out reserve capacity. In contrast conventional strategic bombing on an industry that based its production on an on-time delivery or inventory system, such as those we now find in late-twentieth-century Japan or the United States, would likely have instantaneous if not disastrous results.

Given the heavy losses sustained in the second Schweinfurt raid, the Eighth threw in the towel and accepted, for the time being, that it could not launch unescorted bombers deep into Germany. For the rest of the year, it confined itself to raids in France, the Ruhr, and the German coast—all within the range of Allied fighter escort. On 20 October the Eighth sent out its last bomber mission of the month; eight fighter groups, including one of P-38s, participated. The Americans used Oboe for the first time; however, the equipment failed, leaving 282 bombers to find the city area of Düren on their own. One hundred fourteen bombers attacked, losing nine aircraft.

An answer to the Eighth's situation lay in the expanding pipeline of units and men flowing from the United States to the United Kingdom. After months of development and some good fortune, large numbers of long-range P-38s and P-51s arrived in the first quarter of 1944. The first P-38 group, the 55th, became operational on the day after the Schweinfurt raid. In December P-38s of the 20th Fighter Group and P-51s of the 354 Fighter Group also came on line.

Notes

1. Hinsley, *British Intelligence*, vol. 3, pt. 1, 296.
2. Murray, *Strategy for Defeat*, 225.
3. Speer, *Inside the Third Reich*, 286.
4. Webster and Frankland, *Strategic Air Offensive*, 3:272–75.

Development of the Long-Range Escort Fighter

Any solution to the problem of providing long-range escort of heavy bombers had to overcome two basic challenges. First, the escorts would have to protect the bombers from their home base to the target and back. Second, they would have to match or exceed the performance of enemy interceptors. The YB-40 experiment demonstrated that increasing the integral defenses of bomber formations was unlikely to improve the odds for survival against German interceptors. The solution to the escort problem, then, would have to come from improving the performance of the AAF's fighters. On this point the minds of the world's prewar air staffs locked up. No air force could conceive of a long-range escort aircraft that could carry the fuel and armament required for a long-range escort and still equal the performance of the defender's much lighter and more effective single-engine interceptors. The AAF's thinking at this juncture focused almost entirely on heavily armed, multi-engine bomber aircraft. Its entire strategic doctrine rested on the idea that such aircraft would not need escorts. Hence, the planners and strategists in the AAF had little intellectual capital to invest in conceiving and employing long-range escorts.

As late as October 1941 Spaatz, as chief of the air staff, appointed a board of pursuit and air matériel officers to recommend "the future development of pursuit aircraft." The opinions of the board members, including Eaker and Col Frank O'Driscoll Hunter, illustrated the thinking of the AAF on the eve of war. Eaker played a key role in this board's decisions. He had just returned from England, where he had served as a special air observer until 1 October 1941. Arnold had instructed him to conduct "a broad study of all phases of fighter operations" and to obtain "the best thought now prevalent on the subject of escort fighter protection."[1] Eaker grilled senior RAF officers and came back with copies of reports concerning British and German fighter tactics and performance. He shared the information with the pursuit panel.

The views of the RAF on bomber escort aircraft, as Eaker accurately reported, paralleled those of the AAF. Eaker's visit to England came at the conclusion of Bomber Command's participation in the Circus missions. These short-range operations reinforced the prevailing RAF opinion that a single-engine fighter aircraft could not provide strategic escort. In May 1941 Portal had replied to a query from Churchill on escort fighters by noting, "increased range can only be provided at the expense of performance and maneuverability." He added, "the long-range fighter, whether built specifically as such, or whether given increased range by fitting extra tanks, will be at a disadvantage compared with the short range high performance fighter."[2] On 28

September, Portal repeated this view to Eaker and drew the logical conclusion "that the proper escort fighter will be a ship exactly like the bomber it is going to escort." The commander of the RAF Test, Research, and Experimental Unit spoke to Eaker of the impossibility of the large fighter getting through a screen of small fighters saying, "they will sting it to death."[3]

The organization of the RAF contributed to its inability to conceive of aircraft combining the range of the bomber with the performance of the fighter. The raison d'être of Fighter Command was the air defense of Britain. Its planes, especially the superb Spitfire series, had been designed and built for that purpose alone. They emphasized performance over endurance, which they did not need for the defense of English airspace. Fighter Command had little operational need to develop long-range fighters. Likewise, Bomber Command had committed itself to the strategic bombing of Germany at night. Night operations depended on avoiding and deceiving enemy defenses not fighting through them, which would have required escort aircraft. Bomber Command, too, had little operational need for escort aircraft.

Given the perceived lack of need and the limited resources available, the RAF's refusal to invest in escort aircraft and its failure to pursue technical solutions to extending the range of its fighters was understandable. In fact, the RAF never developed or employed substantial numbers of long-range escort fighters during the war. The strong opinions of a future ally with more than two years of combat experience—confirmed by AAF observers—reinforced the predisposition of the AAF pursuit board against endorsing a fighter-escort. The board members, like the RAF, could not overcome the seeming tautological improbability of the long-range escort fighter achieving success on the aerial battlefield.

The board made no recommendation for procurement of or research on a long-range escort fighter. Instead it suggested a "convoy defender." "Only with the assistance of such an airplane," warned the board, "may bombardment aviation hope to successfully deliver daylight attacks deep inside the enemy territory and beyond range of interceptor support." Yet, the board feared that the size and expense of a convoy defender would interfere with other projects, giving its development a low priority, "The Board is unable to say whether or not the project is worthwhile" and can only point out that if day bombardment is chosen as the method "to gain a decision in war against any other modern power" then those forces will require the "maximum attainable defensive firepower."[4] The board further directed that several ancillary items, such as pressurized drop tanks, be developed; however, it never connected the concept of drop tanks as an add-on to fighters to convert them to long-range escorts.

The US refusal to place a high priority on escort fighters stemmed from doctrine and technical considerations. As an observer in the United Kingdom during the Battle of Britain, Spaatz had seen how the Spitfire and Hurricane outmatched the Bf-110. RAF technical personnel were convinced that a plane capable of long-range combat and successful dogfighting could not be built.

Spaatz and Eaker had seen the British and the Germans resort to night bombing because their bombardment aircraft could not survive in hostile daylight skies. They discounted that experience by calculating that the B-17 flew higher, was more rugged, and carried more and heavier guns than any European bomber. They also assumed, apparently out of pure chauvinism, that the Americans could and would maintain tighter defensive formations than the British or Germans. However, the service threw at least one anchor to windward when, in 1940–41, the AAF began a limited program to extend the range of escort fighters. It expanded the program in 1942.[5]

Even before the experiment with the YB-40 discredited the convoy-defender idea, the Americans had begun to look at increasing the range of fighter aircraft. Five of the most important ways to increase an aircraft's range are air-to-air refueling, increasing internal fuel storage, adding on external fuel tanks, redesigning the airplane, and a combination of the above.

Air-to-air refueling of combat aircraft on a large scale did not exist in 1943; not until after the war would the Americans develop the specialized aircraft and techniques required. Spaatz and Eaker, who pioneered air-to-air fueling in the late 1920s, surely would have adopted it had it been feasible. The addition of several hundred more large tanker aircraft (built at the expense of bombers) taking off from British bases and trolling about in airspace with minimal air control and congested with bombers and fighters would likely have made refueling too difficult. Changing the physical characteristics of existing fighter aircraft, by decreasing weight, reducing the drag coefficient, changing engine settings, or other technological innovations would, in all probability, gain range. However, if such modifications reduced performance or combat worthiness, they could not be justified. Even if the changes did not adversely affect performance, they may have required the production of a new model or variant. If the latter, the appearance of the new model in combat could be delayed for months or longer. Thus, the most practical way to extend a fighter's range in 1942–43 was to put more fuel in or on an aircraft, or some combination of the two. The AAF pursued these options in parallel.

Prewar planners had not foreseen the great demand for drop tanks. Those involved in early deployments and combat in the Pacific filled Arnold's in-basket with requests for range extensions. Soon the same requests came in from North Africa and from Allies flying US-built aircraft. Nonetheless, not until 24 February 1943, did the AAF begin to investigate drop tanks, as opposed to ferrying tanks, for combat aircraft.[6] Constructing drop tanks encountered no insurmountable technical problems but minor setbacks did occur. Drop tanks needed to withstand pressurization up to 25,000 feet and could not affect handling of aircraft. Drop tanks required suitable pumps, braces, and shackles, and they had to withstand excessive warping and leaking. Since they hung from combat aircraft, they needed to be self-sealing. Next came the question of construction: plywood, paper, duckcloth, steel, and so forth. Then came the question of priority within the US war economy. Not every project can be number one or nothing is number one. That very situation had almost stopped the US war effort in World War I. Marshall, Arnold, and even Adm Ernest J. King (US chief of naval operations) did not want to see a repeat of this situation. Eventually, the US program to manufacture steel, 75- and 150-gallon drop tanks came together, and the tanks produced passed the flight and engineering tests. However, the AAF Air Matériel Command did not place the contracts for the procurement of the first 150,000 tanks until mid-September 1943.

In the meantime, the Eighth demonstrated the advantage of drop tanks. It discovered more than 1,000 200-gallon tanks in one of its storage depots and equipped several P-47s with them. On 28 July P-47s equipped with these tanks surprised Luftwaffe fighters as they attacked B-17s returning from a mission. The US fighters downed several German planes. However, because of confused lines of authority, the Eighth failed to notify the British Ministry of Aircraft Production of its requirements for continued production of drop tanks. When the crunch came after the second Schweinfurt attack in October 1943, the Eighth discovered that British production of drop tanks had slipped far behind schedule. Although the Eighth resolved the problem, British production of their 108-gallon paper tank did not meet the Eighth's requirements until December. Moreover, when the AAF supply system learned of the British program, they cut back on the manufacture of drop tanks in the United States for the Eighth.

The AAF reversed this action and increased production of US-assembled drop tanks in September 1943. By then the AAF in the Mediterranean was requesting 23,000 drop tanks a month and the Eighth 22,000.[7] With the upcoming invasion of Europe, these requirements would go higher. The Eighth received the top priority for all drop tanks and modification kits. By the end of the year, because of concerted efforts by manufacturers, each of the Eighth's fighter stations had between 2,000 and 3,000 drop tanks—a 30- to 45-day supply.[8] All American fighter aircraft attached to the Eighth, and later to the Fifteenth Air Force, now had external tanks, which increased their range for greater support of the heavy bombers. For maximum escort range, the AAF needed to join drop tanks with increased internal fuel storage.

In 1941–42 the AAF had two fighter aircraft that might serve as a long-range escort—the P-47 and the P-38. Not only external but higher capacity internal fuel tanks should increase their range. Other pursuit aircraft—the P-39 and P-40—did not have the ceiling or the necessary performance to justify adaptation for either upgrade (drop tanks or larger internal fuel tanks). In April 1943 the AAF began to examine ways of increasing the internal fuel capacity of the P-38, the aircraft considered by the AAF as the most suitable escort fighter. By putting 55-gallon tanks in each wing and a 110-gallon tank behind the cockpit, Lockheed, the plane's manufacturer, brought total internal tankage up to 420 gallons. They delivered the new plane to the AAF proving grounds in November 1943. Before this initiative came to fruition, Arnold, who had followed extending the range of the fighters extremely closely, intervened. At the end of July he sent a personal representative, Maj Gen William E. Kepner, to Lockheed (P-38), Republic (P-47), and North American (P-51) to beg their engineers, almost on bended knee, to do their utmost to extend the range of their aircraft. On 3 September, on a visit to the Eighth, Arnold convinced Marshall, via Atlantic cable, to allocate triple-A priority to range extension. While the P-38 easily accommodated more fuel tanks, the inner construction of the P-47 limited efforts to increase its internal tankage. A 65-gallon internal tank under the pilot required raising the cockpit and changing all bulkheads and fittings in the front part of the fuselage. It took until March 1944 for Republic to incorporate the changes into the production line (P-47D-15). The firm's engineers stayed true to their word. As the war progressed they redesigned the aircraft to weigh less and added another 65-gallon center tank and an internal 100-gallon tank in each wing. With two 100-gallon drop tanks, a late model P-47N had an escort range of more than 2,000 miles.

A better aircraft soon replaced both the P-47 and P-38. As of July 1944 the Eighth had no P-38 groups and only one P-47 group. These heavy and powerful aircraft whose performance compared favorably to their opponents would soon be shifted to another role or another front. The P-47's range increased too slowly and it performed too well as a ground-attack fighter to be converted to an escort. The P-38 lacked the range to reach such targets as Berlin and points east, and its two Allison engines reacted badly to the wintertime combination of bitter cold and high humidity in Europe. They failed too often. While many a pilot owed his life to the P-38's second engine, others lost their lives because the first engine's failure left them vulnerable to the Luftwaffe or caused the second engine to go. More than half the P-38 losses over Germany were traced to its engines. Even before these problems were manifested, the AAF had picked another aircraft as its main escort.

The aircraft that proved the ultimate solution to the long-range escort problem—the P-51 Mustang—had its maiden flight in October 1940. The Mustang was the direct result of a contract between the British government and the North American Aviation Corporation. The contract, signed in January 1940, specified completion within 120 days of a prototype single-engine fighter aircraft. Within 117 days, North American rolled out the plane, complete except for its engine. The design incorporated lessons learned from the early days of the war and included simple lines for ease of production; an in-line, water-cooled engine; and an advanced laminar-flow wing section design for improved performance. The designers had produced a clean-looking airframe with a low drag coefficient. The AAF initially rejected the P-51 because it considered the water-cooled engine more vulnerable to damage than radial, air-cooled power plants. As recompense for giving permission to the British to produce the aircraft in the United States, the AAF took delivery of two of the initial 10 aircraft for testing. Maj Gen Orvill Anderson, the Eighth Air Force chief of bomber operations, recalled his first experience with the P-51 when he served as a junior officer in Washington, DC, "Not having had anything to do with the design, growth, test of the P-51, we looked with disfavor on that airplane." He added that the AAF's own foot-dragging delayed the P-51's deployment for at least nine months.

The original US-produced-and-designed Allison engine, the same used in the P-40, did not provide enough power and limited the P-51's best performance to altitudes below 15,000 feet, an operational ceiling unsuitable for escort of heavy bombers. The British, who appreciated the possibilities of the Mustang's sleek airframe, replaced the original engine with their own powerful Rolls-Royce Merlin 61 engine. The mating of one of the most outstanding piston-driven aircraft engines ever made and a superb airframe resulted in a hybrid of distinguished performance, perhaps the best propeller-driven fighter of World War II.

The Americans, too, made a key contribution to the Mustang's development by increasing its internal fuel capacity, which extended the P-51's escort range to 475 miles—the maximum range of a P-47 with drop tanks. With two 108-gallon drop tanks, the P-51's range expanded to more than 650 miles (to Berlin and beyond). These improvements made the P-51 the preferred escort for the American heavy bombers and the dominant fighter over Europe for the last year of the war. However, it did not come into mass production in the United States until 1942 and did not reach US fighter groups in England until December 1943. The Eighth Air Force received the Mustang just in time to help turn the tide of the air war. Combined with the yeoman-like service of P-47s equipped with their new longer-range drop tanks, the P-51 was instrumental in preventing the US strategic bomber effort from foundering because of excessive losses sustained in unescorted missions deep into Germany.[9] In the Mustang with its internal and external fuel tanks; light, clean, aerodynamically sound air frame; and its powerful Rolls-Royce engine, the Allies had a superb long-range escort with performance exceeding that of its enemies.

Moreover, the aircraft was a financial bargain. In 1943, each P-51 cost $58,824, compared with $105,567 for a P-38 and $104,258 for a P-47.[10] An aircraft privately designed and built in less than four months with no government research and development input cost less, was easier to produce, and outperformed the two aircraft the AAF had spent years bringing to fruition. Perhaps the P-51 was a technological freak aided by wartime combat experience and superior British engine technology, or perhaps the Air Corps aircraft development program limited itself to overly conservative engineering.[11]

Notes

1. Memo, Arnold to Eaker, subject: Additional Instructions on Trip to England, 22 August 1941, AFHSO, microfilm reel A1593, fr. 570.

2. Webster and Frankland, *Strategic Air Offensive*, 2:239.

3. Eaker to chief of the Army Air Forces, subject: Report on Trip to England n.d. (mid-October 1941), AFHSO, microfilm reel A1593, file no. 168.04–6.

4. Report of a Board of Officers, Appointed to Make Recommendations with Respect to Future Development of Pursuit Aircraft, Its Accessory Equipment and Operational Employment, to the chief of the Army Air Forces,

Washington, DC, 27 October 1941, 18 and 46, AFHSO, microfilm reel, frs. 324 and 358.

5. Boylan, *Development of the Long-Range Escort Fighter*, 50–53.

6. Ibid., 115.

7. Ibid., 129–30.

8. Ibid., 128.

9. Swanborough, *United States Military Aircraft Since 1909*, 369–76.

10. *Army Air Forces Statistical Control Digest, World War II*, table 82, 134.

11. See Kelsey, *Dragon's Teeth* (110–12) for a discussion of how Air Corps procurement policy may have encouraged "conservative" designs.

November

1 November: CCS—establishes US Fifteenth Air Force in Italy to bomb strategic targets in the Balkans, Northern Italy, Austria, and Southern Germany. Twelfth Air Force transfers all its heavy bombers, six groups, to the Fifteenth Air Force. Maj Gen James H. Doolittle appointed the Fifteenth's commander.

3 November: Eighth Air Force—dispatches over 500 heavy bombers for the first time. Also marks first use of H2X, the American variant of the British H2S, to lead the attacking force, in this case against Wilhelmshafen.

11–12 November: Fifteenth Air Force—attacks ball bearings plants in northern Italy and southern France.

16 November: Eighth Air Force—attacks heavy water production in Norway.

18 November: Eighth Air Force—attacks airfield in Norway, three bombers crash-land in Sweden.

18–19 November: Bomber Command—"Battle of Berlin" initiated; 15 attacks in the next three months.

25 November: Eighth Air Force—reaches strength of 22 operational heavy bomber groups.

In the first half of November 1943, RAF Bomber Command flew only one major raid in Germany: against Düsseldorf on 3 November. Two other attacks struck marshaling yards in France. On 18 November the command began a new campaign, the Battle of Berlin, with area raids on Berlin and Ludwigshafen. The long nights of winter made penetrations to Berlin and beyond more feasible in one sense but also more difficult because of harsh weather at the command's home bases and along the routes. In launching the battle Harris had the prime minister's support. Churchill had expressed great interest in hitting Berlin since 1942. The air chief marshal also had a deadline he desired to overcome. Current Allied planning specified that, on 1 April 1944, Bomber Command and the Eighth would come under the control of the Allied commander of the cross-channel invasion. If Harris meant to prove that strategic bombing alone could win the war, he had to do so in the next four and one-half months.[1] The first Berlin raid lost a little more than 2 percent, a favorable augury. The mission to Ludwigshafen apparently attracted the bulk of the Luftwaffe's night fighters; the command lost 7.1 percent of its attacking force. The next night (19 November 1943) 232 bombers, using dead reckoning, hit the I. G. Farben chemical plant at Leverkusen. On 22 and 23 November Harris sent his bombers back to Berlin—992 attackers released 4,255 tons of bombs, including 2,200 tons of incendiaries. They lost 46 aircraft, 4.7 percent of the attacking force. After missions to Frankfurt, on the night of 25 November, the command struck Stuttgart, losing six of 162 attackers, and returned to Berlin, losing 28 of 407 attackers (6.9 percent) on 26 November. The major missions of the month over Germany, for the most part, had encountered heavy resistance. The overall rate of Bomber Command losses over Germany hovered perilously close to 5 percent, the figure Harris himself had set as unsustainable in the long run. The "Battle of Berlin" had only begun.

Of the eight large missions dispatched by the Eighth in November 1943, two went to Norway and the other six to Germany. On 16 November the Eighth bombed the molybdenum mine at Knaben and a hydroelectric plant suspected of producing heavy water for German atomic research at Rjuken—both in Norway. Two days afterwards, Eaker sent a diversionary attack to Kjeller outside Oslo to draw German attention from the true target—Rjuken. Nine planes out of 82 attacking aircraft were lost. The six missions into Germany struck seaports and targets in the Ruhr valley under the protective umbrella of P-47 and P-38 escorts; thus, the bomber crews did not encounter significant resistance from the Luftwaffe. Portions of five of the six missions had specific orders from the

Eighth Air Force command to bomb city areas instead of precision targets. The Eighth put up 566 bombers, of which 539 reached the target, to attack the port area of Wilhelmshafen on 3 November. They released 1,450 tons of bombs, more than one-third of them incendiaries, a good mixture for city busting but not necessarily as effective on an industrial area. In the raid the American PFF aircraft first used H2X, the American version of H2S. In late October the Eighth received a dozen H2X-equipped B-17s; they joined the four H2S B-17s to serve as PFF aircraft. The US Radiation Laboratory at the Massachusetts Institute of Technology, which produced the H2X, could supply no more sets for three to four months, which left the Americans dependent on a mere handful of radar aircraft until mid-March. On 5 November small precision raids struck synthetic oil plants in Gelsenkirchen while large raids bombed the city areas of Gelsenkirchen and Münster. The day's bombing was all visual. Two days later, 92 aircraft hit the city areas of Düren and Wessel using Oboe. On 13 November 117 bombers hit the city area of Bremen, the deepest (most easterly) target in Germany assailed during the month. The raid lost 16 bombers, almost 10 percent. The Eighth again struck Bremen on 26 November with 422 bombers, losing 25 bombers (6 percent) and on 29 November with 137 bombers, losing 13 bombers (10 percent). On the last day of the month a PFF aircraft equipped with H2S led 78 bombers to the city area of Solingen. The American effort over Germany suffered an overall loss rate of 4 percent—within tolerable limits. However, the Eighth attacked only targets on the fringes of the Reich, leaving the Luftwaffe with air superiority by day over the German heartland.

US Fifteenth Air Force

The third and newest strategic air force in Europe, the US Fifteenth Air Force, began operations on 1 November 1943. The next day it dispatched its initial strategic mission against the Messerschmidt fighter assembly complex at Wiener Neustadt. As usual the Americans found it a tough nut. They lost 11 out of 113 attackers. For the rest of the month the Fifteenth and No. 205 Group concentrated on marshaling yards, bridges, and transportation viaducts in Italy and southern France. The Fifteenth also bombed German airfields near Athens to assist British operations in the eastern Mediterranean. The Fifteenth and No. 205 Group followed up the Eighth's attacks with strikes on French bearings manufacturers at Annecy, France, and Italian bearings plants at Turin and Villar Perosa, Italy. The plants were not important sources of German bearings, but since the Allies assumed that the raids on Schweinfurt had adversely affected German production and caused shortages, effective strikes on smaller plants could only worsen the enemy situation. As noted earlier, the Germans did face a bearings crisis but not one as severe and prolonged as the Allies estimated. In its first month the Fifteenth made only a modest contribution to the strategic air war. This role would soon change as reinforcements arrived. By May 1944 the Americans planned to have 21 operational heavy bomber groups in Italy—a force capable of launching 1,000 aircraft.

Strategic attacks by the heavy bombers of the Ninth and Twelfth Air Forces on Rome, Ploesti, and Wiener Neustadt in the summer of 1943 strengthened and encouraged Gen Carl Spaatz's conviction that bombers based in his command should participate in raids on Germany. On 13 August, a week after the Wiener Neustadt raid, Spaatz wrote to Robert A. Lovett, assistant secretary of war for air, "I am increasingly convinced that Germany can be forced to her knees by aerial bombardment alone. The process can be accelerated by us [the AAF] if suitable bases are available in the Mediterranean area." He wrote to Gen Henry Arnold that the fate of the air forces after the invasions of Sicily and Salerno concerned him greatly: "If we can establish ourselves in Italy, much of Germany can be reached from there with better weather conditions at our airdromes than prevail normally in England. This would immediately, when applied, force a dispersion of the German fighter and anti-aircraft defenses."[2]

Arnold held different views. In late July he told a member of the RAF delegation in Washington that the fall of Sicily and potential fall of Italy did little for the Allies against Germany. The bombing offensive against Germany must come from Britain and Gen Dwight Eisenhower should return the B-24s loaned to him immediately. The best way to finish the war was to attack the shortest way across the channel. Arnold considered

Spaatz's call for reinforcements an extravagance that could compromise the cross-channel invasion.[3] When the RAF delegation reported these opinions to Air Chief Marshal Charles Portal, he instructed his mission in Washington to present the RAF's case for strategic bombing from Italy, especially from the central (Rome) and north (Po Valley) Italian areas. Portal, like Spaatz, pointed to the advantages of spreading German fighter defenses and placing more vital targets within easy range. He said that without question the Allies should create in Italy the largest bomber force that the logistical base could support.[4]

Sir William Welsh, the head of the RAF delegation, discussed Portal's ideas with Arnold on 1 August and reported back to Portal that the chief of the AAF had modified his views considerably. Arnold had agreed completely on the need for a bomber force flying from northern Italy. A decisive factor in changing Arnold's mind may have been British intelligence indicating significant dispersal of German fighter assembly and manufacturing capacity to Austria and other southern European targets beyond the range of the Eighth Air Force's heavy bombers.[5]

At the Quebec Conference (14 to 25 August), Roosevelt, Churchill, and the Combined Chiefs of Staff (CCS) agreed on "strategic bombing operations from Italian and Central European bases, complementing Pointblank."[6] Portal remarked, "if we could have a strong force of Heavy and Medium Bombers there [northern Italy] in the near future, Germany would be faced with a problem insoluble."[7] Arnold wrote to Spaatz that "a planned and sustained strategic bombing attack on German key industrial targets from Mediterranean bases" warranted the top priority.[8]

Once the CCS accepted Italy as a base for strategic bombing, details of command, control, strength, and coordination with the Eighth Air Force needed attention. By October, Arnold and his staff had drawn up plans for a new strategic air force—the Fifteenth Air Force. On 9 October he submitted to the Joint Chiefs of Staff his design for turning the Twelfth Air Force into a tactical air force and establishing the Fifteenth as a strategic air force. Both forces would operate under the theater commander, but the Fifteenth would occasionally receive directives from the CCS for employment in the Combined Bomber Offensive. The Fifteenth would receive the Twelfth's six heavy groups and 15 more from the continental United States.

Eaker objected vigorously, arguing that the plan diverted forces from Britain and sacrificed the principle of concentration of force, thereby jeopardizing Pointblank and Overlord. The JCS, after discussions with Eisenhower's chief of staff and Spaatz, approved Arnold's plan. They then submitted the matter to the CCS, who had overall control of the Combined Bomber Offensive. The CCS agreed, with a proviso inserted by the British, that if logistical problems prevented the stationing of heavy bomber groups in the Mediterranean, then the excess bombers would go to Britain.[9] The CCS directed Eisenhower to employ the Fifteenth Air Force against strategic targets. They allowed him to use units of the Fifteenth reassigned from the Twelfth Air Force (six heavy bomber groups and two long-range fighter groups) primarily against political targets in the Balkans and in support of land forces in Italy rather than against Pointblank targets, until land forces secured air bases north and east of Rome.[10] At that time the bombers and fighters would then revert to the full control of the Fifteenth for use against strategic targets.

On 22 October, the same day the CCS approved the formation of the Fifteenth, Spaatz reassured Arnold on the logistical capabilities of southern Italy. Spaatz obtained an authoritative statement on logistics from a West Point classmate, Lt Gen Brehon B. Somervell, the crusty commanding general of the Army Services of Supply. Somervell, the Army's chief logistics and supply officer with a status virtually equal to Arnold's, visited the Italian theater and Spaatz at the end of October. Armed with Somervell's estimate and the results of a recent inspection, Spaatz minimized the supply difficulties. Eisenhower appended a staff report that indicated somewhat more soberly that, yes, Italy could support the planned influx of bombers and escorts. Eisenhower's report gave Arnold the ammunition he needed to refuse to discuss the issue when the British again questioned the capability of Italy to support additional strategic groups.[11]

Portal had always favored strategic attacks from Italy because he assumed that the central and northern portions of the peninsula would be available for bases. Hitler's decision to defend Italy south of Rome and Field Marshal Albert Kesselring's successful execution of that policy upset Portal's calculations. In this light he questioned the effectiveness not only of increasing strategic airpower with the addition of more US heavy bombardment groups in the Mediterranean theater but also the basing of bombers at the Foggia fields in the south.[12] In London, Eaker, too, took issue with the rate of the Fifteenth's bomber and fighter group buildup specified in Eisenhower's instructions. Eaker privately protested to the British that the nine heavy bomber groups scheduled to go to Italy in November, December, and January should come to Britain, even if Italy could support them logistically.[13]

On 26 October the British chiefs of staff, reflecting Portal's and Eaker's positions, suggested to the CCS in Washington that the 15 heavy bombardment groups scheduled for Italy be redirected to their original destination, Britain. They further asked that the six heavy-bombardment groups already in Italy be assigned primarily to Pointblank even before the fall of Rome.[14] Churchill seconded these suggestions. He instructed Portal not to allow the strategic buildup to interfere with the battle for Rome but to give the armies and their tactical air support first priority. Churchill emphasized that the goal from Britain must be "saturation" or overwhelming strength for the American daylight attacks.[15]

When the British Joint Staff Mission in Washington presented the British position to the CCS, the Americans brushed it aside. At the 29 October meeting, Arnold, referring repeatedly to assurances given him by Spaatz, said that the buildup of the Fifteenth did not interfere with the strengthening of Eisenhower's tactical air or ground forces. Arnold maintained that bombers in Italy would be more effective than those in Britain and renewed his promise to send to Britain all groups that the Fifteenth could not supply or operate effectively. Gen George C. Marshall reminded the British that Eisenhower himself had called for a strategic air force in Italy, in part to have those forces at his disposal in case of a ground emergency, and that Eisenhower could decide the relative priorities. With the losses during the Schweinfurt mission of 14 October in mind, Marshall observed that strategic forces in Italy would help reduce "very heavy casualties" incurred in daylight bombing over northwest Europe.[16] Having already accepted the creation of an additional US strategic air force, the British could hardly continue to object to the way the Americans divided their own forces, especially in light of assurances that Pointblank remained the prime objective and that the Americans could supply their own forces. The AAF established the Fifteenth Air Force on 1 November 1943.

Notes

1. Webster and Frankland, *Strategic Air Offensive*, 2:197–98.
2. Letter, Spaatz to Lovett, 20 August 1943, Spaatz Papers, Diary.
3. Message, Marcus 914 RAFDEL to Air Ministry (personal for CAS), 23 July 1943, PRO AIR 20/1011.
4. Message, Welsh 78, Air Ministry [Portal] to RAFDEL [Welsh], 26 July 1943, PRO AIR 20/1011.
5. See note by the Air Staff, Welsh to Arnold, 31 July 1943, Arnold Papers, box 274.
6. CCS, 303/3, 17 August 1943.
7. Minutes, CCS 101st Meeting, 14 August 1943.
8. Letter, Arnold to Spaatz, 20 August 1943, Spaatz Papers, Diary.
9. For Arnold's plan see CCS 217/1, "Plan to Assure the Most Effective Exploitation of the Combined Bomber Offensive," 19 October 1943. See also Craven and Cate, *Torch to Pointblank*, 2:564–65, for the course of negotiations. Message JSM1276, Britman, Washington to Air Ministry, 23 October 1943, PRO AIR 20/4419, contained the British side of the decision.
10. Message R-4757/698 (FAN 254), CCS to Eisenhower, 23 October 1943, PRO AIR 20/1011.
11. Memo, Somervell to Spaatz, 30 October 1943; message 3787, Eisenhower [Spaatz] to Arnold, 30 October 1943; message 1420, Arnold to Eisenhower for Spaatz, 31 October 1943, Spaatz Papers, Diary.
12. Message W840, Portal to Welsh, AIR PRO 20/1011.
13. Minute, assistant chief of the air staff (Ops.) to the chief of the air staff, 25 October 1943, AIR PRO 20/1011.
14. Message OZ3387 (COS [W] 908), British chiefs of staff to Britman, Washington, PRO AIR 20/4419.
15. Minute D.191/3, Churchill to chiefs of staff and Portal, PRO AIR 20/1011.
16. Message JSM 1290, from Joint Staff Mission, Washington, to War Cabinet Office, London, 29 October 1943, PRO AIR 20/4419.

December

3–7 December: CCS—Air Chief Marshal Portal informs the Combined Chiefs at Cairo Conference that the American portion of the Combined Bomber Offensive, of which he has overall direction, is three months behind schedule. Arnold expresses displeasure at Eaker's performance. Americans and British discuss command arrangements for Combined Bomber Offensive. British refuse a single Allied strategic air commander and CCS leaves offensive under Portal's direction. Americans decide to set up their own headquarters to coordinate Eighth and Fifteenth.

5 December: Ninth Air Force—P-51s of 357th Fighter Group (under Eighth Air Force control) fly first escort mission from United Kingdom.

13 December: Eighth Air Force—dispatches over 700 heavy bombers for first time, 649 of them attack Bremen, Hamburg, and Kiel. Escorting P-51s (assigned to Ninth AF), without drop tanks, reached the limit of their escort range.

16–17 December: Bomber Command—first intruder raids by Mosquitoes and Bristol Beaufighters. Bomber Command—first attack on Crossbow—German V-weapon sites in France.

20 December: Eighth Air Force—first AAF employment of "Window."

24 December: Eighth Air Force—reaches strength of 26 heavy bomber groups and launches first major Noball mission, 670 heavy bombers attacking 23 V-sites.

28 December: Eighth Air Force—second P-38 group becomes operational.

In December 1943 RAF Bomber Command flew six large raids into Germany: one to Leipzig, one to Frankfurt, four to Berlin. Out of 2,045 bombers reaching Berlin, the command lost 100 aircraft—4.9 percent. Of 1,027 aircraft attacking the other two cities, the command lost 66 aircraft. Casualties in the battle of Berlin remained at the potentially exhausting 5 percent level. On the night of 16 December, the command made its first attacks on V-1 launching sites under construction in France. This mission marked the beginning of Operation Crossbow. The Americans called the bombing of these targets Noball operations.* For the next eight months the bombing of the V-1's launch sites would consume more and more Allied resources and constitute a major strategic diversion.

The Eighth dispatched 12 major missions in December 1943: 10 to Germany and two to France. The raids attacking the Reich conformed to the previous month's pattern, attacks on port city areas and cities on major rivers in western Germany that did not expose unescorted bombers to German daylight fighters. The location of these targets provided H2X operators with a satisfactory land and water differentiation on their radar returns. The raids involved only shallow penetrations into Germany—all under cover of fighter escort. Eight of the 10 attacks—Soligen, Emden, Münster, Osnabrück, Ludwigshafen, and Bremen (three times)—struck city areas. Two other strikes hit U-boat yards at Kiel and Hamburg on 13 December. On the first mission into France on 24 December, 670 of the Eighth's bombers struck Crossbow targets with almost 1,750 tons of bombs. A week later 344 bombers blasted French airfields in the Bordeaux while 120 B-17s attacked two French ball bearing plants in the Paris area. Twelve American fighter groups put up 548 aircraft to escort the bombers. Of the 3,511 effective sorties in the major raids over Germany, the Eighth lost 127 bombers—3.6 percent of the force—once again conceding the high ground to the Luftwaffe. Until the AAF could reach

---

*Crossbow and Noball are essentially the same: Noball refers to attacks on specific targets while Crossbow refers to the bombing campaign against V-rocket sites.

the interior of Germany with losses reduced to an acceptable cost, it could neither knock out German fighter production nor severely damage the German war economy, either by precision bombing or with its freshly adopted policy of area bombing.

The policy of not flying deep into Germany reduced overall bomber losses, because up until late 1943 (and through May 1944) the majority of the Eighth's losses had been at the hands of the enemy fighters. However, the interim policy of attacking targets closer to England put the bombers more frequently over targets with heavier antiaircraft gun defenses. The Germans, naturally, concentrated their antiaircraft defenses at forward targets to defend them and to interfere with bombers flying over the guns on missions deeper into Europe. Forward targets were more likely to be attacked and the Luftwaffe, as a matter of policy, did not routinely commit fighters to defend against bombers with fighter escorts, that is, bombers hitting targets west of Aachen. In December 1943, for the first time in its history, flak inflicted over 30 percent (38 percent) of the Eighth's total heavy bomber losses.[1]

Compared with the Eighth's 24 operational heavy bomber groups, the Fifteenth had only 6 in December 1943. A variety of targets further attenuated the efforts of the Fifteenth and No. 205 Group as they struck the bearings works in Turin, U-boat pens in Toulon, rail yards in Sofia, airfields throughout occupied Italy, and especially marshaling yards, rail bridges, and viaducts in northern Italy. The airfields around Athens also received much attention. In the broad scheme of the war, these actions—never more than 120 bombers—constituted mere pinpricks on the thick German hide. This effect would change as the expanding volume of aircraft output from American production lines began to flow onto the airfields of Foggia, the Fifteenth's home base.

Command of the Combined Bomber Offensive

On 1 August Gen Henry Arnold suggested to the head of the RAF delegation in Washington that the Allied bomber offensive required a single overall commander—a complex matter of great concern not only to the AAF and the RAF but to the theater commanders and the combined chiefs as well. The overall air commander would coordinate the strategic forces in Italy and Britain and prevent overlarge liaison staffs and constant appeals to the CCS for decisions. Air Marshal Sir William Welsh warned Portal that Arnold would bring up the subject at the Quebec Conference.[2]

The theater commanders, Gen Dwight D. Eisenhower in Italy and Lt Gen Jacob L. Devers in Britain, desired total authority over all air forces in their commands. Had the CCS and Allied governments granted complete control of the strategic bombers in their theater of operations to each of the individual theater commanders, it would have hamstrung the coordination of strategic bombing against Germany, especially if both theaters possessed strategic air forces based in their area of responsibility. The CCS, charged with the overall strategic direction of the war, had a stake in the issue. At the conferences in Washington (May 1943) and in Quebec (August 1943), the CCS had decided that an invasion of the continent required a successful strategic bombing campaign. As its first objective, the campaign would damage the Luftwaffe to the extent that it could not contest Allied air supremacy over the invasion area. The equally valid claims of the invasion commanders and ground troops for tactical support for preinvasion preparations, the landings, and postinvasion operations competed with the requirements for strategic bombing.

The AAF and RAF had separate agendas on the issue of command and control. Arnold wanted a single Allied commander of the strategic air force, the Eighth, the Fifteenth, and Bomber Command with headquarters in London and a status equal—presumably to include four-star rank—to that of the European and Mediterranean theater commanders. This idea, if approved, would in a stroke make the AAF and RAF's strategic air forces independent of the ground forces and ground force leaders and allow them the untrammeled pursuit of the strategic bomber campaign against Germany—the raison d'être of both air forces. In addition the incumbent who held the post would emerge with a prestige that at least matched that of the war's other theater commanders, such as Gens Dwight D. Eisenhower and Douglas MacArthur and Adm Chester Nimitz. Arnold assumed that the commander would be a member of the AAF because it would supply the majority of the aircraft. Even if an RAF officer got the job, Arnold would still have taken a large step toward eventual postwar autonomy for the AAF.

Next, Arnold wanted a US strategic air force commander in Europe (also based in London) who would take operational control of the Eighth and Fifteenth Air Forces and administrative control of the US air forces in Britain (the Eighth and Ninth). The AAF would thereby acquire control over all its heavy bombers directed toward Germany. Without such a headquarters, the two air forces, each under a separate theater commander, might well fail to coordinate their efforts adequately. Such a command would equal Bomber Command in prestige and exceed it in numbers. Because this headquarters would be in London, it could still take advantage of British intelligence and cooperate with Bomber Command—a unit already headed by an officer with the equivalent of four-star rank. His opposite US number would probably have to have the same rank and should also gain prestige and fame, which in turn would reflect well on the AAF. By giving the strategic commander administrative control of the Ninth, Arnold continued the current arrangement in the United Kingdom.[3]

By early October, Arnold carried his ideas to Harry Hopkins, President Roosevelt's alter ego, who endorsed them and presented them to the president.[4] A month later, Marshall, who supported Arnold, advised him not to press the question until after the settlement of the more important questions of a unified Mediterranean command proposed by the British and the appointment of a single supreme commander for all Anglo-American forces fighting the Germans.[5]

Arnold persevered. In November 1943 President Roosevelt sailed on board the new battleship USS *Iowa* on the first leg of his trip to the first "Big Three" meeting at Tehran, Iran. The Joint Chiefs of Staff (JCS) traveled with him and added the finishing touches to their plans for the Cairo Conference with Prime Minister Winston Churchill and Chinese leader Generalissimo Chiang Kai-shek (22–26 November) and for the Tehran Conference (28 November to 1 December). During the voyage, Arnold gained the backing of his fellow chiefs and the president for his command scheme. In a JCS memo for the president, dated 17 November 1943, the chiefs stated that the British and American strategic bombers required unity of command.[6]

Next, Arnold obtained JCS approval for the formation of a US headquarters—the US Strategic Air Forces in Europe (USSTAF)—to command and control all US strategic bombers in Europe. The theater commanders retained the right upon notification of the commanding general, USSTAF, to deploy bombers in the event of a tactical or strategic emergency. The JCS also agreed to Arnold's suggestion for a commanding general, Carl A. Spaatz. His name went forward to the president with the rest of the package.[7]

The RAF diametrically opposed Arnold's proposals. It wished, for the most part, to maintain the status quo, which best served its interests. The RAF chief of staff had received from the CCS the task of coordinating the Eighth and Bomber Command effort. On paper, and subject to concurrence by the AAF, the British already directed the Combined Bomber Offensive, while Bomber Command remained independent from the AAF. Maintaining Bomber Command's autonomy was important because the balance of heavy bomber strength, heretofore in favor of the British, would swing dramatically to the Americans in the first six months of 1944, when almost 40 new US heavy bomber groups would arrive in Italy and the United Kingdom. The British also objected, too, that a new command would disrupt the excellent relations between the Eighth and the RAF, create a new unnecessary headquarters staff, and move the responsibility for coordination to Washington from London, which had intelligence and communications personnel trained and ready to work. As for the Fifteenth, the British asserted that tight, direct coordination between that force and the forces in Britain would be impossible and that shuttle bombing was not practical because bombers rapidly lost effectiveness when away from their own ground maintenance and supply echelons.[8]

Once the chiefs of state and their military staffs assembled in Cairo on 23 November, Arnold's proposals encountered stiff opposition from the British. Although Marshall and Roosevelt, on separate occasions, brought up the issue of an overall Allied strategic air force with Churchill, they could not overcome

British resistance. To Roosevelt's observation that "our strategic air forces from London to Ankara should be under one command," Churchill replied that a decision on the matter could be deferred until after Overlord—adding that the current system worked well enough.[9] The Americans and the British did not resolve this dispute until after the Tehran Conference, which dealt mainly with inter-Allied relations and Anglo-American efforts to reassure the Soviets that the Americans and British would open a second front against Germany in the spring of 1944.

At the second Cairo Conference, 3–7 December, the Americans and British settled their chief outstanding differences concerning strategy, strategic priorities, and operations. The Americans abandoned their quest for a supreme Allied strategic air force commander. The Allies did agree to institute the USSTAF. The British declined to interfere in what they regarded as an unwise, but purely American, decision.[10]

USSTAF would employ its strength against Pointblank targets in accordance with directives issued by the CCS, continue to coordinate activities with Bomber Command, and ensure that, in assignment of supplies and services between tactical and strategic operations, Pointblank had first priority. Arnold as commanding general, AAF, would have direct channels to the USSTAF commander "on matters of technical control, operational and training techniques, and uniformity of tactical doctrine." The implementing directive to the American theater commanders and commanding generals, USSTAF stated that it would remain under the direction of the chief of the air staff, RAF, as agent for the CCS, until coming directly under the control of the Supreme Allied Commander Allied Expeditionary Force (SACAEF) for Overlord at a later date. Should a tactical emergency arise, the theater commanders could employ the strategic forces upon notification of the CCS and CG, USSTAF.[11]

The change in command arrangements brought personnel changes, not all of them accepted with good graces, in the AAF's higher ranks. The president and the JCS had already approved Spaatz's appointment to command USSTAF as early as November. On 8 December Arnold obtained Eisenhower's approval. Eisenhower, as the newly appointed commander of the cross-channel invasion, would have control of the heavy bombers at some point before invasion. He required a bomber commander he trusted. At the same time Air Marshal Arthur Tedder, the head of air forces in the Mediterranean, would go to the United Kingdom as Eisenhower's deputy but not his air leader. This left the top air post in the Mediterranean vacant, and Arnold had already obtained British agreement that the position would go to an American. These decisions enabled Arnold to transfer Lt Gen Ira C. Eaker from England to Italy. He had purposely moved Eaker to a more prestigious assignment while removing him from day-to-day control of heavy bombers. Arnold also gained Eisenhower's and Spaatz's agreement to this move on 8 December. In many ways, save perhaps the most important one, the change seemed wise. As Spaatz pointed out, having two of the AAF's most senior officers in the same theater made little sense when those two officers could fill important assignments in different theaters. The new arrangements called for Eighth Air Force headquarters to lose many of its functions to USSTAF. The rump Eighth Air Force headquarters would have far more limited duties and direction of its actions. To have Eaker stay in the United Kingdom and reduce him to the rank of Eighth Air Force commander when he had previously been commander of all AAF forces in the European theater would be an obvious demotion. However, human affairs are almost never so logical. Arnold's moves had not been disinterested and Eaker reacted not only as if he had been "kicked upstairs" but as if he had been kicked somewhere lower on his body.

Simply put, Arnold wanted Eaker removed. At the second Cairo Conference, during a meeting of the CCS on 4 December, Arnold left no doubt in listeners' minds about his unfavorable view of Eaker's efforts and his ability to control a strategic air force. Arnold complained of "lack of flexibility in operations" despite numerous inspections and reports. He noted that Eaker's air units sustained only a 50 percent aircraft availability rate (in an industrialized country) as opposed to 60 to 70 percent in other (more primitive) theaters.[12] Arnold decried Eaker's dispatch of only one 600-aircraft operation in the whole month of November. Arnold said, "the failure to destroy targets was due directly to the failure to employ planes in sufficient numbers. A sufficient weight of bombs was not being dropped on the targets to destroy them nor was the proper priority of targets being followed."[13]

Arnold found that failure intolerable. The hostile tone used in his memoirs to describe his September inspection of the Eighth revealed a growing disenchantment with Eaker's progress. Arnold's wrath surfaced in his memoirs. On his trip to England in September 1943, Arnold described his flight across the Atlantic during which he listened to radio reports of B-17s running out of fuel and crashing into the sea on the ferry route between Gander, Newfoundland, and Prestwick, Scotland. Arnold had worked himself into a heart attack to get those planes and their crews for the AAF and into Eaker's command. Yet these planes were lost before ever reaching combat. "I was not satisfied," Arnold remarked.[14] While Arnold was in England, one large raid by the Eighth misfired over Stuttgart. Not one of the 338 B-17s sent out reached its primary target. Arnold noted darkly, "Certain features of the operation never did find their way into reports sent up through channels."[15] When, in his opinion, the personnel changes offered Arnold a chance for a move that saved the AAF some embarrassment, he took it. He was convinced Eaker was not up to the job as a bomber commander.

Arnold also wanted Spaatz in the United Kingdom. First, Spaatz, unlike Eaker, had Eisenhower's complete confidence and trust. Eisenhower, as the presumed to be successful commander of the invasion of France from England and the following campaign to knock Germany out of the war, would have led the most important operations of the war. Eisenhower and his associates would get the credit for having won the war. Secondly, Eaker had not, in Arnold's opinion, done the job in England, while Spaatz had done well in the Mediterranean. In a highly emotional and confidential letter to Spaatz written in February 1944, Arnold explained some of his reasoning for wanting Spaatz in London. Arnold had advanced the strategic air force for a purely military consideration—unity of command for the British and Italian portions of the bomber offensive. He went on:

> Another, and perhaps equally important, motive behind the formation of the United States Strategic Air Forces in Europe was my desire to

build an American Air Commander to a high position prior to the defeat of Germany. It is that aspect particularly, which has impelled me in my so far successful fight to keep your command parallel to Harris' command and, therefore, parallel to Ike's. If you do not remain in a position parallel with Harris, the air war will certainly be won by the RAF if anybody. Already the spectacular effectiveness of their devastation of cities has placed their contribution in the popular mind at so high a plane that I am having the greatest difficulty in keeping your achievement (far less spectacular to the public) in its proper role not only in publications, but unfortunately in military and naval circles and, in fact, with the President himself. Therefore, considering only the aspect of a proper American share in credit for success in the air war, I feel we must have a high air commander some place in Europe. Today you can be that commander.[16]

On 12 December, when Arnold left Tunis for Washington, he and Spaatz agreed that Maj Gen James H. Doolittle would command the Eighth and Maj Gen Nathan F. Twining would get the Fifteenth. Once back in the Pentagon, Arnold put the changes into effect. Marshall was in the Pacific on an inspection trip.

Eaker, however, almost upset the new arrangements by refusing to accept them lying down. Instead of saluting and flying south, he fired off letters to Arnold, Spaatz, Marshall, Eisenhower, Portal, and his theater commander, Devers, asking to stay and see it through with the Eighth. To Maj Gen James E. Fechet, a former head of the Air Corps and an old friend, Eaker said, "I feel like a pitcher who has been sent to the showers during a World Series game."[17] Eaker's *cri de coeur* (cry from the heart) resonated at the very highest levels. Marshall, who lost the post of commanding the cross-channel invasion to Eisenhower on 6 December 1943, still had the bitter taste of that disappointment in his mouth. When Eaker's letter hit his desk, he reacted with uncharacteristic spleen. He particularly questioned Spaatz's and Tedder's motives for moving to London and implied they were self-serving.[18] Only Eisenhower's assurances that he approved of the moves and that all was, indeed, on the up-and-up, quieted the provoked chief of staff.[19]

Although Portal, who was in a good position to have observed his performance, took up his case, Eaker got little support from his own service.[20] He accepted his new assignment, perhaps with less than his usual good grace, but he accepted it. His temporary rebellion quashed, Eaker left his greatest task of the war and went south, where he continued to serve his country well with his considerable military and diplomatic skills. For his part, Spaatz treated Eaker (his old friend) as if he controlled the Fifteenth and, in an act of courtesy all the sweeter because it was in no way expected or required, he routed all his messages to Twining through Eaker's headquarters.

Notes

1. AAF Office of Statistical Control, *AAF Statistical Digest, World War II*, table 159: "Airplane Losses on Combat Missions in European Theater of Operations, By Type of Airplane and by Cause of Loss: Aug 1942 to May 1945 (Washington, DC: 1945), 225. The *Digest* reports a loss of 65 bombers to flak out of a total combat loss of 172 bombers in December 1943. This figure does not match the actual monthly loss of the Eighth (according to the Eighth's own records), but reflects those documents available to AAF Headquarters. There is usually some discrepancy between the two because of reporting lags between Washington and London. I use this figure to illustrate the trend and not for the exact number of aircraft actually lost.

2. Message, Marcus 133, Welsh to Portal, 2 August 1943, PRO AIR 20/1011.

3. See Joint Chiefs of Staff (JCS) memo to the president (aboard the USS *Iowa*), 17 November 1943, and CCS 400 "Integrated Command of US Strategic Air Forces in the European–Mediterranean Area," 18 November 1943, *FRUS: Cairo-Teheran*, 203–9, plus organization charts, 228–32.

4. Hopkins to FDR, memorandum, 4 October 1943, cited in Sherwood, *Roosevelt and Hopkins*, 764.

5. Copp, *Forged in Fire*, 445.

6. Memo, the JCS to the president, November, *FRUS: Cairo-Teheran*, 203–9.

7. CCS 400, 18 November 1943, *FRUS: Cairo-Teheran*, 228–32.

8. For British arguments against setting up a supreme strategic bombing commander, see CCS 400/1 "Control of Strategic Air Forces in Northwest Europe and the Mediterranean," memo by the British Chiefs of Staff, Cairo, 26 November 1943, *FRUS: Cairo-Teheran*, 432–35. See also Craven and Cate, *Torch to Pointblank*, 2:748.

9. Churchill-Marshall dinner meeting, 23 November 1943, and meeting of the CCS with Roosevelt and Churchill, 24 November 1943, *FRUS: Cairo-Teheran*, 326, 334.

10. Minutes, CCS 134th meeting, 4 December 1943; minutes, CCS 138th meeting, 7 December 1943, *FRUS: Cairo-Teheran*, 681–86 and 756–57.

11. CCS 400/2, "Control of Strategic Air Forces in Northwest Europe and in the Mediterranean," 4 December 1943, *FRUS: Cairo-Teheran*, 787–89.

12. The availability rate is the number of aircraft and crews officially listed as being in the theater or unit divided by the number of aircraft and crews actually available for combat. A 50 percent rate meant that Eaker had only half his planes ready to fight.

13. Minutes of the 134th Meeting of the CCS, *FRUS: Cairo-Teheran,* 685.

14. Arnold, *Global Mission,* 445. See also "Trip to England, August 31, 1943–September 8, 1943," Arnold Papers, Journals, box 271.

15. Arnold, 450.

16. Letter, Arnold to Spaatz, n.d. [late February 1944], AFHSO microfilm reel A1657A, frames 1082–85. Spaatz received this letter on 1 March and returned his copy, one of only two made, with his reply. A copy of Spaatz's copy, with Spaatz's penciled notations faithfully transcribed, found its way into AAF files and thence to microfilm.

17. Letter, Eaker to Fechet, 22 December 1943, Eaker Papers, box 7.

18. Message 5585, Marshall to Eisenhower, [received] 24 December 1943, D. D. Eisenhower Pre-Presidential Papers, Official Cable File, Eisenhower Library, Abilene, Kans.

19. Chandler, *Eisenhower's Papers,* vol. 3, item 1428, message W-8550, Eisenhower to Marshall, 25 December 1943, 1611–15.

20. Letter, Air Marshal W. L. Welch, head RAF Delegation in Washington, to Arnold, 14 December 1943, AF/HSO microfilm reel 34163, frs. 1260–61. This letter contains the text of Portal's message to Arnold and is found in a microfilm copy of the Papers of Gen Laurence Kuter. The originals are part of the collection of the US Air Force Academy at Colorado Springs.

**PART IV
1944**

Overlord and the Strategic Air Forces

In the five months between 1 January and 6 June 1944, the strategic air war in Europe turned in favor of the Anglo-Americans. Bomber Command, which suffered severely from the German night fighter force, halted operations deep into Germany. However, it developed the ability to bomb far more accurately at night than even its commander, Sir Arthur Harris, had conceived possible. The command's accuracy enabled it to take a large role in the preparations for the cross-channel invasion (code-named Overlord). As for the Americans, their aggressive use of long-range fighters and attritional routing of bombers provoked a sustained battle with the Luftwaffe day fighter force, which, in the end, broke the Germans' back. The next five monthly segments address the operations and new battle tactics of the strategic air forces. Two underlying significant subtexts not only had a pivotal influence on the minds and decisions of the ranking airmen, soldiers, and statesmen responsible for Overlord and Pointblank, but also had a direct impact on target selection—the key to any strategic offensive. The command and control of the strategic air forces and the nature of their relationship to the supreme commander of the Allied Expeditionary Force (SCAEF), Gen Dwight Eisenhower, the man charged with executing the cross-channel invasion, constituted the minor or perhaps merely the less contentious theme. The second and major theme, the selection of the specific targets, which the strategic air forces would bomb in support of Overlord, generated a far more sustained controversy. To provide a more complete understanding of the context of preinvasion operations, this section will examine the issues of command and control and target selection for the strategic air forces in the months before D-day.

Command and Control of the Strategic Air Forces

The exact roles that USSTAF under the command of Carl Spaatz and the large RAF metropolitan commands (Air Defense of Great Britain [ADGB], Coastal, and Bomber) would play in supporting the invasion became an issue in January 1944 soon after Eisenhower's arrival in the United Kingdom.[1] He achieved a barely satisfactory solution only after three months of negotiations. At the beginning of 1944, Air Chief Marshal Sir Trafford Leigh-Mallory, commander of the AEAF, had operational control of the Anglo-American tactical air forces—the British 2d Tactical Air Force and the US Ninth Air Force—assigned to support the cross-channel invasion. Leigh-Mallory served directly under Eisenhower. In addition to serving as Eisenhower's air component commander, Leigh-Mallory thought that all air forces assisting the invasion should also come under his control. This assumption met stiff resistance from the independent air leaders, in particular Spaatz and Harris.

At first glance Leigh-Mallory seemed a sound choice as commander in chief, Allied Expeditionary Air Force. He had specialized in army cooperation (that part of the RAF assigned to supporting the ground forces) and in the offensive use of fighter aircraft. In World War I he had served as an army cooperation pilot and, by 1927, he had become commandant, RAF School of Army Cooperation.[2] Shortly before World War II, he transferred to Fighter Command and led No. 12 Group, which defended the Midlands in the Battle of Britain. At the very end of the battle he replaced Air Vice-Marshal Sir Keith Park, a defensive fighter expert, as commander of No. 11 Group, which defended London and southeastern Britain. At that point the RAF switched to the offensive, carrying the air campaign to the Germans via fighter sweeps over France.[3] Eventually Leigh-Mallory became AOC Fighter Command; in November 1943 he officially gained his post as head of the AEAF.

A closer look at Leigh-Mallory revealed weaknesses that hampered his ability to participate in coalition warfare. He has been described "as a man of driving egoism," with a habitually haughty manner[4] and "an assertive temperament."[5] Even his apologists admit that because "Leigh-Mallory was so typically English, [and] sometimes tactless, almost pompous in appearance and naive in character without any finesse," Americans had trouble assessing "his ability, and they did little to try to understand him."[6] Once Leigh-Mallory absorbed an idea it became almost immutable;[7] he defended his own beliefs with a ferocity and an absolute refusal to compromise that exasperated his opponents and embittered his relations with them. This characteristic proved a grave defect, not because Leigh-Mallory adopted impractical ideas but because his obdurate adherence to his own strong ideas about air preparations for Overlord would intensify his conflict with the other air leaders.

Leigh-Mallory had little gift for interpersonal relationships. He did not get along with his American deputies, Maj Gen Hoyt S. Vandenberg and Brig Gen Frederick H. Smith, or with his subordinate air force commanders, Air Marshal "Mary" Coningham and Maj Gen Lewis H. Brereton.[8] After his elevation to the AEAF, the fates dealt unkindly with Leigh-Mallory in supplying his associates. He and Tedder, Eisenhower's deputy supreme commander and a man more distinguished in his own right as an air leader than Leigh-Mallory himself, differed in personality, experience, and outlook. Without informing Leigh-Mallory, Tedder replaced Air Marshal J. H. D'Albiac with Coningham as head of the 2d Tactical Air Force. At the time Leigh-Mallory assumed that the Allied ground forces commander, British general Bernard L. Montgomery, had consented to this change but in fact Montgomery would have picked any air leader over Coningham. Then, Tedder, at Montgomery's insistence, replaced Air Vice-Marshal Harry Broadhurst as commander of No. 83 Group. This group was the largest component of the 2d Tactical Air Force—composed of the fighter and fighter-bomber aircraft assigned to cooperate with the British 2d Army. Leigh-Mallory assumed that Coningham approved of this move but in fact Coningham would have picked any air leader over Broadhurst. Neither Broadhurst nor Coningham had much use for Leigh-Mallory.[9]

The British and American bomber men viewed Leigh-Mallory with suspicion.[10] Leigh-Mallory's natural reserve and somewhat ponderous and inarticulate mode of speech did not endear him to Spaatz and other Americans who mistook his manner for hostility and returned it in kind.[11] Leigh-Mallory's first American deputy, Brig Gen Haywood S. Hansell, was a highly regarded officer and personal friend of Spaatz. Arnold promoted Hansell and sent him to the Pacific to begin B-29 operations. It might have been better for all concerned had

Hansell stayed in London. The American contingent at AEAF headquarters needed high-quality officers to counterbalance the domination of that headquarters by Leigh-Mallory's appointments from Fighter Command. The staffing of Headquarters AEAF called for 150 RAF officers and 80 AAF officers.

AEAF headquarters remained an essentially British organization throughout its existence, which gave the AAF additional reason to view it with suspicion.[12] The Americans either did not understand or refused to acknowledge that one reason Leigh-Mallory had such a large British staff was that he also served as the commander of the home defenses. If his British staff had been equal in number to the American officers assigned to Headquarters AEAF, the British staff contingent would have been vastly overburdened.[13]

Spaatz's and Leigh-Mallory's disparate personalities added a note of personal acrimony to their differences. Their widely divergent views on the employment of airpower and of the place of airpower in the command structure of the Allied invasion force would have brought the two men into conflict in almost any case. The gulf between the two became apparent at their meeting on 3 January when they discussed plans for Overlord. Spaatz noted in his diary, "Apparently he [Leigh-Mallory] accepts [the] possibility of not establishing Air supremacy until landing starts."[14] Spaatz believed that if the Allies delayed the battle for air supremacy until the invasion, it would come too late not only for the invasion but also for the bomber offensive. Spaatz believed that the Luftwaffe must be crushed as soon as possible. If Allied air forces had to fight for supremacy over the beaches, they could provide no support for the ground forces and might fail to provide air cover for the invasion fleet; nor could paratroop drops be guaranteed without air supremacy. In contrast, Leigh-Mallory's perspective came from his four years' experience in successfully defending against Luftwaffe attacks. Since 1941 the Germans had refused to engage in prolonged daylight combat with Fighter Command, which, with its short-range defensive fighters, could not force the Germans to fight if they chose not to. Leigh-Mallory welcomed the thought that the Germans would once more have to fly into territory he defended.

By the time Eisenhower arrived in London on 16 January, the air command arrangements in the British Isles had become a veritable Gordian knot, and the supreme commander seemed as confused as anyone. After meetings with Marshall and Arnold in Washington, Eisenhower warned Maj Gen Bedell Smith, his chief of staff, already in London, on 5 January, that he anticipated trouble in securing the necessary approval for the integration of all forces essential to the success of the cross-channel invasion. Eisenhower noted, "I suspect that the use of these air forces for the necessary preparatory phase will be particularly resisted. To support our position it is essential that a complete plan for use of all available aircraft during this phase be ready as quickly as possible."[15]

Eisenhower assumed that the British would object to placing Bomber and Coastal Commands under the operational control of the supreme commander of the AEAF. Nevertheless, he intended to ensure the employment of every resource, including all airpower in Britain, to achieve the ultimate success of his mission. Eisenhower knew he had Arnold's backing. Arnold confirmed that both USSTAF and Bomber Command should be placed directly under the supreme commander for the "impending operation." Arnold made clear his support, saying "it is my desire to do all that is possible here to further the simultaneous transfer of these two strategic bombing organizations from their present status to your command when you feel this transfer should take place."[16]

Eisenhower also had Spaatz's agreement about the necessity of USSTAF's coming under his operational control. In December when each had learned of his own new appointment, Spaatz had assured Eisenhower that he expected to come under his command at least 60 days prior to the invasion. All the subsequent disputes over preinvasion preparations concerned the means of employing strategic bombers and the place of the bombers under Eisenhower, not the basic principle that the invasion required the support of heavy bombers to succeed.

In the afternoon of 17 January, Eisenhower's first day of work as supreme commander, he met with Spaatz. Eisenhower admitted that he had received no clarification of the "present confused air situation" while in Washington.[17] By the end of January, Spaatz had reaffirmed his personal support for and USSTAF's organizational commitment to placing control of the AAF's heavy bombers in the hands of the commander of the forces assaulting the Continent. This commitment did not mean that Spaatz abdicated his position as the chief proponent in England of strategic daylight precision bombing; rather, it meant that, in practice, Spaatz would employ those techniques in the way that he thought could most effectively contribute to the invasion as a first priority. Spaatz did not abandon the theory that airpower alone could bring about the defeat of Germany, but, as a good soldier, he meant to do all in his power to guarantee the fulfillment of Overlord's objectives. He noted with resignation in his diary: "Launching of [Overlord] will result in the calling off of bomber effort on Germany proper from one to two months prior to invasion. If time is as now contemplated, there will be no opportunity to carry out any Air operations of sufficient intensity to justify the theory that Germany can be knocked out by Air power. . . . Operations in connection with [Overlord] will be child's play compared to present operations and should result in very minor losses."[18]

However, the final form of Eisenhower's control of the heavy bombers was a matter of great concern to Spaatz. Leigh-Mallory's oft stated belief that the decisive battle for air supremacy would occur at the time of the invasion caused Spaatz to doubt Leigh-Mallory's competence as a commander. As a consequence Spaatz made it clear he would not accept any arrangement that subordinated his forces to the command of the AEAF. He informed Eisenhower, "I have no confidence in Leigh-Mallory's ability to handle the job and . . . I view with alarm any setup which places the Strategic Air Forces under his control."[19]

Eisenhower explained to Marshall that he intended to have his "Air Preparation" plan accepted as "doctrine" by everyone under his control, including Spaatz. Eisenhower found General Spaatz's previous complaints concerning Leigh-Mallory worrying.[20] On 17 February Eisenhower met with Spaatz and quietly attempted to change Spaatz's mind. Eisenhower suggested that "proper credit had not been given to Leigh-Mallory's intelligence."

Spaatz stood firm, indicating to Eisenhower that his views "had not and would not change."[21]

On 19 February Eisenhower and Spaatz met again to review the air command arrangements. Eisenhower asked for Spaatz's recommendations about how the current system could be made to work with Leigh-Mallory in his present position. Spaatz replied that no system that left Leigh-Mallory in command of the strategic air forces would work.[22] He recommended as "the only practical solution" the formalization of a joint planning committee—composed of USSTAF, Bomber Command, and the AEAF. This committee was already working on the Pointblank program and on a plan to merge Pointblank into Overlord. After he and Harris had ensured that this plan conformed to the limitations and capabilities of their forces, the CCS could issue a new bombing directive redefining target priorities and transferring the strategic air forces to Eisenhower's direction.[23] Spaatz implied he would not approve any plan that allowed Leigh-Mallory extensive control of all air operations for an extended period prior to the invasion. He conceded, of course, that "plans for the employment of Air in the actual assault of Overlord, including the softening immediately prior thereto, must of necessity be drawn up by Leigh-Mallory, with proper representation from RAF Bomber Command and USSTAF familiar with the capabilities of these forces."[24] Spaatz did not object to Leigh-Mallory's operating within his own area of expertise, particularly if he (Spaatz) had a voice in the use of his own forces.

Eisenhower accepted this plan with two modifications. He asked that Portal have representation on the committee and that, from time to time, the plan be checked against actual bombing results and modified if necessary. These changes brought the RAF chief of staff formally into the process, increasing the probability that the RAF and the CCS would approve any plan drawn up by the committee. Portal would also balance Harris, who tended to operate semi-independently. Eisenhower's second change allowed him flexibility to change the air plans as necessitated by events.[25]

Spaatz apparently assumed that this agreement with Eisenhower would enable him to carry Pointblank a step or two closer to completion. Later that day, Spaatz, after lamenting, "Operations this week insignificant, because of weather," summarized for Arnold the new agreement with Eisenhower. Spaatz emphasized his fear of a "premature shifting from Pointblank to direct preparation for Overlord and its consequent indication of willingness to delay attainment of air supremacy until air battle over beach-head." He also noted that Eisenhower would insist on putting RAF and AAF strategic forces under his own control.[26] In his reply, Arnold wholeheartedly agreed with Spaatz that "premature diversion of Pointblank and failure to achieve air supremacy prior to the assault would have tragic results." Arnold further approved of Eisenhower's gaining some measure of control of the strategic air forces.[27] Fortified with both the support of his chief and his agreement with Eisenhower allowing him to determine the employment of his aircraft, Spaatz prepared to fight for a continuation of the Combined Bomber Offensive.

As Spaatz and Eisenhower reached their agreement, Harris introduced a new complication. Harris appealed directly to Churchill to prevent the subjugation of Bomber Command to the supreme commander of the Allied Expeditionary Force, especially if that meant control by Leigh-Mallory.[28] Spaatz's and Harris's fractious attitudes had so discouraged Eisenhower's second in command, Tedder, that he wrote to Portal on February 22, "I am more and more being forced to the unfortunate conclusion that the two strategic air forces are determined not to play. Spaatz has made it abundantly clear that he will not accept orders, or even coordination from Leigh-Mallory, and the only sign of activity from Harris's representatives has been a series of adjustments to the records of their past bombing statistics, with the evident intention of demonstrating that they are quite unequipped and untrained to do anything except mass fire-raising on very large targets."[29] Tedder warned Portal that if the British chiefs of staff and Churchill continued to withhold Bomber Command from Eisenhower's control, "very serious issues will arise affecting Anglo-American cooperation in Overlord," issues that would result in "quite irremediable cleavage" between the Allies.[30]

On 28 February Eisenhower had dinner at No. 10 Downing Street with Churchill, whom he found impatient for progress on air planning and much disturbed at the thought of Leigh-Mallory's commanding the strategic air forces.[31] Eisenhower explained that he was waiting for a coordinated plan on which all could agree and he asked that the prime minister refrain from acting on the matter. The next morning Eisenhower wrote a memo to Tedder urging him to speed up the planning so that he could have a solid plan for the prime minister before Churchill came "in this thing with both feet."[32] This memo sounded the death knell for Leigh-Mallory's claim to command all airpower cooperating with the invasion. Eisenhower wrote, "I'm quite prepared, if necessary, to issue an order saying I will exert direct supervision of all air forces—through you—and authorizing you to use headquarters facilities now existing to make your control effective. L. M.'s [Leigh-Mallory] position would not be changed so far as *assigned forces* are concerned but those attached for definite periods or definite jobs would not come under his *command.*"[33] [emphasis in original]

Even as Eisenhower signified his willingness to limit Leigh-Mallory to command of only the Ninth and the British 2d, Churchill waded into the air tangle. On 29 February the prime minister voiced his own ideas on Overlord's air organization. Tedder should serve as the "'aviation lobe' of Eisenhower's brain," with the power to use all air forces temporarily or permanently assigned to the invasion in accordance with the plan approved by Eisenhower.[34] Furthermore, Churchill charged Tedder to draw up, with the assistance of Leigh-Mallory's AEAF staff, a plan satisfactory to the supreme commander. Leigh-Mallory would prepare plans and execute orders received from Tedder in Eisenhower's name. As deputy commander, Tedder would be empowered to issue orders to Spaatz, Harris, and Air Chief Marshal Sholto Douglas, head of Coastal Command, for any employment of their forces in Overlord sanctioned by the CCS.[35] This outline would eventually become the command structure the Allies accepted.

Churchill's minutes of 29 February may have suggested the solution for the chain of command for air, but Eisenhower found other sections of it objectionable. Although the minutes admonished that "the 'Overlord' battle must be the chief care of all concerned, and great risks must be run in every other

225

sphere and theater in order that nothing should be withheld which could contribute to the success," Churchill, in the same document, proceeded to violate his own dictum. "There can be no question," he ruled, "of handing over the British Bomber, Fighter or Coastal Commands as a whole to the Supreme Commander and his Deputy." Those commands had other functions as well as those assigned by Overlord. In addition, Churchill felt the CCS should retain the right to vary assignments to the invasion "should overriding circumstances render it necessary."[36]

Upon reviewing these minutes, Eisenhower accepted Tedder's command role and responsibility for drafting an air plan, but Eisenhower balked at having anything less than total operational control of both strategic air forces. Further conversations with Churchill proved unfruitful. In the beginning of March, Eisenhower told Churchill that if Bomber Command did not come under his control, he "would simply have to go home."[37] Eisenhower conceded that Coastal Command, which occupied a lesser place in the invasion planning, could remain under separate control, but he insisted that Bomber Command receive its direction through the headquarters of the supreme commander, as the Combined Chiefs of Staff agreed at Cairo in December 1943. Portal, for his part, denied that the CCS had ever intended to place more than a portion of Bomber Command under Eisenhower. At this juncture, Churchill told Portal to negotiate an agreement with Eisenhower and indicated he would accept whatever arrangement the two men agreed to.[38]

Tedder served as go-between as the British chief of the air staff, Portal, and the American supreme commander, Eisenhower, wrestled to reconcile their different conceptions. Portal, following Churchill's dictates, sought to preserve some autonomy for RAF Coastal, Fighter, and Bomber Commands, whereas Eisenhower wished for complete control, particularly of Bomber Command. By 9 March, Portal produced a draft agreement incorporating elements of both positions. Eisenhower described it as "exactly what we want,"[39] and a day later informed Marshall, "All air forces here will be under Tedder's supervision as my agent and this prospect is particularly pleasing to Spaatz."[40]

Spaatz wrote to Arnold in a similar vein, "I feel that this is a logical workable plan and, under the conditions which exist, cannot be improved upon."[41] Tedder would coordinate the operation of the strategic forces in support of the invasion, and Leigh-Mallory, under Tedder's supervision, would coordinate the tactical air plan. Eisenhower accepted the right of the combined chiefs or the British chiefs to impose additional tasks on the strategic forces if they deemed it necessary. Finally, once the assault forces had established themselves on the Continent, both parties agreed to undertake a revision of the directive for the employment of strategic bomber force.[42]

The British then passed the draft agreement to the combined chiefs. In their covering memos, the British stated that when the air plan for support of Overlord met the approval of both Eisenhower and Portal, acting in his capacity as the agent of the chiefs for the Combined Bomber Offensive, "the responsibility for supervision of air operations out of England of all forces engaged in the program, including the United States Strategic Air Force and British Bomber Command, together with any other air forces that might be made available should pass to the Supreme Commander."[43] Eisenhower and Portal would jointly supervise those strategic forces not used by the invasion in accordance with agreements they previously reached. The British chiefs added that, at present, they had no plans to use the reservations inserted into the agreement, and, if they did, they would immediately inform the US Joint Chiefs of Staff.[44]

The US Joint Chiefs balked at once. This proposal did not give Eisenhower unquestioned control of the strategic air forces. The British protested that the supreme commander himself found the plan acceptable—to no avail. Even Eisenhower had second thoughts and insisted that his control of the strategic bombers for the invasion period be untrammeled. Once again, he thought of resigning if the matter continued to drag on ad infinitum.[45] On 7 April, barely two months before the invasion, the combined chiefs agreed that the strategic air forces would operate under the supreme commander's "direction," apparently a less ambiguous term than allotting to him "the responsibility for supervision." At the same time the combined chiefs approved, with a few exceptions on targets, the air plan developed for the invasion. The formal direction of the strategic air forces passed to Eisenhower on 14 April, confirming the informal command structure already in place.[46]

The Anglo-Americans had settled a delicate matter none too soon, only six weeks remained until the invasion of France. As military men, the participants all accepted the necessity for a defined chain of command, and they each hoped that the eventual chain of command would favor their own interests. The organization chart, which showed a dotted, not a solid, line from the strategic air forces to the Allied Expeditionary Force, did not accurately reflect the human balance of personality and beliefs involved. Fortunately for the Anglo-Americans, Tedder, Spaatz, Harris, Eisenhower, and sometimes even Leigh-Mallory, in his own quixotic fashion, cooperated in the use of the air weapons available to them. Thus, they provided for plentiful support for the invasion and the continuation of the bomber offensive against Germany without letup.

The Dispute over Strategic Targeting

From late January to early May 1944, Spaatz and Harris, supported at times by Churchill, engaged in a heated dispute with Leigh-Mallory, his AEAF staff, and the Overlord planners. The bone of contention was the contribution expected of the strategic air forces in support of the preparation for the invasion of France. Eisenhower and Tedder, as hardly disinterested parties, refereed this dispute with varying degrees of impartiality. Each of the contestants took up distinct positions, which, depending on the fortunes of his own command, his commitment to the invasion, and the imminence of the invasion date, he defended at length. Unlike Harris, Spaatz never questioned the basic premise that, at some point prior to the invasion, his force should come under the direct control of the supreme commander, Allied Expeditionary Force. Naturally, given his personal and professional biases, he differed, at times sharply, with Leigh-Mallory and others over the timing, the direction, and the amount of effort demanded of his forces.

As a first priority, Spaatz insisted that any plan adopted must, at the least, lead to the attainment and maintenance of air parity over the invasion area by the time the troops left their ports to hit the beaches.[47] Spaatz thought that, at a maximum, his forces should begin close assistance to the invasion 60 days before it was launched. Any more time than that would duplicate the effort of and, perhaps, neutralize the effects of his strategic bombing campaign against Germany by preventing follow-up of the blows that he intended to deliver. Spaatz also believed that USSTAF possessed sufficient forces to devote a large simultaneous effort to the invasion and to the strategic campaign. He would resist any invasion plan that he believed would require his forces to participate beyond the point of diminishing returns. Concentrating too heavily on preinvasion operations would threaten the painfully gained momentum of his strategic campaign and thereby deny him the chance to defeat Germany by airpower alone, provided the defeat could be accomplished at all.

Harris held sharper views. Bomber Command's operational limitations made it tactically incapable of hitting night targets save the broad-based area bombing it already pursued. Switching from the current operational program would undo everything achieved to date, allowing Germany the time to harden and disperse its industries as well as giving its production lines an uninterrupted period just before the invasion. Any subordination of Bomber Command to a detailed tactical plan might actually have a detrimental effect on Overlord.[48]

Two events, however, combined to undercut Harris's contentions. His winter bombing campaign over Germany encountered increasingly resourceful, accurate, and costly interception by the German night-fighter force, which by the end of March 1944, had become tactically dominant. Bomber Command losses mounted steeply. It could no longer sustain the demands of this campaign on its aircraft and aircrews.[49] In the first three months of 1944 Bomber Command lost 796 aircraft from all causes as compared with 348 in the same period in 1943.[50] Then, in early March 1944, Portal ordered a series of experimental night precision bombing attacks on targets in France, including railway marshaling yards. These attacks produced outstanding results, unequivocally demonstrating the abilities of Harris's units to pulverize the Overlord targets scheduled for them.[51] By the end of March, Harris had lost much of his credibility and with it a decisive voice in the preinvasion air debate.

Leigh-Mallory, the target of Spaatz's and Harris's fulminations, indomitably and in his own phlegmatic fashion, pressed for the adoption of the preinvasion plan drawn up by the AEAF. The architect of the AEAF bombing plan, Prof. Solly Zuckerman, a personal friend of both Tedder and Spaatz, had returned to London in January 1944 from the Mediterranean, where he had completed his studies of the bombing campaigns in Pantelleria and Sicily. He reached his own judgments about the effectiveness of those campaigns and the ways to improve upon them. Once in London, Zuckerman read the preliminary AEAF plans, which he judged inadequate, and he agreed to work with Leigh-Mallory's staff to prepare a new plan. By the end of January, he had produced a plan fully accepted by Leigh-Mallory.[52]

The Transportation Plan

Zuckerman, like Spaatz, Leigh-Mallory, Tedder, Portal, and most other preinvasion planners, started from the assumption that air superiority over the beachhead was a sine qua non. Therefore, he recognized the necessity for the continuation of Pointblank to promote the attrition of the Luftwaffe fighter force. Similarly, he accepted as a given the diversion of resources to Crossbow. The professor then divided the remainder of the preinvasion bombing plan into three target systems: airfields, coastal defenses, and German lines of communication.

The bombing of communications targets formed the heart of the plan. The Germans, because of their chronic shortage of motor transport, had a far greater dependence than the Anglo-Americans on rail lines for their logistics and long-distance troop transport. German mechanized units committed to stop the invasion would need trains to move their heavy equipment. Otherwise they would have to road march, a slower process that inflicted wear and tear on the tanks' running gear and exposed them to Allied fighter-bombers.

Zuckerman's analysis of the bombing of transportation routes and equipment in Sicily had convinced him that rail yards constituted the pressure point of the rail transportation system. The bombing of a rail yard scatters the tracks, shatters the ties, and flattens roadbeds, all easily repaired, but never quite back to their original condition. More important, bombing smashed or disabled the unique facilities that made a marshaling yard a vital cog in a functioning rail system rather than simply a collection of tracks. Bombing disabled roundhouses, turntables, stocks of spare parts, locomotive and rolling stock maintenance and repair sheds, switches, and boiler cleaning facilities and killed trained personnel of all types. Repeated bombing consumed or destroyed the specialized spare parts needed to make the yard fully functional. Stripping parts from other yards to repair damaged facilities would have diminished the capacity of those yards. It seemed unlikely that the Germans would bring in parts from the Reich to rectify the situation. In any case, production of the parts needed to repair damaged rail yards was not a wartime priority that would ensure speedy replacement of damaged parts and restoration of the targeted rail yard to full capacity. Finally, the bombs pulverized the rail yard's "hump"—a man-made hillock that is central to the operations of a marshaling yard. A yard marshals, or forms, a train by "placing" the rolling stock in the proper order for deliveries up and down the line. This eases loading and unloading in the areas serviced by the yard. The hump efficiently allows the yardmaster to roll cars gently to the correct trains. Losing the hump, and other key facilities, means that the entire system, not just the yard, is affected and loses productivity. Other yards have to sort and resort above and beyond their normal workload. This loss of efficiency compounds with every additional rail yard damaged until the system collapses, strangled by its own rolling stock.

The decimation of the rail yards would aid the final phase of preinvasion air operations. As Zuckerman carefully explained, he had designed his plan to complement preinvasion tactical interdiction operations. The invasion planners had provided for Allied airpower to begin an aggressive interdiction campaign a few weeks before D-day. The damage to locomotives, rolling stock, other rail equipment, and alternative forms of transportation would further devastate the Germans. The planned bombing of

the German transportation system would produce a rail maintenance and repair desert extending to the German border.

The bombing of the airfields 130 miles or less distant from the
beachhead, another key element in the Allied preinvasion
plans, would begin approximately 24 days prior to the invasion.
Zuckerman had not picked this figure at random. Knocking out
all airfields within 130 miles from the beachhead put the Luftwaffe fighters at the same disadvantage as the Allied air forces;
the Luftwaffe fighters would be based at airfields that were as far
from the beachhead as were the Allied air forces. The bombing of
coastal defenses would begin immediately before the assault.
The campaign against communication lines would begin on 1
March, 90 days before the invasion. Zuckerman specified a
lengthy period of preparation because he disagreed with Spaatz
and other air commanders that a final, intense burst of bombing
just before the invasion would suffice. Attrition of the rail system,
in the face of the Germans' well-known ability to make bombing
repairs, would require repeated bombings of the same targets.
Zuckerman allotted 45,000 tons of bombs, out of an entire
preinvasion program of 108,000 tons, to the communications
system. In his estimates of the bomb lift required to neutralize
the system, Zuckerman called for the Eighth to supply 45 percent of the entire preinvasion effort. Bomber Command, with a
bomb lift capacity 60 percent greater than the Eighth's, would
supply 35 percent of the preinvasion effort, and the AEAF would
supply the remaining 20 percent. Zuckerman allotted only 20
percent of the Eighth's effort to Pointblank.[53] He based his decision on the current accuracy and tactics of the Allied air forces.
He allotted the Eighth, with its "precision" day bombing, to carry
a heavier share of the sensitive French targets than Bomber
Command, which specialized in less accurate area bombing.

Zuckerman's planned use of all available airpower appealed
strongly to Eisenhower and Tedder, who were in the position of
having to yoke the AEAF, USSTAF, and Bomber Command into
a single invasion program. Eisenhower needed direct control over
all available planes in Britain to guarantee support for the invasion. He therefore sought a preinvasion air plan that could employ all the air forces available. Tedder agreed. Unlike Leigh-
Mallory, Harris, and Spaatz, each of whom was identified with a

particular type of air warfare, Tedder had not risen to prominence through a fighter or bomber background. Rather, he had come to the fore as a leader of large air forces consisting of all types of aircraft that cooperated closely, both strategically and tactically, with the overall theater command. It was Tedder who first called Zuckerman to the Mediterranean and then dispatched him to London to assist with planning. Tedder accepted the professor's analysis of the lessons learned in the Mediterranean and favored Zuckerman's plan.[54]

On 24 January Zuckerman and Leigh-Mallory presented a draft of the scheme at a preinvasion air planning conference. Everyone agreed on the necessity of bombing the airfields and coastal defenses. However, assigning first priority to the lines of communication or, as all concerned soon called it, the transportation plan, immediately raised USSTAF's dander. Col R. D. Hughes, USSTAF assistant director of intelligence, told Leigh-Mallory that Spaatz had already said "that a large percentage of his available bomber effort was available to assist Overlord." He went on to note that "if it were considered the right course of action," Spaatz was prepared to initiate attacks against rail targets *in Germany* [emphasis added] immediately with a priority second only to Pointblank. Leigh-Mallory then said he would have the Air Ministry issue a directive instructing the strategic forces to bomb such targets in Germany. Leigh-Mallory further stated that he intended to add some French rail targets to USSTAF's list, at which point Hughes began to object: the Eighth did not have the resources to bomb more than the 39 German rail targets assigned to it. Crossbow had priority over northwest France when weather permitted and the French rail targets did not have political clearance. In USSTAF's initial exposure to the plan, Hughes had already stated USSTAF's long-term objections to it.[55]

The Americans did not object to attacking rail yards in Germany. Such targets might lure the Luftwaffe into coming up to fight and could serve as targets of opportunity when weather conditions over the primary targets made bombing impossible. Such a program did not represent a major diversion from Pointblank. Marshaling yards in northwest France yielded none of these advantages. They interfered with USSTAF's secondary priority of Crossbow and, because they were located inland, rail yards did not constitute acceptable targets of opportunity for diverting missions from Crossbow. Nor would the Luftwaffe contest the air over French targets. Finally, bombing French targets would have detrimental political effects for the Allies. When bombs missed the yards and fell into the populated area of French cities, as they surely would, the Germans would gain grist for their propaganda mills while the Allies might earn the opprobrium of an occupied people; the goodwill of these local populations would greatly benefit the invasion.

On 15 February Spaatz attended an air planning meeting at Stanmore, Middlesex, a London suburb and site of Leigh-Mallory's headquarters. At times the meeting became heated. Leigh-Mallory began by presenting a definitive version of the transportation plan. It assigned 41 percent of the total preinvasion bomb tonnage to the transportation plan and only 11 percent of the total preinvasion tonnage to Pointblank. The Eighth would provide 45 percent of the total tonnage on all target systems, with Bomber Command contributing 35 percent. Using a prepared rejoinder, Spaatz sought to skewer the transportation plan. The AEAF plan "did not show a full understanding of the Pointblank operation."[56] Spaatz disagreed with the plan's premise that "air supremacy cannot be assured until the joining of the decisive air battle which will mark the opening of the Overlord assault."[57] Air supremacy must be achieved before the assault, Spaatz said, adding that AEAF had not consulted USSTAF in preparing a plan that called for a massive commitment of strategic forces. He stated that such a plan would not be approved until USSTAF had the opportunity to participate in developing it.

Leigh-Mallory argued that the Luftwaffe would rise to prevent the destruction of the French rail system. Spaatz did not agree. The German fighter force might not take the bait, Spaatz said. If it did not, he had to retain the authority to attack any target necessary to make the Germans fight; otherwise, he could not accomplish his primary task of destroying the German fighter force. Spaatz would not agree to a scheme that allowed Leigh-Mallory to set targets for USSTAF. Leigh-

Mallory then suggested that the CCS and the supreme commander settle the issue.[58]

Spaatz reemphasized the different phases of the Combined Bomber Offensive: (1) destroying the German fighter force, (2) exploiting that destruction to reduce the German will and means to continue the war, and (3) directly supporting the invasion of the Continent.[59] Then Spaatz asked when the strategic air forces would come under Leigh-Mallory's operational control. Leigh-Mallory shot back "1 March." According to Colonel Hughes's minutes of the meeting, Spaatz told Leigh-Mallory that "he could not concur in a paper at cross purposes to his present directive."[60]

Leigh-Mallory and Harris engaged in an equally unproductive dialogue concerning Bomber Command's role. Harris reiterated his prediction that the transportation plan would not succeed and that the army would blame the air forces for its failure. Finally, Spaatz entered the fray once again to reject the tonnage and effort figures in the plan. At this point, Tedder proposed a joint planning committee with representation from USSTAF, Bomber Command, and AEAF "to draw up a plan to suit the capabilities of all concerned."[61] All accepted Tedder's recommendation.

After the meeting, Spaatz and Tedder had more talks in which they agreed not to request a change in the current Combined Bomber Offensive directive until the planning committee produced a scheme acceptable to all parties; meanwhile the current command system would apply. Spaatz also informed Tedder "that Americans would not stand for their Strategic Air Forces operating under Leigh-Mallory."[62] For the Americans the suggestion that they come under Leigh-Mallory's control was not just a function of their mistrust of the commander of the AEAF. The shifting of their priorities to Overlord by 1 March would undercut the strategic bombing campaign. Spaatz had originally assumed that 1 March, which he had accepted as the date of USSTAF's beginning operations under Overlord, would mark a period 60 days before an early May invasion, but the possible postponement of the invasion until June confronted him with a 90-day delay in the strategic campaign if he remained committed to a 1 March date. As of 15 February USSTAF had not yet accomplished even its minimum strategic goals. To have the transportation plan imposed on USSTAF before the Luftwaffe fighter force had been defeated or the destructive effects of bombing on the German economy had been proved was unacceptable. Already frustrated by the weather, which prevented his forces from going after the Germans, and pressured by Washington to push the Combined Bomber Offensive home, Spaatz naturally reacted sharply to another threat to the success of his strategic mission.

The strategic air forces, through their representatives on the Joint Planning Committee for the Overlord air plan, spent much of March arguing as to the merits of Zuckerman's transportation plan and a new plan presented by USSTAF on 5 March 1944 to bomb the German synthetic oil industry (dubbed, of course, the oil plan). The strategic air forces would come into the supreme commander's hands only after USSTAF approved the air preparation plan. Until the airmen could agree on a plan, the formalization of the air command structure would hang fire.

For practical purposes, however, the strategic air commanders had no intention of actually employing their veto. Spaatz and by now even Harris accepted the necessity of some strategic support for the invasion. Moreover, Eisenhower would surely override any veto by appealing to the CCS, who would defer to him in any matter directly touching on the success of the invasion. The most important aspect of their veto power was to give the strategic air commanders leverage in obtaining a command system and a plan for air employment more in keeping with their own ideas than might otherwise have been possible. Although their positions were not invulnerable, Eisenhower would find it difficult and disruptive to replace them with more malleable commanders, who would probably lack the expertise and prestige of Spaatz and Harris.

The Oil Plan

By late February, Spaatz and others had recognized that the Combined Bomber Offensive had progressed to a point, thanks to the attrition inflicted on the Luftwaffe fighter forces in January and February, at which the destruction of targets other than the German aircraft industry was not only feasible but desirable. Therefore, Spaatz formed a USSTAF planning committee to consider future actions. He did so partially in response to the transportation plan that the AEAF had presented to him in February—a plan that USSTAF regarded as unsound. He laid down three guiding principles for the committee: the plan must provide for air supremacy at the time of the invasion; the plan should take into account a possible early collapse of Germany prior to the invasion; and, if Germany did not collapse, the plan should make a maximum contribution to the success of Overlord.[63] With pressure for adoption of the transportation plan gaining momentum every day, Spaatz urgently required a viable alternative on which to base his opposition. He pushed the planning committee to complete its work; the final draft was prepared in a 36-hour period that culminated in the presentation to Spaatz, on 5 March, of a "plan for the Completion of the Combined Bomber Offensive."[64]

The oil plan called for a "re-clarification" of the Pointblank directives and, after examining 10 discrete target systems, selected three German production programs—rubber, bomber aircraft, and oil. To those three, it added the already accepted targets of German fighter production and ball bearings. Oil received top priority followed by fighters and ball bearings, rubber, and bomber aircraft. The plan emphatically rejected railroad transport as a strategic target. Such a system had too many targets; included too much noncritical civilian traffic and long-term industrial traffic that would have to be suppressed or diverted before military traffic would be significantly reduced; and would take too long to have a significant military effect. In contrast, the oil plan required 15 days' visual bombing for the Eighth Air Force and 10 for the Fifteenth Air Force.[65]

In giving oil top priority, the plan assumed that the destruction of only 14 synthetic oil plants and 13 refineries would account for more than 80 percent of synthetic fuel production and 60 percent of the readily usable refining capacity. These losses would reduce the total current German supply of fuel by 50 percent, thereby materially cutting "German military capabilities [by] reducing tactical and strategical mobility and front-line delivery of supplies, and industrial ability to produce weapons and supplies." Furthermore, once the attacks started, USSTAF contended that the Germans would immediately reduce consumption of oil products to conserve their stocks in anticipation of further attacks.[66] This postulate, although logical, could not be verified by intelligence before the attacks. It proved a double-edged weapon. USSTAF insisted that such cutbacks would significantly impact the battle for the beachhead. The oil plan's critics countered by claiming that the resulting reductions of oil would not guarantee a significant impact on German fighting ability before the invasion assault. Almost everyone agreed that the plan might, in the long-range, prove to be devastating to the Nazis. Nonetheless, factors that improved the chances of the imminent invasion appealed more to Eisenhower than schemes promising important but delayed benefits.

The oil industry's configuration added to its suitability as a target system. Ploesti, the enemy's major source of natural petroleum, was vulnerable to the increasing power of the Fifteenth Air Force. Once Ploesti ceased to operate, the synthetic oil plants of Germany would become the enemy's chief source of supply. These plants, most of which were well within bomber range of Britain, constituted a compact target system whose destruction would produce dramatic results before the cross-channel attack, while leaving an adequate reserve of unused force available for containing the aircraft industry or striking at other targets of opportunity.[67]

Bombing the synthetic oil plants presented a practical problem. It was not as important in early 1944, when the strategic airmen had only a minimum of disposable force, as it would become in the winter of 1944–45 when they had enormous bomber fleets. For technical and logistical reasons the Germans had built their synthetic oil plants away from urban areas. The placement of these facilities was a major challenge in that the Americans could bomb the plants only if they could locate them by visual means. The American H2X radar's resolution or return was so inaccurate that it could locate only city areas. Although the synthetic plants were good-sized facilities—the largest measured approximately one square mile—they were considerably smaller than a city. Hence, bombing oil plants meant using the very few days of visual bombing weather to hit targets outside of German cities. In the winter of 1944–45, synthetic oil absorbed all visual bombing days. Thus, the Americans had to resort to H2X-assisted raids on targets within German cities for the majority of their bombing effort. Such attacks had calamitous results on the German civilian population.

The dispute between the adherents of the transportation plan and its opponents, who criticized it on strategic and tactical grounds, continued until mid-May 1944. During a series of meetings held throughout March the transportation plan's detractors mobilized increasing opposition to the plan. Field Marshal Sir Alan Brooke, chief of the Imperial General Staff (CIGS), the equivalent of the US Army's chief of staff, and others questioned the plan's effectiveness, as did segments of the British air staff and Ministry of Economic Warfare.[68] Spaatz, on the day of the AAF's first major raid over Berlin, wrote Arnold enthusiastically: "We do, however, feel sure that a new range of tactical possibilities in operation are open to us, and that it would be a misuse of our force and of the opportunities we have created not to push strategic bombing to its ultimate conclusion, in that period available to us. A concentrated effort against oil, which would represent the most far reaching use of strategic air-power that has been attempted in this war, promises more than any other system, and a fighting chance of ending German resistance in a shorter period than we have hitherto thought possible."[69]

On 16 March the Joint Planning Committee met again. Tedder began the meeting completely in favor of the transportation plan, but the united opposition of the RAF assistant chiefs of staff for plans, bomber operations, and intelligence caused him to waver. He, with Portal and Eisenhower, referred the transportation plan to the British Joint Intelligence Committee for review. Spaatz noted optimistically, "hoped by all concerned here that Tedder will repudiate AEAF Plan of his own accord," an action that would avoid hard feelings all around.[70] Tedder, however, did not abandon the transportation plan, even in the face of the Joint Intelligence Committee Report, which supported the oil plan. The report, according to Tedder, was based on unsubstantiated and invalid assumptions.[71]

In the meanwhile, Eisenhower had reached the end of his tether. If a meeting scheduled for 25 March did not decide between the competing plans, he stated, "I am going to take drastic action and inform the Combined Chiefs of Staff that unless the matter is settled at once I will request relief from this command."[72] During the preceding week, Spaatz and Tedder prepared and circulated briefs detailing their positions and marshaled last-minute agreements to attract further support for their proposals. Apparently Tedder persuaded Portal to back the transportation plan. Harris, too, gave the plan lukewarm support, but he still opposed the oil plan because he disagreed with the concept of designing a strategic bombing strategy around a single target system. Choosing such a "panacea" diverted force from area bombing. In addition, British bomber operations in March had demonstrated the night bomber's surprisingly high capability for precision bombing of marshaling yards. At the same time, the German night-fighter force demonstrated an alarming rise in its effectiveness. It reached its apogee in the winter of 1943–44 and inflicted "prohibitive" casualties on the British.[73] These two factors undercut Harris's original objections that he could not bomb precision targets and that city-busting raids offered a more decisive alternative.

Portal, who chaired the meeting, called on Tedder to present the transportation plan. During the presentation and the ensuing discussion, three salient points emerged. First, all present agreed that the bombing of Luftwaffe targets, including ball bearing producers, had top priority, and, therefore, the meeting would consider the allocation to a specific target system of only the effort remaining after bombing the highest priority system. Second, Tedder believed that only an all-out attack on the transport system would sufficiently disrupt enemy movement before and after D-day to give the invasion the greatest chance of success. Third, Eisenhower said that "the greatest contribution that he could imagine the air forces making" was to hinder enemy movement and "that everything he had read had convinced him that[,] apart from the attack on the G.A.F.[,] the Transportation Plan was the only one which offered a reasonable chance of the air forces making an important contribution to the land battle during the first vital weeks of [Overlord]; [and] in fact he did not believe that there was any other real alternative."[74]

Then the group examined the oil plan. Spaatz presented his case. Several factors affected the manner of his exposition. Spaatz, congenial, even convivial, in his mess or at ease, usually performed woodenly at set-piece conferences.[75] His performance at this meeting proved no exception. Because he had already circulated his views in his brief, he confined himself to reiterating three of its conclusions as follows:

1. Strategic attacks on the railways would not affect the course of the initial battle or prevent movement of German reserves from other fronts, whereas the oil plan might do both;

2. Attacks on the rail system would not, in an acceptable length of time, weaken enemy resistance on all fronts simultaneously, which the oil plan would do while it also hastened the post-invasion success of Overlord; and, most important,

3. Attacks on rail targets would not provoke a strong reaction from the Luftwaffe, whereas attacks on oil targets would.[76]

This spare, straightforward presentation aided the advocates of the transportation plan.

After a British Ministry of Economics (MEW) oil expert stated that the Germans had large reserve petroleum stocks in the west, Portal administered the coup de grâce to the immediate adoption of the oil plan. The MEW statement, said Portal, "showed conclusively that the oil plan would not help Overlord in the first few critical weeks." Portal softened the blow by strongly suggesting that, once the initial invasion crisis had passed, the oil plan had "great attractions." Eisenhower agreed; his concurrence on this point ended the meeting's consideration of Spaatz's alternative to the transportation plan.[77]

Talk then turned to the tactical questions of using the strategic bombers in the transportation plan. Harris doubted that he could carry out precision attacks against all 26 targets allotted to him in the time period before D-day. Despite a rising rate of casualties, Harris wanted to continue his attacks over eastern Germany for as long as he had enough hours of darkness. Eisenhower, conceded that the plan would cause little change in Bomber Command's missions. He noted that "the more important question was whether the 8th and 15th

Air Forces could achieve their part in [the transportation plan]." Spaatz replied that one-half of his visual bombing attacks would have to strike Luftwaffe targets and the other half would have to hit a target system capable of producing "at least some enemy fighter reaction, and so attrition." In fact he [Spaatz] had chosen the oil plan over the transportation plan precisely because the former would guarantee constant air battles and consistent attrition of the Luftwaffe fighter force.

Portal disagreed. He thought that the Luftwaffe would defend the rail system once it realized the Allies had begun an all-out campaign against it. Spaatz emphasized the importance of the location of the targets chosen. He argued that his forces must fly well into Germany to generate the maximum amount of aerial fighting, and for tactical reasons some of the transport targets ought to be in proximity to Luftwaffe targets. Tedder agreed and said he would have no problem coming up with targets to fit Spaatz's requirements. Portal then raised another problem: the large numbers of French civilian casualties almost certain to result from bombing marshaling yards in or adjacent to French towns. He then reserved to His Majesty's government and the cabinet the opportunity to consider the possible consequences of numerous casualties inflicted on an Allied people.[78] This caveat, which few at the time remarked on, would eventually delay complete execution of the transportation plan for several weeks until Churchill could satisfy himself that the bombing would not redound to Britain's discredit.

The meeting ended with Portal and Eisenhower giving Tedder instructions on coordinating the execution of the plan with the air commanders involved.[79] Portal and Eisenhower also stated their intention to put in place the air command arrangements on which they had previously agreed, subject to final approval by the CCS.[80] From that point on, Eisenhower, using Tedder as his executive for air, began to exercise de facto control of the strategic bomber forces.[81] The decision to have Tedder coordinate the execution of the transportation plan had the character of a compromise solution.

Thus concluded what a British official history termed "the historic occasion."[82] Eisenhower chose the transportation over the oil plan, and the air command arrangements agreed on between

Eisenhower and the British went into effect. Critics have disputed the wisdom of the supreme commander's choice ever since. Much ink and emotion have flowed over the actual benefits derived from the transportation plan. On tactical grounds its critics maintain that a campaign of bridge busting and bombing of supply dumps would have consumed less force with equal results.[83] On strategic grounds critics bemoan the "national disaster" of the delay in the oil campaign, which, when executed, severely restricted Germany's ability to wage war.[84]

Spaatz, in March 1944, might have had a hunch that the oil campaign would have immediate crucial results, but he had no proof. He accepted the transportation plan because he would only have to divert, at most, half his effort, much of it on days when weather conditions prevented the Eighth from using usual visual means to bomb Germany. He could employ the remainder of his force with a free hand to continue increasing the Luftwaffe's already ruinous attrition rate. The latest version of the transportation plan assigned RAF Bomber Command 26 rail targets in France, thus ensuring Harris's participation and removing a specter that had troubled Spaatz since the plan's inception.

Spaatz may have lost a round on points, but he had not lost the fight. On 31 March he stepped back into the ring with memos to Portal and Eisenhower titled "The Use of Strategic Bombers in Support of Overlord," in which he accepted the proposition that the French railways required heavy attacks. However, after noting that neither the oil nor the transportation plans had, as yet, a qualitative measure of effectiveness, he rejected an attack on German railways and suggested that oil targets would be just as easy to bomb and more effective in the long run. He wrote, "the effect from the Oil attack, while offering a less definite input in time, is certain to be more far reaching. It will lead directly to sure disaster for Germany. The Rail attack can lead to harassment only. In weighing these two, it appears that too great a price may be paid merely for a certainty of very little."[85]

Spaatz then offered more possibilities to multiply Allied bombing power, thus making the simultaneous execution of both the oil and transportation plans more feasible. Eighth Air Force fighter-bombers could bomb both French railway targets and synthetic fuel plants in the Ruhr. Bomber Command could make daylight attacks against French rail targets or bomb synthetic fuel plants in Stettin or, if they wished, the Ruhr at night. In Rumania the Fifteenth Air Force might bomb transportation targets, and the Russians might advance far enough to send their limited-range planes against Ploesti. To Spaatz, bombing the transport lines around Ploesti was the key. Attacking these targets would hamper German military operations in the Balkans and the southern USSR, restrict the flow of refined and crude petroleum from Ploesti, and contribute to the general dislocation of the German rail system. If the Soviets could take or neutralize Ploesti, the Germans would be extremely vulnerable to air attacks on the synthetic fuel plants, Hitler's only remaining significant source of oil. "These possibilities," in Spaatz's opinion, "therefore, lend weight to the advantage of early attack upon the synthetics . . . to obtain the earliest possible threat. That impact might well be far earlier than currently estimated."[86] Finally, Spaatz recommended the following target priorities, in order of importance, for his two air forces:

For the Eighth:

1. The Luftwaffe and ball bearings,

2. The nineteen rail targets already selected in occupied countries, and

3. The thirteen major synthetic oil plants.

For the Fifteenth:

1. The Luftwaffe and ball bearings,

2. Rail transport in Rumania and selected targets in southern France,

3. Synthetic oil plants in southern Germany, and

4. Political targets in the Balkans.[87]

The Oil Plan Revived

During April 1944 Spaatz managed to gain the partial acceptance of oil as a high-priority target. He had recognized as early as May 1942 that the bombing of the Rumanian oil fields and refinery complex at Ploesti was the logical first step of an oil campaign[88] and a prerequisite for the bombing of synthetic oil plants.[89] The elimination of the 25 percent of German petroleum production derived from the Rumanian fields would wipe out all reserves in the Axis oil network and render the Axis oil supply even more vulnerable to the bombing of the hydrogenation plants. Spaatz, however, had difficulties with the British when it came to freeing the Fifteenth Air Force from its other responsibilities to enable it to neutralize Ploesti. The latest combined bomber offensive directive pertaining to the Fifteenth, issued by Portal on 17 February, limited its targets to "cities, transportation targets and other suitable objectives in the Balkans and in the Satellite countries of southeastern Europe whenever weather or tactical conditions prevent operations against 'Pointblank' objectives or in support of land operations in Italy."[90] Portal interpreted this clause in a manner that forbade attacks on Ploesti oil targets. Later Portal added Balkan and Hungarian political targets to the Fifteenth's strike list.

Portal's refusal to target Ploesti stemmed from the ongoing confrontation in London over the oil versus transportation plans. Because Ploesti produced such a large percentage of total Axis production, it was the single most lucrative target in any oil campaign. Conversely, it made little sense to damage Ploesti, forcing the Germans back on their synthetic production, and then ignore the remaining highly vulnerable synthetic oil plants in Germany proper. A successful raid on Ploesti would put a high trump in Spaatz's hand and might well allow him to gather enough support to carry the day for oil. Thus Spaatz adamantly pressed for a strike on Ploesti, and Portal just as adamantly resisted it.

On 5 April the Fifteenth went after Ploesti to attack its marshaling yards, but the bombs actually fell on oil targets; each refinery complex had its own commercial railway yard, and sloppy bombing of the yards would surely inflict damage on the oil centers. As AAF official historians state, "it was thought wise to begin the undertaking surreptitiously . . . bombing transportation targets supporting German forces . . . facing the Russians." With some satisfaction the history went on to note, "Most of the 588 tons of bombs, with more than coincidental inaccuracy, struck and badly damaged the Astra group of refineries near by."[91]

Twice more, on 15 and 26 April, hundreds of US heavy bombers returned to Ploesti, where they inflicted "incidental" damage to oil refineries. These raids alerted the Germans to their danger. By the time the Fifteenth obtained Portal's official permission in May 1944 to blast Ploesti, the Germans had greatly intensified their artificial smoke screen, antiaircraft artillery, and fighter defenses. As a result, H2X bombing and a much greater expenditure of effort were required to achieve the accurate delivery of the required amount of high explosives on target.[92] German imports of finished oil products, mostly from Rumania, fell from 186,000 tons in March to 104,000 in April to 40,000 tons in June.[93] The April raids obviously had inflicted great damage.

The Fifteenth's clandestine oil offensive set the stage for attacks on the synthetic plants. Churchill, meanwhile, continued to hold up implementation of the transportation plan. When the prime minister and the British War Cabinet reviewed it on 3 April, they blanched at an attached Ministry of Home Security, Research and Experiments Department, Section 8 (RE8) estimate predicting 80,000 to 160,000 French and Belgian civilian casualties, one-quarter of them fatalities.[94] RE8 specialized in bomb damage assessment; its reputation for no-nonsense, cautious analysis made its work relatively authoritative.[95] It could not help but influence the government. Churchill, who well remembered the disastrous affect on Anglo-French relations of the decision to bombard the French fleet in July 1940, regarded these figures with apprehension.[96] He began a monthlong series of Defence Committee meetings in which he questioned the necessity for the transportation plan. In the meantime he wished to limit transport attacks to those with estimated civilian casualties of no more than 100 to 150 in each raid.[97] With the full execution of the transportation plan on hold, Spaatz and USSTAF perceived an opening for the implementation of the oil plan.

Even as Spaatz prepared to reopen the oil plan with Eisenhower, another diversion threatened the strategic effort. In mid-April, the British concern about V-1 launch sites intensified. On

15 April, at an air leaders meeting, Tedder informed Spaatz that Crossbow had become the Eighth's second priority after the Luftwaffe and before the French marshaling yards. When Spaatz stated such a priority would prevent him from fulfilling his transportation plan bombings, Tedder said the British were willing to accept the consequences.[98] Four days later Tedder notified Spaatz's deputy for operations that the British government, alarmed at recent intelligence, had declared V-1 site construction as a matter affecting the security of the British Isles and moved Crossbow up to number one priority, even over destruction of the Luftwaffe.[99] This may have been the final straw for Spaatz. Not only did Tedder propose to divert his forces from Pointblank, but he proposed to do it for a target system chosen almost entirely for British domestic political considerations. Spaatz immediately notified Doolittle, "[Crossbow] missions will be placed on first priority until further notice."[100] He then proceeded to do his best to get that directive revoked.

Earlier that day, 19 April, Spaatz had decided to ask Eisenhower for permission to bomb oil targets during the next two days with suitable visual weather conditions.[101] Spaatz based the decision on several factors. He felt that German fighter opposition had appreciably lessened.[102] On 18 and 19 April two strikes of more than 775 heavy bombers each, directed against Berlin and Kassel, respectively, had lost a combined total of only 15 bombers.[103] Instead of pleasing Spaatz, Doolittle, and Fred Anderson, this new development inspired apprehension, if not alarm.

They feared that the Germans may have adopted a policy of conservation of their fighters for the purpose of staging truly formidable interceptions or more likely for commitment against the coming invasion. It is possible that unreleased Ultra intercepts might shed some light on the exact state of the US appreciation of the German situation. However, if the Luftwaffe would not rise to protect its own industrial infrastructure, as was apparently the case on 18–19 April, then USSTAF needed even more valuable targets to prod the Germans into fighting. Eisenhower had made Spaatz's first and most important task the destruction of the Luftwaffe.

In keeping with this mission, Spaatz wished to experiment with the oil targets to see whether such strikes would force the Luftwaffe to rise in defense of vital targets, thereby leading to further attrition of German air force fighters.[104] Spaatz still believed that oil should have priority second only to the destruction of the Luftwaffe.[105] Finally, the morale of Spaatz's command needed boosting.[106] If oil bombing proved as effective as Spaatz suspected, his men would see that their efforts were contributing greatly to the defeat of Germany. If Spaatz could not gain Eisenhower's approval, he feared that the entire AAF strategic effort in Europe might fail, or at least fail to keep the Luftwaffe out of the air over the invasion beaches.

That evening, Spaatz took his dissatisfaction to Eisenhower. The two had a stormy meeting in the supreme commander's personal quarters. First, they dealt with the foolishness of one of Spaatz's general officers, Maj Gen Henry F. Miller, commander, Ninth Service Command. The previous evening Miller had gotten drunk at Claridge's, a swank London nightclub, and had loudly, profanely, and, worst of all, publicly proceeded to take bets that the invasion would occur before 15 June. Spaatz called Ninth Air Force headquaters and had Miller arrested. Eisenhower sent Miller back to the states as a colonel. Spaatz reopened the oil plan debate by pleading for permission to conduct two experimental raids on oil targets to test Luftwaffe reaction. He may also have revealed, although it is improbable that he had any solid intelligence to back his conclusions, that his "clandestine" bombing of Ploesti on 5 April and the beginning of the Danubian mining campaign by No. 205 Group on the night of 8 April had already begun to limit German oil supply from Rumania—a prerequisite for bombing the hydrogenation plants.

Eisenhower apparently pointed out that Spaatz had not yet begun bombing his transportation targets. The supreme commander may have noted further that the British interest in the V-1, however silly from a military standpoint, rested on legitimate political concerns for the Churchill government. Foot-dragging on bombing V-1s would certainly antagonize the American's hosts. Spaatz strongly protested Tedder's decision to give Crossbow overall priority. As he told Tedder later in the evening, Spaatz thought that if the rocket sites so upset the British, they should send the RAF to get them.[107] Eisenhower supported Spaatz's basic position: Pointblank had priority over Crossbow, but also apparently upheld Tedder's request for Crossbow attacks.[108] In any case, convinced either by the logic or the vehemence of his arguments, Eisenhower gave Spaatz verbal permission to take the two days he needed.[109] It must have seemed a small price to pay given the possibly disruptive consequences of strictly adhering to the transportation plan. During the meeting Eisenhower may also have taken Spaatz to task for his laggardly performance on behalf of the transportation plan. As of 19 April the Eighth had not bombed a single one of its assigned rail targets.

Eisenhower and Spaatz recognized that the weather seldom allowed the bomber forces to undertake visual attacks on targets deep in Germany and on the French coast during the same day. Eisenhower kept no record of the meeting, and Spaatz's diary merely lists the points under discussion, giving little hint of any conversation or emotions. He laconically noted, "received permission from Eisenhower to use two days of visual target weather to attack oil targets for purpose of determining Germans' willingness to send up defensive fighters against our bombers—must find some way to force them into the Air so that the strength of the German Air Force can continue to be decreased by knocking them down."[110] As the official AAF history stated, "somehow it seemed important to the two U.S. leaders not to go on record as taking the initiative in opening this new offensive."[111]

On the morning of the next day, 20 April, Spaatz went to Tedder's office where the two reached a decision on Crossbow's priority. At first Tedder insisted that the bomber force make the V-1 sites its primary objective. At Spaatz's urging, he agreed to a compromise. On the first suitable day the Eighth would bomb Crossbow targets; on the next two suitable days it would attack oil targets.[112] That very day Spaatz and Doolittle sent 892 B-17s and B-24s against Crossbow sites in France. The Luftwaffe offered no opposition; the Eighth lost nine bombers to antiaircraft fire.[113] Not until 12 May would the right combination of weather over bases and targets allow the first blow against oil. During the interim, the Eighth conducted nine Crossbow missions, sending out 2,941 sorties; it lost 33 bombers—some to flak and some were scrapped as nonrepairable aircraft.[114] Two days after his meeting with Eisenhower, Spaatz sent the Eighth over its first transportation target, Hamm, Germany, the largest rail marshaling yard in Europe. This action may have partially fulfilled his bargain with the supreme commander.

Churchill Delays the Transportation Plan

By 1 May, five weeks after Eisenhower had endorsed it, Churchill still had not approved the transportation plan. The latter remained worried about the potential political side effects arising from the killing and maiming of French civilians. French civilian losses troubled Spaatz, as well. In a conversation with Eisenhower, Spaatz pointed out the necessity for all air forces to give direct support to Overlord, but he observed, "The use of these forces in a manner which involves so much destruction to our Allies on the Continent may far outweigh the advantages gained by the attacks as planned. We must evolve a scheme of employment of our Air Forces which better achieves the basic aim of maximum direct assistance to Overlord." He suggested studying possibilities of cutting rail and road lines at points outside town centers and of the results of attacking concentrations of German troops, their supply and ammunition depots, and their tank parks.[115] Eisenhower replied that he had examined the problem and understood the political repercussions in a postwar Europe, but he argued that the primary consideration was the absolute necessity of winning the war quickly.[116] Although not completely convinced by Eisenhower's rejoinder, Spaatz acquiesced to Eisenhower's wishes.[117]

Spaatz accepted the continuation of the transportation plan but did what he could to mitigate its consequences for French civilians living near the targets. He emphasized to his subordinates the importance of taking great care in all operations against targets in France: only the best lead bombardiers would be used, no indiscriminate bombing and no H2X bombing would be permitted. "The crews must be impressed with the need for air discipline in order to avoid needless killing of French personnel."[118]

The prime minister, whose political senses were perhaps more acute than those of the US generals, delayed his final decision. On the night of 19 April, Churchill still doubted that the suffering that would be caused by the transportation plan justified its results. He raised the possibility of attacking synthetic oil, but Portal and Tedder repeated their opinion that such a tactic could not succeed by D-day.[119] Even after the British chiefs of staff asked for a speedy decision, Churchill demurred. Although he admitted that the longer the decision remained in question, the stronger the case for the transportation plan became.[120]

On 26 April the prime minister, after further questioning of the transportation plan, agreed to put the matter before the War Cabinet. Portal drew up a list of targets, the bombing of which would cause no more than 100 civilian casualties each. At its meeting the next day, the cabinet agreed to revise the transportation plan to include only attacks that would inflict no more than 150 civilian casualties each. Churchill was to visit Eisenhower and then send a message to Roosevelt for a definitive American opinion.[121]

On 29 April Churchill suggested to Eisenhower that USSTAF, perhaps in conjunction with the Air Ministry, should produce a plan for employment of the heavy bombers in a manner causing the sacrifice of no more than 100 French lives per attack. If this plan failed to inflict sufficient damage to the key portions of the French rail system, arguments in favor of the full transportation plan, whatever the cost to civilians, would be strengthened.[122] Slowing or delaying movement of German ground units toward the beachhead had to have priority over other considerations. Eisenhower remained adamant. To abandon the transportation plan at this juncture was unthinkable. He wrote to Marshall, "There is no other way in which this tremendous air force can help [the] U.S. during the preparatory period, to get ashore and stay there. The Prime Minister talked to me about bombing 'bases, troop concentrations and dumps.'"[123]

On 2 May Eisenhower sent Churchill a detailed reply. He patiently reviewed the rationale behind the transportation plan—

that it was intended to weaken and disrupt the rail network at a critical time, rather than to choke it off entirely. Next Eisenhower took note of the 25 March meeting and of USSTAF's alternative suggestions. USSTAF had "fully and sympathetically considered" those propsoals but rejected them because they did not "in any way constitute a plan by which our air power can, in the final stages, effectively delay and disrupt enemy concentrations." After noting that a limitation of 100 to 150 casualties per mission would "emasculate" the transportation plan, the reply concluded with Eisenhower's typical reaction to any challenge of his plans, "The 'Overlord' concept was based on the assumption that our overwhelming Air Power would be able to prepare the way for the assault. If its [airpower's] hands are to be tied, the perils of an already hazardous undertaking will be greatly enhanced."[124]

The War Cabinet considered Eisenhower's response. Churchill spoke of the hazards of interfering with Eisenhower's plans for political reasons, yet he said he had not realized "that our use of air power before 'Overlord' would assume so cruel and remorseless a form."[125] The cabinet agreed that the prime minister "should consider further the air plan for support of 'Overlord.'"[126] On 3 May the British Defence Committee met a last time on the subject. "The transportation plan," said Churchill, "will smear the good name of the Royal Air Force across the world." Churchill asked whether the plan could be implemented at a cost of fewer than 10,000 dead. Tedder expressed his hopes of keeping the number of French dead below that number, but he could make no guarantees. After reviewing the intelligence about the transportation plan's current effectiveness, the committee considered a suggestion from Lord Cherwell that bridges might be better alternative targets than rail centers. Tedder rejected the suggestion out of hand. In the end, the committee decided to instruct Tedder to review the execution of the transportation plan to ensure no more than 10,000 French dead and to report the course of the discussion and conclusion to Eisenhower.[127]

On 7 May Churchill informed Roosevelt of the British government's concern over the "slaughter" of French civilians, which might "leave a legacy of hate behind them." He noted "the great differences of opinion in the two air forces—not between them but crisscross about the efficacy of the 'railway plan' as a short-term project." Then he asked for Roosevelt's opinion: "It must be remembered, on the one hand, that this slaughter is among a friendly people who have committed no crimes against us, and not among the German foe, with all their record of cruelty and ruthlessness. On the other hand we naturally feel the hazardous nature of 'Overlord' and are in deadly earnest about making it a success. Whatever is settled between us, we are quite willing to share responsibilities with you."[128] Roosevelt replied on 11 May, "However regrettable the attendant loss of civilian lives is, I am not prepared to impose from this distance any restriction on military action by the responsible commanders that in their opinion might militate against the success of 'Overlord' or cause additional loss of life to our Allied forces of invasion."[129]

This ended the matter. Having received no support from the CCS or the president and having been opposed by Eisenhower, Churchill allowed the transportation plan to proceed without interference. Happily, civilian casualties from rail center and bridge attacks before D-day proved less than predicted; approximately 5,750 were killed. Attacks on rails and bridges after D-day probably doubled that figure. For 1944 as a whole, the French suffered 36,000 dead from Allied air strikes.[130]

Almost as an afterthought the British and the Americans finally asked an official representative of Gen Charles de Gaulle's Free French government in exile about its opinions on the killing of French civilians. On 16 May Eisenhower sent his chief of staff, Bedell Smith, to call on the commander of the French forces in Britain, Maj Gen Pierre Joseph Koenig. After Smith explained the situation, Koenig grimly replied, "c'est la guerre [This is war]." He added, "people will be killed. We would take twice the anticipated loss to be rid of the Germans."[131]

The long and tedious fight over strategic targeting resulted in the usual bureaucratic and management compromises. Organizations with the most clout or outside support achieved positions that satisfied their minimum acceptable goals. In even the most autocratic of schemes, such struggles are endemic, although more hidden. As a corollary, when organizations clash and a decision is made, at least one participant will refuse to accept the situation and continue to campaign for substantial modification. The dispute over targeting illustrates

another truism; each organization having input into target selection, or almost any form of planning, will seek to have its own
choices added to the list and with the highest priority. In this
particular affair, Harris and Leigh-Mallory quickly lost out;
Leigh-Mallory because of his personality and consequent lack
of support (How did this man ever make four-star rank?) and
Harris because the capabilities of his force so obviously fit the
approved transportation plan (he had no effective counteroption
to offer). Portal and Tedder did well with relatively weak hands.
They believed in the transportation plan and helped it carry
the day. Portal succeeded in keeping the ADGB and Coastal
Command under British control, and he handed over his position as titular head of the Combined Bomber Offensive to another British officer, Tedder. Portal further refused to give
ground to Churchill's worries over civilian casualties. Portal
advanced the cause of his service, his country, and the Allied
coalition. Much the same can be said of Tedder; he served his
two masters, Eisenhower and Portal, faithfully, while showing
rare flexibility.

Eisenhower, of course, had the trump hand—the complete
support of his government, the complete support of the US
JCS, including the incomparable General Marshall, and the
majority of the troops and personnel. He too showed diplomatic skill and flexibility, which he used more to soothe feelings after he had triumphed than to obtain compromises that
did not fulfill his goals. Unlike the airmen, he had other large
problems to confront, some with the Allied ground forces (Patton and Montgomery to name two) and with logistics. Ike was
a very tough customer when it came to the success of the
cross-channel invasion.

When it came to airpower in the United Kingdom in the spring
of 1944, Spaatz had as much or more of it than almost all of the
rest of the airmen put together. He had the most to give, but
much was wanted from him. Spaatz's dogged stubbornness
showed in his refusal to serve under Leigh-Mallory, his refusal to
lower the number one priority of destroying the Luftwaffe, and
his successful campaign to institute the bombing of German
synthetic oil. Spaatz covered his mulishness with a generous
helping of congeniality. In the affairs of mankind the power of

congeniality is one of the most underrated. In a one-on-one situation Spaatz usually came away with much of what he wanted. Who else could walk into Eisenhower's home, about to be hammered for lack of performance, and leave with permission to begin bombing synthetic oil? Eisenhower had turned Spaatz down in public a month earlier. Who but Spaatz could go into Tedder's office the next day and convince him that Spaatz needed flexibility to help with "a matter threatening the security of the U.K.?"

To the pilots flying daily into the danger, the above tales of command and control, target selection, and the doings of high rank probably made little difference. They tended to keep their attention tightly focused on whatever would keep them alive. For those coming after them it is important to know who ordered the pilots on their missions and what made a particular target worth the sacrifice of their lives. By answering those questions in this section, this work gives the sections on operations more context and meaning for the reader.

Notes

1. When the RAF formed the 2d Tactical Air Force, that air force absorbed much of the strength of Fighter Command. As a consequence the RAF reorganized the rump Fighter Command as the ADGB.

2. Terraine, *Time for Courage*, 196.

3. Richards, *Fight at Odds*, 194.

4. Terraine, 196.

5. Weigley, *Eisenhower's Lieutenants*, 59.

6. Kingston-McCloughry, *Direction of War*, 121.

7. Terraine, 196.

8. Numerous entries in Vandenberg's diaries, Papers of Hoyt S. Vandenberg, Manuscript Division, Library of Congress, Washington, DC; interview, Gen Frederick H. Smith, by James C. Hasdorff and Brig Gen Noel F. Parrish, USAF Oral History Collection, 7–8 June 1976, AFHRA File No. K239.0512-903; D'Este, *Decision in Normandy*, 214, 222–25; entry for 10 December 1943, in Brereton, *Brereton Diaries*, 228.

9. Kingston-McCloughry, 120.

10. Weigley, 58–59.

11. D'Este, 210.

12. Weigley, 59.

13. AHB Narrative, *Liberation of North-western Europe*, vol. 1, *AEAF Planning and Preparation*, 25–27.

14. Entry for 3 January 1944, Command Diary, Spaatz Papers, Diary.

15. Chandler, *Eisenhower's Papers*, vol. 3, item 1472: message 6490, Eisenhower to Smith, 5 January 1944, 1651–52.

16. Letter, Arnold to Eisenhower, 17 January 1944, Arnold Papers, Correspondence.

17. Entry for 22 January 1944, Command Diary, Spaatz Papers, Diary.

18. Entry for 21 January 1944, Command Diary, Spaatz Papers, Diary.

19. Draft message, Spaatz to Arnold, 7 February 1944, Spaatz Papers, Diary.

20. Chandler, vol. 3, item 1539, Message, Eisenhower to Marshall, 9 February 1944, 1715.

21. Entry for 17 February 1944, Command Diary, Spaatz Papers, Diary.

22. Ibid., 19 February 1944.

23. Message, K3769, Spaatz to Arnold, 19 February 1944, Spaatz Papers, Diary.

24. Entry for 19 February 1944, Command Diary, Spaatz Papers, Diary.

25. Ibid.

26. Message, K-3769, Spaatz to Arnold, 19 February 1944, Spaatz Papers, Diary.

27. Message, F-347, Arnold to Spaatz, 20 February 1944, Spaatz Papers, Diary.

28. Butcher, *My Three Years with Eisenhower*, 498–99; Hastings, *Bomber Command*, 274–75; Craven and Cate, *Argument to V-E Day*, 3:80.

29. Tedder, *With Prejudice*, 508.

30. Ibid., 8–9.

31. Chandler, vol. 3, item 1575, memo, Eisenhower to Tedder, 29 February 1944, 1755–56.

32. Ibid.

33. Ibid.

34. Ibid.

35. Tedder, 510–11.

36. Ibid.

37. Butcher, 498–99.

38. Pogue, *Supreme Command*, 124.

39. Butcher, 499.

40. Chandler, vol. 3, item 1585: message B-252, Eisenhower to Marshall, 20 March 1944, 1766–67.

41. Letter, Spaatz to Arnold, 1 March 1944, AFHSO microfilm reel A1657A, frs. 1079–89, AFHRA File no. 168.491.

42. Pogue, 124.

43. Message, COS (W)1210, Air Ministry to British Military Mission, Washington, DC, 13 March 1944, Spaatz Papers, Diary; and CCS 520, "Control of Strategic Bombing for Overlord," 17 March 1944, AFHSO microfilm reel A5535, frs. 377–79.

44. Pogue, 125.

45. Ibid.

46. Ibid.

47. Draft message, Spaatz to Arnold, 7 February 1944, Spaatz Papers, Diary.

48. Webster and Frankland, *Strategic Air Offensive*, 3:24-25.

49. Hastings, 263–68; Murray, *Strategy for Defeat*, 216–22.

50. Murray, 220.

51. Webster and Frankland, 3:27.

52. Zuckerman, *Apes to Warlords*, 216–20.

53. AEAF/MS 22007/Air Ops., "'OVERLORD' Employment of Bomber Forces in Relation to the Outline Plans," 12 February 1944, Spaatz Papers, Diary.

54. Rostow, *Pre-Invasion Bombing Strategy*, 46–47, 50. See also Tedder, 489.

55. Memo, Assistant Director of Intelligence, USSTAF [Hughes] to Deputy Commander for Operations, "Planning Conference at Norfolk House," 25 January 1944, Spaatz Papers, Diary. I have found no indication that USSTAF or the Eighth had access to a copy of the transportation plan, either an earlier draft, or one for comment, before this meeting.

56. Memo, Assistant Director of Intelligence, USSTAF [Hughes] to CG, USSTAF [Spaatz], subject: "Conference Held at AEAF Headquarters, Stanmore 15 February 1944," 15 February 1944, Spaatz Papers, Diary.

57. AEAF/MS 22007/Air Ops., 12 February 1944, 1, Spaatz Papers, Diary.

58. Memo, Hughes to Spaatz, 15 February 1944, Spaatz Papers, Diary.

59. Ibid.

60. Ibid.

61. Ibid.

62. Entry for 15 February 1944, Command Diary, Spaatz Papers, Diary.

63. Col R. D. Hughes, interview by Bruce Hopper, 20 March 1944, Spaatz Papers, Subject File 1929–1945.

64. Ibid.

65. "Plan for the Completion of the Combined Bomber Offensive," 5 March 1944, Spaatz Papers, Subject File 1929–1945.

66. Ibid.

67. Rostow, 31.

68. Pogue, 128.

69. Letter, Spaatz to Arnold, 6 March 1944, Spaatz Papers, Diary.

70. Teletype conference, Spaatz to AAF Headquarters, Washington, DC, 16 March 1944, Spaatz Papers, Diary.

71. Tedder, 518–19.

72. Chandler, vol. 3, item 1601: memo, 22 March 1944, 1782–85.

73. Webster and Frankland, 3:28.

74. CAS/Misc/61, Spaatz Papers, Diary.

75. Middleton, "Boss of the Heavyweights." See also Hamilton, *Master of the Battlefield*, 582.

76. CAS/Misc/61, Spaatz Papers, Diary.

77. Ibid.

78. Ibid.

79. Ibid.

80. Letter, Eaker to Arnold, 8 April 1944, AFHSO microfilm reel A1658, frs. 893896, AFHRA File no. 168.491.

81. Craven and Cate, *Argument to V-E Day*, 3:81.

82. Webster and Frankland, 3:32. See also Rostow, 52.

83. See Lytton, "Bombing Policy in the Rome and Pre-Normandy Invasion Aerial Campaigns of World War II," 53–58; Kindleberger, "World War II Strategy," 39–42; Rostow, "Controversy over World War II Bombing," 100–101.

84. Hastings, 277, cites conversation with Air Commodore Sidney O. Bufton of the Air Ministry Planning Staff.

85. Memo, Spaatz to Portal, "Use of Strategic Bombers in Support of OVERLORD," 31 March 1944, Spaatz Papers, Diary.

86. Ibid.

87. Ibid.

88. Entry for 14 May 1942, Command Diary, Spaatz Papers Diary.

89. Draft letter, Spaatz to Arnold [ca. 6 March 1944]. Annotated "Draft" with no indication that Spaatz ever sent it as finished copy to Arnold, Spaatz Papers, Diary.

90. Message, AX-621, Air Ministry to USSTAF, 17 February 1944, Spaatz Papers, Diary.

91. Craven and Cate, 3:174.

92. Col. R. D. Hughes, interview by Bruce Hopper, 13 June 1944, Spaatz Papers, Subject File 19291945.

93. Webster and Frankland, appendix 49 (table 38), 4:516.

94. Ibid., 3:34.

95. Hinsley, *British Intelligence*, 2:515.

96. Ismay, *Memoirs*, 349.

97. Tedder, 522–29.

98. Memo for the record, subject: Meeting of 15 April, n.d. [ca., 15 April 1944], Spaatz Papers, Diary.

99. D/SAC/TS.100, Letter, Tedder to Spaatz, 19 April 1944, Spaatz Papers, Diary.

100. Message, U61140, Spaatz to Doolittle, 19 April 1944, AFHSO microfilm reel A5885, fr. 773.

101. Maj Gen F. L. Anderson's Official Journal, entry for 19 April 1944, Spaatz Papers, USSTAF file.

102. Ibid.

103. COPC/S.501/10/INT, 8 May 1944, AFHSO microfilm reel A5219, fr. 1425.

104. F. L. Anderson's Official Journal, entry 19 April 1944, Spaatz Papers, USSTAF file.

105. Draft of teletype text to be sent to Arnold, 8 April 1944, Spaatz Papers, Diary, marked "never sent."

106. Craven and Cate, 3:3067.

107. Entry for 19 April 1944, Command Diary, Spaatz Papers, Diary.

108. Transcript of telephone conversation, Spaatz-Anderson, 20 April 1944, Spaatz Papers, Diary.

109. Entry for 19 April 1944, Command Diary, Spaatz Papers, Diary.

110. Ibid. Also see, message, U61161, Spaatz to Doolittle, which informed the Eighth Air Force that, "By verbal direction of the Supreme Allied Commander the German oil system will be attacked on the next two days of visual weather." AFHSO microfilm reel A5885, fr. 1053.

111. Craven and Cate, 3:175.

112. Entry for 20 April 1944, Command Diary, Spaatz Papers, Diary. Also see, message, U61173, Spaatz to Doolittle that informed Doolittle that, "Temporary 1st priority of CROSSBOW installations directed in our U61140 is no longer in effect." AFHSO microfilm, reel A5885, fr. 772.

113. COPC/S.501/10/INT, 8 May 1944, AFHSO microfilm reel A5219, frs. 14121413.

114. Compiled from Freeman, *Mighty Eighth War Diary*.

115. Draft letter, Spaatz to Eisenhower, 22 April 1944, Spaatz Papers, Diary—annotated "shown to General Eisenhower unsigned."

116. Entry for 23 April 1944, Command Diary, Spaatz Papers, Diary.

117. Ibid.

118. Notes of meeting at General Wilson's headquarters, 30 April 1944, Spaatz Papers, Diary.

119. Tedder, 526.

120. Ibid., 526–27.

121. Ibid., 528.

122. Ibid.

123. Chandler, vol. 3, item 1658: message, Eisenhower to Marshall, 29 April 1944, 1838–39.

124. Ibid., 1842–44.

125. Tedder, 529.

126. Ibid, 530.

127. Ibid., 530–31.

128. Churchill, *Closing the Ring*, 466–67.

129. Ibid., 467.

130. AAF Evaluation Board in the European theater of operations, "Effectiveness of Third Phase Tactical Air Operations in the European Theater," August 1945, appendix G, "Deaths Resulting from Air Attacks," 164, AFHRA 138.4-37. This study based its figures on statistics supplied by the *Defense Passive*, the French organization responsible for calculating casualties resulting from air attacks.

131. Message, S-51984, Smith to Marshall, 17 May 1944, W. B. Smith Papers, Eisenhower Presidential Library, Abilene, Kans.; W. B. Smith, *Eisenhower's Six Great Decisions*, 38; Chandler, vol. 3, note 3 to item 1630, 1810.

January

1 January: United States Strategic Air Forces in Europe (USSAFE)—established in London by Lt Gen Carl A. Spaatz. Has operational control of the Eighth and Fifteenth Air Forces. On 4 February 1944 the abbreviation for headquarters changed to USSTAF, which shall be used hereafter.

3 January: Fifteenth Air Force—Maj Gen Nathan F. Twining assumes command.

4 January: Eighth Air Force—begins flying supplies to resistance forces in Western Europe, code-named Carpetbagger.

6 January: Eighth Air Force—Maj Gen James H. Doolittle assumes command. General Eaker becomes commanding general, Mediterranean Allied Air Force.

7 January: Eighth Air Force—one B-24 interned in Switzerland.

8 January: Fifteenth Air Force—achieves strength of eight heavy bomber groups.

11 January: Eighth Air Force—first use of H2S on B-24.

16 January: Supreme Headquarters Allied Expeditionary Force (SHAEF)—General Eisenhower named as Supreme Commander Allied Expeditionary Force to direct the cross-channel invasion.

21 January: Eighth Air Force—General Doolittle frees his escort fighters from the passive restrictions of flying close escort of the bombers and orders them, instead, to attack German interceptors whenever possible. This wrecks the Luftwaffe's antibomber tactics and results in a battle of attrition between

260

the German day fighter force and the more numerous long-range fighter escorts of the Eighth Air Force.

22 January: Allies invade Anzio area south of Rome.

25 January: SHAEF—Transportation Plan introduced. It calls for attritional bombing of French and Belgian rail centers to aid invasion.

Bomber Command continued the Battle of Berlin in January 1944. Its winter campaign focused on the German capital but directed raids at other German cities as well. It dispatched nine major attacks for a combined total of almost 4,350 effective heavy bomber sorties into Germany, six against Berlin and one each against Stettin, Magdeburg, and Hannover. They dropped 11,865 tons on Berlin, 2,500 on both Magdeburg and Hannover, and 1,258 on Stettin. Weather limited follow-up photographic reconnaissance for many of these raids. Harris assumed that his bombers had inflicted important damage. However, German defenses extracted a stiff payment for the command's efforts. Of the bombers sent to Berlin, 202 failed to return; the command listed 111 aircraft missing from the three other missions. The overall loss rate of 7 percent of the effective sorties meant that the command averaged almost no gain in the number of crews available for the month. Men had stepped forward to replace the fallen, but the fresh flyers, whatever their undoubted courage and enthusiasm, lacked seasoning. A continued drain of experienced aircrew would result in diminished performance, increased battle casualties, and higher accident rates—the dread of any air commander. Of all the modern armed services it may well be that air forces are the most susceptible to harm when training levels spiral downward.

As noted above, Bomber Command reported 313 bombers lost over Germany. German night fighters claimed the bulk of the kills. Ground controllers directed the fighters to the bomber stream and supplied "running commentary" on the action. The German controllers adopted this tactic as an expedient to cope with Bomber Command's use of Window (chaff) in late July 1943. The Luftwaffe combined the technique with mass control of its fighters; one or two ground controllers would direct the Luftwaffe's entire night fighter force against the aerial invaders. Mass control helped resolve one of the most difficult problems—locating the bombers. Previous attempts to control individual fighters proved uneconomical. Placing a high concentration of fighters in the bomber stream ensured more contact and kills. Within four months, the Luftwaffe had almost perfected the tactic in spite of RAF attempts at jamming German ground controllers using "tinsell" (another form of chaff), disrupting the radio and telephone frequencies of the fighters using airborne countermeasures (airborne control or ABC—Cigar), and broadcasting fake instructions to German fighters (Corona). Bomber Command could reduce its casualties only by confusing the Germans as to the actual target or by choosing a target not well defended by night fighters. For example, a feint by Mosquitoes toward Berlin tricked German ground control into sending the Luftwaffe against bombers that were not there. This deception enabled Bomber Command to reduce its casualties in its 5 January 1944 attack on Stettin, the actual target. During the month Bomber Command's Mosquitoes continued harassing the Germans through raids on bearings plants, steel facilities, and numerous cities. Flying at high speeds, high altitudes, and alone or in small packets, they remained nearly invulnerable to German fighter and flak defenses, as evidenced by a loss rate of just one-half of one percent (0.5 percent).

On 1 January 1944 American strategic air operations in Europe entered into a new era as the air command and personnel changes agreed to by the Allied leadership in December 1943 began to take effect. In London Lt Gen Carl A. Spaatz, who had relinquished his previous position as commander of the North African Air Forces, took over the former US Eighth Air Force headquarters and changed it to USSTAF. A few days later, Maj Gen (soon to be Lt Gen) James H. Doolittle left his post as commander of the US Fifteenth Air Force in the Mediterranean theater of operations and assumed command of the Eighth. He took over the former VIII Bomber Command

and turned it into the new US Eighth Air Force headquarters. Lt Gen Ira C. Eaker moved from his position as commanding general of the US Eighth Air Force to take over the newly activated MAAF, which oversaw all Allied airpower in that theater. Maj Gen Nathan F. Twining assumed command of the US Fifteenth Air Force.

Spaatz had operational control of the Eighth, based in Great Britain, and Fifteenth, based in Italy, but not the US Ninth Air Force, a tactical air command based in Great Britain. Spaatz and Eaker agreed that, although Spaatz had operational control of the Fifteenth, all his communications to it would go through Eaker's MAAF Headquarters. As the AAF history stated: "On paper this arrangement promised many opportunities for disagreement, but actually there was no trouble at all. Eaker and Spaatz were in full agreement on the overriding priority that should be given to strategic bombing."[1] Spaatz had administrative control of all AAF personnel in Great Britain, including the Eighth and Ninth Air Forces but no administrative control over the Fifteenth (that belonged to Eaker). General Knerr, Spaatz's deputy for logistics and former head of VIII Air Force Service Command, coordinated the air logistics for the massive AAF force in England. By raising logistics to the level of operations, Spaatz recognized that modern airpower required professional support.

Doolittle and the Eighth Air Force

Immediately after assuming command of the Eighth, Doolittle began to put his stamp on its operations and tactics. In its new commander the Eighth Air Force had one of the most extraordinary air officers ever produced by the United States or any other country. While in the Air Corps he earned a master's degree and doctorate in aeronautical engineering in a total of two years from the Massachusetts Institute of Technology. They were the first such degrees ever awarded by MIT and, perhaps, in the nation. The PhD hanging on his wall bespoke of scientific curiosity and mental discipline. Not only was he brilliant but the Medal of Honor that hung around his neck denoted the recognition of unusual physical courage that he demonstrated in leading the raid on Tokyo.

263

Doolittle, the short, stocky, 47-year-old son of a carpenter, projected a devil-may-care image that masked a man of surprising substance. In the 1920s and 1930s, he won several international airplane speed races, including the Schneider Trophy for seaplanes in 1925 and the first Bendix Trophy for transcontinental speed in 1931. In taking the Thompson Trophy in 1932, he again set a new speed record. As one of the most famous pilots of his day, he had the same aura of technological mystery and death-defying courage that clings to modern-day astronauts.

Doolittle showed bad judgment at times. On a trip through South America in 1926, when he was under the influence of alcohol during a stopover in Santiago, Chile, he fell from a second-story window ledge and broke both ankles. Yet Jimmy Doolittle finished the journey, including air shows and stunts, by flying in leg casts. On other occasions Doolittle engaged in wing walking or sat on a biplane's wheel spreader or axle while it landed.

Unlike much of the AAF's leadership, Doolittle was not a career officer or a West Pointer. He had joined the Army in April 1917, transferred to the Aviation Section, and served for 13 years until early 1930 before resigning to join the Shell Oil Company. At Shell, Doolittle worked to develop 100-octane aviation fuel, a prerequisite for the advanced and more powerful piston-driven engines that would equip US aircraft in World War II. Recalled to duty as a major on 1 July 1940, he acted as a troubleshooter at various aircraft plants. In late January 1942 Arnold assigned Doolittle, now a lieutenant colonel, to command Special Project No. 1, a combined Army-Navy effort to bomb Tokyo with Army bombers flying from a Navy aircraft carrier.

"Doolittle's Tokyo Raid," 16 B-25s launched from the USS *Hornet* on 18 April 1942, catapulted Doolittle into national prominence. He again demonstrated his great physical courage by leading the flight and taking off with the shortest run. When a Japanese picketboat spotted the Navy task force before the planned launch time, he displayed the willingness to take a calculated risk and demonstrated the moral courage needed for command by accepting the responsibility of ordering the flight to leave early, thus lengthening the journey by

250 miles. He lost all his aircraft, but, nonetheless, the very fact of the raid raised US morale. It also caused the Japanese army, the service responsible for air defense of the Home Islands, to lose face. The humiliation of the Imperial Army was intensified by its being forced to extend the air defense perimeter farther out from the Japanese coastline. Additionally, the army had to capitulate to the Imperial Navy by withdrawing its objections to the Midway operation. Just as the RAF's first bombing of Berlin loosened the pebble that unleashed a landslide of Allied action against the fatherland, so too did the AAF's first bombing of Tokyo unleash a tidal wave that brought the battle to the Japanese.

Awards, recognition, and honors for Doolittle followed. The AAF and the nation, saddened by the surrender of US and Filipino forces in Bataan in early April, rejoiced over a genuine hero. By 5 May, the day before the surrender of Corregidor in Manila Bay, Doolittle was jumped to brigadier general. On 19 May President Roosevelt hung a Medal of Honor around his neck. When the Anglo-Americans agreed on the North African invasion, Arnold reassigned Doolittle to command its American air support. The Twelfth Air Force, which in the initial planning was not large, grew substantially as the overall invasion force grew. Doolittle was definitely a man of parts, most of them excellent.[2]

During his service in the Mediterranean in 1942 and 1943, he gained the trust of Spaatz and Eisenhower. When Spaatz became commander of USSTAF and Eisenhower commander of Overlord, they orchestrated Doolittle's transfer to the United Kingdom to the take command of the Eighth. Throughout his life Doolittle had confronted hard choices and developed the ability to make them. Soon after taking up the Eighth he ran headlong into another.

After arriving in England in January 1944 and throughout the first three months of 1944, Spaatz and Doolittle had insisted at every opportunity that the Eighth had to go after the Luftwaffe, especially the German day fighter force, which directly opposed US strategic bomber operations. Maj Gen William Kepner, the head of VIII Fighter Command, said in July 1944, "the minute Spaatz and Doolittle came here they directed that I take such steps as I felt necessary to lick this German Air Force. If it meant getting out and scouring the skies, even by thinning down the escort, that would be okay with them."[3]

On 21 January, in one of his first meetings with his subordinate leaders in the Eighth Air Force, Doolittle announced the new theme,[4] which he based on his experience in the Mediterranean.[5] He emphasized that although "the role of protecting the bombardment formation should not be minimized," fighters "should be encouraged to meet the enemy and destroy him rather than be content to keep him away."[6] Spaatz agreed with this view. A year earlier in North Africa, when Spaatz had confronted a situation of air parity or slight inferiority, he had codified some personal principles on air employment. One principle addressed close escort of bombers: "*Do not give close support to Heavy Bombers* [emphasis added]. This was not followed in early days of operations, causing heavy losses in fighter units, particularly P-38's."[7] Before January 1944 the Eighth's standard procedure had tied US fighters to bomber formations; they were forbidden from deserting the bombers to pursue German fighters.[8] Doolittle's order of 21 January freed the long-range escort fighters from the restrictions of close escort that heretofore had applied.

The order contradicted approved official doctrine. AAF Field Manual 1-15, *Tactics and Technique of Air Fighting*, 10 April 1942, made the task of close escorts clear: "Their mission precludes their seeking to impose combat on other forces except as necessary to carry out their defensive role." When it addressed the recommended tactics for escorts, the manual stressed their defensive nature: "Forces in special support counterattack immediately when hostile fighters make direct attacks on the defended formation. When possible withdrawal from combat will be made when threat against the defended formation has been removed." It would seem that Eaker and his fighter commander, Maj Gen Frank O. Hunter, hampered by insufficient numbers of escorts, poorly trained bomber and fighter groups, and inadequate range for the fighters they did possess, had erred chiefly in following "the book" too closely. As Field Manual 1-15 acknowledged, "Distance from the supported force will be influenced by relative speeds, escort strength, and visibility conditions."[9] Spaatz, Doolittle, and Kepner had the escort strength their predecessors lacked. They could place their fighters in loose escort.

Doolittle and Spaatz went well beyond loose escort. They introduced a doctrine of ultimate pursuit that stood official doctrine on its head. It turned the escorts into aggressors, which attacked rather than counterattacked and did not withdraw from combat but pursued from the tops of the clouds to the tops of the trees. The change in tactics failed to please everyone in the Eighth. The bomber commanders immediately understood what loose escort and ultimate pursuit implied for them—they became the worm on the hook, bait left out on the line for the enemy to snap at. It was an extremely uncomfortable feeling and would decline only in direct proportion to decreases in bomber losses.

By the end of January, the Eighth abandoned pure close escort, substituting a system based on the doctrine of "ultimate pursuit," which allowed the US fighters to follow the enemy, wherever he might be, until they destroyed him in the air or on the ground. By the end of February, the escorting fighter groups spread out in formations of 25 to 30 miles wide and frequently sent a squadron or more directly ahead to sweep the routes before the bomber formations.[10] If no enemy aircraft attacked the bombers or hovered nearby, two-thirds of the fighters were permitted to search both flanks and above and below the bombers for enemy fighters. As a result, combat took place at all altitudes, and small formations of US fighters returned from Germany at a low level, which encouraged them to shoot up targets of opportunity en route.[11]

Doolittle and Spaatz recognized this change in daily operations and adopted a brutal strategy to maximize its effects. Ultra intercepts reinforced their decision. Starting in late 1943, even before the American low altitude operations started, decoded messages revealed a series of key items of intelligence. When taken together these items showed that the Luftwaffe was having extreme difficulty in supplying experienced pilots to its frontline daylight fighter/interceptor units. First, in December 1943, the Germans curtailed reconnaissance flights and required test and ferry pilots to operate fighters against American day raids. Second, in January 1944, Hitler ordered a cutback in the flights of the Luftwaffe meteorological service and a reduction of the recuperation period allowed to pilots.[12] Finally, a series of intercepts revealed that frontline Luftwaffe fighter units were refusing to release experienced pilots to training programs. This demonstrated that frontline units were short of experienced aircrew and implied that new pilot training would be hampered through lack of experienced instructors.[13]

Spaatz's and Doolittle's new strategy of demanding air-to-air combat whenever and wherever possible attacked the German daylight fighter force at its weakest link—its ability to man the fighter force with an adequate level of experienced pilots. This was a strategy of annihilation, not merely aerial domination. The two American air leaders meant to kill the German daylight fighter force by destroying the Luftwaffe's leadership cadres. Because the Germans were not rotating veteran pilots out of frontline units, they exposed those veterans to constant attrition and inevitable loss (and denied their training base the benefit of experienced instructors). Consequently, as the veterans died, their replacements would have even less experience and even less chance of survival. By the beginning of 1944 each Luftwaffe fighter group may have had, perhaps, one or two survivors of Hitler's war with 60 or 80 kills and also may have had a few skilled pilots of 15 to 25 kills. A German daylight fighter squadron might have an ace with five kills. But the bulk of the pilots, young men with at least 150 hours' training time less than their American counterparts, had yet to fly or had hardly ever flown in combat.[14] Kill or maim the veterans, kill or maim the skilled pilots, destroy the aces, and nothing would remain but the easy meat. The Luftwaffe's best were not supermen; sooner or later the odds would overcome them and the Luftwaffe daylight fighter force would enter a final dive induced by lack of trained personnel. Brutal, undoubtedly, but effective—pitilessly so.

Luftwaffe general Adolph Galland, commander of the German day fighter force, offers perhaps the most telling description of the devastation wrought by the Americans' change of tactics. He recorded the effect of the new US tactics in his postwar memoirs:

[The American fighters] were no longer glued to the slow-moving bomber formation, but took action into their own hands. Wherever our fighters appeared, the Americans hurled themselves at them. They went over to low-level attacks on our airfields. Nowhere were we safe from them, and we had to skulk on our own bases. During take-off, assembling, climb and approach to the bombers, when we were in contact with them, on our way back, during landing, and even after that the American fighters attacked with overwhelming superiority.[15]

The Eighth's operations in January 1944 soon demonstrated the fundamental change in its tactics introduced by its new commander. During the month it sent out nine major raids, two against Noball (V-1) targets in France, and seven into Germany. The Luftwaffe made no effort to defend the V-sites under construction. Noball bombing constituted a drag on the entire Allied air effort. These strikes were directed against inappropriate or, at the least, less valuable targets since they impeded a project that might not ever come to fruition. Also, because they took place in the middle of winter, these strikes frittered away men and aircraft by imposing the normal winter wastage rates on those sorties flown. Wastage, the average day-to-day attrition of aircraft and crews lost to all causes, was greater in the winter—the perils of harsh northern European weather compounded losses to other causes.

The raids dispatched into Germany confirmed the dramatic nature of the change in the Eighth's circumstances and leadership. The first two raids, 4 and 5 January, came before Doolittle's arrival. They struck the shipyards in Kiel and conformed to the timid pattern of November and December 1943—attack of a target on the fringe of the German heartland under full escort. Giving the Eighth's planners the benefit of the doubt, these raids may have been launched because they were safe. It is usually considered bad form to present your new commander with a catastrophe. One gleam of the new pattern of operations did show through. On 5 January the Eighth's single group of operational P-51s launched 41 aircraft and claimed 16 Germans with a loss of seven of their own.

On 7 January, the day after Doolittle assumed command, the Eighth made its first deep penetration into Germany since the second Schweinfurt mission. Of 502 dispatched, 417 bombed the city area of Ludwigshafen under orders and using H2X. If their primary target, the massive I. G. Farben chemical complex, had appeared through the clouds they would have bombed it instead. The Luftwaffe did not rise to offer serious opposition to the raid. The weather may have kept it on its fields.

Four days later the Eighth again went well into north central Germany to attack aircraft plants at Oschersleben and Halberstadt. Harsh weather forced most of the 2d and 3d Bombardment Divisions to bomb targets of opportunity short of their targets and left the bomber groups of the 1st Bombardment Division separated from each other and escorted by only four groups of P-47s and one of P-51s. The German ground-to-air controllers concentrated their fighter aircraft on the 1st Bombardment Division and, as they intended, the Luftwaffe ran up a large score. Of the 266 B-17s of the 1st Bombardment Division making effective sorties, the Germans shot down 42. The only bombers from another division to strike their primary target that day lost 16 out of 47 aircraft. In all the Eighth Air Force counted 60 bombers missing for the day—a loss rate of 11 percent.

The Americans had lost heavily once again, but they had taken the enemy's best shot and had suffered, in terms of percentage, only half as badly as they had at either battle of Schweinfurt. The loss rate for bombers on this mission was unsustainable in the long run, but the Eighth sent an ominous message to the Luftwaffe. The message was straightforward: US fighter-escorts were becoming a formidable foe and would exact higher penalties from the Luftwaffe's defenses. The 1 AD's escorts (177 P-47s and 44 P-51s) had performed well. They claimed 29 sure kills and 11 probables. Of that number the single P-51 group, the 354th, shot down 15, while one of its members, Col James H. Howard, won the Medal of Honor for providing the sole protection for an embattled B-17 wing.

For more than two weeks, losses, Noball, and bad weather kept the Eighth out of Germany. On 29 January flying conditions improved, allowing the Eighth to cast 863 heavy bombers towards Frankfurt. Over 800 of them released 1,866 tons of bombs (including 525 tons of incendiaries) on the city area. They lost 34 bombers (4 percent), but their fighter escorts claimed 47 kills for a loss of only 15 of their own planes. The next day the Eighth pummeled the city areas of Brunswick and Hannover with 742 effective sorties. The force lost 20 bombers (3 percent), but the American fighters claimed 45 German fighters downed with a loss of only four US escorts.

In November 1943 when new drop tanks extended the P-47's range, American fighters claimed to have brought down approximately 110 German interceptors in engagements over German targets. This extension of the P-47's range initially caught the Luftwaffe unaware. German losses fell in December to 65 as the Luftwaffe adjusted to the new range of the P-47s. However, this downtick was only temporary. The Luftwaffe lost 180 fighters in January (one half on 29 and 30 January alone) as the P-51 and P-38 came online and as Doolittle freed the fighters from having to fly escort missions in close contact with the bomber formations.

In the south the Fifteenth reached a strength of eight heavy bomber groups. Allied ground operations, however, continued to affect strategic air operations negatively. The Allied invasion at Anzio to the south of Rome on 22 January 1944 (Operation Shingle) forced the Fifteenth to divert its strategic effort to the bombing of airfields, marshaling yards, rail and highway bridges, and other key lines of communication to slow down and harass the German reaction to the invasion. These attacks became even more important when Ultra intercepts revealed far stronger than anticipated German ground forces were rushing to counterattack.[16] The Luftwaffe staged its strongest intervention in Italy in months, bombers from Greece and close air support aircraft from throughout the theater concentrated attacks against the Allied beachhead. Operations by the RAF's 205 Group followed the same pattern as those of the Fifteenth.

The Fifteenth mounted two missions of strategic interest. On 3 January 53 of its B-17s attacked the Italian ball bearing plant at Villa Perosa with 156 tons of high explosives. On 10 January 142 of its B-17s executed a city-area attack on Sofia (the capital of Bulgaria) dropping 420 tons of high explosives. Following this raid and three earlier raids by the Fifteenth in November and December 1943, the capital's population fled the city in a mass exodus; the Bulgarian government too took flight, moving to a safer location.[17] The aim of these attacks, which the Allies repeated during subsequent months, apparently was to force the Bulgarian Council of Regents to the peace table.[18]

Notes

1. Craven and Cate, *Argument to V-E Day*, 3:328.

2. Doolittle badly deserves a good biography. The current works on him range in quality from execrable to acceptable. The most useful biography is Thomas and Jablonski, *Doolittle*. See also, if you must, Reynolds, *The Amazing Mr. Doolittle*; and Glines, *Jimmy Doolittle, Daredevil Aviator and Scientist*. Doolittle's autobiography, *I Could Never Be So Lucky Again*, written in extreme old age, has less new information than the 1970 interview done by three uniformed members of the USAF—interview of Lt Gen James H. Doolittle by Lt Col Robert M. Burch, Maj Ronald R. Fogleman, and Capt James P. Tate, 26 September 1970, AFHRA K239.512-0793. For a series of memorial articles occasioned by Doolittle's death, see *Air Power History*, vol. 40, no. 4 (Winter 1993): 2–35.

3. Kepner interview by Bruce Hopper, 15 July 1944, Spaatz Papers, Subject File 1929–1945.

4. Minutes of Commanders' Meeting, 21 January 1943, AFHSO microfilm reel A5871, Fr. 1217, AFHRA file no. 520.1411.

5. Air Force Oral History Project interview of Gen Earle E. Partridge, 23–25 April 1974, AFHRA File no. K239.0512729, 239. Partridge served as Doolittle's deputy commander from January to May 1944. In June 1944 he took over the Eighth's 3AD from Maj Gen Curtis Lemay. Before going to Britain, Partridge spent eight months as the operations officer and chief of staff of the Twelfth and Fifteenth Air Forces in the Mediterranean.

6. Minutes of Commanders' Meeting, 21 January 1943, AF/HSO microfilm 520.141-1 "Commanders' Meetings," reel A5871, Fr. 1217. For examples of Doolittle's earlier thinking, see Report, Doolittle to Arnold, subject: Escort Fighters, 22 May 1943, and Report, Doolittle to Arnold, subject: Long Range Fighters, 23 May 1943, both in Doolittle Papers, box 19. In these documents Doolittle speaks of sending fighters on low-level sweeps ahead of escorted bomber formations to catch enemy aircraft on their fields and to strafe and bomb the fields. He implied an aggressive stance on the part of the escorting fighters by noting their capabilities of either preventing attacking fighters from "getting set" or of driving away heavily armored twin-engine fighters.

7. Command diary, entry for 3 February 1943, Spaatz Papers, Diary.

8. AAF Evaluation Board, ETO, "Eighth Air Force Tactical Development, August 1943–May 1945," n.d.[ca. September 1945], AFHSO microfilm reel A1722, Fr. 203.

9. Army Air Force Field Manual 1-15, *Tactics and Technique of Air Fighting*," 10 April 1942.

10. AAF Evaluation Board, ETO, "Eighth Air Force Tactical Development, August 1943–May 1945," n.d. [September 1945], 127, AFHRA 168.6005-192.

11. Letter, Spaatz to Arnold, subject: Long-Range Fighter Sweeps, 10 April 1944, AFHSO microfilm reel A1658, frs. 1065-1070, AFHRA File no. 168.491.

12. Hinsley, *British Intelligence*, 317.

13. [Haines], *Ultra History USSTAF*, 77.

14. Murray, *Strategy for Defeat*, table 70: "Flying Hours in British, American, and German Training Programs," 314.

15. Galland, *First and the Last*, 276. This is a reprint of the 1955 British edition.

16. Hinsley, vol. 3, pt. 1, 185–96.

17. Message PZ 861, from the Air Ministry [British] Joint Intelligence Committee to FREEDOM [CINC Mediterranean], 16 February 1944, Air Force History Support Office (AFHSO), microfilm reel A6068.

18. The death in August 1943 of the 49-year-old King Boris, an able if somewhat slippery ruler and politician, forced a regency. The regents had neither the skill nor courage of King Boris. Although pro-Western, they continued to dither about surrendering to the Western Allies until the Red Army crossed their border (in early September 1944) and they lost all.

February

8 February: Fifteenth Air Force—reaches strength of 10 heavy bomber groups.

8–9 February: Bomber Command—617 Squadron drops first Bomber Command 12,000-pound bomb.

11 February: General Arnold rescinds policy on the return of aircrews after a set time period or number of combat missions flown.[1] Eighth Air Force—combat tour for heavy bomber crews extended to 30 missions.

15 February: Fifteenth Air Force—bombs Monte Cassino Benedictine abbey at the request of Allied ground forces.

15–16 February: Bomber Command—heaviest attack on Berlin—2,960 tons.

17 February: Fifteenth Air Force—reaches strength of 12 operational heavy bomber groups.

20 February: Eighth and Fifteenth Air Forces—commence Operation Argument, a systematic and coordinated attack on the German fighter aircraft industry and fighter airfields. On this date for the first time the Eighth sent out over 1,000 heavy bombers.

20–25 February: Eighth and Fifteenth Air Forces—continue Argument, known as "Big Week." Results convince American strategic air commanders that time has come to attack other targets. Germans decide to disperse their air industry.

23–24 February: Bomber Command—Mosquitoes drop 4,000-pound bombs for first time.

25 February: Eighth Air Force—one B-17 lands in Switzerland. Fifteenth Air Force—one B-24 lands in Switzerland.

Bomber Command launched five major operations into Germany in February 1944 and none into France. However, Bomber Command Mosquitoes served as Oboe pathfinders for forces of the Allied Expeditionary Air Force (AEAF) attacking airfields and V-rocket launch sites in France. No. 617 Squadron attempted two night precision attacks in France. They first attacked the undefended Gnome et Rhone aeroengine plant at Limoges on 8 and 9 February. Flying at 50 to 100 feet and using 12,000-pound bombs, which obliterated machine tools as well as buildings, the bomb aimers landed five of them on the factory and put it out of action for the remainder of the war.[2] On 12 February the squadron struck the Antheor rail viaduct, a crucial link between France and Italy. They found the target, the object of many previous Allied attacks, alertly and heavily defended. This sally achieved nothing.

The command's first major raid of the month went to Berlin on the night of 15 February. A mammoth force of 806 effective sorties disturbed the dreams of the citizens of Hitler's capital with the largest total tonnage that British bomb bays would ever spew upon them—2,960 tons (including 1,582 tons of incendiaries). Berlin may have crumbled but never burned with the hell of a firestorm. The city's wide avenues and stone or brick architecture prevented the quick spread of fire and saved the capital for a worse fate. The raid lost 43 bombers, or 5 percent, a sustainable but expensive figure. The bombs were dropped through complete cloud cover with the aid of H2S. Crew reports indicated good bombing, and Mosquitoes flying over the city a few hours later reported smoke up to 20,000 feet. Such reports raised morale but had virtually no meaningful intelligence value.

In his next raids over Germany, Harris responded to requests from the Americans and pressure from his own air staff and the Germans. As will be discussed below, the US strategic air forces had planned an all-out attack on the German air industry. This operation (Argument) would require precision bombing, several days of clear weather, and coordinated Bomber Command area raids against German cities associated with fighter production. As they awaited a sustained break in weather, the Americans dispatched repeated area raids into Germany and bided their time. The RAF air staff wanted Harris to follow Allied plans. As early as 14 January 1944, the RAF air staff had brought to Harris's attention his lack of cooperation with the targets specified in the Pointblank directive. His continued intransigence brought an RAF air staff order to strike six targets (in order of priority): Schweinfurt, Leipzig, Brunswick, Regensburg, Augsburg, and Gotha as soon as practicable. Instead, Harris launched four straight major attacks on Berlin.[3] At the end of February, when the weather finally cleared and the Americans commenced Operation Argument, Harris and Bomber Command dropped the first bombs in the operation. It would seem that Harris, like Spaatz, had merely continued other operations while waiting his crack at the German air industry.

For the Americans' struggle with the Luftwaffe day fighter force to succeed, they had to send bombers to targets the Germans would defend. Doolittle smashed at German targets whenever possible. From 3 February on, he sent out eight major raids: three to France and the rest to Germany. Of the raids sent to France, one hit V-rocket launch sites, while the other two struck numerous German fighter fields. On 3 February 552 effective sorties using H2S bombed Wilhelmshafen. The next day 474 heavy bombers struck Frankfurt; four days later another 123 smashed the city. On 10 February 138 bombers drove deep into Germany to hit aircraft plants in Brunswick. Because the target was cloud covered, they dropped their bombs on their secondary target, Brunswick's city area. The command lost 29 bombers. On 11 February 88 bombers struck Frankfurt again and, using H2S, hit the city center. Another 111 aircraft overshot Frankfurt and attacked the "industrial areas" of Saarbrücken and Ludwigshafen using visual sighting. The standing order for every single raid, except the last two, was to bomb the city area as a primary or secondary target. If clouds covered the primary and the PFF aircraft were using H2X, then the city area became the secondary target. The raids lost 70 bombers, but American fighters claimed 118 German fighters while losing 34 of their own. Ultra intercepts showed that within less than a month of

Doolittle's freeing of the fighters, the new tactics had imposed serious losses on German single-engine day fighters and forced Luftwaffe twin-engine day fighters to fly with the single-engine escorts. The AAF could afford this rate of attrition. The Luftwaffe could not. When weather cleared on 20 February, the Eighth, in spite of its own heavy losses, was well on its path to victory.

While Bomber Command and the Eighth waited to go, the Fifteenth found itself mired in the thick Italian mud of its air bases and in the requirements of the Allied ground forces for air support. In February the Germans rushed reinforcements to the Anzio beachhead and mounted two serious counterattacks. From 1 through 9 February weather limited the Fifteenth to only two days of bombing Italian marshaling yards, airfields housing Luftwaffe bombers and close support aircraft, and the Antheor viaduct. On 10 February it sent 110 bombers to hit tactical targets on the Anzio battlefields. Two days later 50 bombers struck tactical targets on the Anzio battlefield while 58 planes hit nearby highway junctions. On 14 February it sent a force of 224 aircraft to bomb rail yards and airfields in central and northern Italy. No. 205 Group also concentrated on vital rail and highway links during the period.

On 15 February the Fifteenth Air Force flew its most controversial mission of war. Only the two A-bomb strikes on Japan and, perhaps, the attack on Dresden embroiled the AAF in greater moral debate. Maj Gen Nathan A. Twining—commander of the Fifteenth Air Force and a subordinate to Lt Gen Ira Eaker, who headed all Anglo-American airpower in the theater as the commander of the Mediterranean Allied Air Forces—sent 172 of his aircraft to destroy the 1,000-year-old Benedictine monastery, the Abbey of Monte Cassino. Forty-one of the aircraft overshot and bombed 11 miles behind Allied lines. The remaining 136, aided by medium bombers of the Twelfth Air Force and heavy artillery (203 and 240 mm howitzers) of the US Fifth Army, reduced the abbey to rubble. According to the British official intelligence history, not a single scrap of intelligence placed German soldiers on the grounds of the institution before its destruction.[4] The US Army official history agreed, citing a desire on the Germans' part to maintain good relations with the Vatican and a German judgment that the abbey did not offer positions of greater military advantage than those they already held.[5]

The decision to bomb the monastery was not universally endorsed and did not split solely on international or service lines but crisscrossed them. Lt Gen Mark Clark (US Fifth Army commander), Maj Gen Geoffrey Keyes (head of US II Corps), and Keyes' two division commanders, who had all just finished a bruising battle before the Cassino line with the monastery looming in the heights above their positions, opposed destroying the monastery. However, Lt Gen Jacob Devers (the deputy Allied theater commander and the commander of all US ground forces in the Mediterranean theater of operations) and the Allied air commander, Ira Eaker, personally flew over the monastery, at 200 feet, and claimed to have seen German military going in and out of the building. They saw no reason not to bomb.[6] In the end, however, it came down to one man: Gen B. C. Freyberg, commander of the Provisional New Zealand Corps, under Clark's command. Upon examining the terrain, the commander of Freyberg's 4th Indian Division declared that he could not fulfill his mission while the monastery remained intact. Freyberg could not have agreed more. He insisted on elimination of the monastery by air attack. Clark hesitated to enforce his will on his non-American corps commander. In the meantime the matter went to higher authorities. Sir Harold Alexander, the British army group commander supported Freyberg, a notoriously touchy individual—hero of both world wars and the New Zealand political representative in the theater. The decision went well beyond bombing to the internal politics of future commonwealth relations. The same considerations influenced the Allied theater commander, Sir Maitland Wilson. The British had yet to live down the loss of an Australian division at Singapore and a South African one at Tobruk. If Freyberg believed that smashing the monastery would save his men's lives, let it be so.[7]

Initially Freyberg had requested only three dozen planes. The plan expanded, as plans so often do, as the Allied Air Forces and ground gunners vied to give the Indians what they felt they needed whether the Indians had asked for it or not. In fact the Indians had to withdraw from some positions out of fear of short rounds. Although the bombing leveled the monastery, much of the ordnance missed its target, causing 40 casualties among the Indians. Eaker witnessed the bombing and termed it "amateurish."[8] Once the Allies had proclaimed in front of the world their intention to treat the monastery as a military target by pulverizing it in front of newsreel cameras, which, in turn, spread pictures of the bombing of a Roman Catholic shrine throughout the world, the Germans, of course, occupied the ruin and used it as a defensive position and observation post. The Allies gained nothing of military value from the operation and received a self-inflicted black eye in world opinion. The bombing of the monastery quickly became an icon to those who criticized the Anglo-American Allies' methods of combat operations. In the opinion of the critics, the Allies, especially the uncultured Americans, valued the lives of military men (by implication a lower sort of person anyway) over the unique art and cultural treasures of western civilization created by generations of European artists and craftsmen. Afterwards, the Fifteenth returned to conventional operations. On 16 February 225 bombers hit nine transportation targets in Italy. The next day the same number of bombers attacked tactical targets on the Anzio battlefield.

"Big Week"

On 19 February 1944 USSTAF's weather forecasters predicted the breakup of the cloud cover over central Europe for an extended period, an event eagerly awaited by the leaders of the American heavy bombers in Europe. Headquarters USSTAF ordered Operation Argument to begin the next day. This operation, planned since early November 1943, called for a series of combined attacks by the Eighth and Fifteenth Air Forces against the Combined Bomber Offensive's highest priority objectives. During these attacks, RAF Bomber Command agreed to make nighttime area bombing attacks on the same targets. Harris's participation marked Big Week as the first air battle in which all three Allied strategic air forces fought together.

Because the plans called for efforts by the Eighth and Fifteenth, USSTAF took direct responsibility for mounting the attacks. Spaatz alerted Eaker to the implementation of Argument, requesting that Eaker's forces bomb the Regensburg and Augsburg aircraft assembly plants or the ball bearing works at Stuttgart. Spaatz directed, "All forces of the [Fifteenth] Air Force should use an area attack on Breslau as their secondary mission."[9] An attack by the Fifteenth's 12 heavy bomber groups and four fighter groups or even a diversionary attack on Breslau, the alternative target, would prevent some of the German defenders from concentrating on the Eighth coming from England and give it a better chance of successful bombing.

Eaker informed Spaatz that the Fifteenth could not fly its scheduled strategic mission. A German counterattack at Anzio had come dangerously close to driving the Allies into the sea. Eaker believed that if the Fifteenth did not support Anzio, the Allied theater commander, Wilson, might declare a ground emergency and exercise his right to take control of the Fifteenth from USSTAF for the duration of the critical situation. Eaker wished to avoid that declaration. It robbed him of all flexibility and established a troublesome precedent. He also objected because his forecasters predicted overcast skies for the Fifteenth's targets in Germany. The Fifteenth lacked H2X equipment and, thus, could not bomb its assigned targets effectively in nonvisual conditions.[10]

Spaatz disagreed. Pointblank, too, had reached a climactic stage. He and Maj Gen Frederick Anderson had agreed previously to accept extraordinary risks to ensure the completion of Argument before 1 March, even if it meant the loss of 200 bombers in a single mission.[11] Spaatz went to Portal.[12] Portal, in turn, consulted Churchill, who ruled that all available forces should support the Anzio battle. Portal told Spaatz that he [Portal] could not agree to other missions for the Fifteenth.[13]

Even while Spaatz faced marginal weather conditions for his first day's attack, Bomber Command assailed Leipzig (a center of German aircraft production) 270 miles beyond the Rhine in eastern Germany. Of Bomber Command's 730 effective sorties, 78 failed to return, a loss rate of almost 11 percent. German night fighters accounted for the bulk of the losses. They had changed tactics and made many kills over the English Channel as the bombers flew to their targets. The Germans did not pursue their foes after the bombing. This raid, coupled with the earlier raid on Berlin on the night of 15 February, caused significant changes in Bomber Command tactics. It began to rely more heavily on spoof attacks, feints, and misdirection and splitting the main force into two bodies. The command also shifted its deep attacks to more southerly targets, which had less sophisticated night defenses.

Failure to obtain support from the Fifteenth Air Force added to the tension at Spaatz's headquarters on the night of 19 February. Even as RAF Bomber Command mounted a heavy strike over Leipzig, one of the Eighth's principal targets for the next day, Spaatz's subordinates debated the wisdom of following up the RAF's effort with their own Sunday punch. The meteorologists of the Eighth and Ninth Air Forces had arrived at a forecast less optimistic than that of USSTAF. This information led Doolittle and Lt Gen Lewis H. Brereton, commander of the Ninth Air Force, to doubt the feasibility of a large-scale raid for the next day.[14] Maj Gen William Kepner (VIII Fighter Command) believed the expected conditions would produce icing on the wings of his fighters, cutting the efficiency of the P-38s in half and lowering the efficiency of his P-47s and P-51s as well.[15]

The P-38, on which great hopes rested, was beginning to prove itself unsuited for operations over Europe. Its engines reacted badly to the combination of extreme cold and high humidity encountered in winter operations. On 17 February VIII Fighter Command reported that 40 percent of its P-38 force was affected by engine trouble.[16] In all more than half the P-38 losses in the theater were attributable to engine malfunction.[17] Gen Fred Anderson vehemently opposed the naysayers.[18]

The decision rested squarely on Spaatz's shoulders. Brig Gen Charles P. Cabell, formerly commander of the 45th Bomb Wing but at that time serving on Spaatz's staff, told Brig Gen Haywood S. Hansell, "finally, when the last moment for action had arrived, the decision was left in the lap of General Spaatz. The risks were so great and the conditions so unfavorable that none of the subordinate commanders was willing to take the responsibility for the launch. General Spaatz quietly and firmly issued the order to go."[19]

Sixteen combat wings of heavy bombers (more than 1,000 bombers), all 17 AAF fighter groups (835 fighter planes), and 16 RAF squadrons (to assist in short-range penetration and withdrawal escort) began their takeoff runs, assembled, turned to the east, and headed for 12 major assembly and component plants that constituted the heart of Hitler's fighter production. As part of the largest force dispatched to date by the Eighth, six unescorted bomber wings flew a northern route to bomb targets near Posen and Tutow. The rest of the bomber force, escorted by the entire fighter force, flew toward Leipzig and Brunswick in central Germany. They would show up on German radar screens in time to attract the bulk of the fighter reaction to themselves and away from the northern force. In addition 135 medium bombers from the Ninth Air Force, two-thirds of which aborted because of weather, assisted by attacking airfields in western Europe.

The mere fact that the Eighth intended to hit 12 German targets in one mission, which meant breaking the main bombing force into several small portions, bespoke the confidence of its commanders and their determination to strike hard. By early 1943, the Eighth Air Force Operational Research Section had confirmed the unsurprising conclusion that the first two groups of bombers (45–75 aircraft) over the target did the most accurate bombing. Later bombers had to contend with alerted defenses and smoke from earlier bombing.[20] By assigning 16 bomb groups to 12 targets, Doolittle had maximized potential destruction.

In contrast to the loss of 60 bombers against the same targets on 11 January, only 21 heavy bombers of the 889 that reached their targets (2.4 percent) failed to return to base. The Baltic force encountered clouds over its targets. It bombed the city area of Rostok (using H2X) and Tutow using visual dead reckoning, the most inefficient method possible. The main force bombed visually, hitting eight aircraft plants in the Brunswick and Leipzig areas and 11 targets of opportunity, such as rail marshaling yards and industrial areas. They seriously damaged four plants manufacturing Ju-88 (Junkers night fighter-bomber) aircraft and two plants manufacturing Me-109s (day fighters). The AAF official history, basing its assertions on examination of postwar records, cited a delay of one month's production of Ju-88s and severe damage to about 32 percent of Me-109 manufacturing capacity. However, official historians admitted that the raids, like most AAF raids, damaged the machine tools less severely than the buildings that surrounded them. When the plants were cleared of rubble and dispersed to other parts of Germany, those tools could still be used to continue to produce more aircraft.[21] American fighters claimed 61 German fighters destroyed while sustaining a loss of four of their own.

The next night, 20 February, Bomber Command hit Stuttgart, a city with ball bearing and aircraft industries. It lost only nine bombers out of 552 effective sorties. That same night the command sent intruders against six night fighter bases in Holland. On 21 February the Eighth attacked 14 targets (factory airfields and aircraft plants) in central Germany with 30 bomb groups and 15 fighter groups (including a second P-51 group, the 357 FG). Of 762 effective sorties, the Eighth lost 16 bombers while its escort fighters claimed 33 of the enemy at a cost of three planes. On the next day the Fifteenth joined the fray, sending 151 of its bombers to strike German aircraft plants at Regensburg. Another 42 bombed the rail yards at Olching—a target of opportunity. The Fifteenth, with no escorts all the way to the target, lost 14 bombers (almost a 7 percent loss rate).

For a third straight day, 22 February, the Eighth dispatched 800 or more bombers. Clouds and strong winds scattered the mission, forcing the recall of the 3d Bombardment Division (3 BD); 333 B-17s targeted Schweinfurt. The 2d Bombardment Division's B-24s had already entered German airspace, so they sought targets of opportunity. Seventy-four American bombers attacked the Dutch towns of Enschede, Arnheim, Nijmegen, and Deventer after misidentifying them as German, killing many civilians. Another group (the 92d) of 64 bombers detailed to attack the airfield at Aalborg, Denmark, found the target cloud covered, and did not release their ordnance out of fear of harming friendly civilians. Both groups of attackers lost three bombers each. The 1 BD penetrated deep into Germany with 151 effective sorties. Some sorties struck an aeroengine plant at Halberstadt and Ju-88 assembly and component plants at Aschersleben and Bernberg; out of 97 aircraft, the attackers lost 19 bombers. The 1 BD suffered heavily from a large Luftwaffe response. Its bomb groups had become so widely dispersed that the escort fighters had trouble trying to provide cover for them. Several of the formations sought targets of opportunity. One combat wing, which dropped its bombs on the town of Bunde, lost 11 out of 29 attackers. Nineteen bombers struck the town of Wernigerode and lost four aircraft. In all the 1 BD lost 35 bombers. Sixteen fighter groups—two P-38s, 12 P-47s, and two P-51s (659 fighters total) sought out the Luftwaffe. They claimed 59 German aircraft as definite kills while losing 11 of their own number.

Weather scotched operations for the Eighth on 23 February but was conducive for the Fifteenth flying missions from the south. For flights into Austria and Germany, the Fifteenth did not fly over the Alps—too high and treacherous. Instead they formed up over the Adriatic Sea near their bases in southern Italy and then proceeded up the Adriatic. They flew over the former Yugoslav province of Slovenia and turned left into Austria or Germany. This route skirted the highest portion of the Alps and avoided the mountains of Italy. The Fifteenth sent 150 effective sorties to attack the Diamler-Puch aeroengine plant at Steyr, Austria. They lost 17 aircraft, more than 11 percent of the attacking force.

On 24 February the Fifteenth attacked the same target with 114 effective sorties. The Fifteenth suffered heavily, losing 17 heavy bombers—a 15 percent loss rate. Bomber Command's No. 205 Group followed this raid with an attack that night on the same target. It lost six out of 40 bombers or 15 percent. Neither organization could afford such casualties indefinitely. No. 205 Group, because of worn-out or second-line aircraft and lack of priority for new equipment, almost always absorbed a severe beating when it attacked Germany without escort.

The Eighth also suffered heavy losses, but it sent out more than 800 bombers and 767 fighters. The 3 BD, assigned to destroy air plants near Rostock and flying without fighter escort, found the targets clouded over and bombed the city area instead. They lost but five aircraft out of 236 because the Luftwaffe concentrated its efforts elsewhere. The B-24s of the 2 BD attacked the Bf-110 assembly plants in Gotha. The obsolescent, twin-engine Bf-110 made up a significant portion of the German night fighter force and the daylight heavy fighter and rocket-firing day fighter force. Some of the division aircraft bombed the city area of Eisenach as a target of opportunity. The 2 BD absorbed heavy losses, 33 bombers out of 213 effective sorties, or 15.5 percent.

The attack of the 1 BD, however, demonstrated how the tide had turned against the German defenders. The Eighth dispatched a force of 266 aircraft to finish the ball bearing plants at Schweinfurt—a somewhat smaller but comparable force to those aimed against it in the two previous attacks on that target. This force represented only one-third of the Eighth's overall strength—not a maximum effort against one target. The force faced no highly contested fight from the moment it entered German airspace. Rather 238 of its aircraft reached the ball bearing plants. They incurred a loss of 11 aircraft instead of 60—a loss of 4.6 percent instead of 20 percent. For the entire day the Eighth lost 49 bombers out of 746 effective sorties, a 6.6 percent loss rate. The Luftwaffe snapped at the bait. The American fighters escorting the bombers claimed 38 sure kills against a loss of 10 of their own. On the night of 24 February, Bomber Command followed up the Eighth's daylight raid by finally attacking Schweinfurt. Harris had refused to attack the city since its inclusion on the strategic target list in June 1943 because he believed that his bombers lacked the accuracy to strike the city of 60,000 effectively. Bomber Command dropped 2,534 tons of bombs, including 1,160 tons of incendiaries, in the assault. It lost 33 bombers out of 662 effective sorties, a 5 percent loss rate. In all of the attacks on the town that had once produced 45 percent of Germany's ball bearings, the Allies dropped more than 3,000 tons of bombs and lost 44 heavy bombers. They did not know at the time that Germany had already dispersed 34 percent of the ball bearing industry. Still, the cumulative effect of the raids on Schweinfurt and other plants reduced German ball bearing manufacturing by 50 percent.[22]

The weather held for one last day, enabling the Allied strategic air forces to hit targets in southern Germany. The Fifteenth and Eighth launched a combined mission against the Messerschmidt assembly plants in the Regensburg area. Allied intelligence credited the plants with the assembly of one-third of Germany's Me-109s. The Fifteenth came into the target area first and suffered cruelly. Of 116 effective sorties, it lost 32 bombers, a loss rate of almost 28 percent, the highest for any US mission of more than 100 bombers for the war. The 5 BW lost 22 of its B-17s, while the 301 BG lost 13. Lack of escorts allowed the German fighters, a combined force of single- and twin-engine fighters, to intercept the 301 BG at its landfall over Yugoslavia and to follow it, through flak, all the way to the target and for part of the return flight. The crews of the 5 and 47 BWs amply demonstrated that the larger and older strategic air forces had no monopoly on gallantry and the will to press on to the target.

The Eighth's 3 BD came over the target area approximately one hour later. The fighters that had hurled themselves at the Fifteenth were either refueling or still in pursuit. The Eighth lost only 12 bombers out of 267 effective sorties—a loss rate of 4.5 percent. Bomb photos indicated that the 889 tons of bombs dropped by both air forces damaged their target. The 1 BD went after the huge Messerschmidt development and experimental complex at Augsburg and the VKF ball bearing plant at Stuttgart. Of 246 effective sorties, it lost 13 aircraft—5.3 percent. The 2 BD put 161 B-24s over the Bf-110 assembly center at Fürth—losing six bombers, a 3.7 percent loss rate. For the last day of the Big Week a new P-51 group, the 363 FG, joined the action as the Eighth and Ninth put up 899 fighters. This armada claimed only 26 sure kills while losing three of its aircraft. The presence of so many of the bomber's "little friends" inhibited the German reaction. Although there would be bad days in the future, the Luftwaffe would not tamely roll over and play dead. The Americans had proved that they could fly into the worst the Luftwaffe could muster, as long as they had fighter escort, and they could do so with an overall loss rate of less then 5 percent. Soon the Fifteenth would get its share of P-51s, including the all-black 332 FG. Bomber Command not only dropped the first bombs of Big Week but it dropped the last. On the night of 25 February, it brought down the curtain by following up the Eighth's attack on Augsburg with one of its own. It dropped 2,048 tons, including 890 tons of incendiaries, on the city area—losing 21 of 528 effective sorties, a 4 percent loss rate.

The Fifteenth Air Force, which lacked P-51s, lost 89 bombers, compared with 158 lost by the Eighth, but the Fifteenth suffered a higher percentage loss.[23] In all USSTAF lost at least 266 heavy bombers; 2,600 aircrew members (killed, wounded, or captured and in German hands); and 28 fighters.[24] Almost half those losses occurred on the last two missions when the Germans took advantage of mistakes that left the bombers unescorted or underescorted.[25] In February the Eighth wrote off 299 bombers, one-fifth of its force,[26] whereas the Luftwaffe wrote off more than one-third of its single-engine fighters and lost almost 18 percent of its fighter pilots.[27]

The AAF official history states that the damage inflicted by the week's missions caused a two-month delay in German fighter aircraft production.[28] At the end of February, Field Marshal Erhard Milch (the Luftwaffe officer in charge of aircraft production) informed Albert Speer (the German minister for armaments production) that he expected the March production figures to equal only 30 to 40 percent of the February total.[29] As a result of this meeting, the two set up a fighter staff to push through a large increase in fighter production. The head of the fighter staff, Karl-Otto Saur, estimated that, at the time of its establishment on 1 March 1944, 70 percent of the original buildings of the German aircraft industry had been destroyed. Damage to machine tools was at much lower levels.[30]

The delay in German fighter production was even more significant than the actual number of fighters never produced. By the time the aircraft industry recovered in late spring and early summer, the situation had changed totally. The Eighth Air Force's attacks on German synthetic oil—begun in May 1944—produced severe shortages in aviation gasoline, which resulted in catastrophic curtailment of training programs and operations. By July 1944, hundreds of newly assembled fighters were grounded by a lack of fuel. If those new fighters had gone into operation in April or May when the Germans still had sufficient fuel available, they might have made Pointblank or even the cross-channel invasion more risky undertakings.

Big Week also affected replacement production by persuading the German leadership and aircraft industry to undertake an immediate, large-scale dispersal program. They divided the 29 major aircraft producers into 85 airframe factories and scattered aeroengine production to 249 sites.[31] This program eventually rendered the aircraft industry relatively invulnerable to bombing. However, it caused more production delays, increased indirect labor costs by 20 percent, robbed the German air industry of the advantages of economic scales of production, and heightened the demand on the German railway system by forcing elevated levels of shipment and transshipment of materials, assemblies, subassemblies, and components.[32] This situation further strained the economy and left aircraft production dependent on uninterrupted rail transportation.[33] By October 1944 the German air industry employed 450,000 workers, 103,000 of them women, with 48 percent of the workforce native Germans, 36 percent foreigners, and the remaining 16 percent Jews, prisoners of war, and political prisoners. The fighter staff also instituted, at last, double factory shifts and a seven-day, 72-hour workweek.[34]

Although postwar research has shown that the missions between 20 and 25 February accomplished less than originally estimated by the Allies, what made Big Week "big" was not only the physical damage inflicted on the German fighter industry and frontline fighter strength, which was significant, but also the psychological effect it had on the AAF. In one week Doolittle dropped almost as much bomb tonnage as the Eighth had dropped in its entire first year. At the same time, the RAF Bomber Command conducted five heavy raids on Combined Bomber Offensive targets losing 157 heavy bombers—a loss rate of 6.6 bombers per 100 bomber sorties, which slightly exceeded the American rate of six bombers per 100 sorties.[35] In trial by combat the AAF had shown that precision bombing in daylight not only performed as claimed, but also at no greater cost than the supposedly safer and less accurate night area bombing.

What is more, USSTAF, thanks to its fighter escorts, claimed to have destroyed more than 600 enemy aircraft; Bomber Command could claim only 13.[36] Of course, the US claim of 600 German fighters destroyed was a vast exaggeration. Such a claim could be approached only by counting not just the sure and probable kills by US fighters but also the numbers claimed by the American bomber crews. As noted earlier,

American bomber gunners, aided by faulty intelligence debriefing evaluation techniques, killed, at best, only one-tenth of the enemy fighter aircraft that they claimed and were credited with. Fragmentary Luftwaffe sources do not allow a specific breakout for the Big Week, but they support a conclusion that the Germans lost between 225 and 275 aircraft,[37] a close approximation to the 241 sure and probable kills claimed by the American fighters.[38]

In their own minds General Spaatz and other high-ranking American air officers had validated their belief in their chosen mode of combat. Spaatz fairly glowed in a letter he sent to Arnold summarizing the month: "The resultant destruction and damage caused to industrial plants of vital importance to the German war effort, and to the very existence of the German Air Force, can be considered a conspicuous success in the course of the European war." Spaatz went on to compare the relative contributions of the month by the AAF and RAF. The Eighth flew 5,400 more sorties than Bomber Command and dropped some 5,000 tons more bombs, all with a lower loss rate. The AAF had come of age; the long buildup in Britain had produced results at last. "During the past two years as our forces slowly built up and the RAF carried the great part and weight of attack, some circles of both the Government and the general public have been inclined to think that our part in the battle was but a small one. I trust that this brief comparison of effort will enable you to erase any doubts that may exist in some minds as to the great importance of the part now being played by the United States Army Air Forces in Europe in the task which has been sent us—the destruction of Germany's ability to wage war."[39]

Although the Luftwaffe fighter force actually increased its bomber kills in March and April, the Big Week—in the minds of Spaatz and others in the AAF—was the beginning of the end for the German daylight fighter. Most of the senior American Airmen in Europe probably agreed with USSTAF's assistant director of intelligence, Col R. D. Hughes, who said three weeks later, "I consider the result of the week's attack to be the funeral of the German Fighter Force." Hughes added that USSTAF now realized that it could bomb any target in Germany at will—a realization that led USSTAF and Spaatz to begin the hunt for the one crucial target system to bomb now that the first objective, the suppression of the Luftwaffe, seemed to have been accomplished.[40] In short order they agreed on the German synthetic oil industry as that critical target system.

United States Wins Daylight Air Superiority

Doolittle's freeing of the fighters changed the attitude of American fighter pilots. Although some would say that Doolittle's decision merely gave free rein to the already existing attitude of American fighter pilots, the new philosophy required a tactical framework that allowed some freedom of operation for the fighter pilot while providing reasonable protection for the bombers. The new system quickly coalesced around four points:

1. Freeing US fighters from the restrictions of close escort.

2. Arrival in-theater of large numbers of US long-range fighter aircraft.

3. Development of the relay system of fighter escort.

4. Increased strafing of German ground targets by US fighter aircraft.[41]

Coincident with the arrival of Spaatz and Doolittle, large numbers of long-range P-38 and P-51 fighter aircraft appeared in the theater while the range of the P-47 (already present in large numbers) was increased by 100 miles. This increase in numbers and range enabled the Americans to refine their escort technique. Large numbers of aircraft and an average of almost two pilots per plane permitted constant use of fighters. On any given day Doolittle could put several hundred fighters into the air. Such numbers helped spur development of the relay system and buffered the casualties absorbed in ground strafing. Spaatz also had administrative control of all AAF forces in the United Kingdom, which allowed him to change P-51 allocations from the Ninth to the Eighth (giving the Ninth P-47s, an excellent ground-attack aircraft, in its place) and to ensure that Ninth Air Force fighter groups flew escort for the Eighth. The influence of numbers should not be underrated; they enabled all else. Spaatz's authority included the power of promotion, a weighty club to hold over the heads of recalcitrant Ninth Air Force personnel.

The differing escort ranges of the Eighth's fighter aircraft greatly influenced the system eventually adopted. The escort ranges of the fighters in comparison with the manufacturer's specifications represented only a fraction of the aircraft's rated capabilities. Several factors—the necessity to provide for an emergency combat reserve for each plane; the fuel consumed by delays in takeoffs, landings, and forming up; and less than optimum weather conditions—combined to limit a plane's range to, at best, three-eighths of its rated maximum. Escort imposed further range restrictions because of the speed difference between the bombers and their little friends. On penetration the bombers, usually carrying their full wartime emergency weight overload, averaged an indicated airspeed of 150 mph. The fighters, throttled back for optimum gas consumption, averaged at least 100 mph (indicated airspeed) faster. For example, P-47s that were not flying escort duty conducted sweeps well beyond Berlin—far beyond their escort range. To maintain stations with the bombers, the fighters had to zigzag, which subtracted from their straight-line range.

To maximize the amount of escort available to medium- and long-range missions, the Eighth Air Force developed a relay escort system. In this system instead of a single fighter group escorting a single bomber formation all the way to and from the target—an impossibility given a fighter group's range—a fighter group would fly straight to a prearranged rendezvous point with the bombers and escort them 150 to 200 miles to yet another rendezvous point where a second fighter group would pick them up, while the first group flew straight home.[42] This tactic minimized the fuel consumed while weaving back and forth thus extending the fighter's escort range. It was also the only way to provide escort all the way to and from the target. As the deep penetration raids flown in 1943 had shown, if the bombers did not have escort all the way to their target, the Luftwaffe would simply wait until the bombers had flown beyond the escort's range and then attack. At first glance this system had the apparent disadvantage of using several times more fighters than necessary for a given mission. Instead, this relay system maximized escort throughout the entire mission. During the first half of 1944, before it had converted all but one of its fighter groups (the 56th Fighter Group) to P-51s, the Eighth employed three types of fighter aircraft, each with a different range, in relays. P-47s escorted the shallow leg or initial penetration of the mission, P-38s provided the escort on the middle leg, and P-51s flew escort for deep penetration and support over the target.[43] This system proved of special value in February and March when the shorter-range P-47s formed the bulk of the available escort aircraft. Using the P-47, P-38, and P-51 in relays allowed the long-range fighter groups to double the protection of the bombers for a few minutes or enabled one group to leave the bombers five minutes early, drop down to low altitude, and sweep all parts of western, central, and southern Germany.[44]

Until the end of March 1944, RAF Spitfire squadrons supplemented the fighters of Eighth and Ninth by providing the escort for initial penetration and the final withdrawal leg of the heavy bomber missions. With the support from the RAF, the Americans were able to extend the range of their own escort fighters during early 1944 and provide fighter cover all the way to the target. By the end of March, the increase in the number of available American long-range escorts, the decline in the efficiency of the Luftwaffe fighter force, and the Germans' tactic of concentrating their fighter defenses over Germany itself permitted the Americans to release the RAF fighters back to Air Chief Marshal Sir Trafford Leigh-Mallory of RAF Fighter Command.[45] He now regained the use of these resources after having been forced to delay training for ground support for the Ninth and the British 2d Tactical Air Force.

German ground controllers almost never managed to get all the Luftwaffe fighters available to them massed for a single blow, so the Eighth's escort seldom had to deal with overwhelming numbers of defenders. The Germans depended on carefully timed assaults by intact formations to knock down the heavy bombers. A group of Luftwaffe fighters attacking in formation could mass their firepower, downing several aircraft on each pass. However, a relatively few escorts, even if they shot down no enemy fighters, could disrupt the German formations and timing, causing them to lose much of their effectiveness. Even in the worst case, the Germans would have time for only one or two passes against the B-17s and B-24s before escorts arrived. It took brave, determined, and skilled pilots to make a successful solo attack on a heavy bomber formation.

The escort relay system led directly to the increased strafing of German ground targets by US fighters. On 9 February 1944 General Kepner issued the following instruction to his fighter pilots: "Any target of opportunity within the boundaries of Germany can be attacked."[46] With this encouragement individual fighter pilots, high on bravery and low on a sense of survival, began to fly on the deck (very low level) on their return relay flights and to strafe German aircraft, facilities, and other targets of opportunity.[47] To stimulate this practice and to invite the pilots to focus on Luftwaffe fields and facilities, the Eighth began to record official kills for planes destroyed on the ground. In March VIII Fighter Command routinely ordered all fighters to descend to low altitude and conduct fighter sweeps on their return trips.[48] In effect, Doolittle, Spaatz, and Kepner created a system that employed fighters simultaneously in the primary role of escort with a usual and secondary role of ground attack on counterair targets. Because the Germans soon supplied their airfields with liberal amounts of light flak, ground strafing became a battle of attrition on both sides. By then, however, the Eighth had established air superiority over Germany and could afford the losses.

In the relay system, as elsewhere, Ultra and other signal intelligence greatly aided the US fighters' efforts. In March Ultra intercepts revealed the damage done by the low-level fighter attacks. On 8 March Allied intelligence intercepted a Luftwaffe message stating, "the enemy has recognized our own tactics of taking off and getting away from the airfield with all serviceable aircraft before attacks on our ground organization. . . . He has recently put aside a part of the escorting force to attack these aircraft and has achieved successes in this connection."[49] Sixteen days later, as Allied fighter pressure increased, the command organization of the Luftwaffe's home fighter forces reported repeated attacks on aircraft landing on airfields in the home war zone. The report further noted of American tactics: "They imitate the landing procedures of German fighters or effect surprise by approaching the airfield in fast and level flight. The difficulty of distinguishing friend from foe often makes it impossible for flak artillery to fire on them."[50] Given such direct encouragement the Eighth had decided in April to launch pure fighter sweeps in weather unsuitable for bombers to keep up the pressure over western and central Germany. In addition to the ground attack sweeps, the Americans began to launch "free sweeps" toward suspected concentration areas of German fighters to disperse them before they could mount attacks on the US bombers.[51]

Tactical signal intercepts gave further impetus to the new tactics. RAF "Y" Service, a tactical intercept organization, cooperated fully with the Eighth. Upon detecting large concentrations of German fighters assembling to attack the bombers by means of intercepts of in-the-clear transmissions by German ground controllers to concentrations assembling to attack the bombers, "Y" Service vectored groups out on sweeps into the German formations.[52] By the end of March, although the Germans had ceased to use radio telephones, British intelligence had worked out new methods of timing the P-51 sweeps. The British intelligence official history claims that these new methods "contributed a good deal to the Eighth Air Force's success in its policy of deliberately seeking out German fighters and forcing them to accept combat."[53]

The policy of attacking German ground targets took a heavy toll on American fighter pilots, who suffered five times more casualties in strafing than in air-to-air combat with German fighters.[54] By the end of March, Spaatz reported that USSTAF was 500 fighter pilots short of its goal of two pilots per plane,[55] which would allow increased use of the planes without pushing individual pilots to the breaking point. Throughout March and for the rest of the air war against Germany, US fighter escorts accompanied the bombers so efficiently that large US losses resulted only when navigational or timing errors by bombers or fighters caused them to miss their rendezvous, or when a small contingent of the escorts was overwhelmed by large numbers of enemy fighters, which then broke through to attack the bombers.[56]

Notes

1. Letter, Arnold to Twining, 11 February 1944, Library of Congress, Manuscript Division, Papers of Ira C. Eaker (appended to the Papers of Carl A. Spaatz), Box 22. Arnold sent this letter announcing the new policy to all of the AAF numbered air force commanders. He noted that the practice of relief after a arbitrary number of missions, without regard to the replacement situation, was "a serious factor which is causing a critical shortage of crews." He stated, "If you have made any policies or understandings that combat personnel will be returned to the United States after fulfilling such arbitrary conditions as I have just described, those policies will be suspended at once."

2. Webster and Frankland, *Strategic Air Offensive*, 2:292.

3. Air Historical Branch (AHB), *Bombing Offensive*, 5:135.

4. Hinsley, *British Intelligence*, vol. 3, pt. 1, 193, see footnote.

5. Blumenson, *Salerno to Cassino*, vol. 11, pt. 3, 407.

6. Ibid., 408.

7. Ibid., 397–418, provides for a good account of this incident.

8. Letter, Lt Gen Ira C. Eaker, CINC, MAAF, to Maj Gen Nathan Twining, CG, Fifteenth Air Force, 17 March 1944, Nathan F. Twining Papers, Manuscript Division, Library of Congress, Washington, box 17, folder: personal correspondence.

9. Message IE-129 CS [Redline], Spaatz to Eaker, 19 February 1944, Spaatz Papers, cables file.

10. Craven and Cate, *Argument to V-E Day*, 3:32.

11. Ibid., 31. See also letter, Spaatz to Arnold, 23 January 1944, Spaatz Papers, Diary; interview of Col R. D. Hughes by Dr. Bruce C. Hooper, London, 20 March 1944, 1, Spaatz Papers, Subject File 1929–1945; Hughes stated, "We were all resigned to losing 150–200 heavies on the first initial show."

12. Message, Spaatz to Eaker, 19 February 1944, Spaatz Papers, Diary. Spaatz cancelled the message before transmission to Eaker.

13. Command Diary, entry for 19 February1944, Spaatz Papers.

14. Craven and Cate, 3:32.

15. Ibid.

16. Boylan, *Development of the Long-Range Escort Fighter*, 180.

17. Freeman, *Mighty Eighth War Diary*, 134–35. Kelsey made the first P-38 test flight, served as the project officer for the P-38's development, and in 1943–1944 commanded the Eighth Air Forces Operational Engineering Section. In his view the performance of the P-38 in Europe was also hampered by their pilot's poor opinion of their aircraft's performance. An opinion not shared by P-38 pilots in other theaters of operation.

18. Col C. G. Williamson, assistant deputy commander for operations, interview by Bruce C. Hopper, London, 14 June 1944, Spaatz Papers, Subject File 1929–1945.

19. Hansell, *Air Plan that Defeated Hitler*, 181.

20. McArthur, *History of Mathematics*, 35.

21. Craven and Cate, 3:34.

22. Webster and Frankland, 3:272–75.

23. Compiled from Bomb Group Mission reports found in Freeman, 183–88.

24. Murray, *Strategy for Defeat*, 242; and Craven and Cate, 3:43.

25. Combined Operational Planning Committee, Third Periodic Report on Enemy Daylight Fighter Defenses and Interception Tactics, Period 15 February 1944–2 March 1944, 26 March 1944, Spaatz Papers, Subject File 1929–1945.

26. Murray, 242.

27. Murray, 234.

28. Craven and Cate, 45.

29. AHB, vol. 5, *Full Offensive, February 1943 to February 1944* (G.225497/DEW/9/49), n.d. [ca. 1949], 164.

30. Ibid., 165.

31. Edward R. Zilbert, *Albert Speer and the Nazi Ministry of Arms*, 242.

32. AHB, vol. 5, 165.

33. Craven and Cate, 45–47; and Murray, 253–55.

34. Zilbert, 247.

35. Craven and Cate, 43–44.

36. Letter, Spaatz to Arnold, n.d. [early March 1944], Spaatz Papers, Diary.

37. Hinsley, vol. 3, pt. 1, 317, see footnote.

38. Freeman, 183–88.

39. Letter, Spaatz to Arnold, n.d. [early March 1944], Spaatz Papers, Diary.

40. Hughes interview.

41. Discussed above, in January 1944 essay.

42. European theater of operations (ETO), "Eighth Air Force Tactical Development, August 1942–May 1945," 52.

43. Director of operations (AD), minute 20849, subject: "American Long-Range Fighter Tactics, 26 April 1944," PRO AIR 20/860.

44. Letter, Spaatz to Arnold, subject: Long-Range Fighter Sweeps, 10 April 1944, AFHSO microfilm reel A1658, frs. 1065-1070, AFHRC File no. 168.491.

45. Letter, Doolittle to Leigh-Mallory, 22 March 1944, Doolittle Papers, box 19.

46. Message, 8FC F67AE, CG, VIII Fighter Command to COs 65th, 67th, and 70th Fighter Wings, 9 February 1944, AFHSO A5885, fr. 812.

47. Boylan, 181–82.

48. CG, VIII Fighter Command to CG, Eighth Air Force, subject: Tactics and Techniques of Long-Range Fighter Escort (E-A-58), memorandum, 25 July 1944, *AFHSO* microfilm reel B5200, frs. 142–61.

49. Murray, 244.

50. Ibid.

51. ETO, "Eighth Air Force Tactical Development, August 1942–May 1945," 127.

52. Ibid., 50.

53. Hinsley, vol. 3, pt. 1, 320–23.

54. Freeman, 72. The Operational Research Section of Headquarters VIII Fighter Command reported that the loss rate per 1,000 sorties for ground staffing was 3.6 times higher than that of bomber escort and that figure did not include staffing losses associated with Eighth Air Force fighter bombing missions. See, Rpt. No. 66-44, M.A., London, 8 September 1944, AFHSO microfilm, reel A5883, fr. 151.

55. Letter, The Air Surgeon, Maj Gen N. W. Grant, to Arnold, 29 March 1944, Arnold Papers, Official Decimal File, box 91.

56. Memo, "Tactics of Long-Range Fighter Escort," 25 July 1944, AFHSO microfilm reel 5200, 2.

March

1 March: Germans establish a special fighter staff to increase production. Speer gains control of fighter aircraft procurement.

4 March: Eighth Air Force—first attack on Berlin.

5 March: USSTAF—presents oil plan to aid cross-channel invasion by knocking out German synthetic fuel production.

6 March: Eighth Air Force—sends first major mission over Berlin. Severe air battle results in the loss of 69 heavy bombers, the highest number lost by the Eighth in a single day. Four bombers interned in Sweden.

6–7 March: Bomber Command—begins experiments bombing transportation plan targets. Accuracy is much higher than expected by Air Chief Marshal Harris.

9 March: Eighth Air Force—for the third time in four days launches a major attack on Berlin. Unlike previous two missions German air opposition is negligible. One bomber interned in Sweden.

15 March: Fifteenth Air Force—bombs town of Cassino.

16 March: Eighth Air Force—four B-17s and three B-24s land in Switzerland.

18 March: Eighth Air Force—12 B-24s and four B-17s down in Switzerland.

19 March: Fifteenth Air Force—reaches strength of 14 heavy bomber groups.

22 March: Eighth Air Force—one B-24 interned in Sweden.

25 March: SHAEF—General Eisenhower selects the transportation plan over the oil plan.

29 March: Fifteenth Air Force—sends out largest raid to date, almost 400 heavy bombers.

30–31 March: Bomber Command—loses 96 out of 795 heavy bombers dispatched to bomb Nürnberg. Reduces heavy bomber operations over Germany.

For Bomber Command, March 1944 marked the closing of the Battle of Berlin. Whereas the Battles of the Ruhr and Hamburg had resulted in stupendous destruction and some loss to the German war economy, the Battle of Berlin ended in a whimper with Berlin still standing, the city's production rate still climbing, and the command suffering its worst night of the war. The weather, the distance, and above all the high level of efficiency achieved by the German night fighter force combined to thwart Bomber Command. During the month, Harris launched seven large raids—4,971 effective heavy bomber sorties and 21,978 tons of bombs—into Germany. Numerous Mosquito raids complemented those of the main force. The first two raids, 1 and 15 March, attacked Stuttgart. The first mission lost four out of 502 (less than 1 percent) and the second lost 37 out of 813 (4.6 percent). The next two missions on the nights of 18 and 22 March went after Frankfurt; out of 1,543 aircraft, they lost 55 bombers, only 3.6 percent of the force. The tactics adopted after the Leipzig mission of 19 February seemed to work as long as Bomber Command did not penetrate far beyond the Rhine. On 24 March, the last heavy bomber raid on Berlin during the Battle of Berlin, German controllers guessed the target almost immediately. Only high winds, which dispersed the bomber stream, prevented an even worse debacle. What happened was bad enough. When the bombers scattered, they drifted over flak positions, which took an unusually high toll. In all Bomber Command lost 72 out of 726 heavy bombers engaged (a 10 percent loss rate). Two nights later Harris sent the force to Essen, an easy target within Oboe range. He lost only 9 of 677 bombers, a loss rate of 1.3 percent.

Then came the infamous Nürnberg raid. On the night of 30 March the main force of Bomber Command took off to attack the city famous for hosting the widely publicized and propagandized Nazi Party rallies of the 1930s. A harbinger of things to come occurred almost immediately. German night fighters made their first kill over English soil before the bombers even reached the channel, where more went down to the guns of the Luftwaffe.[1] Strangely, the mission planners abandoned the recent tactics adopted to reduce casualties and sent the bombers on an almost straight course to their target. The death ride of Bomber Command had begun. When it ended the RAF had lost 95 out of 710 attacking bombers, a loss rate of 13.4 percent—one out of every seven and one-half aircraft and aircrews. It was the highest number of heavy bombers lost on any mission during the war. The combined loss of more than 167 bombers in the two missions deep into Germany led Bomber Command to discontinue such dangerous raids for several months. Aircrews shot down over Germany or its occupied territories where they could not be recovered represented a total loss to the Anglo-American air services. About 40–50 percent of the crews survived the initial shoot-down to become prisoners of war—another advantage for the defender. Aircrews lost over friendly territory could be recovered.

While events in the night sky over Germany cast doubts on Bomber Command's ability to operate on deep missions, the command found a new and unexpected role over France. Except for 617 Squadron (an elite unit), Harris had stoutly resisted any notion that his force possessed the bombing accuracy necessary to use any method other than area bombing to hit a target. As Sir Arthur Tedder, Eisenhower's deputy, phrased it, Harris seemed intent on proving "that Bomber Command could undertake nothing other than 'mass fire raising on very large targets.'"[2] As Bomber Command's winter operations continued, the RAF air staff became increasingly skeptical of Harris's opinions on bombing accuracy. For his part, Harris tended to view the air staff as excessively academic and inexperienced. This conviction did not fit the facts. The air staff had within its ranks men of considerable operational experience in leadership positions from all segments of the RAF, including Bomber Command. At the beginning of March 1944, Portal, who suspected that Harris's views on accuracy were influenced, in some part, by his desire to avoid commitment to the transportation plan, issued a special directive to Bomber Command.

The directive of 4 March specified Pointblank and Overlord targets for the moonlight periods of March, April, and May and noted that attacks on these targets were "most likely to be of assistance to 'Pointblank' and 'Overlord' either through the actual destruction of supplies and equipment of use to the enemy or by providing opportunity to obtain experience of the effects of night attack of airfields, communications centres and ammunition dumps, before operation 'Overlord.'"[3] In particular the directive instructed Harris to attack Friedrichshafen, important for its tank engine, tank gear, and radar manufacturing, as both an industrial Pointblank target and as an Overlord target—destruction of its radar production would be of "direct assistance" to Overlord. It next listed targets in France, including six marshaling yards: Trappes, Aulnoye, Le Mans, Amiens-Longueau, Courtrai, and Laon. Bomber Command was to attack these targets at night "using a ground marking technique to provide data for the final detailed planning of 'Overlord' and in order to contribute materially to the requirements of 'Overlord' during periods when 'Pointblank' night operations are not practicable."[4] The fact that the air staff went so far as to require a specific technique, rather than allowing the operational commander, Harris, to use his discretion, clearly indicated that the air staff wanted to test the command's accuracy. Once these raids had determined Bomber Command's capabilities, then those capabilities could be used to plan further missions in support of the cross-channel invasion.

The rail yards—small, undefended targets near populated areas—constituted a literal trial-by-combat of bombing accuracy. By the end of March, Bomber Command had not only struck the six rail yards but it hit two of them twice and added a seventh. Of the nine raids, Bomber Command had outstanding success on five, which heavily damaged their targets and killed relatively few French civilians (110—an average of 22 civilian deaths per raid). In one of the less successful strikes, Courtrai on 26 March, 252 civilians died.[5] Nonetheless, Bomber Command proved, at least in the opinion of the RAF air staff, that it could accurately strike small targets at night. In fact these raids demonstrated that the command could bomb more accurately at night against small targets (and, by logical extension, against any and *all* targets) than could the US Eighth Air Force during the day.

The raids had significant consequences for the Combined Bomber Offensive. Harris never gave up his belief that strategic bombing, when properly applied, could win the war alone. Bomber Command's high losses from going deep into the Reich coupled with its newly proven ability to conduct precision attacks on French rail yards completely undercut all of Harris's practical objections to the transportation plan. In fact the roles of the Eighth and Bomber Command in the transportation plan were reversed. By the day of the invasion, 6 June, Bomber Command had dropped more than three times the tonnage on transportation targets as the Eighth—46,000 to 13,000. This result eased some of Spaatz's fears that the Americans would be dragged into transportation bombing, which would deny him the chance to destroy the Luftwaffe day fighter force before the invasion and leave him without enough strength to continue the strategic bombing of Germany.

In March 1944 the Eighth forced the Luftwaffe to continue the unequal battle between the two. It began the month with the equivalent of 30 groups of heavy bombers—a force of 1,156 bombers ready for combat.[6] Signal intelligence and combat reports clearly indicated the rising rate of German losses and led the Americans to adopt "Verdun" tactics.[7] The Eighth went over the top by suspending its attacks on the German air industry for two weeks and routing its formations directly into German fighter defenses rather than seeking to avoid them.[8] It also stopped the practice of flying bombers on diversions. Henceforward, all heavy bombers would go after the primary objectives. For the month the Eighth sent out 20 missions of 100 or more effective sorties. The increased operations rate in a winter month reflected Doolittle's insistence on operating when at all possible and with the use of H2X—which justified increased activity by giving the missions the ability to hit something, even through clouds. The Americans selected Berlin as a target likely to provoke a strong Luftwaffe response. First, they knew from the RAF's experience that the Germans had defended their capital tenaciously by night. Second, the city contained many major military and industrial targets such as ball bearing, tank, and aeroengine manufacture. Finally, as the capital of the German homeland, Berlin was of great importance in the sense that successfully attacking the city could raise the morale of Allied aircrews and the public at home while perhaps adversely affecting the morale of German people. On 3 March the Eighth dispatched 748 bombers towards Berlin and its industrial suburbs, but weather broke up the raid, leaving three groups to bomb targets of opportunity. The next day the Eighth tried again, but of 502 bombers dispatched, only one bomb wing, the 13th, pushed through the weather to the Reich's capital. The 13th's 43 bombers became the first Americans to attack Berlin; they lost five of their number.

On 6 March the Americans again attacked Berlin. Doolittle abandoned all pretense of dissimulation; he lined up 730 heavy bombers into one 125-mile-long column and hurled them straight at Berlin. Seventeen groups of American fighters (801 aircraft) flew escort: three groups of P-38s, 11 groups of P-47s, and four groups of P-51s. One of the P-51 groups, the 4th—the Eighth's most experienced fighter group—had converted from P-47s less than a week earlier. One bomber column on a single directional heading simplified navigation problems for the fighter pilots and the workings of the fighter relay system—nor could the Germans fail to find it. They reacted to the American challenge in full force, inciting one of the deadliest air battles of World War II. Of 672 effective bomber sorties, the Eighth lost 69 aircraft—a loss rate of 10.3 percent, the highest number of American bombers lost in any single engagement of the war. An additional 347 bombers suffered various degrees of damage, including six written off as unflyable. They did not hit the targets. Clouds covered the city, forcing the Americans off their industrial targets and back to their secondary target, the Friedrichsstrasse (the center of the city).[9] However, postraid photoreconnaissance showed that the bombers' crews had failed to land a bomb within five miles of the city's center.[10] These disappointing results were offset somewhat by the success of the US fighters. They claimed 81 sure kills while losing only 11 planes of their own. The P-51 pilots dealt with the Germans making last-ditch attacks over the capital, scoring 43 of the kills.

With all the finesse of a sledgehammer, the Eighth went back to Berlin on 8 March. This time the Eighth heavily damaged the Erkner ball bearing plant, and 30 aircraft bombed the city's center. The Eighth lost 37 of 539 effective sorties, a 7 percent loss rate. Nineteen US fighter groups (six of them P-51s) supported the raid and claimed 79 sure German kills with a loss of 18 US escorts. The next day, when clouds completely covered the Reich, two-thirds of the Eighth (B-17s of the 1 and 3 BD) hit Berlin while the other third (the B-24s of 2 BD) bombed in central Germany. The Luftwaffe put up little resistance possibly because it may have wished to avoid excess losses caused by bad weather operations. Given the minimal effort by the Luftwaffe, the Eighth lost only six of its 239 bombers over Berlin, mostly to flak. Almost two weeks later on 22 March, 657 bombers and 817 fighters, including six groups of P-51s, participated in another raid on Berlin. They suffered a loss of 12 bombers and 12 fighters and met no resistance from the Luftwaffe. Clouds covered the intended industrial targets, forcing the bombers to hit their secondary target, the city's center.

Other hard-fought missions of the month included two pointed at air industrial targets in southern Germany: against Augsburg and Friedrichshafen (16 March) and against Munich, Freidrichshafen, and Oberpfaffenhofen (18 March). They lost 66 out of 1,343 effective sorties, a 5 percent loss rate. Their escorts claimed 113 sure kills while losing 15 of their own planes. A mission into north-central Germany on 23 March ignited another fierce melee with 28 of 707 bombers downed and four fighters lost while scoring 20 sure claims.

The remaining missions, including those over France, met little or no opposition. The Luftwaffe could no longer oppose each deep penetration and was forced into a policy of conserving and picking its engagements with care. If it had not yet lost air parity over the fatherland during the day, one more month of such losses would have swung the battle to the Americans. For the month the Eighth wrote off 349 heavy bombers (24.6 percent of those on hand as of 1 March) and almost 3,500 air-crew members, but the overall loss rate per credited sortie dropped from 3.6 percent in February to 3.3 percent in March. The Eighth's fighters suffered a loss rate of only 1.6 percent. The strain also began to tell on the AAF's personnel programs. At the end of March 1944, Arnold reduced the training period for bombardment crews from three to two and one-half months and informed Spaatz that he would be sending some Training Command instructor pilots out as combat replacements. Arnold intended to replace the instructor pilots with aircrews returning from combat tours.[11]

The Luftwaffe day fighters sustained heavy casualties during the month, writing off 56.4 percent of single-engine fighters available on 1 March and losing 511 pilots, 22 percent of those present on 29 February. The delay in aircraft production caused by the "Big Week" strained replacement of lost aircraft, while the inadequacies and shortfalls of the German pilot training program became more obvious. As predicted, the Luftwaffe's irreplaceable leadership core also suffered. In March two Geschwader commanders with 102 and 161 kills lost their lives in operations.[12]

German Response to the Eighth's New Tactics

In the same month that the German night fighter force defeated RAF Bomber Command and forced it to curtail its night operations deep into Germany, the Luftwaffe's day fighter force was well on its way to losing its battle to drive the Americans from the Reich's daylight skies. The increasing intensity of the US daylight, heavy bomber offensive and the new tactics of the fighter escorts posed an insoluble problem to the Luftwaffe day fighter forces. In addition the Luftwaffe day fighter forces labored under the self-imposed handicaps of faulty organization and incompetent higher leadership. From October 1943 through March 1944, Hermann Göring, the commander in chief of the Luftwaffe, attempted to cope with the deteriorating air situation by strictly enforcing a policy of ignoring the fighter escort in favor of attacking the heavy bombers.[13] Gen Adolf Galland, the commander of the Luftwaffe day fighter force, protested vociferously against this directive, claiming that it unnecessarily handcuffed his pilots. German pilots under orders to avoid American fighters were put on the defensive and robbed of the aggressiveness needed for successful fighter-to-fighter combat.[14]

Other German wartime critics advocated attacking the US escorts at the earliest possible point after their takeoff to force them to jettison or "strip" their drop tanks, thus, considerably reducing their range.[15] This apparently simple stratagem demonstrated the depth of the German defensive problem. From what location would the Luftwaffe launch such preemptive strikes, France or Germany? The Luftwaffe could not have based substantial numbers of fighters in western and central France because they would have been vulnerable to harassing Allied countermeasures such as raids from medium and fighter bombers and radar-vectored fighter sweeps. The strategic and tactical air forces of both the RAF and the AAF in Britain could supply large numbers of aircraft for both tasks. German air bases in France would require additional manpower to man heavy antiaircraft defenses, provide ground defense against partisans, and to secure their supply dumps. Forward basing and maintenance of those facilities would further stretch already strained logistical links as well as offer additional targets to the Allies. The Germans simply did not have the resources to permit forward basing of fighters. In fact by the spring of 1944 the Luftwaffe had withdrawn most of its forces from France to conserve its existing strength.

The German fighters would have to scramble from western Germany or eastern France to engage the American escort fighters. However, before engaging the escorts or the fighter groups, they would first have to determine whether the American and British groups were flying radar- and ground-controlled counterair sweeps and, then, avoid those fighters to engage the escorting fighters. Of course, if too few Germans reached the escorts, then the escorting American fighter group might counter by having only one squadron drop its tanks and engage the enemy, while the other two squadrons continued the escort mission. If, on the other hand, a large number of Germans broke through to the escorted bombers, so what? The escort fighters' first priority was to kill German fighters, not to protect the bombers. If all the US escort fighters accompanying a bomber wing then attacked a large formation of German fighter aircraft, the bombers (and US fighters) would be no worse off than if the encounter happened deep in Germany. Once the fighter melee ended, the Americans would drop to the deck for targets of opportunity and return to their bases. In contrast the Luftwaffe might well have to fight their way through sweeping Allied fighters and returning US fighters that were attacking the German landing and refueling bases.

The Eighth's fighter groups actively sought combat with the Luftwaffe, whether still flying bomber escort or having broken off their escort. The Luftwaffe tactic of forcing the Eighth's fighters to jettison fuel tanks early would have played directly into Spaatz and Doolittle's hands by provoking air battles not only within range of all AAF fighters but also within the reach of short-range RAF fighters as well. If the Luftwaffe wished to begin the battle over France instead of deep over the Reich, all the better. Given the growing technical inferiority of German aircraft, the relative lack of training and experience of the fighter pilots, and the superior numbers of Allied fighter aircraft, such a tactic could have only one result: even greater disaster for the Luftwaffe.

After March 1944, when the situation had become far worse, Göring authorized one fighter group from each fighter division to attack and divert American escorts.[16] Granting permission for diversionary operations instead of all-out attacks on American fighters did not return the initiative to the German fighter pilots, but his decision did show more flexibility on his part than his subordinates tended to attribute to him. At the end of March, Göring responded to the pleas of his subordinates by consolidating the three defensive air commands facing the American bombers. He gave operational control of three of the most important of the Reich's western air defenses to the Luftwaffe's I Fighter Corps.[17] Before then the I Fighter Corps (responsible for the northern air defense sectors, coastal areas devoted to naval operations, the Berlin area, and the industrial districts of the Rhineland, Westphalia, and central Germany), the Luftwaffe's 7th Fighter Division (responsible for the defense of southern Germany, especially the industrial areas of Frankfurt, Mannheim, Stuttgart, Nürnberg, Munich, and Augsburg), and Fighter Command Ostmark (charged with defending vital Austrian targets such as Vienna, Wiener Neustadt, Steyr, and Linz) had operated semiautonomously. Each had forces inadequate to defend its sector, but there was no central operational control mechanism capable of forcing the commands to cooperate with each other. This shortcoming was an important factor in the Luftwaffe's inability to concentrate all its defensive strength on the attacking US forces. The shortage of fighters to marshal against its opponent was as much a function of the Luftwaffe's own inefficiency as it was a result of the heavy losses inflicted by the Americans.

Ever larger numbers of American long-range escorts wrecked the combined interceptor tactics the Germans had developed to combat bomber penetrations deeper into Germany. During 1943 and up to February 1944, the Germans almost always waited to attack the bomber formations until the escort had left the bombers to return home. Waiting to attack until after the bombers had committed to a specific route and destination, Luftwaffe fighters could gather without having to fend off enemy fighter attacks. During the Schweinfurt missions and later, German twin-engine fighters had stayed beyond range of the bombers' defensive armament and shelled them with 210 mm rockets—adapted from the German rocket mortars known as the screaming meemie to the ground troops. When the bombers dispersed to avoid rocket explosions, the single-engine fighters would attack the attenuated formation. In the face of vigorous escorts this tactic would not work. Not only were the Luftwaffe fighters vulnerable to attack at their areas' assembly points but so, too, were their home airfields. The performance of the American single-engine fighter escorts so outclassed the twin-engine German heavy fighters that the latter became virtually helpless against the US planes. If the Germans wished to employ their heavy twin-engine fighters at all, their lighter single-engine fighters had to escort them, much to the detriment of German pilot morale and total firepower directed against the bombers. By the end of March the twin-engine fighter seldom arose to defend against American daylight raids.[18]

The increasing numbers of American escorts also forced the Luftwaffe to modify its single-engine fighter tactics. As early as mid-December 1943, map exercises at the I Fighter Corps head-quarters had demonstrated that commitment of individual single-engine fighter groups alone had little chance of success against the attacking bombers; a single group would become too involved in fighter-to-fighter combat with the escorts. On 29 December 1943 I Fighter Corps ordered future attacks on Allied heavy bomber formations to employ a wing formation of at least three closely aligned groups to ensure that at least one group of fighters penetrated to the bomber stream.[19] These larger formations required longer time to marshal, offered easier targets for Allied air controllers to identify, and proved difficult for the increasingly inexperienced German fighter pilots because they had to fly with less space between individual aircraft, which increased the threat of accident.

The Luftwaffe could do almost nothing to reverse its decline. The Me-262 jet aircraft, if introduced in sufficient number ear-lier in the conflict, might have made life difficult for the Anglo-Americans. In actual employment, however, it never proved more than a nuisance and never shot down more than 10 bombers in a single engagement (18 March 1945). It was a classic case of too little, too late. One could also balance the development of the Me-262 against that of the He-177 bomber, a technological flop that consumed far too many resources and, since it was never deployed, it doomed the German bomber fleet to permanent obsolescence.

In the largest sense the Luftwaffe suffered from more funda-mental shortcomings, ones that it shared with the entire Nazi state. Of Germany's three regular armed services (the Waffen-SS forms a strange case of its own), the Luftwaffe was the most iden-tified with the Nazi leadership. Its head, Hermann Göring, was not only the commander in chief of the Luftwaffe but also Hitler's heir designate for the Nazi Party and the German state. In every instance Göring placed his own interests ahead of those of the Luftwaffe. What doomed the Luftwaffe was what doomed the Nazi state, the utter self-interest of its leadership and the complete fecklessness of that leadership when faced with rational wartime production decisions. If one has any doubt of Hitler's basic irrationality and of the ignorance of the goons and thugs attracted to him, one need only look at their supervision of the German war economy to disprove them. Of all the World War II leaders, only Hitler tried to fight with an economy geared to butter and guns; not until the end of 1942 did the Germans finally begin to make substantial cuts in consumer production. By that time the Americans, British, and Soviets were each too far ahead in production of war matériel to be caught.

Luftwaffe fighter pilot training provides additional evidence of the German failure to anticipate wartime needs. Through the summer of 1942 the German air force ran its fighter pilot training course under peacetime conditions, including time off for dancing classes and ski holidays. Since the course showed no dramatic growth in size during this time frame, the Luftwaffe apparently maintained its rigorous prewar policies as to physical fitness and other qualifications, thus, greatly restricting the recruiting base. This lack of urgency might also have reflected overconfidence in the effectiveness of the Luftwaffe and, thus, showed that its leadership saw no need to increase throughput. For the year, the frontline units received 1,662 pilots. The demands of the 1942 German summer offensive in Russia and the disastrous battles in Stalingrad and Tunisia disrupted this idyllic existence. Increased allotments of fuel for training and better management doubled the size of the class to 3,276 in 1943. However, wastage on the battlefronts—2,870 pilots lost in combat—almost swallowed this increment in one piece. The need on the front for modern aircraft also meant that the new pilots trained on obsolescent aircraft and received less than half the flight hours of their Anglo-American counterparts.[20] A surplus of 400 pilots a year rendered Speer's labor to produce thousands of extra fighter aircraft, above those lost in normal attrition, a cruel misdirection of effort. What need is there for more aircraft when one does not have the pilots to fly them? And how can the force structure increase dramatically, no matter how many aircraft one has on hand, if the personnel pipeline only supplies a few pilots more than those expended by the existing force each year?

When the Eighth began its campaign of attrition, the Luftwaffe operated on a narrow margin. The Eighth, for its part, benefited from a massive US training program. AAF graduates from advanced single-engine flight training numbered 1,786 in 1940; 6,853 in 1941; 13,885 in 1942; and 49,503 in 1943.[21]

For March 1944, No. 205 Group and the Fifteenth Air Force reverted to routine attacks on German airfields and marshaling yards in Italy. For the Fifteenth, its increasing strength began to make its rail yard attacks more devastating; it could now send two or three bomb groups, instead of one, to complete the mission—the number of bombers involved grew from 30–35 aircraft to 100 or more for each target. Even though bombing accuracy may not have improved, increased tonnage in ordnance dropped meant more damage to the target (and more bombs that missed the target causing greater collateral damage, as well). As the month progressed, the US strategic bombers became heavily involved in Operation Strangle, a large-scale interdiction campaign directed against all German rail and road communications in Italy. Although the campaign failed in its objective to starve the Germans out, it kept their supply situation tight and hindered their movements.[22] The operation lasted until the beginning of May. The Fifteenth also attacked tactical targets. On 2 March it struck targets in the Anzio area to help snuff out the last major counterattack by the Germans. On 15 March it bombed the city of Cassino, which the Germans had incorporated into their frontline defenses to commence the third Battle of Cassino. The Fifteenth flew 263 effective sorties, which reduced much of the city to rubble and provided the tough German paratroops defending it with even more suitable defensive terrain. Forty-three aircraft from two newly arrived groups missed Cassino and bombed targets of opportunity—all behind Allied lines. Some of the bombs killed 28 Allied soldiers while 10 miles away other bombs struck the town of Venafro, killing 17 soldiers and 40 civilians and wounding 79 soldiers and 100 civilians.[23] A last stick of bombs demolished the personal headquarters of Lt Gen Sir Oliver Lesse, the commander of the British Eighth Army. (Lesse followed Field Marshal Bernard Montgomery as commander of the Eighth Army.) On 17 March the Fifteenth made its first visit to a target it would strike more often than any other—Vienna, Austria. Vienna was called the capital city without a country because many of its monuments and structures belonging to the Hapsburg Empire had been destroyed under the terms of the peace settlement of 1919. This raid rudely introduced the residents of Vienna to World War II when 126 effective sorties were flown against the city area while 87 more hit the He-219 ground attack aircraft assembly plant in the Schwechat district of the city.

The mission against aircraft plants in Vienna conformed to the Pointblank priorities, but Spaatz had wanted to hit what he considered a more important target—the refinery complex at Ploesti. On 5 March he asked Air Chief Marshal Charles Portal for permission to attack it but received no answer. When the weather cleared on 17 March, Spaatz twice asked to strike Ploesti. Portal instructed him to direct the Fifteenth's activities toward the Balkan capitals of Budapest, Bucharest, and Sofia and, after consulting with Churchill, ruled Ploesti off limits.

Strategic Bombing and the Balkans

Portal's decision reflected the struggle in London between targeting oil production and transportation facilities and the agreed upon Anglo-American bombing policy directed towards Bulgaria, Rumania, and Hungary. If Portal allowed the Fifteenth to plaster Ploesti, that decision would strengthen the case for the oil plan. It made little sense to curtail the Germans' supply of natural petroleum, forcing them into greater reliance on synthetic oil production if the Allies were not then prepared to knock out the synthetic plants. Portal gave his reasons: first, the Ploesti refineries were widely scattered targets so bombing them would require more visual days (clear weather) than would likely to be forthcoming, and, second, given the air resources available, an attack on Bucharest would probably have a more adverse effect on Rumanian oil exports than the same scale of effort applied to refineries in Ploesti. In addition an attack on the Rumanian capital would have a more damaging effect on German political interests.[24] His directive that the Fifteenth devote more of its efforts towards the capitals of Hitler's Balkan allies added teeth to a policy already implemented by the British and Americans. Anglo-American strategic air operations directed towards the Balkans combined political and military objectives. Even more so than with Italy, strategic operations against these three minor powers might also validate prewar strategic bombardment theories concerning the ability of bombing to break the will of an opposing power and force it to surrender.

Bulgaria, which had declared war on Great Britain and the United States, but not the Soviet Union, was the first of the Balkan powers subjected to Anglo-American coercion through strategic bombing. Although Bulgarian forces did not take the field directly against the western Allies, at least eight Bulgarian divisions helped the Germans occupy Yugoslavia and Greece and took part in antiguerilla activities, which freed German troops for operations against the Allies. On 19 October 1943, Churchill, who was habitually more inclined to use strategic airpower for political purposes than his American partners, chaired a meeting of the Defense Committee. The committee concluded,

> We cannot tolerate any longer these activities of [the] Bulgarian jackals however much they may be under the heels of the Germans. We consider that a sharp lesson should be administered to Bulgaria with the primary object of forcing them to withdraw their divisions from Yugoslavia and Greece, thereby adding to Germany's difficulties and helping our campaign in Italy.
>
> We have carefully considered the best method of bringing Bulgaria to heel. All agree that surprise air attack on Sofia, accompanied by leaflets citing fate of Hamburg and Hannover, would have best and most immediate effects warning in advance of bombing not favored because it will risk increased losses. Better to do it well first and then threaten repetition on a larger scale.
>
> Relatively small diversion of air resources required for above would be well worth while [sic] if Germany has to choose between replacing Bulgarian divisions or quitting Greece.
>
> Sofia is the centre of administration of belligerent Government, an important railway centre, and has barracks, arsenals and marshalling yards.[25]

The committee further suggested that the attacks on Bulgaria begin with an American daylight heavy bomber raid followed by an RAF night raid. The next day the British representatives to the CCS in Washington requested American concurrence and that Eisenhower be instructed to carry out the raids at the "first favorable opportunity."[26] The American chiefs agreed, but proposed that, in light of Eisenhower's responsibilities for Pointblank, Overlord, and operations in Italy, he be allowed to choose his own time for the attack rather than being instructed to make it his highest priority air task.[27] The British agreed.

As with so many other strategic bombing initiatives, implementation fell far behind the intent. Instead of administering a "sharp lesson," Eisenhower supplied little more than a somewhat tardy demonstration. On 14 November 1943 90 B-25s of the Northwest African Tactical Air Force (NATAF) attacked Sofia's marshaling yards with 139.5 tons of high-explosive bombs. The Fifteenth Air Force followed up this strike with three small B-24 raids on the marshaling yards: one of 17 bombers on 24 November, another of 31 bombers on 10 December; and the last of 37 bombers on 20 December. The total tonnage of all operations in November and December against Sofia amounted to only 352 tons of high explosives. On 4 January 1944 bad weather caused the Fifteenth to abort a B-17 attack, although one group hit the marshaling yard in the small Bulgarian town of Dupnitsa, 30 miles south of Sofia. However, on 10 January the Mediterranean Allied Strategic Air Force (MASAF), which succeeded NASAF in December 1943, at last delivered the trashing that Churchill had called for more than 10 weeks earlier. That day, 142 B-17s of the Fifteenth, bombing through more than seven-tenths overcast, delivered 419.5 tons on the city; that night 42 Wellingtons of No. 205 Group followed up with 73 more tons of high explosives. Two weeks later a force of 40 B-17s frustrated in their attempt to reach Sofia dropped 117 tons of high explosives on the rail yards at Vrattso, 50 miles north of the capital.

This investment of 960 tons of bombs and only one concentrated raid produced disproportionately spectacular results. A large portion of Sofia's population, including government bureaucrats, fled the city, greatly disrupting the administration of the country. According to a report of the British Joint Intelligence Committee, the raids stimulated opposition to the government's pro-German policy, reduced Bulgaria's modest contribution to the German war effort, and increased German anxiety as to Bulgaria's stability. The bombing also caused the German's to divert flak and 100 single-engine fighters to the defense of Bulgaria and supply modern aircraft to the Bulgarian air force.[28] On 6 February 1944 the Bulgarian minister to Turkey, just returned to Istanbul from Sofia, contacted American Col Angel Kouymoumdjisky, an agent of the Office of Strategic Services—the US foreign intelligence agency. The Bulgarian minister stated that he had attended a conference with the regents, the prime minister, and the chief leaders of the opposition and was authorized to initiate talks with the United States with a view to join Bulgaria to the Allies. He also asked that the Allies give some form of guarantee that they did not intend to end the national existence of Bulgaria. As a last point he requested that air raids over Bulgaria be stopped for 10 days to permit the Bulgarian mission to reach Istanbul.[29] Upon being informed of this démarche, British general Maitland Wilson, who had replaced Eisenhower as Allied commander in chief in the Mediterranean, ordered the suspension of bombing, although he specified that the Bulgarians not be informed of it.[30] This contact was the first of a long, twisted series of negotiations that led to the eventual surrender of Bulgaria in September 1944.

Although Allied bombers would not appear again over Bulgaria for another six weeks, the continuing threat of their action led the Bulgars, on 20 February, to ask the Turkish government to intervene with the Anglo-Americans to bring about the discontinuance of the bombing of Sofia and other cities.[31] The Turks declined. It would appear that the Allied bombing deeply concerned the Bulgars, and it is not a great leap to assume that Allied bombing had been a factor, perhaps a critical one, in their decision to seek a means of leaving the war. However, once negotiations had begun, geographic and political considerations prevented a speedy Bulgarian capitulation. If the Bulgars were to turn their coats, they would need a good deal of immediate assistance from the Anglo-Americans to prevent a German takeover. Given what occurred in Italy and Hungary after those two governments negotiated a peace with the Allies, the Bulgarians' fears were not unfounded. The Germans occupied three-fourths of Italy after its surrender in February. In

315

Hungary in March 1944, the Germans successfully staged a coup to bring down a government that was wavering in its allegiance to the Axis. Since Bulgaria had no common border with any of the United Nations and was almost surrounded by Axis allies or Axis-occupied nations, the Anglo-Americans could not give the practical guarantee of quick assistance with ground forces that the Bulgarians required. This point proved a snag in future negotiations.

Even before the Bulgarian peace feeler, the success of the initial results of the bombing of Sofia led the Anglo-Americans to extend their bombing to Hungary and Rumania. On 4 February the CCS authorized Portal to target those countries, provided the effort did not interfere with Pointblank and the support of land operations in Italy.[32] On 15 February Portal sent his target priorities, in order of importance, to Wilson: Bulgaria, Budapest, and Bucharest.[33] When Wilson queried if this message meant that he should resume bombing of Bulgaria forthwith, he was answered in the affirmative.[34] The British Joint Intelligence Committee bolstered Portal's directive by advising Wilson that the Allies had received "a number of Bulgarian offers of surrender [and] approaches from [Rumania]," and that "there are abundant signs that the Hungarian government is seriously concerned at the bombing of Sofia and Helsinki." Although uncertain as to the genuineness of these initiatives, the committee recommended to Wilson that the MAAF bomb the Bulgarian towns of Plovdiv (a communications center), Burgas (a transit port for German imports of Turkish chrome), and Varna (a German navy and sea transport base) for political and economic reasons until the Bulgarians made "an authoritative approach." The committee further advised the bombing of Bucharest and Budapest to produce "panic and administrative confusion." The committee added, "it is important that the first bombing [of Budapest] should be effective and perhaps for that reason Anglo-American bombing should precede Russian."[35] Wilson could not act on the new priorities until mid-March because the Big Week, the needs of the Anzio Beachhead, the requirements of the third Battle of Cassino, and the start of Operation Strangle (a massive air interdiction campaign over occupied Italy) had first call on his resources.

Meanwhile, as Anglo-Americans awaited the opportunity to hit Balkan targets, events unfolding on the Soviet-German front dramatically changed the perceptions of those involved. In the second phase of their winter offensive, which began 4 March 1944, the Soviets drove the Germans from the Ukraine, almost destroying two German armies and part of another. On 7 March the Red Army cut the Lvov–Odessa rail line and entered Rumanian territory. By 15 April the Soviets had closed up to the Rumanian border and established bridgeheads over the river Bug. In the weeks after that the Soviets cleared the Crimea, in the process destroying the German Eighteenth Army, inflicting heavy casualties on the Rumanians and taking Sebastopol on 9 May.

The Russian advance made the Rumanians and Hungarians even more anxious to quit the war, while cutting the Lvov–Odessa line forced the Axis to shift their line of communications for the southern portion of the Russian front from the direct route through Poland to a new and far more circuitous artery via Prague, Budapest, and Bucharest. This line detoured far to the west around the barrier of the Carpathian Mountains, which were pierced by no major railways, and was hundreds of miles longer and over systems far less capable than the main line in Poland. The new route, which was the only source of supply and only route of retreat for 40 German divisions, placed yet more strain on the German railway system and, unlike the former one, lay within range of Anglo-American heavy bombers staging from the Mediterranean theater. In the eyes of some Allied commanders, particularly Portal and Wilson, this presented the western Allies with a golden opportunity to attack the Germans at a vulnerable point and aid the Soviets.

On 9 March 1944 Portal informed Spaatz and Wilson of the latest bombing priorities for the Mediterranean theater: towns in Bulgaria (including Sofia, Varna, and Burgas) subject to political considerations; Bucharest; and Budapest.[36] Two days later the British chiefs of staff detected "some hope that [a] heavy air attack on Bulgaria, coordinated with diplomatic pressure, political warfare, and action by the S.O.E. [British Special Operations Executive] and O.S.S. organizations, if carried out without delay, would force the Germans to occupy

Bulgaria if she is to be kept in the war." They urged that Wilson be instructed to deliver one or two heavy attacks on Sofia "at the earliest possible date."[37] The American chiefs refused to alter the existing priorities. In this decision they relied on the report of the American Joint Planning Committee, which stated, "we are of the opinion that a 'collapse' of Bulgaria to an extent requiring the employment of additional German ground forces will take place only when the United Nations are in a position to place forces into Bulgaria . . . collapse of Bulgaria will not be hastened by further air attacks."[38]

However, events in Hungary and the continuing defeats of Axis forces by the Soviets led to rapid and seemingly conflicting revisions of Balkan bombing directives. Within Hungary the approach of the Red Army sparked an internal political conflict between factions who believed that the time had come to quit the war and gain the best terms possible from the Anglo-Americans—the Hungarians were terrified of Soviet occupation—and those who felt that the current crisis demanded continued cooperation with the Germans. Adm Miklos Horthy, the regent of Hungary and head of state, seemed inclined to support the anti-German factions although he was not willing to make any overt moves to change current Hungarian relations with Germany. Hitler decided to take no chances on losing vital Hungarian oil and other resources or in having the defense of the east disrupted. On 19 March the Germans occupied Hungary and forced Horthy to appoint a pro-German regime, which would operate under the eye of a German plenipotentiary. At that point, the British War Cabinet, to aid anti-German elements in Hungary then in communication with His Majesty's Government, forbade Allied air operations over Hungary.[39] On 22 March Wilson asked the Fifteenth to move in the greatest possible strength against marshaling yards in Bucharest, Ploesti, Sofia, and other suitable Bulgarian and Rumanian targets. However, he placed Budapest on the restricted list.

Whereupon Spaatz, the officer with operational control of the Fifteenth, vigorously protested to Arnold and the US joint chiefs that "too many agencies are giving orders to the 15th AF," and, by implication, diverting it from its primary mission—the bombing of Germany. He added, "I cannot accept responsibility for the direction of the Fifteenth Air Force unless this situation is clarified. All orders for the attack of targets other than those effecting [sic] the battle situation in Italy must be processed through my headquarters or the 15th Air Force must be deleted from my command . . . unless positive and definite action is taken by the Combined Chiefs of Staff as to command channels and is properly impressed on all concerned, I believe that the efforts of the U.S. Strategic Air Forces will be emasculated."[40] Arnold promised to bring the matter up with the combined chiefs and pointed out to Portal that all orders to the Fifteenth must go through Spaatz, and, in spite "of the many attractive targets in the Balkans," the higher priority of the Pointblank targets should be observed.[41] Portal in his reply regretted the difficulties and promised to prevent a recurrence but pointed out that he forecasted such problems in his objections to the establishment of USSTAF at the Cairo Conference in December 1943. He explained that it was essential to notify Wilson of the strategic bombing priorities because, in addition to his theaterwide responsibilities, he controlled the MAAF's medium bombers (No. 205 Group under NASAF and American mediums in NATAF), which played a larger role in strategic operations in the Mediterranean than in the European theater. Portal followed with his justification for requesting more Balkan bombing:

> When USSTAF was created it was stated that the theater commanders would at their discretion be authorized to utilize the Strategic Air Forces for purposes other than their primary mission, should a strategical or tactical emergency arise requiring such action. It has been recognized by the Combined Chief [sic] of Staff that the situation in Italy has constituted an emergency which justified their effort to targets in Italy. In my opinion and in that of the other British Chiefs of Staff, the situation in [Rumania] and Bulgaria now ranks as a strategical emergency though it is the Germans and not we who are threatened. We believe the Germans are temporarily at any rate in a very serious predicament on the south Eastern front and that any action on our part which will add suddenly and substantially to their difficulties in that area at this time may yield incalculable to the Allied war position as a whole and therefore to our prospects for [Overlord]. . . . We feel convinced that the effect on operations in other areas would be very small, since weather is rarely suitable for more than one area at a time. . . .

> I urge you to consider my views sympathetically and to give your agreement to our treating the present situation in South East Europe as an emergency warranting a temporary and largely theoretical departure from the general order of priority.[42]

Reluctantly Arnold agreed but with the proviso that Portal insure that Balkan bombing would occur only on days in which weather did not permit strikes on Pointblank and Overlord targets.[43] Portal agreed that the prevailing weather conditions were such that the targets were mutually exclusive and assured Arnold "that no instructions will go out authorizing diversions from targets of primary importance on the priority list unless really important results can be expected."[44] Portal's arguments carried the CCS. On 24 March they authorized Portal "to instruct Spaatz and Wilson to depart from the agreed order of priority in order to deliver one or two heavy attacks on suitable objectives in Southeast Europe when the situation warrants it and results of great importance may be expected," and the CCS also told Portal that they expected only a minimum of diversion from Italian operations and Pointblank.[45] The next day Portal set the revised bombing priorities for the Mediterranean: "Bucharest railway centre, Budapest railway centre (existing ban on Hungary is hereby cancelled), and Sofia and other towns in Bulgaria."[46] Portal had prevailed upon the War Cabinet to remove the ban on Hungary when it became obvious that Hungarian resistance, such as it was, had collapsed.[47]

It was within the above context that No. 205 Group and the Fifteenth attacked Bulgarian targets during March. On the night of 15 March, No. 205 Group attacked the Sofia marshaling yard. The next night the group returned to the same aiming point, and two nights later the group struck the marshaling yards at Plovdiv. On the night of 29 March, the British attacked Sofia one more time, dropping 149 tons. The next day the American's hit Sofia; 246 bombers attacked the marshaling yards, 88 bombers attacked the center of the city, and 32 bombers hit the city's industrial area. In all the Fifteenth's crews dropped 1,070 tons of bombs (including 278 tons of incendiaries, the second highest total of such bombs ever dropped by the Fifteenth in a single raid). In terms of the Fifteenth's total wartime operational pattern, this was clearly a city-area raid. One source reported that this raid caused a firestorm.[48] Given the inaccuracy of the Allied bombing—neither No. 205 Group or the Fifteenth had as yet received electronic aids, the residents and bureaucrats of Sofia had again been touched by the war. On 17 April 250 American heavy bombers made their last major raid on Sofia, hitting its marshaling yard and industrial areas. Another 34 bombers struck the rail yards at Plovdiv (90 miles southeast of Sofia on the main rail line to Turkey) the same day.

Four hundred and fifty of the Fifteenth's heavy bombers hit a Budapest marshaling yard and an armaments work in the built-up area of the city on 3 April. The Americans returned 10 days later, attacking airfields and Me-410 fighter component plants in Budapest with 336 bombers and industrial targets in Gyor (halfway between Vienna and Budapest) with 162 heavy bombers. No. 205 bracketed this raid with missions of 53 bombers on 12 April and 64 bombers on the night of 16 April on the Budapest rail yards.

As for Rumania, the government of Marshal Ion Antonescu and its opposition had already made peace overtures. On 13 October 1943 the Rumanian military attaché in Ankara approached the British Embassy with a proposal from Antonescu. In mid-November Iuliu Maniu, head of the National Peasant Party and the most internationally respected and influential Rumanian opposition leader, also approached the British. They insisted that any negotiations include the Americans and Soviets on an equal basis. Maniu's representative, apparently with the knowledge of Antonescu, arrived in Ankara on 3 March 1944 and continued on to Cairo where he began substantive negotiations with Soviet and Anglo-American officials.[49] On the advice of the joint chiefs, the US government concluded that it would pursue these talks to remove Rumania from the Axis no matter what the eventual cost might be to the Rumanians and, by implication, with little regard for the eventual postwar situation in the Balkans.[50] As the Soviet winter offensive pulverized the German forces blocking their path to the Rumanian border, 313 of the Fifteenth's heavy bombers dropped 866 tons of high explosives (no incendiaries) on Bucharest marshaling yards. These actions had no connection other than timing. Neither the Anglo-Americans nor the Soviets conducted their military operations against the Rumanians in coordination with the other. Of course, this circumstance may have been lost on their mutual enemy.

On 11 April the CCS, noting the transfer of German forces from France to the eastern front and the increased dependence of Germany on Rumanian armed forces, stated, "In [Rumania], central control of country weakening and [Rumanian] Government apparently losing confidence in ability of Germans and own ill-equipped troops to hold Russian advance." Consequently the CCS directed, through Portal, that "maximum possible bombing effort on the Balkans until further notice should be concentrated on [Rumania] where German military position [is] weakest, German economic interests [are] greatest, and the Government [is] most shaken." Portal set the new Balkan priorities:

- Bucharest (particularly railway centre),

- Ploesti railway centre,

- other Rumanian railway targets (much lower in importance for the time being and *only* [emphasis in original] if weather [was] unsuitable for bombing in [Rumania]), and

- Budapest railway centre.[51]

At the same time Portal informed Spaatz and Wilson that towns in Bulgaria "were of little importance." The following week Portal added the Hungarian communication centers of Szolnok and Szeged, both on the main rail line to the southern front, to the priority list.[52] On 12 April the United Nations presented their armistice terms to Rumania. Three days later, 257 heavy bombers dropped 598 tons of high explosives on the Bucharest city area using radar and dead reckoning. On 24 April 209 heavies hit Bucharest with 477 tons. As Arnold informed Spaatz, these attacks were not only to disrupt rail communications but also were "intended to weaken the position of the Balkan states."[53]

Given the extent of Rumania's cooperation with the Germans, the Allies, breaking with their stated intention of unconditional surrender for the Axis powers, offered generous terms, including a pledge not to occupy Rumania and a promise of the reversal of the Vienna Award of 1940, by which Hitler had deprived Rumania of Transylvania.[54] However, Maniu, a man known for his indecisiveness, procrastinated. He waited, in vain, for some conjunction of events that might ameliorate the consequences of his country's war against the three most powerful nations in the world. On 27 April the Allies tightened the screws, demanding a yes or no response to their terms by sending a 72-hour ultimatum to both Maniu and to the Antonescu government (which was to some extent informed of developments by Maniu). When the time limit expired, with no response from Antonescu and only excuses for inaction from Maniu, an exasperated Churchill received a report from Foreign Minister Anthony Eden on the status of the talks. The prime minister's reply, written at a time when he was delaying pre-Normandy air operations out of concern for French civilian casualties, revealed an all-too-human capacity to hold two contradictory thoughts at the same time. He noted, "It is surely a case of more bombing," a statement that would seem to demonstrate a lack of equal concern for innocent Rumanians.[55]

No. 205 Group sent night raids to Bucharest on 3, 6, and 7 May, but the Fifteenth dealt the heaviest blows. On 5 May 550 bombers hit Ploesti. On 6 May more than 667 bombers assailed rail yards and aircraft plants in five different Rumanian cities. On 7 May 481 heavy bombers dropped 1,168 tons (including 164 tons of incendiaries) on rail yards in Bucharest. These attacks had a military purpose of denying the Germans oil, snarling communication with the eastern front, and adding to the burden on the rails imposed by the Danube mining campaign. Given Churchill's pique, the Allies also intended the bombing as reminder of the consequences of continued delay. Unfortunately, the Bucharest raid of 7 May partially missed its intended target and struck a crowded industrial slum. Ira Eaker reported that the Rumanians informed him that his attack killed 12,000 civilians.[56] This was typical of the exaggerated losses often attributed to strategic bombing. The official report of the Rumanian air staff on the raid indicated only 231 killed, 28 wounded, and 1,567 dwellings destroyed or damaged.[57] This spasm of bombing did not push Rumania into switching sides. The Soviet offensive had ground to a halt by 15 April, not to resume until August. The lessening of immediate pressure lowered the Rumanians' sense of urgency and eased German supply requirements.

On 16 May in a new directive obviously influenced by the inaugural raid of the Eighth Air Force on German synthetic oil production on 12 May and the Fifteenth's sub-rosa bombing of Ploesti, Portal revealed another change in Allied bombing policy, placing more emphasis on economic objectives. The directive maintained priority for Rumanian and Hungarian rail centers and added as a secondary objective: "the remaining refinery capacity at Ploesti and the refineries at Budapest and Vienna." The chief of the air staff further encouraged continued mining of the Danube and suggested bombing a factory supplying the Germans with radio tubes in Budapest.[58] Three weeks later, 6 June 1944, Portal made the refineries of Rumania (Ploesti), Hungary, and Austria first priority and mining of the Danube and operations against the river port of Giurgiu and the Iron Gates—a lock system on the Danube—second priority. Speaking for the CCS, he acknowledged the lack of measurable success in the earlier transportation and political bombing campaign and placed such operations on the lowest priority: "During present lull in fighting on Eastern Front [sic] . . . we feel that bombing directed at dislocating rail communications in Rumania and Hungary with resources likely to be available for the time being relatively black. . . . If made they should in our opinion be confined to important centres such as Budapest and Bucharest where resultant administrative chaos offers additional advantages."[59] At the end of July the CCS took cognizance of the improving Allied situation in the Balkans by toughening bombing restrictions:

(a) Strategic priorities for bombing operations in satellite countries (Hungary, Bulgaria and Rumania) should, as in the past, be confined to targets of military importance and the selection of these targets will be made with due regard for the probable scale of incidental casualties.

(b) Bombing objectives selected in Greece, Yugoslavia and Albania should be of demonstrable military value and targets will be attacked with careful avoidance of civilian casualties.[60]

This guidance standardized Allied policy for bombing occupied territory in western and eastern Europe. Greater Germany would receive the harshest treatment. Its Axis Allies would receive somewhat less harsh treatment. Countries occupied by the Germans would be treated with care.

Oil continued to retain the top priority until the end of August 1944, when the Rumanians switched sides. This volte-face allowed the summer offensive of the Red Army direct land access to Bulgaria, Yugoslavia, and Hungary. At that point the Anglo-Americans suspended bombing Bulgarian and Rumanian territory, unless coordinated with the Rumanian and Soviet high commands, and made the bombing of oil targets in Hungary and Czechoslovakia first priority with bombing communications in Hungary, Yugoslavia, and Greece as second.[61] Bombing of Hungarian and Czech targets continued into April 1945—portions of those countries remained under German control.

In their negotiations with the Balkan Axis governments, the Anglo-Americans maintained a solid diplomatic front with the Soviets. This close consultation reassured Stalin and recognized geopolitical and diplomatic realities. No lasting settlement in the Balkans could be achieved without Soviet participation. The Rumanians continued with the Axis until late August. Ultimately, as with the Bulgarians, they delayed until it was too late to make an agreement with the western Allies. They also ended up in the belly of the Soviet wolf. By missing their chance to deal with the Allies as a whole, the Axis satellites were eventually forced to come to terms with the Soviets almost one on one, much to their disadvantage.

The results of bombing Bucharest and other Balkan capitals did not seem to have produced significant political results. Given the weak morale of the Balkan nations' leadership and populations, they would seem to have been excellent candidates for the prewar air theories that advanced the principle that strategic bombing could panic a state's leadership into surrender. That such did not occur says much about the thinking of air theorists, who tend to emphasize the potency and potential of airpower without adequate consideration of the entire spectrum of diplomatic and military factors involved in warfare. The Red Army, not Anglo-American strategic airpower, forced the leaders of Hitler's Balkan satellites to capitulate to the Allies. Soviet ground force—when available and no matter how threatening to the satellite regimes—could protect them from Nazi revenge. Airpower acting alone could not do so. On the other hand the psychological effects of strategic bombing defy exact measurement. The Balkan bombings may well have contributed to defeatism and to a desire to limit commitments to their German partners.

Notes

1. Webster and Frankland, *Strategic Air Offensive*, map 15, "Nuremburg Operation 30th–31st March 1944," 2:208.

2. Ibid., 3:21.

3. Ibid., appendix 8, document xxxviii, 4:166.

4. Ibid., 4:166.

5. Richards, *Hardest Victory*, 227.

6. AAF Office of Statistical Control, "AAF Planning Controls," (SC-SS-1636), European Theater Basic Operating Statistics.

7. I owe this vivid term to Prof. Wesley Phillips Newton of Auburn University.

8. Hinsley, *British Intelligence*, vol. 3, pt. 1, 317–18.

9. Eighth Air Force, *Narrative of Operations*, "250th Operation: 6 March 1944," Air Force History Support Office (AFHSO) microfilm, reel A5959A, fr. 107.

10. Eighth Air Force, *Interpretation Report*, S.A. 1137, "Attack on Berlin on 6.3.44," AFHSO microfilm, reel A5960, fr. 111.

11. Letter, Arnold to Spaatz, 29 March 1944, in Spaatz Papers, Diary.

12. See Murray, *Strategy for Defeat*, 236–45, for an excellent discussion of Luftwaffe and AAF attrition during this period.

13. Air Ministry, *The Rise and Fall of the German Air Force, 1933–1945*, 288. See also Boylan, *Long-Range Fighter Escort*, 203–4.

14. Air Ministry, *Rise and Fall of the German Air Force*, 296.

15. Boylan, 208–10.

16. Schmid and Grabmann, *Struggle for Air Supremacy over the Reich*, 2:82. General Schmid commanded the Luftwaffe's I Fighter Corps during 1944. His force had responsibility for the defense of central Germany. This unpublished work is part of the USAF's German air generals' monograph project, which produced 42 studies dealing with various aspects of the war from the Luftwaffe perspective.

17. Schmid, *Air Battles over the Reich's Territory*, 3:4.

18. Air Ministry, *German Air Force*, 292–93; Murray, *Strategy for Defeat*, 230–31.

19. Grabmann, *German Air Force Air Defense Operations*, 735–36.

20. Murray, 254.

21. AAF Statistical Control Section, "AAF Statistical Digest for World War II," table 47: Flying Training Graduates, By Type of Course, 64.

22. See Mark, *Aerial Interdiction*, chap. 5, "Operation Strangle," for the most recent scholarship on this subject. Mark argues that the operation was not as successful as heretofore seen.

23. Blumenson, *Salerno to Cassino*, 441, n. 215.

24. Message, OZ 1638, Portal to Gen Sir John Dill, chief, British military mission to the US and UK Representative to the CCS, 25 March 1944, in Arnold Papers, Official File, Box 49.

25. CCS 376, subject: "Bombing of Sofia," 20 October 1943, NARA, RG 218, Geographic File, CCS 373.11 Bulgaria (10-20-43), Box 18.

26. Ibid.

27. Ibid.

28. J. I. C. (44) 37 (0) (Final), London, 29 January 1944, subject: Effect of Allied Bombing of Balkans on Balkan Situation, attached to JIC Memorandum for Information No. 38, 11 February 1944, NARA, RG 218, Geographic File, CCS 373.11, Balkans (2-3-44).

29. Message 274, [Edward] Stettinius, acting secretary of state [Washington], to [Averrell] Harriman, ambassador to the Soviet Union [Moscow], 10 February 1944, in US Department of State, *FRUS, 1944, The British Commonwealth and Europe*, 3:300.

30. Message, MEDCOS 35, CinC Med to British chiefs of staff, 9 February 1944, NARA, RG 218, Geographic File, Folder CCS Bulgaria 092, O.S.S. Plan to Detach Bulgaria from the Axis (8-2-43), sec. 1.

31. Message 301, [Laurence] Steinhardt, ambassador to Turkey, to the secretary of state, 21 February 1944, *FRUS*, 301.

32. CCS 482, subject: "Bombing of Axis Satellite Countries," 4 February 1944: NARA, RG 218, Geographic File, CCS 373.11 Balkans (2-3-44).

33. Message COSMED 33, British chiefs of staff to CinC Med, 15 February 1944, NARA, RG 218, Geographic File, 373.11 Balkans (2-3-44).

34. For Wilson's query, see message, MEDCOS 51, CinC Med to British chiefs of staff, 17 February 1944. For the British Chiefs reply, see message, COSMED 38, British Chiefs of Staff to CinC Med, 18 February 1944, both in NARA, RG 218, Geographic File, 373.11 Balkans (2-3-44).

35. Message PZ 861, from the Air Ministry from the JIC to FREEDOM [Allied CINC Mediterranean], 16 February 1944, AFHSO microfilm reel A6068.

36. Message COSMED 55, Portal to Wilson, 9 March 1944, NARA, RG 218, Geographic File, CCS Bulgaria 092 (8-2-43), sec. 1, OSS, Plan to Detach Bulgaria from the Axis.

37. CCS 517, subject: "Bombing of Bulgaria," 11 March 1944, NARA, RG 218, Geographic File, CCS Bulgaria 092 (8-2-43), sec. 1, OSS, Plan to Detach Bulgaria from the Axis.

38. JPS 410/1, subject: "Bombing of Bulgaria," 14 March 1944, NARA, RG 218, Geographic File, CCS Bulgaria 092 (8-2-43), sec. 1, OSS. Plan to Detach Bulgaria from the Axis.

39. Message, OZ 1638.

40. Message U 60045, Spaatz to Arnold, 23 March 1944, Spaatz Papers, Diary. See message, U 60100, Spaatz to Arnold, 24 March 1944, Spaatz Pa-

pers, Diary, where Spaatz strongly states his fears that the theater commanders are being granted too much authority to direct strategic air forces and as a consequence, "opportunities will be lost that we cannot afford to throw away in the brief time before Overlord."

41. Message 13235, Arnold to Portal (through Spaatz), 23 March 1944, Spaatz Papers, Diary.

42. Message AX 779, Portal to Arnold, 25 March 1944, Spaatz Papers, Diary.

43. Message 14086, Arnold to Portal, 25 March 1944, Spaatz Papers, Diary.

44. Message AX 902, Portal to Arnold, 26 March 1944, Spaatz Papers, Diary.

45. Message J.S.M. 1592, CCS to Portal, 24 March 1944, NARA, RG 218, Geographic File, 373.11 Balkans (2-3-44).

46. Message COSMED 71, Portal to Wilson and Spaatz, 25 March 1944, NARA, RG 218, Geographic File, CCS 373.11 Balkans (2-3-44), Bombing of Axis Satellite Countries.

47. Message OZ 1638.

48. Schaffer, *Wings of Judgment*, 56.

49. For the American side of these negotiations, see Department of State, *FRUS, Diplomatic Papers 1944, Europe*, 4:133–289.

50. See folder, CCS 387 Rumania (10-23-43), Section 1, Rumanian Cooperation with Anglo-American Forces, NARA, RG 218, Geographic File.

51. Message COSMED 87, Portal to Wilson and Spaatz, 11 April 1944, NARA, RG 218, Geographic File, CCS 373.11 Balkans (2-3-44), Bombing of Axis Satellite Countries.

52. Message COSMED 89, Portal to Wilson and Spaatz, 18 April 1944, NARA, RG 218, Geographic File, CCS 373.11 Balkans (2-3-44), Bombing of Axis Satellite Countries.

53. Message WARX 20129, Arnold to Spaatz, 7 April 1944, NARA, RG 218, Geographic File, CCS 373.11 Balkans (2-3-44), Bombing of Axis Satellite Countries.

54. Message Yugos 84, Department of State to US Ambassador to the Greek and Yugoslav government in exile, Lincoln MacVeagh, in *FRUS, 1944, Europe*, 4:170. MacVeagh was the US representative in these Rumanian negotiations.

55. Minute, W. S. C. to Anthony Eden, 29 April 1944, PRO FO 371/43999/R 6819.

56. Letter, Ira C. Eaker to H. H. Arnold, 17 September 1944, U.S. Library of Congress, Manuscript Division, Washington, D.C., The Papers of Henry H. Arnold, folder "Letters to General Marshall," Box 44. Arnold also sent a copy to the president (see box 45, folder "Letters to FDR").

57. Section II-a, *Statul Major al Aerului*, Nr. 30.543D, 10 May 1944, Subject: *Dare de Seama Recapitulativa asupre Bombardament Lor Aeriene Inamice Dela 5–8 Mai 1944*. Rumanian State Archives, Bucharest, Rumania. This report places the civilian dead from all Anglo-American bombing of Ruma-

nia from 5–8 May at 820. This document supplied by Dr. Eduard Mark of the USAF History Office, Bolling Air Force Base, DC.

58. Message COSMED 109, 16 May 1944, NARA, RG 218, Geographic File, CCS 373.11 Balkans (2-3-44), Bombing of Axis Satellite Countries.

59. Message COSMED 124, Portal to Spaatz and Wilson, 6 June 1944, in NARA, RG 218, Geographic File, CCS 373.11 Balkans (2-3-44), Bombing of Axis Satellite Countries.

60. Message JSM 166, British Joint Staff Mission (Washington) to British chiefs of staff, 29 July 1944, in NARA, RG 218, Geographic File, CCS 373.11 Balkans (2-3-44), Bombing of Axis Satellite Countries.

61. Message COSMED 176, CCS to Wilson and Spaatz, 29 August 1944, in NARA, RG 218, Geographic File, CCS 373.11 Balkans (2-3-44), Bombing of Axis Satellite Countries.

April

1 April: Eighth Air Force—mistakenly bombs Swiss city of Schaffhausen. One B-24 interned in Switzerland.

2 April: Fifteenth Air Force—reaches strength of 16 heavy bomber groups.

5 April: USSTAF—General Spaatz informs General Arnold that Eighth Air Force fighters are briefed "to strafe anything that moves in Germany."

9 April: Eighth Air Force—three B-17s and seven B-24s interned in Sweden.

10 April: Soviets take Odessa.

11 April: Eighth Air Force—nine B-17s interned in Sweden.

13 April: Eighth Air Force—10 B-17s and three B-24s interned in Switzerland.

14 April: Bomber Command and Eighth Air Force come under General Eisenhower's "direction."

18 April: Eighth Air Force—one B-17 interned in Switzerland.

19 April: SHAEF and USSTAF—General Eisenhower agrees to allow two Eighth AF missions against synthetic oil.

21 April: Eighth Air Force—bad weather cancels first oil mission.

22 April: Eighth Air Force—bombs first transportation plan target.

22–23 April: Bomber Command—drops first 30-pound J incendiary bombs on Brunswick.

24 April: Eighth Air Force—13 B-17s and one B-24 interned in Switzerland.

25 April: Eighth Air Force—two B-24s land in Switzerland. Fifteenth Air Force—one B-24 lands in Switzerland.

29 April: Eighth Air Force—one B-17 interned in Sweden.

30 April: Fifteenth Air Force—reaches strength of 19 heavy bomber groups.

In April 1944 Bomber Command possessed an average daily strength of 614 Lancasters, 353 Halifaxes, 58 Stirlings, and 72 Mosquitoes.[1] The command launched 11 major raids during April 1944: five bombed French targets, three bombed German targets, and three hit targets in both countries. Two raids into cities deep into Germany (Schweinfurt on 26 April and Friedrickshafen on 27 April), lost 23 out of 217 and 19 out of 309 effective sorties, respectively, a combined loss rate of 8 percent. Deep attacks on Munich (24 April) and Brunswick (22 April) lost only nine of 255 and three of 256 for a loss rate of 2.3 percent. Attacks on cities not deep inside Germany, Aachen (11 April) and Essen (26 April), lost 14 of 811 (1.7 percent), while equally close in raids on Karlsrühe (24 April) and Düsseldorf (22 April) lost 50 of 1,165 bombers (4.3 percent). Whenever Bomber Command staged double main-force attacks, the German controllers singled out one raid and concentrated on it. The only single raid dispatched, to Friedrichshafen, suffered 6 percent losses.

Over France, Bomber Command carried on its string of successful raids (low casualties, minimal collateral damage, and measurable destruction of key facilities and equipment) on transportation targets. Harris encouraged the development of more accurate marking techniques and attack procedures by encouraging competition between No. 5 Group and the Pathfinder force (PFF). The command hit 13 transportation targets: 11 in France, one in Belgium (the Ghent rail yard) and one in Germany (the Aachen railway station). Most of the raids caused heavy damage, but some involved significant collateral damages. A mission of 227 heavy bombers to Lille on 9 April dropped almost 1,200 tons of bombs and killed 456 civilians. A mission of 124 aircraft the next night dropped 689 tons of bombs on Ghent but killed 482 citizens.[2] Although Bomber Command would suffer the low loss rate of only 1.8 percent for all its attacks on German transportation, the Luftwaffe night fighter force had by no means lost its edge. On the night of 27 April, German night fighters intercepted a raid on the Montzen rail yard in Belgium and shot down 15 of 134 bombers. Still, the command had begun to wear down the French rail system, forcing the Germans to curtail operations down to a point that they would have to cut into their own requirements because they already had suppressed completely the needs of the French economy and people.

On 19 days in April 1944, the Fifteenth Air Force flew major missions in the Balkans. The majority of them struck Pointblank targets. Three missions (on 2, 12, and 23 April) struck the air industry and ball bearing manufacture. Following the German occupation of Hungary and the installation of a pro-German government, the Allies removed restrictions on bombing targets in Hungary. On 3 April the Fifteenth bombed the main Budapest marshaling yards and a components plant for Me-410s. The psychological component of these raids, which reminded the Hungarians that the Western Allies could punish them even before the Red Army arrived, may have outweighed the actual damage inflicted. Ten days later the Fifteenth again attacked a components plant in Budapest and motor transport and air plants at Gyor—about 50 miles southeast of Vienna. The Fifteenth staged a raid of 217 bombers on 17 April against Sofia's marshaling yard, reminding the Bulgarians of their vulnerable position. Five other raids hit rail, road, and airfield targets in Italy.

Six more raids struck Rumanian targets. On 5, 15, and 24 April, large missions attacked marshaling yards in Ploesti. Each refinery complex had its own rail yard. As the US official history noted, with some satisfaction, the bombs "with more than coincidental accuracy" fell on the refinery complexes. The Americans did not acknowledge the beginning of an oil campaign even in their classified intelligence reports and documents.[3] This bombing had a significant affect on Ploesti's production. German imports of finished oil products, mostly from Rumania, fell from 186,000 tons in March to 104,000 tons in April.[4]

Rumania, Hungary, and Bulgaria had a different legal standing with the Anglo-Americans than occupied Italy and Yugoslavia. By becoming a cobelligerent with the Allies, Italy had converted its territory occupied by the Germans from enemy territory to occupied territory. The German occupation of Yugoslavia and its breakdown into its constituent parts meant that the Allied recognition of King Peter's government in exile made Yugoslavia an occupied country. Rumania, Hungary, and Bulgaria had formally declared war on the Anglo-Americans. As enemy states, a different set of rules applied. Whereas Allied Airmen sought to limit civilian casualties in occupied countries, they felt less obligation to do so in belligerent countries. For example, in the raids of 15 April on the Ploesti and Bucharest marshaling yards, 395 American bombers found their targets covered with clouds. According to their orders they diverted their mission and attacked the city centers as secondary targets. In addition to its efforts in the Balkans, the Fifteenth attacked the submarine pens in Toulon, France (29 April).

The Eighth maintained the pressure on the Luftwaffe day fighter force and German industry in April. In spite of its casualties in March, it fielded an average of 109 more heavy bombers a day in April (1,156 to 1,265). Crews available for operations also increased.[5] During the month the Eighth launched 17 major operations: four into France, one into Belgium, and 12 into Germany. Large losses, uncooperative weather, and downright peculiar circumstances made for a difficult month. The raids on April Fools' Day set the tone. Doolittle dispatched all three of the Eighth's bombardment divisions to Germany. The 1st Bombardment Division encountered heavy clouds and returned to base. Of the 440 bombers credited with missions in the other divisions, 275 returned without making attacks. The PFF aircraft leading the 165 remaining bombers of the 2 BD suffered equipment failure and due to navigation errors ended up 100 miles south of its intended course. Since they could not locate their primary targets, they bombed, according to Eighth Air Force policy, the city centers of secondary targets and targets of opportunity. Pforzheim received the attention of 101 bombers and Grafenhausen nine, but other bombers wandered out of Germany. Seventeen bombers mistook the French city of Strassbourg for Mannheim and bombed the city center; 38 others, using H2X and chancing upon a hole in the clouds, mistakenly identified the Swiss town of Schaffhausen as a German city—the municipality is practically surrounded on all sides by German territory—and accidentally bombed it. Most of the bombs, with perverse accuracy, struck the town. The bombing killed at least 37, seriously injured 48 more, smashed a wing of the city museum, damaged the city hall, and struck the railroad station, the power plant, and several factories.[6] Two days later Spaatz and the US ambassador to Great Britain, John G. Winant, personally visited the Swiss legation in London to express their regrets.[7] The United States apologized and paid an immediate $1,000,000 indemnity followed by $3,000,000 on 11 October 1944, and, as a final settlement for all bomb damage of Swiss territory during the war, of which Schaffhausen was the most egregious example, 62,176,433.06 Swiss francs, including interest, in October 1949.[8] The mission lost 12 bombers; its escort claimed five kills in the air and 13 on the ground.

On 8 and 9 April missions to central Germany and the Baltic coastline produced heated resistance. The first mission lost 34 bombers (30 of them B-24s from the 2d Division), but the escorts claimed 88 in the air and 65 on the ground. The second mission lost 32, including 10 interned in Sweden, by pilots who claimed they had left their planned return routes and landed damaged bombers in Sweden out of fear that their aircraft were too badly injured to continue the flight all the way to Great Britain. The Swedes kept the aircraft and treated the crews well. They returned the personnel late in 1944 in exchange for Allied military aircraft. The Eighth's escort claimed 20 Luftwaffe fighters in the air and 19 on the ground for both missions; however, the escort lost a total of 33 fighters. A mission to northern Germany on 11 April ran into a hornet's nest; 64 bombers were lost (9 down in Sweden). The escort claimed

51 air victories and 65 German fighters destroyed or damaged on the ground while losing but 16 of their own fighters. Attacks on 13 April on Schweinfurt, Augsburg, and other targets lost 38 bombers. The Schweinfurt force lost 14 of 153 effective sorties. The escort claimed 42 air and 35 ground kills while incurring losses of only nine. On 18 April 729 of the Eighth's bombers attacked He-177 production near Berlin. One group of 41 bombers missed their escort and lost 11, most to German fighters. The remaining bombers, many of whom were scattered by high winds and operating singly or in small formations, lost only eight aircraft, most to ground antiaircraft guns. American fighters lost five planes while claiming four air-to-air kills and putting 16 more Luftwaffe aircraft on the ground out of action.

Most Eighth Air Force observers, in evaluating the day's reports, noted that although the Luftwaffe had had one instance of effectiveness against a single bomb group, on the whole, it inflicted few casualties. In fact the bulk of the US bomber force had hit several dozen scattered targets while operating in small formations over a wide area with almost no loss. The American air commanders interpreted this as a strong indication that the Luftwaffe day fighter effort had weakened appreciably. Of course, there will always be instances in any fight when the enemy through skill or luck may land a blow, but for the German day fighter force those opportunities had begun to decline in February 1944 and would diminish for the remainder of the war. The next day more than 700 bombers attacked aircraft industry facilities in Kassel and airfields in central Germany. They lost five bombers; their escort of 17 fighter groups claimed only 16 sure kills in the air while suffering a loss of but two planes. That the Luftwaffe effort was able to inflict so few losses on the Allied bombers and escorts indicated that its strength had gone down yet another notch.

As noted earlier, this development alarmed Spaatz, Doolittle, and Maj Gen Frederick Anderson. They feared that the Germans might have adopted a policy of conservation of their fighters. Instead of assuming that the Luftwaffe could not defend valuable targets because it was exhausted, the American generals surmised that it would not defend such targets because it was husbanding its strength for more important duties, such as disrupting the forthcoming Anglo-American invasion of France. However, if the Luftwaffe would not rise to protect its own industrial infrastructure, then USSTAF needed even more valuable targets to prod the Germans into fighting. At this point, the British government introduced pressure from a new direction. It proclaimed a national security emergency and insisted that Allied airpower make Crossbow its first objective. Spaatz objected to bombing the V-1 sites on principle; arguing that the V-1 launch sites represented a waste of effort that could be spent better elsewhere. He further objected to bombing them because he had not yet achieved his overriding objective of destroying the Luftwaffe. Spaatz wanted targets the Luftwaffe would have to defend, not ones on the coast of France that the Luftwaffe had no intention of protecting. He arranged for a meeting with Eisenhower on the evening of 19 April. The two reached an agreement. Spaatz received permission to bomb oil on the next two clear days over those targets; he promised to devote greater effort to the transportation plan and to V-1s. Spaatz was good to his word. The next morning the Eighth dispatched 824 bombers to strike V-sites in the Pas-de-Calais. On 22 April 653 bombers struck the largest marshaling yard in Europe—Hamm, Germany—with 1,550 tons of bombs. A few days later, on 27 April, 476 bombers struck 22 V-targets in France.

For the remainder of the month the Luftwaffe chose its engagements carefully. On 22 April out of 779 effective sorties, the bombers lost five to all causes, but as the 2d Division landed in the dark, German intruders infiltrated the pattern and shot down an additional 14 bombers for a total of 19 losses. Strangely the Germans never pursued this tactic further even though their early warning radar for two years had observed and timed the bombers forming up after takeoff and dispersing for landing. Because American pilots spent a good deal of time after takeoffs and during landings positioning themselves into and out of formation, they feared this tactic above all others. They were more vulnerable to interception at this point than at any other time in their mission. The crowded airspace at these two moments during a mission made fighter escort impossible.

On 24 April the Eighth attacked air industry targets in southern Germany with more than 700 aircraft. It lost 40 bombers, including 14 interned in Switzerland after crashing or landing there due to damage; one plane was shot down by friendly fire from a runaway gun turret on another bomber. The raid, coupled with a Bomber Command attack on 27 April, badly damaged the plants, which produced one-half the drive gear assemblies for Panzer (Pz) IIIs, IVs, and Vs, and half of all engines for Pz IVs, Vs, and VIs. It took three to four months to disperse the work to other firms and created a 30 percent production drop for the critical months of May and June 1944.[9] The escorts claimed 66 air victories and 58 aircraft damaged or destroyed on the ground while incurring a loss of 17 fighters. Heavy overcast kept the Luftwaffe on the ground on 26 April, as 344 American bombers attacked the city centers of Brunswick and Hannover. No bombers and but five fighters were lost during this mission. The Eighth's escorts claimed no German aircraft kills.

On 29 April Spaatz and Doolittle had hoped to launch the Eighth's first raid on German synthetic oil production, but cloud cover over the target forced a diversion of the mission to their alternate target, Berlin. As noted earlier, H2X could not pinpoint the synthetic oil plants because of their relatively small size. The plants could only be bombed visually and, again because of their relatively small size, only on days that allowed clear views of wide areas of the ground. Such days occurred only a few days a month. In short, to be effective, the bombers required optimum conditions to damage oil plants. On this day the Luftwaffe chose to make a stand. Of 618 effective bomber sorties, the Eighth lost 64 bombers in combat, wrote off two as damaged beyond repair, and listed 432 as damaged. One bomb wing went off course and bombed the city center of Magdeburg; out of 25 effective sorties, the wing suffered 18 of the day's 64 losses. The rest of the force released bombs despite cloud cover over the city center of Berlin. Seventeen groups of escort fighters, including six of P-51s, claimed 16 kills in the air and six on the ground at a cost of 13 escorts. For the month, the Eighth wrote off 420 heavy bombers.

The loss rate for its bombers increased from 3.3 percent in March 1944 to 3.6 percent in April. The fighter loss rate was only 1.4 percent. The Eighth's opponent suffered even more drastically, losing 20.1 percent (447) of its pilots to all causes. The commands responsible for the defense of Germany, Luftflotte Reich and Luftflotte 3, lost 34 percent and 24 percent of their fighter pilots, respectively.[10] Such losses intensified the pressure on Luftwaffe units outside Germany to surrender their experienced pilots for the defense of the homeland.

Mining of the Danube

In April No. 205 Group began its most significant task in the war—the aerial mining of the Danube River. The Danube, one of the world's great rivers, wends its way more than 1,700 miles from the foothills of the Swiss Alps and the Black Forest through some of the foremost cities of central Europe and the Balkans—Augsburg, Munich, Linz, Vienna, Budapest, and Belgrade—and thence along the Rumanian-Bulgarian border before turning north and emptying into the Black Sea. It is commercially navigable for most of its course, from the Black Sea to Regensburg. During WWII, the Danube served as a vital link in the German southeastern transportation system, allowing them to transport an estimated 8,000,000 tons of goods into Germany from 1942 to 1944.

The mining began on the night of 8 April in the Yugoslavian Danube and it continued until the night of 10 September, by which time the group's Wellingtons and Liberators had dropped a total of 1,315 mines in Hungarian, Yugoslav, and Rumanian waters. Out of 372 sorties on 8 April, the British lost nine aircraft and laid 693.2 tons of mines. The naval mine, like its land counterpart, attacks not only the enemy's men and matériel but his psyche as well. River captains delayed sailings until assured that their paths had been swept. The Germans had to create a mine-sweeping force from scratch by training a new force or transferring trained personnel from North German waters. Given wartime shortages, ships lost to mines represented a permanent loss to the river's freight-carrying capacity.

British intelligence, probably Ultra, stated that between April and July 1944 tonnage carried on the Danube declined by 35 percent from the average of the preceding 8 months and that the mining campaign sank approximately 100 river steamers. The same source further noted that before the mining began the major portion of the tonnage on the river consisted of oil products from Rumania. By June 1944 Rumanian goods tonnage on the river had decreased by 75 percent. Oil tonnage accounted for all the decrease in river freight, although cereals and food from Rumania's abundant granaries made up some of the difference.[11]

By forcing a shift of oil traffic from the river to the rail system, mining the Danube added one more burden on the already strained German state railroads. The new load proved particularly difficult to bear because it fell on a specialized portion of the rolling stock, oil tank cars. The mining campaign caused an unknown, but likely significant, portion of the drop in German oil imports that had first begun following the Fifteenth's bombing of Ploesti in April 1944. This reduction in the flow of oil imports left the oil output from Rumanian facilities in vulnerable storage facilities where subsequent attacks by the Fifteenth torched it.

Given the ratio of resources expended versus results achieved, the mining of the Danube ranks as one of the most effective strategic bombing campaigns of World War II. This offensive exploited a weak point the Germans hardly even realized they had, and it did so in a manner that left them scrambling to counter it and its effects. The riverine operations on the Danube demonstrated, in a classic manner, the great leverage of strategic operations when applied to an appropriate target set and equipped with the correct weapon. Less than 400 sorties flown by castoff aircraft and only 1,315 mines scattered from Rumania to Hungary, over a period of five months, disrupted a vital communications line for several months and cut the imports of the commodity most valuable to the German war machine, oil. The results of the campaign suggest that modern air forces might do well to develop a family of nonmetallic, smart naval mines for deployment in future conflicts.

Notes

1. Webster and Frankland, *Strategic Air Offensive*, 3:124n.
2. Richards, *Hardest Victory*, 227.

3. Craven and Cate, *Argument to V-E Day*, 3:174.

4. Webster and Frankland, appendix 46 (table: xxxviii), 4:516.

5. AAF, "Planning Controls."

6. Note, Swiss minister to the US to the secretary of state, 7 April 1944, US Department of State, *FRUS, 1944, Europe*, 4:796–97.

7. Message 2687, US ambassador to the United Kingdom to the secretary of state, 3 April 1944, *FRUS, 1944*, 4:793.

8. *FRUS, 1944*, 4:800.

9. Murray, *Strategy for Defeat*, 279.

10. Ibid., 278.

11. Fifteenth Air Force, Intelligence Section, Draft Study: "Mining of the Danube: A General Summary of Operations and Results," n.d. [c.a. October 1944], AFHSO microfilm reel A6116, fr. 27, AFHRA file no. 628.3071.

May

3–4 May: Bomber Command—begins attacks on German airfields in France.

5 May: Fifteenth Air Force—reaches strength of 20 heavy bomber groups and sends out largest force to date, more than 640 bombers, to attack Ploesti marshaling yards and other targets.

8 May: Eighth Air Force—two B-17s crash-land in Sweden.

9 May: Eighth Air Force—begins offensive against German airfields within range (130 miles) of site of cross-channel invasion. Red Army captures Sevastapol.

9–10 May: Bomber Command—makes first major attack on coastal batteries in Pas-de-Calais.

10 May: Fifteenth Air Force—reaches planned strength of 21 heavy bomber groups.

11 May: Eighth Air Force—two B-24s crash in Switzerland.

12 May: Eighth Air Force—launches first attack on German synthetic oil, loses 46 bombers.

Fifteenth Air Force—sends out largest force to date, almost 730 heavy bombers, to assist offensives by Allied ground forces.

12–13 May: Bomber Command—Mosquitoes lay sea mines for first time—Kiel Canal.

15 May: Germans begin sending Hungarian Jews to Auschwitz, where they are systematically murdered.

19 May: Eighth Air Force—one B-17 lands in Sweden.

21 May: AEAF and Eighth Air Force—unrestricted strafing on French railroads begins (such missions soon dubbed "Chattanooga Choo Choos," after hit song of period).

27 May: Eighth Air Force—three B-17s and two B-24s land in Switzerland.

28 May: Eighth Air Force—makes second attack on synthetic oil, 32 bombers lost.

29 May: Eighth Air Force—attacks synthetic oil a third time, 34 heavy bombers lost. Two B-17s and six B-24s land in Sweden.

In May 1944 the tempo of preinvasion air operations quickened. Bomber Command concentrated its efforts in France and Belgium. Of 18 major missions in May, only four penetrated German airspace. However, hundreds of nuisance raids by nearly invulnerable Mosquitoes to every part of the Reich kept the German population awake and irritable and defenses at some stage of alert. The command kept up its attacks on French and Belgian rail yards, smashing facilities in a wide arc from Ghent to Tours. The command also began attacks on German barracks, airfields, and coastal defenses. At the end of the month it initiated action to take out German radar countermeasures facilities. Attacks on hardened coastal facilities did little damage. In contrast strikes on rail yards and Luftwaffe airfields inflicted significant, cumulative damage. Bomber Command, conducted the lion's share of the attacks with support from the Eighth and the AEAF. The authorization of unrestricted strafing of trains on 21 May (until then aircraft could only attack goods trains) introduced a new tactic that added considerably to the German repair backlog. Locomotives whose steam chambers and/or boilers were punctured in these attacks (as shown in the gun cameras of the Allied fighters) could be patched relatively easily if repair facilities could service them. Trains that carried explosives normally were so severely damaged during these attacks that they could not be returned to service. The French train crews, who had no desire to be machine-gunned or scalded to death, deserted en masse, forcing the Germans to bring in crews from the fatherland to drive the trains. Here again, rapidly deploying experienced personnel from one area to a different front set up yet another sector of the German war machine for a precipitous decline in capability.

The destruction of its base structure in France shattered the Luftwaffe's plans for opposing the invasion. These forward bases were vital to its plans to stage quick counterattacks on the beaches. By the end of May, Ultra intercepts revealed the extent of the devastation.[1] What little chance the Luftwaffe had of mounting a major counterattack had vanished. Bomber Command suffered a loss rate of only 1.8 percent in its raids over France from April through June, and the number of crews and aircraft on hand increased considerably.

Nonetheless, despite their numerical disadvantages, German night fighters could still prove effective. For example, on the night of 3 May, the night fighters downed 42 bombers out of a force of 331 bombers that hit an armored division barracks at Mailly-le-Camps, France. The Luftwaffe thus avenged some of the 200 noncommissioned officers killed. The losses inflicted on the Allies also exacted a measure of balance for several dozen armored fighting vehicles destroyed in the bombing.

Missions into Belgium and Germany, locations more within range of the German night fighter force suffered heavily on occasion, but the overall loss rate of 3.9 percent (more than twice that for operations over France) was acceptable. Of 1,235 heavy bombers sent into Belgium in May, Bomber Command lost 48 aircraft. Harris launched four major raids into Germany. Two of the raids—24 and 27 May—made minimal forays into Germany to attack rail targets in Aachen; both raids used Oboe guidance. The command lost 27 of 408 aircraft on the first, while the second lost 12 out of 165 attacking bombers, a combined loss of 6.8 percent. The other two raids suffered losses of more than 5 percent. On 21 May Bomber Command made an Oboe-guided attack on Duisburg, a familiar target in the Ruhr, losing 29 of 488 bombers (5.9 percent). The next night the Bomber Command undertook a two-pronged mission; one force attacked Dortmund (another familiar target in the Ruhr), losing 17 of 326 bombers (5.2 percent) while a second formation pressed into central Germany to bomb Brunswick. The command lost 14 of 211 bombers (6.6 percent) in the latter attack. Loss figures for missions over Germany offered little encouragement for resumption of large-scale Bomber Command operations. In the meantime its yeoman service against targets identified in the transportation plan contributed to the success of the D-day invasion and freed the Americans not only to carry on their duel with the Luftwaffe but also to attack oil.

The Fifteenth Air Force reached its authorized strength of 21 bombardment groups and a full complement of 1,512 heavy bombers in May. In keeping with the polyglot nature of its theater of war it carried out 22 major missions against targets ranging from the south of France to Rumania. It further provided direct support for the Allied 15th Army Group's spring offensive and Marshal Josef Broz Tito's Yugoslav partisans. Nine of the missions supported the ground offensive of the American Fifth and British Eighth Armies in Italy, which began on 12 May. General Twining directed 3,500 of the approximately 4,800 heavy bomber sorties flown over Italy towards rail targets and ports to interdict movement of German supplies and troops. His aircraft flew 682 sorties in direct support of the ground forces. Twining's bombers attacked cities close to the frontlines; these missions were supposed to create choke points to slow any German retreat by both Kesselring's and the German Tenth Army headquarters. Twining's air forces lost but 16 bombers (a loss rate of .03 percent) and showed how the air battle over the center of Hitler's empire had drained the periphery of sufficient Luftwaffe strength to counter the Allied air effort there. Preparations for the cross-channel invasion intruded into the Fifteenth's operations with a requirement to strike rail facilities in southern France to delay movement of reinforcements to Normandy. On 25, 26, and 27 May, Twining expended 1,621 effective sorties on 15 marshaling yards and two airfields. Yards struck included

Toulon, Grenoble, Nice, Lyon, Marseilles, and Montpellier. The raids had losses of less than 1 percent.

The Fifteenth's direct support for Tito's forces reflected the bloody-minded nature of the war in Yugoslavia, which combined the traditional struggle against the outside occupier with elements of a civil war of communists against conservatives. It also reflected the virulent ethnic conflict between Serbs, Croats, and Slovenes and between Muslims and non-Muslims. Simply put, Tito wished to deprive his enemies of shelter and labor. Consequently, his representatives to the Allies requested the bombing of cities housing Germans and their collaborators. There is little evidence that the Anglo-Americans examined these requests for hidden motives or attempted to investigate the ethnic or political leanings of populations in Tito's chosen targets. Apparently it sufficed that Tito attested to the necessity of it. Beginning on 5 May the Fifteenth attacked Podgorica and 11 other Yugoslav towns, including two attacks on Bihac. As a rule only one or two groups attacked each target; their instructions forbade use of H2X. For the month, Twining's aircrews conducted 509 effective sorties and delivered 1,088 tons of bombs without loss.

The raids were of somewhat dubious legality. According to international law, a country's recognized government has the right to bombard any of its cities occupied by enemy forces. The Anglo-Americans still recognized the government in exile of King Peter, which was rapidly disintegrating. In all likelihood the king and his threadbare cabinet did not authorize the raids. The Allies had not recognized Tito's shadow government as legitimate although they seemed to have acknowledged, at least to themselves, that he and his forces would dominate postwar Yugoslavia. International law does sanction the bombing of enemy garrisons in occupied countries, but only if the attacking party does not employ disproportionate force—for example, dropping 1,000 bombs when 100 would accomplish the job. The Fifteenth seems to have met those requirements by requiring visual bombing and sending small forces—usually 40 or fewer bombers. In this instance, as in others, politics overpowers ordnance. Since the bombing advanced the partisan cause, the Allies' acceptance of the request from Tito's hands represented a step away from King Peter and towards Tito's cause and ideals. The symbolic power of the heavy bomber, apparently at Tito's beck and call, served to make the Allies' political position clear and was more significant than any damage inflicted by their bombs.

The AAF had not breathed life into the Fifteenth for the sole purpose of aiding ground forces in winning the war. The Fifteenth also would support the larger air war in setting the stage for the coming invasion of the continent. In May it hit Pointblank targets. At the beginning of the month, Portal eased his restrictions on the bombing of Ploesti and the Americans struck the city and refineries three times: 5, 18, and 31 May.[2] Although the 1,293 effective sorties dispatched against Ploesti suffered a loss of 52 aircraft (4 percent), the missions became steadily more difficult as the Germans increased flak and passive defenses. Anti-aircraft fire unnerved aircrews; it typically reduced bombing accuracy by 50 percent. The smoke screen over Ploesti, the densest in Europe, forced the bombardiers to revert to H2X. These combined defenses forced the Fifteenth to devote many more sorties to Ploesti to ensure a sufficient number of bombs on target.

The Fifteenth sent strategic missions north into Austria as well. These trans-Alpine missions encountered fierce resistance as the Luftwaffe defended the aircraft component and assembly plants upon which its existence depended. For each of the four raids (10, 24, 29, and 30 May) the loss rate grew less as opposition weakened. The mission of 10 May against Me-109 plants at Wiener Neustadt lost 31 of 406 aircraft (8 percent), but the raid of 30 May against Me-109 component plants lost five of 420 effective sorties (1 percent). Out of 1,855 sorties sent to Austria, 78 failed to return—an overall loss rate of 4.2 percent.

In May 1944 the Eighth dispatched more effective sorties and lost more heavy bombers than Bomber Command or the Fifteenth. In all it sent out 13,674 effective sorties, losing 292 bombers in combat for a loss rate of 2.1 percent—less than two-thirds that of the previous month. It sent out 23 major missions almost equally divided against Germany, France, and the Low Countries. With 40 bombardment groups, 1,688 heavy bombers, and 1,423 crews available for operations plus the long northern European days, the Eighth sometimes launched two major attacks in one day—the first into Germany and the second against France. On 9 May the Eighth joined the campaign against Luftwaffe airfields. By the end of the month, it had expended 49 strikes on French and German airfields and committed more than one-fifth of its effective sorties and 6,700 tons of bombs to the effort. An additional 1,299 strikes hit aeroengine manufacture and Me-109 and FW-190 component and assembly plants.

On 25 May, in accordance with Prof. Solly Zuckerman's transportation plan, Lt Gen James Doolittle began to dispatch his bombers against German coastal fortifications. This effort intensified in June. Almost one-third of the Eighth's bombing—3,569 effective sorties and 9,800 tons of bombs—landed on or near marshaling yards in France, western Germany, and Belgium. On 21 May the British government withdrew its restriction of strafing passenger trains in France. The AEAF and the Eighth's fighters claimed hundreds of trains. One pilot of the 352d Fighter Group claimed 25 cows—an indication that American fighter pilots took their orders to shoot everything that moved literally.[3] (Much eyewitness testimony within the Reich indicated that the Allied fighter pilots did not limit themselves to targets of the bovine persuasion.) The attacks on Crossbow targets consumed a further 771 sorties and 2,600 tons. In total the above missions lost 114 bombers for a loss rate of 1.4 percent.

None of the above raids met the Eighth's first priority mission, the destruction of the Luftwaffe. The diversion of its strategic bombers to other targets nagged at the Eighth's command structure. The Germans would not employ their fighters to defend occupied Europe. The Luftwaffe's strategy of husbanding its aircraft to the defense of the heartland greatly worried Spaatz. On 10 May 1944 he wrote to Arnold:

> Your concern over the reaction of the GAF [German air force] when [Overlord] is launched is shared by me. He is undoubtedly attempting to ration his forces to the greatest extent possible at this time in order to maintain an adequate force against a threat of invasion from the West. I have stressed in all my conferences with Eisenhower, Tedder, and others that a continuation of [Pointblank] operations is vital in order to maintain wastage of the GAF. The primary purpose of these [Pointblank] operations to date has been the depletion of the GAF. At

> this time it is the sole purpose. Targets selected are those which we an-
> ticipate will force the GAF into the air against us.[4]

Only two targets—Berlin and synthetic oil—brought the Luftwaffe into action. In the case of Berlin, its considerable value
as a manufacturing center for war matériel may have played a
secondary consideration in the minds of the Luftwaffe's leadership to its propaganda and administrative worth. Unopposed
attacks on Berlin would have further undercut Göring's weakening position within the Nazi hierarchy. The Eighth launched
four raids on Berlin (7, 8, 19, and 24 May). Almost all 1,861
effective sorties attacked the city area dropping 4,277 tons of
bombs through overcast skies using H2X.

In association with the raids of 7, 8, and 19 May, the Eighth
attacked additional German cities. On 7 May 312 bombers
struck Osnabrück and Hannover; the next day 336 bombers
struck Brandenburg. Finally, on 19 May, a force of 273 bombers
struck the city center of Brunswick. For the month, 3,287 of the
Eighth's effective sorties—all authorized by AAF policy—hit German city areas with 7,800 tons of bombs. For the first time, the
Eighth had dispatched more area sorties into Germany than
Bomber Command. Doolittle lost 119 bombers, most because of
escort foul-ups in these area attacks for a loss rate of 3.6 percent.

The most spectacular of the Eighth's effort in May 1944 were
the long-awaited, at least by Arnold, Spaatz, and Doolittle, experimental attacks on German synthetic oil on 12, 28, and 29
May. They consumed a little less than 10 percent of the Eighth's
total effort for the month: 1,315 effective sorties and 2,930 tons
of bombs. Weather conditions on 12 May finally permitted a full-
scale visual attack on several crucial synthetic oil plants. Aside
from two costly strikes on 29 April and 8 May over Berlin,
which produced heavy German reaction, this attack attracted
the heaviest opposition in three weeks. Fifteen combat wings—
886 heavy bombers plus 735 escorting fighters—left Britain to
bomb their targets. The leading division, the 3d Bombardment
Division, not fully defended because one of its assigned fighter
groups mistakenly rendezvoused with a trailing division, had its
remaining escort swamped by a large force of German fighters.
The 3 BD received the brunt of the German attack. Attempted
attacks on targets of opportunity—rail yards at Gera and

Zwickau—demonstrated how deadly the Luftwaffe had become. Of 16 bombers attacking Gera, 12 went down; at Zwickau, 10 of the 14 attacking bombers went down. Out of 59 aircraft going after an air repair facility at Zwickau, only 50 returned. The division lost 32 bombers to the Luftwaffe. Direct attacks on the oil plants lost only 13 bombers (most to flak) out of 679 effective sorties. The Luftwaffe had not come up to defend oil. The Germans, having no way of knowing an oil attack was in the offing, took off to oppose a deep penetration, just as they did for raids on Berlin. The other two bombardment divisions lost only two bombers to enemy fighters, whereas antiaircraft fire accounted for the remaining 12 bombers lost.[5] The Eighth wrote off an additional nine bombers as irreparable.[6] (See CD-ROM graphics: maps.pdf.) The American escort lost four P-47s and three P-51s, but claimed 61 German aircraft destroyed and 11 damaged in the air as well as five destroyed and two damaged on the ground. German records confirmed the accuracy of the fighter claims. They counted 28 pilots dead, 26 injured,[7] and 65 aircraft lost.[8]

The surviving bombers dropped 1,718 tons of bombs through ground haze and low clouds on synthetic oil plants at Zwickau, Merseburg-Leuna, Brux, Lutzkendorf, Bohlen, and Zeitz. Unknown to the Allies until after the war, the raid destroyed a building at Merseburg-Leuna that housed heavy-water [D_2O] experiments for Germany's atom bomb program.[9] Albert Speer, the Nazi minister of armaments and war production, spoke of USSTAF's work that day in his postwar memoirs: "I shall never forget the day the technological war was decided. Until then we had managed to produce approximately as many weapons as the armed forces needed, in spite of their considerable losses. However, with the attack of 935 daylight bombers of the American Eighth Air Force upon several fuel plants in central and eastern Germany, a new era in the air war began. It meant the end of German armaments production."[10] A week later Speer reported to Hitler, "the enemy has struck us at one of our weakest points. If they persist at it this time, we will soon no longer have any fuel production worth mentioning. Our one hope is that the other side has an air force General Staff as scatterbrained as ours!"[11]

Weather, in addition to commitments to Crossbow and Over-lord, delayed the next mission against oil targets until 28 May, when 400 heavy bombers attacked plants at Ruhland and Magdeburg and again struck Merseburg-Leuna, Zeitz, and Lutzkendorf. The next day the Eighth sent 224 B-24s to bomb the synthetic plant at Politz; the rest of the force bombed air-craft industry targets deep in eastern Germany and Poland. Once again, on 28 May, aircraft involved in direct attacks on the oil plants suffered relatively lightly, losing only 10 bombers out of 410 effective sorties. In contrast a group of 36 bombers striking the city of Dessau lost 15 aircraft. Only in the raid on Politz on 29 May did the force attacking an oil plant suffer more than 5 percent losses. Combined totals of 66 bombers and 19 fighters were lost in the two raids. The American es-corts claimed 100 destroyed, two probables, and 11 damaged in the air as well as 21 destroyed and 22 damaged on the ground.[12] Only the month's raids on Berlin and the previous oil raid met opposition of similar intensity. The total of all the deep raids to Berlin and against oil showed US fighter claims of 378 sure kills in the air versus a loss of 80 fighters. For the month the Luftwaffe lost 25 percent (578) of its pilots, more than any month since the year began. In the first five months of the year, its pool of fighter pilots suffered a turnover of 99 percent—no force could survive such casualties for long and retain any semblance of effectiveness. The air battle had deci-sively turned against the Luftwaffe.

The oil bombing had an immediate and profound effect on both sides of the conflict. The Ultra organization intercepted an order, dated 13 May, showing that the previous day's mis-sion greatly alarmed the Germans. This order, from the Luft-waffe operations staff in Berlin, stripped heavy and light anti-aircraft guns from the eastern front and fighter manufacturing plants at Oschersleben, Leipzig-Erla, and Wiener Neustadt to protect hydrogenation plants at Zeitz and Politz.[13] A history of USSTAF and Ultra called this intercept "one of the most deci-sive and timely pieces of intelligence received in this war."[14] It gave proof that the Germans regarded oil as the target system of paramount importance—even above the production of fighter aircraft. A week later the Allies intercepted an order directing the German armed forces to convert an even higher percentage of their motor transport to power supplied by highly inefficient wood fuel generators.[15] When he learned of these messages, Tedder dropped his opposition to the oil plan and is reported to have remarked, "I guess we'll have to give the customer what he wants."[16]

After the war, captured documents from Speer to Hitler revealed the dramatic and almost instantaneous effect of the May bombings. On 30 June Speer reported the state of production of aviation fuel to Hitler. In April the Luftwaffe consumed 156,000 tons of the 175,000 tons of aviation gasoline manufactured by the synthetic plants; the average daily production in April was 5,850 tons. The attack of 12 May reduced that average to 4,821 tons, but production had recovered to 5,526 tons a day by 28 May when the Allies completely knocked out the plant at Leuna. The 29 May attack stopped all production at Politz, and the two strikes combined dropped daily production to 2,775 tons. The total May output of 156,000 tons fell 14,000 tons short of essential planned consumption. In June, thanks to more attacks, production rose above 3,000 tons on only two days.[17] On 7 June Ultra deciphered the following message, dated 5 June, from the Luftwaffe operations staff: "As a result of renewed encroachment into the production of a/c [aircraft] fuel by enemy action, the most essential requirements for training and carrying out production plans can scarcely be covered with the quantities of a/c fuel available. In order to assure the defense of the Reich and to prevent the readiness for defense of the GAF in the east from gradually collapsing, it has been necessary to break into the strategical reserve."[18]

Portal sent a copy of this decryption to the prime minister saying, "I regard this as one of the most important pieces of information we have yet received." Portal also recommended a concentrated bombing attack by all Allied strategic bombers on synthetic oil as soon as they could be spared by the invasion. Piecemeal attacks spread over a long period by small forces, warned Portal, would only allow the enemy time to increase his flak and smoke defenses. Churchill replied, "Good."[19] On 4 June Eisenhower's headquarters publicly proclaimed the existence of the oil offensive.[20] Once Eisenhower released the Eighth from its invasion support requirements, the American's campaign against oil would begin in earnest.

Notes

1. Murray, *Strategy for Defeat*, 279.
2. Message AX-119, Portal to Bottomley, 3 May 1944, Spaatz Papers, Diary.
3. Freeman, *Mighty Eighth War Diary*, 246.
4. Letter, Spaatz to Arnold, 10 May 1944, Spaatz Papers, Diary.
5. Hinsley, *British Intelligence*, vol. 3, pt. 2, 105; memo, Maxwell to Spaatz, 16 May 1944; COPC/S.501/10/INT., Combined Operational Planning Committee, "Sixth Periodic Report on Enemy Daylight Fighter Defenses and Interception Tactics, Period 1 May 1944–31 May 1944," 29 June 1944, Spaatz Papers, Subject File 1929–1945.
6. Hinsley, 105; and Maxwell to Spaatz, 16 May 1944.
7. Freeman, 243; and Murray, 273.
8. Galland, *First and the Last*, 280.
9. Craven and Cate, *Argument to V-E Day*, 3:176–77.
10. Speer, *Inside the Third Reich*, 346.
11. Ibid., 346–47.
12. Freeman, 252–54.
13. [Haines], *Ultra History of USSTAF*, 98–99. This study was completed by USSTAF no later than 24 September 1945.
14. Ibid., 99.
15. Ibid.
16. Ibid.
17. Webster and Frankland, appendix 32, 4:321–25.
18. *Ultra History of USSTAF*, 104. For a full and personal appreciation of the value of Ultra to USSTAF, see Putney, *Ultra and the Army Air Forces in World War II*. For the issue of targeting the oil plants, see pages 35–38. This is an interview with US Supreme Court Justice Lewis F. Powell Jr., who served as an Ultra liaison officer attached to Spaatz's headquarters.
19. Hinsley, vol. 3, pt. 2, 502–3.
20. Craven and Cate, 3:179.

June

2 June: Fifteenth Air Force—General Eaker leads first shuttle flight of 130 AAF heavy bombers from Western Europe to the USSR.

3–4 June: Eighth Air Force—attacks coastal defenses in the Pas-de-Calais region.

4 June: Allies enter Rome.

5 June: Eighth Air Force—attacks defenses in Normandy and Pas-de-Calais.

5–6 June: Bomber Command—Normandy invasion, 1,333 night sorties flown.

6 June: Eighth Air Force—reaches peak strength of 40 heavy bomber groups. It launches four separate missions in support of D-day for a total of 1,726 heavy bomber missions and 3,596 tons of bombs. Caen and 10 French towns are bombed to cause choke points for German reinforcements.

6–7 June: Bomber Command—sends over 1,000 aircraft to attack communications behind the battlefront.

8 June: USSTAF—General Spaatz makes synthetic oil the first priority for strategic bombing.

8–9 June: Bomber Command—drops first 12,000-pound "Tallboy"—Samur Railway tunnel.

12–13 June: Germans begin launching V-1 jet-propelled, pilotless bombs against the United Kingdom. Most are aimed at London.

13 June: Fifteenth Air Force—two B-24s and one B-17 land in Switzerland.

14 June: Bomber Command—begins a series of day heavy bomber raids over France. First daylight raid since 31 May 1943.

Mid-June: Request by Slovakian Jewish community for bombing of rail lines leading to Auschwitz received by US authorities in Switzerland.

15–16 June: Fifteenth Air Force—attacks numerous oil targets in Balkans and Austria.

18 June: Eighth Air Force—launches large attacks against refineries in Germany. One B-24 lands in Sweden.

20 June: Eighth Air Force—20 B-24s land in Sweden after missions into Germany. Speer ministry gains control of Luftwaffe arms production.

21 June: Eighth Air Force—conducts large attack on Berlin. Part of force, 144 heavy bombers and escort, continues on to the airfields in the Ukraine. Thirteen heavy bombers land or crash in Sweden after mission to Berlin.

21–22 June: Luftwaffe—in one of its last effective actions, carries out a night attack on Poltava airfield; destroys 47 bombers, damages over 20 more, and inflicts heavy damage on supplies and stores.

23 June: Soviet summer offensive begins.

28 June: Eighth Air Force—one B-24 lands in Switzerland.

At the beginning of June 1944, thick black storm clouds mounted higher and higher on both the eastern and western fronts. The Anglo-Americans prepared to undertake their cross-channel invasion and the Soviets massed for their summer offensive. The Germans braced for the expected tempest. The question of "if" the storm would break had long since become "when" and they knew the answer, "soon."

Preinvasion Operations

In June 1944 the pace of bombing operations reached its wartime peak as the Anglo-Americans geared their entire tactical and strategic air effort directly towards ensuring the success of Operation Overlord. Unfortunately overcast, rain, and wind during the first week of June forced the Eighth to conduct much of its bombing in France using H2X, which reduced its overall accuracy and effectiveness. At night Bomber Command made extensive use of the far more accurate Oboe in its operations over France.

As the air preliminaries for the invasion proceeded, Leigh-Mallory laid the groundwork for the final phase of the preinvasion air preparations. In the week before the invasion he would have control of all air forces assisting the invasion, including the Eighth and Bomber Command. By the end of May, the USSTAF had still not completed the details of its participation in the first day of the invasion. All agreed that USSTAF's first bomber mission of the day would saturate the invasion beaches just before the assault forces landed. USSTAF and the AEAF parted company, however, on the objectives for the remaining missions of the day. On 1 June Leigh-Mallory rejected as operationally unsound USSTAF's proposal to strike enemy troop and road movement behind the front lines from an altitude of 15,000 feet. He argued that the bombers could never locate the German troops in the thickly wooded countryside of Normandy, and they would further congest the already crowded airspace. The AEAF wanted USSTAF to stick to the original plan of bombing designated villages and towns to block the roads with rubble and thereby impede German movement.[1] As the USAAF leadership realized, the creation of urban choke points meant blowing the rubble of destroyed buildings, including civilian residences, into streets to slow, detour, or prevent passage. It meant employing the area bombing technique for a specialized purpose. Spaatz and

Doolittle insisted the bombing would not slow the Germans and objected mightily to the needless bombing of French civilians. So did Harris. Bomber Command's records, which had no compunction about listing raids over Germany as area raids, show a reluctance to designate the raids on these French cities as such. The Bomber Command Monthly Summary for June 1944 placed three raids in the target category "omitted" (Bomber Command shorthand for a city strike on an occupied city) and two in the "communications center" target category, an almost unique designation in the command's target list. Subsequent ground investigation of the results of those attacks in August 1944 tended to support the air leaders' protestations that the bombings did not appreciably slow German units. One observer noted that the only delay imposed on the enemy was the few minutes it took to post detour signs around the stricken city.[2]

However, Leigh-Mallory had Tedder's and Eisenhower's approval for the choke point plan. Reluctantly, Maj Gen Hoyt S. Vandenberg, Leigh-Mallory's American deputy, signed the order for an attack on 11 French cities.[3] The Allies added three more cities to the list before the invasion. They could only hope that leaflets dropped two hours before the bombing would save lives. Early Monday morning, 5 June, Eisenhower, despite marginal weather conditions, made his fateful decision to commit his forces to the assault the following day, 6 June.

As the air generals and marshals fought over the last details of the plans, preinvasion operations proceeded in their set course. Allied heavy bombers switched from the French railway system and airfields to put the bulk of their effort into bombing coastal fortifications and defended localities. On 2, 3, 4, and 5 June, in spite of foul weather, the Eighth bombed coastal fortifications using H2X; Bomber Command, using Oboe, joined the battle. Together they flew 3,876 sorties and dropped 18,110 tons of bombs.

The bombing of coastal fortifications formed part of Operation Fortitude, the Anglo-Americans' strategic deception plan to misdirect and mislead the Germans as to the place and timing of the invasion. In order not to reveal the Normandy area as the site of the invasion, the air portion of Fortitude required that Allied aircraft drop two bombs outside of Normandy for each bomb dropped in the invasion area. Three quarters of the Eighth's preinvasion bombing, more than 14,000 tons, fell on the Pas-de-Calais, the narrowest part of the English Channel, and the area in which the Germans had stationed their Fifteenth Army, their strongest and most heavily armored force in France.

The importance of Fortitude to the invasion cannot be underestimated, nor, unfortunately, can it be quantified. Although many Germans have stepped forward to claim after the war that they knew all along that the Allies would come ashore in Normandy, when the invasion's naval bombardment commenced, its location caught virtually every German high-level commander by surprise.

Each segment of the Allied air forces took its own distinctive part in the operations on D-day. Bomber Command hit coastal fortifications, some near the British invasion beaches, with 1,058 effective sorties and flew 111 diversion sorties. The IX Troop Carrier Command began the American assault with airborne drops during the night of 5 June. Eighth Fighter Command began patrolling the outer perimeter of the operating area as the troop carriers and night bombers withdrew. The Eighth's fighters kept up the patrols until the landings. Then they moved to an area just outside the beachhead to patrol and to attack any legitimate targets. The IX Fighter Command and the RAF (with their shorter range and endurance fighters) covered the beaches and provided fighter-bomber support. Five groups of P-38s, one from the Ninth Air Force and four from the Eighth, maintained an all-day umbrella over the invasion convoys delivering the ground assault troops to the beaches. Just before H hour the first wave of the heavy bombers of the Eighth, which on 6 June reached its peak strength of 40 heavy bomber groups, and medium bombers of the Ninth attacked the beach defenses.[4] Low clouds forced the Eighth's bombers to employ H2X. Given the well-known inaccuracy of H2X, Eighth Air Force Headquarters ordered the bombardiers to delay their releases for 10 to 30 seconds after the indicated drop point to avoid bombs falling short into the invasion fleet and landing craft. This restriction put the bombs between three-fourths and one and one-half miles beyond the beaches, almost completely wasting 3,000 tons of bombs. In addition the Americans used instantaneous fused bombs to prevent excessive cratering. Even if the bombs had hit the beach defenses, they would not have penetrated concrete structures.[5] The medium bombers came in under the clouds to drop their payloads, exposing themselves to heavy coastal antiaircraft fire. For 6 June, the Eighth and Ninth launched 8,722 sorties and lost 71 aircraft, mostly fighters, to flak.[6]

Weather interfered with the second wave of the first mission. The Eighth dispatched 528 bombers of which only 37 reached their target, Argentan. The second mission of the day also consisted of two waves; the first 56 out of 73 dispatched bombed a choke point in the city of Caen, an important objective on the left of the British front line. In the second wave 450 heavy bombers released their bombs, all by H2X, on 13 choke point cities. That night 707 planes from Bomber Command again attacked six of the choke points while 215 bombers hit key railroad junctions. All but one attack used Oboe. On 7 June the Eighth restruck five of the choke points. That ended the Anglo-American area attacks on French towns. Other than Bomber Command's area attacks, authorized by the War Cabinet, on Lorient during the anti U-boat offensive, they were the only intentional area bombing of the French. The Allies expended 1,692 sorties, dropped 5,586 tons of bombs, and lost 10 bombers. The author could locate no Anglo-American source that estimated or stated the actual number of French civilian casualties inflicted by these missions.

For both the Eighth and Bomber Command, their work in the week before the invasion mattered less than their accomplishments in the preceding months. From the beginning of March 1944, Bomber Command carried the transportation plan on its broad shoulders. Using evolving techniques of bombing accuracy, its attacks shredded the enemy's rail system. Its large bombs did immense damage, which no other force could have duplicated. By wrecking the rail yards, Bomber Command squeezed German logistics capacity to a minimum or below and forced enemy units into time-consuming night road marches or day marches exposed to Allied airpower. Bomber Command's execution of the transportation plan was a decisive contribution to the invasion's success.

While Bomber Command's contribution became more obvious each day after the invasion, the Eighth's manifested itself at once. The Anglo-Americans had air supremacy over the beachhead, in part because RAF Fighter Command had spent four years wresting control of the air over western France from the Luftwaffe, and in part because the Eighth had either knocked out the German day-fighter force or compelled the Germans to concentrate their defenses over the homeland. Indeed, the Germans attempted an air response to the invasion but the woebegone status of the Luftwaffe rendered it ineffective. Within the Eighth's oil campaign lay the doom of any last chance of German victory. It also proved complementary with the transportation plan. Lack of fuel compromised Luftwaffe training, which meant, in the final analysis, no air cover for German ground units or their transportation system. Lack of fuel for the ground units and supply trucks made for even more dependency on rail transport. After only seven weeks of hard fighting in excellent defensive terrain, the Allies broke through and the German defenses in the west collapsed, done in as much by lack of strategic mobility (AEAF's fighter-bombers ensured no daylight tactical mobility) and shortness of supply as any other factors.

As for the Luftwaffe, it mounted barely 100 sorties (70 by fighters) on the first day of the invasion and only 175 more completely ineffectual sorties on the night of 6 June. In all of France it possessed 815 aircraft, including 325 bombers, 170 single-engine fighters, 45 twin-engine fighters, and only 75 ground-attack aircraft.[7] As Spaatz stated in late June 1944, "the concentrated attacks on the Luftwaffe, production and product, has paid the dividends that we have always envisioned, the dividend being beyond expectation. During the entire first day of the invasion, enemy opposition in the air, either fighter or bomber, was next to nil."[8]

The battle for air supremacy over the beachhead on D-day never occurred because the USAAF had already defeated the Luftwaffe in the skies over Germany. The subsequent feeble Luftwaffe reaction in the weeks following the invasion amply proved Spaatz's oft-repeated contention that the greatest contribution the US Strategic Air Forces could make to Overlord was smashing the Luftwaffe fighter force. This offensive air achievement ranks with the defensive victory of the RAF in the Battle of Britain as one of the most decisive air battles of World War II.

Postinvasion Operations

For the last three weeks of June, the weather was adequate, the range short, and the need intense. The weather allowed operations on most days, while the extended daylight hours of the summer solstice and the brief flight time to nearby northern France allowed the Eighth to mount two or three operations a day. The abbreviated northern European nights and the necessity to bomb V sites and invasion targets forced Bomber Command to undertake day as well as night raids with its heavy bombers.

Before the invasion Spaatz had agreed to aid the assault phase of the operation. For that critical phase the Eighth Air Force ceased its attacks directed against German industry and devoted its efforts to the bombing program called for in the preinvasion and invasion deception plans. From 30 May (when it struck aircraft production targets in Germany) until 18 June (when it resumed missions against industrial targets in Germany), the Eighth flew exclusively in support of the invasion. In June the Eighth dropped 44,209 tons of bombs on France—almost 76 percent of its effort for the month.[9]

The Germans, too, meant to put their maximum airpower into the skies over the beachhead. To that end, in the four days following D-day, the Luftwaffe attempted to mount a fierce defense against Allied air operations in France. In addition to the 170 aircraft already in France (to fly ground support for the troops battling the Allies), they sent more than 300 single-engine fighter aircraft from the fighter force charged with defending the homeland into the fray to defend against the air attacks above Normandy.[10] This action failed disastrously. These fledgling pilots— recent replacements from bases inside Germany for veteran pilots killed or disabled in the spring—had minimal training in antibomber operations and none in ground support. In flying to forward airfields, they suffered an accumulation of losses not only from Allied fighters who knew their flight plans from signal intelligence,[11] but also from their own faulty navigation and from bad landings on unfamiliar fields.[12]

The Luftwaffe literally telegraphed its punches to the Allies. Throughout this phase of the campaign in the west, Ultra read and distributed Luftwaffe messages at least as quickly as the intended recipients.[13] The Luftwaffe Enigma machine was simpler than its army and navy equivalents in that it possessed one less code-setting wheel or rotor. Consequently, Ultra had fewer difficulties in deciphering Luftwaffe messages than those of the other German armed forces. By 1430 on 6 June, Ultra learned that 18 fighter groups had left Germany for France; seven more groups had arrived by 8 June.[14] Ultra immediately determined their exact locations and passed that intelligence on to Allied units. By 12 June, Ultra learned that the fierce pressure exerted by the Allies had forced the Luftwaffe to suspend fighter bombing when it deciphered an order instructing the Luftwaffe to remove bomb racks and convert aircraft back to their pure fighter configuration.[15] Eliminating the capacity to deliver bombs meant that the Luftwaffe had abandoned its ground-support role and had assumed a defensive stance against Allied air attacks. By the end of the first week, Luftwaffe strength stood at 1,100 fighters—its highest numbers of the campaign.

British air intelligence (AI) overestimated this force at 1,615 aircraft but noted a very low serviceability rate, 33 percent for fighters and 16 percent for fighter-bombers. The average daily fighter effort ranged from 250 to 300 sorties. Air intelligence noted that German bomber groups operated at only 65 percent of authorized strength.[16] Heavy attacks by the Eighth on Luftwaffe airfields on 14 and 15 June—based on information from Ultra intercepts—applied the coup de grâce. On 16 June the Luftwaffe withdrew five shattered fighter groups to Germany for refitting and replacement of lost pilots and aircraft. Their replacements at the front, also drawn from domestic air defense duties, fared little better. During the month of June 1944, the total fighter force available for German home defense fell from 700 to 370.[17]

The Allies could not avoid diverting the Eighth and Bomber Command from the strategic bombing campaign of targets in Germany to the immediate support of the invasion. The Luftwaffe, however, failed to use the temporary halt in Pointblank to any advantage. Instead, Hitler and Göring stripped the homeland of half of its defending aircraft to send them into the maelstrom over Normandy, where overwhelming Allied airpower quickly decimated the Luftwaffe forces. When the Combined Bomber Offensive resumed, it encountered much less opposition.

On 13 June the Eighth ended the German war economy's two-week respite from Allied strategic bombing by sending 200 bombers to strike the Misburg oil refinery near Hannover. The bomber force suffered no casualties. Five days later more than 1,200 effective sorties sent to bomb oil refineries in the north German ports and Hannover encountered deteriorating weather conditions and, for the most part, bombed the city areas instead of their intended targets. They lost 11 bombers, many to flak. Two days later, in good visual conditions, the Eighth again attacked eight refineries in northern Germany and synthetic oil plants at Politz and Magdeburg. The raid on Politz lost 31 planes (including 20 that landed or crashed in Sweden) of 245 effective sorties, while the Magdeburg mission lost five out of 99 bombers; for the day the Eighth suffered an overall loss of 45 bombers of 1,607 sorties. Flak brought down more than half of the bombers lost—a trend that would continue until the end of the war.

The next day, 21 June, the Eighth sent 965 effective sorties to strike Berlin and its industrial suburbs. More than 600 of the bombers had explicit orders to attack "Berlin (Center of the City)."[18] Harris had planned to join in this raid but backed off at the last second because he feared that the Eighth could not spread its escorts to cover both Bomber Command and the Eighth. It would appear that the Allies had meant this raid on Berlin to be special. The records give no clue as to what extra meaning the raid may have had—retaliation for the V-1 attacks, perhaps, or aid for the imminent Soviet summer offensive? In any case the Eighth paid a high price of 45 bombers for the effort, again more than half of those losses were to flak.

An additional 145 bombers attacked the synthetic oil plant at Ruhland before proceeding to airfields prepared for them in the Soviet Ukraine. They would attack enemy targets from the east when they returned to England later in the month. Since the aircraft shuttled between fields in England and the Ukraine these operations were known as shuttle bombing missions. The code-name for the overall operation was "Frantic." The Allies intended it to serve several purposes. It would confront the Germans with a strategic air threat from a new direction. It would demonstrate to the German, Allied, and Soviet civilian populations that Germany's foes could cooperate in actions against the Reich. And it was supposed to foster better relations between the Soviets and the western Allies. Like many grandiose schemes it proved difficult to implement. It failed to distract the Germans and on a person-to-person basis probably did more harm to inter-Allied relations than good. The American aircrews reacted badly to the strict wartime security the Soviets applied to the operation, which included isolation from the local Soviet population. In any case, a few hours after the first mission landed in the USSR, the Luftwaffe launched a night attack on the airfield at Poltava, Ukraine, and cut the American force to ribbons. US hopes that Frantic would effectively divert the German air defenses to defending a second front in the air war died that night along with the bombers and stores destroyed there.

On 24 June approximately 300 B-17s attacked both the city and oil targets in Bremen without loss. Finally, on 29 June, 705 effective sorties attacked targets in the Leipzig area, including bearing factories, airfields at aircraft production plants, FW-190 and Ju-88 component plants, and aeroengine plants, including the Volkswagen plant at Fallersleben. The Eighth, spread out at one point in the day in a column 200 miles long, encountered little aerial resistance, suffering only 15 losses (mostly to flak). On the four large raids deep into Germany in June, the Eighth suffered a bomber loss rate of 2.8 percent. For all bomber operations during the month it had a loss rate of 1.1 percent.

Meanwhile Bomber Command's Mosquitoes pestered the enemy and Harris sent his heavies into the Ruhr where they could use Oboe to their advantage to knock out synthetic oil targets. Far from disdaining the oil offensive, Harris, at this point, cooperated with the desires of both the RAF air staff and the SHAEF staff. Harris sent 276 effective sorties against the

Nordstern plant at Gelsenkirchen (losing 17 aircraft) in the command's first attack on oil production and storage facilities on 12 June. The second attack against the Holten plant in Sterkrade lost 32 of 300 sorties; the third attack against the Buer plant in Gelsenkirchen lost only eight of 121 aircraft; and the last, a visual attack, against the Union Rheinische facility in Wesseling lost 37 of 118 planes. The 11.5 percent loss rate incurred in these attacks gave every indication that the weakness of the Luftwaffe day fighter force had not yet been extended to the night fighters. Until it did so, Bomber Command could not execute frequent missions deep into Germany without excessive losses.

However, during the month, Bomber Command and Harris again showed their flexibility. For the first time during the war, the command began to send its heavy bombers out on attacks of 100 bombers or more during the day. During the month the command dispatched 16 major attacks and several minor ones for a total of 2,380 effective daylight heavy bomber sorties, which dropped 11,576 tons of bombs. Both figures represented one-sixth of the command's monthly effort. Harris employed these attacks cautiously, aiming them only at targets in France, mostly V sites and marshaling yards. On the last day of the month, at the request of the ground forces, he put 258 of his bombers over the bocage (woodlands) near Villiers in a midlevel daylight attack on a panzer unit. In all the daylight attacks in June lost only 12 aircraft. These boosted the command's experience in a new method of attack, daylight target marking, which further increased their accuracy.

The cross-channel invasion and its aftermath pushed the Fifteenth and its co-combatants in the Mediterranean theater out of the limelight and into a supporting role, at least in the judgment of the Anglo-American public media. Ironically, in the month of June 1944, the Fifteenth picked up much of the strategic effort left undone by the Eighth and Bomber Command. For the first time in its existence, the Fifteenth flew more effective sorties against strategic targets (oil storage, refineries, and synthetic oil) than against communications targets (rails, highways, bridges, marshaling yards, and ports). It flew north across the Alps to Munich on 9 and 13 June, where it attacked BMW aircraft engine plants, factory airfields, marshaling yards, and the city center. On 16 and 26 June, it struck marshaling yards, synthetic oil plants, refineries, and oil storage facilities in Vienna. The Fifteenth attacked Ploesti three times (6, 24, and 25 June) and refineries, marshaling yards, and the city of Bucharest on 28 June. In an effort to deny the Germans alternate refining capacity, the Fifteenth hit refineries in Hungary, Yugoslavia, Italy, France, and Czechoslovakia. For the month, the Fifteenth lost 188 bombers out of 9,813 effective sorties, a loss rate of 1.9 percent.

Crossbow

Within a few days of the invasion, another major diversion of the strategic bombing forces began. On the night of 12 June, the first V-1 robot bomb—designated by the Germans as *Vergeltungswaffe eins* (hence V-1, translates as reprisal weapon no. 1) and called, among other names, "flying bomb," "buzz bomb," or "doodlebug" by the Allies—struck England. In the next few days, the rate of the attack, directed mainly toward London, increased. In retrospect this weapon caused much more alarm among the English populace and their political leadership than its actual results warranted. Nonetheless, at the time the V-1, characterized by near-total unpredictability and coupled with a buzzing sound that shut off just before impact, was unnerving to the British people, provoked extraordinary anxiety, and put intense pressure on the Allied military to reduce the threat.

In all, between 13 June and 1 September 1944, when the last V-1 fell on British soil, 5,890 flying bombs had landed in England. They killed 5,835 and seriously injured an additional 16,762 individuals. London suffered 90 percent of all casualties.[19] Each weapon that struck England killed, on the average, one person and seriously injured three more. In contrast, during the 10-day Battle of Hamburg in July 1943, the RAF and the AAF killed almost 45,000 German civilians, most as the result of a single firestorm on the night of 27 July.[20] (See CD-ROM graphics: maps.pdf.)

Since the Allied armies were bogged down in Normandy, they could not capture the launching sites, which were farther up the French coast, and, because they needed the tactical air forces for their own support, the burden of countering the V-1 fell to the strategic air forces. The British advocated two methods to defang the threat. They wanted to obliterate the launch sites and conduct counterterror raids on the German populace. The Americans objected to both. Previous bombings of launch sites had proved ineffective, and terror bombing of Germany did not justify the abandonment of precision bombing techniques.

At first the Allies did not act, but the impact of 300 buzz bombs on the night of 15 June necessitated countermeasures. On 18 June Churchill persuaded Eisenhower to designate the V-1 sites as chief targets of the strategic air forces.[21] Eisenhower emphasized to all air leaders the seriousness with which he viewed the situation. He approved the use of USSTAF and Bomber Command and every other "means practicable for stopping the pilotless aircraft."[22] He told Maj Gen Fred Anderson to carry the word to Spaatz that Crossbow would "receive first priority over all other targets, either in France or Germany." Eisenhower called Spaatz that afternoon, who, in turn, promised to set aside a small force for exclusive use against the V-1 sites.[23]

Spaatz and Doolittle responded promptly. They had already resumed Crossbow strikes on 16 and 18 June. On 19 June they stepped up their effort by sending 703 heavy bombers out to hit the V-1 launch sites. During six of the remaining 11 days of the month, the Eighth sent out Crossbow missions of at least 125 planes each. In addition to hitting the launch sites, the Eighth broadened its attack to include the electrical switching and power stations that supplied the weapons as well as their storage areas. Bomber Command took even stronger measures and the Ninth contributed 1,500 medium bomber sorties starting on 23 June. For the latter half of June, Allied airpower dispatched 8,310 bomber sorties and dropped 23,431 tons against the V-1 target system. As the AAF official historians acknowledged, "Crossbow operations during the second half of June indicated that the Germans had again created for the Allies a diversionary problem of the first magnitude."[24]

From the beginning, Spaatz voiced objections to the effort devoted to V-1s. He believed that mass bombing of the launch sites accomplished little. The Germans had hardened the large sites, making them impervious to even the largest bombs. Moreover, the enemy had, for the most part, abandoned the large sites to concentrate on small, well-camouflaged positions that were almost impossible to spot and hit from the air. Spaatz wished to bomb the electrical system in the Pas-de-Calais area, which would stymie the functioning of the large sites and supply areas. The British, who controlled V-1 targeting, incorporated these proposals into their plans but did not emphasize them.[25] They continued to expend most of the heavy-bomber effort on launch sites, with negligible results. Finally, Spaatz offered two suggestions closer to his true purpose—maintaining the Combined Bomber Offensive. He offered to bomb the German factories making the V-1's gyroscopes and the large, recently discovered V-1 storage depots in France. The bombing of factories in Germany would serve the twofold purpose of halting the V-1 attacks and luring the Luftwaffe into the sky.

On 29 June Spaatz asked Eisenhower to approve the following policy: "On those days when weather conditions over Germany are favorable for visual bombing, such operations should have overriding priority over all others." Spaatz allowed two exceptions—a major emergency involving the ground forces and operations against the large installations being prepared to launch the German rocket-propelled V-2 weapon. The Allies feared the advent of the V-2, a supersonic rocket, even more than that of the V-1. No defense, save the destruction of its takeoff platform, could work against it. Spaatz did not consider operations against V-1 firing sites sufficiently decisive on any one day to justify the diversion of the strategic air forces from their primary tasks on the few days during which the weather conditions were favorable over Germany. As for the use of heavy bombers in support of the ground forces, Spaatz noted, "in the absence of a major ground force emergency, I do not believe that the results from the tactical use of heavy bombers will constitute as much support to [Overlord] as the use of the same force against critical German targets." In any case Spaatz explained that the "normal weather cycle" ensured enough unsuitable weather over Germany to provide a large proportion of the available heavy bomber effort for employment against tactical objectives in Normandy.[26]

Although Eisenhower privately regarded the V-1 as "very much of a nuisance," his ranking of air priorities differed from Spaatz's.[27] He realized that by 20 September good flying weather over Europe would cease. Therefore, for the next 60 to 90 days, he ranked "direct attacks against Germany" sixth in priority below normal close support of the ground army, disruption of communication lines, neutralization of Crossbow, airborne operations, and supply of troops by air. Eisenhower, however, allowed an escape clause: "In any event there will unquestionably be sufficient days, when other types of operations are impracticable, to continue the striking [air] assault upon Germany, and there will be days during the winter when this can likewise be carried out."[28] On 29 June Eisenhower issued a bombing directive that gave Crossbow top priority but at the same time acknowledged as "an overall policy that, when we have favorable conditions over Germany and when the entire Strategic Air Force cannot be used against [Crossbow], we should attack—a. Aircraft industry; b. Oil; c. Ball bearings; d. Vehicular production."[29] Given that he did not abuse the authority, Spaatz had clearance for strategic operations against Germany.

Spaatz's resentment of and resistance to the Crossbow diversion continued into July. When the Eighth received an allocation of targets giving it 68 Crossbow targets as compared to 30 for Bomber Command and only six for the AEAF, he strongly protested to Eisenhower, saying, "the implementation of our strategic bombing plans will be seriously hindered."[30] At the forefront of Spaatz's objections lay the realization that the long summer days provided unparalleled opportunities for his own forces but denied them to Bomber Command, which could not penetrate deeply into Germany during the short summer nights in northern Europe. A short winter's day later in the war could not replace a long sunlit July day that gave the US bomber formations license to penetrate as deeply as possible into German-occupied Europe. Spaatz pointed out to Eisenhower: "It must be borne in mind that the U.S. Strategic Air Force is the only force presently in a position to make deep penetrations in strength beyond the Ruhr and therefore must be responsible for the largest share of the strategic task of denying to the enemy the means with which to effectively continue resistance."[31]

Spaatz noted that Crossbow would interfere with USSTAF's tactical target assignments (bridges, POL [petroleum, oil, and lubricants] dumps, and airfields). Because of the "present restricted operational capabilities" of Bomber Command and the limited range of the tactical air force, he recommended that Bomber Command maintain a fixed percentage of their force for Crossbow. For his part, Spaatz promised to put in a strong effort against the V sites when he could not fly over Germany. "Such an arrangement," he stated, "should insure adequate effort against the Crossbow installations and yet will not force one command to carry a greater burden than another to the detriment of the other priority tasks and the war effort as a whole."[32]

During July and August, until Allied ground troops overran the last launching site on 1 September, Bomber Command, USSTAF, and the AEAF rained bombs on the entire identified V-weapon target system—from the German experimental rocket research station at Peenemünde on the Baltic through the manufacturing plants at Rüsselshiem and Ober Raderach and the power stations and electric switching sites in France to the storage areas and launching sites in Pas-de-Calais. The campaign lasted 77 days. In just two months—July and August—the Allied air forces expended 16,566 sorties and one-fourth of their total overall tonnage on Crossbow targets, all to little avail, however.[33] The rate of V-1 firings continued "essentially unhindered" and the AAF official historians concluded that "the Crossbow campaign of the summer of 1944 must be regarded generally as having failed to achieve its objectives.[34] Indeed it seems to have been the least successful part of the over-all effort."[35]

Reprisal Bombing and Thunderclap

The failure of Crossbow to reduce the rate of V-1 firings by early July 1944 intensified demands for retaliation or counter-terror raids over Germany. The idea of reprisal raids for the V-1, once started, gained a life of its own. Churchill raised the subject at a British chiefs of staff meeting on 1 July. He suggested that the British announce their intention to flatten the lesser German cities in turn if V-1 attacks continued. The British chiefs agreed to postpone action to allow for a thorough study—a classic bureaucratic method of pigeonholing an unattractive idea. In the meantime Churchill took up the matter with Bedell Smith, who approved it, and Tedder, who considered the policy ineffective and "wickedly uneconomical."[36] At the chiefs of staff meeting on 3 July, Portal spoke against retaliatory bombing, saying it would provide "invaluable proof" to the Germans that their V-1 policy had succeeded and amounted to entering into negotiations with the enemy. Portal doubted that the Germans would alter their plans for the sake of unimportant towns and noted that such bombing would divert Allied resources from more important communications and oil targets.[37]

That evening Churchill overrode his chiefs and ordered them to take up the matter the next day. Portal presented further arguments. He favored adding V-1 attacks to the list of war crimes. He also feared that the Germans might resort to counterreprisals, such as murdering downed aircrews from the British reprisal raids. "We could not hope to keep pace with the Germans in a campaign of reprisals," he concluded. The chiefs agreed to conduct a study of all aspects of retaliatory bombing, including the use of poison gas.[38]

The study reflected Portal's views. "No threat," he reasoned, "is likely to deter Hitler in his present fix. Indeed it may well encourage him to order more F.B.'s [flying bombs] and make still further efforts to increase the scale of attack." A threat to bomb the towns implied a guarantee not to bomb them if Hitler stopped his V-1 campaign. Such a circumstance would open the door to the Germans with respect to negotiations on other aspects of bombing. Portal acknowledged, "Actually, London with its vast production, its communications centres, and the seat of Government is (under the conditions prevailing in the present war) a perfectly legitimate target for the sort of 'browning' [night nuisance] attacks which we are making by instruments on Berlin."[39] The final report repeated Portal's arguments recommending rejection of the policy.[40] This action did not end the matter. On 5 July the chiefs of staff agreed "that the time might well come in the not too distant future when an all-out attack by every means at our disposal on German civilian morale might be decisive." They recommended to Churchill "that the method by which such an attack would be carried out should be examined and all possible preparations made."[41]

A working committee with the air staff, Foreign Office, Ministry of Economic Warfare, and USSTAF representatives met to determine the ideal approach to conducting attacks specifically designed to weaken civilian morale. On 22 July the committee issued a preliminary report. It concluded that the object of such attacks was "to influence the minds of the German authorities in such a way that they prefer organized surrender to continued resistance." When the time came for an assault, it would need to be coordinated with Allied propaganda policy and directed against the German High Command, the army, and the civilian population. Because of Berlin's importance as a center of population, industry, communications, and administration, the committee selected that city as the target of its campaign. Such bombing would disrupt governmental services and communications at a critical juncture as well as dishearten minor civil servants and would lead to an overall breakdown of public morale. Berlin could be attacked on short notice, in part because its size made it easy to locate on radarscopes; weather was not a factor in staging such attacks because both air forces knew the route to and the defenses of the city. The committee proposed to deliver 20,000 tons of bombs in a four-day and three-night operation against the administrative center of Berlin.[42]

The committee's final draft, submitted to the British chiefs of staff on 3 August, placed even greater emphasis on bombing population centers. They named their plan Thunderclap. The operational details called for 2,000 Eighth Air Force bombers to drop 5,000 tons under visual conditions on a two-and-one-half square-mile area of central Berlin estimated to contain a daytime population of 375,000. The bomb density of 2,000 tons per square mile would produce approximately 137,500 dead and 137,500 seriously injured. If necessary, the Fifteenth Air Force could participate and Bomber Command could follow up with a night incendiary raid.[43] Arnold objected strongly when the British proposal to attack civilian morale reached his desk. He preferred not to direct the attack solely at Berlin or the German people. He suggested a six-day-long series of sweeps by all available fighters and heavy bombers over all of Germany.[44]

When RAF air staff presented Thunderclap, it suggested that the War Cabinet's joint planning staff prepare an additional study on a possible assault on the Nazi machinery of repression, particularly the SS (*Schutzstaffel*) and the Gestapo (*Geheime Staatspolizei*). This attack would occur in coordination with, but not at the same time as, Thunderclap to weaken Nazi control of the populace.[45] However, two weeks later, when it reviewed a draft of the plan to bomb the security forces, the air staff rejected the plan. Instead, the air staff reiterated the virtues of bombing Berlin and produced a bloodcurdling analysis of the advantages of Thunderclap, noting that "a spectacular and final object lesson to the German people on the consequences of universal aggression would be of continuing value in the post-war period. Again, the total devastation of the centre of a vast city such as Berlin would offer incontrovertible proof to all peoples of the power of a modern air force." The air staff suggested that "such a proof would appreciably ease the task of policing the occupied areas largely by means of Air Forces. Moreover, it would convince our Russian allies and the Neutrals of the effectiveness of Anglo-American air power." Finally, the analysis concluded, "when allied forces had occasion to occupy, or neutral representatives to visit Berlin, they would be presented with a long continuing memorial to the effects which strategical bombing had produced in this war and could produce at any time again."[46]

The final plan for the attack on the German government machinery went forward on 17 August. The joint planning staff, because of the wide dispersion of targets and doubts as to exact locations, did not consider the scheme "likely to achieve any worthwhile degree of success."[47] The RAF staff had additional concerns. The German government was not vulnerable. The selected small targets required visual bombing, and the RAF had insufficient intelligence. In addition raids on complexes with concentration camps would produce casualties among the "internees."[48] Churchill agreed on the plan's impracticality. He suggested instead drawing up a short list of war criminals, 50 to 100 high-ranking Nazis, who would be executed if they fell into Allied hands. Publishing such a list, he speculated, would open a gap between the individuals named and the populace. He observed, "at the present moment, none of the German leaders has any interest but fighting to the last man, hoping he will be that last man. It is very important to show the German people that they are not on the same footing as Hitler, Göring, Himmler, and other monsters who will infallibly be destroyed."[49]

Later in August, SHAEF headquarters began to discuss Thunderclap.[50] Spaatz, who apparently had second thoughts, gave Eisenhower his opinion of the plan, "I am opposed to this operation as now planned. We are prepared to participate in an operation against Berlin, but in doing so will select targets for attack of military importance." Spaatz added, "U.S. Bombing Policy, as you know, has been directed against precision military objectives, and not morale."[51] Eisenhower noted that the operation would occur only under a limited set of conditions and added that, although he had always insisted that USSTAF bomb precision targets, he was "always prepared to take part in anything that gives real promise to ending the war quickly." Eisenhower promised Spaatz, "the policies under which you are now operating will be unchanged unless in my opinion an opportunity arises where a sudden and devastating blow may have an incalculable result."[52]

Spaatz expressed stronger views to Arnold, who, unlike Eisenhower, did not require his subordinates to eschew inter-Allied bickering: "I have been subjected to some pressure on the part of the Air Ministry to join hands with them in morale bombing. I discussed this matter previously with [Robert A.] Lovett when he was here and have maintained a firm position that our bombing will continue to be precision bombing against military objective [sic]." While admitting that a case could be made for bombing Berlin, Spaatz stated flatly, "I personally believe that any deviation from our present policy, even for an exceptional case, will be unfortunate. There is no doubt in my mind that the RAF want very much to have the U.S. Air Forces tarred with the morale bombing aftermath, which we feel will be terrific."[53] The prediction of 137,500 dead and an equal number seriously wounded as a result of American bombing during Thunderclap was apparently too much for him.

Eisenhower had the last word. On 9 September he asked Spaatz to have Doolittle ready to bomb Berlin at a moment's notice. Spaatz complied, instructing the Eighth to drop plans to hit military objectives and be ready to drop bombs "indiscriminately" on the city whenever Eisenhower gave the order.[54] Eisenhower may have been holding Thunderclap as a last card to play in the faltering drive across France. Only the last-gasp Operation Market-Garden paratroop drop in Holland, scheduled for mid-September, seemed to offer hope of a quick breakthrough. If the paratroopers had succeeded in establishing a bridgehead over the Rhine, the moment for launching Thunderclap might have arrived. Instead, Market-Garden proved a costly failure.

Ironically, the British and the Americans may have missed their opportunity. One can only speculate on the results of an anti-morale raid coming on the heels of the 20 July assassination attempt on Hitler. For a brief instant before Hitler savagely and sadistically retaliated against the plotters, confusion reigned. If nothing else, a raid at that time would have further roiled an already boiling pot. The Allied breakout from the Normandy beachhead, which would have occurred at approximately the same time, might have added the final push. Talk of Thunderclap subsided with the capture of the V-1 sites and the stalemate of the Allied ground forces on the western front in September 1944. Different circumstances four months later would resurrect it.

The conception and planning of Thunderclap illustrated the staying power of the prewar confidence in the striking power of bomber fleets. Between the wars, Western airpower experts and general publics alike subscribed to the view that a massive strategic bombing attack, delivered in a sudden stroke at the beginning of hostilities, might quickly end a war between major powers. This so-called bolt from the blue would totally disrupt daily life and inflict such horrific casualties on civilians as to compel the recipient power to capitulate. Yet, long after Chinese, British, and, especially, German civilians had demonstrated a capacity to withstand the heaviest of aerial bombardments, Allied air planners still seriously proposed a back-breaking, 72-hour operation of Thunderclap's magnitude. The operation's estimated casualty figures were more akin to those predicted in 1937 by the RAF air staff (150,000 for the first week of the bombing of London) than were those to be expected in 1944. Even the operation's code name evoked the image of the prewar bolt-from-the-blue mentality.

Notes

1. Diary, entry for 1 June 1944, Vandenberg Papers, Library of Congress, Manuscript Division, Washington, DC, Diaries, box 1.

2. AAF Evaluation Board, ETO, "The Effectiveness of Third Phase Tactical Air Operations in the European Theater: 5 May 1944–8 May 1944," 5 August 1944. The Evaluation Board apparently based its conclusions on joint Eighth and Ninth Air Force target team reports prepared in August 1944. This question is not well documented. However, the loss of French bridges, which were more difficult to go around or to substitute, probably delayed the Germans more than the bombing of minor cities. Like a rail marshaling yard, if all that one wants is a single line or path through the rubble, enough forced labor can clear a route in half a day even though it will not make entire a working rail yard or whole a French town.

3. Diary, entry for 2 June 1944, Vandenberg Papers, Diaries.

4. H hour, the time when the first assault craft would land and release its troops onto the beach, was 6:30 AM for the American invasion beaches (Omaha and Utah) and 7:00 and 7:30 AM for the British landings. Among the factors dictating selection of H hour were at least an hour of daylight before it (for preliminary bombardment) and tide at half-flood (to expose German obstacles) and rising (to insure two high tides in daylight for maximum unloading of supplies).

5. McArthur, *Operations Analysis in the Eighth Air Force*, 158–60.

6. Letter, Spaatz to Giles, 27 June 1944, Spaatz Papers, Diary; Craven and Cate, *Argument to V-E Day*, 3:188–93.

7. Air Ministry, *German Air Force*, 329.

8. Letter, Spaatz to Giles, 27 June 1944, Spaatz Papers, Diary.

9. Eighth Air Force, Monthly Summary of Operations, June 1944, n.d. [July 1944], AFCHO microfilm reel A5874, fr. 1398.

10. Air Ministry, *German Air Force*, 329–30.

11. Hinsley, *British Intelligence*, vol. 3, pt. 2, 220.

12. Ibid. Also see Haines, *Ultra: History of US Strategic Air Forces Europe*, 197–206.

13. Haines, 197.

14. Ibid., 196.

15. Ibid., 201–2.

16. Hinsley, 220–21.

17. Air Ministry, *German Air Force*, 332–33.

18. Eighth Air Force, INTOPS Summary No. 52, 21 June 1944, AFHSO, microfilm reel A5976, fr. 1636.

19. Pogue, *Supreme Command*, 252.

20. Terraine, *Time for Courage*, 546–47.

21. Chandler, *Eisenhower's Papers*, vol. 3, item 1758 n., 1933.

22. Diary, entry for 18 June 1944, Vandenberg Papers, Diaries, box 1.

23. Command Diary, entry for 18 June 1944, Spaatz Papers, Diary.

24. Craven and Cate, *Argument to V-E Day*, 3:528.

25. Ibid., 3:531.

26. Letter, Spaatz to Eisenhower, 28 June 1944, Spaatz Papers, Diary. Craven and Cate, 3:880. Note that the copy of the document available to them [Craven and Cate] carried the notation, "Carried to General E. by Gen. S., June 29, 1944."

27. Chandler, *Eisenhower's Papers*, vol. 3, item 1763, message, Eisenhower to Marshall, 19 June 1944, 1936–1937.

28. Ibid., item 1771, memo, Eisenhower to C/S, SHAEF [Smith], 23 June 1944, 1946–47.

29. Ibid., item 1786, memo, Eisenhower to DSC, SHAEF [Tedder], 29 June 1944, 1960–61.

30. Letter, Spaatz to Eisenhower, 10 July 1944, Spaatz Papers, Diary.

31. Ibid.

32. Ibid.

33. Craven and Cate, 3:533.

34. Ibid., 3:534.

35. Ibid., 3:540.

36. Minutes, VCAS 1803, VCAS to CAS, subject: Crossbow, 2 July 1944, PRO AIR 8/1229.

37. Extract from COS (44) 219th Meeting (O), 3 July 1944, PRO AIR 8/1229.

38. Extract from minutes, COS (44) 220th meeting (O), 4 July 1944, PRO AIR 8/1229.

39. Minutes, CAS (Portal) to DCAS (Bottomley), 5 July 1944, PRO AIR 8/1229.

40. COS (44) 598 (O), subject: Crossbow: Question of Retaliation, 5 July 1944, PRO AIR 8/1229.

41. 222d Meeting of the British chiefs of staff, cited in memo, Brig Gen L. S. Kuter to Arnold, 9 August 1944, Spaatz Papers, Diary.

42. Memo by the Air Staff, subject: Attack on German Civilian Morale, 22 July 1944, PRO AIR 20/3227.

43. COS (44) 650 (O), Attack on German Civilian Morale, 2 August 1944, PRO AIR 20/4831. See attached note "Operation THUNDERCLAP," 1 August 1944.

44. Letter, Kuter to Anderson, 15 August 1944; memo for Maj Gen F. L. Anderson, subject: Attack on German Civilian Morale," from Col Charles G. Williamson, 12 September 1944, Spaatz Papers, Diary.

45. Extract from COS (44) 257th Meeting (O), 3 August 1944, PRO AIR 8/1229.

46. Draft D. B. Ops comments on Attack on the German Government Machine, Outline Plan by Joint Planning Staff, J.P. (44) 203 (O), Revised Preliminary Draft, 15 August 1944, PRO AIR 20/4831.

47. J. P. (44) 203 Final, Attack on the German Government Machine, 17 August 1944, PRO AIR 20/8152.

48. B. Ops. 1, to Wing Commander Ford-Kelsey, [Comments on] Attack on German Government Machine, 6 August 1944, PRO AIR 20/4831.

49. COS (44) 774 (O), minute (D (K) 4/4) by the prime minister, Attack on the German Government Machine, 28 August 1944 [minute dated 23 August 1944], PRO AIR 20/8152.

50. Craven and Cate, 3:638–39. The author of this chapter, John E. Fagg, demonstrated no understanding of the background of Thunderclap and presented a somewhat confused account of the proposed operation.

51. Letter, Spaatz to Eisenhower, 24 August 1944, Spaatz Papers, Diary.

52. Ibid.

53. Letter, Spaatz to Arnold, 27 August 1944, Spaatz Papers, Diary.

54. Entry for 9 September 1944, Command Diary, Spaatz Papers, Diary.

July

7 July: Bomber Command—bombs Caen to support advance of British 2d Army, resultant rubble blocks all roads but one.

11 July: Eighth Air Force—three B-17s and five B-24s land in Switzerland after mission to Munich.

12 July: Eighth Air Force—six B-24s and four B-17s land in Switzerland after mission to Munich.

13 July: Eighth Air Force—four B-17s and one B-24 land in Switzerland after mission to Munich.

16 July: Eighth Air Force—one B-17 lands in Switzerland after mission to southern Germany.

18 July: Eighth Air Force—three B-17s land in Sweden after mission in Baltic. Fifteenth Air Force—one B-17 lands in Switzerland after mission to Munich. Bomber Command and Eighth Air Force—support Operation Goodwood, unsuccessful British 2d Army attempt to break out of beachhead.

19 July: Eighth Air Force—two B-17s land in Switzerland after mission to southwestern Germany. Fifteenth Air Force—two B-24s crash-land in Switzerland after mission to Munich.

20 July: Eighth Air Force—one B-17 lands in Switzerland after mission to Leipzig. Fifteenth Air Force—five B-24s land in Switzerland after mission to Friedrichshafen. Attempt on Hitler's life and anti-Nazi coup by German dissidents fails.

21 July: Eighth Air Force—eight B-24s land in Switzerland after missions to southern Germany. Two other damaged bombers fly to Italy.

22 July: Fifteenth Air Force—attacks Ploesti and sends 134 fighters to Soviet bases. Hitler appoints Joseph Göbbels, German minister of propaganda and long-time advocate for a greatly increased war effort, Reich's commissioner for total mobilization of resources for war.

24 July: Eighth Air Force—scheduled to participate in Operation Cobra, US First Army attempt to break out of the beachhead. Over 350 bombers miss bad weather recall and attempt to bomb designated section of German front lines. Short bombs kill 25 men and wound 131 of the US 30th Infantry Division.

25 July: Eighth Air Force—sends 1,581 heavy bombers to execute Operation Cobra.

26 July: US First Army—makes decisive breakout from the Normandy beachhead.

26 July: Red Army captures Lublin and takes Majdanek death camp intact. Soviets make available to the world physical evidence of the German extermination policies.

31 July: Eighth Air Force—two B-17s land in Switzerland after mission to Munich.

For the second month in a row Bomber Command delivered more than 64,000 short tons of bombs. Of those, three-fourths (47,000 tons) struck targets in France, falling predominately on Crossbow sites, but also on marshaling yards and in support of three attacks by British ground forces. The command expended 6,109 daylight heavy bomber sorties in France. Many of these attacks in France took place in daylight—more than 45 percent of the command's monthly total. A command comparison of night and day bombing raids in occupied countries showed, as one would expect, the accuracy of daylight bombing exceeded the accuracy of nighttime sorties by almost one-third.[1]

Air Marshal Sir Arthur Harris launched 10 major raids into Germany: five directed against synthetic oil targets in the

Ruhr and five area raids on German cities. Between 18 and 25 July, five missions (753 sorties) attacked the Ruhr, suffering a loss of 33 bombers (a loss rate of 4.3 percent). Some raids had no casualties or only a few, while other raids lost between 5 and 13.7 percent. Of the five area raids, two struck fringe targets along the German coast: Kiel (612 bombers, four lost) and Hamburg (300 bombers, 23 lost). The remaining three penetrated into Germany to attack Stuttgart (1,511 effective sorties, 72 aircraft lost). The loss rate of 4.8 percent on the deep missions approached the unacceptable point but the overall loss figure, far below that of operations over Germany in the preceding month, suggested that night operations over Germany were once again possible, but expensive.

The Eighth's situation in July 1944 reversed that of Bomber Command. Of the 43,700 tons of bombs that the Eighth dropped in the month, only 14,000 tons fell on French targets. Of those bombs released over France, the bulk were directed at Crossbow objectives with 3,100 tons going to support ground attacks by American and British troops. The remaining two-thirds of the Eighth's bombs and 11,800 effective bomber sorties went to Germany, escorted by hundreds of P-51s. Doolittle launched three large raids against the air industry and factory airfields in central and southern Germany, expending 2,100 sorties, dropping 5,160 tons of bombs, and losing 61 bombers. For the month another 1,065 sorties and 2,980 tons of bombs went to marshaling yards, the bulk by means of H2X sightings on Saarbrücken, the rail gateway from Germany to France. The city's proximity to the Saar River made it a good H2X target. Oil targets—Merseberg, Bohlen, and Lutzkendorf—received their share of attention: 1,692 sorties, 4,080 tons, and 26 bombers lost. Only one of the oil attacks used H2X sighting.

The Eighth concentrated the largest percentage of its efforts against Munich and other German city areas. The Eighth directed almost 4,200 sorties and 10,000 tons of bombs (losing 92 bombers) against city areas of 14 different cities. On 11, 12, 13, 16, and 31 July, the bombers set out to attack industrial targets such as the BMW aeroengine factory in Munich, as well as the center of that city. When they encountered clouds, all crews dropped their ordnance on the city center using H2X. Munich had a special symbolism to the Germans and the Allies. It was the home of the Nazi Party and the beer-hall putsch—the city that had nurtured the party and enabled it to grow. Munich also served as the administrative center of the party. Wrecking some of the party's machinery of control, which the Allies presumed stiffened the will of the general public, might make Germany collapse all the sooner. There seems to have been no connection between this bombing and the 20 July plot against Hitler. The Eighth struck only one other city area with more than 100 bombers. On 16 July 261 bombers using H2X hit Stuttgart. Twelve other cities suffered when one or two combat boxes could not attack their primary targets and chose targets of opportunity instead.

In the midst of this effort, Maj Gen Frederick Anderson, Spaatz's deputy for operations, issued a policy statement to the Eighth and Fifteenth on bombing with H2X. Anderson noted Spaatz's oft reiterated and continuing intention to direct bombing toward precision targets and categorically denied any intention to area bomb. However, having denied the intention, he (Anderson) proceeded to authorize the practice: "We will conduct bombing attacks through the overcast where it is impossible to get precision targets. Such attacks will include German marshaling yards whether or not they are located in German cities."[2] As Anderson and Spaatz well knew, bombs dropped on targets in cities using overcast bombing techniques would cause great collateral damage. Apparently it was acceptable to the Americans to bomb German civilians if they lived in cities with military targets, but not acceptable to make German civilians a target in and of themselves. The reports of the bomb groups and bombardment divisions often did not bother with such niceties as distinguishing between collateral damage and purposefully attacking civilians.

So fast and furious had the operational pace been in May, June, and July that the US air forces experienced a temporary shortage of aviation fuel. Toward the end of July, Spaatz ordered the Eighth and Ninth Air Forces to reduce nonoperational and nontraining flights to a minimum. He further ordered his forces to reduce the size of formations dispatched against a single target and against single aiming points within a target. Since the Luftwaffe day fighters had been defeated, he instructed Lt Gens James Doolittle and Lewis Brereton to reduce the number "of sorties dispatched under conditions promising relatively small return."[3]

In July 1944 the Fifteenth Air Force became a full partner in the strategic bombing. As the Germans retreated up the Italian peninsula, they shortened their supply lines and lines of communication, which diminished the strategic benefits of continued attacks on such targets. The Fifteenth used only 1,250 effective sorties in Italy and half hit strategic targets such as bearings manufacture in Turin, oil refineries in Trieste, and oil storage sites in Aviano. However, Italy was near the bottom of the Fifteenth's priority target list. It topped only Yugoslavia, the object of only 361 sorties, aimed mostly at the marshaling yard at Brod. In France, the Fifteenth began preparations for the invasion of southern France by hitting the submarine pens at Toulon and the marshaling yards and railroad bridges at Avignon, Tarascon, and Nimes with 1,276 sorties and 3,254 tons of bombs. In Germany, the Fifteenth attacked synthetic oil targets at Blechhammer (its first bombing mission near the infamous Auschwitz death camp) on 7 July while the Eighth attacked targets in central Germany. On 18 July the Fifteenth attacked a tank engine plant in Friedrichshafen. On 19 July, in conjunction with a full-force Eighth Air Force mission into southern Germany, most of the Fifteenth attacked Munich. The bombers found clear conditions and damaged the BMW plant, other air plants, and the ordnance depot at Milbertshoven. The next day the Fifteenth returned to Friedrichshafen to restrike the Maybach armored fighting vehicle (AFV) plant and aircraft plants. The Eighth coordinated operations by trying to launch a thousand bombers into central Germany. Operations in Germany cost the Fifteenth 1,459 sorties, 3,663 tons of bombs, and 77 bombers. The Fifteenth's 5.3 percent loss rate, given the coordinated strikes with the Eighth, indicated that the Fifteenth needed additional P-51s.

The Fifteenth pummeled Austria with four large raids on 8, 16, 25, and 26 July. The first two missions concentrated on the many oil refineries in Vienna. On 25 July the Fifteenth dropped 1,110 tons of bombs on the Hermann Göring steel works at Linz, losing 24 bombers (14 to atrocious weather). The next day the

Fifteenth struck various airfields. In all, the Americans expended 1,578 sorties, 3,978 tons of bombs, and 76 aircraft (a loss rate of 5 percent). The Fifteenth needed more escorts to go deep. Nearly as much effort was aimed at Hungary as at Austria—1,572 sorties, 3,934 tons of bombs, and 35 bombers. The 2.2 percent loss rate reflected the weakness of the Hungarian air defenses. Almost 80 percent of the bombs during the three major raids of 2, 14, and 27 July fell on targets near or in Budapest (the capital): airfields, refineries, marshaling yards, fighter assembly plants, and the Manfried Weiss armaments firm.

Rumania was first on the Fifteenth's hit parade. Its bombers flew 2,785 effective sorties and dropped 7,244 tons of bombs on the country at a cost of 91 bombers lost. Two-thirds of the effort was directed against the refineries of Ploesti (1,783 sorties, 4,667 tons of ordnance; 76 bombers lost); the Fifteenth struck Ploesti's oil facilities five times. The Fifteenth carried out another 362 sorties on refineries, oil storage, and locomotive works in Bucharest. The remainder of the missions attacked oil storage refineries and rail targets throughout the country. In spite of this pounding, German imports of finished oil products rose in July to 56,000 metric tons from 40,000 metric tons in June. How much of this increase, if any, came from Rumania cannot be determined from available sources. Despite the fall of Ploesti on 22 August, German-finished oil imports (as opposed to production in occupied territories) either remained steady or increased for the remainder of the year.[4] Apparently, the Germans exploited Hungarian capacity to the hilt.

The Fifteenth's attacks on oil targets throughout the region, including 350 bombers sent to the large synthetic oil plant at Brux, Czechoslovakia, on 21 July, damaged alternate or excess refinery capacity available to the Germans. The damage inflicted on the oil industry in German satellites was not the only cause for the diminished output from these facilities. Although German firms had built these facilities, these refineries had to stand in line behind German refineries to obtain spare parts for repairs and other materials. The cumulative effects of the Fifteenth's attacks on the oil production and storage facilities on the periphery of the German state made the Eighth's punches on the homeland more effective. The Fifteenth paid a price for its operations.

The loss rate over Italy had run under 1 percent, but in July 1944 its losses (3 percent) exceeded that of both the Eighth (1.2 percent) and Bomber Command (2 percent). In absolute numbers the Fifteenth lost 317 bombers, Bomber Command 305, and the Eighth 224. RAF No. 205 Group flying at medium level in its obsolescent Wellingtons and unwanted Liberators continued the Danube mining, dropped leaflets, and attacked refineries in Yugoslavia, Italy, and Rumania. It suffered the highest casualty rate of all, 4 percent, losing 44 bombers out of 1,180 effective sorties.

Heavy Bombers in Close Support of the Ground Forces

At the request of Gen Bernard Law Montgomery, the Allied ground commander in the Normandy beachhead, Bomber Command and the Eighth bombed German defensive positions in support of the Allied ground efforts. These missions were the first instance, but not the last, of heavy bombers being used in direct support of the ground forces during the campaign. Bomber Command dropped 6,000 half-ton bombs directly on northern Caen and on targets 6,000 yards beyond the British front lines, on the night of 7 July 1944. The raid devastated about two and one-half square miles, leaving practically contiguous craters, none of which measured less than 20 feet across. These bomb craters blocked all the roads to Caen, save one.[5] These sorties seem to have inflicted little harm on the defenders. The Eighth bombed bridges and tunnels beyond the German lines. According to Zuckerman, who observed and prepared a detailed report soon afterward, the bombing failed to demoralize or materially affect the Germans, but at least there were no Allied casualties.[6]

On 18 July Bomber Command and the Eighth Air Force provided direct support for the next British assault. At dawn Bomber Command dropped 6,000 half-ton bombs and 9,600 500-pound bombs on three target areas. Medium bombers of the Ninth Air Force swept over the battlefield, but many could not drop their bombs because of clouds of smoke left behind by Bomber Command. B-24s of the Eighth's 2d Bombardment

Division, 570 strong, dropped almost 13,000 100-pound and 76,000 20-pound fragmentation bombs (1,410 tons in all) on a key tactical feature, Bourguebus Ridge. In all 4,500 Allied aircraft beset the Germans. Once again the bombing did not completely clear the way for the ground forces.

Bomber Command did the most accurate bombing. It bombed first in the remarkably clear morning, hitting most of its targets squarely. Even four months later a British Bombing Analysis Unit reported that one area "resembled the surface of the moon."[7] Only a small proportion of the B-24s' fragmentation weapons fell on their targets; most scattered over the countryside. In the ensuing ground assault, Allied troops encountered particularly stiff resistance in the American target areas.[8] Bomb bursts had cratered the terrain over which they traveled, hindering the advance of some units; and the bombing failed to knock out entrenched German antitank guns and panzers. Furthermore, the Germans, anticipating the attack, had prepared defenses in depth; many of the deeper defense positions had not come under fire. Operation Goodwood, like its predecessors, soon ground to a bloody halt.[9]

The failure of Montgomery's ballyhooed attack led to a round of recriminations among top Allied leaders. The airmen, in particular, expressed keen disappointment. The normally unflappable Air Chief Marshal Sir Arthur Tedder began to agitate for Montgomery's dismissal and wrote to his old friend Lord Trenchard (founder of the RAF) that he and Eisenhower had been "had for suckers" by Montgomery.[10] At a high-level SHAEF staff meeting on 21 July, Tedder asked Lt Gen Bedell Smith when the army would get to the V-1 launching sites in the Pas-de-Calais region of France. When Smith replied it would not be soon, Tedder sarcastically remarked, "Then we must change our leaders for men who will get us there."[11] Air Chief Marshal Sir Trafford Leigh-Mallory felt "bitterly disappointed, for it does not seem to me that the breakthrough which we produced has been exploited and pressed to a conclusion."[12] Eisenhower fumed as well. He acidly noted that the air forces had dropped a thousand tons of bombs for each mile of Montgomery's advance and wondered whether the Allies could afford to advance through all of France paying that price.[13]

The Eighth's next ground support mission proved both its most effective in terms of supporting the ground forces and its most controversial, because some of its bombs dropped short of the intended target area, landing among American troops, killing more than 100 and wounding hundreds more. The plan for Cobra, an operation designed to achieve a breakthrough of the American First Army at the St. Lo sector on the right flank of the Allied beachhead, came almost solely from Gen Omar Bradley. He presented it to his staff and corps commanders on 12 July. Cobra differed from the pattern of other American offensives. Once the First Army secured a key portion of the road between St. Lo and Periers, the offensive's jump-off point, VIII Corps would use its combat-experienced reserve of two US armored divisions and the fully motorized US 1st Infantry Division to launch a narrow and concentrated attack on the German front line. The concentration on a narrow front departed from the wide front operations US ground forces usually conducted.[14] Bradley meant to pierce the enemy lines rather than continue the attritional struggles of the earlier phases of the campaign. Ultra intercepts fueled Bradley's determination. The enemy units opposite him, II Parachute Corps and LXXXIV [84th] Corps, reported heavy losses before 10 July and continuing heavy losses during the next two weeks. The senior German officers on the scene expected a breakthrough at any moment.[15]

Bradley inserted a second unusual feature by insisting that a heavy aerial bombardment immediately precede Cobra. Bradley intended that the air bombardment include the use of heavy bombers. "Realizing the great power we had in our Air Force, I wanted to secure someplace where we could use a great mass of power to virtually wipe out some German division opposing part of our line and then punch a hole through." The air bombardment, in Bradley's mind, offset the lack of artillery firepower available to him. Lack of artillery ammunition, at least as much as lack of artillery pieces, prevented an extensive land bombardment. The Allied supply situation—restricted to supplies that had come over on the initial landings on the beaches on D-day (they had not yet captured a working French port)—did not include a surfeit of shells.[16]

Bradley required that the air bombardment fall into a rectangular area approximately four miles long and one and one-half miles deep—7,000 yards by 2,500 yards—approximately four and one-half times the size of New York City's Central Park.[17] The rectangle covered the entire front of his attack. Bradley directed that the bombers carry only 100-pound fragmentation bombs to prevent excessive cratering that would hamper the advance of the infantry and, more important, the mechanized forces.[18] He also wanted the air bombardment conducted rapidly; if it stretched out over several hours, it would lose its massive shock effect.

He recognized that the aircrews would prefer to approach the target box at a right angle to the front, flying from north to south, first crossing over the American lines and then dropping their bombs on the Germans to minimize their exposure to antiaircraft fire. Bradley, however, wished the bombers to fly parallel to the front (along the German lines) rather than perpendicular to it to provide a greater security margin for his troops. The bombers could attack from the east to the west, during the morning, putting the sun in the eyes of the antiaircraft gunners, or reverse the course of attack in the afternoon.[19] On 19 July he met the Allied air leaders and received a commitment for 1,500 heavy bombers, almost 900 medium bombers, and 350 fighter bombers.[20] Bradley agreed to withdraw his troops 1,200 yards and the heavies would not strike the first 250 yards of the target box.[21] Bradley insisted that the bombers fly parallel to the front; some of the Eighth's representatives that were present agreed.[22]

The completed air command arrangements for Cobra were a bizarre mishmash that excluded USSTAF and the Eighth from most command decisions and left the heavy bombers subject to the orders of men who understood little of the technical difficulties involved in their operation. Tedder, who had approved the mission in the first place, would provide top-level supervision; Leigh-Mallory would set the time and date of the operation; Lt Gen Lewis Brereton would plan the bomber attack; and Maj Gen Elwood R. Quesada, commanding general of the IX Tactical Air Command, the AAF unit cooperating with the First Army, would coordinate the air attack with the ground forces.[23]

Inclement weather delayed Cobra from 21 to 24 July. This postponement allowed the Eighth to send a 1,100-bomber raid against German aircraft production plants on 21 July and a 280-bomber attack on French airfields on 23 July. On the evening of 23 July, AEAF's meteorologists predicted suitable weather for the next day. USSTAF's weathermen had a different forecast. They predicted clouds for 24 July and better conditions for 25 July in the St. Lo area. They foresaw good bombing weather over Berlin and central Germany on 24 July.

Late on 23 July, Spaatz's deputy for operations, Maj Gen Frederick Anderson called Leigh-Mallory for an immediate decision as to the target. The Eighth needed to know which bombs to load—500-pound, general-purpose bombs and incendiaries for Berlin or fragmentation bombs for St. Lo. Leigh-Mallory, relying on his own forecasts, set the starting time for the Cobra air bombardment at 1000. On the morning of 24 July, AEAF's meteorologists revised their estimates and called for slowly breaking clouds from 1100 to 1300. Leigh-Mallory delayed the attack for two hours, rescheduling it for 1200.[24] Despite the unease of the Eighth's own weathermen, 1,586 B-17s and B-24s left their bases to participate in Cobra. The skies stayed heavily overcast with a ceiling of only 5,000 feet, leaving Leigh-Mallory with no choice but to call off the mission and reschedule for the next day.

The last-minute timing of this cancellation caused tragedy and confusion. Incredibly, the ground forces had no direct communications link to the bombers in the air. Leigh-Mallory's halt order went back to Stanmore by radiotelephone, where the order's receipt produced immediate consternation in the daily air commanders' meeting. Tedder, Spaatz, Harris, and Doolittle were nonplused. Doolittle said that the bombers would arrive over their target in only seven minutes and could not be recalled now. He assumed that the planes would return fully loaded if they could not bomb visually.

Over St. Lo the first of the Eighth's three bombardment divisions made no attack because of poor visibility. One group (35 bombers) in the second bombardment division to pass released its bombs after making three runs to identify its target. The third bombardment division to arrive over the target box found weather conditions slightly improved; 317 bombers loosed their loads—550 tons of high explosives and 135 tons of fragmentation bombs—before finally receiving the recall order.[25] All the heavy bombers had approached and bombed at a right angle, or perpendicular, to the front line. Some had dropped short, directly onto their own troops, killing 25 men and wounding 131 more of the US 30th Division. The performance enraged Bradley, who felt that the air leaders had given him an ironclad promise for a parallel approach. His troops had to fight hand-to-hand to regain the start line.[26] The German LXXXIV Corps defending St. Lo optimistically (and prematurely) reported it had shot the American offensive into the ground with a great expenditure of artillery ammunition.[27]

On the evening of 24 July, Lt Gen Hoyt S. Vandenberg informed Spaatz that all the meteorologists had agreed on 1000 for the next day's mission over St. Lo.[28] Spaatz was irked not because of bombing short but for the waste of effort for 1,600 of his bombers. The late decision to cancel had cost him a day of visual bombing conditions over Berlin and central Germany.[29] Vandenberg talked to the Eighth's headquarters and informed them of Bradley's desire for bombing parallel to the troops. The Eighth replied that as long as Bradley required that the bombers attack in as short a time as possible, they could not fly parallel. Funneling more than 1,500 bombers through the short side of the target box would take two and one-half hours, if it could be done at all. Such an approach required the Eighth to form a column stretching all the way to Holland. General Anderson of USSTAF emphasized that the time factor controlled the direction of attack. He suggested that Bradley might want to extend the time allowed. Before Vandenberg could pass this message on to Leigh-Mallory, the latter informed him that he had just spoken to Bradley and that Bradley could not accept a lengthier attack and therefore had accepted "the additional risk of perpendicular to the road bombing."[30] What clinched the decision for Bradley was Leigh-Mallory's latest weather forecast, which noted that a low-pressure area would move into the St. Lo area in the afternoon of 25 July carrying with it several days of bad weather. In addition, at an earlier command conference, Bradley and his subordinates had decided to wait only one or two more days for air support. Bradley added that he would have pulled his troops farther back had he known the bombers' approach route in advance.[31]

The status of the enemy troops facing his attack added to Bradley's anxiety. Signal intelligence decrypts from 14 and 21 July revealed that the German LXXXIV Corps and II Parachute Corps had reported serious disorganization as a result of earlier American attacks. The commanders of both corps doubted that they could continue a successful defense. Further messages on 22, 24, and 25 July detailed the steadily depreciating combat value of II Parachute Corps. An extraordinary opportunity beckoned if only Bradley's forces could go forward—the blow could not be long delayed. A message from the German Seventh Army Luftwaffe liaison, dated late 22 July and decrypted at 0818 on 23 July, urgently requested reconnaissance of powerful new US forces with tanks (Patton's Third Army) opposite the 17th SS Panzer Grenadier Division.[32] This request indicated that the Germans had recognized their vulnerability in this section of the beachhead. (See CD-ROM graphics: maps.pdf.)

On the morning of 25 July, the Eighth began its bomb drop. The dispatch of 1,581 B-17s and B-24s equaled the effort of the previous day. Unlike 24 July, when only a few bombers attacked, most of the heavies (1,503 of them) released their high-explosive cargo and sent it hurtling toward the front line. Their 3,300 tons of explosives plus 870 tons dropped by the medium bombers and fighter-bombers crashed into the greatly understrength German Panzer Lehr Division. These attacks killed 1,000 men, destroyed three of its battalion command posts, knocked out all but a dozen of its armored fighting vehicles, and wiped out an attached parachute regiment.[33] Lt Gen Fritz Bayerlein, the division's commander, described the Normandy scene in a postwar interrogation. "It was hell. . . . The planes kept coming overhead like a conveyor belt, and the bomb carpets came down. . . . My frontlines looked like a landscape on the moon, and at least seventy percent of my personnel were out of action—dead, wounded, crazed or numb."[34] At 1000 Bayerlein reported to his superiors that the air bombardment heralded an American breakthrough attempt and urgently requested Luftwaffe assistance.[35]

Despite this punishing blow and the artillery barrage that followed, the well-disciplined and well-trained German survivors, in a last-gasp effort, managed to prevent the American breakthrough for one more day. By the night of 25 July the American assault had advanced only a mile south of Periers road, still within the target box. The general gloom and disappointment that surrounded the first day's action did not affect Lt Gen Lawton J. Collins, the VII Corps commander. He sensed that the attack had broken through the German lines. The signal intelligence of the Germans' weakened state even before the offensive, which Bradley undoubtedly shared with Collins, and the early morning decryption of Bayerlein's plea for help must have confirmed his feelings. Ultra intercepted a message dated before dawn on 26 July in which LXXXIV Corps reported a shortage of 88 mm antitank ammunition, heavy casualties, and a deteriorating situation.[36] On the evening of 25 July, Collins summoned his armor to the front with orders to push through the last German defenders and exploit the breakthrough.[37] The German forces in Normandy—bled white by seven weeks of attrition, their attention focused on the Caen sector by Montgomery's repeated attacks, and their mobility curtailed by Allied control of the air—did not react quickly or forcefully enough to the threat of Bradley's offensive. On 26 July Collins' troops burst through the thin screen of Germans opposing them. An ingenious and simple idea of welding iron shears to the front of their tanks allowed the Americans to plow through the hedgerows into the clear terrain beyond. VII Corps armor had gained a tactical advantage over the Germans, who were largely road-bound. The race through France to the German border had begun.

On the afternoon of 25 July, however, the long-awaited breakthrough seemed as far away as ever. In addition to the surprisingly stout German defense, more short bombings had shaken the advancing troops. Friendly fire killed 111 Americans, including Lt Gen Lesley J. McNair (the highest-ranking Allied officer to die in the campaign), and wounded 490 more.[38] Eisenhower, at Bradley's headquarters for the first day of the offensive, seemed more dismayed by the short bombing than Bradley. Eisenhower said of the performance of the heavy bombers: "I don't believe they can be used in support of ground forces. That's a job for artillery. I gave them a green light this time. But I promise you it's the last."[39]

In fact, many bombardiers, well aware of the first day's tragedy, took great pains not to bomb short on the second day. One-half of the 1st Bombardment Division, approximately 150 to 200 bombers, delivered their loads beyond the target box. Unfortunately, 2 to 4 percent of the bombers again dropped short. One bombardier had trouble with his bombsight and re-computed visually, with poor results; another failed to identify vital landmarks properly; and a command pilot failed to observe the order to drop by bomb group and ordered "bombs away" when his wing leader, flying in the lead group several hundred yards ahead of the trailing group, dropped his bombs.[40] As the breakthrough progressed and the troops and commanders had a chance to assess the damage inflicted on the Germans, emotions cooled. On 28 July Bradley wrote to Eisenhower: "This operation could not have been the success it has been without such close cooperation of the Air. In the first place the bombardment we gave them last Tuesday was apparently highly successful even though we did suffer many casualties ourselves."[41]

General Montgomery requested another heavy bomber mission for early August to assist an offensive by his newly established 1st Canadian Army. The air leaders agreed to supply American and British heavy bombers. On 8 August the Eighth dispatched 678 bombers to follow up the initial bombardment by 637 Bomber Command aircraft on the night of 7 August.[42] This combined attack incorporated several lessons learned from St. Lo and earlier bombardments. Bomber Command did not bomb directly ahead of the troops. Instead, the British heavy bombers delivered large bombs with their accompanying cratering effect, on both ends of the German line facing the assaulting Canadians. The British employed this tactic to isolate the area under attack and keep German reinforcements from moving laterally down the German lines on either side of the assault area. The RAF, departing from its practice in earlier close support missions, attacked at night when the Canadians began their own assault. The ground attack penetrated the first two German lines and gained five kilometers. The army commander then committed two inexperienced armored divisions, the 4th Canadian and the 1st Polish, to exploit the attack.[43]

Early in the afternoon of 8 August, the Eighth arrived to bomb its targets. Scouting planes had preceded it to check weather conditions and the state of the target areas, marked by smoke shells and flares. As planned, the bombers delivered their attack flying north to south parallel to the lines of the attacking troops, a tactic forcing a long flight over enemy territory and, of course, magnifying the usual problems of operating in congested airspace. The Canadians and the Poles withdrew only 1,500 yards; they, like Bradley, apparently preferred to chance casualties rather than give up too much ground and momentum.

The bombardment struck its targets in turn, in the manner of a creeping barrage. The bombers flew straight and level down 40 miles of the German lines and received intense heavy flak for the entire distance. Of the 681 attacking bombers, seven were lost with four more written off as not repairable; 107 had major damage and 187 minor damage. They dropped 1,275 tons of bombs. Two of their four aiming points were well covered. Clouds of dust prevented the bombing of one point and allowed only 30 percent of the bombers to drop on the other.[44] Two 12-plane formations bombed short, killing 65 and wounding 265 Canadians and Poles. Their bombs fell on areas packed with unsuspecting members of the 1st Polish Armored Division and the 3d Canadian Infantry Division. Many were sitting in moving vehicles or waiting to move up to the front.[45] The disorder caused by the shorts, the five-minute safety delay between the bombardment and the renewal of the ground assault, the 1,500-yard safety margin, and the inexperience of the two divisions caused the attack to bog down. It halted on 9 August after gaining 13 kilometers.[46]

Army Air Forces after-action reports revealed the near impossibility of preventing such short bombing. In one bomb group an antiaircraft round hit the lead plane just after it had decided to bypass the primary target because it was obscured by smoke. The round caused a fire in the bomb bay. The pilot, fearing for the lives of his crew and his own life, salvoed his bomb load. The rest of the formation followed his lead. Their bombs landed in the friendly city of Caen. In a second instance, the lead bombardier and pilot, confused by a course change to avoid intense flak, performed "exceedingly poorly." They misidentified their targets, dropping the formation's bombs just to the south of Caen.[47] Such errors were inevitable on any large mission. The only way to keep them from adversely affecting the friendly assault troops was to bomb so far behind the enemy front line that any direct advantage the troops might gain was eliminated.

Five days later, on 14 August, a daylight Bomber Command bombardment preceded another 1st Canadian Army lunge, this time toward Falaise. The RAF dropped short, causing 400 casualties among Commonwealth troops, including 65 killed and 91 missing. Many were blown to bits. A recent history of the RAF explained why: "It appeared that someone had omitted to inform Bomber Command that the Canadians standard color for marking their positions was yellow; this was Bomber Command's target-indicating colour, and 77 aircraft which had gone astray proceeded to bomb on yellow marks (the more the troops burnt yellow flares to show their position the more the errant aircraft bombed them)."[48] In a twist of fate 44 of the bomber crews dropping short were Canadian; the Poles suffered along with the Canadians. The RAF, adding insult to injury, almost killed one of its own; Air Marshal Sir Arthur Coningham and a Canadian corps commander were in the midst of one of the concentrations of short bombs.[49]

Allied heavy bombers did not fly another close support mission until 16 November 1944 when they participated in the preliminary bombardment of Operation Queen, a US First Army offensive in the Huertgen Forest region near Aachen. The overall performance of the heavy bombers in the close support role during the campaign in northwestern Europe indicates that they were not entirely suitable weapons. They did not belong on the tactical battlefield unless all the other ground or tactical air firepower available was insufficient for the contemplated task. A flyswatter and a sledgehammer can both kill flies, but the ease of use of the former made it far easier to control and more effective than the sound and force of the latter. In three out of four cases, close support of the ground troops, although spectacular, achieved little compared with the effort involved. The ground troops did not achieve a breakthrough. In the fourth instance, St. Lo, the heavy bombers expedited the success of a massive ground offensive by undercutting German resistance and probably reducing American casualties.

The attacks in support of Montgomery, who faced the bulk of the Germans' high-quality armored formations, could do little because Montgomery did not have the preponderance of strength necessary to overwhelm the troops facing him. Sheer weight of fire cannot make up for lack of manpower against a first-class opponent. The Panzer Lehr Division held on for one more day despite its drenching from the air. Had the Germans had reserves available, they might well have delayed the breakthrough for days. The decisive factors in the St. Lo breakthrough were Bradley's massing of four divisions on a single division front and the Germans' total lack of reserves to respond. This blow would have succeeded in any case, but the heavy bomber attack helped the assault penetrate the German lines more quickly and with fewer American casualties.

Notes

1. Webster and Frankland, *Strategic Air Offensive*, appendix 48, table: Small Targets in Occupied Territory March–September 1944, 4:462.

2. Memo, Anderson to director of operations, 21 July 1944, Spaatz Papers, Subject File 1929–1945.

3. Memo, Spaatz to CGs Eighth and Ninth Air Forces, subject: Aviation Fuel, 28 July 1944, AFHSO microfilm reel A1879-1, fr. 2037.

4. Webster and Frankland, appendix 49, Table 4: Monthly German Production and Imports of Finished Oil Products, January 1944–March 1945, 516.

5. AHB Narrative, *The Liberation of North-West Europe*, vol. 4, *The Breakout and Advance to the Lower Rhine, June–Sept 1944*, PRO AIR 41/67, 23.

6. Zuckerman, *Apes to Warlords*, 276.

7. See Webster and Frankland (3:166–73) for a discussion on the improvement in British accuracy for the last year of the war. Much of this improvement came from Bomber Command's use of electronic bombing aids such as Oboe and GH. The accuracy of both guidance systems surpassed

that of the H2X employed by the Americans. For similar coverage and a comparison of the average bomb weight carried by US and British heavy bombers, see the report of the BBSU, *Strategic Air War against Germany 1939–1945*, 42–50. A copy of this work can be found in the files of the AFHRA, Maxwell AFB, Ala., 512.552-11(c). Effectiveness is a combination of accuracy and bomb damage. The evidence indicates that Bomber Command, on the whole, delivered more of its bombs closer to its aiming points than USSTAF. In any case, many British bombs were much larger than American ones and, when on target, inflicted a higher degree of damage. German reports of damage to oil targets after AAF and RAF raids speak of the greater damage caused by the heavier British ordnance.

8. AHB Narrative, *Breakout and Lower Rhine*, 4:52. This monograph has detailed examinations of several of the heavy bomber ground support operations.

9. D'Este, *Decision in Normandy*, 370–78. This book offers particularly good insights into British methods, performance, and personalities during the Normandy campaign.

10. Tedder, *With Prejudice*, 571.

11. D'Este, 385.

12. Leigh-Mallory, Diary, 18 and 19 July 1944, PRO AIR 37/784.

13. Ambrose, *Supreme Commander*, 439.

14. Bradley, *Soldier's Story*, 330; Weigley, *Eisenhower's Lieutenants*, 137.

15. Bennett, *Ultra in the West*, 99–101.

16. Blumenson, *Breakout and Pursuit*, 220. Blumenson's account of Cobra is by far the most detailed, accurate, and objective published to date.

17. Ibid.

18. Bradley, 341.

19. Blumenson, 220. See also the report by Col Harold W. Ohkle to CG, USSTAF, 14 August 1944, subject: "Report on Investigation," Spaatz Papers, Subject File 1929–1945.

20. Bradley, 341.

21. Diary, entry for 19 July 1944, Vandenberg Papers, Diaries.

22. USAF Oral History Program Interview, Gen Elwood R. Quesada, 12–13 May 1975, AFHRA, file no. K239.0512-838.

23. Blumenson, 221.

24. Special Report on Operations 24 and 25 July, Headquarters, Eighth Air Force, n.d. [ca. 9 August 1944], AFHSO microfilm reel B 5050, frame 1185; Diary, entry for 23 July 1944, Vandenberg Papers, Diaries.

25. Craven and Cate, *Argument to V E Day*, 3:230.

26. Blumenson, 231.

27. Hinsley, *British Intelligence*, vol. 3, pt. 2, 229.

28. Diary, entry for 24 July 1944, Vandenberg Papers, Diary, box 1, Manuscript Division, Library of Congress, Washington, DC.

29. Memo for Gen Spaatz's Diary, subject: Operation Cobra from Maj Gen Frederick L. Anderson, 24 July 1944, Spaatz Papers, Diary.

30. Diary, entry for 24 July 1944, Vandenberg Papers, Diary.

31. Bradley, 347–48; Bradley's memo for the record of 25 July 1944, Hanson Collection, Military History Institute, Carlisle, Pa.

32. Hinsley, 228.

33. Blumenson, 240.

34. D'Este, 393. See also Air P/W Interrogation Detachment Report, APWIU (Ninth AF Adv.) 63/1945, 29 May 1945, Spaatz Papers, Subject File 1929–1945. Bayerlein was a favorite of postwar American interrogators because his excellent English enabled him to present his case more sympathetically than some of his compatriots.

35. Hinsley, 231.

36. Bennett, 102.

37. Blumenson, 246.

38. Ibid., 236. Blumenson bases his figures on a USSTAF report of 14 August 1944. A possible contributing factor to McNair's death was his complete deafness. He may not have heard the dropping bombs until it was too late to take cover.

39. Blumenson, 236.

40. Special Report on Operations, 24 and 25 July 1944, Col Walter K. Todd, deputy chief of staff for operations to commanding general, Eighth Air Force, n.d. [ca. 8 August 1944], AFHSO microfilm reel B5050, frs. 1181–1204.

41. Letter, Bradley to Eisenhower, 28 July 1944, US Army Military History Institute, Carlisle, Pa., Bradley Papers, Correspondence with Eisenhower.

42. Craven and Cate, 3:250–51.

43. Weigley, 204.

44. Letter, Doolittle to Spaatz, 10 August 1944, Doolittle Papers, box 18; Freeman, *Mighty Eighth War Diary*, 319.

45. Stacey, *Official History of the Canadian Army*, vol. 3, *Victory Campaign*, 223–24.

46. Weigley, 204. Hamilton, *Master of the Battlefield* (785) contains a misleading account of the Eighth's performance on 8 August. In this hagiography of Montgomery, the author claims that, after the brilliant initial Canadian breakout, bombers of Spaatz's Eighth Air Force ran amok, bombing their own troops and causing more casualties than on the first day of Cobra, when Collins had to close down the offensive and start again the following day.

47. Report of Bombing Results by Units of 1st Bombardment Division, 8 August 1944, n.d. [ca. 10 August 1944], AFHSO microfilm reel B5050, frames 1647–1657.

48. Terraine, *Time for Courage*, 661.

49. Stacey, 3:243–45.

The Combined Bomber Offensive
and the Holocaust

All that was needed was to bomb the train tracks. The Allies bombed the targets nearby. The pilots only had to nudge their crosshairs. You think they didn't know? They knew. They didn't bomb because at that time the Jews didn't have a state, nor the political force to protect themselves.

> —Benjamin Netanyahu, Israeli prime minister
> Auschwitz Death Camp
> 23 April 1998

On 2 July 1944 the Fifteenth Air Force put 509 heavy bombers and 1,200 tons of bombs over targets in or near Budapest. The raid, the largest single day's concentration of heavy bombers over Hungary during the Second World War, underlined the Allies' ability to bomb any Hungarian target at any given time. The Fifteenth's effort that day had an unintended but extremely beneficial side effect.

American B-17s and B-24s not only savaged their assigned targets, refineries, rail yards, and airfields, but they also struck the mind of the Hungarian Quisling regime. The timing of the mission coincided, apparently quite unintentionally on the part of either Spaatz or Twining or other portions of the US government, with an Anglo-American diplomatic initiative. The Allies had learned of the Hungarian government's acquiescence in and support of the liquidation of Hungary's Jews at the hands of the Germans. Both Allied governments had threatened the Hungarians with retribution unless they stopped transporting their Jews to the German-operated death camp at Auschwitz. On 4 July the Hungarian prime minister informed the German minister in Budapest that Allied threats to bomb rail lines to the death camp and to attack government ministries in Budapest involved with the shipment of Jews alarmed his government.[1] Transportations stopped on 6 July, after carrying approximately 435,000 Jews to Auschwitz since 15 May 1944.

Three hundred thousand Jews remained in Hungary. Many succumbed from suffering experienced in German-established ghettos, from German-inspired anti-Semitism, and from the fighting between the Red Army and Axis forces, but relatively few met their fate in a death camp—the final portion of most Jews in the hands of the Germans. As for their brethren already gassed and cremated in Poland, one can only speculate on whether or not a threat to the Hungarian government, backed up by a mass raid of all 700 of the Fifteenth's bombers on the administrative center of Budapest, would have ended the transports sooner. Since the slaughter at Auschwitz during the Hungarian shipments averaged over 8,300 persons per day, every minute was precious.

The 2 July attack, although flown against unrelated targets and for unrelated motives, was the only bombing raid of the war with a direct and significant effect on the holocaust. It would appear to have succeeded because it struck the weak government of an Axis satellite. Hungary still retained some autonomy, and, within its governmental ranks, there was no consensus of opinion in cooperating with the SS in the destruction of its Jews. For example, Adm Niklos Horthy, regent of Hungary, had successfully resisted handing over Hungary's Jews until the coup of March 1944 effectively ended his control of his country's government. Even afterwards, Horthy, who remained the titular head of state until October 1944, and other elements within the regime continued to oppose extermination of Hungary's Jews, perhaps from principle or from fear of postwar Allied reprisals. However, the Allies possessed no such leverage over Hitler's government within Germany or its occupied territories.

The question of why the Anglo-Americans did not use their air superiority over Europe to intervene in the slaughter of millions of innocents has become a matter of intense and emotional debate. How can anyone with knowledge of the Nazi death apparatus remain emotionally detached from its horrific practices or arrive at a completely objective synthesis of this subject? From the perspective of over half a century, I believe that Pres. Franklin D. Roosevelt and Prime Minister Winston S. Churchill erred in not ordering the bombing of Auschwitz. It is my judgment that by July 1944 the Anglo-Americans had the knowledge and capability to begin the destruction of the Birkenau Death Camp. This task, which would have taken several weeks to accomplish, would have sent an unmistakable message to the Nazis to halt their genocide and may have prevented the extermination of tens of thousands of individuals.[2] Furthermore, fulfillment of that single task, undertaken in the summer of 1944 when the US Army Air Forces had reached their full European deployment of 62 heavy bombardment groups, would not have constituted a significant diversion of force from the ultimate Allied goal of winning the war. I also believe the destruction of the gas chambers and crematoria would have been a gesture toward posterity in the sense that it might have lessened the charges that the Allies did nothing to help Hitler's victims and may have provided a precedent for even stronger actions against future examples of man's inhumanity toward man in Cambodia, Rwanda, and Yugoslavia.

The bombing of Auschwitz is the focus of this essay because it was one of the most dramatic examples of the Anglo-Americans' failure to intervene. An analysis of the capabilities of Allied airpower, when compared to the course of the holocaust, further reveals that the bombing of Auschwitz in the summer of 1944 has become the central point of this attention because airpower could not have effectively struck that or any other death camp earlier.

By July 1942 the Nazis had established six death camps in Poland for the extermination of Jews and others. The Germans built all these camps far from the prying eyes of western Europeans and, except for Chelmno, out of range of Allied bombers flying from and returning to airfields in Great Britain. From 1939 to 1945 Royal Air Force Bomber Command, stationed in England, hit only one target in Poland—the port of Gydnia—once in March 1942 and twice in December 1944. It could have struck only one death camp, Chelmno, approximately 85 miles south of Gydnia and then only in the unlikely event that it could have located that camp during a night mission. But there is no evidence that the RAF knew of the camp's existence. Flying from and returning to English bases from August 1942 through May 1945, the US Eighth Air Force struck Gydnia twice (October 1943 and April 1944); Posen, 180 miles west of Warsaw, twice (April and May 1944); and Krzesinski, near Posen, once (May 1944). From 21 June through 18 September 1944, the Eighth conducted a series of shuttle-bombing missions called Operation Frantic, from English airfields to Soviet bases in the Ukraine. These missions could have hit both Auschwitz and Majdanek, the only death camps operating during that period.

Two of the Eighth's Frantic missions have a particular interest for students of the holocaust. On 8 August 1944, 55 bombers, flying from Soviet fields, dropped 109 tons of bombs on the refinery at Trzebinia, about 20 miles from Auschwitz. On 18 September 1944, 107 B-17s, departing from English fields and landing in the Soviet Union, dropped supplies—most of which fell in German hands—on Warsaw to aid the Polish Home Army, which had risen against the common enemy. This raid, and other supply drops on Warsaw flown by Allied air forces in the Mediterranean, demonstrated that the Anglo-Americans had some capability to aid groups in occupied German territory, if they had the desire to do so. One might also note that these raids were personally ordered by Churchill and Roosevelt over the objections of their airmen, who regarded the missions as militarily ineffective and too costly in casualties.[3] The 18 September mission to Warsaw ended Operation Frantic. Stalin refused to authorize any further missions, while the Americans lost interest, in part because of political differences with the Soviets and partly because the Soviet summer offensive had already overrun most of the eastern targets intended for the operation.

Heavy bombers flying from England could have had little impact on the holocaust before the summer of 1944, but as David Wyman and others have indicated, Anglo-American heavy bombers flying from Italy had the range to reach Auschwitz. However, the American heavy bombers of the US Fifteenth Air Force, created in November 1943, and medium and heavy bombers of RAF No. 205 Group did not deploy from North Africa to Italy until December 1943. RAF No. 205 Group would have had the same problem as Bomber Command in locating and attacking Auschwitz at night. Although the Fifteenth had Auschwitz in reach by December 1943, it did not have the long-range escort fighters that enabled it to operate deep into enemy territory with acceptable losses until the end of March 1944.[4] It began operations against Hungary by attacking the Budapest rail marshaling yards on 3 April 1944. The next day, the Allies

401

flew their first photoreconnaissance sortie over the I. G. Farben synthetic oil and rubber plant at Auschwitz and began sustained operations over Rumania by attacking the Bucharest marshaling yards.[5] By then, all the Polish death camps had discontinued operations, save Majdanek, liberated by the Russians in July 1944, and Auschwitz.

On 7 July 1944 the Fifteenth dispatched its first raids to targets near Auschwitz: 448 bombers and 1,150 tons of bombs against the refinery complexes at Odertal and Blechhammer, 60 miles northwest of the death camp. The Americans continued to attack these targets through 26 December 1944, expending almost 4,200 sorties and 9,250 tons of bombs. Six weeks later, on 20 August, the Fifteenth sent the first of three raids against the I. G. Farben Industries at Auschwitz, using 127 bombers and 334 tons of bombs. The Americans followed up these raids on 13 September (96 bombers, 236 tons), 18 December (49 bombers, 109 tons), and 26 December (95 bombers, 170 tons). From 29 August through 19 December, the Americans also bombed two Czechoslovakian targets within 40 miles of the camp: Moravska Ostrava (286 sorties, 708 tons) and Bohumin (34 sorties, 75 tons).

Birkenau ceased its mass killing operations in mid-November 1944. For each and every day before that date, the complete destruction of its crematoria/gas chamber complexes might have saved more than 1,000 lives every 24 hours. But this does not alter the fact that 95 percent of the 5.8 million Jews and millions of others who died in Hitler's death camps, concentration camps, executions, and ghettos died before the Allied airpower had both the knowledge and capacity to interfere.

Next is the question of the feasibility of conducting a bombing raid aimed at the gas chambers and crematoria of the Birkenau Death Camp. The target was a factory complex, albeit one that produced and disposed of corpses rather than one that manufactured war matériel. In addition to its above-ground facilities, made of modern brick construction designed to support heavy machinery and resist heat and fire, it contained below- or slightly-above-ground-level structures with dirt-covered concrete roofs of undetermined thicknesses. The target was in close proximity to workers' housing, and those workers, although many of them were technically enemy nationals, would have to be considered pro-Allied. Consequently, its destruction would require an accurate bombing attack designed to minimize damage to friendly civilians. (The Allied airmen planning raids on Auschwitz would assuredly have been unaware of the psychological outlook of the prisoners, who would have gladly accepted their own deaths at the hands of American or British airmen, as long as it resulted in the destruction of the camp.) Auschwitz could not be attacked at night because it was too small to appear on the British H2S radar carried in RAF bombers and was also beyond the range of ground-based electronic night-bombing aids such as Oboe and GH. Night bombers would have difficulty identifying the target and even greater problems in hitting it without destroying nearby barracks, which would be jammed to overflowing at night. Day bombers attacking Auschwitz in cloudy or overcast conditions would encounter similar problems. The target required a daylight, clear-weather assault.

Unlike David Wyman or Stuart Erdheim, who suggest that the Allies should or could have employed RAF Mosquito attack aircraft to attack this target complex, I believe the nature of the facilities would tend to rule out attack by such aircraft and their crews, especially by units reserved for "special operations," such as the support of espionage and partisan organizations in occupied Europe, or by units trained in conventional low-level attacks. Examples of such operations were the Mosquito attacks on the Amiens Prison, the Dutch records facility, and Gestapo headquarters in Oslo and Copenhagen. These missions, consisting of a few aircraft, struck a single structure at low altitudes and followed routes largely over water, where they would not be detected and tracked until close to their targets. Such would not be the case for a long land route from the Adriatic Sea to southern Poland. The use of 40 such fast aircraft to attack several buildings from slightly differing headings at approximately the same time, or in closely coordinated waves, would have presented a daunting, perhaps insurmountable, problem in coordination and mission planning. In addition, a close examination of the tactics employed in low-level Mosquito attacks shows that, with the single exception of experimental tactics unsuccessfully used on V-1 launching sites, they always attacked above-ground facilities and then only with straight-ahead or shallow-dive approaches.[6] Such tactics, although highly accurate against walls and the sides of buildings, would be less effective against the gas chambers at Auschwitz, which were below or only slightly above ground level. As long as the chambers were operational, the SS could dispose of bodies they produced by burning them in pyres composed of rails and ties, such as the Germans used at Auschwitz during the Hungarian transports whenever the daily number of bodies produced surpassed the capacity of the crematoria.

As Wyman and Erdheim have further suggested, American P-38 fighter-bombers flying at extreme range could have attacked the death camp. Those aircraft employed steeper diving angles than the Mosquitoes and would have had a better chance of landing bombs on the gas chambers. However, what is feasible is not necessarily what is practical. The 10 June 1944 raid of the 82d Fighter Group, which Erdheim identifies as a prime example of P-38 capability, was a one-time special mission flown to attack the highest-priority target in Europe, a relatively undamaged refinery complex at Ploesti that had escaped many previous heavy-bomber attacks. There was no need to fly such a specialized mission to Auschwitz until other, more conventional, attacks had been tried. In addition, the 82d Fighter Group's attack on Ploesti assigned one squadron to each of three aiming points, only one of which sustained major damage. Given the substantially weaker defenses at Birkenau, one might expect a P-38 raid to land bombs on at least two or all three of its aiming points. Even so, the raid would have to be repeated at least three times to hit all four crematoria and all four gas chambers.

B-25 medium bombers and B-17 and B-24 heavies, all equipped with the same Norden bombsight, could have attacked with their standard medium- or high-altitude tactics. Their bombs, angled to drop straight down—provided they possessed the necessary penetrative force and weight—could have destroyed both the crematoria and the gas chambers. Although the twin-engined B-25 medium bombers may theoretically have had the range with a minimum bomb load to attack Auschwitz and return, the Americans rarely employed them at such extreme ranges. They were more vulnerable to flak and to fighter defenses along the route because of their lower operating altitudes. Nor, despite Erdheim's example of the B-25 attack on Toulon, is there any evidence to suggest that American medium bombers were, on average, substantially more accurate than American heavy bombers. Also, American medium bombers in the Mediterranean belonged to the Twelfth, not the Fifteenth, Air Force. Their use would have required an entirely different chain of command. There is no reason to suppose that going through British general Maitland Wilson, the Allied theater commander in the Mediterranean, and American lieutenant general Ira C. Eaker, commander of the Mediterranean Allied Air Forces, would have posed more of a problem than going through Gen Dwight D. Eisenhower, the Allied commander for the European theater, and Lieutenant General Spaatz. However, no research has yet shown that either Wilson or Eaker were ever approached on the use of the B-25s to bomb the death camp. There would have been no reason to do so.

The four-engined B-17s and B-24s not only carried heavier bomb loads than the B-25s, but they also, at over 600 miles, counted Auschwitz as a target well within their range. In addition, the Fifteenth Air Force, as compared to the Twelfth, had infinitely greater experience in planning and conducting long-range strikes against industrial targets. The Fifteenth already had prepared a target folder for the I. G. Farben synthetic complex at Oswiecim supported by the Auschwitz slave-labor complex, a mere seven miles from the Birkenau Death Camp. When the Fifteenth attacked these targets with one of its bomb wings, composed of five or more groups of heavy bombers (approximately 175 bombers), it would not have been an insurmountable problem to give two of those groups primary visual aiming points in the death camp. Furthermore, it seems logical that the Fifteenth would have handled the issue of collateral damage (the death of prisoners within the camp from Allied bombs) in the same manner as the American Eighth Air Force dealt with the bombing of transportation targets within French cities in April, May, and June 1944, where General Spaatz instructed his aircrews to take all reasonable precautions to avoid hitting friendly civilians.[7] Had the Anglo-

Americans chosen to bomb Birkenau, the American heavy bomber would have been their weapon of choice.

Heavy-bomber missions against Auschwitz may have even offered the opportunity to send the strongest possible message to the Nazis. Given the permission of Soviet dictator Joseph Stalin—and who can judge if this would have been granted?—a raid on the death camp could have been conducted as part of Operation Frantic, American shuttle bombing from bases in the Soviet Union. Such a mission would have sent a combined Anglo-American–Soviet warning to the Germans and given a strong indication to the people of occupied Europe and the Allies' own populations of the desire to end the holocaust.

In any case, it seems unlikely that a single raid by any type of Allied aircraft could have destroyed all the facilities at once and halted the exterminations. At least three, if not four, separate strikes would probably have been required. Had one of those strikes encountered overcast at Auschwitz, then it would have had to divert to another target, necessitating the scheduling of additional missions.[8] The history of strategic bombing has repeatedly shown that targets are often far more resilient than expected. German industry, for example, maintained production in plants with roofs blown off and outside walls breached. Could the crematoria have continued to function with their chimneys down, or their roofs blown away, or an outside wall collapsed? Were the ovens sturdy enough to survive all but a direct hit? As for the gas chambers, would one or two holes through their roofs, quickly repaired with a steel plate and two feet of earth, have made them any less deadly? It is possible that Birkenau might have been far less vulnerable to bomb damage than the proponents of bombing have acknowledged, even to themselves. Furthermore, how quickly could the Nazis have repaired damage? They had a virtually unlimited supply of slave labor on site. Also, the Allies would not have sent these strikes on consecutive days. Their standard operating pattern would have been to space the raids two or three weeks apart to confuse the enemy, carry out other priority missions, assess bomb damage, and wait for optimum weather. Therefore, the destruction of Auschwitz could have stretched over a period of six to eight weeks from the date of the first strike. As already noted, from 7 July 1944, the last of the Hungarian transports, through late November 1944, when Himmler ordered the SS to discontinue exterminations, the camp averaged somewhat over 1,000 murders per day, a fraction of its daily physical capacity of 6,000. The first raid or two would have knocked out excess capacity but may not have slowed the killing process in the least.

If destruction of the extermination facilities required a minimum of four missions of approximately 75 effective heavy-bomber sorties each, would those 300 sorties have constituted a significant diversion of force? In July 1944 the Fifteenth launched 10,716 effective heavy-bomber sorties and dropped 27,400 tons of bombs; in August, it sent out 10,708 effective heavy-bomber sorties and dropped 26,200 tons of bombs. Three hundred sorties and 900 tons of bombs, or even twice that number, would not have been a substantial diversion of this total effort. Even if one assumes that the 300 sorties, because of their deep penetration into German-occupied territory, would all have come at the direct expense of the Fifteenth's highest-priority target, the German oil supply, the effort expended on Birkenau would have amounted to about 7 percent of that effort. In July and August 1944—a period of very heavy attacks on Ploesti, Rumania—the Fifteenth directed 5,059 sorties and 12,054 tons against oil targets. Although the Anglo-American air leaders would have certainly begrudged any diversion of their forces from their already assigned targets, it would seem that the amount of force required to have put Birkenau's gas chamber and crematoria facilities out of action would not have seriously delayed the accomplishment of other goals.

This could not be said about a campaign to destroy the German transportation net leading to Auschwitz. As this study notes in its examination of the pre–D-day and winter 1944 transportation bombing campaigns, such an effort requires repeated heavy raids to gradually wear down a transportation system to the point where it can no longer carry an appreciable wartime load. Such a campaign could never completely halt all traffic. Given the nature of the Nazis' effort concerning the holocaust, it seems likely that they would have insisted on continuing to push the shipment of Jews to the death camp. Such a campaign would have consumed far more effort than a direct attack on the camp, with no guarantee of success. It would have required a diversion of effort and scale that would have invoked the greatest resistance from Allied air leaders.

Destruction of the death camp with a direct attack was a limited and attainable task. However, expansion of that priority into one implementing a systematic bombing campaign against the vast SS organization of camps and industrial enterprises that had metastasized throughout Nazi Europe would have required a significant diversion of force. Allied air leaders would have strenuously objected to such an effort, and it seems unlikely that Roosevelt or Churchill would have overruled them.

To answer the question of when the Anglo-Americans could have begun attacks on the death camp, one must first satisfy two more queries: (1) When did the Allies have the physical capability to launch a sustained series of attacks against the camp? and (2) When did the Allied leadership (Roosevelt, Churchill, and their combined chiefs of staff) possess authoritative knowledge of Auschwitz's purpose and location? The first of the two questions is easily answered. Fifteenth Air Force, for reasons noted earlier, could not have begun a series of operations against Birkenau until the beginning of April 1944. It is unfortunate that it did not do so, because a series of successful bombing attacks on the death camp in April 1944 would probably have disrupted the mass transportations of the Jews of Hungary, and saved, at least momentarily, hundreds of thousands of lives.

However, in April 1944 the Anglo-American leadership had not yet come to a complete appreciation of Auschwitz's function and location. Richard Breitman, of course, presents an irrefutable case that portions of the Allied governments possessed all the information necessary to deduce the exact site and role of the camp by mid-1943, if not before. He fails to make the case that the Allies had fully analyzed and appreciated this information. For example, the Ultra code breakers at Bletchley Park had known about and routinely decrypted the series of German police reports that contained detailed data on the course of the holocaust. However, Ultra had limited resources and other intelligence-collection priorities. Consequently, it concentrated on bomb damage assessment data in the police messages and on other series of messages that had a more direct influence on military strategy and operations. Breitman does not show that those Allied leaders in a position to affect bombing policy were made aware of all the necessary information and were then confronted with a decision as to take action.

Naturally, some intelligence of the holocaust did reach the leadership, and they reacted by authorizing various declarations and radio broadcasts denouncing it. Two additional circumstances, when joined with already-held knowledge, finally prodded Churchill to intervene on 7 July 1944. First, the Vrba-Wetzler Report, not available to Anglo-American governments until June 1944, not only provided explicit, authoritative details of the horrors at Birkenau, but it also actually reached the hands of the highest leadership. Second, the Allied leadership knew of the Hungarian Jewish transports, begun mid-May 1944, and could now visualize their fate. Hence, Allied airmen could not have been ordered to commence planning the raid until the beginning of July or later, after the decision had worked its way through the British Foreign Office and Air Ministry and the US State Department and War Department. In addition, both Roosevelt and Churchill would have to have given their approval, probably on the record, to this politically significant change in bombing policy and priorities. Given a minimum of two weeks of planning, which includes prompt access to the necessary aerial photo-reconnaissance, bombing could not have begun until after the Hungarian transports had stopped. As noted above, high-priority oil targets near Auschwitz, known to Allied targeteers long before June 1944, were not attacked by the Fifteenth before 7 July 1944. Given the six to eight weeks needed to physically destroy the gas chambers and crematoria and assuming the Germans did not invest in an effort to rebuild them, Auschwitz may have ceased to function by 1 September 1944.

Of course, there is no way to calculate how many of the lives spared by bombing of Birkenau might have succumbed later in improvised extermination facilities, labor camps, and ghettos before the end of the conflict. Nor is there a way to know what the Nazi leadership's reactions may have been. After all, a prime rationale for bombing the camp was to send a message to the Nazis to end their policy of genocide. Who can state with assurance that the leveling of that death camp would have halted an insane policy supported by a demented ideology? In this instance, I must agree with Gerhard L. Weinberg, who stated, "The idea that men who were dedicated to the killing program, and who saw their own careers and even their own lives tied to its continuation, were likely to be halted in their tracks by a few line cuts in the railways or the blowing up of a gas chamber is preposterous."[9] One might even ask the hard question: of Is an indication that the Allies are willing to devote hundreds of aerial sorties to stopping the extermination an incentive for the Nazis to halt the process, or does it encourage them to proceed in hopes of diverting yet more Allied airpower from oil and armaments plants? We will never know the answer to these speculations because the Allies failed to act, allowing the tragedy of the death camp to continue.

If a bombing campaign of six to eight or more weeks were to be effective against Auschwitz, it probably would have begun in mid-July and would had to have begun no later than mid-September. Not only would beginning the bombing in October 1944 have been too late to save many lives, but also the weather in that month was so bad that the Fifteenth flew only 5,800 sorties—the least of any month since March 1944. Nor should one lose sight of the dramatic sweep of events occurring elsewhere on the continent. On 6 June 1944 only a few days before the Vrba-Wetzler Report reached the Allied leadership, the Anglo-Americans commenced the cross-channel invasion from Great Britain to France. The Normandy invasion was the Western Allies' single most important military operation of the war. If it failed the war might have been extended for years as the Germans would have been freed to devote far more resources to the eastern front, where they might have gained a stalemate or convinced the Soviets to seek a separate peace. At the same time as the invasion, the Anglo-Americans had apparently broken the deadlock on the ground in Italy: taking Rome on 4 June and advancing north. The Eighth Air Force found itself tied to supporting the Normandy invasion until 21 June, and for much of the rest of summer devoted a substantial effort to combating the German V-1 pilotless bomb menace (of large, perhaps inordinate, concern to the British home front and leadership) or attacking its prime objective, German oil. The Fifteenth extended some support to ground operations in Italy, but expended its primary effort in the summer of 1944 in attacks on Axis oil installations. The bombing of the German oil industry, in postwar analysis, proved to have been the single most effective Allied bombing campaign of the war. It grounded the German air force and denied the priceless asset of mobility to the German ground forces. Without this campaign the Nazis may well have extended the war (and their genocides) by many months. The Soviet summer offensive began on 25 June 1944. Within a month it destroyed a German army group of some 50 divisions, and by 19 August 1944 it placed the Red Army at the gates of Warsaw and the borders of Hungary.

The window of opportunity for bombing the Auschwitz Death Camp opened just as these actions unfolded. For most of July 1944 the Air Ministry mulled over its options on Auschwitz and inexcusably delayed contacting General Spaatz, whose headquarters was only a few miles from the ministry building, until 2 August.[10] Spaatz expressed sympathy for the effort and asked for aerial photography of the camp.[11] However, he never received the appropriate intelligence, and, on 6 September 1944 (when the opportunity for bombing Birkenau had almost passed), the Air Ministry informed him that he no longer should consider the project.[12] Here again, our focus on the death camp should not obscure the events surrounding it. On 26 July, a week before Spaatz learned of a possible operation against Auschwitz, the Allies broke out of the Normandy beachhead. By mid-August the Germans were in full retreat from France, and on 25 August, amid scenes of tremendous emotion and excitement, the Allies liberated Paris. At almost the same instant, Rumania switched sides, trapping an entire German army unit and capsizing the entire German position in the Balkans. Bulgaria and Finland surrendered to the Soviets in early September. Finally, on 10 September, spearheads of the US Army reached the Franco-German border.

It appeared to many in the West, especially in light of Germany's collapse under somewhat similar circumstances in the First World War, that the conflict might end within weeks. Even in late October 1944, after the Allied ground forces had stalled in Poland, Italy, and northwest Europe, US Army chief of staff George C. Marshall informed Eisenhower that the US chiefs of staff contemplated issuing "at an early date" a directive for a supreme effort to end the war in Europe by 1 January 1945.[13]

With the advantage of hindsight we now know that the war would not end for many months and that the Allies should have attacked Birkenau as soon as possible. I do not offer the above review of events as an excuse for Allied inaction. I do, however, suggest that the reader should understand that in the minds of many Allied decision makers in late July through mid-September 1944, the urgency of combating the holocaust was subsumed in a larger hope that victory was in the offing.

The Allies *could* have bombed and destroyed Auschwitz, and they *should* have bombed and destroyed Auschwitz. Why didn't Roosevelt order it done? And why didn't Churchill follow up his interest expressed to Foreign Minister Anthony Eden on 7 July 1944, when he instructed him, somewhat cryptically, to write the Air Ministry and ask the Air Staff to examine the feasibility of bombing Auschwitz and to "get anything out of the Air Force you can and invoke me if necessary"?[14]

We cannot know; Roosevelt died before the question arose and, even had he lived, who can say how the "Sphinx of the Potomac" would have replied? Churchill never followed up his instructions to Eden. Probably because, given the context of his comments to Eden, Churchill was more concerned with stopping the Jewish deportations from Hungary than in actually bombing the death camp as a statement of policy. Hence, when the Hungarian government halted shipment of its Jews, Churchill had reached his objective and saw no need to pursue the matter. After the war, Churchill was apparently never asked why he did not act. (Martin Gilbert, one of the world's leading Churchill scholars and an expert on the holocaust, who, if anyone, would know if this occurred, offers us nothing on this point.)

As a Gentile I am uncomfortable with the implication that anti-Semitism is the most obvious and leading cause of the West's inactivity. But, as a historian I must acknowledge that anti-Semitism is a recurrent theme in Western civilization and that some decision makers in both the British and American governments were anti-Semites. If the holocaust stood alone as the sole instance of genocide in the twentieth century, anti-Semitism might have accounted for the world's inactivity. But anti-Semitism does not explain the world's inaction to the other genocides of the modern era. Benjamin Netanyahu came closer to an answer when he noted that European Jewry lacked political force or leverage in the Anglo-American governments to protect themselves. Western leaders made decisions affecting the lives and deaths of millions of souls every day. Perhaps, in the midst of the noise of a total war, it was only natural that they listened most closely to those with the nearest and loudest voices. This would also appear to apply to the victims of the other mass exterminations of the twentieth century. The Armenians, Cambodians, Rwandans, and Yugoslavs have had no greater, and possibly less, constituency within the West than did the Jews of Europe.

Notes

1. Martin Gilbert, *Auschwitz and the Allies* (New York, NY: Holt, Rinehart, and Winston, 1981), 266.

2. The number of lives spared at Birkenau Death Camp would depend on the precise date on which the camp ceased operations and whether or not the Germans resorted to alternate methods of execution and corpse disposal other than gas chambers and crematoria. It would appear that the average daily death rate at the camp from 7 July 1944 (when the mass Hungarian deportations ceased) and early November 1944, when the Germans discontinued mass killings) was between 1,100 and 1,400. German policy forbade the retention of records within the camp of the precise number of killings. The inmates kept an oral record of the arriving trains, but could only estimate the numbers selected for death. See David S. Wyman, *The Abandonment of the Jews: America and the Holocaust, 1941–1945* (New York: Pantheon Books, 1984), 304, who puts the figures at 50,000 deaths between 7 July and 20 August and 100,000 deaths between 21 August and November. Also see Gilbert, *Auschwitz and the Allies*, 326, who states that 34,000 died in October 1944. Wyman cites several sources, none dated later than 1970, for his estimates. I accept Wyman's numbers of those exterminated, at face value, although I would argue that not all of them would have been saved unless, by some unlikely miracle, the camp ceased operations entirely on 7 July 1944.

Immediately after the war the Soviet government announced that four million people may have died at the camp (Norman Davies, "Auschwitz," in I.C.B. Dear, *The Oxford Companion to World War II* [New York: Oxford Uni-

413

versity Press, 1995], 77). In 1981 Gilbert, *Auschwitz and the Allies*, 343, put the total of Jewish deaths at the camp, from June 1942 through June 1944, at 1.5 million. Finally, in 1991 the Auschwitz museum issued a revised total death count, all types of victims, as 1.2 to 1.5 million victims, 800,000 of which were Jews (Dear, *Oxford Companion to WW II*, 77). Clearly, there can never be an authoritative death total.

3. For a detailed description of the air operations in support of Warsaw, see Neil Orpen, *Airlift to Warsaw: The Rising of 1944* (Norman, OK: University of Oklahoma Press, 1984).

4. During Big Week (20–25 February 1944), when the Americans lacked sufficient long-range escort fighters in Italy, 657 of the Fifteenth's heavy bombers attacked aircraft manufacturing targets in southern Germany and Austria. Eighty-eight bombers fell victim to the German defenses, a loss rate of 13.4 percent, far in excess of the 5 percent loss rate that the AAF considered unsustainable. On 25 February, the Fifteenth lost 25 percent of its attacking aircraft, a loss rate above that suffered by the Eighth in its famous attacks on Schweinfurt.

5. Gilbert, *Auschwitz and the Allies*, 191.

6. See C. Martin Sharp and Michael J. F. Bowyer, *Mosquito* (London: Crecy Books, 1995), chap. 13, "Day Bombers," 143–45, and chap. 16, "Fighter Bombers," 235–59. The detailed discussion of attack tactics and missions flown by Mosquitoes in daylight bombing raids in these two chapters convincingly demonstrates that Mosquitoes did not use the steep-angle dive bombing (which would allow bombs to penetrate below ground level) and invariably struck only targets such as above-ground buildings, rail facilities, and industrial plants.

7. Notes of meeting at General Wilson's headquarters, 30 April 1944, Spaatz Papers, Diary.

8. Clouds over the target forced half the American sorties sent against the nearby Blechhamer synthetic complexes to use H2X radar. According to wartime operations analysis reports of the Eighth Air Force, visual bombing was 70 times more accurate than was radar bombing through 100 percent clouds. See Operational Analysis Section, Eighth Air Force, Report on Bombing Accuracy, Eighth Air Force, 1 September 1944 through 31 December 1944, 20 April 1945, USAF History Support Office, Bolling AFB, Washington DC, microfilm reel A5883, starting frame 566.

9. Gerhard L. Weinberg, "The Allies and the Holocaust," in Michael J. Neufeld and Michael Berenbaum, *The Bombing of Auschwitz: Should it Have Been Attempted?* (Lawrence, KS; University of Kansas Press, 2000).

10. Minutes, AM Norman Bottomley, deputy chief of the RAF staff, to the vice-chief of the RAF Staff (Intelligence), 2 August 1944, reproduced in the documentary appendix of Neufeld and Berenbaum, *Bombing of Auschwitz*.

11. Spaatz may even have turned the matter over to his target-planning officers. Forty-six years later former US Supreme Court justice Lewis F. Powell, Jr., one of Spaatz's intelligence officers, while admitting that after such a long time "memories grow dim," hinted as much when he wrote:

I do not recall any real interest at General Spaatz's headquarters in bombing Auschwitz or any other German death camp. To the extent that there was discussion, we were concerned that more internees would be killed than Germans. Our objective was to bring the war to an early end. This was far more important than bombing any particular German death camp. (Powell, to Richard G. Davis, letter, 5 July 1990).

Given Spaatz's request for photography, what information did Spaatz's headquarters examine in determining that a raid would cause too much collateral damage? Is it possible that they already had some photos of the camp available to them in London?

The official "Target Information Sheet" on the Monowitz facility, dated 18 July 1944 and prepared by RAF Intelligence, based on the 4 April 1944 overflight covers only the plant, not Birkenau. It would have been of little value to Spaatz's people. (For a copy of this "Target Information Sheet," see AF/HSO microfilm, reel A5286, frs. 156–63.)

12. Minutes, Bottomley to Spaatz, 6 September 1944, in the documentary appendix, Neufeld and Berenbaum, *Bombing of Auschwitz.*

13. See Forrest Pogue, *The United States Army in World War II*, subseries: *The European Theater of Operations*: *The Supreme Command* (Washington, DC: OCMH, GPO, 1954), 307.

14. Minutes, W. S. Churchill to Anthony Eden, 7 July 1944, in the documentary appendix to Neufeld and Berenbaum, *Bombing of Auschwitz.*

August

1 August: Polish Home Army in Warsaw rises against the Germans. Soviets refuse aid.

3 August: Fifteenth Air Force—one B-24 and one B-17 land in Switzerland after mission to Friedrichshafen.

4 August: Fifteenth Air Force—at the direct request of the Soviets' two fighter groups attack Focsani Airfield and land in Frantic bases. Eighth Air Force—two heavy bombers crash-land in Sweden after mission to Baltic targets. First Aphrodite (radio-controlled, war-weary B-17 mission) attacks V-Sites.

6 August: Eighth Air Force—attacks fourteen targets in Germany and sends second shuttle force, 75 B-17s and escorts, to Frantic bases in the USSR. Two heavy bombers land in Sweden. Fifteenth Air Force—fighters return from USSR.

8 August: Bomber Command and Eighth Air Force—aid British 2d Army lunge forward. American short bombs kill 65 Poles and Canadians and wound 265 more.

11 August: Eighth Air Force—one B-17 lands in Switzerland after mission to Saarbrücken.

12 August: Eighth Air Force—bombers return from Frantic mission.

13 August: Eighth Air Force—first use of TV-guided, 2,000-pound bomb.

14 August: Bomber Command—supports British 2d Army; short bombs kill 65 Poles and Canadians, 91 more are missing.

13–16 August: Fifteenth Air Force—bombs coastal installations and transportation targets in southern France in support of Allied invasion.

16 August: Fifteenth Air Force—one B-24 lands in Switzerland after mission to Friedrichshafen.

22 August: Soviets take Ploesti.

23 August: Rumania surrenders to the Allies.

24 August: Eighth Air Force—two B-24s land in Sweden after mission to central and north central Germany. Göbbels issues total mobilization decree for Germany. It conscripts women into the workforce, imposes a 60-hour workweek for all industry, and severely limits travel, amusements, printing, and publishing. An additional decree instructed all males between 16 and 60 to join the People's Army (Volksturm). Full mobilization of the war economy comes too late to affect the war's outcome.

25 August: Allies enter Paris. Eighth Air Force—five B-17s and one B-24 land in Sweden.

27 August: Bomber Command—first major bomb raid by day on Germany—Homburg synthetic oil plant.

29 August: Eighth Air Force—begins to employ two B-24 groups to "truck" medical supplies, critical spare parts, and gasoline from United Kingdom to continental bases close to American front lines.

31 August–1 September: Fifteenth Air Force—evacuates Allied POWs from Rumania.

In August 1944 the Eighth flew more than 18,000 effective bomber sorties and lost 218 bombers. Of the 47,000 tons of bombs dropped, 20,800 fell on France and 23,500 fell on Germany. The loss rate over Germany, 1.9 percent (174 bombers out of 9,200 sorties), reflected an increasing number of losses to flak and decreasing losses to fighter aircraft. In France it bombed Noball targets until, by the end of the month, the Allied ground forces finally overran those sites and rail targets. It hit the rail targets more to discommode the German retreat than to delay reinforcements. Over Germany, the Eighth expended almost two-thirds of its effort against air targets: 3,103 tons on airfields, 5,232 tons on assembly and components plants, and 2,358 on aeroengines (including 375 tons on Me-262 jet engines). It aimed another 6,152 tons of bombs at German oil facilities. These raids over some of the most heavily defended spots in Germany cost 116 heavy bombers—a loss rate of 1.7 percent. For all operations for the month, the Eighth lost 218 bombers (1.2 percent).

The bombs rained down on the air industry had little effect on output (the number of finished aircraft rolled out of the final assembly point). In August 1944 the Germans produced 3,020 single-engine fighters, their second highest total of the war. In September they would produce 3,375 fighters.[1] The Germans had dispersed their air industry, making it a difficult target. The bombs falling on oil facilities vitiated the productivity of the German aircraft industry. The number of fighters Germany pushed out the factory door became irrelevant because the amount of aviation gasoline Germany produced had fallen from approximately 165,000 tons in April to approximately 15,000 tons in August 1944.

Not only did the lack of fuel limit the number of operational sorties flown by the Luftwaffe interceptors, but also it forced the Luftwaffe to eliminate flight training. In September 1944 the German air force prohibited all flying except combat missions. In the last few months of the war, German pilots went into action with but 40 to 45 hours of training.[2] These poorly trained pilots had high accident and wastage rates, thus contributing to the diminishing combat readiness of the German air force. Since it did not have the fuel to fly them or adequate pilots to man them or even move them from their point of production, the number of new fighter aircraft the Luftwaffe possessed was meaningless. Many of the new aircraft produced quickly fell victim to Allied bombing and strafing on their factory or dispersal airfields without ever seeing combat. In this instance, as in others, critics of strategic bombing point to the rise in fighter production as an indication of the failure of bombing without placing that figure into the overall context of the strategic effort.

Bomber Command's delivered bomb tonnage—74,330 tons—in August 1944 exceeded the previous month by 10,000. Of the 16,543 effective sorties flown, the command sent 10,255 to France, 4,719 to Germany, and the rest to the Low Countries. Noball targets, with an emphasis on V-1 supply depots, dominated the command's efforts over France. However, it did fly two large missions in support of Montgomery's troops and other missions against the fortifications guarding Brest as well as the ships blocking the mouth of its port. After the Allied breakout from the Normandy peninsula, Hitler had ordered the garrisons of the major French ports, largely second-line troops to stay put. These forces, with no transportation and very weak organic structures, would have been swept up and destroyed had they joined in the general retreat of the mobile forces to Germany. By staying in place, the garrisons retained the support structures and fortifications of the port cities. They also would have ample opportunity to thoroughly wreck port facilities and block channels. The stand-fast order for the port garrisons reflected Hitler's never retreat attitude. More importantly, however, this stratagem kept the French ports closed to the Allies and forced them to funnel their supplies through a single entry point: Normandy. Because of the closure of the ports and the bottleneck at Normandy, the Allies literally ran out of gas at the German border and could not follow up the German retreat into Germany proper. The Allies responded by surrounding the ports with their own second-line troops, units of the reconstituted French army. The new French units were not equipped with large amounts of artillery; thus, when the Allies decided to make their move on a port, the French would need airpower for fire support.

As for the Reich, Bomber Command spread 946 Mosquito sorties, about 30 each night, from Berlin through virtually every major German city. They followed a pattern of one large concentration over a single target while dispatching one or two aircraft to other cities. The 4,000-pound "cookies" they delivered ruined many a night's sleep. Bomber Command also greatly increased the number of heavy sorties over Germany. During the month it launched 13 main force raids; including, on 27 August, its first major daylight raid over Germany, an attack on the Meerbeck benzoyl plant in Homburg. The 220 bombers on that raid suffered no losses. Another daylight raid hit synthetic oil sites and a third attacked the American General Motors (Opel) plant at Rüsselsheim. The remaining 10 main force attacks struck the city areas of Brunswick and Rüsselsheim (12 August), Stettin and Kiel (16 August), Bremen (18 August), Darmstadt (25 August), Kiel and Königsberg (26 August), and Königsberg and Stettin (29 August). Overall the night raids sustained a loss rate of 4.2 percent.

Closer examination reveals that raids on fringe targets, the North Sea ports, the Ruhr, and Darmstadt lost 37 bombers out of 1,795 effective sorties (2 percent). The losses would have been fewer had the German controllers not concentrated the night fighters on the force attacking Kiel on the night of 26 August (which lost 17 of 367 bombers) and missed or ignored the much smaller force attacking Königsberg. The 1,758 sorties making deeper penetrations into central Germany and the Baltic lost 114 bombers (6.5 percent), a figure that indicated that the German night fighter force still was a potent weapon. For all its operations in the month, the command lost 229 bombers (1.4 percent). However, the liberation of France would present Harris with new advantages and enable him to reduce the command's casualties still further.

The destruction of the German early warning radar system in France spelled the end of large, coordinated night fighter responses. The tactical depth that France had given the Luftwaffe defenses allowed the necessary time for the night fighters to become airborne and to concentrate as directed. But now the air controllers would have less time to identify and separate the main threats from Mosquitoes and less time to marshal their fighters against main-force thrusts. Interception operations that involved combat over France and the English Channel became far more difficult, while the bombers' exposure to the night defenses lessened considerably. The same problems confronted the Luftwaffe day fighters.

In August 1944 the Fifteenth Air Force bombed targets in nine different countries. Of the 26,000 tons of bombs it dropped, the largest quantity (5,970 tons) hit targets in France. This bombing supported the Anglo-American invasion of southern France on 14 August 1944. The Fifteenth struck marshaling yards, airfields, and beach fortifications. With slightly more than 20 percent of its effort, the Fifteenth tightened the thumbscrew on German oil. It struck refineries and oil storage facilities in Austria, Hungary, and Germany as well as synthetic oil in Czechoslovakia. The Fifteenth pounded Ploesti and other Rumanian oil refineries until the day that country switched allegiance from the Germans to the Allies. It also attacked German air units near Bucharest that had bombed the Rumanians in an attempt to keep them loyal to Germany.

At the end of the month, the Fifteenth evacuated Allied prisoners of war from Bucharest, almost all of them airmen. The prisoners reported that those taken in the low-level raid on Ploesti on 1 August 1943 had fared well. The Rumanians had admired their courage. Aircrews of the Fifteenth who participated in the high-altitude mass bombings of Ploesti and Bucharest reported less favorable treatment. The Rumanians had resented the collateral damage inflicted by high-level bombing.

Other targets were the synthetic oil and rubber plants at Oswiecim and Monowitz. On 20 August the Americans attacked the plant, flying tantalizingly close to the Auschwitz death camp—only seven miles away. The aircrews, the photoreconnaissance pilots, the photo interpreters, and mission planners concentrated their attention on the oil plant. It is unlikely that any of them knew of Auschwitz or its function. The oil raids cost the Fifteenth 119 bombers, for a loss rate of 3.4 percent; overall the Fifteenth's loss rate of 2 percent exceeded both the Eighth's and Bomber Command's. RAF 205 Group, whose sorties followed the same pattern but not necessarily the same timing as the Fifteenth's, again sustained the highest loss rate—4 percent.

Notes

1. Webster and Frankland, *Strategic Air Offensive*, appendix 49, table, Number of German Aircraft Produced by Types, Annually 1939–1944 and Monthly 1941–1944, 4:495.

2. USSBS, *Oil Division Final Report*, 2.

September

5 September: Eighth Air Force—one B-24 and one B-17 land in Switzerland.

8 September: Bomber Command—last raid by Stirlings. Germans begin launching V-2 rockets.

10 September: Eighth and Fifteenth Air Forces—begin bombing ordnance depots and AFV plants. US troops reach German border near Aachen.

11 September: Eighth Air Force—sends shuttle mission of 75 B-17s and escorts to Frantic bases in USSR.

12 September: Fifteenth Air Force—three B-24s land in Switzerland after mission to Munich.

13 September: Eighth Air Force—one B-17 lands in Switzerland.

14 September: Bomber Command and USSTAF—are removed from General Eisenhower's direction. General Spaatz gains more control over his target selection. General Spaatz and Air Marshal Norman Bottomley, deputy chief of the RAF air staff, agree on Strategic Bombing Directive No. 1.

15 September: Fifteenth Air Force—begins evacuation of Allied POWs from Bulgaria.

17 September: Eighth Air Force—supports Operation Market-Garden, a corps-sized airborne drop in the Low Countries, with largest fragmentation bomb attack of the war on 117 German antiaircraft batteries. Frantic mission returns via Italy.

18 September: Eighth Air Force—dispatches 250 B-24s to drop supplies for airborne troops. An additional 110 B-17s plus escorts drop supplies for the Polish Home Army in Warsaw and proceed to Frantic bases.

22 September: Eighth Air Force—last Frantic mission returns via Italy. Fifteenth Air Force—two B-24s land in Switzerland after mission to Munich.

23 September: Fifteenth Air Force—one B-17 lands in Switzerland after mission to Brux.

23–24 September: Bomber Command—breaches Dortmund-Ems Canal.

In September 1944 Harris discovered that France still had the capacity to provide a significant distraction for Bomber Command's efforts. Of the 58,500 tons of bombs dropped by the command in the month, slightly more than half (29,550) fell on occupied France. More than 95 percent of them fell on the port defenses of Brest, Le Havre, Boulogne, and Calais. The Allies needed these ports to expand the flow of their logistics into the continent.

Allied logistical planners had counted on the capture of the large, modern port of Brest to fulfill the supply needs of the Allied armies on the continent. The channel ports would provide closer ports, which required fewer trucks and trains to transport supplies to the front. However, when Brest fell, on 25 September, the Allies discovered that the Germans had completely demolished the port. This was more than offset by the capture of the ports of Antwerp, Amsterdam, and Rotterdam intact. Germany's failure to wreck these ports, especially Antwerp, constituted a strategic error of the first magnitude. Antwerp alone could support 50 divisions from a distance only one-third as long as that from the Breton Peninsula. The Germans also failed to inflict long-term damage on the port of Marseilles in southern France. It, too, could support up to 50 divisions and proved instrumental in keeping the Allied 6th Army

Group in supply. The Anglo-Americans required intact ports with heavy-lifting cranes because supplies from the United States—in the fall of 1944 and afterwards—arrived crated and unassembled in freighters to save shipping space. In the summer vehicles and other supplies had arrived combat loaded and assembled for quick unloading from landing ships. The rougher waters produced by winter weather created problems for the specialized assault landing ships, such as the landing ship tank (LST), and, in any case, they were needed in the Pacific and in Southeast Asia for operations against Japan.

Harris increased operations and tonnage over Germany by 40 percent but decreased total tonnage throughout the theater by 20 percent. Command accuracy on long-distance missions increased as Oboe transmitters and other electronic aids displaced forward into France from Britain. Bomber Command made eight major daylight attacks on synthetic oil, flying 1,078 effective sorties, dropping 4,482 tons, and losing 19 bombers. One major raid attacked a marshaling yard, Osnabrück (406 tons, 80 sorties, no losses); another (99 sorties, 573 tons, 14 lost) flying at 8,000 feet and below breached the Dortmund-Ems Canal, one of the most heavily used commercial waterways in Germany, near Münster. But the bulk of Bomber Command's effort over Germany went into area raids. After subtracting approximately 950 Mosquito sorties, Harris launched 14 area attacks comprising 3,330 sorties, 59 lost bombers, and 15,000 tons of bombs. The attack on Bremen on 16 September left 30,000 homeless; the mission against Kaiserslautern on 26 September destroyed one-third of the town; and a raid on Darmstadt on 11 September killed 10,000; and left 70,000 homeless.[1] In addition the command hit the town of Neuss with almost 3,000 tons in a single night, and struck Frankfurt, Kiel, and Karlsruhe with over 1,000 tons each. The loss rate from these raids, 1.8 percent, demonstrated the collapse of the German night fighter control system and gave Harris no incentive to discontinue the policy of area bombing.

Eighth Air Force dropped only 2,075 tons of bombs on France during September. On 3 and 5 September the Americans struck the defenses of Brest with 1,467 tons, and on 25 September, 214 bombers mistook Strasbourg for Ludwigshafen and released 608 tons on the wrong city. During the month the Eighth expended almost 90 percent of its efforts over Germany (12,831 sorties, 34,191 tons, and 243 lost aircraft). It dispatched 2,141 sorties, dropped 5,562 tons, and lost 83 bombers against synthetic oil and oil refineries. German production of aviation gasoline temporarily came to halt in mid-September while all oil production reached a low point for the year. The oil plants also produced byproducts of great value to the German war economy. By September 1944 the shutdown of the Luena and Ludwigshafen plants deprived the Germans of 63 percent of their synthetic nitrogen (the most vital component for making explosives), 40 percent of their synthetic methanol (a key component for advanced explosives), and 65 percent of their synthetic rubber. Diversion of the remaining nitrogen to the military resulted in no production of fertilizer for the 1945 harvest.[2]

The bombing effort against the air industry continued with approximately 5,000 tons directed toward those plants, half against Me-262 production. The Eighth sent an equal amount against tank production. High German losses in armored fighting vehicles (AFV) on both fronts led the Allies to conclude that the Germans were desperately short of AFVs. Technical intelligence tended to confirm this surmise. Studies of manufacturing dates on captured equipment determined that the Germans sent finished tanks to the front within a month of completion—an indication of a lack of reserve equipment. Using the same reasoning, Doolittle added another 594 sorties, 13 lost bombers, and 1,450 tons on ordnance depots. Marshaling yards in western Germany absorbed 12,000 tons of bombs—8,861 tons dropped by H2X and 3,219 dropped visually. In both cases the bomb loads contained an overall bomb mix of 80 percent high explosives and 20 percent incendiaries. But on days where the Eighth apparently anticipated cloudy conditions, the large missions usually carried a higher percentage of incendiaries. The Eighth attacked a catchall target category, "industrial areas," with approximately 2,450 tons of bombs.

In August 1944 after General Anderson's late July prohibition of city raids, the amount of such strikes declined to a small fraction of July's total. In July the Eighth dropped more tonnage on cities than in any other month of the war. However, in September the total of area bombings, openly acknowledged in American records, began to climb. Ninety percent of the area bombing used H2X. In late September, during a spate of poor weather, the Eighth launched four major raids: 25 September, Frankfurt, 1,097 tons, including 170 tons of incendiaries (an unsuccessful experiment with the British-developed Braddock firebomb); 27 September, Cologne, 1,212 tons, including 76 tons of incendiaries; 28 September, Magdeburg, 891 tons, including 184 tons of incendiaries; and 30 September, Münster, 840 tons, including 174 tons of incendiaries. Raids on AFVs and ordnance depots carried almost 40 percent incendiaries and dropped 80 percent of their total by H2X, most into major cities such as Kassel and Bremen.

Even the bombing of synthetic oil showed unusual bomb loads. Seventy percent of synthetic oil bombing used H2X. However, the Eighth firmly believed that oil facilities did not burn. In bombing such facilities when anticipating visual conditions, the bombers carried only high explosives. Even when anticipating unfavorable conditions, they carried few, if any, incendiaries. The Eighth was highly disciplined in loading the proscribed bomb mix for the target. For example, Noball targets required high explosives; a review of the Eighth's bomb loads for that target category demonstrates the air force's complete control over bomb loadings—out of 31,000 tons of bombs, nil incendiaries. But the September figures for synthetic oil bombing with H2X contain an anomaly. They include five raids on the Ludwigshafen synthetic plant, which was situated inside a large chemical complex bordered by workers' housing and near a major city. Germany's other oil plants were not located near built-up areas. The three largest raids carried an average of 30 percent incendiaries. On 8 September a raid on the associated chemical plant carried no incendiaries.

It would seem that there may be a relationship between H2X-assisted sighting, the use of bomb loads that include a large percentage of incendiaries when attacking targets in cities, and a desire to take advantage of H2X's known inaccuracy to maximize urban destruction. Bomber Command's statistics strengthen this correlation. In its first raids on a city, the command carried anywhere from 40 to 50 percent or higher incendiaries—standard procedure. Once fire-raising attacks had burnt out major sections of the city, creating firebreaks and lessening the area that ARP personnel had to patrol, the command switched to bomb loads mostly composed of high explosives. No target system other than city areas consistently required or received a bomb mix high in incendiaries. Although by this stage in the conflict, the command used Oboe, H2X, GH, and MH electronic guidance aids, most of the crews bombed on markers laid down by highly skilled pathfinders. The PFF crews, expert in the use of the electronic aids, could fly in at low level, mark the target (an art the RAF had mastered), and oversee and correct the attack. The Americans, too, made use of advanced electronic aids but not to the same extent as their British colleagues. The AAF used H2X for the bulk of its missions when bombing through overcast.

In September 1944 the Eighth, the Fifteenth, and Bomber Command participated in an unusual mission for heavy bomber aircraft—airlifting supplies to the continent. As noted above, the Allies' inability to open the French ports constricted the supply line of the Anglo-American ground forces pursuing the Germans. As the Americans, British, and Canadians closed to the German border, they literally ran out of gas and other vitally needed supplies. At the beginning of September, Allied airpower undertook to deliver gasoline, spare parts, medicine, and food to bases close to the front. Bomber Command flew 437 sorties into Melsbroek Airfield at Brussels. Harris probably limited his command's participation in the supply mission because of its heavy obligations to opening the ports by bombing their defenses. The Fifteenth flew 401 sorties into Lyon Airport. The Eighth flew 2,183 supply sorties into several fields, including Lille, Orleans, and Florennes, behind American lines. At one point Doolittle devoted 224 B-24s—one-fifth of the Eighth Air Force—to the task. In all the Eighth delivered 1,627 tons of supplies and 8,226 tons (2,703,255 gallons) of gasoline.[3] The Ninth Air Force's IX Troop Carrier Command (TCC), with its aircraft designed for hauling, delivered more than 20,000 tons of supplies and materials. For the heavy bombers it was another matter. Placing cans of gas and other objects not designed to fit in or to stay in bomb bays proved frustrating and tiring to the ground crews and supply personnel manhandling the goods.

The Eighth, Bomber Command, and the IX TCC had yet another joint task in the middle of the month—the support of Market-Garden, a three-division parachute drop into Holland. The Allies hoped to seize and hold a string of bridges from their front line all the way across the Rhine. Unfortunately the paratroopers failed to gain the last bridge. The miscarriage of the operation cost a British division and caused a Polish reinforcement brigade to be cut to ribbons. As to why Market-Garden did not succeed, the usual reasons apply: underestimating the enemy, failing to heed accurate intelligence, having inexperienced staff planners, and allowing politics rather than experience to select the placement of units. The two American parachute divisions, the 82d and the 101st Divisions, had relatively light casualties. Their ready status would make them the most available theater reserves when the Germans launched their Ardennes counter-offensive (the Battle of the Bulge) in December 1944.

The operation, of course, locked up the theater's air transport assets. According to an inter-Allied agreement, IX TCC supplied lift for the Americans and the British. For the first four days, 17–20 September, the Eighth committed fighters and bombers to support. On 17 September a force of 834 bombers dropped 2,859 tons of fragmentation bombs (a one-mission record) on flak sites near Arnheim, while 703 fighters strafed the countryside. The next day 254 B-24s dropped supplies and 575 fighter-escorts strafed. Light flak shot down eight bombers and 20 fighters; nine more were written off as irreparable. Not only was the operation expensive in fighters, their commitment to Holland limited the rest of the Eighth to shallow penetrations into western Germany until 26 September. Doolittle estimated that Market-Garden cost the Eighth "four major and two minor heavy bomber missions in September."[4]

On 18 September the Eighth flew another significant supply mission to a different destination. A force of 107 B-17s dropped canisters of supplies to the beleaguered Polish Home Army in Warsaw. On 1 August the Poles had risen against the Germans when the Soviet summer offensive had reached a point on the Vistula River, only a few miles from Warsaw. But the Soviet offensive halted ("out of supplies," said the Soviets; "in order to let the Germans snuff out the anticommunist Home Army," said the Poles). This left the Poles surrounded and at the mercy of the Germans, who showed none. In the meantime the Polish government in exile in London, recognized by the Anglo-Americans, exerted all its energy into pressing the Allies for relief supplies for Warsaw. By the time of the drop, the Germans had compressed the defenders into a small pocket and most of the supplies fell on the Germans. This was the last Frantic mission. Soviet premier Stalin refused to allow further flights, in part because the Allies made it clear they intended to use them to aid the Poles. Frantic, an excessively costly exercise, probably lost more goodwill than it was intended to gain. The end of Frantic and the fate of the Polish Home Army contributed to the growing disenchantment of the Anglo-Americans with their Soviet ally.

For the Fifteenth Air Force September 1944 marked a shift in operations. On 9 September a communist-dominated coup overthrew the government of Bulgaria. Shortly thereafter Bulgaria joined the war against the Axis. The volte-faces of Rumania and Bulgaria and the advance of the Red Army through both those countries made the German occupation of Greece untenable and gravely threatened their hold on Yugoslavia. In Yugoslavia Josip Broz Tito's partisans went over to the offensive. In Hungary the Red Army had reached and, in some places, breached the Carpathian Mountains, the last natural defensive barrier between the USSR and Budapest. Axis units rushed east to stem that flood. For their part the Germans attempted to save as many of their troops as possible from the Balkans.

During the month the Fifteenth flew 2,125 effective sorties against Hungary. Of those, 1,025 dropped 2,589 tons on railroad bridges and 923 dropped 2,365 tons on marshaling yards. Another 1,810 sorties placed 4,677 tons on bridges, highways, and marshaling yards in Yugoslavia. Greece absorbed 817 sorties and 1,742 tons on airfields, ports, and rail targets. The last third of the Fifteenth's total monthly tonnage went to transportation targets in Italy (2,739 tons) and to synthetic oil (for a cost of almost 6 percent losses) and to the air industry in Germany (2,498 tons). Missions to Munich resulted in almost 500 tons of area bombing on that city. Finally, oil, rail, and ordnance targets in Vienna received 660 tons on 10 September. Clouds caused one wing to area bomb the center of the city with another 188 tons of high explosives. September also saw the final change in the command structure for the strategic bombing offensive.

Strategic Air Forces Removed from Eisenhower's Direction

On the afternoon of 30 August, Spaatz, after consultations with Eaker, discussed with Eisenhower the organization of the US Army Air Forces in the European theater of operations. The next morning he held further discussions with Tedder and Eisenhower, and that afternoon he met with Portal. At the meetings a consensus developed that the AEAF ought to be disbanded. In his meeting with Spaatz, Portal not only had indicated a willingness to dispense with the AEAF but also raised the issue of a change in the command arrangements between Eisenhower and the strategic air forces. Overlord's obvious success had led Portal to decide that the time had come to invoke the provision, previously agreed upon by the CCS, of the preinvasion air agreements that called for the independence of Bomber Command and USSTAF after the establishment of the Allies on the continent.[5] Instead of supporting this move, as might have been expected, Spaatz opposed it on two grounds.

First, Spaatz assumed Portal intended "to attempt to obtain a decision for the return of the strategic forces to the status existent 1 January 1944,"[6] and he had no wish to have Portal resume his role as chief interlocutor of the Combined Bomber Offensive. Before Overlord, Spaatz had objected strenuously to several of Portal's actions, especially his refusal to authorize the bombing of the Ploesti oil facilities. In the months since then Spaatz had become accustomed to serving under Eisenhower's congenial hand and had no wish to exchange an American master for a British one. Spaatz warned Arnold that "under no conditions should RAF Bomber Command be consolidated with the US Strategic Air Forces." He foresaw continued heavy RAF nighttime losses or extensive disruption of his own fighter cover if they operated by day. Spaatz realized that Bomber Command would not accept an overall American strategic bombing commander; as for USSTAF, he added, "It may not be fully appreciated by you how strongly our American Air Force personnel feel about serving under British Command."[7] Instead, Spaatz suggested to Portal that Eisenhower should have both operational control and direct command of the heavy bombers.[8] Second, Spaatz objected because he preferred a slight modification of the current status of command relations. He and Eisenhower, whom Spaatz had completely won over to his views on reversion to Portal's control on 1 September, worked together well; neither saw any need to change the current arrangements.[9]

At Spaatz's urging, Eisenhower sent messages to both Marshall and Arnold detailing their objections. Saying that he "would regard any change as a serious mistake," Eisenhower told Marshall that he needed to retain control of the strategic forces in order to keep the greatest possible force available for the "penetration" of Germany. So far there had been no disputes between his headquarters and the British chiefs of staff concerning the bombers. Moreover, strategic priorities and bombing missions needed careful coordination with the ground battle by planners in his headquarters. To facilitate such coordination, Spaatz had moved his headquarters on 1 September to the continent next to Eisenhower's. Air Chief Marshal Harris, head of Bomber Command, sent his own liaison officers. Thus, Eisenhower said, USSTAF should stay under his own control. For the same reasons Eisenhower would resist separation of Bomber Command from his control. Reversion of Bomber Command to Portal's direction would make it difficult to coordinate the two strategic commands.[10]

On 3 September Eisenhower told Arnold that USSTAF should remain with him. "All of us," Eisenhower stated, "are striving to keep the heavies on normal tasks, but emergency use in battle must be assured by continuation of the command system."[11] Arnold replied, "With regard to the Strategic Air Force command situation, I agree *wholeheartedly* [emphasis in original] with the view expressed in your recent cables that the control now vested in your headquarters should not be changed to revert to Chief of

Air Staff but instead that all strategic air forces should be placed under your command."[12]

At the Second Quebec Conference, 12–17 September 1944, Arnold, however, "flopped over" on the issue of independence for the heavy bombers.[13] During the conference, which dealt with European occupation policy and the war against Japan, Portal gained Arnold's consent and the approval of the CCS to detach the strategic air forces from Eisenhower's control. This air issue had meant more to Portal than to any of the other chiefs. By bringing Harris back under control of the Air Ministry, Portal hoped to rein him in; he had enjoyed, like Spaatz, comparative freedom under Eisenhower's lenient yoke.[14]

In August Harris had obtained Tedder's and Eisenhower's permission to mount 12 area attacks on German cities when his forces were not required elsewhere. In a single attack on Königsberg on the night of 29–30 August, for example, only 175 Lancaster heavy bombers left 134,000 people homeless.[15] Portal and the air staff, however, disapproved of such attacks. They had at last seized on the oil plan with the enthusiasm only a convert can generate,[16] and they hoped to redirect Harris's efforts toward the synthetic plants and refineries.[17] Paradoxically, Harris probably operated with more freedom than before after the command change from Eisenhower to the Air Ministry.[18] He happily stepped up his program of area bombing on Germany's cities.[19] At Quebec, Portal apparently felt so strongly about regaining control of Harris that he was willing to pull Bomber Command out from under Eisenhower and leave USSTAF under SHAEF if the Americans refused to cooperate.[20]

Arnold and Marshall initially resisted Portal's suggestions, but the next day, 13 September, the British and American chiefs agreed to the substance of Portal's new command arrangements.[21] The CCS directive to Spaatz and Air Marshal Sir Norman Bottomley, the deputy chief of staff for operations, RAF, announced the new command structure and specified certain target priorities. The CCS vested joint executive responsibility for the control of strategic bomber forces in Europe in the chief of staff, RAF, and the commanding general, AAF, who, in turn, designated Bottomley and Spaatz as their representatives for the purposes of providing control and local coordination through consultation. The directive required direct support of ground and naval forces and charged Spaatz and Bottomley with the task of coordinating their actions with the theater tactical air forces. After accepting the current target priorities, it added six broad objectives:

1. Counter air force action consisting of policing current production facilities;

2. Direct support of land and naval forces whenever the Supreme Commanders called for it;

3. The bombing of important industrial areas when weather made other targets impractical, including the use of blind-bombing techniques if necessary;

4. Attacks in support of the Soviet armies, when authorized by the CCS;

5. Continued support for British Special Operations Executive/American Office of Strategic Services operations;[22] and

6. Targets of opportunity, such as the German fleet or submarines.[23]

These objectives reflected the concerns of all the combined chiefs. The first three points were already part of current directives to the bomber forces. Before accepting the change, both the American and British chiefs had ensured that the heavy bombers would be available for other purposes if needed. Point 3 authorized RAF area bombing, while point 4, inserted at the behest of the British, introduced an entirely new consideration, which was of little importance until January and February 1945.[24]

Why did Arnold revise his stance on the issue of command change for the strategic air forces? In a letter to Spaatz shortly afterwards, he explained that he had "found it expedient to agree to having the responsibility for the direction of the U. S. Strategic Air Forces vested in me." The reason, he implied, was that Portal had formulated a plan to make the RAF and the AAF equal by making them co-directors of the Combined Bomber Offensive.[25] A few days later, Arnold explained further:

I went to Quebec with a firm conviction that we should not change the control of the Strategic Air Forces, RAF and AAF, but after I went into the matter more thoroughly and saw that there was no control lost by the United States Higher Command and that provisions could be made for General Eisenhower to get strategic bombing missions upon request, I flopped over. In my opinion the advantages of having you as my representative determine the targets and objectives for the Strategic Air Force on a co-equal status with Portal give U.S. a position in the scheme of things that we have never had before.[26]

The Quebec Conference also approved the demise of the AEAF. Because Leigh-Mallory had become heavily involved in the air operations surrounding Market-Garden, the Allied paratroop drop designed to seize a series of bridges and break through across the Rhine, Eisenhower delayed his release until 15 October.[27] On that date AEAF ceased to exist.

The new command structure made no difference to the congenial relationship already established among Spaatz, Tedder, and Eisenhower. As Eisenhower moved SHAEF to Granville, Normandy, thence to Paris, and finally to Reims, Spaatz, after momentarily deciding in the first flush of command change that his presence might be more useful in London,[28] marched in lockstep, keeping his personal headquarters next to the supreme commander's. On 1 October Spaatz informed Lovett, "We have moved an advance headquarters of USSTAF to the vicinity of Paris and very close to Eisenhower's main headquarters. . . . I expect to spend practically all of my time here in order to be close to Eisenhower."[29] Spaatz left Fred Anderson in London to ensure coordination of operations. This propinquity facilitated Spaatz's administrative control of the large AAF contingent in France and maintained short and speedy lines of coordination between the strategic air force and the supreme commander.

In theory each half of the bomber offensive was independent of the other, with both being responsible ultimately to the CCS. However, the excellent working relationship established between the RAF air staff and USSTAF continued. And in the persons of Spaatz and Bottomley, as the representatives of Arnold and Portal, the direction of targeting policy and coordination of operations flowed smoothly with far less contention than in the preinvasion period.

Notes

1. Richards, *Hardest Victory*, 256.

2. USSBS, *Oil Division Final Report*, 3.

3. Memo for CG, Eighth Air Force, subject: "Cargo Trucking Operations, 29 August–30 September," n.d. [October 1944], AFHSO microfilm reel A5875, frs. 1149–54.

4. Letter, Kuter to Giles [AAF chief of staff], 3 November 1944, AFHSO, manuscript and collected material for proposed volume on the correspondence of Gen H. H. Arnold, European Theater, item 220, 540–42. This letter summarizes the reports of Col Sidney F. Griffin and Lt Col Arthur C. Carlson, who visited General Doolittle after Market-Garden.

5. Letter, Spaatz to Arnold, 1 September 1944, Spaatz Papers, Diary.

6. Ibid.

7. Letter, Spaatz to Arnold, 27 August 1944, Spaatz Papers, Diary.

8. Letter, Spaatz to Arnold, 1 September 1944, Spaatz Papers, Diary.

9. Command Diary, entry for 1 September 1944, Spaatz Papers, Diary.

10. Chandler, *Eisenhower's Papers*, item 1930, message FWD-13605, Eisenhower to Marshall, 2 September 1944, 4:211.

11. Chandler, item 1931, message FWD-13657, Eisenhower to Arnold, 3 September 1944, 4:2112–13.

12. Letter, Arnold to Eisenhower, 6 September 1944, Spaatz Papers, Diary.

13. Letter, Arnold to Spaatz, 29 September 1944, Spaatz Papers, Dairy.

14. Matloff, *Strategic Planning, 1943–1944*, 511.

15. Hastings, *Bomber Command*, 302.

16. Webster and Frankland, *Strategic Air Offensive*, 4:47, 50–51.

17. Terraine, *Time for Courage*, 672.

18. Webster and Frankland, 3:80.

19. Hastings, 323–37. See also Webster and Frankland, 3:80–93.

20. Webster and Frankland, 3:60, n. 1.

21. Ibid., 58–59.

22. The British Special Operations Executive (SOE) and the American Office of Strategic Services (OSS) were Allied intelligence organizations heavily involved with resistance movements in German-occupied Europe. They also engaged in other types of covert intelligence operations directed against the Germans.

23. Message, Octagon 29, Portal and Arnold to Bottomley and Spaatz, 15 September 1944, Spaatz Papers, Diary. See also Webster and Frankland, appendix 8, table 39, 4:170–72.

24. Webster and Frankland, 3:62.

25. Letter, Arnold to Spaatz, n.d. [c.a. 19 September 1944], Spaatz Papers, Diary. This is misfiled in Spaatz's papers having been erroneously annotated "23 October?" Spaatz's reply to this letter is dated 30 September 1944. This letter appears to be Arnold's letter to Spaatz of 19 September cited in Craven and Cate, *Argument to V-E Day*, 3:622, n. 80.

26. Letter, Arnold to Spaatz, 29 September 1944, Spaatz Papers, Diary.

27. Chandler, item 1986, letter, Eisenhower to A. H. M. Sinclair (secretary of state for air), 2 September 1944, 4:2180.

28. Craven and Cate, 3:622.

29. Letter, Spaatz to Lovett, 1 October 1944, Spaatz Papers, Diary.

October

4 October: Fifteenth Air Force—one B-24 lands in Switzerland after mission to Munich.

12 October: Fifteenth Air Force—supports US Fifth Army ground offensive (Operation Pancake).

14–15 October: Bomber Command—conducts its largest night operation of the war.

28 October: USSTAF—General Spaatz and Air Marshal Bottomley agree on Strategic Bombing Directive No. 2.

In October 1944 Bomber Command turned its main effort on Germany with a vengeance. Harris's forces flew 12,419 effective sorties over and dropped 57,679 tons on the fast shrinking Reich. Eighty percent of the bombs struck cities as the command used area bombing in 20 large raids (18 of them over or near 950 tons of bombs). The command's confidence in daylight operations had grown so much that nine of the city raids took place during the day. The command's first ever daylight area raid occurred against Wilhelmshafen on 5 October 1944. It used H2X because clouds and smoke screens concealed the port. By the end of the month, daylight raids had begun to use GH radar over Germany. Most of the raids hit the Ruhr, ports, and targets close to the Rhine. On 14 October Harris subjected Duisberg, a familiar target to his command, to two large raids within 12 hours; a daylight raid smashed the city with 5,029 tons, and a night raid, carrying the largest night tonnage of the war, followed up with 5,093 tons. The record of more than 10,100 tons of conventional explosives dropped on a single target in a day probably still stands. In contrast the daylight missions against Saarbrücken on 5 October and against Kleve and Emmerich on 7 October came at the request of the Allied ground forces. The 1,079 effective sorties and the area bombing technique came from Bomber

Command, but the onus for ordering city-area bombing falls on the ground forces. In its selection of the size of the attacking forces, Bomber Command determined the proportionality of force for each attack, a key consideration in international law. The request for bombing certainly demonstrated that the ground forces had yet to learn one fundamental lesson of city fighting. The more artillery and bombing pulverize a city, the easier it is for the enemy to create stronger defensive positions—in this case, the more accurate the bombing, the greater the advantage to the German defenders (other than the fact that they have lost another perfectly good city). Casualties measured 32 lost for 3,449 daylight sorties (less than 1 percent) and 47 lost for 6,335 night sorties. After subtracting the not insignificant contribution of the Mosquitoes (1,944 sorties and 1,329 tons), Bomber Command dropped 49,667 tons of bombs on German cites. The renewed area bombing campaign, which had begun in July and had steadily increased in August and September, made a large jump in tonnage and sorties.

Bomber Command's concentration on area bombing left little attention for other targets. For instance, against the Allies' highest priority target system, synthetic oil, the command expended 817 sorties and 4,088 tons—about one-twelfth of the resources devoted to area bombing. In Harris's judgment oil targets required relatively small daylight attacks.[1] Its largest raid on transportation, the marshaling yard at Saarbrücken, on 5 October occurred as part of an area raid. The attackers flew in with the main force, which was attacking Saarbrücken, with the mission of striking the yards. Chemical plants received only 885 tons.

In October fortification targets in the Netherlands absorbed 9,700 tons as British and Canadian troops sought to clear the Scheldt River estuary from German troops in fortified positions in Flushing, Westkapell, and other locations. As long as the Germans remained in place, they blocked access to the port of Antwerp. Missions against U-boat pens and units of the German fleet in Norway consumed another 1,050 tons of bombs.

In October 1944 the Eighth Air Force achieved a unique distinction. It became the first of the Allied strategic air forces to drop all its bombs on Germany, 43,194 tons of them.[2] Weather greatly affected USSTAF operations in the autumn of 1944. In mid-December Spaatz ruefully commented in a letter to Lovett, "We have been facing unusual handicaps from weather in our operations."[3] On the same day he wrote to Arnold, "Weather is, of course, the serious handicap in any operation at this time of year. Practically all of our bombing for the last two months has been PFF [blind bombing]. The amount of rainfall exceeds, in the opinion of experts to whom we have talked, any experienced for the last thirty years."[4]

Spaatz did not exaggerate the problem. The AAF official history noted that in the last quarter of 1944, 80 percent of the Eighth's and 70 percent of the Fifteenth's missions employed, at least in part, blind-bombing devices.[5] An Eighth Air Force operational analysis section report on the bombing accuracy for the period 1 September to 31 December 1944, graphically depicted the effects of weather on operational performance. Of the 73 days in the period in which the Eighth conducted heavy-bomber operations, visual means could be used on only 26 days. Only 14 percent of the Eighth's bombing was done by visual means under good visibility. Even in good visibility (no cloud cover, no German smoke screens, or haze), high altitude and smoke from previous bombing meant that only 30 percent of the bombs landed within 1,000 feet of their aiming point. Thirty-five percent of the bombing employed H2X through complete cloud cover. The possibility that bombs would land within 1,000 feet of the aiming point was 150 times greater with good visibility than with H2X through 100 percent clouds.[6]

Even for visual targets, bombing accuracy in the fourth quarter of the year fell a dramatic 40 percent—a drop that the report attributed to more heavily defended targets, longer missions, and poor flying conditions. More flak at the target meant increased altitudes and decreased accuracy. Given the abysmal results obtained (58 percent) from the bombing employing H2X, an official postwar survey admitted, "It cannot be said that this equipment [H2X] was in any sense a precision bombing instrument."[7]

The German synthetic oil industry particularly benefitted from cloud cover and man-made smoke screens, which reduced bombing accuracy. Large-scale visual attacks in mid-September brought the production of aviation fuel to a virtual halt.[8] For that month, the 14 chief hydrogenation plants produced only 5,300 tons, one-thirtieth of their May 1944 production.[9] In October, however, the Eighth dropped more tonnage on military equipment targets (AFVs, motor transport manufacturers, and ordnance depots), 5,597 tons, than on oil, 3,256 tons. It also conducted only three raids on oil targets relying completely on visual means. As a result, aviation gas production tripled to 16,400 tons.

Of the 16,400 sorties the Eighth flew over Germany, it directed 6,600 against marshaling yards. The average raid carried 28 percent incendiaries; 95 percent of the raids employed H2X-assisted sighting. In attacks mounted on 14, 15, 17, and 18 October, the Eighth bombed Cologne, employing for the most part H2X radar. In one of the far more accurate raids, the attackers relied on the GH radar/ground beacon system. It directed the attacks at four of Cologne's marshaling yards and the Ford Motors tank plant. These raids, plus raids on Hamm and RAF raids on Duisburg and Wedau on 14 October, almost shut down the coal railroad gateways leading from the Ruhr. They temporarily cut coal traffic by 80 percent. Any long-term loss of coal would drastically affect the entire German economy. The railroads would stop and power generation would fall to a small fraction. German industry was far more dependent on cogeneration of power (power generated on site as a by-product of industrial processes) than was Allied industry. A shortage of coal would delay and upset all industrial planning and timetables as factories went online and offline depending on the status of their coal supply. The 14 October strike by US planes at Cologne not only damaged the yards but, by a stroke of extraordinary chance, set off the demolition charges affixed to the Cologne–Mulheimer Bridge. The 13,000-ton suspension span, roadway intact, collapsed into the Rhine River blocking navigation. Only unusually high water later in the winter allowed a few days of traffic to float over the wreckage.[10] On 29 October Ultra revealed this debacle to the Allies.[11] By the end of October as a result of Allied bombing, Germany's three most important western waterways—the Rhine, the Ruhr, and the Dortmund-Ems Canal—had become unnavigable at a time when river traffic was at its annual peak before the winter freeze.

Area bombing ranked second in frequency behind attacks on rail targets. The Eighth conducted 2,247 sorties and dropped

5,850 tons in area attacks. It launched five large city raids, all using H2X, in the month: Kassel (2 October), Nürnberg (3 October), Cologne (5 October), Schweinfurt (9 October), and Mannheim (19 October). Excluding the Schweinfurt mission—for which the bombers were loaded with high explosives to hit an industrial target, the missions averaged 37 percent incendiaries (adding in Schweinfurt reduces the average percentage to 31 percent incendiaries). The attacks followed an unwritten policy, the Eighth and its bombardment divisions often recognized in their orders to the units: if your primary military target, for example, a tank factory or marshaling yard, was cloud covered, then make your secondary target the center of the city associated with your primary target. Striking secondary targets when the primary target was unidentifiable reflected the limitations of H2X. Aircrews were often unable to locate a specific target on the fringe of the city, but they could find the city itself. In eight instances individual groups and squadrons (no more than 35 bombers at any one time) attacked cities as targets of opportunity—half employed H2X. The AAF became the first air force to area bomb Dresden when 30 of its bombers dropped 72.5 tons on the city on 7 October.

In October 1944 the Fifteenth Air Force shifted its focus from the Balkans to Central Europe. The fall of Belgrade to Tito's partisans on 20 October marked the liberation of most of Yugoslavia. The Fifteenth dropped only 266 tons, most on transportation targets in that country. The Germans finished their evacuation of Greece and were driven out of most of Rumania and Bulgaria into Hungary by the advancing Soviets. Of the 2,100 tons of bombs dropped on Hungary, almost 80 percent were aimed at marshaling yards and other rail targets. The Fifteenth dropped 3,325 tons of ordnance on Italy. This tonnage included 1,400 tons against rail targets, much of it along the direct rail line to Germany, which ran through the Brenner Pass into Austria and thence to Bavaria. The Fifteenth also assisted an American Fifth Army offensive in the Bologna area, dropping 1,109 tons of high explosives and 184 tons of fragmentation bombs on the German front lines. The Fifteenth continued to blast Italy's remaining war industry capacity. On 20 October the Americans struck Milan with visual bombing aimed at the Isotta Fraschini, Alfa Romeo, and Breda plants.

More than half of the Fifteenth's effective sorties went beyond the Alps. It delivered a total of 3,182 tons in 1,377 sorties with a loss of 66 aircraft (4.8 percent loss rate) in Austria. Targets included AFV and aeroengine, aircraft, and armaments plants. Nine hundred tons went to rail targets, while oil absorbed another 1,139 tons. The Fifteenth raided Czechoslovakia in the middle of the month, striking at the Brux synthetic oil plant (416 tons), the Skoda Works at Pilsen (307 tons), and miscellaneous rail yards. Bombing in Germany followed the pattern set in Austria. In a total of 1,473 sorties, the Fifteenth dropped 3,439 tons and lost 53 bombers (3.6 percent). Almost 1,600 tons were directed against oil; 1,300 tons were dropped on rail targets. The Fifteenth initiated a new tactic late in October. It asked its H2X aircraft to perform double duty as pathfinders for day raids and as harassment bombers at night. On 28 and 30 October, H2X-equipped aircraft made night attacks on Munich and Klagenfurt.

Search for a New Targeting Policy

As noted earlier, the CCS had removed the strategic bombers from Eisenhower's control in mid-September 1944, placing Bomber Command under Portal's direction and USSTAF under Arnold. Arnold delegated his authority to Spaatz while Portal delegated his responsibilities to Air Marshal Sir Norman Bottomley, his deputy chief of the air staff, rather than to the Bomber Command's Air Marshal Sir Arthur Harris. In effect these arrangements placed Spaatz in complete control of American target and priorities selection since Arnold rubber-stamped all of Spaatz's decisions. However, the British arrangements left the RAF in some disarray. Bottomley gave great weight to Portal's opinions, but he [Bottomley] had little control over Harris, whose views did not always coincide with those of Portal. By the end of September, Spaatz and Bottomley had agreed on instructions for the strategic air forces.

On 25 September Bottomley issued a "Directive for the Control of Strategic Bomber Forces in Europe," to Harris.[12] Spaatz had earlier agreed to this directive, later designated "Strategic Bombing Directive No. 1." In referring to important industrial areas [area bombing], the document stated, "when weather or tactical conditions are unsuitable for operations against specific primary objectives, attacks should be delivered on important industrial areas, using blind-bombing techniques as necessary." Given the temper of the times, no one could have justified keeping idle the heavy bomber fleets, on which so much national treasure and effort had been heaped, merely because thick clouds or darkness necessitated their delivering cargoes of destruction against built-up areas rather than specific targets.

The joint directive provided for the periodic issuance of a separate list of strategic targets. The list would specify the targets best calculated to achieve the goals of the bomber offensive and set relative priorities among them, noting that the priorities "will be adjusted from time to time in accordance with the situation." Interestingly enough, the first list of targets and priorities lumped attacks on the German rail transport system in a secondary category with missions against the Luftwaffe. Both types of attack would occur "from time to time." In the meantime oil targets remained first priority. Second priority went to ordnance, tank, and motor transport depots; tank assembly plants; and motor transport assembly plants—in that order. Apparently the Allied air leaders felt that the immediate denial of tactical equipment to the German ground forces would still pay a greater dividend than a protracted series of strategic attacks on transport. This view, which emphasized short-term results, mirrored the still prevalent hopes that the Germans would collapse with one more good push. Eisenhower's headquarters in particular placed the highest priority on the Wehrmacht's major ordnance depots.[13]

Within a week this optimism had evaporated. Allied air leaders began to search for new ways to employ their forces. The bombing results of September and October had shown the inconclusiveness of the campaign against ordnance, tanks, and motor transport. Oil targets had absorbed most of the visual bombing days, which meant that USSTAF employed blind-bombing techniques for a part of most raids against military equipment targets. However, blind bombing produced less accurate bombing. Meanwhile the German frontline troops showed no equipment shortages attributable to the bombing, and postwar analysis revealed no major effects. By the end of October, the Allies were ready to try different target systems.[14]

The British air staff, for its part, wanted a new directive that would enable it to gain better control over Harris. Since the CCS directive of 14 September placing him again under Portal, Harris had proceeded on his own course, and he continued to do so at least until the beginning of 1945. During the last three months of 1944, Bomber Command dropped 53 percent of its bombs on cities, 15 percent on railways and canals, 18 percent on miscellaneous targets, and only 14 percent on oil targets.[15] Harris, who enjoyed personal access to Churchill and great prestige from Bomber Command's status as both the largest component of the RAF and the most successful punisher of the Germans, rebuffed Portal's repeated attempts to have him concentrate his strikes on oil targets. By late January 1945 the dispute between Harris and Portal over oil targeting culminated in Harris's threat to resign. Although he had the authority to accept Harris's resignation, Portal chose not to because he would have had to justify Harris's removal to Churchill and the British people, who, at that time, regarded Harris as a war hero. However, in declining Harris's gesture, Portal lost any sanction he might have held, and, consequently, Harris persisted in flouting Portal's authority until the end of the war. In any case Bomber Command had delivered only 6 percent of its bombs against oil targets in October, a figure Portal and Bottomley wanted greatly increased.[16]

Portal solicited Tedder's views on new instructions for the heavy bombers.[17] Tedder replied on 25 October with a tightly reasoned brief favoring transportation as the primary target system.[18] After referring to the current operations of the strategic and tactical air forces, Tedder said, "I am not satisfied that on these lines, we are using our airpower effectively. The various types of operations should fit into one comprehensive pattern, whereas I feel that at present they are more like a patchwork quilt." Tedder believed that the one common factor underlying the entire German war effort, from political control to troop supply, was communications. He argued, "our primary air objective should be the enemy's communications.

Road, water, and rail are interdependent and complementary, and our air operations should play on that fact. The present oil plan is the key to movement by road or air, and, moreover, directly affects operations in the battle area."

Tedder integrated the oil plan into his own concept, adding two factors that he believed should make this anti-transportation system effort even more telling than the one that had preceded Operation Overlord. First, all loss of transport traffic would be a dead loss to the German war effort. Unlike France, where the Wehrmacht required only 20 percent of the rail traffic, with much of the remainder going to support the French economy, in Germany any loss of transportation would eventually produce a shortage or delay in the German war effort. In Germany bombed-out transport lines could be replaced only at the cost of other vital programs. In contrast in France the Wehrmacht could use a large portion of the remaining 80 percent of the excess capacity to replace bombed-out capacity.

Second, noted Tedder, "in France and Belgium the programme of attacks on rail centres was severely limited, both as regards selection of targets and as regards weather conditions, by the need to avoid civilian casualties; no such limitations affect attacks on German rail centres." Tedder concluded that by concentrating heavy bombers over marshaling yards, oil targets, the canal system, and "centres of population" in the Ruhr, and backing up that concentration with the tactical air force operations against trains, rail embankments, and selected bridges, the Allies "would rapidly produce a state of chaos which would vitally affect not only the immediate battle on the West Wall, but also the whole German war effort."

British intelligence buttressed Tedder's arguments. As early as July 1944, the British Joint Intelligence Committee detected diversion of essential war freight from the overstrained railroads to the inland water transport system. By the end of August, the Allies perceived an overall weakening of the German transport system demonstrated by more diversion to water transport and delay in the delivery of war production matériel. Intelligence from high-grade intercepts in October revealed the worsening German situation. A 10 October decryption of a 2 October message to Tokyo from the Japanese naval attaché reported gradually increasing havoc on the German lines of communications and confusion in the transport of coal and munitions from the Rhineland. A particularly telling decryption on 24 October of a four-day-old message from Hitler's headquarters quoted a report from Albert Speer that destruction of traffic installations and lack of power had brought from 30 to 35 of all armament factories to a standstill.[19] Lack of power meant lack of coal to fire the generating plants—a sign of serious, if not catastrophic, rail disruption. This intercept can only have convinced the Allied air leaders both of the efficacy of bombing the transportation network inside Germany and of the diminishing capacity of the Germans to absorb more of it.

On 28 October Spaatz and Bottomley issued Strategic Directive No. 2. It deleted the military equipment targets except when specifically requested by the ground forces. This deletion left only two target systems: the petroleum industry and lines of communications, the latter with second priority. Spaatz and the British air staff had maintained top priority in oil targets but had also seen the advantages of Tedder's campaign against communications.[20]

Meanwhile, Harris had an escape clause as wide as an autobahn. Strategic Directive No. 2 authorized the bombing of "important industrial areas"—a useful euphemism for area bombing—whenever weather or tactical conditions were unsuitable for the two main objectives. Bottomley did modify the clause slightly by adding language requiring that these alternative attacks contribute, as far as possible, to the destruction of the oil and transport systems. He also wrote a cover letter to Harris—to little avail—emphasizing the importance of oil. Harris believed in neither oil nor communications targets. He dryly annotated his copy of Bottomley's letter, "here we go around the Mulberry bush."[21] In November, however, Harris did increase his strikes on petroleum sites to 24.6 percent of his total effort, a figure not far from the Fifteenth's 28.4 percent. In November the Eighth Air Force dropped 39 percent of its bomb tonnage on oil targets.[22] This directive remained in effect until it was modified and replaced by Strategic Directive No. 3, issued on 12 January 1945.

Spaatz had sound technical reasons for striking marshaling yards. The terrible weather of the fall of 1944 compelled his forces to bomb blind, which meant bombing targets that could be picked up on H2X. As mentioned earlier, the Germans had located synthetic oil plants away from cities. Although large, these facilities were not large enough to give a consistently identifiable return on the H2X radar. Hence, they had to be bombed by visual means to achieve a reasonable return on the effort invested to get them. Bombs that missed the synthetic plants usually fell in open country where they did little harm. However, H2X had no trouble locating cities and the marshaling yards within them and, given any break in the clouds, the yards would be well hit. But therein lay the tragic conundrum of the strategic bombing campaign: a well-hit marshaling yard meant a well-hit city, with block upon block of residential areas gutted, families left homeless, small businesses smashed, and workers and others—including women and children—blown to bits or, more likely, burned or crushed by the hundreds, if not the thousands.[23]

Notes

1. Richards, *Hardest Victory*, 257.
2. This figure includes only bombs purposely released over Germany. The AAF did not normally count bombs jettisoned for various reasons as purposeful releases during wartime, although some postwar compilations did so.
3. Letter, Spaatz to Lovett, 13 December 1944, Spaatz Papers, Diary.
4. Ibid.
5. Craven and Cate, *Argument to V-E Day*, 3:667.
6. Headquarters Eighth Air Force, Operational Analysis Section, "Report on Bombing Accuracy Eighth Air Force, 1 September–31 December 1944," 22 April 1945, Spaatz Papers, Subject File 1929–1945, 5–7.
7. USSBS, Military Analysis Division, *Bombing Accuracy: USAF Heavy & Medium Bombers in the ETO*, vol. 63, 4.
8. Webster and Frankland, *Strategic Air Offensive*, appendix 32, table 4, Report of 5 October 1944, Speer to Hitler, 4:335.
9. Ibid., appendix 49, table 39, 4:517.
10. Alfred C. Mierzejewski, "Wheels Must Roll for Victory: Allied Air Power and the German War Economy, 1944–1945" (PhD diss., University of North Carolina, Chapel Hill, N. Car., 1985), 207–8.
11. Hinsley, *British Intelligence*, vol. 3, pt. 2, 526.
12. See Webster and Frankland, vol. 4, appendix 8, table 40, for a complete copy of the text of this directive.
13. TLM/F/S. 34, "Notes of the 100th Air Commanders' Meeting," 26 September 1944, Spaatz Papers, Diary.

14. Craven and Cate, 3:647–49.

15. Terraine, *Time for Courage*, 675.

16. Webster and Frankland, 3:84, n. 3.

17. Ibid., 68.

18. DCS/TS.100, "Notes on Air Policy to be Adopted in View to a Rapid Defeat of Germany," Spaatz Papers, Diary.

19. Hinsley, vol. 3, pt. 2, 526.

20. See Webster and Frankland, appendix 8, table 43 (b), 4:178–79 for a complete copy of this directive.

21. Ibid.

22. Webster and Frankland, 3:84, n. 3.

23. Everyone in Germany had heard, in one form or another of the old grandfather who had gone into city "X" with five coffins for his son, daughter-in-law, and their three children, all killed in an Allied bombing raid, only to return with the remains of all in a single bucket.

German Cities, Occupied Europe, and Allied Bombing Policy

The adoption of a target directive that, at least by implication, specified the bombing of marshaling yards by H2X or area methods must necessarily bring to the fore the question of the Anglo-Americans' policies concerning collateral damage and area bombing. Because of the highly charged emotions surrounding this question, the following section of this work will depart from earlier practice and employ heavy use of extensive citations from original documents. This will allow readers to independently assess the intent of Allied policies.

The British, victims of heavy German bombing, adopted a policy of city-area bombing early in the conflict. A 9 July 1941 directive, as did subsequent directives, authorized Bomber Command to make area attacks against the German workforce. On 29 October 1942, the RAF, as discussed earlier, codified its policies on bombing occupied and enemy countries in a policy letter to all its commands. The letter drew a sharp distinction between the bombing of German-occupied territory and Germany itself; it supplied an extensive listing of military objectives in occupied countries authorized for attack. The letter addressed a British problem never shared by the Americans: home territory occupied by the Germans—namely, the Channel Islands. The letter limited attacks to those "necessitated by operational considerations of real importance" and confined those attacks only to objectives which were specified in orders. The letter added a last restriction: "Owing to the difficulty of discriminating between troops and civilians, machine-gun attacks on personnel are not to be made."

The concern for their own citizens and the people of their subjugated Allies did not extend to the enemy. "Consequent upon the enemy's adoption of a campaign of unrestricted air warfare, the Cabinet have [sic] authorized a bombing policy which includes the attack of enemy morale. The foregoing rules governing the policy to be observed in enemy occupied countries do not, therefore, apply in our conduct of air warfare against German, Italian, and Japanese territory, except that the provisions of the Red Cross Conventions are to be continued to be observed."[1] This policy remained in effect until the end of the war.

As Air Marshall Sir John Slessor observed, the Germans' own actions heavily colored the views of the prime minister and the average Briton. In the course of the war, the Luftwaffe, V weapons, and long-range guns killed more than 60,000 British civilians. The bombing "blitz" of 1940–41 alone killed 43,000 and wounded 139,000. Many persons in and out of the government not only wanted to give back as much as they had gotten but instead wanted to give back more. Some clerics and individuals with exceptionally forgiving and discriminating consciences— never more than a small, uninfluential minority—opposed area bombing on ethical and humanitarian grounds.

American policy towards collateral damage and area bombing lacked the clear and concise definition of British policy and procedure. United States Strategic Air Forces and the Eighth and Fifteenth Air Forces Headquarters' records on this topic are sparse. Whether this is by accident or by design, such as a refusal to record such matters or from a pruning of the files, cannot be determined, at least not by this author, from a remove of more than 50 years.[2] Nonetheless, remaining records and mission reports submitted by lower headquarters, particularly the Eighth's three bombardment divisions and the Fifteenth's five bombardment wings, allow a definition of American policy both by inference and by watching what they did, not what they said.

Up until the end of September 1943, the Eighth conducted all of its bombing by the sole means available—visual with the Norden bombsight. In their raids on occupied Western Europe and on Germany, the Americans invariably used tactics of the high-altitude, visual attack. Given the incomplete training of some crews, active German defenses such as fighters and guns (as a rule of thumb the Eighth calculated that flak near and over the target reduced accuracy by 50 percent), passive German defenses such as man-made smoke screens, the relatively compact nature of some targets, and, finally, smoke and dust thrown up by previous bombing, the Eighth's efforts were at best inconsistent. Their methods contrasted sharply with the RAF, whose No. 2 Group sent small forces of five to 20 light and medium bombers in at low levels to hit war-related facilities in the occupied countries. These low-level attacks greatly increased accuracy and usually came and went before the surprised defenders could react. Citizens of the attacked French, Belgian, and Dutch towns naturally felt the Americans were taking insufficient precautions with their lives. In France, the saying "Up with the RAF and down with the Americans" became prevalent. The Eighth apparently took what precautions it could, such as briefing the crews to identify the proper target, refusing to authorize the selection of alternate targets in occupied countries, and selecting approach angles that directed bombs away from populated areas. The basic inaccuracy of their bombing method betrayed their good intentions.

However, the Eighth did not engage in indiscriminate bombing over occupied Europe. The Eighth had considerable independence in its day-to-day selection of targets and in determining its bombing priorities, but approval of its overall priorities came from the combined chiefs of staff, who designated the RAF chief of the Air Staff ACM Portal as their executive agent charged with direction of the Combined Bomber Offensive. The British exercised tight control over targets in occupied Europe, and Portal applied these controls to the Eighth as well. On 10 June 1943, Portal's assistant chief of the Air Staff (operations), Air Vice Marshal (AVM) Sir Norman Bottomley, issued the formal Pointblank directive to Lt Gen Ira Eaker. In addition to specifying target priorities, it contained a list of 13 French, five Belgian, and one

Dutch targets that were "cleared" for attack once radio broadcasts and leaflets had notified the surrounding populace.[3] Twelve of the targets were aircraft overhaul and maintenance facilities, one was a naval storage depot, four were rail yards or locomotive shops, and three were motor transport factories. No other targets, except airfields in use by the Luftwaffe, were cleared for attack. By 27 June 1943, the RAF notified the Eighth that all the target areas had received their warnings and specified that "you should continue to observe the principle that all possible measures be taken to keep to an absolute minimum the risk of casualties to the civilian population consistent with ensuring the effectiveness of your attacks."[4] The Eighth's implementing directive somewhat diluted this strict standard, "In planning operations in enemy occupied countries, care should be taken to spare as many civilian casualties as is practical."[5] By implication any target not on the cleared list was excluded from attack. Throughout 1943, Eaker and his bomber commander, Maj Gen Fred Anderson, and fighter commander, Maj Gen William Kepner, observed a verbal arrangement that required both subordinates to clear any attacks on occupied territory with their commander before executing them.[6]

The British continued to limit attacks throughout 1943 and the first of 1944. The target list changed over time. Temporary targets, such as blockade runners (ships attempting to carry extremely high-value cargoes between Germany and Japan) appeared on the list in November 1943, while targets heavily damaged or put out of action disappeared from it. Crossbow and Noball added a large number of new targets. Temporary prohibitions were added to the list as warranted. For the week of 16 to 23 October 1943, the Allies exempted the German Baltic ports of Sassnitz and Swinemunde from attack to safeguard a British–German exchange of prisoners. On 26 November 1943, the British suspended bombing and strafing attacks on all electrical power installations in France and the Low Countries because they would produce no immediate or large effect on the enemy's war effort, and "on the other hand [would] create much distress among the civilian population [that] may prejudice the success of our future military operations in those countries."[7] On the same day, the Allies also discontinued fighter attacks on "the railway transportation system, particularly locomotives, trains, and signal boxes in occupied North-West Europe," but noted that such attacks in conjunction with support of the cross-channel invasion could be planned and would be authorized when appropriate.[8] By 20 May 1944 the Allies had resumed fighter attacks on all trains, including passenger trains, in occupied territory. After the invasion of France, demands of the ground forces and their associated tactical air forces necessitated the attack of so many communications, Noball, and combat-related targets that the system of tight control of bombing in occupied countries in northwest Europe disappeared.

Over Germany, the Eighth employed a looser set of rules. The Eighth's "Bombardment Directive" of 27 June 1943, issued to implement Pointblank, stated, "Any target in Germany is cleared for attack at any time."[9] The Americans had an option normally unavailable to Bomber Command, which tied its bombers to the two or three locations physically marked for bombing. If during a daylight mission an American aircrew could not hit its primary target, the crew, using either "eyeballs" or radar, was authorized to hit a designated secondary target or any target of opportunity. Bomber Command crews normally did not have this same level of discretion. The Eighth and the Fifteenth normally had four target priorities for each mission:

1. Primary: Visual attack on a war plant, rail facility, or military target. Chosen by the Air Force Headquarters in accordance with current bombing directives.

2. Secondary: usually chosen by Air Force Headquarters in accordance with current bombing directives, with its location coordinated with the bombers' planned route and fighter protection.

   a. Visual: an alternative target similar to the primary.

   b. Nonvisual: area attack on city associated with either of the above.

3. Last-Resort Target: a tertiary target with the same qualifications as a secondary target.

4. Target of Opportunity: A target selected by the mission or individual bomber formation leaders, while in the air, when they are unable to attack any of the above targets. If weather or enemy action scatters a formation, all leaders and pilots are encouraged to seek targets of opportunity within specified limits. Forbidden over occupied territory and either visual or radar over greater Germany.

The first area raid noted in Eighth Air Force records occurred on 12 August 1943 when 106 bombers visually attacked the city of Bonn as a target of opportunity with 243 tons of bombs. Almost three weeks later 28 bombers made visual-opportunity attacks on four different German cities. With the introduction into American service of the RAF's H2S radar-bombing device—with all its inherent inaccuracy—the Eighth began systematic area bombing of Germany, but not to the same scale as the RAF. Nonetheless, under nonvisual conditions it could only hit and locate built-up areas. On 27 September 1943, the Eighth used H2S for the first time. As the employment of H2S on this raid would suggest, planners expected the raid to encounter clouds. The mission (Eighth Air Force Mission No. 104) found the objective, the city of Emden, completely covered and dropped 506 tons through the clouds.[10] It was the Eighth's first intentional, or ordered, area bombing of a city. Brig Gen Fred Anderson, commanding general, VIII Bomber Command, who authorized the raid, had been instrumental in the procurement, installation, and use of H2S and the subsequent employment of H2X.[11]

Within a week of this initial ordered area bombing, the data sheets of Eighth Air Force planners specified the following objectives for a raid on Frankfurt-am-Main: primary, "Frankfurt (city proper)"; secondary, "any industrial target in Germany." Aircraft from the raid struck the primary target "Frankfurt (city proper)"; and targets of opportunity: "Wiesbaden, Saarlautern (city), Sarreguemines (city proper), and Saarbrücken (city proper)."[12] On 10 October, the Eighth, employing visual sighting, struck the city of Münster as a primary target and the German city of Coesfeld and the Dutch city of Enschede as targets of last resort.[13] The day after this raid General Anderson outlined American target priorities for officers of the 3d Bombardment Division as follows: first, destruction of the Luftwaffe, its factories, and planes; second, essential German industries; and third, the cities themselves.[14]

Anderson was also responsible for another change in Eighth Air Force policy, which took effect at the same time as the introduction of H_2S—a large increase in the Eighth's use of incendiaries. General Anderson had begun to encourage the Eighth's bombardment wings to employ more firebombs soon after his promotion in July 1943 from command of the Eighth's Fourth Bombardment Wing to that of VIII Bomber Command, which made him the officer in charge of all bomber operations.[15] The 27 September Emden mission was the first of the Eighth's missions to load more than 20 percent incendiaries, while the 2 October mission against Emden was the Eighth's first strike to deliver more than 100 tons of firebombs on a single target. Henceforth, the Eighth would not only conduct intentional area bombing, it would do so using area bombing techniques, especially in the expenditure of incendiaries against urban areas.

The dividing line for visual and area bombing was as unpredictable as the weather. For instance, the Eighth's bombers participating in the second battle of Schweinfurt on 14 October 1943 went into the combat with orders specifying Schweinfurt Ball Bearings Works as the primary target, Schweinfurt city center as the secondary target, and chemical works of I. G. Farben Industries A. G. in Ludwigshafen, as the target of last resort.[16] Had weather stopped the mission short, it would have gone down in history as a footnote, an abortive mission against ball bearings plants. Had the bombers arrived over Schweinfurt and dropped their tonnage by dead reckoning onto a city of only 50,000, what would the reaction have been?[17] Would postwar analysis have turned one of the AAF's most gallant and expensive missions into something akin to a war crime?

Immediately after Schweinfurt, bombing policy changed. On the next mission, 18 October, VIII Bomber Command instructed its bombers to hit Duren, center of city, as the primary target and designated the secondary targets as "any German city which may be bombed using visual methods without disrupting fighter support."[18] The new formulation for secondary targets reflected both operational and political facts of life for the Eighth. The accidental attack (the aircrews identified it as a German town) on Enschede on 10 October had angered the Dutch; hence, the restriction to German cities and the prohibition against H2X bombing on secondary targets. Also, the instructions recognized that the bombers could not operate over Germany without escort. These orders made any German city within the limits of the range of P-47s eligible for visual city bombing. Units of the Eighth, using visual bombing, dropped 209 tons of ordnance during the raid on Duren. On 30 October the Eighth amended the bombing instructions for secondary targets to "any German city which may be bombed without disrupting [Allied] fighter support."[19] In October 1943 the Eighth dropped 2,672 tons on German cities. Eliminating the restrictions on nonvisual bombing may have stemmed from the arrival of a dozen H2X-equipped B-17s and from the onset of winter weather, which was normally too adverse to allow visual bombing. On 30 November 1943 the rules were changed to restrict bombing to any positively identified industrial city in Germany. The term *industrial* tended to be a distinction without difference as almost any city in Germany could be considered industrial. In November 1943, the Eighth dropped 3,219 tons on German cities. By the end of Eaker's tenure with the Eighth, the formulation for secondary city targets had reverted to "any city positively identified as being in Germany which can be attacked without disrupting fighter support."[20] On 16 December 1943 under this new definition, 528 bombers of the Eighth, using H2X, hit the city of Bremen as a primary target with 1,006 tons of high explosives and 514 tons of incendiaries. The exact wording of the field orders may have changed from mission to mission, but the Eighth's intent to authorize area bombing in a broad range of circumstances remained constant. For the month of December the Eighth dropped 7,562 tons in area attacks on German cities.

Upon their arrival, Spaatz and Doolittle continued the Eighth's area bombing. On 29 January 1944 the Eighth dispatched 763 effective bomber sorties to Frankfurt-am-Main, with the city's marshaling yard as their primary target. As a secondary target, or target of last resort, the field order authorized attacks on "any city or industrial area positively identified as being in Germany [and] which can be attacked without disrupting fighter support."[21] During this raid, the Eighth dropped a total of 1,866 tons using H2X on Frankfurt, which, according to the Eighth's records, was the primary target. The next day, 701 effective sorties attacked Brunswick, but weather prevented an attack on their primary targets—Bf 110 assembly facilities. They instead dropped 1,681 tons on the city of Brunswick, their secondary target. Their instructions for targets of last resort reflected the Eighth's drive, in the winter and spring of 1944, to destroy the Luftwaffe. These orders authorized attacks on "any *airdrome* [emphasis added] in enemy territory or any city or any industrial area positively identified as being German and which can be attacked without disrupting fighter support."[22] In January 1944 the Eighth delivered 6,568 tons in area raids on German cities. American bombing in February 1944, which included "Big Week" stressed precision bombing of targets. However, the Eighth still conducted area bombing on German cities with 3,703 tons of bombs. The orders to the Eighth's fighters echoed those to the bombers. On 9 February 1944 Kepner informed his fighter pilots that "any target of opportunity within the boundaries of Germany can be attacked."[23]

The introduction of H2X into the Fifteenth Air Force occasioned a memo from Spaatz to Eaker, dated 3 February 1944, on "Objectives for Area Attack." It established the following priorities:

    a. First Priority. Cities or towns which complement the precision first-priority Pointblank targets, such as Regensburg, Schweinfurt, Steyr, Augsburg, Stuttgart, and so forth.

    b. Second Priority. Towns not necessarily directly connected to the precision first-priority Pointblank targets but which, if bombed, will contribute in other ways to the mission of the Strategic Air Forces. These, in order of priority, are

        (1) Budapest,

        (2) Sofia,

        (3) Bucharest, and

        (4) Vienna.[24]

Before issuing this list Spaatz apparently coordinated it with the British Joint Intelligence Committee and Air Chief Marshal Portal.

On 21 February, six days after the bombing of the Monte Cassino Abbey, Twining issued an order to all bombers under his command, including No. 205 Group. He stated that he wished to ensure that "historic and religious buildings of permanent value to civilization are not destroyed *unless their destruction is essential to successful operations* [emphasis added]." He placed Rome, Fiesole, Florence, Venice, and Torcello off-limits for bombing unless approved by Headquarters Fifteenth Air Force. Twining listed 21 towns, including Ravenna, Pavia, Aosta, Como, and Split, as having no military objectives that necessitated bombing and directed that they not be bombed unless necessary. He listed 24 towns that either contained or had located near them important military objectives "which are to be bombed and any consequential damage accepted." Cities eligible for attack included Pistoia, Modena, Brescia, Pisa, Verona, Bologna, Ferrara, Vicenza, Piacenza, and Perugia. Twining laid down the following guidelines in the event it became necessary to attack towns in the second and third categories:

> a. If the town is in the actual zone of ground operations and is occupied by the enemy, no restrictions whatsoever are to be accepted, and the sole determining factor will be the requirements of the military situation.

> [If a town were not in a ground combat zone, the following restrictions applied:]

> b. Military objectives will not be bombed if they are obscured by cloud in either day or night. Bombing through less than 10/10 cloud is at the formation leader's discretion.

> c. At night markers must be placed with reasonable certainty, and crews must attack the target rather than releasing bombs in the target area.

> d. Briefings will ensure that aircrews understand the location of historical monuments.

In his conclusion he noted, "Unnecessary damage is of no advantage, and should be avoided if that is possible without increased cost."[25]

Although one might disagree with Twining's selections as to the sanctity of individual cities, his instructions did attempt to draw a distinction between Italy's irreplaceable art treasures and the needs of combat. The cities that were included in the "may be struck" portion of his list consisted of some of Italy's largest industrial towns and towns with key marshaling yards and/or bridges necessary for German supply and movement. Certainly the bombing limitations set for occupied Italy at least equaled those followed by the Eighth for France and the Low Countries.

On 7 March 1944, the day after its units dropped 840 tons into the center of Berlin using H2X, Doolittle clarified the Eighth's bombing policy by issuing a new set of standard operating procedures (SOP) on bombing. The document bore the singularly unfortunate designation "Indiscriminate Bombing." Doolittle established the following three bombing zones:

a. Unrestricted Areas. Any military targets in Germany proper more than 50 miles from occupied territory may be attacked under any conditions provided the mission instructions of the field order are followed.

b. Restricted Areas. Military targets in Germany proper that are in a zone less than 50 miles from occupied territory may be attacked if they can be positively identified, bombed visually, and attacked without any risk of bombs falling in occupied territory.

c. Occupied Territory. Only those targets listed in the field order for the particular operation may be attacked in occupied territory. When these targets are so obscured that normal bombing accuracy cannot be expected, the bombs will not be released.

Doolittle added, "Specific admonition that grave consequences will ensue for errors in identification will be repeated and emphasized in the pre-mission briefing of all combat crews."[26]

The key to understanding this document rests on the definition of "military target." Was it expansive, such as that given the Fifteenth a month earlier, which allowed area bombing of cities associated with Pointblank targets, or did it revert to a policy of precision bombing? Since the Eighth would continue to employ H2X until the end of the conflict, this memo can hardly be a reversion to precision bombing. An examination of the Eighth's targeting in the following weeks showed that however exclusive the definition of military target might be, it did not exclude area or city bombing. In a little over three weeks after Doolittle declared most of Germany an unrestricted bombing zone, the Eighth hit the cities of Brunswick (15, 23, and 29 March), Augsburg (16 March), Friedrichshaven (16 March), Berlin (22 March), and Frankfurt (24 March) with 150 or more bombers. During the 22 March raid on Berlin, the Eighth sent 621 sorties to bomb industrial plants in its suburbs, with the secondary target for this mission as "Berlin—Friedrichstrasse Main Line and Underground Stations." The bombers dropped 1,374 tons on the secondary targets: the subway in the heart of the administrative and residential center of Berlin. On April Fools' Day the Eighth set out to bomb the I. G. Farben chemical plant at Ludwigshafen with a secondary of "Ludwigshafen—City."[27] Deteriorating weather caused two-thirds of the force to turn back and the rest to bomb targets of opportunity, which they proceeded to do with a vengeance. Most of the aircraft hit the German town of Pforzheim, but others mistook Strassburg for Mannheim and dropped in the center of the French city. Worse yet, two other groups of B-24s released on the Swiss towns of Grafenhausen and Schaffenhausen. All the day's bombing employed H2X. Clearly the planners and the combat crews of the Eighth Air Force considered any city a military target. In March 1944 the Eighth Air Force adopted the so-called Verdun strategy of attritional attacks on targets the Luftwaffe had to defend. In these area attacks, especially on Berlin, units of the Eighth released 8,466 tons on German cities.

On the last day of March, when Doolittle informed Spaatz's headquarters of his operations plans for the first half of April, he further stated his policy for use of force in overcast conditions. His policy explicitly established the link between city-area bombing and H2X. Doolittle stated, "When overcast bombing technique must be employed, attacks will be directed against Munich, Berlin, and other large German cities."[28]

Upon receiving Doolittle's proposal, General Anderson added the following requirements for overcast bombing:

a. Flush the German air force.

b. Do vital damage to the enemy.

   c. Provide training for Pathfinder crews.

   d. Create a yardstick by which the capabilities of bombing through overcast techniques can be assessed and material for critique can be obtained.

   e. Be free from other types of bombing which would confuse assessment of results of Pathfinder attacks.

   f. Be in areas where photographic coverage can be obtained in order to get the greatest benefits out of requirements c, d, and e.

Next, Anderson assigned three targets, including Huls and Leverkusen, most likely to meet the above requirements. In spite of his desire to investigate the concrete effectiveness of bombing through overcast, Anderson did not deny current methods of employment. He stated, "This list is not intended to prevent selection by you of additional targets of equal value, nor is it intended to deny the attack on German cities when major results such as attrition of the German Air Force can be expected."[29]

By July 1944 USSTAF intelligence had compiled a list of cities and towns for H2X attacks. The list consisted of 100 targets for the Eighth (53 cities judged "suitable" and 47 cities judged as "poorer targets") and 16 for the Fifteenth.[30] The list included the French city of Strassburg, which the Eighth area bombed on two occasions. Perhaps someone in the Eighth's headquarters having knowledge of geography failed to reflect the return of this city, annexed by Germany in 1871, to France after World War I.

In April 1944 American area bombing in Germany fell to 3,668 tons as good bombing weather allowed strikes on primary military targets and Crossbow diverted the bombing efforts to France. In May 1944, however, in spite of the bombing of synthetic oil, Crossbow, and the transportation plan, the Eighth's area bombing of German cities more than doubled to 8,214 tons. A majority of the Eighth's deep penetrations into Germany encountered clouds, forcing them to divert to secondary targets (the associated city). Strikes on oil production and storage facilities during two days of clear weather came at the expense of other bombing in Germany. The Eighth spent the first three weeks of June 1944 assisting the Normandy invasion and bombing Crossbow targets. On 6 and 7 June, at the direct order of Eisenhower and over the objection of Spaatz and Doolittle, the Eighth engaged in its only area bombing of French targets, dropping

2,956 tons on French towns whose destruction would impede German reinforcements. Once the Eighth resumed operations over Germany, it delivered 3,992 tons on German cities.

In July 1944 the Eighth dropped approximately 26,000 tons on Germany. In that month the Eighth reached its wartime high of area bombing with 10,033 tons dropped on Germany— 80 percent on Munich (the home of the Nazi Party), including its administrative machinery and an important manufacturing point for aero engines. Given the attempted coup against Hitler and the Nazis on 20 July and the completely coincidental planning within the RAF Air Staff for Thunderclap and for an attack on the controlling machinery of the Reich, the raids on Munich may indicate that the bombing of a police state for the purpose of toppling the regime cannot succeed.

The increase in area bombing did not go unnoticed at USSTAF headquarters where Spaatz waged a fight to avoid entanglement in British V-1 retaliation schemes and against openly acknowledged area bombing. As Spaatz noted to Lovett, "There is no doubt in my mind that the RAF wants very much to have the US Air Forces tarred with the morale bombing aftermath, which we feel will be terrific."[31] On 21 July, a date on which six separate groups of the Eighth's bombers visually attacked cities as targets of opportunity, Anderson sent a new bombing policy memo to Doolittle and Twining. Anderson pointed to Spaatz's oft reiterated and continuing intention to direct bombing toward precision targets and categorically denied any intention to area bomb. Despite having denied the intention, he proceeded to authorize the practice: "We will conduct bombing attacks through the overcast where it is impossible to get precision targets. Such attacks will include German marshalling yards whether or not they are located in German cities."[32] In August the Eighth's area bombing of Germany dropped to a mere 401 tons, all of it freelance choices by seven already airborne groups and none at the direction of higher headquarters. With Allied armies racing across France and the defeat of Germany almost imminent, the Eighth concentrated on air targets and oil in Germany, not cities.

For the first three weeks in September, as the hopes for a quick Allied victory ebbed, the area bombing pattern followed that of the previous month. Individual aircrews conducted target of opportunity bombings (bombings not specifically directed by higher headquarters) for a total of only 670 tons on city areas. In the last week of September, after the failure of Market–Garden when the Germans had achieved a stalemate on the western front, the Eighth launched nonvisual area attacks on Frankfurt (25 September), Cologne (27 September), Magdeburg (28 September), and Münster (30 September). These attacks, all authorized by higher headquarters either as primary or secondary targets, brought the September area bombing total to 4,716 tons.

In October 1944 the Eighth's area bombing total increased to 5,850 tons. Bad weather forced more bombing of secondary targets. At the end of the month the Eighth Air Force issued a new SOP, "Attack of Secondary and Last-Resort Targets." It increased the likelihood of area bombing by setting the following criteria:

1. No towns or cities in Germany will be attacked as secondary or last-resort targets, targets of opportunity, or otherwise, unless such towns contain or have immediately adjacent to them, one (1) or more military objectives. Military objectives include railway lines; junctions; marshalling yards; railway or road bridges, or other communications networks; any industrial plant; and such obvious military objectives as oil storage tanks, military camps and barracks, troop concentrations, motor transport or AFV parks, ordnance or supply depots, ammunition depots; airfields; etc.

2. Combat crews will be briefed before each mission to insure that no targets other than military objectives in Germany are attacked.

3. It has been determined that towns and cities large enough to produce an identifiable return on the H2X scope generally contain a large proportion of the military objectives listed above. These centers, therefore, may be attacked as secondary or last-resort targets by through-the-overcast bombing technique.[33]

Almost every city or town in Germany with a population exceeding 50,000, and a few below that figure, met the foregoing criteria. This policy made it open season for bombing Germany's major cities in any weather. Those cities fortunate enough not to show up on H2X could still be bombed by visual or visually assisted means. If the AAF had not abandoned its precision techniques for area and terror bombing in this memo, it came perilously close.

A week later Twining issued an equally draconian set of instructions to his bomber crews:

1. The present war situation demands that every effort be made to bomb military targets in GERMANY.

2. Any military installation, communication line, or industrial plant, no matter how small, adds to the German war strength, and almost any one of the numerous GERMAN towns contains such a target. Bombardment crews may select such targets as alternate targets of opportunity in the event that primary targets or assigned alternate targets cannot be bombed. It is imperative that every bomb carried into GERMANY be dropped to achieve maximum results. Under no circumstances will bombs be returned to bases after being carried over German territory.[34]

At the same time Twining repeated orders he had given in May 1944: "Targets without military value will not be bombed or strafed," and "unnecessary bombing or strafing of the civilian populace of Axis-occupied countries will be scrupulously avoided to prevent unnecessary casualties and to avoid the development of resentment and hatred on the part of these peoples toward the Allied war effort." Twining placed no such restrictions on attacks in Germany.[35] He further instructed that, in the cases of Yugoslavia and Albania, "Care will be exercised to see that jettisoning of bombs is done over the sea except when extreme emergency dictates otherwise."

The severity of European weather in November and December 1944 exceeded that of the previous four decades, but such circumstances did not lead to increased area bombing. November did not include a single day of visual bombing on oil sites. As a consequence the Eighth devoted a large percentage of its effort to oil production and storage facilities in a vain attempt to keep production down. Ground support missions for the US First and Third Armies siphoned aircraft away from bombing missions elsewhere. In November the Eighth dropped a mere 332 tons in area attacks. As for December 1944, severe weather and the ground crisis caused by the German counteroffensive in the Ardennes kept the Eighth concentrated on oil, both to reduce the supply of fuel for the counteroffensive and marshaling yards in western Germany and to interfere with direct logistical support to the counteroffensive. It released only 1,066 tons in area attacks during December. Of the 19 area attacks in December, 18 were against targets of opportunity.

Notes

1. Air Ministry, C.S.15803/A.S.P.1., to all AOCs, letter, "Bombardment Policy," signed AVM J. C. Slessor, A.C.A.S. (Policy), 29 October 1942, enclosure to Air Commodore Bufton, to Spaatz, letter M.P./6496/D.B.Ops, "[USSTAF] Bombardment Policy in Regard to Enemy-Occupied Territories," 22 January 1945: AF/HSO microfilm, reel A5616, frs. 16 and 17. Bufton states that the Slessor letter remained in force up until the date of his letter. There is no reason to suppose it was withdrawn before the end of hostilities.

2. The Eighth issued its bombing policy guidelines in SOP format. The recordkeeping instruction for SOPs specified the destruction of the previous procedure when a new one replaced it. This practice had kept everyone on the same page, avoiding reference to outdated procedures. This procedure may account for lack of a consistent turn of bombing policy memos in the Eighth Air Force records for wartime operations.

3. S.46368/A.C.A.S. (Ops), Bottomley, to Eaker, 10 June 1943, AF/HSO microfilm, reel A5885, frs. 617–19.

4. Message, AX837, Air Ministry, to commanding general, Eighth Air Force and AOCs, Bomber and Fighter Commands, 22 June 1943 cleared French targets; Message, AX751 (15 June 1943) and message, AX 166 (25 June 1943), Air Ministry, to same addressees, cleared the Dutch and Belgian targets; AF/HSO microfilm, reel A5885, frs. 622–23, and 632.

5. Brig Gen C. C. Chauncey, chief of staff Eighth Air Force, to CG, VIII Bomber Command, and CG, VIII Fighter Command, memorandum, "Bombardment Directive," 27 June 1943; AF/HSO microfilm, reel A5885, fr. 615.

6. Col George W. Jones, Jr., Eighth Air Force A-2 Operational Intelligence Unit, to Col William N. Cleveland, Eighth Air Force Executive, A-3 Section, memorandum, "Restrictions on Bombing in Enemy-Occupied Countries in Northwest Europe," 27 January 1944; AF/HSO microfilm, reel A5885, fr. 870.

7. S.46368/IV/A.C.A.S. (Ops), AVM W. A. Coryton, to commanding general, USAAFUK, and AOCs, Bomber Command and Allied Expeditionary Air Forces, "Attacks on Electrical Installations in Occupied Countries in N.W. Europe," 26 November 1943; AF/HSO microfilm, reel A5885, fr. 687.

8. S.3119/A.C.A.S. (Ops), AVM W. A. Coryton, to AOC Allied Expeditionary Air Force (copies to commanding general, USAAFUK, and AOC, Bomber Command), "ADGB and Tactical Air Force Offensive Operations," 26 November 1943.

9. Chauncey, to commanding general, VIII Bomber Command, and commanding general, VIII Fighter Command, memorandum, "Bombardment Directive," 27 June 1943; AF/HSO microfilm, reel A5885, fr. 615.

10. HQ, VIII Bomber Command, Report of Operations, 27 September 1943, Mission 104, p. 2, reel A5940, fr. 908. Also see HQ, VIII Bomber Command, Narrative of Operations, 27 September 1943, p. 2, reel A5940, fr. 657.

11. Charles W. McArthur, "Operations Analysis in the US Army Eighth Air Force," vol. 4, *History of Mathematics* (Providence, RI: American Mathematical Society, 1990), 69.

12. Eighth Air Force Planners' Data Sheet, Mission 108, n.d. [kept in diary format], AF/HSO microfilm, reel A5873, fr. 462.

13. Eighth Air Force Planners' Data Sheet, Mission 114, n.d., AF/HSO microfilm, reel A5873, fr. 460.

14. Headquarters Eighth Air Force, Office of the Commanding General, 1st Lt E. D. Whitley, to Lt Col Agan, memorandum, "Visit to 3rd Bomb Division Critique of Bremen, Marienburg-Gydnia and Munster Missions, Held 11 October 1943," n.d. [c.a. 12 October 1943], AF/HSO microfilm, reel A5883, fr. 1944.

15. McArthur, "Operations Analysis," 65. For examples of Maj Gen Frederick Anderson's interest in incendiaries, see his receipt of a special US National Defense Research Committee report on European industrial plants as incendiary targets [Lt Col George W. Jones, Jr., VIII Bomber Command, Operational Intelligence, to Brig Gen Frederick L. Anderson, commanding general, VIII Bomber Command, memorandum, 17 July 1943, AF/HSO microfilm, reel A5500, fr. 1058], and his circular to the Eighth's heavy bomber wing commanders on the usefulness of incendiary attacks [commanding general, VIII Bomber Command, to commanding generals, 1st, 2d, and 4th Bombardment Wings, memorandum, "Effectiveness of Incendiaries," 9 September 1943, AF/HSO microfilm, reel B5549, fr. 1492.]

16. Planners' Data Sheet, Mission 115, AF/HSO microfilm, reel A5873, fr. 461.

17. Schweinfurt was too small to provide an accurate H2S picture. No H2S aircraft accompanied the raid.

18. Planners' Data Sheet, Mission 116, AF/HSO microfilm, reel A5873.

19. Planners' Data Sheet, Mission 119 A [Aborted], AF/HSO microfilm, reel A5873, fr. 457.

20. Planners' Data Sheet, Mission 156, AF/HSO microfilm, reel A5873, fr. 438.

21. Planners' Data Sheet, Mission 198, AF/HSO microfilm, reel A5873, fr. 418.

22. Planners' Data Sheet, Mission 200, AF/HSO microfilm, reel A5873, fr. 417.

23. Message, 8FC F67AE, commanding general, VIII Fighter Command, to commanding officers, 65th, 67th, and 70th Fighter Wings, 9 February 1944; AF/HSO microfilm, reel A5885, fr. 812.

24. Spaatz, to Eaker, memorandum, "Objectives for Area Attack," 3 February 1944, AF/HSO microfilm, reel A5616, fr. 45.

25. Fifteenth Air Force, to Commanding Generals et al., Instruction (File No. 384.3), "Bombing Limitations," 21 February 1944, AF/HSO microfilm, reel A6436, fr. 560.

26. Memo 55-2, HQ Eighth Air Force, SOPs, Operations, "Indiscriminate Bombing," 7 March 1944, AF/HSO microfilm, reel A5616, fr. 119.

27. Planners' Data Sheet, Mission 287, AF/HSO microfilm, reel A5873, fr. 379.

28. Doolittle, to Spaatz (attn: Anderson), memorandum, "Tentative Operations Plans, Eighth Air Force," 31 March 1944, HSO microfilm, reel A5885, fr. 1063.

29. Ibid.; 1st ind., USSTAF, deputy commander for operations, 8 April 1944, HSO microfilm, reel A5885, fr. 1064.

30. Dr. David Griggs, advisor special group [Radar], to General McDonald [USSTAF director of intelligence], memorandum, 5 July 1944, Spaatz Papers, Subject File 1929–1945, Targets.

31. Spaatz, to Arnold, letter, 27 August 1944, Spaatz Papers, Diary.

32. Anderson, to director of operations, memorandum, 21 July 1944, Spaatz Papers, Subject File 1929–1945.

33. Operations Memo 55-24, Headquarters Eighth Air Force, Office of the Commanding General, Standard Operating Procedures, "Attack of Secondary and Last-Resort Targets," 29 October 1944, Air Force Historical Research Agency, Maxwell AFB, Ala., File no. 519.5991-1.

34. Operations Memorandum 5-11, Headquarters Fifteenth Air Force, "Operations Planning, Targets of Opportunity," 7 November 1944, AF/HSO microfilm, reel A6430, fr. 59.

35. See Operations Memo 5-11, Headquarters Fifteenth Air Force, "Operations Planning, Targets of Opportunity," 3 May 1944, AF/HSO microfilm, reel A6430, fr. 111. This memo makes no mention of German targets.

November

9 November: Eighth Air Force—sends 800 heavy bombers to hit fortifications at Metz in support of US Third Army offensive.

12 November: Bomber Command—sinks German battleship *Tirpitz*.

16 November: Bomber Command—supplies close support, in daylight, to American troops by bombing Jülich, Düren, and Heinsberg. Fifteenth Air Force—two B-24s land in Switzerland after mission to Munich. Eighth Air Force—sends almost 1,200 heavy bombers to support offensive by US First and Ninth Armies.

25 November: Eighth Air Force—assigns 36th Bomb Squadron to establish permanent airborne RCM screen for attacking bombers and to protect primary VHF fighter to bomber frequencies.

27 November: Germans launch 750 interceptors, their largest number of the war, their "Big Hit" (*Grosse Schlag*) fails to produce significant results.

In November 1944 clouds covered the synthetic oil plants for the first 29 days of the month. All three of the strategic air forces (Eighth and Fifteenth Air Forces and Bomber Command) attempted to overcome the inaccuracy associated with bombing through cloud cover with sheer quantity in hopes of placing some bombs on the vital area of the targeted plants. The Eighth devoted 41 percent of its bombing effort (16,023 tons) for the month to oil facilities. The Fifteenth added 35 percent (4,690 tons) of its efforts, and Bomber Command contributed 24 percent (14,244 tons) of its missions to the total effort. Nonetheless, German aviation gasoline production doubled from the previous month to 35,400 tons. The upswing in production came at a steep cost. Speer and his chief subordinate, Edmund Geilenberg, had to establish a slave labor force of 350,000 to keep the plants in working order. The plants were defended with hundreds of high velocity antiaircraft guns (the plant at Bohlen had more guns than Berlin), thousands of tons of shells, and many thousand gunners. The Eighth suffered a 2 percent bomber loss rate in operations against the oil plants, more than triple its loss rate for all other missions.

During the month the Eighth dropped a total of 37,799 tons on Germany and 2,607 tons on France. The Eighth spent more than a third of its monthly effort against marshaling yards, rail viaducts and bridges, and canals (15,160 tons). Most of that bombing attacked marshaling yards in the Ruhr and western Germany. The bulk of its remaining bombs assisted two American ground attacks. On 9 November the Eighth assisted a US Third Army assault on the fortifications surrounding Metz. It devoted 751 bombers and 2,586 tons of bombs to this effort—most of the aircraft used GH radar bombing. Lt Gen George S. Patton, the Third Army's commander, was pleased with the results, telling General Spaatz, "This morning I was in the Verny group of forts which, if you remember, was the no. 1 priority in the bombing attack you put in on the 9th [of November]. One of the forts was completely removed—I have never seen so many large chunks of concrete in my life."[1]

A week later the Eighth began Operation Queen, a US First and Ninth Army offensive near Aachen, with an attack by 1,191 bombers, all using GH or MH radar-assisted aiming. They released 25 tons of high explosives and 3,847 tons of fragmentation bombs on positions a little to the rear of the German front lines. This precaution minimized the chance of bombs falling on Allied frontline troops. Bomber Command also joined in the attack, striking key road junctions in three towns close to the front—Düren, Jülich, and Heinsburg—with 1,130 heavy bombers, 5,787 tons of high explosives, and 584 tons of incendiaries. Bomber Command attacked visually. It was the largest close air support mission ever flown in terms of bombers and tonnage. The bombing went almost perfectly; only one bomber encountered a problem, causing it to release its bombs several miles short. Although it caught and hammered a German infantry division that was in the open and moving to the front, this attack produced little gain on the ground. Unlike the bombing at St. Lo in July 1944 the attack had not shaken the German troops manning the front line, nor did the ground forces assigned to Queen have the more than four to one strength advantage that the Americans possessed in Cobra. Perhaps the ground commanders should have asked for heavier ordnance delivered on the front line and taken the risk of short bombs.

In November 1944 Bomber Command expended more than 99 percent of its effort (12,193 sorties and 58,870 tons of bombs) against Germany. Its bombers applied the remainder against targets in Norway. The command accomplished one of its most famous achievements there. The surrender of Finland to the USSR and the subsequent Soviet pursuit of retreating German units into northern Norway rendered German naval bases in the north of Norway untenable. The pride of the German fleet, the battleship *Tirpitz*, was forced south to an anchorage at Tromsö Fjord, which put it into the range of Bomber Command's Lancasters. On 5 November in daylight hours, 32 Lancasters, each carrying a 12,000-pound bomb, attacked and damaged the ship, leaving it unable to sail from the fjord. A week later, on 12 November, 30 Lancasters with 12,000-pound bombs attacked again. When the smoke cleared the RAF had lost a bomber and the Kriegesmarine a battleship.

Strategic Directive No. 2 set oil facilities as the top priority and, as noted, Harris placed a quarter of his bombs in that category. The directive set transportation as the second priority. Bomber Command attacked the Mittelland and Dortmund-Ems canals with 2,508 tons and seven marshaling yards with 2,942 tons—9 percent of the command's monthly total. Harris sent almost 60 percent of his sorties (7,194) and bombs (32,251 tons) against city areas. Twelve of the raids, four conducted in daylight, exceeded 1,000 tons, including 5,023 tons released over Düsseldorf on the night of 2 November. The heavies suffered a loss rate of 1.2 percent during these raids. Bomber Command employed an average of 14 percent incendiaries in its bomb loadings for area bombing and a much smaller percentage for attacks on marshaling yards.

In accordance with the Strategic Directive No. 2, the Fifteenth put much of its strength into attacking oil facilities (35 percent of its sorties and 4,690 tons) and transportation bombing (6,817 tons and 51 percent of its sorties). Of the attacks on transportation, approximately 1,100 tons hit Austrian rail targets, while 2,500 tons struck German targets, and 1,000 tons hit the Brenner Pass. The other 14 percent of the month's bombing fell on scattered targets, such as ordnance depots in Vienna, Italian airfields, and, at the request of Marshal Josip Tito's Yugoslav forces, towns and roads.

By the end of the month the attrition inflicted on the German Reichsbahn began to reach critical proportions. The Reichsbahn had great reserves: rolling stock and locomotives looted from the entirety of Europe; an abundance of tracks for alternate routes; and well-trained, relatively numerous repair crews. All this did not suffice. By the first week of November, 50,000 "workers" from Holland reinforced German repair crews. By mid-November the Germans committed 161,000 workers—95,000 of them in the Ruhr. Marshaling yards had top priority. On 29 November Hitler allowed Speer to send 150,000 laborers, taken from all sections of the country, including some engaged in fortification work, to the Ruhr. Others may have come from the infamous Auschwitz death camp. After a killing frenzy in October 1944, that piece of hell on earth began to dismantle its ovens and crematoria and to ship its inmates to the interior of Germany for slave labor in November. The approach of the Red Army and the need for more labor created by the bombing offensive may have indirectly saved some of the death camp's intended victims. However, enormous inputs of unskilled labor could not substitute for exhausted trained crews. Repairs to constantly bombed yards consumed spare parts, signals, switches, and rails. Bombs churned up the earth making it unable to support the rail loads. Bombs also flattened the switching humps, dramatically decreasing the yards' ability to marshal cars into proper trains.[2]

Unable to use wrecked or unrepaired telecommunications equipment, Reichsbahn and German industrial managers, who had their production disrupted by late or failed deliveries, made fatal recourse to their code machines, an action that proved fatal. By November 1944, the British Government Code

470

and Cypher School—the Ultra organization—had broken two Reichsbahn Enigma keys (code-named Blunderbuss and Culverin) for Germany and the West and some armament industry Geheimschreiber settings (code-name Fish).[3] An 8 November decryption called for more use of waterways. Other decryptions spoke of increased antiaircraft defenses for traffic installations, and a 1 January decryption stated that fighter-bomber attacks (from the Ninth Air Force) in the area between the Moselle and the Saarland had ruined weeks of repair work, eliminated telephone facilities, and made it impossible to reroute trains.[4]

This cumulative destruction of the yards took its toll on the economy. Items of military necessity such as troop and vital supply trains could get through on a single track. Although some routes could be opened in a few hours or days, point-to-point travel times in Germany lengthened, but one through line did not a functioning marshaling yard make. Raid after raid, repair after repair (each not quite as good as the last), reduced the capacity of the yards in an ever-descending spiral dooming the German war economy. The thousands of separate items needed for production, not to mention coal, piled up at the factories and shaft heads or lay idle in marshaling yards or sidings, as the trains to haul them could no longer be put together. By November the Reichsbahn got a chilling glimpse of its future. It could not even keep its fireboxes full. Instead of the normal 20-day supply of hard coal, the system's supply stood at 11 days on 5 November, 10 days on 11 November, nine on 18 November, eight days on 20 November, six days on 1 December, and five days on 12 December. The east suffered just as badly as the west, and in the south, cut off from the Ruhr by shattered rail lines, empty bins testified to a complete coal famine.[5]

When the Reichsbahn resorted to brown coal for its fuel, locomotive power dropped, repair intervals tripled, and a much larger smoke cloud made the engines easier targets for roving Allied fighter-bombers and fighters. Reduced to a hand-to-mouth fuel situation in one of the greatest coal-producing countries in the world, and unable to marshal the necessary trains, the Reichsbahn imposed further embargoes on cargo. In the western areas, only coal and Wehrmacht troop and supply shipments were allowed; not even food or armament production trains could be placed. The railroads even refused a plea from the Ministry of Food and Agriculture for additional car space for the harvest.[6] Clearly the economic life of Germany was ebbing away. Yet, like the Wehrmacht and the Luftwaffe, the Reichsbahn was capable of one last effort, which Hitler demanded and squandered in his futile Ardennes counteroffensive.

Notes

1. Letter, G. S. Patton, CG Third Army, to C. Spaatz, CG USSTAF, 19 November 1944.
2. Mierzejewski, "Wheels Must Roll," 282–83 and 287.
3. The Geheimschreiber was a more advanced machine than the Enigma. It was used for Hitler's and other high-ranking officials' traffic.
4. Hinsley, *British Intelligence*, vol. 3, pt. 2, 527.
5. Mierzejewski, 298–99.
6. Ibid., 304.

December

9 December: Fifteenth Air Force—one B-24 lands in Switzerland, after mission to Regensburg.

16 December: Germans begin Ardennes counteroffensive (Battle of the Bulge). Assign all fighter aircraft flying air defense of Germany to support of the ground attack.

18 December 1944–13 January 1945: Eighth Air Force—concentrates on transportation targets in Western Germany and near the battle zone.

24 December: Eighth Air Force—dispatches over 2,000 heavy bombers to attack airfields, communications centers, and cities close to front in support of American defenders in the Battle of the Bulge.

25 December: Fifteenth Air Force—one B-24 crashes in Switzerland after mission to Innsbruck.

31 December: Bomber Command—Mosquitoes attack Gestapo headquarters in Oslo.

The German counteroffensive in the Ardennes broke upon the Allied ground troops on 16 December. The attack presented the strategic air forces with "the ground emergency" that their directives had always anticipated. Harris and Spaatz redeemed their pledge to supply aid in characteristic fashion.

In December 1944 the Eighth flew 15,542 effective bombing sorties over Germany and released 41,092 tons of bombs. Forty-five percent of that effort took place between 1 and 16 December. In that first half of the month, the Eighth continued the bombing pattern established in November. Two H2X sighted attacks, 6 and 12 December, on Merseberg placed over 2,100 tons on synthetic oil sites; another raid using H2X put 400 bombers over and 943 tons on the Tegel section in Berlin on 5 December. A day before the counteroffensive the Eighth struck the Henschel tank factory at Kassel. Two-thirds of the Eighth's effort in the first half of December was against marshaling yards. It showered them with more than 12,600 tons (5,900 tons sighted by H2X) before the German attack through the Ardennes.

The Germans, out of a healthy respect for Allied tactical air-power, had chosen to launch their attack in a period of severe winter conditions to limit air attacks on their advancing forces. However, within 24 hours the Eighth began a series of counter-strikes on the German ground units. On 18 December 400 bombers struck marshaling yards in Cologne, Koblenz, and Mainz. The next day small groups of bombers, employing radar assisted sighting, hit eight small centers of communications—such as Bitburg and Stadtkyll—leading to the front and the mar-shaling yards of Erhang and Koblenz. The Eighth returned to the attack on communications centers on 23 December. On Christ-mas Eve the weather cleared and Doolittle dispatched 2,046 heavy bombers, the largest bomber force ever dispatched in one day for one set of missions. One hundred sixty-two crews aborted before reaching their targets; the remaining 1,884 effec-tive sorties used visual sighting on their bomb runs and smashed numerous airfields, marshaling yards, and communi-cations centers. The relentless bombing did not cease. In the last half of December 1944 the Eighth dropped 2,150 tons on air-fields, 3,000 tons on communications and detraining centers; 10,200 tons on marshaling yards; and 4,616 tons on railroad bridges. The chance of hitting a bridge, employing even the rela-tively more accurate GH and MH radar systems, was minuscule. This bombing came at the expense of other priorities—oil targets received only 880 tons.

Bomber Command reacted to the German counteroffensive at Ardennes by halting almost all bombing of city areas. From 2 to 17 December, Harris sent his heavies out to strike six city areas and to employ area bomb techniques against four other cities and their marshaling yards. This campaign expended 3,700 sor-ties and 16,000 tons of the month's total of 11,341 sorties and 51,132 tons over Germany. Four of the raids exceeded 2,000 tons: Hagen (2 December), Karlsruhe (4 December), the com-mand's last major raid on Essen (12 December), and Duisburg

(17 December). A raid of 1,248 tons on the rail facilities and town of Heilbronn on 4 December reportedly killed 7,000 people and destroyed 80 percent of the town.[1] Harris maintained the pressure on the oil and chemical industry with 5,446 tons before 17 December and 2,600 hundred tons afterwards. The command's attack on the largest synthetic oil facility, the Leuna Plant at Merseburg, halted the facility's operations until the end of the war. The larger British bombs proved far more damaging than the smaller American bombs. In a series of four raids during daylight hours, the command sought to help the Allied ground forces by breaching the Heimbach Dam on the River Urft. Sorties by 341 bombers (two aircraft lost) dropped 2,237 tons of bombs between 3 and 11 December. These bomb strikes failed to destroy the dam, leaving the Germans with the ability to open the sluice gates and isolate Allied spearheads if they so wished. Before the counteroffensive kicked off, Bomber Command had unleashed 5,206 tons on German marshaling yards, including 2,072 tons on Soest by night and 1,008 on Duisberg by day. Starting on 21 December the command more than doubled that figure with 13,414 tons and five raids of more than 1,000 tons. Most of the tonnage of the six daytime raids and ten night raids concentrated on yards serving the battlefront, such as Koblenz, Cologne, Bingen, and Rheydt. As it had from the beginning of the conflict, the command maintained its mining program with 202 sorties. It concentrated its mines in the Baltic Sea and Norwegian fjords housing the remnants of the German fleet. The command also maintained its support of special operations. On Christmas Eve the command sent 424 effective sorties and 2,048 tons against German airfields. Finally, in the second half of the month, the command spent 3,303 tons in direct support of the ground forces support by bombing road junctions at St. Vith and Houffalize and attacking Trier, the closest marshaling yard to the front. On the last day of 1944, eight Mosquitoes attacked Gestapo headquarters in Oslo.

December's poor weather also affected the operations of the Fifteenth Air Force; two-thirds of its missions during the month used H2X. It concentrated more than 80 percent of its total effective sorties against Greater Germany (including Austria and portions of Czechoslovakia), hitting marshaling yards and locomotive shops serving the German eastern and Italian fronts with 6,000 tons; the Fifteenth also struck oil facilities, especially in Vienna, with more than 7,000 tons. Rail facilities in Italy and rail viaducts in the Brenner Pass came in for another 1,500 tons. The RAF's No. 205 Group added 800 more sorties, the bulk flown to aid Tito's forces in Yugoslavia.

Its raids against strongly defended oil and other targets put the Fifteenth's heavy bombers into the sights of enemy heavy flak guns. Here the Fifteenth's ratio of two B-24 groups to each B-17 group (the reverse of the Eighth's ratio) increased its casualties, for the Fifteenth exposed comparatively more of the lower altitude B-24s to enemy guns. In December the Fifteenth lost 152 heavy bombers in combat for a loss rate of 2.1 percent, twice that of Bomber Command (0.9 percent or 117 bombers) and three and one-half times that of the Eighth (0.6 percent or 98 bombers).

German defenses could extract a toll from each major operation, but they could no longer prevent the Anglo-American bomber forces from roaming at will throughout the Reich. No amount of antiaircraft artillery (the principal killer of Allied bombers since July of 1944) could protect the vast economic infrastructure exposed to Allied air attack. A year earlier the Eighth refused to mount deep penetration raids into Germany, the Fifteenth had barely begun operations, and the scales had tipped against Bomber Command in the Battle of Berlin. Now American fighter escorts pounced on almost every German aircraft. The Eighth and the Fifteenth could field almost 3,000 heavy bombers a day and had permanently reduced synthetic oil production by 80 percent. Bomber Command not only had increased its bomb lift and vastly improved its accuracy but also had commenced to conduct up to 20 percent of its operations in daylight.

Note

1. Richards, *Hardest Victory*, 260.

Part V
1945

January

1–2 January: Bomber Command: breaches Mittelland Canal.

12 January: Soviet winter offensive begins, soon overruns important industrial area of Silesia in Eastern Germany.

16 January: USSTAF—General Spaatz and Air Marshal Bottomley issue Strategic Bombing Directive No. 3.

26 January: Prime Minister Churchill prods RAF air staff to order attacks on major cities and transportation centers in Eastern Germany. All ground lost in Battle of the Bulge regained by Allies.

27 January: Red Army liberates Auschwitz death camp.

In January 1945 weather plagued air operations, hitting the Fifteenth Air Force with particular virulence. The Fifteenth launched only 2,808 effective heavy bomber sorties—its lowest total since February 1944. It directed 60 percent of its sorties against Austria and 15 percent each against Italy and Yugoslavia. Of the 5,860 tons of bombs it dropped, the Fifteenth aimed 98 percent at two target systems: oil facilities (1,795 tons) and rail transportation (3,921 tons). Once again the Fifteenth Air Force suffered the highest loss rate of all strategic air forces operating in Europe. It lost 79 heavy bombers out of 2,808 sorties, or 2.8 percent, as compared to Bomber Command's loss of 125 aircraft out of 9,225 sorties (1.4 percent) and the Eighth's 90 out of 14,288 (0.6 percent). Fifty-seven percent of its bombing employed H2X.

Of the 31,394 tons of bombs Bomber Command expended in January 1945, it hit the French town of Royan with 1,780 tons of ordnance. This bombing caused some controversy. Unlike other German forces blocking other French ports, the garrison commander of Royan, located at the head of the Bordeaux estuary, had, either out of altruism or from a desire to cut his rations list, allowed civilians who wished to leave the opportunity to do so. Assured that their bombs would cause a minimum of civilian casualties, the Allies rewarded this "good deed" by planning to deliver a massive air strike on the city— to be delivered when conditions did not suit operations over Germany. Harris duly delivered Bomber Command's last blow against the Germans in France on the night of 4 January. Not only did the town continue to resist until the end of the war but the bombing, nonetheless, killed several hundred civilians who had refused to leave either out of fear of their compatriots in liberated France, sickness, or simply inertia.

Over Germany, Bomber Command stepped up its bombing of oil targets, concentrating on the large synthetic plants, such as Zeitz and Merseburg. The Eighth's focus on supporting the army prevented it from hitting those targets. In all Bomber Command dropped one-third of the month's effort (10,112 tons) on oil targets. Nor did Harris ignore his obligations for direct support of ground forces. His forces flew 1,545 sorties and dropped 7,000 tons; more than 20 percent of the month's total on German marshaling yards that were sustaining the Ardennes counteroffensive or the German attack in Alsace. More than 40 percent of the command's bombs, 12,993 tons, went to the area bombing of German cities. Main-force attacks averaging more than 2,500 tons each smashed into Nürnberg (2 January), Hannover (5 January), and Munich (6 January). Other raids averaging 1,400 tons each struck Hanau (6 January), Magdeburg (16 January), and Zuffhausen (28 January). The loss rate on these raids, 2 percent, doubled that of other operations. Of the 5,250 tons of incendiaries dropped by the command in January, 4,780 fell on cities. A main-force raid showered 1,367 tons on the I. G. Farben chemical plant in Ludwigshafen, a target associated with residential areas. Bombers dropped an additional 238 tons of incendiaries, which accounted for almost all of that type of bomb not expended by the marking forces. The conclusion of the Battle of the Bulge freed the command from the necessity of raiding western Germany. The collapse of the German night fighter defenses allowed Bomber Command to conduct almost uncontested raids deep into greater Germany against oil targets such as Brux. Harris's continued adherence to area bombing set the stage for the command's February operations into eastern Germany.

In January 1945 Eighth Air Force flew more effective sorties (14,288) than Bomber Command and the Fifteenth Air Force combined. More than two-thirds of the sorties employed some form of radar-assisted bombing. The Eighth's bomb tonnage (35,335) exceeded Bomber Command's and almost sextupled that of the Fifteenth. However, little of that effort resulted in damage to intended strategic targets: only 1,100 sorties and 2,850 tons—more than 80 percent aimed at refineries and benzene plants—actually hit oil targets. Another 560 sorties hit steelworks, aluminum plants, and arms and tank plants. The bulk of the Eighth's exertions went against the German transportation system. The Eighth launched 1,165 sorties and 3,227 tons to mount 32 attacks on communications centers directly supporting the German counteroffensive at Ardennes. Rail and highway bridges and viaducts absorbed another 2,650 sorties and 7,460 tons. Finally, the Eighth literally rained bombs onto marshaling yards in western Germany, conducting 7,650 sorties and dropping 20,660 tons of ordnance in more than 50 attacks throughout the region.

In this case, at least, the Eighth had the unique opportunity to hit not just two but three targets with the same bomb. Destruction of rail and highway systems provided direct tactical aid to Allied ground forces by denying German ground forces uninterrupted use of their transportation system. The Germans, who relied heavily on railways for logistical support, were forced to detrain almost 100 miles before their anticipated arrival points, straining their inadequate motor transport beyond its capabilities, which in turn caused the premature breakdown of armored vehicles fresh from the factories that had not yet been adequately broken in. This effort's success was invaluable in halting the German offensive and advancing the overall Anglo-American strategy of the defeat of German ground forces and their subsequent occupation of Germany. The destruction of the transportation system in western Germany, including the Ruhr, fulfilled the transportation priority of the Combined Bomber Offensive. The simultaneous loss of the Silesian and Ruhr coalfields, one through ground operations and the other solely by airpower, dealt a fatal blow to German industrial capacity.

Even as the three strategic air forces continued to operate in the pattern set in December, the strategic and political context changed. Soviet advances in the east and the Anglo-American repulse of the Ardennes counteroffensive allowed Allied forces to renew the ground offensive in the west. These developments tightened the vise on Germany. The situation seemed increasingly chaotic within that stricken land as waves of refugees threatened to overwhelm relief organizations, while spreading panic and defeatism to every corner of the country. A US-UK-USSR summit meeting at the highest levels of Allied leadership that would decide the fate of eastern Europe for decades to come was scheduled for the end of the month. It consumed the efforts of the three Allied leaders: one a dying man, one the leader of an exhausted state, and one the paranoid dictator of a devastated but powerful police state. All these forces conjoined to force reconsideration and sometimes abrupt shifts of strategic bombing priorities.

Targeting Priorities and "Strategic Directive No. 3"

The Battle of the Bulge brought about a reappraisal of long-range goals in USSTAF. Two weeks after the offensive started, General Arnold, reflecting the thinking in Washington, wrote to General Spaatz: "General Marshall . . . has been pressing in Washington for any and every plan to bring increased effort against the German forces. . . . Periods of about *sixty days* [emphasis in original] have been discussed."[1] Arnold went on to state that he could not view, "with complacency," estimates that the war in Europe would not end until the summer of 1945.

In Paris, meanwhile, Spaatz and the USSTAF staff had adopted a somewhat longer perspective. By the end of 1944, they foresaw a war of several more months' duration if strategic airpower did not return to the oil campaign and if German jet production continued unabated. In fact bombing oil facilities did hinder the German ground forces and conventional piston-engine aircraft but not the Me-262. Its jet engines used low-grade fuels, such as kerosene, that the Germans could produce relatively easily. The specter of hundreds of twin-engine Me-262 jets, each armed with four 30 mm cannons, launched against the slower American escort fighters and lumbering heavy bombers, severely haunting Spaatz's calculations.

As mentioned, the concentration of the Eighth on tactical bombing related to the Battle of the Bulge had eased the pressure on Germany's oil industry. Also, early in 1945 a new mass-produced, faster, snorkel-breathing U-boat had begun to enter service. These new submarines might allow the Nazis to successfully reopen the Battle of the Atlantic, jeopardizing the Allies' supply lines from the United States. The Allies had also completely lost their capability to decipher U-boat signals.[2] A change in German code procedures had deprived the Allied navies of much of their knowledge of the locations and intentions of the enemy. This loss accounted in part for the panic in Allied naval circles that led to pressure on the airmen to prevent submarines from getting to open waters by bombing their construction yards. As for tanks, intelligence indicated that, upon manufacture, they reached the front in less than a month. The Germans had suffered severe tank losses in the Bulge, and the anticipated Soviet winter offensive would cause more. A campaign against tank plants would hamper the Germans' ability to replace losses. As Spaatz and Doolittle told Eisenhower, all these factors meant that the Eighth should return to strategic targeting at once. Eisenhower disagreed; the critical ground battle situation, he insisted, still required all the strategic bomber help that Spaatz could spare.[3]

Spaatz, however, did not give up. Latest intelligence, he said, had shown that the Germans would produce more oil than their minimum requirements in January, if unmolested by the Eighth. He probably expressed the general feeling in USSTAF that continuing to bomb marshaling yards and other tactical targets west of the Rhine would only lengthen the war by relieving German industry of the pressure of strategic bombardment.[4]

On 6 January, Spaatz gained Eisenhower's permission for two-thirds of the bomber force to resume oil attacks as a top priority, followed by tank plants and jet production if necessary.[5] One-third of his force, the 2d Air Division (equipped with GH), would assist the ground forces. Three days later on 9 January, Spaatz gained SHAEF's consent to use visual bombing techniques to bomb enemy jet production on the same priority as oil facilities.[6]

Spaatz's concern about being overcommitted to tactical bombing reached the newly constructed Pentagon in Washington. In a letter to Arnold dated 7 January he expressed the general pessimism and widespread fear of jets that was prevalent within USSTAF: "Our estimate of the situation concerning the whole German war proposition does not lead up to the conclusion that German strength will crack in the near future." As for oil targets, Spaatz's intelligence estimates indicated that the Germans could operate along defensive lines if they practiced the strictest economy. He predicted German resistance to the bitter end and concluded, "unless our ground armies succeed in obtaining a significant victory over German ground armies west of the Rhine in the reasonably near future, it will be necessary to reorient ourselves and prepare for a long drawn out war."[7]

On 11 January at the weekly air commanders' conference, Spaatz, Anderson, and Doolittle reviewed the strategic bombing situation. "From the strategic point of view," lamented Anderson, "the picture is very sad!" The strategic air forces "were paying a tremendous price by concentrating on helping ground forces." Oil, ball bearings, aircraft factories, and submarine yards would have to be hit again. Doolittle backed up Anderson "100 percent or possibly even more." Unless the bombing of strategic targets resumed at once, German jets would prevent deep-penetration raids after July. Spaatz took note of Eisenhower's agreement to release two-thirds of the Eighth to attack oil and jets. He suggested specific U-boat targets as well as armored fighting vehicles as the second priority.[8] Support for the vehicle plants had originated in Eisenhower's headquarters and reflected the needs of the ground forces.[9] Spaatz probably added them as part of his agreement with Eisenhower allowing USSTAF partial resumption of the strategic offensive.

General Spaatz and Air Marshal Sir Norman Bottomley agreed on a new strategic bombing policy, "Directive No. 3 for the Strategic Air Forces in Europe," on 12 January and issued it on 16 January. In his cover letter to Arnold, Spaatz stated simply, "a new directive is necessary at this time, since we have recently had to revise our estimate of VE day [Victory Day in Europe], and consequently must include the attack of target systems with a longer range application."[10] After identifying oil, transportation, and important industrial areas as priority targets, the new directive added both the authorization to employ "the necessary amount of strategic effort" required to neutralize jets and the instruction that the U-boat organization "will be attacked whenever possible by marginal effort or incidental to operations covered by the proceeding priorities."[11] In this case the marginal effort would provide a substantial amount of bombs for submarines because missions diverting from visual targets could obtain excellent H2X resolution from coastal targets.

The Air Staff in Washington found the directive a "much too conservative approach to the problem." They asked Spaatz to consider raising the priority of attacking U-boats and providing ground support.[12] Portal, who did not agree that jets constituted a threat because he did not believe that the war would drag on, accepted the directive as temporary. He hoped to revise it during the CCS meetings at Malta at the end of January.

Notes

1. Letter, Arnold to Spaatz, 30 December 1944, Spaatz Papers, Diary.
2. Hinsley, *British Intelligence*, vol. 3, pt. 2, 853.
3. Command Diary, entry for 5 January 1945, Spaatz Papers, Diary.
4. Message, Anderson to Spaatz, 5 January 1945, Spaatz Diary. See also Vandenberg's Diary, entry for 7 January 1945, Vandenberg Papers, Diary, box 1; memo for the record, Lt Gen Giles, 5 January 1945, on conference with Anderson and Winant, AFHSO microfilm reel A1658, frs. 146366.
5. SHAEF Meetings, 6 January 1945, Robb Papers, RAF Museum.
6. Command Diary, entries for 8 and 9 January 1945, Spaatz Papers, Diary.
7. Letter, Spaatz to Arnold, 7 January 1945, Spaatz Papers, Diary. This letter is a reply to Arnold's of 14 December 1944.
8. Notes of the Allied Air Commanders Conference held at SHAEF, Versailles, on Thursday, 11 January 1945, at 1130 hours, Spaatz Papers, Diary.

9. Minutes, USSTAF Staff Meeting, 16 January 1945, Spaatz Papers, Diary; and message, Air Staff SHAEF to Chairman Combined Strategic Targeting Committee, 13 January 1945, AFHSO microfilm reel A5543, Fr. 229.

10. Letter, Spaatz to Arnold, 16 January 1945, Spaatz Papers, Diary.

11. Directive No. 3 for the Strategic Air Forces in Europe, Spaatz Papers, Diary.

12. Memo for General Kuter, subject: Comments on Strategic Directive No. 3 by AC/AS Plans, AF/HSO microfilm reel A1658A, frs. 1471–1472, AFHRC File no. 168.491.

February

3 February: Eighth Air Force—executes Operation Thunder-clap—anti-morale bombing of center of Berlin in hopes of collapsing Nazi government.

5 February: Fifteenth Air Force—one B-17 crashes in Switzerland after mission to Regensburg.

7–8 February: Bomber Command—attacks Kleve and Goch in support of British ground offensive.

13–14 February: Bomber Command—796 Lancasters bomb untouched city of Dresden and ignite a firestorm that kills 35,000 persons.

14 February: Eighth Air Force—311 B-17s hit Dresden center of city.

15 February: Eighth Air Force—210 B-17s strike military targets in Dresden.

16–19 February: BC—attacks Wesel in preparation for British ground offensive.

20–21 February: BC—begins first of 36 consecutive night raids on Berlin by Mosquitoes.

22 February: Allied strategic and tactical air forces—execute Operation Clarion—the bombing of dozens of small marshaling yards and rail junctions in small, untouched German towns to demonstrate the reach and destructiveness of Allied airpower to all Germans.

25 February: Eighth Air Force—three B-17s crash in Switzerland after mission to Munich.

27 February: Fifteenth Air Force—two B-17s and six B-24s land in Switzerland after mission to Augsburg.

In February 1945 improved weather allowed the Fifteenth Air Force to more than triple its number of effective sorties to 10,535 and drop almost four times as many bombs—22,593 tons—as in January. Slightly more than 50 percent of the raids used visual sighting. Eighty percent of the bombing went beyond the Alps to Austria and Germany; German supply lines into Italy received most of the remainder. On 8 February the Fifteenth conducted one of its largest area raids with 113 heavy bombers. One of its combat wings could not locate its primary target and bombed its secondary target, the center of Vienna instead. On 22 February, in conjunction with the two other strategic air forces, the Fifteenth participated in Operation Clarion. For the month the Fifteenth directed two-thirds of its bomb lift to marshaling yards and other rail targets and a further 20 percent towards oil facilities. The remainder consisted of attacks on airfields and armament plants. In all its bombing the Fifteenth used no incendiary bombs whatsoever. As usual the Fifteenth's loss rate of 1.4 percent, although low, exceeded that of both the Eighth (0.5 percent) and Bomber Command (1 percent).

The Fifteenth's bombing by and large followed the pattern of its previous operations. The Eighth Air Force and Bomber Command spent much of February attacking relatively new targets in eastern Germany in hopes of disrupting German defenses on the eastern front, or in attacking old targets for different reasons. On 3 February the Eighth once again attacked Berlin, not so much to engage the Luftwaffe, which no longer offered an effective threat, but to damage east-west communications, aid the Soviet advance, and, perhaps, precipitate the fall of the Nazi state.

Thunderclap

Even as General Spaatz and Air Marshal Sir Norman Bottomley issued Directive No. 3, events overtook it. The Soviets opened their winter offensive on 12 January. Overwhelming the German defenders, they drove hundreds of thousands of German refugees before them and conquered Silesia's industrial area (Germany's last intact, unbombed production base). This region included large coal deposits. The Soviets reached the Oder River, 45 miles east of Berlin, on 31 January. As the Red offensive steamrolled forward, the Western Allies prepared to renew their own ground offensive. Meanwhile, the Anglo-American and Soviet high commands and political leadership completed arrangements for a series of Anglo-American and Tripartite conferences at Malta and Yalta. The conjunction of these events changed strategic bombing priorities and led directly to an attack on marshaling yards and cities in eastern Germany. This bombing campaign included an assault on Dresden on the night of 13 February. At least 35,000 died in these bombings.

The Allies' decision to bomb cities in eastern Germany stemmed from the Anglo-Americans' desire to support the Soviet offensive by knocking out transportation centers serving Germany's eastern front. Another objective was to prevent the rapid shifting of forces among sectors along the eastern front and impede the transfer of troops from west to east. Berlin was the administrative center of the nation and it served as a transportation nexus for a large section of the eastern front. As such, Berlin was an obvious target for this effort. Accordingly, on 16 January, Spaatz's chief of staff ordered Doolittle to take a new look at Operation Thunderclap and begin planning its execution.[1]

As mentioned earlier, the Allies first conceived of Thunderclap as a combined Bomber Command–United States Strategic Air Forces (USSTAF) daylight mission on Berlin in response to the German V-1 offensive during the summer of 1944. Because of opposition from Spaatz and others, it had been planned but not carried out. By early September 1944 USSTAF planners had filed it away for reconsideration when the situation in Germany deteriorated to the extent that one large blow on Berlin might shock its government into surrender. With the Germans' Ardennes counteroffensive turned back and the Soviets' shattering of the front in the east, Spaatz believed that the crucial moment might come soon.

The British, too, began to consider Thunderclap. On 22 January Air Commodore Sidney O. Bufton suggested the launching of the operation while the Soviet offensive was in full stride.[2] Bufton served as director of bomber operations and chairman of the Combined Strategic Targeting Committee, a combined USSTAF and British air staff agency that selected specific strategic targets and ranked them for bombing by the strategic air forces. He feared that the psychological moment would pass if the Allies did not execute the operation before the Soviets' momentum slowed.[3] Bottomley agreed, noting that "German radio has recently shown signs of hysteria in broadcasts to the people, and a heavy air attack on the capital and other big towns now might well ruin an already shaky morale."[4]

Thunderclap soon gained adherents on the British Joint Intelligence Committee (JIC), which, while discounting its effects on morale, suggested adopting the operation to assist the Soviet offensive. In a detailed examination of Thunderclap's possible repercussions, the JIC on 25 January 1945 observed that Thunderclap would "create great confusion, interfere with the orderly movement of troops to the front, and hamper the German military and administrative machine."[5] The committee suggested that attacks on Berlin might have a "political value in demonstrating to the Russians, in the best way open to us, a desire on the part of the British and Americans to assist them in the present battle."[6]

On the same day Harris and Spaatz received notice that the time for Thunderclap had come. Bottomley, after perusing the JIC's findings, telephoned Harris. Harris suggested supplementing the main attack on Berlin with strikes against Chemnitz, Leipzig, and Dresden. These cities, like Berlin, had their communication links stretched thin by refugees from the east. They had also so far escaped relatively untouched from Bomber Command's area bombing campaign.[7] Both officers agreed that Spaatz must be consulted. Meanwhile in Paris, at the weekly air commanders' conference, the airmen examined the possible uses "of the Heavies in the new military situation." At the end of the discussion Tedder asked whether the time had come to stage Operation Thunderclap; presumably, he had either read the JIC report or had heard about it from

Bufton directly. Spaatz agreed, saying that he "felt that this operation should be held in instant readiness, but not ordered until the Russians were either on the Oder in strength, or across it." Tedder accepted Spaatz's recommendation.[8]

Spaatz's consent to Thunderclap did not mean that he wholeheartedly favored adoption of a policy of area bombing. As will be seen, he did not believe that Thunderclap would end the war, although he hoped it might. However, he did feel that a large raid on Berlin would demonstrate solidarity with the Soviets and disrupt the city's capability to aid the defense of the eastern front. Spaatz followed events there closely and stated, "I don't think we are paying nearly enough attention to what is happening in the East. We are using the wrong end of the telescope."[9]

On the evening of 25 January the prime minister jumped into the question of bombing cities in eastern Germany. Part of his concern may have sprung from a British Joint Intelligence Subcommittee report ("German Strategy and Capacity to Resist") prepared for his eyes only. The document predicted that Germany might collapse by mid-April if the Soviet offensive overran the Germans at their eastern defenses before they could be consolidated. Alternatively, the Germans might hold out until November if they could stop the Soviets from conquering Silesia.[10] Any help given the USSR on the eastern front would shorten the conflict. Churchill asked Sir Archibald Sinclair, the secretary of war for air, what plans the RAF had made for "blasting the Germans in their retreat from Breslau."[11] Sinclair passed Churchill's inquiry to Portal. The latter, who was hard at work preparing for the coming CCS meetings, replied cautiously that oil, subject to the demands of the jet assembly factories and submarine yards, should continue to have top priority. However, he reluctantly allowed that the Allies should use the "available effort in one big attack on Berlin and attacks on Dresden, Leipzig, Chemnitz, or any other cities where a severe blitz will not only cause confusion in the evacuation from the East but will hamper the movement of troops from the west."[12] Portal further recommended that the CCS, Spaatz, and Tedder all have a chance to approve the new suggestion.

Portal's reply failed to assuage the prime minister, who shot back: "I did not ask you last night about plans for harrying the

German retreat from Breslau. On the contrary, I asked whether Berlin, and no doubt other large cities in East Germany, should not now be considered attractive targets. I am glad that this is under 'examination.' Pray report to me tomorrow what is going to be done."[13] This sarcastic missive prodded Bottomley, who had begun acting as chief of the air staff because of Portal's scheduled departure for the Mediterranean, to inform Harris of Portal's and Churchill's desires. "I am, therefore, to request that subject to the qualifications stated above and as soon as moon and weather conditions allow, you will undertake such attacks with the particular object of exploiting the confused conditions which are likely to exist in the above mentioned cities during the successful Russian advance."[14] Bottomley issued this unequivocal order before consulting Spaatz or the CCS. He notified Churchill that operations against cities in eastern Germany would begin as soon as conditions permitted (the moon would not allow deep penetrations until 3 or 4 February).[15]

The next day, 28 January, Spaatz flew to England to celebrate the third anniversary of the Eighth's formation. He lunched with Bottomley. The American did not agree to bomb any cities in eastern Germany except Berlin. Spaatz verbally gave Doolittle the following priorities (and method of attack): oil (visual), Berlin (visual or blind), the Ruhr, Munich, and Hamburg. Spaatz further ordered the Eighth's fighters to cover the bombers, strafe oil targets, and interrupt "traffic from West to East toward Berlin and Dresden."[16] This order clarified a previous one given to Doolittle on 24 January that had stated, "anticipating that the enemy will attempt to reinforce the Russian Front by rail movement of units which have been engaged recently on the Western Front, it is desired that your fighters be used until further notice to assist in an interdiction program by strafing rail lines."[17] Also, on 28 January, Spaatz's headquarters delivered the Thunderclap plan to the Eighth. Primary aiming points included the German air ministry, Gestapo headquarters, and the Alexanderplatz railway station—all in the governmental and administrative center of Berlin. At this point USSTAF still envisaged full implementation of the plan, including a follow-up raid by the RAF on the night after the American bombing.[18]

After meeting Spaatz, Bottomley visited Tedder in Paris. According to Tedder they agreed to maintain oil as top priority when visual conditions allowed, with first Berlin, then Leipzig, and, finally, Dresden as the next targets in order of priority.[19] In the meantime Spaatz had already put in train a large operation over Berlin. On 31 January Bottomley radioed the new priorities to Portal.[20] After noting their first priority remained the main synthetic oil plants, he stated, "Next in order of priority for Air Forces operating in the UK is attack of Berlin, Leipzig, Dresden, and associated cities where heavy attack will cause great confusion in civilian evacuation from the east and hamper movement of reinforcements from other fronts."[21] The next day Spaatz read the same message to the weekly air commanders conference. No one present questioned it.[22] According to an intelligence briefing at the same conference, the German Sixth SS Panzer Army had left the West and was presumed headed toward the East.

Even as Spaatz agreed to this new directive, the subject of strategic air targets became a topic of discussion at the Malta and Yalta conferences. A severe heart attack in early January temporarily removed Arnold from AAF affairs, depriving Gen George C. Marshall, the Army chief of staff, of his most trusted and influential airpower adviser. The AAF was left scrambling to fill the leadership void created by Arnold's absence.

Events at the Malta Conference reinforced Spaatz's determination to bomb Berlin. Lt Gen Barney M. Giles, AAF chief of staff and acting AAF commander in Arnold's absence, observed in a telegram to Maj Gen Laurence S. Kuter in Malta on 31 January, "Indications are that pandemonium reigns in Berlin as a result [of] Soviet advances in the East. Suggest that you propose action to have all available day and night heavy-bomber aircraft directed against Berlin for the next few days with a view towards accentuating this condition."[23] Kuter replied that "the Allies had scheduled the operation to begin as soon as weather permitted."[24]

At Malta, Marshall expressed views on airpower that Arnold would have disagreed with. At the CCS meeting on 30 January, Marshall suggested skip-bombing the entrances of underground German manufacturing plants. The airmen present discouraged the idea. Next, he reportedly expressed "his desire to see attacks over all of Germany, by fighters, in accordance with [what] he called the Quesada plan, which he said had been turned down by his air advisers in Washington—and he still didn't know why."[25]

Outside the formal meetings he indicated his desire to bomb Berlin and other cities—without offending the Soviets.[26] Gen Fred Anderson, whom Spaatz had informally attached to the AAF delegation from Washington to ensure that USSTAF's views had adequate representation, took advantage of these informal discussions to tell Marshall of USSTAF's upcoming plans and pointed out that USSTAF had rejected the Quesada plan in favor of its own Operation Clarion.[27]

The Quesada plan, named for its originator, Maj Gen Elwood Quesada, commander, IX Tactical Air Command, called for the establishment of a force of 500 fighter-bombers under the control of the strategic air forces to bomb and strafe strategic targets and communications far beyond the tactical air force zone of operations immediately on or behind German lines. The plan met a cool reception in AAF headquarters. The US Air Staff noted that the allocation of an additional 500 aircraft plus support troops was "not within our current AAF capabilities."[28] Because the plan provided no new forces, Spaatz turned it down.[29] He hoped, instead, to implement Clarion. By attacking numerous transportation and communications targets in small towns throughout Germany that heretofore remained unbombed, Clarion would demonstrate the might of Allied airpower to millions of Germans who had not yet witnessed it. The operation would also overwhelm Reichsbahn repair crews and damage the infrastructure of the transport system. According to General Anderson, Spaatz's exposition of USSTAF's plans, including rejecting the Quesada plan, "greatly reassured" Marshall.[30]

Marshall and Anderson discussed Bottomley's message giving Berlin, Leipzig, and Dresden a priority second only to oil targets. Marshall emphasized that the Soviets must receive notification through current liaison channels (i.e., the US military mission in Moscow). He also suggested that, in addition to the attacks on Berlin and other eastern cities, "attacks on

Munich would probably be of great benefit because [they] would show the people that are being evacuated to Munich that there is no hope."[31] Although this suggestion did not necessarily imply that Marshall supported indiscriminate bombing of civilians, it certainly indicated his willingness to bomb urban targets to demoralize the population in general and Nazi leadership in particular.

The next day Spaatz ordered Twining to attack Munich when weather and other priorities permitted, observing that the city was valuable not only as a communications target but also as a destination for evacuations that "may take place from Berlin and Eastern Germany . . . as [a] result of Russian advance."[32] Spaatz confirmed that the Soviet General Staff had been notified of the Berlin mission.[33] Weather and concentration on oil and transportation prevented the Fifteenth from carrying out this order. Not until 24 March did the Fifteenth bomb Munich, but under strategic circumstances much different from those at the beginning of February.[34] Spaatz further noted to Twining that the 31 January revision of target priorities represented the usual division of labor between Bomber Command and USSTAF. Spaatz explained that the Eighth would attack Berlin, while Bomber Command had plans "to attack other large communications targets such as Leipzig and Dresden."[35]

The upcoming mission to Berlin was not part of Thunderclap because it was not a combined RAF-AAF round-the-clock attack. It was out of the ordinary, however, in that its purpose was to kill or injure up to 275,000 people. Doolittle had no hesitancy in bombing Berlin, but he vehemently objected to Thunderclap's targets in the center of the city. He stated: "There are no basically important strictly military targets in the designated area." He pointed out that to bomb the center of the city accurately his crews would have to bomb visually and fly over almost all the 300 heavy guns defending the city. This approach would subject his low-flying B-24s to heavy casualties. He also questioned the effectiveness of Thunderclap or any bombing attack aimed at morale. In his opinion the people of Berlin would have plenty of warning to take shelter; thus, "the chances of terrorizing into submission, by merely an increased concentration of bombing, a people who have been subjected to intense bombing for four years is extremely remote." Finally, Doolittle, who also opposed the mission as well as Thunderclap appealed to Spaatz saying, "we will, in what may be one of our last and best-remembered operations regardless of its effectiveness, violate the basic American principle of precision bombing of targets of strictly military significance for which our tactics were designed and our crews trained and indoctrinated." He recommended to Spaatz that area bombing be left to the RAF and that the AAF confine itself to picking precision military targets to assure an effective mission with a minimum of losses.[36] He felt the proposed raid on Berlin would definitely cross the line separating incidental damage caused by an attack on military targets and area bombing for morale effects.

Spaatz sent Doolittle a somewhat ambiguous reply. He did not mention Thunderclap; instead, he restated his target priorities. Visual attacks on synthetic oil plants, especially those in the Leipzig area, had first priority. He anticipated that any bombing of Berlin would not be visual, but that city "at this time" had a priority second only to oil. In closing Spaatz observed, "with that in mind, anticipate that you will hit Berlin whenever conditions do not, repeat not indicate possibility of visual bombing of oil targets but do permit operations to Berlin."[37]

On 2 February bad weather forced the Eighth to postpone the Berlin mission by 24 hours. Weather forecasts indicated marginal weather with only a chance for a shallow penetration the next day. That evening Spaatz's headquarters called the Eighth and insisted on a Berlin mission. The Eighth's planners drew up two plans: Plan A, a raid by all bomb divisions on Berlin's industrial areas of Spandau, Tegel, and Seimenstadt; and Plan B, raids on oil and transportation targets in western and central Germany if inclement weather prevented a deep penetration. The weather deteriorated, ruling out visuals for most of Germany. At USSTAF's insistence the Eighth drew up two more plans: Plan C, "a Berlin attack by all BDs [Bombardment Divisions] on the heart of the 'official' city, east of the Tiergarten," and Plan D, "a similar attack on Dresden."[38] At the same time Spaatz recommended to Doolittle that his combat camera unit should send still and motion picture cameramen on the raid and that he offer to allow "any qualified correspondents" who were available on short notice to accompany the mission. Spaatz further recommended that flash news summaries and mission communiqués stress the point that the objective of the mission was "to disrupt reinforcement of [the] Eastern Front and increase administrative confusion."[39] This language indicated he did not wish to broadcast Thunderclap's tertiary goal—causing the German government to collapse. He may have felt a public claim for such a goal might be counterproductive and stiffen the German will to resist. Or, if the effort did not succeed, Spaatz may have felt that its failure would expose the AAF to criticism for having once again promised more than it could deliver. Instead, he emphasized the practical aspects of the raid. Pressure from AAF Headquarters and Marshall must have added to his desire to punish the German capital posthaste.

Doolittle complied, sending four combat cameramen with two groups and a BBC correspondent with a third group. Six more combat cameramen covered the ground activities at three bases. The Eighth planned to develop the film quickly and to title it "Inter-Allied Cooperation: Eighth Air Force Strategic Heavies Tactically Bomb Berlin for Soviets." Once it developed the film, the Eighth would rush it to the combat camera unit headquarters in New York City and offer prints for the newsreels in London. The Eighth even went so far as to take sound film of the target officer, the bomber controller, and the fighter controller who was briefing Doolittle.[40]

Before he received Spaatz's press recommendations, Doolittle double-checked Spaatz's priorities. Almost desperately he asked, "Is Berlin still open to air attack? Do you want priority oil targets hit in preference to Berlin if they definitely become visual? Do you want center of city hit or definitely military targets, such as Spandau, on the Western outskirts?"[41] Spaatz replied by phone annotating his copy of the message, "Told Doolittle to hit oil if visual assured; otherwise, Berlin—center of the city."[42]

Spaatz's answer clearly demonstrated his and the AAF's order of importance in targeting vital military objectives—targets such as oil having first priority. He and Doolittle apparently disagreed over what constituted a "definitely military target." From his location close to Eisenhower's headquarters and as chief, US air forces in Europe, Spaatz would naturally take a more expansive view of military targets than Doolittle, who concentrated solely on operations. To Spaatz a demonstration of support for the Russians and the disruption of government and rail yards in Berlin were justifiable goals. Doolittle thought the raid would tarnish the AAF's reputation and expose his crews to too much danger for too little return. Spaatz thought that targeting eastern Berlin would show the ability of the AAF to cooperate at the highest levels of the alliance while retaining independent control of its forces. The raid pushed the definition of military target to the limit; Spaatz anticipated a nonvisual attack and, therefore, knew the raid would be wildly inaccurate. Nonetheless, it would seem that Spaatz hoped—albeit faintly—that a heavy raid on Berlin just might crack the morale of the German High Command and produce a surrender.[43] In this context Spaatz took note that Mussolini's ouster in July 1943 followed the first bombing attack on Rome by nine days. When in command of the Pacific strategic air forces in August 1945, Spaatz had recommended dropping a third A-bomb, when it became available, on Tokyo.

The next day, 3 February, the Eighth struck Berlin with more than 1,000 B-17s. Of these, 932, employing mostly visual methods but hampered by the need for violent evasive action to avoid intense flak, dropped 2,279 tons of bombs (including 250 tons of incendiaries). The attacking bombers lost 23 of their number to flak but none to German fighters. The 1st Air Division, which led the attack, bombed visually. The 3d Air Division followed and bombed visually but used H2X to aid in finding their targets. Postattack photographic reconnaissance showed severe damage to the Anhalter rail station and moderate damage to the Tempelhof marshaling yard and the Schlesischer rail station (secondary aiming points on the Thunderclap target list).

Industrial and residential property in the center of the city suffered severe damage, while government offices along the Wilhelmstrasse, including the Air Ministry, Reichs Chancellory (Reichs Kanzlei), Foreign Office, and Gestapo headquarters (primary aiming points on the Thunderclap target list) received numerous hits.[44] However, many bombs missed the aiming points and fell into the city's residential areas.[45] For the 10th and last time, the Eighth had bombed the civil and military government area of Berlin.[46] Doolittle employed only his B-17s in the strike on Berlin; the more vulnerable B-24s bombed the Magdeburg synthetic oil plant in keeping with Spaatz's verbal directive to send at least 400 bombers against oil whenever possible. Of 434 B-24s dispatched, 116 bombed the oil plant. Most of the rest bombed the Magdeburg marshaling yard, using H2X when clouds obscured the primary target.

A postraid report prepared by the Eighth Air Force's Operations Analysis Section characterized the raid, in terms of concentration of bombs around the aiming point, as "undoubtedly one of the outstanding operations conducted by this air force." Eighty percent of the bomb patterns of the 1st Air Division, which bombed using entirely visual methods, averaged a circular error probable of 4,400 feet from the aiming point. Two-thirds of the 3d Air Division bombed with visually assisted H2X because of smoke from earlier bombing and increasing cloud cover. Thirty-three percent of its bomb patterns were more than three miles from the target. The centers of the patterns of the remaining bombers averaged 8,500 feet from their aiming points. Given this level of inaccuracy, most of the 3d Division's bombs fell on built-up areas surrounding the area covered by the bombs of the previous division. Of the 2,279 tons of bombs dropped, the report estimated that only 90 tons fell within 1,000 feet of the aiming point and 720 tons within one mile. The bomb density using 500-pound bombs for a 1,000-foot circle, an area of 72 square acres, around the aiming point was five per acre (an area the size of an American football field).[47] As this report clearly demonstrated, even an "outstanding" bombardment mission will place a good many bombs quite far from the intended target. The larger the force flown over a particular target, the greater the number of misses. Given the technology of the time, an attack of several hundred bombers on an urban area, even using the most accurate techniques, would invariably result in severe collateral damage up to five miles from the aiming point.

The Germans, in accordance with their standard policy, declared the Berlin raid a terror-bombing attack. Stories in their own papers and in neutral newspapers claimed 20,000 dead.[48] In this instance the German government and propaganda organs had been hit where they hurt. The AAF official history uncritically accepts a figure of 25,000.[49] Recent figures based on records of the Berlin city archives and the Bundesarchiv (German federal government archives) indicated losses of 2,893 dead; 729 heavily injured; 1,205 lightly injured; and 120,000 left homeless.[50] Given the relative accuracy of the visual bombing employed and the sparing use of firebombs by the Eighth on this mission, the lower figures were probably closer to reality. This mission, unusual because of its accuracy and low volume of firebombs, apparently struck its assigned targets—rail junctions and the center of government. However, the heavy damage inflicted on residential areas showed that even under favorable conditions, AAF precision attacks on city areas had considerable "spillage" into the civilian population. Damage reports indicated that some groups managed to miss the 883 square miles of Berlin altogether.[51] The Berlin Chamber of Commerce called this raid the worst yet experienced and cited heavy damage to the southwestern and southeastern business sections, which caused a significant drop in industrial production.[52]

That this mission greatly aggravated the calamitous situation in Berlin cannot be doubted. There was no proof one way or the other, however, that it significantly delayed rail movement or added to the administrative confusion of the capital. To the world the AAF emphasized both the "direct tactical aid" given to Marshal Gregory Zhukov's advancing armies and the damage to the rail stations and government buildings.[53] The *New York Times* reported that "the raid was designed to fan the flames of German civilian discontent, but even more important, to snarl the enemy's administrative machinery, disrupt his communications, and disorganize his control of the Reich's military forces as they poured eastward to man the Oder River line."[54]

Berlin remained centered in the Eighth's sights. On 5 February Spaatz told his staff that Berlin retained its priority after oil and before transportation.[55] Later in the day, Spaatz received word from General [Frederick] Anderson at Yalta that the Soviets had formally requested air attacks against Berlin and Leipzig.[56] Spaatz replied, "all-out effort will be placed against targets mentioned whenever weather conditions permit."[57] In response to Marshall's request, the Eighth planned a raid by all three air divisions on the center of Munich on 5 February but cancelled it because of the weather. On 6 February weather again caused cancellation of a mission to Berlin.[58]

That same day Spaatz wrote to Arnold informing him of the plans for Clarion, which Spaatz hoped would paralyze all traffic in Germany. Spaatz rejected the Quesada plan but noted, "for the past two weeks we have been using the returning escort fighters in a Jeb Stuart role with the intention of preventing rapid movement of German troops from the Western to the Eastern front by strafing rail traffic." As for J. E. B. [James Ewell Brown] Stuart, Thunderclap, and Clarion, Spaatz observed, "your comment on the decisiveness of results achieved by airpower leads me to believe you might be following the chimera of the one air operation which will end the war." Spaatz no longer believed such an animal existed. He spoke of the difficulty of exploiting and measuring the results of air operations. Only in the aggregate could one see that Allied airpower had badly damaged the German economy and denied oil to the German military.[59]

Dresden

In the meantime Bomber Command maintained its support of British ground forces by conducting area attacks on Munich-Gladbach and Mainz. On the same night, 1 February, the command struck the cities and marshaling yards of Siegen and Ludwigshafen using area techniques. All four attacks carried 30 percent or more incendiaries. Harris had supplied tactical support to the British army before and would do so again. These attacks came at the direct request of the army. Of the 24 joint attacks on the cities and marshaling yards on Bomber Command's books, four occurred in December 1944 before the German counteroffensive, and the remaining 20 took place in February 1945. Does the command's designation of these raids imply that they were instigated at higher levels (the air staff and the prime minister) or simply that they belonged to an aspect of the transportation campaign applied to eastern Germany? The command hit the yards and cities of Wiesbaden on the night of 2 February and Bonn on 4 February with high percentages of incendiaries. Also on the night of 2 February, the command conducted a regular area attack on Karlsruhe, dropping 1,325 tons of explosives—two-thirds of them incendiaries. On 8 February the command attacked the yards at Hohenbudberg at the army's request; it employed no incendiaries other than marking bombs. Harris kept up a steady effort on oil for the month, launching 22 attacks and expending almost 30 percent of his sorties and tonnage against oil facilities. Harris had not forgotten his pleas of November 1944 to be allowed to strike Chemnitz, Leipzig, and Dresden, in lieu of oil.[60] Furthermore, the amended strategic directive of 31 January 1945 explicitly authorized him to hit those cities when practicable. With the demise of the German night fighter force only the weather protected those cities from Allied bombers.

On 6 February the Eighth attempted to attack oil targets only to find clouds over the synthetic plants, which meant that more than 1,300 bombers hit targets of opportunity or secondary targets, including more than 400 each on the Chemnitz and Magdeburg marshaling yards. On 9 February another 1,300-plane mission against the same targets was again thwarted by the weather. Two hundred fifty bombers struck their secondary target, the Magdeburg rail yards, while others struck targets of opportunity. On 13 February USSTAF called the Eighth to report that the weather would be "beautiful" over Dresden and Chemnitz. The Eighth drew up three plans: Plan A—in case of marginal weather, a short mission over western Germany; Plan B—the 1st and 3d Air Divisions to bomb Dresden and the 2d Division to bomb Chemnitz (after these cities' names, the planners noted, "Beat'em up"); and Plan C—the 1st and 3d Air Divisions to bomb Dresden and the 2d Division to bomb transport and jet targets in central Germany in case it could not climb over the clouds to eastern Germany.[61] After postponing the attack for 24 hours because of the weather, 1,377 B-17s and B-24s set out on 14 February to bomb the city of Dresden, marshaling yards in Magdeburg, and Chemnitz.

Three hundred eleven B-17s of the 1st Air Division, using visually assisted H2X, dropped 771 tons of bombs (including 294 tons of incendiaries) on Dresden.[62] The orders issued by the 1st Division to its bombers clearly defined mission objectives:

- Primary Target-Visual: Center of built-up area Dresden.
- Secondary Targets: Visual-M/Y Chemnitz, H2X. Center of Dresden.
- Last Resort: Any military objective positively identified as being in Germany and east of the current bomb line.[63]

The 1 AD was escorted by 281 P-51s. The fighters had permission "to strafe rail and road transportation on withdrawal if no enemy aircraft had been encountered."[64]

Several eyewitnesses in Dresden never even noticed the American bombs.[65] Harris and Bomber Command had beaten the 1st AD to the punch. On the previous night, 13 February, Bomber Command Lancasters, in a two-wave attack of 772 bombers, released 2,646 tons of bombs, including 1,181 tons of incendiaries, into the very heart of the city and its marshaling yards. Much of Dresden's antiaircraft defense, including almost all the heavy guns capable of reaching high altitudes, had been moved to serve as antitank units on the eastern front or to supplement flak defenses at points hit more often by the Allies. Thus, the British and American raids met no opposition. The British, in particular, benefited from the lack of interference because their airborne controller could bring his planes in undisturbed and direct them to drop their bomb loads in a newly developed fan-shaped pattern that maximized the coverage and effect of incendiary bombs. Unlike Hamburg, the RAF intended to create a firestorm from the beginning. The first wave of Lancasters carried the greatest weight of incendiaries. Their attack ignited the dry medieval center of the city like a huge torch. The second wave carried a larger proportion of high explosives to kill firefighters and disrupt fire-control efforts. The RAF conducted a technically perfect fire-raising attack on the city.[66]

By early morning on 14 February, Ash Wednesday, a firestorm engulfed the middle of Dresden, causing staggering loss of life. Estimates of the death toll range from a low of 35,000, now accepted as the best guess, to a high of 250,000. No one will ever know the exact figure with certainty, because Silesian refugees, evacuees from other bombed cities, slave laborers, and other displaced persons had jammed into the city, which previously had been almost untouched by Allied bombing. Few of the city's residents and recent arrivals had ever experienced a major bombing attack. They had little idea of how to protect themselves.[67]

The 311 American B-17s, which, for this mission, carried approximately the same percentage of firebombs as the Lancasters, attacked at 1223 hours. After releasing 771 tons of ordnance, the crews reported a low-lying haze of smoke that prevented them from seeing the bombs fall. Nevertheless, immediate postraid analysis of strike photos taken by the attacking bombers indicated "that the majority of the bombs dropped fell into heavily built-up areas of the city" and stated "damage to the city should be severe."[68]

Other units of the 1st Air Division lost their way and failed to reach Dresden. In their zeal to complete the mission, they misidentified several Czech cities as their targets. Sixty B-17s dropped 153 tons into the center of Prague while 25 attacked Brux and 12 struck Pilsen. Bombers of the 3d Air Division also wandered into Czechoslovakia. Thirty-eight of its B-17s attacked the town of Eger, and 24 more hit Tachau. In all the Eighth dropped 397 tons on Czech territory. The 2d and 3d Air Divisions had orders to attack marshaling yards with no mention of city areas; they made "area like" attacks that day. However, the 2 AD did hit one of the desired targets, the Buckau marshaling yard at Magdeburg, with 333 B-24s carrying 799 tons (31 percent incendiaries), and some of the 3d Division struck the Chemnitz marshaling yard with 306 B-17s carrying 747 tons (27 percent incendiaries). Both attacks used radar-assisted sighting.

The next day at the weekly conference of air commanders, Doolittle reported that in Dresden "the fires lit by Bomber Command the previous night had been rekindled," and, he noted with "greatest reticence" because of the expanse of the devastation, that the smoke had risen to 15,000 feet.[69] That same day 210 B-17s, unable to bomb their primary target—the synthetic oil plant at Ruhland—diverted to their secondary target, "military installations, [at Dresden]."[70] The Eighth had never used "military installations" as a description for a target in Germany before this mission nor would it do so again. Eighth Air Force records supply no information as to which specific military installations were located within Dresden or how a raid dropping bombs through clouds could be expected to hit them. Using H2X, the 1st Division's bombers dropped 461 tons of bombs, all high explosives, on the stricken city.[71] For the month of February 1945, the Americans had flown 521 heavy-bomber sorties and dropped 1,232 tons of bombs on Dresden in February 1945. Their bombs mattered little, for the RAF had already virtually leveled the city. As a result of these raids, the AAF official history, relying in part on immediate postmission aerial photography, stated, "if casualties were exceptionally high and damage to residential areas great, it was also evident that the city's industrial and transportation establishments had been blotted out."[72] Harris expressed his assessments less matter of factly. "Dresden was a mass of munitions works, an intact government centre, and a key transportation point to the east. Now it is none of those things."[73]

The Dresden raids, like earlier missions against Berlin, evoked bitter accusations of terror bombing from the German propaganda machine and strong reaction in the neutral press. A 17 February broadcast by the German Overseas Service in English for North America awarded Spaatz the "Order of the White Feather" for "acts of exceptional cowardice in bombing German cities filled with pitiful refugees."[74]

Clarion

In the week after the Dresden mission, Bomber Command launched three missions against oil facilities. It also attacked Wessel on 16, 18, and 19 February in support of ground forces. The raids carried no incendiaries. The night after Dresden, Bomber Command sent 671 sorties to attack the city and marshaling yards of Chemnitz with 2,329 tons (over 60 percent of them incendiaries). The night of 20 February, Bomber Command dispatched an area raid of 513 effective sorties carrying 904 tons of high explosives and 1,615 tons of incendiaries to Dortmund. Next, Harris directed two raids, one by 617 Squadron, on the Mittelland Canal overpass at Gravenhorst on 20 and 21 February. On the 21st the command struck the marshaling yards and cities of Chemnitz (1,055 tons) and Worms (1,828 tons); both raids carried more than 55 percent high explosives. Between 13 and 20 February Bomber Command carried out eight area raids.

The Eighth undertook raids against its second priority target, transportation, with vigor. Radar directed raids averaging 150 heavy bombers struck at Cottbus on 15 February; Rheine, Osnabrück, and Hamm on 16 February; Frankfurt on 17 February; and Siegen, Münster, Osnabrück, and Rheine on 19 February. None of these raids carried a significant amount of incendiary bombs. On 20 February the Eighth sent 859 heavy bombers in an area raid against marshaling yards in Nürnberg, a city heretofore relatively untouched by bombing. This mission carried 1,869 tons of ordnance, 26 percent incendiaries. The next day the Eighth sent a maximum effort—its largest raid against a single target of the entire war—against Nürnberg's marshaling yards. This "area" raid of 1,198 bombers drenched the city with 2,889 tons of bombs, including 1,169 tons of incendiaries. In the latter raid weather had given planners a choice between Berlin and Nürnberg. They chose Nürnberg only moments from take-off. Both Nürnberg raids used H2X.

On 21 February 1945 Allied weather forecasters predicted clear skies over much of Germany for the next day, whereupon the Allied air leaders, at the request of Eisenhower's headquarters, scheduled Operation Clarion for execution.[75] The plan had a gestation stretching back to mid-September 1944 when the Allies sought to deliver a blow to break German will. The idea of a wide-ranging offensive had continued to grow. Spaatz, in particular, embraced the plan and continued to advocate it. He hoped to repeat it frequently. By the end of December 1944, Clarion provided for attacks in visual bombing weather by all available Allied strategic and tactical airpower on unbombed smaller German rail and water communications centers in the hope of disrupting economic life and the tactical situation at the front line. The plan had also gained Tedder's support. However, Bottomley, speaking for the RAF air staff, did not judge the time propitious. In a bit of irony the air staff hurled at Spaatz the cry he had so often used himself—Clarion would interfere with bombing German oil targets.[76] Within Spaatz's own staff some dissented. General [Frederick] Anderson's deputy wrote that Clarion would cause little dislocation in Germany's rail system because of its redundancy. "There is," he added, "absolutely no basis for the hope that such an operation would cause disorder among the civil population of Germany by the feeling of fear." He felt, however, that such bombing might cause disorder leading to the maltreatment of American aircrews and other POWs. Before recommending the plan not be executed, he had a further observation, "Operation [Clarion] constitutes open war against civilians, [who] would react badly in [those] states and . . . place our forces in a defensive position before the world."[77]

Eaker strenuously objected as well. His response emphasized the constant ambivalence of the AAF's leadership towards the subject—area bombing. Eaker, when he commanded the Eighth, had initiated US area bombing in the fall of 1943.[78] Writing on 1 January, as the Battle of the Bulge still raged and before the Soviet winter, he begged Spaatz not to order implementation of area bombing, stating: "It will absolutely convince the Germans that we are the barbarians they say we are, for it would be perfectly obvious to them that this is primarily a large-scale attack on civilians as, in fact, it of course will be. Of all the people killed in this attack, over 95% of them can be expected to be civilians." He also objected to operational aspects of the plan, especially its low-level, small formation tactics and to the diversion of effort from the oil campaign. Next came a remarkable passage:

> If the time ever comes when we want to attack the civilian populace with a view to breaking civil morale, such a plan as the one suggested is probably the way to do it. I personally, however, have become completely convinced that you and Bob Lovett are right and we should never allow the history of this war to convict us [of] throwing the strategic bomber at the man in the street. I think there is a better way we can do our share to defeat the enemy, but if we are to attack the civil population I am certain we should wait until its morale is much nearer the breaking point and until the weather favors the operation more than it will at any time in the winter or early spring.[79]

In fact the Americans did not intend to kill German civilians as much as they hoped to damage their psyches. SHAEF's proposed psychological war plan to accompany Clarion aimed to stress to the German people, especially train crews and yard workers, the necessity of avoiding railway stations, tracks, freight yards, and similar facilities.[80] Shortly before initiating the operation and after the American press furor over Dresden, Spaatz issued specific instructions as follows: "In planning for Operation [Clarion] it is important that Public Relations and Communiqué Officers be advised to state clearly in communiqués and all press releases the military nature of all targets attacked. Special care should be taken against giving any impression that this operation is aimed at the civilian population or intended to terrorize them. In addition to the above care must taken to insure that all crews are thoroughly briefed that attacks will be limited to military objectives."[81]

By attacking numerous unbombed targets near small cities and towns, the Allies hoped to impress upon millions of Germans their helplessness in the face of Allied air superiority. British and American fighters and bombers would spread out all over Germany blasting transport targets such as grade crossings, stations, barges, docks, signals, tracks, bridges, and marshaling yards. The plan purposely selected targets near small towns heretofore untouched by the war and therefore not likely to have strong antiaircraft defenses. To heighten their accuracy, the Eighth's and the Fifteenth's heavy bombers came in at unusually low altitudes. Some of them bombed from 6,000 feet, while the Ninth's medium bombers buzzed up and down the rail lines destroying locomotives and disrupting traffic. Britain's 2d Tactical Air Force joined in the operations with more than 1,600 sorties, and Bomber Command made four attacks. In Italy the British 1st Tactical Air Force and the American Twelfth also joined in. In all more than 3,500 heavy bombers and 4,900 fighters took part. The bombers attacked 219 transportation targets while the fighters claimed to have destroyed or damaged 594 locomotives and 3,803 railcars.[82] The Allies lost 90 bombers. Eleven of Eighth Air Force's 13 fighter groups strafed targets of opportunity. In an Eighth Air Force daily intelligence and operations summary, the AAF made a rare admission. This document recorded that the ground strafing had killed three civilians.[83]

Eisenhower's headquarters had requested Clarion to assist an offensive by Lt Gen William G. Simpson's US Ninth Army, scheduled to begin the night of 22 February. The Ninth Army staged an assault that would cross the Roer River, clear the Cologne plain, seize Cologne itself, and close up to the Rhine, all of which it accomplished by 7 March. Spaatz had been itching for months to go ahead with Clarion. On 1 February at the weekly air commanders' conference, he had pressed for immediate execution of Clarion.[84] On 2 February Spaatz informed Twining and Eaker of his intention to order Clarion when conditions allowed. When Twining objected to the special tactics called for in the plan but not the concept behind it, Spaatz accommodated him with some slight modifications to provide more safety for the heavy bombers.[85] On 5 February Spaatz told Arnold that Clarion was cocked and primed; he noted that he no longer expected any single air operation to win the war.[86]

The results of Clarion justified Spaatz's caution. The operation, which took place on 22 February and which the Eighth alone repeated the next day, failed to achieve its lofty goals. It did not precipitate a crisis among railway workers nor did it overwhelm the Reichsbahn's repair facilities, disrupt the railways enough to affect the frontline troops immediately, or drive the war home to the German people. Clarion did, however, destroy a considerable amount of rolling stock and lowered the throughput capacity of several main rail lines for the duration of the war. The operation added further strain and attrition to a system already collapsing from the cumulative effects of the destruction being rained upon it.[87]

The bombing itself proved remarkably accurate. The combination of lower altitude and smaller attacking formations produced good results. Of the 124 squadrons dispatched by the Eighth, 96 bombed visually; the Eighth Air Force operational analysis section plotted 76 of those bomb patterns and compared them to the average of operations from 1 September 1944 through 31 January 1945. Clarion's bomb patterns were considerably more compact with one-third as many gross errors (8 percent as compared to 28 percent). In addition 26 percent of Clarion's visually aimed bombs fell within 500 feet of the aiming point, and 82 percent fell within 2,000 feet as opposed to only 12 percent falling within 500 feet and only 57 percent landing within 2,000 feet for the winter's general bombing campaign.[88] Relatively few of Clarion's bombs fell on populated areas, and for its entire effort during this operation, the Eighth loaded less than two-tenths of one percent (0.02 percent) incendiary bombs—an unequivocal sign that the Americans did not intend for Clarion's raids to attack civilians or city areas. The Fifteenth Air Force chipped in with 48 squadron-sized or smaller attacks on rail targets in Germany, Austria, and Italy, while medium bombers of the Ninth Air Force dropped 850 tons on 11 marshaling yards and 44 other rail targets. Fighter bombers from the Ninth's three tactical air commands hit rail targets with an additional 376 tons of ordnance and conducted armed reconnaissance along trackage from Düsseldorf to Giessen. Although Maj Gen Frederick Anderson probably spoke for all of USSTAF when, a month later, he proclaimed Clarion to be "singularly effective,"[89] neither USSTAF nor the rest of the Allied airmen repeated the operation—first, because it required a special set of weather conditions and, second, because it required all the Allied air forces to give up their primary missions to concentrate on a special project with unquantifiable results.

The operation demonstrated yet again the impossibility of completely controlling the actions of the aircrews. In spite of the admonitions some crews, either because of cloud cover or failure to understand bombing policy for Clarion, bombed city areas as targets of opportunity. Thirteen aircraft, bombing visually, placed 39 tons on Grabow, and 77 bombers, employing H2X, put 233 tons on Ulm. Most embarrassing of all, a lone bomber strayed into Switzerland and bombed Basel.

Clarion provided yet another example of the inability of airpower to fatally loosen a police state's internal control of its populace. The concentrated assaults on Berlin and Dresden on 3, 14, and 15 February failed as did the broad attack, which proved equally unsuccessful, and the combination of both tactics. It may further have confirmed the military axiom against spreading one's forces too thinly in an attempt to accomplish too broad an objective. Napoléon and Gen Robert E. Lee practiced their wiles on the minds of either a single person or a few individuals, such as Mack in 1805 and Gen Joe Hooker in 1863. However, in the aggregate of modern warfare and intelligence, such moves are likely to be less than successful.

Clarion did, however, provide the opportunity for USSTAF to stage a press blitz to counteract reporting of the Dresden bombing. USSTAF had a United Press International correspondent at Eighth Air Force headquarters to cover the planning; briefed the press in London and Paris; sent a planeload of reporters to front-line airfields to cover the story; and sent its own combat camera crews out to get movie and still footage of the operation. The Eighth promptly released this footage and gained a 15-minute news spot on the National Broadcasting Company network.[90]

After Clarion, both the Eighth and Bomber Command continued their pounding of Germany's urban areas. On 23 February 1945 Bomber Command sent a daylight main-force raid against its most heavily bombed target, Essen, dropping an additional 1,313 tons, including 878 tons of incendiaries, on that city. That night Harris smashed the last of the 63 German cities of more than 100,000 population that he had placed on his target list. Three hundred sixty-eight heavy bombers blasted Pforzheim with 1,739 tons of ordnance, including 919 tons of incendiaries, starting a firestorm that may have killed up to 17,000 persons.[91] Harris boasted to his fellow air commanders, "that whole place has been burned out. This attack had been what was popularly known as a deliberate terror attack." He said that he knew "that in certain quarters, the value of these area attacks was disputed. Pforzheim was a town that contained innumerable small workshops for the manufacture of precision instruments. This attack must have destroyed the 'home-work' of the population and their equipment." Harris finished by noting, "Bomber Command had now destroyed 63 German towns in this fashion."[92]

The Eighth hit two marshaling yards in Munich on 25 February. Although executed visually, this raid otherwise fit the pattern of the other "area-like" missions of the month; its 561 effective sorties dropped 1,652 tons of bombs, 45 percent of them incendiaries, in a possible response to General Marshall's urgings earlier in the month. The next day the Eighth sent all three of its air divisions over the capital of the Reich (Berlin), where 1,089 effective sorties employed H2X to drop 2,778 tons of bombs, 44 percent of them incendiaries, through 10/10 clouds. Each division attempted to hit a separate rail station. The Schlesischer, Alexanderplatz, and Berlin-North stations were all located within two miles of the center of Berlin. The bombing started large fires and killed many civilians. RAF Mosquito night-intruder bombers attacking 12 hours later reported fires still burning.[93] After the 26 February mission, with its 500,000 fire bomblets, the typical Berliner, with reason, would have been hard put to distinguish between RAF area bombing and AAF precision bombing. The mission lost only three bombers. The next day both strategic air forces continued the assault. Bomber Command hit the city and yards of Mainz with a daytime main-force attack that released 1,734 tons of explosives, including 1,033 tons of incendiaries. As that raid took place, 314 of the Eighth's bombers hit the yards at Halle with more than 700 tons of ordnance—15 percent incendiaries—while 717 bombers smashed the main marshaling yard at Leipzig with an area-like raid that dropped 1,933 tons, 24 percent incendiaries. Both raids used H2X. Finally, on the last day of the month the Eighth conducted an area-like attack on the yards at Kassel. Three hundred sixty effective sorties, with the aid of H2X, dumped 1,217 tons of bombs, 39 percent incendiaries, on the city. On the first day of March the assault continued with an area-like attack (353 bomber, 988 tons, 34 percent incendiaries) on the rail yards at Ulm.

There can no longer be any doubt that the US Army Air Forces purposely bombed the city area of Dresden. These attacks were certainly part of the Anglo-Americans' campaign against cities and transportation centers in eastern Germany and, perhaps, as part of an attempt to push Germany into surrender. Taken as a whole, many of February's strategic bombing operations were conducted with the seeming purpose of breaking the German will to resist. Like strategic operations in the Gulf War 47 years later, they illustrated the difficulty, if not the impossibility, of bringing down a police state with bombing alone.

Notes

1. Message U-68114, Curtis (signed Spaatz) to Doolittle, 16 January 1945, AFHSO microfilm reel B 5046, fr. 1819.
2. Webster and Frankland, *Strategic Air Offensive*, 3:99.

3. Minutes, D. B. OPs (Bufton) to DCAS (Bottomley), 22 January 1945, PRO AIR 20/3227.

4. Minutes, ACAS (Ops.) to DCAS, 23 January 1945, PRO AIR 20/3227.

5. Webster and Frankland, 3:100.

6. Ibid.

7. Thunderclap itself referred to only the one raid on Berlin. The linking by Harris of other cities in eastern Germany to the operation has led to some misunderstanding by later historians, such as David Irving, who incorrectly apply the operation's designation to the entire bombing campaign in eastern Germany.

8. Webster and Frankland, 100.

9. SHAEF Meetings, 24 January 1945, Robb Papers, RAF Museum.

10. JIC (45) 22 (O) (Final), subject: German Strategy and Capacity to Resist, 21 January 1945, PRO PREM 3/193/6A.

11. Webster and Frankland, 3:101.

12. Ibid.

13. Ibid., 3:103.

14. Ibid., appendix 28, letter, Bottomley to Harris, 27 January 1945, 4:301.

15. Ibid., 3:104.

16. Command Diary, entry for 28 January 1945, Spaatz Papers, Diary. See also A-2 [Intelligence] Planning Notes for the Eighth Air Force, 28 January to 3 February 1945, AFHSO microfilm reel A5884, frs. 1639–41. These notes centered on planning for oil missions if visibility allowed. Otherwise they concentrated on a Berlin strike. The note for 3 February spoke of a "verbal USSTAF directive that requires 400 aircraft on any of the four active synthetic oil plants" (fr. 1641).

17. Message SP-184, Spaatz to Doolittle, 24 January 1945, Spaatz Papers, Diary.

18. Message UA-53417, Spaatz to Doolittle, 28 January 1945, Spaatz Papers, Cables; and [Thunderclap Target List], 28 January 1945, Spaatz Papers, Subject File 1929–1945.

19. Tedder, *With Prejudice*, 659.

20. Message S-77217, Bottomley to Portal, 31 January 1945, AFHSO microfilm reel A5543, frs. 1405–6.

21. Ibid.

22. Notes of the Allied Air Commanders Conference held at SHAEF, on 1 February 1945, at 1130 hours, Spaatz Papers, Diary.

23. Message War-29863 (Hearth 88), Giles to Kuter, signed Arnold, 31 January 1945, War Department Classified Message Center (WDCMC), Washington National Records Center, Suitland, Md., microfilm reel 1347.

24. Message Cricket-35, Kuter to Giles, 1 February 1945, AFHSO microfilm reel A5543, fr. 1372.

25. Letter, Anderson to Spaatz ("Eyes Only"), 2 February 1945, Spaatz Papers, Diary; *The Conferences at Malta and Yalta 1945*, 46869; minutes of the 182d Meeting of the Combined Chiefs of Staff, 30 January 1945.

26. Letter, Anderson to Spaatz ("Eyes Only"), 2 February 1945, Spaatz Papers, Diary.

27. Ibid.

28. Excerpts from memo, Kuter to Arnold, 11 January 1945, enclosed in letter, Arnold to Spaatz, 14 January 1945, Spaatz Papers, Diary.

29. Letter, Spaatz to Arnold, 5 February 1945, Spaatz Papers, Diary.

30. Letter, Anderson to Spaatz, ("Eyes Only"), 2 February 1945, Spaatz Papers, Diary.

31. Message Cricket-40, Anderson to Spaatz, 1 February 1945, AFHSO microfilm reel A5543, fr. 1354.

32. Message UAX-53637, Spaatz to Twining, 2 February 1945, Spaatz Papers, Diary.

33. Minutes, [USSTAF] Staff Meeting, 2 February 1945, Spaatz Papers, Diary.

34. However, on 25 February, the Eighth hit Munich's marshaling yards with almost 400 heavy bombers and over 1,100 tons of bombs.

35. Message UAX-53637, Spaatz to Twining, 2 February 1945, Spaatz Papers, Diary.

36. Message CS-93-JD (Redline), Doolittle to Spaatz, 30 January 1945, AFHSO microfilm reel B5046, fr. 1808. For Doolittle's opinions on the shortcomings of the B-24 as compared to the B-17 see letter, Doolittle to Barney M. Giles, 25 January 1945, AFHRA file no. 168.491, AF/CEO microfilm reel A1657A, frs. 827–31. Doolittle noted that the B-24 flew at 24,000 feet compared to the B-17's 28,000 feet, and, therefore, suffered higher losses to flak.

37. Message JD-104-CS (Redline), Spaatz to Doolittle, 30 January 1945, AFHSO microfilm reel B5046, fr. 1818.

38. [Eighth Air Force] A-2 Planning Notes, 30 January 1945, AFHSO microfilm reel A5884, fr. 1639, AFHRA file no. 520.321. Also see message D-61064, Doolittle to Spaatz, 2 February 1945; message D–61068, Doolittle to Spaatz, 2 February 1945, AFHRA File no. 519.332, 1–19 February 1945.

39. Message UA-53649, Spaatz to Doolittle, 2 February 1945, AFHSO microfilm reel B5046, fr. 1809.

40. Memo (D-W-33), Maj J. Rifkin, assistant D/Ops, to DCS Ops, 2 February 1945, AFHSO microfilm reel B5046.

41. Message CS-96-JD (Redline), Doolittle to Spaatz, 2 February 1945, Spaatz Papers, Cables.

42. Ibid. This notation is signed C. S. (Carl Spaatz).

43. It is possible that Spaatz may have recalled portions of the prewar AWPD-1 plan in connection with bombing Berlin. AWPD 1 (tab 3, 3) had stated, in August 1941, "Immediately after some very apparent results of air attacks on the material objective listed above [power plants, oil, and transportation] or immediately after some major set-back of the German ground forces, it may become highly profitable to deliver a large scale, all-out attack on the civil population of Berlin. In this event any or all of the bombardment forces may be diverted for this mission."

44. Eighth Air Force Monthly Summary of Operations, February 1945, AFHSO microfilm reel A5875, fr. 333; Freeman, *Mighty Eighth War Diary*, 432–33; "THUNDERCLAP Target List," Spaatz Papers, Subject File 1929–1945.

45. Memo D-M-8, Headquarters 1st Air Division, Office Director of Intelligence, subject: Immediate Interpretation Report No. 229, 4 February 1945. AFHRA file no. 525.332, AFHSO microfilm reel B5287.

46. Eighth Air Force Target Summary: Statistical Summary of All Bomber Attacks, 31 May 1945, AFHSO microfilm reel A5875, frs. 618–19, AFHRA file no. 520.3084-1, 7–8.

47. Report, Eighth Air Force Operations Analysis Section, subject: Analysis of Attack on Berlin [on] 3 February 1945, dated 24 February 1945, AFHSO microfilm reel A5680, frs. 445–47.

48. *New York Times*, 6 February 1945, citing Swedish news service stories based on reports from returning plane passengers.

49. Craven and Cate, *Argument to V E Day*, 3:726.

50. Figures cited by Professor Doctor Olaf Groehler, Akademie der Wissenschaften der DDR, Zentralinstitute für Geschichte, Berlin, in a letter to Mr. Herman Wolk, Office of Air Force History, 6 March 1990. Given the number of homeless, Professor Groehler assessed the raid as the heaviest single raid to hit Berlin during the war.

51. Third Air Division Mission Report of 3 February 1945, n.d. [ca. early February 1945], Eighth Air Force Mission Reports, RG 18, NARA, Modern Military Field Branch, Suitland, Md.

52. USSBS, Area Studies Division, "A Brief Study of the Effects of Area Bombing on Berlin, Augsburg, Bochum, Leipzig, Hagen, Dortmund, Oberhausen, Schweinfurt, and Bremen," (Washington: January 1947), 35–36.

53. Translation of Allied propaganda leaflet dropped on Holland, "The Flying Dutchman No. 101," 5 February 1945, AFHSO microfilm reel A5823, frs. 150–51.

54. Sydney Gruson, "3000-Ton Blow Hits Berlin in Steady Bombing of Reich," *New York Times*, 4 February 1945, 1 and 5.

55. Minutes of [USSTAF] Staff Meeting, 5 February 1945, Spaatz Papers, Diary.

56. Message Argonaut-23, Anderson to Spaatz, 5 February 1945, AFHSO microfilm reel A5544, fr. 703.

57. Message USSTAF-MAIN-IN 15905, Spaatz to Anderson, 5 February 1945, AFHSO microfilm reel A5544, fr. 699.

58. A-2 Planning Notes, AFHSO microfilm reel A5884, fr. 1640, AFHRA file no. 520.321.

59. Letter, Spaatz to Arnold, 5 February 1945, Spaatz Papers, Diary.

60. Webster and Frankland, 3:82.

61. A-2 Planning Notes, 13 February 1945, AFHSO microfilm reel A 5884, fr. 1643, AFHRA file no. 520.321.

62. Freeman, 439; Eighth Air Force Summary of Operations, February 1945, AFHSO microfilm reel A5875, frs. 313–82.

63. Report, Headquarters 1st Air Division, subject: "Report of Operations, DRESDEN, 14 February 1945," dated 25 February 1945, AFHSO microfilm reel B5018, fr. 642.

64. Tactical Command Report, Field Order 1622A, 14 February 1945, from Col Fred C. Grey, director of fighters, AFHSO microfilm reel B5018, fr. 688.

65. McKee, Dresden 1945, 211–43, in particular, 225.

66. See USSBS, "Area Studies Division Report," vol. 31 (Washington, DC: GPO, January 1947), 5, for an excellent discussion of Bomber Command's new techniques and increased accuracy.

67. The bombing of Dresden has given birth to a large body of literature, both of accusation and justification. In addition to the previously cited works by David Irving and Alexander McKee, both highly critical of Allied policy, one should read the official AAF historical study on Dresden, "Historical Analysis of the 14–15 February 1945 Bombing of Dresden," prepared by chief historian Charles Angell in 1953, which can be found in the AFHSO Dresden Subject File; and Melden E. Smith, "The Bombing of Dresden Reconsidered: A Study in Wartime Decision Making" (PhD diss., Boston University, Boston, Mass., 1971).

68. Headquarters 1st Air Division, Office of the Director of Intelligence, "Immediate Interpretation Report No. 232, 0530 hours, 15 February 1945." AFHRA file No. 525.332, AFHSO microfilm reel B5288, fr. 676.

69. Notes of the Allied Air Commanders Conference held at SHAEF, Versailles, on Thursday, 15 February 1945, at 1130 hours, Spaatz Papers, Diary.

70. Report, Headquarters 1st Air Division, Report of Operations, BOHLAN, 15 February 1945, dated 25 February 1945, AFHSO microfilm reel B5018, fr. 988. It is interesting to note that of the individual bomb groups of the 1st Division only one reported that it had struck "military installations." Most of the groups stated merely that their target was "Dresden." However, the 91st BG reported its target as the "City of Dresden" (Report of the Operations Officer to CO 91st BG, 16 February 1945, AFHSO microfilm Reel B5019, fr. 353); the 385th BG reported its target as "Dresden" (Center of Industrial Area) (Headquarters 385th BG, Narrative Report of Operation, 16 February 1945, AFHSO microfilm reel B5019, fr. 421).

71. Eighth Air Force Monthly Summary of Operations, February 1945, 22; Freeman, 440.

72. Craven and Cate, 3:731.

73. Saward, Bomber Harris, 292, citing letter, Harris to Bottomley, 29 March 1945.

74. Excerpts of broadcast of 17 February 1945, Spaatz Papers, Diary.

75. Craven and Cate, 3:732.

76. Message AX 991, Bottomley to Spaatz, 26 December 1944, AFHSO microfilm reel A5687, fr. 660.

77. Memo for General Anderson, subject: Operation CLARION, Col Thetus C. Odum, asst deputy commander, operations, USSTAF, 9 January 1945, AFHSO microfilm reel A5687, fr. 779.

78. From 27 September 1943 through 22 December 1943, the Eighth conducted 24 authorized city area raids, dropping 12,000 tons of bombs, 40 percent of them incendiaries.

79. Letter, Eaker to Spaatz, 1 January 1945, AFHSO, Dresden Reference File.

80. Memo to CG, USSTAF, from Gen Robert A. McClure, chief, Psychological Warfare Division, SHAEF, subject: Psychological Warfare Operations in Connection with CLARION, 16 January 1945, AFHSO microfilm reel, fr. 637.

81. Text of the message, as received by Eighth AF, see message UAX 64613, Spaatz to Doolittle, Eaker, Twining, Vandenburg [sic], Saville [sic], 21 February 1945, AFHSO microfilm, reel B5047, fr. 722. A repeat of this message from Ninth Air Force headquarters back to USSTAF, after the execution of the operation, contained the following text as the last sentence of the message, "this is extremely important for the safety of our crews in case they should be shot down in enemy territory," which would seem to emphasize Spaatz's intention to avoid collateral damage. (See message USSTAF-MAIN-IN 20170, Advanced HQ Ninth AF to HQ, USSTAF, 28 February 1945, AFHSO microfilm reel A5616, fr. 92.)

82. "Summary of CLARION," Spaatz Papers, Diary.

83. Eighth Air Force, INTOPS Summary No. 268, 22 February 1945, 5, AFHSO microfilm reel B5019, fr. 1731.

84. Notes of the Allied Air Commanders' Conference, 1 February 1945, Spaatz Papers, Diary.

85. Message XVAF E-0695, Twining to Spaatz, 3 February 1945, AFHSO microfilm reel A5544, fr. 827.

86. Letter, Spaatz to Anderson, 5 February 1945, Spaatz Papers, Diary.

87. USSBS, Transportation Division, *The Effects of Strategic Bombing on German Transportation*, vol. 200, 16; USSBS, Military Analysis Division, *The Impact of the Allied Air Efforts on German Logistics*, vol. 64a, 60–61.

88. Report, Eighth Air Force Operations Analysis Section, subject: "Report on Attacks against Enemy Rail Communications—22 February 1945," 8 March 1945, AFHSO microfilm reel A5923, fr. 48.

89. Letter, Anderson to Brig Gen Joe L. Loutzenheiser, chief, Operational Plans Division, Headquarters AAF, 20 March 1945, AFHSO microfilm reel A5534, frs. 344–45.

90. Message, Anderson to Spaatz, 22 February 1945, Spaatz Papers, Diary.

91. Richards, *Hardest Victory*, 277.

92. Notes of Allied Air Commanders Conference, 1 March 1945, Spaatz Papers, Diary.

93. Eighth Air Force, Monthly Summary of Operations, February 1945, AFHSO microfilm reel A5875, fr. 333.

March

4 March: Eighth Air Force—bombs Swiss cities of Zurich and Basel.

7 March: US troops capture the Ludendorf Bridge over the Rhine at Remagen, Germany.

14 March: Bomber Command—drops first 22,000-pound "Grand Slam" bombs on Bielefeld Viaduct, target destroyed.

15 March: Eighth Air Force—raids German atomic energy research facility at Oranienburg, a suburb of Berlin, to keep it from falling into Soviet hands.

23-24 March: Bomber Command—supports British ground assault on Wesel.

24 March: Bomber Command—Grand Slams destroy new U-boat shelter at Farge. Fifteenth Air Force—One B-24 lands in Switzerland after mission to Munich.

27-28 March: Last V-2s land in the UK.

In March the strategic air forces maintained the furious pace they had established at the end of February. Bomber Command led the way with 75,000 tons of bombs and 18,200 effective sorties. Harris expended almost 30 percent of his command's effort on oil targets, launching 4,400 sorties and 21,200 tons in 32 attacks of over 400 tons each. He launched another 775 sorties and 3,450 tons of ordnance on U-boat yards, hitting Hamburg with 940 tons on the night of 8 March and again with 2,503 tons and 454 heavy bombers using H2S on 31 March. The command flew 11 more missions, seven by day and four at night, attacking cities in support of the ground forces: 2,002 sorties, 9,007 tons of bombs (7 percent incendiary bombs [IB]). Six daylight missions struck marshaling yards at the army's request: 726 sorties, 3,394 tons (less than 1 percent incendiaries). Another eight daylight missions sought to bring down bridges targeted by the land forces: those missions required 360 sorties 2,019 tons (no incendiaries). For the month, the Eighth Air Force conducted 3,088 sorties and dropped 14,420 tons of bombs.

Most of the raids supported the 21st Army Group's set-piece assault crossing of the Rhine. Bomber Command used another 260 sorties on mining harbors to prevent easy submarine access to still active German U-boat bases; 180 against German shipping at Sassnitz; and 213 on the Dortmund-Ems Canal at Ladbergen, where an elevated aqueduct carried the canal. The remaining 45 percent of Bomber Command's effort demonstrated Harris at his most implacable.

During March 1945 Bomber Command conducted 17 main-force area raids and continued the full-scale harassment of cities still in German hands with thousands of night Mosquito sorties. Starting on 1 March with a daylight raid of 926 tons of high explosives (HE) and 1,299 tons of IB on Mannheim and ending with 40 Mosquitoes dropping 55 tons at intervals throughout the night on Berlin, Harris hurled 8,994 effective sorties and 33,125 tons at German city areas. One thousand daylight bomber raids, accomplished with frontline aircraft only and employing H_2S, smashed Essen on 11 March—Bomber Command's second largest raid of the war. On 12 March, in its largest raid of the war, Bomber Command struck Dortmund. Neither Essen nor Dortmund had any combustibles left to burn, so the bomb mix of more than 5,000 tons each consisted of high explosives and virtually no incendiaries. Both raids took place in daylight. This meant that the rest of the month's area attacks averaged almost 50 percent incendiaries. Thirteen other cites received more than 1,000 tons of bombs as main-force attacks continued through 27 March.

The next day Churchill began to question the entire policy of area bombing. Whether the prime minister demurred because of conscience, fear of possible domestic and international political repercussions, concern over postwar Europe, or a desire to preserve his historical reputation cannot be determined at this remove. On 28 March in a note to Portal, Churchill questioned the need for continued area bombing:

> The moment has come when the question of bombing German cities simply for the sake of increasing the terror, though under other pretexts, should be reviewed. Otherwise, we shall come into control of an utterly ruined land. The destruction of Dresden remains a serious query against the conduct of Allied bombing. I am of the opinion that military objectives must henceforward be more strictly studied in our own interests rather than that of the enemy. The Foreign Secretary has spoken to me on this subject, and I feel the need for more precise concentration upon military objectives such as oil and communications behind the immediate battle zone, rather than on mere acts of terror and wanton destruction, however impressive.[1]

This minute, with its implication that the airmen were running amok, rocked Portal, who found it unacceptable.[2] Given Churchill's support of Harris, his methods throughout the war, and his bullying of the air staff into bombing east German cities, one of which—as Churchill was specifically informed—would be Dresden, the minute seemed at best churlish and at worst an attempt to shift the entire responsibility for the policy of area bombing from the civilian to the military leadership. Portal suggested that Churchill withdraw the minute.[3] Portal also asked Bottomley to obtain Harris's comments immediately. Bottomley wrote of Churchill's note to Harris, "I am sure you will agree that [it] misinterprets the purpose of our attacks on industrial areas in the past, and appears to ignore the aim given by the Combined Chiefs of Staff in their directives which have been blessed by the Heads of Government."[4]

Harris, after three years of implementing official policy, erupted in anger. He termed Churchill's note "abusive" and "an insult both to the bombing policy of the Air Ministry and to the manner in which that policy has been executed by Bomber Command." Not satisfied with that observation, Harris argued that area bombing ought to continue precisely because the Germans no longer had the ability to recover from it. He added: "I therefore assume that the view under consideration is something like this: no doubt in the past we were justified in attacking German cities. But to do so was always repugnant and now that the Germans are beaten anyway we can properly abstain from proceeding with these attacks." Harris said that he could never agree to such reasoning: "Attacks on cities, like any other act of war, are intolerable unless they are strategically justified. But they are strategically justified insofar as they tend to shorten the war and so preserve the lives of Allied soldiers. To my mind, we have absolutely no right to give them up unless it is certain that they will not have that effect."

Harris then paraphrased Bismarck, "I do not personally regard the whole of the remaining cities of Germany as worth the bones of one British Grenadier." Besides, Harris pointed out, technical factors, such as a shortage of HE bombs but ample supplies of IBs also meant either the continuation of area bombing or standing down the entire force. Finally, Harris mentioned Japan. "Are we going to bomb their cities flat" to help the army? "Or are we going to bomb only their outlying factories, largely underground by the time we get going, and subsequently invade at the cost of 3 to 6 million casualties?"[5]

On 30 March Churchill withdrew the original minute, substituting on 1 April a much milder one that merely requested the air staff to investigate whether "our attacks do more harm to ourselves in the long run than they do to the enemy's immediate war effort."[6] On 4 April Portal replied, "at this advanced stage of the war no great or immediate additional advantage can be expected from the attack of the remaining industrial centres of Germany."[7] The air staff, however, did reserve the right to use area bombing to assist the advance of the Allied armies or to meet any stiffened German resistance. The air staff recommended no change in current strategic directives.

USSTAF's primary comment on the British discontinuation of area bombing revealed the contradictions in its own policies: "The U.S. Strategic Air Forces in Europe have not at any time had a policy of making area bombing attacks upon German cities. Even our attacks against the Berlin area were always directed against military objectives." However, USSTAF acknowledged that "our Pathfinder [H2X] attacks against communications centers have often resulted in an area type of bombing because of the inaccuracy of this type of bombing."[8]

In fact the Eighth's bombing in March 1945 raised some of the same questions as that of Bomber Command's. For the month the Eighth dispatched 27,985 effective sorties and

521

dropped 73,750 tons of bombs, 10,550 tons of them incendiaries. During the month the Eighth conducted four major area bombings, dropping 1,014 tons visually on the city of Plauen (19 March) and employing H2X to release 1,039 tons on the Berlin suburb of Spandau (28 March); 1,166 tons on Hannover (28 March); and 730 tons on Brandenburg (31 March). Other large raids on rail targets in city areas carried large percentages of incendiaries: Ulm (1 March), 30 percent; Frankfurt (9 March), 30 percent; Berlin (18 March), 50 percent; and Brunswick (31 March), 22 percent.

On 4 March the Eighth sent out 1,028 bombers, of which 671 succeeded in attacking their targets. Clouds forced the 2d Air Division off its primary targets—Me-262 airfields (targets not suitable for radar bombing)—leaving the division to seek targets of opportunity. Using H2X and visual sighting, 62 B-24s bombed Stuttgart with 146 tons (41 tons incendiaries), 14 B-24s hit Offenburg with 32 tons (19 tons incendiaries), and 11 B-24s struck Tuttlingen with 27 tons (five tons incendiaries). In addition, a combat box of the 1st Air Division, using GH, put 228 tons (105 tons incendiaries) into Ulm. However, the bombers of the Eighth had not finished their search for targets.

Two small formations of B-24s crossed into neutral Switzerland. Nine B-24s, using visual sighting, bombed Basel, located on the Swiss border where it meets the Franco-German border, with 22 tons of bombs, while six more B-24s flew approximately 25 miles into central Switzerland and attacked Zürich, using H2X, with 13 tons of bombs. In both instances the crews identified their target as the German city of Freiburg, approximately 30 miles north of Basel. The raids killed five and injured 19. Quite naturally they infuriated the Swiss as they did General Marshall, who ordered Spaatz to travel to Switzerland to apologize personally to the Swiss government and people. On 8 March Spaatz arrived in Bern. He agreed to prohibit bombing without his express permission within 50 miles of the Swiss borders and to set up a zone from 50 to 150 miles from the Swiss border in which he would forbid attacks without positive identification. In keeping with their strict policy of neutrality, the Swiss would not disclose this agreement, so the

Germans could not profit from it by moving industrial and military facilities closer to the Swiss border.[9]

On 7 March troops of the 6th Army Group seized the Ludendorf railroad bridge across the Rhine River at Remagen, Germany. They quickly established a bridgehead that obviated the need for a planned assault crossing of the Rhine. This feat was one of the greatest disasters to the German defenders on the western front. The Eighth Air Force quite unintentionally facilitated the capture of the bridge. In six raids previous to 7 March, it expended 246 effective sorties and 700 tons of high explosives to bring the bridge down. Ironically, the ineffectiveness of these raids left the bridge intact for its subsequent capture.

For the month the Eighth dropped more than 40 percent of its bombs on rail targets, almost 19 percent of which were incendiaries. It expended most of its remaining bombs on targets supporting Germany's last modern weapons. From 20 to 24 March the Eighth's bombers dropped more than 6,600 tons on German jet airfields; its fighters followed up with strafing attacks. During the month the Americans also attacked Me-262 assembly and component production plants using 2,900 tons of ordnance. The Americans devoted almost 6,500 tons against armored fighting vehicle production and another 3,800 tons against U-boats. Doolittle did not neglect oil facilities; his forces spent 9,400 tons, or 13 percent, of the Eighth's effort against these targets.

Two of March's heaviest raids occurred at the request of the Manhattan Project, the US military-controlled scientific team charged with designing, manufacturing, and exploding the first atomic weapon. Maj Gen Leslie R. Groves, commander of the project, revealed to Spaatz that Allied intelligence indicated that a German laboratory—hereafter sometimes called one of the "atomic" targets—in Oranienburg, a suburb of Berlin, had undertaken experiments with two radioactive elements: thorium and uranium. According to the Yalta agreements, the Berlin area would form part of the Soviet zone of occupation and would, therefore, be unavailable for exploitation by Western scientists. Consequently, Groves requested that Spaatz destroy the facility to keep it from falling intact into Soviet hands.[10] Ironically, Groves was unaware that Soviet intelligence had already penetrated many vital areas of his project, including the fact that a test of an atomic bomb might occur by June 1945.[11]

On 15 March, a day when the Eighth's meteorologists predicted clear weather over what remained of Nazi Germany, the Eighth's planning officers began to lay out an assault on their highest priority target system—oil. Instead, Spaatz's headquarters intervened directly, an unusual action. USSTAF selected the force (a maximum effort of 1,300 bombers), targets, bomb fusing, and axis of attacks for two targets in the Berlin area: the marshaling yards at Oranienburg, to the northwest of the capital city, and the general headquarters of the German army at Zossen to the southeast of the city.[12]

The attack on Oranienburg began at approximately 1450 hours. It took the 617 attacking aircraft, bombing visually, 45 minutes to pass over the target and deliver their 1,552 tons of high explosives and 178 tons of incendiaries. Immediate photographic reconnaissance, although hampered by clouds, reported severe damage to the marshaling yard and showed that "more than 100 H.E. bursts [500 and 1,000 lbs], mixed with I.B., blanket the industrial area."[13] In accordance with USSTAF's instructions, the raid carried an unusually large percentage of delayed-action bombs. Such fusing allowed the weapons to penetrate roofs instead of exploding on impact and to more thoroughly damage equipment within structures. Delayed-action bombs also slowed firefighting, salvage, and repair of facilities. Some of the weapons overshot their targets and destroyed barracks in the nearby Sachsenhausen concentration camp. By 19 March, Spaatz could report to Marshall that the Eighth had destroyed the "atomic" targets.[14] As a marshaling yard raid, it ranked as the third largest ever conducted by the Eighth as well as the largest conducted in visual conditions. It seems unlikely that significantly more than 600 bombers releasing through the smoke and haze would have inflicted further critical damage on this relatively small target— a consideration that applied to the raid on Zossen too.

The attack on Zossen, apparently chosen as part of the cover for the assault on the atomic targets, had its own intrinsic value. In selecting it Spaatz avoided the formidable flak defenses guarding Berlin proper. During the 3 February raid in clear weather the Eighth lost 24 bombers to flak. Of all those targets near

Berlin, Spaatz chose another attack on the German leadership. He sent 573 effective sorties (using both visual and H2X sighting and carrying 811 tons of high explosives and 581 tons of incendiaries) over the German army's general headquarters, its administrative establishment, barracks, and the adjacent Maybach tank training depot. The high concentration of incendiaries reflected the nature of the target, many aboveground administrative structures. A postraid photographic reconnaissance report, although hampered by haze and smoke, noted that four concentrations of high explosive and incendiary bombs blanketing the headquarters area heavily damaged barrack areas 6, 7, and 8 and damaged administrative buildings. On a less satisfactory note the report confirmed that the majority of the bombs fell in open spaces within the complex and in adjacent wooded areas. Some landed more than five miles from the target. The Eighth had hit the target with its average accuracy. By a stroke of sheer chance the raid caused some turmoil in the top German leadership, although not in the way Spaatz may have hoped. It wounded Colonel-General Heinz Guderian, chief of the German general staff, removing him from active duty and leading to the appointment of a less forceful individual in his stead.

In March 1945 the Fifteenth Air Force flew 12,739 effective sorties and dropped 28,010 tons of bombs, including 1,900 tons of fragmentation bombs, but not a single pound of incendiaries. It lost 134 heavy bombers, a 1 percent loss rate—compared to Bomber Command's 207 bombers lost (1.1 percent), and the Eighth's 121 lost bombers (0.4 percent). The Fifteenth expended 17,400 tons—more than 60 percent of its total tonnage for the month, concentrating its efforts on marshaling yards and rail targets in Italy, Hungary, Yugoslavia, Czechoslovakia, Germany, and Austria. This continued constriction of the German's lines of communication weakened their forces in Italy and the eastern front. The Fifteenth devoted another quarter (6,400 tons) of its energies to oil targets, most in Vienna. At the end of the month the Fifteenth joined the Eighth in an antiair campaign directed at Me-262s. The Fifteenth laid down 2,700 tons, including 1,900 tons of fragmentation bombs, on airfields in its area of operations. Its best-known raid of the month occurred on 24 March, when a force of 148 bombers escorted by its own P-51s made the long trip north to Berlin to hit a Diamler-Benz tank factory on the city's outskirts. The raid demonstrated the Fifteenth's capability to strike almost anywhere. The loss of 12 bombers (8 percent) discouraged any further such demonstrations.

In March 1945 the Combined Bomber Offensive reached its apogee in terms of tonnage dropped. In a month of virtually unconstrained attacks, the three strategic air forces rained bombs onto the rapidly shrinking Nazi state. German oil production had almost ceased, and its transportation system functioned only sporadically. German war production had collapsed from lack of coal, raw materials, and subassemblies.

Even as it reached the peak of its of effectiveness, the doctrine of strategic bombing, as practiced by the AAF and the RAF, came into question. The revulsion of the American public against the civilian casualties at Dresden and Churchill's attempt to distance himself from area bombing were harbingers of increasing disapproval from the public, scholars, and the ruling elite. Dropping atomic bombs on Japan, the logical conclusion of World War II strategic bombing, has come to represent an entire range of ideals never imagined or intended by those participating in the decision to drop the weapons or in the chain of command that ordered the atomic attacks. The disapprobation directed at Allied strategic bombing has hindered its objective study. The Anglo-Americans' use of incendiaries to purposely raze German cities is one of the major analytic themes of this work. The following section establishes the factual base for the author's reasoning.

Strategic Bombing, Targeting, and the Implications of the Bomb Mix

As discussed earlier, aircraft in a successful bombing attack must be able to locate their target, concentrate their effort, and release their bombs accurately on the intended aiming point. All this can be for very little result or even for naught if the weapons employed by the attacker are inappropriate for the nature of the target struck. The direct hit of six tons of ordnance, in the form of 300 forty-pound fragmentation bombs, on the 12-foot-thick hardened concrete roof of a submarine pen will have no effect on the target. Yet a single hit by specially designed 12,000-pound bomb, may well penetrate that roof and destroy the sheltered submarines and other vital facilities. Yet that same 12,000-pound bomb, when dropped on frontline enemy troops in field fortifications, might only destroy one or two foxholes, while leaving behind a crater so large that it impedes the advance of friendly armored vehicles. Obversely, 300 fragmentation bombs might heavily damage the defenders while leaving only small craters that would not slow the movement of friendly mechanized units. Hence, the bomber force must carry munitions, or a combination of munitions whose weight, penetrating force, and destructive properties optimize the effect of their strike.

Anglo-American strategic bombers employed three basic types of ordnance: high-explosive, magnesium or flammable jelly-filled incendiary, and fragmentation bombs. Each of these basic types came in varying weights with each weight and type of bomb designed to destroy a specific range of targets. HE bombs ranged in weight from 100 to 22,000 pounds and destroyed targets with their blast effects. The American bombers could not carry individual weapons of more than 2,000 pounds, and their high-explosive weapons of choice were the 500- and 1,000-pound general-purpose bombs. These bombs were effective against most targets, other than fortified structures with several feet of hardened concrete.

The British also used considerable numbers of 500- and 1,000-pound bombs, but many of their bombers, especially those employed in the last half of the war, could carry the large 4,000- to 16,000-pound "blockbuster" bombs. By the end of the war, a few late-model Lancasters could carry a 22,000-pound bomb, and the light Mosquito bomber could carry 4,000-pound weapons. Most of the larger British munitions were designed for blast effect, although some variants had special purposes, such as breaching dams and penetrating hardened concrete. High-explosive types constituted 85 percent of all bombs dropped in the Combined Bomber Offensive and comprised the majority of bombs employed against every target system. For example, when one subtracts Bomber Command's marking pyrotechnics, the Anglo-Americans hit the V-1 target system with 104,000 tons of bombs—all high explosives.

As their name suggests, fragmentation bombs destroy targets by propelling hundreds of small pieces of steel (shrapnel) throughout the vicinity of the impact. These shrapnel-producing weapons, usually between 40 and 250 pounds, were the sole province of the American bombers. They used them against airfields, where they shredded aircraft, ground support equipment, and personnel. They also used them in direct support of ground operations, where they slashed apart field fortifications and personnel but left the terrain uncratered. Of the 1,000,000 tons of bombs dropped by the Americans in Europe, fragmentation weapons accounted for less than 4 percent.

IBs comprised 15 percent of the strategic bomb mix: 20 percent of Bomber Command's, 10 percent of the Eighth Air Force's, and less than 3 percent of the Fifteenth Air Force's mix. The typical firebomb, dropped individually or in clusters of up to 500 pounds, consisted of a two-pound stick of magnesium, which burns at high temperature, an igniter, and a two-pound steel cap. (When in compound with manganese, magnesium is water resistant.) The cap gave the weapon a terminal velocity sufficient to penetrate a slate, wood, or metal sheet roof and start a fire that would destroy or damage the target. Obviously, the amount of combustibles in a particular target determined its vulnerability to incendiary attack. Fortifications, troops in the field, bridges, and ships were poor targets for firebombs since they had little flammable material or because they had sufficient manpower to quickly douse small fires before they could become conflagrations. In an industrial manufacturing or assembly plant the target was machinery, often the machine tools that turned out parts needed to assemble the final product. A direct hit by a high-explosive bomb would likely destroy a machine tool. As the Allies learned after the war, the collapse of a wall or roof alone on a factory machine usually inflicted little permanent damage. However, an extensive, hot fire would warp the machine out of tolerance, which would either make it unworkable or, more likely, make it unable to turn out parts to the precise dimensions required for assembly into modern weapons or new goods. The fire needed to destroy or severely damage a machine tool must feed on other material, most commonly a wood roof and/or floor. A new factory with a metal roof and framing, concrete floor, and internal fire partitions presents a much less attractive target for incendiaries than an older facility with wooden roof, floor, and frame, a facade of brick, and surrounded by other equally ignitable structures.[15] By January 1943 RAF analysis of its bombing of industrial zones indicated that, ton for ton, fire damage inflicted by incendiary bombs far exceeded that of high explosives.[16]

Unlike RAF Bomber Command, which expended half its efforts in city-area bombing and only 13 percent on industrial facilities,[17] the American strategic air forces aimed at least 26 percent of their bombs at economic targets.[18] Against the air industry the Eighth Air Force employed incendiaries at a 28 percent rate. Most aircraft facilities were of relatively recent construction, and by the fall of 1944 the Germans had so dispersed their air industry that it, as a whole, no longer presented a practical target. The Eighth used a similar ratio of incendiaries against armored fighting vehicle and motor transport targets and a ratio of 22 percent on armaments plants and ordnance depots. The Eighth reserved its heaviest ratio of incendiaries, 37 percent of its bomb mix, for the ball bearing industry, much of which was established in older, less fireproof facilities. Many of the aircraft plants and a majority of the arms and vehicle plants were situated in urban areas. Allied attacks on these targets, when directed by airborne radar (H2S or H2X), would invariably scatter a large percentage of high explosives and firebombs into nearby residential areas. As for the larger and isolated industrial plants, initial postwar investigations summarized the effect of incendiaries as "variable and not clear cut."[19]

However, none of the Allied strategic air forces employed an overall bomb mix of higher than 3 percent incendiaries against oil targets. That ratio shrinks to almost nil when one subtracts Bomber Command's marker bombs and the Eighth's raids on the Ludwigshafen synthetic oil plant and refineries in Hamburg and Bremen. Unlike the other plants, which stood alone in isolation from major urban areas, the Germans had built the Ludwigshafen oil plant as part of a gigantic I. G. Farben industrial chemical complex, closely associated with large blocks of workers' housing and in the middle of a highly populated district.[20] At first glance, the Allies' decision not to use incendiaries seems counterintuitive. Strategic bombing veterans, such as Maj Gen Ramsey Potts (director of targets for the Eighth Air Force) and Col Jacob Smart (a heavy-bomber group commander) have stated to the author that they and their contemporaries were convinced that "refineries don't burn." This surmise was apparently a distillation of a judgment prevalent in the Eighth and Fifteenth Air Forces.

The following passage taken from a report prepared by the American National Defense Research Committee (NDRC) and made available to VIII Bomber Command, in July 1943, provides the rationale for their position:

> In both oil refineries and synthetic petroleum plants almost any section of the plant constitutes a vital target because of the continuous nature of the process. Contents of the plant are highly inflammable, but most of the equipment is of such heavy construction that extensive fire damage to it would probably only accompany a major conflagration. The heavy construction of the equipment likewise protects the inflammable contents from ignition, unless high explosives damage has first broken up part of the installation and released the combustibles. The petroleum industry consequently does not constitute a target which is vulnerable to incendiary bombardment.[21]

In April 1944 the Bombs and Fuzes Subsection of the Eighth's Operational Research Section (ORS) prepared an analysis of ordnance needed for attacks on synthetic oil plants to support a proposed campaign against them.

The ORS study reinforced the conclusions of the NDRC. It identified the key component of the plant as the "water-gas" generator units, which could be destroyed by 100-pound HE bombs. The subsection added, "No incendiary bombs are recommended because there is sufficient heat involved in most of the processes to ignite the inflammable materials once the installations are broken open by high explosives and because gasoline and gases in storage can be ignited by hot fragments. It is also possible for H.E. bombs to cause destructive secondary explosions in the equipment of some of the processes and in gas storage tanks."[22] The thrust of both statements was not that "refineries don't burn," but, because of the highly inflammable nature of oil plants, one would not need incendiary weapons to torch them.

However, we learned that refineries do burn. Bomb photos of refineries and synthetic plants, not to mention civilian experience, show smoke clouds up to several thousand feet from such facilities and their associated tank farms. The most systematic and exhaustive analysis of the effects of strategic bombing on Germany, the postwar *United States Strategic Bombing Survey* noted that, "the large and efficient fire-fighting squads which were found in every [chemical and oil] plant investigated by the Survey in Germany bear witness to the ever present fear of fire." It concluded that "uncontrollable" fires in oil and chemical plants could have been started if: "(a) delayed-action incendiaries were used or fire bombs were dropped after high-explosive attacks had opened up lines, vessels, etc., and released inflammable materials and (b) anti-personnel bombs were dropped to keep plant protection forces under cover."[23] Despite evidence to the contrary, the Anglo-Americans erred in their assessment of the vulnerability of oil facilities to firebombs, and they persisted in that error until the end of the conflict.

Although firebombs proved destructive against industrial concerns, they reached the height of their effectiveness against cities. The British had received their initial experience at the hands of the Luftwaffe during the Blitz of 1940–41. Analysis of German area attacks, which used firebombs as the primary weapon, showed the British "that weight for weight, incendiaries caused at least five times more damage than H.E.; moreover, the damage sustained was more complete and permanent in character."[24] The first ordered British area attack of the war, against Mannheim in December 1940, consciously imitated German fire-raising techniques. Within two years the student had far surpassed the teacher.

German residential districts proved no less vulnerable to incendiaries than English ones. From January 1942 through May 1945, Bomber Command expended one-half of its total effort in area attacks on German cities, dropping more than 512,000 tons (37.8 percent or 193,500 tons of incendiaries). Of every 100 tons of incendiary bombs it released, Bomber Command aimed 92 tons of them against city areas. Of the remaining eight tons of incendiaries, at least half were marking devices, not weapons.

531

The US Eighth Air Force allotted 22 percent of its effective sorties towards city areas and area-like attacks.[25] This effort, 147,000 tons in total, included 48,000 tons of firebombs for a 33 percent ratio. Area attacks consumed one-half off all incendiaries dropped by the Eighth. An expert fire-protection engineer, who served on the NDRC, and as a consultant to both US Civil Defense authorities and the Eighth Air Force, as well as heading the fire analysis section of USSBS's physical damage Division, confirmed that the British experience of the Blitz held true for the Third Reich: "incendiaries were effective in city areas. The photo studies of damage indicated that, ton for ton, incendiaries were 4.8 times as effective as high-explosive bombs on residential areas and against the smaller industrial and mercantile properties. This was due, of course, to combustible contents, wood floors, and roofs."[26]

The vast majority of the area raids were directed at German cities. Of the 48,000 tons of American incendiaries dropped in city-area and area-like raids, 47,816 fell on Germany and 184 fell on cities in occupied Europe mistakenly identified by the bomber crews as lying in Germany. Of the almost 200,000 tons of firebombs dropped in area raids by Bomber Command, 95 percent hit German city areas. Of the remaining incendiaries, half fell on the city areas of another power, Italy, at war with Great Britain, and half fell on the French cities of St. Nazaire and Lorient in a campaign expressly authorized by the British War Cabinet to destroy the cities supporting German U-boat pens. Clearly, firebombs destroy cities. Just as clearly, the Anglo-Americans recognized that fact and used them accordingly.

This is not a new or original conclusion. The RAF never attempted to conceal or deny the intention and method of its attacks on Germany. The AAF, in spite of its efforts to change the record and to disavow any intention to area bomb, has been tarred, correctly, with the same brush. This study merely confirms what has long been known and assumed.

Allied Bombs and German Cities

The AAF and the RAF strategic air forces operated under quite different policies and they pursued totally dissimilar tactics. The statistical nature of this study tends to blur those differences, yet at the same time it can point to some insightful similarities. Area bombing of cities is one example of the problems and benefits of statistical study.

On 27 September 1943 the first American bombing mission was sent out with specific orders to bomb the center of a German city (Eighth Air Force; target Emden). The last attack by the Eighth was on Inglostadt, Germany, on 21 April 1945. During this period, the Eighth Air Force launched 111 area attacks, 105 of 30 or more heavy bombers, either conducted by the direct order of a superior headquarters or authorized by orders as a secondary target. Twenty-nine of the attacks took place between 27 September 1943—the date of the initial introduction of radar-assisted bombing—and 7 January 1944. All attacks were shallow penetrations of German territory because the Eighth could not fly deep into Germany without excessive casualties, and most encountered poor weather. The Eighth conducted another 33 area attacks between 29 January and 30 April 1944, including 16 in March 1944. These attacks coincided with the Eighth's offensive against the German fighter force and involved deep penetrations to Berlin and beyond. The attackers often ran into clouds, which necessitated radar bombing. These helped to force the Luftwaffe into the air. In May 1944 the Eighth launched 11 area attacks, including four against Berlin.

Once freed from full-time support of the Normandy invasion, the Eighth conducted 12 area raids in June and July. These missions included a series of large attacks on Munich in July 1944, which was the month in which it spent its largest tonnage on city targets. Near the end of the month, USSTAF issued orders stating:

1. The Commanding General has reiterated and reemphasized the firm policy under which the United States Strategic Air Forces in Europe have operated; that is, we have in the past, and will continue to do so in the future, directed our efforts toward precision targets.

2. We will not, at any time, direct our efforts toward area bombing.

3. We will conduct bombing attacks through the overcast where it is impossible to get precision targets. Such attacks will include German marshalling yards whether or not they are located in cities.[27]

Not surprisingly the number of city attacks recorded in the Eighth's records fell after the receipt of this order.

No area attacks occurred between 1 August and 25 September 1944. They resumed at the end of September and continued until early December. Seventeen occurred between 25 September and 9 December 1944, with nine in October. Several of these missions, such as the attack on the Ford plant at Kassel on 2 October and the assault on the Maschinenfabrik Augsburg-Nürnberg (MAN) tank plant on 2 October, could not hit their precision targets because of cloud cover and so bombed the city area instead. For all of 1945 the Eighth conducted only 11 documented area attacks: one in January, four each in February and March, and two in April.

The average Eighth Air Force area attack, excluding those smaller than 30 bombers, consisted of 277 bombers carrying 441 tons of high-explosive bombs, 237 tons of incendiaries (35 percent), and five tons of fragmentation bombs.[28] Each raid lost an average of eight bombers (3.2 percent). More than six out of seven of the raids used radar sighting, and of the raids using visual sighting, only three of more than 100 aircraft took place after 5 January 1944: Berlin (21 June 1944), Berlin (3 February 1945), and Plauen (19 March 1945). In all, not excluding raids under 30 bombers, the command area raids accounted for 29,176 effective sorties, 915 lost aircraft, 46,570 tons of high explosives, 24,936 tons of incendiaries, and 576 tons of fragmentation bombs, for a total of 72,082 tons of bombs.

In addition to ordered area bombing, Eighth Air Force crews seeking targets of opportunity attacked an additional 124 German cities and towns.[29] Thirty-eight of those attacks exceeded 30 heavy bombers, but only two—Stuttgart (16 July 1944) and Chemnitz (5 March 1945)—exceeded 100 heavy bombers. The number of these attacks remained fairly constant for the last 20 months of the war, and they coincided with poor weather units to divert from their primary and secondary targets to strike more accessible targets. The average opportunity raid averaged about one-eighth the size of a command area raid, 32 aircraft. This force, on the average, lost one bomber and carried 60 tons of high explosives and 19 tons of incendiaries (24 percent). In all opportunity bombings accounted for 3,940 sorties, 82 lost heavy bombers, 7,437 tons of high explosives, 2,345 tons of incendiaries, and 64 tons of fragmentation bombs, for a total of 9,846 tons. The impromptu nature of the opportunity raids is confirmed by their method of sighting. Slightly more than 50 of them employed visual methods, an indication of bombers roaming in search of a target, rather than proceeding to bomb the precision primary as an H2X secondary.

In comparison, from 27 September 1943 through 30 April 1945, the Eighth Air Force as a whole conducted 1,501 attacks on Germany, including area bombings of 30 bombers or more. These 1,501 attacks averaged 123 bombers, 258 tons of high explosives, 57 tons of incendiaries (18 percent), and six tons of fragmentation bombs. Each attack lost two heavy bombers, and 60 of the attacks employed some type of radar sighting, usually H2X. Command and opportunity area attacks of over 30 bombers comprised roughly 10 percent of the Eighth's efforts. They also included area bombings of 30 or more aircraft. Each of these attacks was confirmed by the Eighth's own documentation. Given the association between command city raids, use of H2X, large numbers of attacking bombers, and a high percentage of incendiaries, other similar raids conducted by the Eighth must certainly have had the effect of an area attack.

Not until the end of February 1945 did USSTAF issue a formal bombardment policy. The necessity for it arose from a mission of the Fifteenth Air Force. On 20 November 1944 the 5th Bombardment Wing could not penetrate through adverse weather to its primary target, the synthetic oil facility at Blechhammer. The force diverted to an alternate target and 158 B-17s employing H2X released 311 tons on the marshaling yard at Brno, formerly in Czechoslovakia. Brno presented an excellent picture on an H2X scope, one of the reasons for its selection as an alternate target. A factory area and ordnance plant were adjacent to the yard.[30] Although photographic reconnaissance revealed a good concentration in the factory area, an Ultra intercept noted that the raid killed 200, severely wounded 140, and slightly wounded 27. Ultra further revealed hits on the ordnance factory (repaired in 24 hours), the destruction of 20,000 fuses, and permanent destruction of textile plants apparently converted to assist the ordnance plant.[31] There the matter stood until January 1945, when a member of parliament inquired to the secretary of state for air "as to the policy of the Allied Air Forces in regard to the bombardment of targets in Czechoslovakia and the instructions given to the crews before they attack such targets." The member referred in particular to the attack on Brno. The RAF, as does any bureaucratic organization whose funding depends on legislative approval, reacted with alacrity. Its own policy had not changed since October 1942, but it sent an immediate query to USSTAF for American policy.

The British request caught USSTAF flatfooted. A search of its files found no comprehensive or even an incompletely formulated draft of a bombing policy. Queries to the Eighth, Ninth, and Fifteenth Air Forces produced standard operating procedures but no useful policy statements. However, MAAF Operations Instruction No. 88, dated 16 November 1944, which Eaker forwarded to USSTAF stated, in part:

> a. When weather or tactical conditions are unsuitable for operations against the systems of objectives mentioned in the preceding paragraphs, attacks are to be delivered on important industrial areas, with blind bombing technique as necessary. As far as operational and other conditions permit, these attacks are to be directed so as to contribute to the maximum destruction of the petroleum industries and the dislocation of German lines of communication. . . .
>
> b. Attacks on targets of opportunity, by blind bombing technique, should be made in Poland and Czechoslovakia *only* [emphasis in original] on particularly important targets well suited to PFF attack. If such installations do not appear on the scope, bombs should *not* [emphasis in original] be released.[32]

Events in February—for example, Thunderclap, Dresden, and Clarion—heavily influenced USSTAF's formulation of a bombardment policy. The American public's negative reaction to Dresden and the flap it created in AAF headquarters led to a spate of telegrams back and forth between Washington and London—Giles and Arnold demanding details of USSTAF's policies with General [Frederick] Anderson explaining them (Spaatz was in the Mediterranean for meetings with Eaker).[33] By 21 February, in preparation for Clarion, USSTAF issued a policy for the bombing of Czechoslovakia. The Sudetenland, annexed by Germany in 1938 as part of Greater Germany, would be treated as German territory. In the provinces of Bohemia, Moravia, and Slovakia, air forces would select visual targets "with due regard to risk to civilian population" and limit PFF attacks "to targets whose military importance clearly outweighs hazards to population."[34]

On 1 March USSTAF finally promulgated its only coordinated and comprehensive statement on American bombing policy. Anderson also rescinded any subordinate air force's policies in contradiction to it. The policy grouped Germany, Austria, the Sudetenland, and Hungary (whose territory not occupied by the Soviets was controlled by a Fascist regime that was formally at war with the Allies) into one grouping. The policy provided for their attack under the following conditions:

a. By visual sighting method.

    (1) Military objectives will be assigned for attack so as to best fulfill the objectives outlined in current directives as amplified by priority target lists.

    (2) Military objectives may be attacked as targets of opportunity if attack on the assigned targets proves to be impracticable.

b. By instrument bombing method.

    (1) Military objectives will be assigned for attack so as to best fulfill the objectives outlined in current directives as amplified by priority target lists.

    (2) If attack of the assigned targets is not practicable, military objectives may be attacked as targets of opportunity by instrument bombing technique. These attacks will be made against military objectives outlined under the current bombing directive.

Missions against Norway, Denmark, Belgium, Holland, France, Poland, Yugoslavia, Albania, Italy, and non-Sudeten Czechoslovakia would operate under more restrictive conditions.

a. By visual bombing method.

    (1) Military objectives will be assigned for attack so as to best fulfill the objectives outlined in current directives as amplified by priority target lists.

    (2) The attack of targets of opportunity is prohibited, and crews will be briefed to insure that no such attacks are made.

b. By instrument bombing method.

    (1) Military objectives will be assigned for attack when their military importance is so great that the risk of causing civilian casualties by bombing with normal accuracy is warranted.

(2) The attack of targets of opportunity is prohibited, and crews will be briefed to insure that no such attacks are made.

The policy went on to forbid H2X attacks within 50 miles of neutral countries and to require that aircraft have "positive and distinct" GH, MH, and visual fixes before bombing within the 50-mile zone. Some general admonitions and definitions concluded the document:

In all cases bombing will be done by precision methods when practicable and by instrument technique only when conditions of weather or tactical requirements dictate. In no case will targets be attacked unless the following requirements have been satisfied:

a. The target must be a military objective.

b. The identity of the target must be established beyond doubt.

The policy defined a military objective as "any objective the continued existence of which will materially contribute to the enemy's ability to wage war."[35]

This policy, for all its draconian tone, in actuality established less expansive bombing guidelines than its predecessors. It explicitly recognized the inaccuracy of radar attacks, limiting their application to occupied countries but not to Greater Germany. An early draft had incorporated Doolittle's formulation of 29 October 1944, which authorized radar attacks on any German city.[36] USSTAF struck this out and limited such attacks to those in current directives. Doolittle had defined military objectives loosely: any transport facility, any military installation, or any factory. The new policy defined a military objective as providing material aid to the enemy. A judgment call, perhaps, but one whose implication was clear—control indiscriminate bombing practices.

The rapidly changing situations of the final months of the war in Europe meant that modifications of the bombardment policy came quickly. The bombings of Switzerland on 4 March led to a prohibition on 6 March of attacks on targets of opportunity within 50 miles of a neutral country.[37] The next day USSTAF notified the air force commanders that Frankfurt, Würzburg, Nürnberg, and Regensburg were excluded from the restricted area surrounding Switzerland.[38] At the end of the month, 29 March, SHAEF sharply limited attacks on Denmark and occupied Hol-

land for humanitarian reasons. Only road and rail traffic definitely identified as military should be attacked and only road and
rail centers directly connected to the ground battle should be
struck. Attacks on V-2 sites near residential areas would require
specific SHAEF approval.[39] On 2 April Spaatz forbade attacks
within 25 miles of Berlin.[40] Spaatz went further the next day, ordering that henceforth, all targets would be cleared through
USSTAF.[41] The actual effect of these moves on bombardment
policy and on operations was minimal. In March the Eighth
reached its all-time highs for tonnage dropped and sorties flown.
The command (Eighth Air Force) conducted four area bombings
in March and two in April. The old ways die hard and some evidence indicates that some aircrews may well have continued the
past practice until almost the end of the war.

The Fifteenth Air Force either employed a different area bombing policy than the Eighth, or it simply was more assiduous in
pruning its records of direct references to instances of city bombing. The mission folders of the Eighth's three bombardment divisions and the Fifteenth's five bomb wings show a difference between the two forces. The Fifteenth may have been more
disciplined in defining its raids according to official regulations
but, for the most part, it quite simply fought a very different war.
The Fifteenth relied on finesse far more than the Eighth, which
had the bombers and escorts in numbers large enough to over-
power its adversary. The Fifteenth's 1,340 attacks of more than
30 aircraft, 47 percent of the US total after 27 September 1943,
averaged 85 heavy bombers, 183 tons of high explosives, five
tons of incendiaries, and 12 tons of fragmentation bombs, for a
total of 200 tons. Each raid lost one bomber; only 18 of them employed H2X. The ability to bomb in one or two group formations,
a luxury afforded by the relative lack of opposition by aircraft or
heavy flak covering most of its targets, far better weather (witnessed by the somewhat sparing use of H2X), and the lack of
ground haze generated by large conglomerations of heavy industry allowed the Fifteenth to bomb with much greater accuracy
than the Eighth. However, even daylight precision bombing as
practiced by the AAF in World War II, could still result in considerable collateral damage. The Fifteenth was more accurate
than the Eighth, but that is a relative not an absolute measure.

Of the 291 "city" attacks in the Fifteenth's records, only 60 exceeded 30 or more aircraft. Of those 60 the Allied ground forces or Tito's partisans requested 14 (11 by Tito, three by the 15th Army Group). In the remaining 44 attacks, the Fifteenth struck Rumania 16 times, Austria eight times, Italy seven times, Germany four times, Bulgaria and Yugoslavia three times each, Czechoslovakia twice, and Hungary once. The attacks, made up of more than 30 aircraft, averaged only 55 heavy bombers, less than a fourth of the size of the Eighth's comparable attacks, and used only 4 percent incendiaries, one-ninth of the Eighth's ratio of incendiaries to total bomb load.

The noticeably high number of city attacks on Rumania—12 on Ploesti and four on Bucharest—have a simple explanation. Aircraft assigned to destroy the refinery complexes at Ploesti had a secondary target, Ploesti itself, if their primary target was cloud or smoke covered. Bucharest contained refineries, marshaling yards, locomotive repair facilities, and the governmental and administrative center of the nation. The Fifteenth struck the city using visual dead reckoning through clouds, the most inaccurate bombing of all, with its first and continuing use of H2X, and visually. Bombers missing their targets often bombed the city itself. Fifteenth Air Force delivered more city tonnage on Rumania, (2,152 tons) than on any other country.

Of the eight city raids on Austria, six were against Vienna. On some occasions, but by no means all, aircraft sent to bomb its marshaling yards, ordnance depots, refineries, aircraft plants, and industrial areas had orders to hit the center of the city if they could not locate their primaries. Of the four area attacks on Germany, three hit Munich and one Plauen. Counting the 14 ground requested attacks, city raids of over 30 bombers dropped 7,860 tons, only 4 percent of them incendiaries.

The above facts confirm that the Fifteenth had followed a policy quite similar to that of Eighth. Units or individual aircraft seeking targets of opportunity had permission to attack cities, towns, or villages. However, these attacks averaged only five aircraft (1,172 total sorties) and 12 tons of bombs (2,790 tons total) each. In all the Fifteenth's 291 city raids accounted for 4,494 effective sorties, lost 102 bombers, and 10,704 tons dropped—a little over 3 percent of the Fifteenth's total effort.

Analysis of the 11 most heavily hit targets of each of the American strategic air forces reveals useful data on how they approached the problem of bombing accuracy. See the list of top targets below. The Fifteenth's target lists show all those attacked with 5,000 or more tons of bombs. The Eighth's list includes targets bombed with 10,000 tons or more. This includes all but two of the German targets, Hamm (10,000 tons) and Münster (10,280 tons), that it bombed with 10,000 tons or more.

For both air forces the tonnage released on the top 11 target areas represents precisely one-third of the total effort for the Fifteenth and for the Eighth one-third of its total effort against Germany after 27 September 1943.

The nature of the bombing of these targets says much about American bombing practice. The Fifteenth bombed the submarine pens and coastal defense in Toulon, with 1,969 effective sorties, using only high-explosive bombs and no H2X. The bomb mix reflected the nature of hardened concrete targets and a desire to avoid unnecessary damage to a city in occupied Europe. The Eighth and the Fifteenth each had one target not associated with a large city: synthetic oil plants at Blechhammer (north and south of the town) and Merseberg.

Top Targets

Fifteenth Air Force (targets, tons of explosives)	Eighth Air Force (targets, tons of explosives)
Vienna, 30,122	East Berlin, 23,070
Ploesti, 12,804	Ludwigshafen-Mannheim, 17,796
Linz, 8,962	Hamburg, 16,909
Budapest, 8,370	Cologne, 15,165
Munich, 7,801	Bremen, 14,022
Blechhammer, 7,082	Kassel, 12,980
Regensburg, 5,815	Merseberg, 12,953
Wiener Neustadt, 5,274	Frankfurt, 12,197
Toulon, 5,247	Munich, 11,541
Bucharest, 5,117	Kiel, 10,888
Graz, 5,047	Munster, 10,280

Source: Compiled by author from historical records.

Each demonstrated remarkable discipline in bomb loading that exhibited the American belief that oil targets did not burn. The Fifteenth dropped 139 tons of incendiaries (2 percent) on Blechhammer, and the Eighth only 10 tons on Merseberg. In their attacks on the 22 targets, both air forces employed H2X at a greater than average rate. Out of 62,250 sorties expended in the 348 attacks by the Eighth on its top 11 targets, 45,180 (73 percent) employed some form of radar bombing. Bremen had the lowest ratio of 66 percent, while Cologne, with its four marshaling yards, had 91 percent of the effective sorties flown against it directed by radar. So wild was the bombing that this produced that when the Eighth Air Force operations analysis section examined the results of approximately 2,000 sorties flown in late September and October 1944, its bomb plots revealed that only 12 aircraft had struck the target area. Another 550, or more, planes missed the target area by more than five miles. The report noted, however, that even the slightest of breaks in the clouds could reduce such gross errors by 300 percent.

Of the bombs aimed at Cologne's central yard, fully 60 percent hit the city's built-up area. The report concluded that, at least on theoretical grounds, the optimum aiming point for H2X raids that would produce, on the average, the greatest damage to all the marshaling yards was the center of the city![42] Cologne also had the distinction of sustaining the largest number of separate American attacks of any city in Europe—56 aerial raids of 30 or more heavy bombers.

On nine of its targets the Eighth used a ratio of 34 percent incendiaries, a figure equal to its area-bombing statistics. This ratio excludes two targets, Merseberg and Hamburg. The Eighth's bomb mix for Hamburg consisted of only 1,060 tons of incendiaries or 6 percent of the total. This low total has a practical, if grim, explanation. First, after Bomber Command's great fire raids of July 1943, the city had little left to burn. Secondly, much of the American effort struck oil refineries with no incendiaries and U-boat yards, which required few incendiaries. The ports of Kiel and Bremen absorbed a far greater percentage of firebombs, 28 and 26 percent, respectively. The Eighth's bomb mix for these targets dramatically illustrated the relationship between H2X and firebombs. For each target, save Kiel and Merse-berg, the ratio of firebombs was higher for H2X bombing than visual bombing. Munich and Berlin showed the greatest disparity. Both cities were hit with an overall ratio of incendiaries to total bombs dropped of 40 percent. But for both targets the H2X raids dropped fully 80 percent of all incendiaries. Ludwigshafen-Mannheim, a contiguous urban region separated by the Rhine River, had 82 percent radar bombing, with 95 percent of the firebombs released during radar-directed raids. For each target, excluding Hamburg and Merseberg, the Eighth employed large numbers of aircraft, a higher than average use of H2X, and a greater than average ratio of firebombs—all the necessary ingredients for area bombing.

When asked what European city was subjected to the greatest tonnage of American bombs, one is likely to respond by naming Berlin, Hamburg, or even Dresden. In fact that honor, if honor it be, belongs to Vienna. One out of every 10 bombs released by the Fifteenth Air Force fell on targets in that city or its environs. The city had served as the capital of the Austro-Hungarian Empire from the 1600s to 1918, of a rump Austrian state from 1918 to 1937, and from 1937 to 1945 of a province of Hitler's Greater Germany. Its citizens wryly referred to it as the capital without a country. Nonetheless, Vienna retained many of the accouterments of its glory days when it had served as the military, administrative, industrial, transportation, and commercial center of a major European power. Its very size and location on the wide Danube River made it as easy a target as any H2X operator could ask for. The river, navigable from the Black Sea almost to Switzerland, helped to turn the city into a giant entrepôt for grain, oil, and manufactured goods of all sorts and eased the strain on the German railway system. In addition the city offered a rich target selection. It contained numerous marshaling yards, train stations, and locomotive works. It had nearby airfields and an extensive aircraft industry producing and assembling aircraft engines, He-219s, and Me-109s. It also manufactured motor transport and armaments and contained ordnance depots. Finally, it served as a major oil center with five large refineries, benzoyl plants, and storage facilities. The Fifteenth attacked each of those in the course of 125 raids of more than 30 aircraft.

As noted above, the Fifteenth conducted only 18 percent of its sorties with H2X; for Vienna the figure was 60 percent (31 percent of all H2X sorties flown by the Fifteenth). Raids of more than 30 aircraft on Vienna averaged 20 percent more bombers than the usual such raid by the Fifteenth, 103 bombers to 85. Although the Fifteenth was anything but a firebomb-dropping force, it hit Vienna with more incendiaries than any of its other targets. The amount totaled 1,216 tons, 18 percent of all incendiaries used by the Fifteenth, but only 4 percent of the bombs released over the city. The long flight from the heel of Italy and the return, as well as German defenses, took a heavy toll of American heavy bombers. Three hundred and seventy-seven failed to return, almost one out of every five such aircraft lost in combat by the Fifteenth. Discounting firebombs, the raids on Vienna exhibited a high usage of H2X and larger than average attacks. Vienna, like its German counterparts, undoubtedly suffered from the area bombing.[43]

Bucharest and Budapest, two capitals with many targets similar to Vienna's, received different treatment. Of the Fifteenth's top 11 targets, the two cities had received the fewest number, save Toulon, of H2X sorties applied against them, 3 and 6 percent, respectively. However, their status as communications, administrative, and manufacturing centers attracted comparatively large bomb tonnages. The large amount of visual bombing of marshaling yards, oil refineries, and armaments works and railroad bridges in Budapest and locomotive works in Bucharest produced minimum, but still substantial, collateral damage. The Rumanians, in particular, seemed to feel that they had suffered undue punishment. As for the Hungarians, the house-to-house fighting in their capital at the end of 1944 showed them conclusively that bombing was the lesser of several evils. Ploesti, the Fifteenth's second most heavily hit target, was that air force's raison d'être. Spaatz and Arnold had established it for the prime purpose of knocking out the German's main source of natural oil. The controversy over oil versus transportation targeting in London delayed the Fifteenth's first mission against Ploesti until 5 April 1944. From that point on, the Fifteenth made 65 attacks of 30 or more aircraft on the refinery complex. The long delay in mounting the air offensive on Ploesti gave the Germans and Rumanians time to perfect smoke screens and install heavy flak. The passive defenses of the refineries and occasional clouds forced the forces attacking Ploesti to employ H2X 40 percent of the time. While flak and fighter aircraft downed 226 bombers, a loss rate of 4 percent, those defenses did not prevent the raids from demolishing the refinery complex and severely damaging the adjoining city.

The Fifteenth shared two of its top 11 targets—Regensburg and Munich—with the Eighth. The Fifteenth flew 19 attacks of 30 or more bombers and 2,500 sorties in all operations against Regensburg. During Big Week in February 1944 it directed 270 sorties at the Messerschmidt fighter factories. In late 1944 and 1945 the Fifteenth returned to attack Regensburg's marshaling yards and oil storage facilities. Its location on the Danube and at the nexus of several rail lines made Regensburg an important communications center for Italy and Hungary. The Danube attracted bombs as well as commerce. After subtracting the February 1944 raids, when the Fifteenth had not yet acquired H2X, the percentage of radar sighting for the remaining raids came to 82 percent. H2X reconnaissance flights, which took pictures of the scope images of targets, aided the regular bombardiers, especially in water and land contrast.

Munich, on the Isar River, a tributary of the Danube, was the only city on the top 11 lists of the Eighth and Fifteenth. The Eighth systematically area bombed it in July 1944. The Fifteenth added 32 more attacks of 30 or more aircraft, including three area attacks, and flew 3,270 sorties in all against the city. It attacked marshaling yards, ordnance depots, airfields, and the BMW aeroengine plants at Allach, a suburb of Munich. Forty percent of the bombing used H2X. The Fifteenth's bombing added to the suffering in the Bavarian capital, but determining the damage inflicted by each air force proved difficult. One thing is certain, USSTAF dropped 19,342 tons on Munich and 8,307 on Regensburg.

In addition to Vienna three other Austrian cities were among the Fifteenth's top 11 targets: Graz, Linz, and Wiener Neustadt. The bombing of all three followed a similar pattern. In the first five months of 1944, the Fifteenth attacked aircraft component, assembly, and engine plants in each of the cities as part of USSTAF's counterair campaign. After a hiatus of bombing in the summer of 1944, the Fifteenth began a series of heavy attacks from November 1944 through April 1945 on the marshaling yards and associated facilities of the cities. These raids came as part of the Fifteenth's participation in the second offensive by Allied strategic air forces against transportation targets. In each case the use of H2X against each target exceeded the Fifteenth's average, reaching 37 percent for Wiener Neustadt (excluding pre-H2X raids), 47 percent for Graz, and 65 percent for Linz. Including all raids of over 30 aircraft, the Fifteenth struck Wiener Neustadt and Graz 19 times each and Linz 32 times. Given the relatively high percentage of H2X sorties, these cities, in the words of Gen F. L. Anderson, can be said to have sustained "an area type of bombing."[44]

The patterns established in these large bombings were repeated in many of the other cities suffering more moderate attacks. The Eighth dropped 5,000 tons or more of ordnance on the cities of Nürnberg, Hannover, Koblenz, Leipzig, Mainz, Münster, Osnabruck, and Saarbrücken. The Eighth's bombers used firebombs and H2X in ratios similar to the targets on its top 11 list. The Fifteenth delivered more than 2,000 tons each on the industrial and communications centers of Northern Italy: Turin, Verona, Genoa, Bologna, and Ferrara. In Austria the Fifteenth hit industrial plants and marshaling yards in Innsbruck and Klagenfurt; in Czechoslovakia, Brux. Its bombers hit Sofia, Belgrade, Brod, and Maribor with more than 2,000 tons of bombs.

Bomber Command and its air officer commanding, of course, made no bones about area bombing. From 27 September 1943—the midpoint of Sir Arthur Harris's tenure as head of the command and a time when the Battle of Hamburg had begun to wind down and the Battle of Berlin had yet to start—to May 1945, the command conducted 213 heavy bomber attacks on Germany using area bombing techniques. This total includes 26 attacks in support of army operations support attacks and 24 raids on cities and rail facilities. Only eight of the raids had consisted of less than 30 aircraft. The greater bomb lift of Harris's aircraft and the marking techniques that directed the bombers to a single target gave the command the ability to concentrate its attacks. The problems encountered during daylight bombing forced the Americans to strike multiple targets, an option for the most part denied to the RAF at night. The 173 regular area attacks averaged 378 heavy bombers, lost 12 aircraft, and released 1,044 tons of high explosives and 639 tons of incendiaries, a 38 percent ratio, for a total of 1,683 tons. The army support attacks averaged 227 bombers, lost one bomber on each mission, and released 1,058 tons of high explosives and 72 tons of incendiaries, a ratio of 6 percent, for a total of 1130 tons. The transportation attacks (city and rail targets) averaged 384 bombers, lost six aircraft, and dropped 844 tons of high explosives and 751 tons of firebombs, a ratio of 47 percent, for a total of 1,595 tons. The attack on Dresden fell in the category of city and rail targets. Over the same period Bomber Command flew more than 23,000 sorties using Mosquitoes to harass the Germans. Bomber Command dropped 49,000 tons of high explosives while losing 121 aircraft.

The city and rail facility attacks were indistinguishable from regular city attacks as to technique and aiming points. For the remainder of this discussion they will be considered as a part of ordinary city-area bombing. From 27 September 1943 to 3 May 1945, the command devoted 63 percent of its total heavy bomber effort—70,500 effective sorties out of 109,550 and 312,100 tons of bombs out of 497,800—to city-area bombing of cities. City attacks in support of army actions fall into a specialized category. The army, knowing that Bomber Command used large bombs, wanted the air attacks for two purposes; either to root out dug-in German defenders or to crater city and surrounding roads to hinder German retreats or movement of reinforcements. Both tasks required a bomb mix high in explosives and low in incendiaries. Firebombs had no concussive, blast, or cratering effects. The raids met no notable success, but on at least one occasion their aftermath slowed the advance of Montgomery's forces. The effort cost the command 6,200 sorties and 30,900 tons, 6 percent of its total bombing.

Because Bomber Command's city-area raids are acknowledged as such, they serve to validate the relationship between greater than average forces, radar aiming, and a high ratio of firebombs to total bombs delivered. From late September 1943 until the end of the war, the command flew a grand total of 376 heavy bomber raids of 30 or more aircraft, averaging 289 planes. Each raid lost seven aircraft and dropped a total of 1,313 tons of ordnance: 976 tons of high explosives and 337 tons of incendiaries, a ratio of 26 percent. If one subtracted the 197 area raids, then this average would shrink dramatically. In any case RAF area raids exceeded the average number of aircraft deployed by at least 30 percent. The target locating and marking methods of the AAF and the RAF differed so widely as to make comparison between the two difficult. However, for approximately 75 percent of the command's night area attacks, the marking forces used some form of instrument aid, usually H2S for deep targets and Oboe for those in western Germany, to locate the objectives. Once they had identified the point of the attacks the marking force would use its own specialized techniques to direct the bomber stream to the release point. In the matter of bomb mixes, Bomber Command, as with its American counterparts, showed superb discipline. Of the 126,000 tons of firebombs dropped by the command after September 1943, city-area raids consumed 95 percent of them, or 120,750 tons, for a ratio of 39 percent. Large force, heavy use of instrument-assisted sighting, and the dropping of high numbers of fire bombs equals area bombing. Hence, hypotheses confirmed.

A list of Bomber Command's top 11 targets further confirms its ability to concentrate its attacks. All attacks on Berlin, Essen, Hannover, and Frankfurt-am-Main were city-area attacks. The Bomber Command achieved the totals cited in the table below with remarkably few attacks of 30 or more aircraft: Berlin—16, Essen—nine, Cologne—12, and Düsseldorf—only four. The sheer weight of heavy ordnance and firebombs rapidly delivered and concentrated on or near the markers made a Bomber Command raid a thing of awesome power and destructiveness. No one who lived through the experience was likely ever to forget it. The command expended 41 percent of its total heavy bomber effort against the above targets.

Although Harris pursued area bombing, Harris had other responsibilities imposed on him from outside forces, particularly the oil campaign and the second transportation campaign. Including bombing marshaling yard raids at the request of the 21st Army Group to interdict German movement and logistics, the command flew 8,450 sorties and released 41,000 tons of bombs—8 percent of its total bombing—on those targets. As opposed to the Eighth, which placed a mix of 16 percent incendiaries on rail yards, Bomber Command used a mix of only 4 percent firebombs. Attacks on oil facilities, Bomber Command's second most heavily bombed target system, consisted of 16,900 effective heavy bomber sorties and 77,500 tons, 15 percent of Harris's total effort. Four targets systems—cities, oil, marshaling yards, and city bombing requested by the army—93 percent of the Command's energy applied towards Germany.

Bomber Command's Top Targets and Tonnage

Targets	Tonnage
Berlin	41,374
Essen	25,955
Cologne	23,249
Duisburg	22,448
Hamburg	22,360
Dortmund	19,904
Stuttgart	19,432
Gelsenkirchen	18,343
Frankfurt-am-Main	14,017
Kiel	13,951
Hannover	12,441
Düsseldorf	11,385
Total	244,859

The US Army Air Forces never officially acknowledged that it bombed German city areas as a matter of policy. Analysis of the Eighth's and Fifteenth's bombardment policies, their employment of large raids, H2X, and incendiary bombs, and their targeting of city areas clearly demonstrates that, despite denials, the AAF engaged in the deliberate bombing of German population centers. There were only two discernible but important differences between the AAF's practice and the RAF's admitted policy.

First, unlike RAF Bomber Command under the direction of Harris, the AAF did not consider cities its chief and preferred targets. Whereas Harris repeatedly and sarcastically scoffed at any other target system as a "panacea," the AAF preferred to bomb oil and other recognizable and identifiable target systems whenever visual methods would allow. Spaatz correctly believed that the bombing of crucial oil and transportation targets would end the war sooner, with less loss of life, than area bombing.

Second, the AAF in Europe never trained for the use of nor developed or employed the specialized fire-raising techniques used by Bomber Command. To do so would have openly acknowledged a city-area bombing policy. Nonetheless, under nonvisual bombing conditions (night or heavy overcast), however, the points of attack and the bomb loadings of the RAF and the AAF were virtually indistinguishable, as were their results.

Notes

1. Webster and Frankland, *Strategic Air Offensive*, 3:112.
2. Ibid., 117.
3. Ibid.
4. Letter, Bottomley to Harris, 28 March 1945 in Saward, *Bomber Harris*, 291–92.
5. Letter, Harris to Bottomley, 29 March 1945, in Saward, 292–94.
6. Minute, Churchill to chief of the Air Staff, 1 April 1945, in, Saward, 294–95.
7. Note by the Air Staff, COS(45)238(0), Portal to Churchill, "Area Bombing," in Saward, 295–97.
8. Memo, Frederick L. Anderson, subject: Comments Re Cablegram WAR 65558 (USSTAF IN-28993), 10 April 1945, AF/HSO, microfilm, reel A5616, fr. 154.
9. Letter, Spaatz to chief of staff, US Army, "Report on Visit to Switzerland 7–8 March 1945," 10 March 1945, Spaatz Papers, Dairy.
10. V. Jones, *Manhattan*, 287–88; Groves, *Story of the Manhattan Project*, 230–31.
11. Holloway, *Stalin and the Bomb*, 105. Also see, Albright and Kunstel, *Bombshell*, which notes the existence of several Soviet spies in the Manhattan project including Ted Hall, Saville Sax, Klaus Fuchs, the Rosenbergs, and at least six persons identified in Soviet records only by their code names. Among other secrets these spies passed a detailed design of the "Fat Man" bomb to the Soviets.
12. Headquarters, Eighth Air Force, subject: "Planning for Mission of 15 March 1945," 16 March 1945, AF/HSO microfilm, reel B5023, fr. 29.
13. Interpretation Report S.A. 3397, "Attack on Oranienburg Marshalling Yard on 15 Mar 1945," 16 March 1945, AF/HSO microfilm, reel B5022, fr. 2328.

14. Message SP-201, Spaatz to Marshall, 15 March 1945, and message UAX-66143, Spaatz to Marshall, 19 March 1945, Spaatz Papers, Diary.

15. For a discussion of the vulnerability of industrial concerns by expert fire-prevention engineers, one of whom participated in the Eighth Air Force's target planning, see Bond and McElroy, "Some Observations and Conclusions," in Bond, *Fire and the Air War*, 246–47.

16. Memorandum, Headquarters VIII Bomber Command, Operational Research Section, subject: Effectiveness of Incendiaries, 9 September 1943; AFHSO microfilm, reel B5549, fr. 1492. This memo is the Eighth's analysis of a RAF report of January 1943 entitled "Incendiary Attacks on German Cities."

17. Industrial facilities comprise the following target systems: the air industry (engines, components, assembly, and repair); steel; ball bearings; chemical plants; armaments, motor transport, and armored fighting vehicle factories; oil facilities (pumping stations, refineries, synthetic oil plants, and storage areas); and general industrial plants. Bomber Command devoted 10 percent of its entire effort from 1942 to 1945 to oil targets and less than 3 percent to all other industry.

18. The Fifteenth Air Force spent 29 percent of its efforts, including 19 percent against oil, on industrial targets, while the Eighth Air Force directed 26 percent, including 13 percent against oil. These calculations do not include incendiaries expended against airfields. Many of the air fields attacked by these two air forces were directly associated with Axis aircraft assembly plants and the bombs dropped on them were also intended for adjacent portions of the air industry.

19. "Fire Attacks on German Cities," in Bond, *Fire and the Air War*, 80.

20. The 75,000 tons that the Eighth aimed at oil targets included only 1,984 tons of firebombs. Of those 1,984 tons of firebombs, 918 tons fell, in five raids, on Ludwigshafen; 522, in two attacks, on refineries in Hamburg; and 176, in a single attack, on a refinery in Bremen. In Hamburg and Bremen the refineries were associated with a much larger port and industrial area.

21. NDRC, "Memorandum on European Industrial Plants as Targets for Incendiary Bombing," 5 June 1943, attached to memo, Headquarters VIII Bomber Command, Lt Col George W. Jones, Jr., Operational Intelligence, to Brig Gen Frederick L. Anderson, 27 July 1943; AF/HSO microfilm, reel A5500, fr. 1058. Bomber Command agreed with this reasoning. Although Bomber Command Pamphlet "B.C. 45 (rev. ed. 1943): Types of Bomb (and Fusing) for the Attack of Various Land Targets" [AF/HSO microfilm, reel A5500, fr. 1001], specified all types of incendiaries for petroleum products stored in "light and heavy oil tanks," it recommended only high explosives for "Liquid Fuel Production Plants, Synthetic Rubber Works, and Chemical Works."

22. Memorandum, Headquarters Eighth Air Force, Operational Research Section, subject: Selection of Bombs and Fuzes for Attacks on Synthetic Oil Plants, 10 April 1944, AF/HSO microfilm, reel 5500, fr. 996.

23. USSBS, *Oil Division Final Report*, 2d ed., vol. 109, 129.

24. Memorandum, HQ VIII Bomber Command, Operational Research Section, subject: Effectiveness of Incendiaries, 9 September 1943; AFHSO microfilm, reel B5549, fr. 1492. This memo is the Eighth's analysis of an RAF report of January 1943 entitled "Incendiary Attacks on German Cities."

25. For the purposes of this work "area-like" raids are defined as American raids of 100 or more heavy bombers, carrying a ratio of 20 percent or more incendiaries, and attacking by means of H2X.

26. Bond, 80.

27. Memo to director of operations, from Maj Gen F. L. Anderson, deputy commander, operations, 21 July 1944. Annotated by hand "directive to 8th and 15th [Air Forces]."

28. The eight area raids by the command for raids of less than 30 bombers total only 126 sorties and 222 tons of bombs.

29. I did not include data for opportunity raids on Bonn (106 bombers; 243 tons) on 12 August 1943 and Karlsruhe (17 bombers; 31 tons) on 6 September 1943.

30. Message D-2333, Fifteenth Air Force to USSTAF MAIN, 28 November 1944, AFHSO, microfilm reel A5616, fr. 47.

31. Intercept CX/MSS/T378/51 of message HP 7691, 24 November 1944, cited as enclosure no. 10 in Maj Robert F. Prokop Jr., USA, "ULTRA's Impact to the European Strategic Bombing Campaign of World War II," thesis, Joint Military Intelligence College, Bolling AFB, DC, December 1996.

32. Memo, Col Alfred R. Maxwell, director of operations, to Maj Gen F. L. Anderson, deputy commander for operations, USSTAF, subject: Attacks on Czechoslovakia, 18 February 1945; AFHSO, microfilm reel A5616, frs. 40–41.

33. See Davis, *Spaatz* (558–62) for a more detailed examination of the transatlantic exchange.

34. Message UAX 64650, USSTAF to Fifteenth Air Force, 21 February 1945, AFHSO, microfilm reel A5616, fr. 81.

35. Headquarters USSTAF, Office of the Deputy Commander, Operations, Bombardment Policy, 1 March 1945; AFHSO, microfilm reel A5616, frs. 95-97.

36. Enclosure No. 8, "Amended Bombardment Policy," to memo, Col Alfred R. Maxwell, director of operations, to Maj Gen F. L. Anderson, deputy commander for operations, USSTAF, subject: Attacks on Czechoslovakia, 18 February 1945; AFHSO, microfilm reel A5616, frs. 49–50.

37. Message UAX 65405 USSTAF to MAAF, 6 March 1945, AFHSO, microfilm reel A5616, fr. 109.

38. Message UAX 65454, USSTAF to MAAF, 7 March 1945, AFHSO, microfilm reel A5616, fr. 118.

39. Message A 277, air staff SHEAF Forward to USSTAF, 29 March 1945, AFHSO, microfilm reel A5616, fr. 140.

40. Message UAX 66845 USSTAF to Eighth Air Force, 2 April 1945, AFHSO, microfilm reel A5616, fr. 144.

41. Message UAX 66900, USSTAF to Eighth Air Force and Fifteenth Air Force et. al., 3 April 1945, AFHSO, microfilm reel A5616, fr. 145.

42. Memo, HQ Eighth Air Force, Operations Analysis Section, subject: H2X Operations Against Cologne in September and October 1944, 21 November 1944, AFHSO, microfilm reel A5994, frs. 1517–21.

43. A "poor man's" assessment of the damage inflicted on Vienna can still be seen in Orson Wells' superb movie *The Third Man*, parts of which were filmed on location in Vienna in 1946–1947. Some of the background footage reveals uncleared rubble and unrepaired damage to residential areas more than two years after the war.

44. Memo, F. L. Anderson, subject: Comments re Cablegram WAR 65558 (USSTAF IN-28993), 10 April 1945, AFHSO, microfilm reel A5616, fr. 154.

April

6 April: Bomber Command—Area bombing officially discontinued, unless in exceptional military situations.

8 April: Fifteenth Air Force—two B-24s land in Switzerland after mission to Vipiteno, Italy.

12 April: USSTAF—General Spaatz and Air Marshal Bottomley issue Strategic Bombing Directive No. 4, which ended the strategic air war and ordered the strategic air forces to give direct assistance to the land campaign.

14–15 April: Bomber Command—sends 512 heavy bombers against Potsdam.

14–16 April: Eighth Air Force—sends 3,200 heavy bomber sorties to hit German defensive installations around Bordeaux in support of French army ground assault. One raid, 860 bombers, is the sole operational use of napalm by the Eighth. It is judged ineffective.

15–18 April: Fifteenth Air Force—bombers support US Fifth Army attack by hitting German front lines, supply dumps, and headquarters.

20 April: Fifteenth Air Force—one B-17 lands in Switzerland after mission to Vipiteno.

22 April: Bomber Command—sends 767 heavy bombers against Bremen in preparation for British ground assault.

25 April: Eighth Air Force—last heavy bomber combat mission strikes Skoda Armaments at Pilsen, Czechoslovakia, and various marshaling yards. Bomber Command—sends 320 heavy bombers against Berchtesgaden, Hitler's personal retreat.

25–26 April: Bomber Command—last operation by heavy bombers—oil refinery at Tonsberg, Norway.

26 April: Bomber Command—Operation Exodus, repatriation of British POWs, begins.

29 April: Operation Manna, food for the Dutch, begins.

30 April: Hitler commits suicide.

By the beginning of April 1945 the Anglo-American strategic bomber commanders could scarcely find a target in the detritus of the Nazi state that justified the expense of mounting an operation against it. On 5 April USSTAF acknowledged that, except for U-boat yards, all targets "should now be regarded as tactical targets." Of the tactical targets, USSTAF accorded first priority to the Luftwaffe and second priority to communications centers in central and southern Germany.[1]

On 10 April, Tedder, noting that the strategic air forces had agreed that their primary objective was now direct support of the land campaign, requested Spaatz put full effort on enemy rail communications, especially those in central Germany.[2] Apparently Tedder and Eisenhower hoped to prevent effective north-to-south as well as west-to-east transfers of German men and matériel. Spaatz ordered Doolittle to give enemy communications top priority and push airfield bombing back a notch. Spaatz added hopefully, "Wherever suitable, [Clarion] low-altitude, small formation technique[s] should be used to obtain maximum effectiveness."[3]

At last, on 12 April, Spaatz and Bottomley, after consulting Tedder, agreed on a final directive, Strategic Directive No. 4, which brought the strategic air war in Europe to a close. They designated the top-priority mission of the strategic air forces as giving "direct assistance to the land campaign." Operations to support the Soviet armies would occur only if directly requested by the Soviet High Command. Second priority went to oil supplies, particularly gasoline in storage depots, enemy lines of communications, and "such other missions as may be requested by the Supreme Commanders." The directive next allowed policing attacks against the Luftwaffe and provided that the marginal effort would remain concentrated on U-boats. The area bombing catchall category "Important Industrial Areas" disappeared, as did the requirement to support clandestine intelligence activities.[4]

Four days later, Spaatz formally signaled the end of the strategic effort to Doolittle and Twining: "The advances of the Ground Forces have brought to a close the Strategic Air War waged by the United States Strategic Air Forces and the Royal Air Force Bomber Command. It has been won with a decisiveness becoming increasingly evident as our armies overrun Germany. From now on, our Strategic Air Forces must operate with our Tactical Air Forces in close cooperation with our armies."[5] The operations of the three strategic air forces mirrored the new priorities from somewhat different angles.

The Fifteenth Air Force reduced its number of sorties by approximately 10 percent and its tonnage to 27,347, down from 28,010. The new emphasis on transportation made little difference to a force that was already spending the bulk of its effort in that area. During April 1945 the Fifteenth dropped 6,700 tons on marshaling yards, 360 tons on motor transport repair, 7,690 tons on rail bridges, junctions, and viaducts, and 2,500 tons on highway bridges. The result of this bombing, plus that of the Allied tactical air forces in Italy, immobilized the German Tenth and Fourteenth Armies, reducing them to the expedient of moving motorized equipment with teams of oxen. When the Allied ground forces broke through the German lines, they quickly overran their defeated foes and forced the surrender of German forces in Italy before the end of April. The Fifteenth aided the final Allied ground assaults with attacks on German lines. On 9 and 10 April the Fifteenth used more than 3,100 tons of fragmentation bombs. On 15 through 19 April it used 4,000 tons of high explosives and 500 tons of fragmentation bombs on tactical targets.

During the month the Fifteenth became the first air force to employ proximity-fused bombs in combat. The fuse, built around a small radar transmitter/receiver, could be set to detonate at a fixed height from the ground—airbursts would prove deadly to personnel with insufficient top cover or protection. The Fifteenth used the fuse against German flak because they had to expose themselves in order to fire. One could also speculate that the use of such a potentially destructive weapon against the men who had personally tried to kill the aircrews from the first day of battle onwards gave the men of the Fifteenth a certain extra satisfaction.

While the Fifteenth made little change in its operations, Bomber Command took the opposite tack. Its monthly tonnage fell by around 50 percent, from 74,970 to 38,630. Harris followed his orders in letter and spirit by completely discontinuing the area bombing of cities. Bomber Command's use of incendiaries fell from 11,300 tons in March to 500 tons in April, almost all of it used by the Pathfinders and other marking forces. However, Bomber Command did maintain its night harassing attacks with Mosquitoes, which flew 1,600 sorties and dropped 2,200 tons on 13 German cities. Neither the weary nor the wicked found ease in Germany's remaining cities. Bomber Command invested a further 6,100 tons in oil targets, most against storage and re-fineries. Its last heavy bomber raid of the war was against a Norwegian refinery at Tönsberg, Norway, on 25 April 1945. The command pasted some familiar targets, the U-boat yards in Kiel and Hamburg, with 6,800 tons.

More than half of Bomber Command's tonnage, approximately 21,000 tons, went to support the operations of 21st Army Group. Marshaling yards designated by SHAEF as supplying a potential German national redoubt in Bavaria, such as Leipzig, Plauen, Beareth, Nürnberg, and Pilsen, absorbed 5,900 tons. German military bases, such as Nordhausen, received 1,700 tons, and facilities on the fortified island of Helgoland garnered 4,700 tons, including a massive raid of 3,800 tons on 18 April. A daylight raid, employing GH, placed 1,100 tons on Bremen (22 April) and on 25 April a visual daylight raid put 2,500 tons on the island of Wangerooge. All the above missions advanced, in some measure, the needs of the ground and sea forces.

It is possible that on two other missions Harris may have "cooked the books" and used the cover of ground forces support to pursue his own agenda. On 14 April he dispatched 490 heavy bombers to attack the barracks and marshaling yards at Potsdam, a southwestern suburb of Berlin. The town had a close association with the kings of Prussia, particularly Frederick the Great, and in both German and non-German minds was symbolically tied to the phenomena of German/Prussian militarism. The raid's 1,960 tons of high explosives flattened much of the town. A second raid, the last daylight raid by Bomber Command's heavy bombers, suggested by Harris and approved by SHAEF, went into the command's records as a city attack in support of the army.[6] It struck directly at the symbolism of the Nazi state. Three hundred twenty-five effective heavy bomber sorties attacked the SS Barracks, the marshaling yard, and both parts of Hitler's mountain residence—the chalet and the "Eagles Nest"—at Berchtesgaden in the Bavarian Alps. Nazi propaganda films had made much of Hitler's relatively few hours of relaxation at the spectacularly beautiful mountain setting. This created a false impression that he had a close bond with the residence and succeeded in identifying the dictator with the house in the minds of the Allied and German publics. This act of aerial de-nazification wrecked two barracks and the residence of the SS commandant. No. 617 Squadron assaulted and damaged the chalet with nine Lancasters, while three Lancasters missed the Eagles Nest, which Hitler had only visited a half dozen times.

By the end of the month, the command's heavy bombers had abandoned their bombs for more humanitarian cargoes. In Operation Manna the command dropped food to the famine-stricken people of the Netherlands. In Operation Exodus the bombers began to repatriate British and Commonwealth prisoners of war. The Mosquitoes continued their bombing into the next month.

The Eighth Air Force also lowered its rate of operations. It reduced its sorties by 10,000 to 17,950 and bomb tonnage by 26,500 tons to 47,250. But it did not change its mode of operation to the same extent as the other strategic air forces. The Fifteenth used no incendiaries, and Bomber Command dropped only 500 tons, enough to mark its attacks and little more. The Eighth employed almost 5,400 tons in April 1945. It expended almost 1,500 tons in a single attack on the German defenders of the isolated French city and area of Royan. This raid on 15 April

1945 prepared the way for a French assault on the area. The US aircrews dropped 1,050 tons of high explosives in addition to incendiaries. The Eighth used napalm (jellied gasoline) for the first and last time. After-action studies judged the use of the fiery chemical cocktail as ineffective. Counting a raid on the previous day, the Eighth expended over 7,500 tons on Royan. During the first two weeks of the month, the Eighth maintained its suppression attacks on the ghost of the Luftwaffe with almost 3,000 sorties and 7,500 tons, including 870 tons of incendiaries. Bombing of the thoroughly smashed oil industry declined to a mere 1,824 tons, 4 percent of the Eighth's effort, as its heavy bombers concentrated on the few intact oil storage facilities. The Eighth attacked U-boat yards in Kiel, employing H2X for the majority of the attacks and dropping twice as much tonnage—3,676 tons—on that target. It also put almost 3,100 tons, including 988 tons of incendiaries on ordnance depots to prevent them from issuing their last stocks of weapons to depleted German units or to guerilla bands that might stay behind.

Marshaling yards and railroad targets consumed the largest portion of the Eighth's tonnage—19,225 tons, including 1,439 tons of incendiaries. Forty percent of the effort was directed to the Eighth's last area raids. On 5 April 148 heavy bombers, using H2X, hit Plauen with 344 tons of explosives including 17 tons of incendiaries; on 21 April, 212 heavy bombers navigating by H2X dropped 374 tons of high explosives and 147 tons of fragmentation bombs on Ingolstadt.

Notes

1. Notes of Allied Air Commanders Conference, Reims, France, 5 April 1945, Spaatz Papers, Diary.

2. Message, FWD-18890, Tedder to Spaatz, signed Eisenhower, 10 April 1945, Spaatz Papers, Diary.

3. Message, UA-67340, Spaatz to Doolittle, 11 April 1945, Spaatz Papers, Diary.

4. Directive No. 4 for the Strategic Air Forces in Europe, April 1945, AFHSO microfilm reel A1658, fr. 857, AFHRA File no. 168.491.

5. Message, JD-117-CS (Redline), Spaatz to Doolittle, 16 April 1945, Spaatz Papers, Diary.

6. Richards, *Hardest Victory*, 286.

May

1 May: Eighth Air Force—begins dropping food to alleviate famine in the Netherlands. Fifteenth Air Force—2d Bomb Group flies last heavy bomber combat mission in Europe against Salzburg marshaling yards.

2 May: Soviets take Berlin. Bomber Command—126 Mosquitoes attack Kiel, releasing 173 tons of high explosives. Last strategic air force combat mission in Europe.

8 May: Germans surrender to the Allies at Reims, France.

9 May: Germans surrender to the Soviets in Berlin.

On 1 May 1945 27 B-17s of the Fifteenth Air Force's 2d Bombardment Group flew the last heavy-bomber combat mission of the war in Europe. Using H2X, they dropped 78 tons of high explosives on the main marshaling yard of Salzburg. Ironically, seven years earlier one of its squadrons had been equipped with 13 B-17s—the entire Anglo-American inventory of four-engine heavy bombers. Within a little more than 90 days, events at Hiroshima and Nagasaki would make this mighty flotilla of bombers almost obsolete. Within a year or two, the bulk of the aircraft that had literally laid low much of Germany was in the scrap heap or the boneyard. The next evening, 2 May, 126 Mosquitoes of No. 8 Group flew Bomber Command's last combat mission of the war in Europe. The group dropped 173 tons of high explosives. This last operation, like so many flown over German cities, was an area raid, albeit on a small scale.

Even as the 2d Bombardment Group and No. 2 Group made their last attacks, the heavy bombers of the Eighth Air Force and Bomber Command became aerial plowshares. For the first time they brought life, not death. The Eighth flew 2,000 sorties over the Netherlands, dropping food to the famine-stricken Dutch. The Germans and wrecked transportation infrastructure (roads, bridges, canals, and the like) had cut their rations to starvation level. Bomber Command added more than 1,600 food sorties to the Eighth's totals. The two air forces also continued to take care of their own by repatriating thousands of Allied POWs to England.

PART VI
CONCLUSION

New Perspectives
and Enduring Realities

The Anglo-American Combined Bomber Offensive was a unique historical event. From September 1939 through May 1945, the four-engine bombers of the US Army Air Forces and the strategic bombers of the British Royal Air Force flew 410,000 and 300,000 effective sorties, respectively. Each air force dropped more than 1,000,000 tons of bombs on enemy targets in Europe, the Mediterranean, and North Africa.[1] So complex have modern aircraft become that never again will fleets of massed heavy bombers using iron bombs make strategic or tactical attacks on enemy targets. In constant procurement dollars, one B-2 bomber costs as much as 600 B-17s.[2] The B-2 may make up that difference in lowered personnel and support costs—three trained aircrew members versus 6,000 (10 for each B-17) and one hangar and ground staff versus 600. Not only costs but the advent of precision-guided munitions and nuclear weapons have lessened the requirement for large numbers of aircraft to deliver the required amount of destructive force to the target.

The air war in Europe in World War II has generated several bomber loads of written material. The US Eighth Air Force and its related interests alone inspired approximately 3,000 books and articles as of 1981, with many hundreds, if not thousands of works, inspired by the 50th Anniversary of World War II produced since.[3] Nonetheless, a reexamination of the original wartime records of both the RAF and the AAF and their compilation into a homogeneous whole has removed the detritus of over 50 years of revisionism and denial to reveal new perspectives concerning one of the most intriguing aspects of the Second World War.

Research in and the compilation and reconciliation of the original records have produced new insights into the nature of the Allied bomber offensive. These fresh perspectives fell into four broad and sometimes overlapping categories: the role of the US Fifteenth Air Force in the offensive; the possible effects of strategic bombing on Axis decisions and decision makers;

the actual conduct of bomber operations as opposed to wartime and postwar disputes and agendas; and the relationship of targets bombed to strategic and target priorities and to technological limitations.

The US Fifteenth Air Force fought a much different war than the American and British strategic air forces based in the United Kingdom. The Anglo-Americans established the Fifteenth on 1 November 1943 and based it at the great airfield complex at Foggia in southern Italy. Its purposes were to further the bomber offensive by stretching German air defenses to cover operations from the south, to bomb key strategic targets beyond the range of heavy bombers based in England (especially the Rumanian oil center of Ploesti and other Balkan targets), and to support Allied ground forces in the Mediterranean.[4]

Unlike the Eighth or Bomber Command, which devoted more than two-thirds of their effort to attacking targets in Greater Germany, the Fifteenth expended only 40 percent of its energy against the main foe.[5] Nor did the Fifteenth wield incendiary weapons in area bombing. While the Eighth devoted 13 percent of its bombs to city attacks and Bomber Command 51 percent, the Fifteenth weighed in with only 4 percent of its bombs on city areas. Likewise, the city-killing incendiary bomb constituted only 2 percent of the Fifteenth's entire bomb mix, but it composed 15 percent of the Eighth's and 21 percent of Bomber Command's bomb loads. The Fifteenth conducted only 17 such strikes, out of more than 3,100, using more than 100 tons of firebombs and none of more than 400 tons per strike. The Eighth ran 253 such attacks, out of 5,500 strikes, including 36 of more than 400 tons. Bomber Command, which specialized in city-area raids, laid down 349 such attacks, out of 6,865 strikes, including three raids of more than 2,000 tons, 49 raids between 1,000 and 2,000 tons, and 138 raids between 400 and 1,000 tons of firebombs. The Fifteenth specialized in striking the transportation and oil target systems towards which it expended two-thirds of its bombs. Its attacks on oil knocked out the Germans' chief source of natural petroleum, the Ploesti oil fields, and suppressed several synthetic oil plants and refineries, especially those in Vienna.

This strategy had a decisive and negative impact on the overall German oil position. Its transportation system attacks, towards which the Fifteenth sent 45 percent of its bombs, narrowed the supply lines of the German armies in Italy and interfered with the movement of Axis troops in the Balkans and with the shipment of raw materials to the Reich. Although they increased the overall strain on the German state railway system, the Fifteenth's attacks on transportation infrastructures appear to have been more in the nature of interdiction raids than a direct attack on the railways themselves.

New perspectives on strategic bomber operations come quickly from the ability to make speedy comparisons of data by using electronic spreadsheets (table 1). This tremendous analytical tool facilitates a fresh look at one of the enduring controversies of the era: the contribution of Harris and Bomber Command to the Anglo-American campaign against German oil, a system whose destruction meant the end of effective German military operations. The US Eighth Air Force and Bomber Command had access to the same targets, encountered the same weather conditions, and responded to the needs of the same ground forces. The US Fifteenth Air Force attacked different targets under much different circumstances. Twining based his decisions on whether or not to attack oil targets during a specific period on very different criteria than those of Harris and Spaatz. Spaatz and Doolittle treated oil as the primary strategic target from 12 May 1944, the date of the first systematic American attack on German synthetic oil, to the end of the war. However, Harris's commitment to oil bombing, especially when it competed with his city-area campaign, was questioned during the war by his service chief, Air Chief Marshal Charles Portal, and afterwards by numerous critics, all of whom contend he could have done far more against the oil target system. One of Harris's most severe critics stated the charge most clearly, "Having made allowances for all these elements, there were still many mornings when Harris sat at his desk confronted with a long list of targets of every kind, together with a weather forecast that—as usual throughout the war—made the C-in-C's decision a matter of the most open judgment. Again and again, Harris came down in favor of attacking a city rather than an oil plant."[6]

Although the statistical record cannot address Harris' reasoning for the selection of targets bombed, it does show what

Table 1. The Bomber Offensive, January 1942 to May 1945*

Air Force	Aircraft Attacking	Aircraft Lost	High-Explosive Bombs (Tons)	Incendiary Bombs (Tons)	Fragmentation Bombs (Tons)	Total Tonnage
Eighth	273,841	4,182	570,293	96,775	19,984	687,052
Ninth	3,923	96	9,338	64	55	9,457
Twelfth	11,064	104	23,811	73	3,008	26,892
Fifteenth	128,496	2,189	280,131	7,011	16,192	303,334
Total AAF	*417,324*	*6,571*	*883,573*	*103,923*	*39,239*	*1,026,735*
Bomber Command	277,695	7,094	800,726	210,784		1,011,510
205 Group	23,953	352	45,989	1,245		47,234
Total RAF	*301,648*	*7,446*	*846,715*	*212,029*		*1,058,744*
Grand Total	**718,972**	**14,017**	**1,730,288**	**315,952**	**39,239**	**2,085,479**

*This table includes all bombing, mining, leaflet, special operations, radar counter-measure, and supply missions.

he bombed. From 1 June 1944 to 8 May 1945 Bomber Command devoted 15 percent of its total sorties, 22,000 out of 155,000, against oil targets and dropped 99,500 tons on them. Both these figures exceeded those of the Eighth Air Force, which devoted 13 percent of its effective sorties, 28,000 out of 220,000, and dropped 73,000 tons of bombs on oil targets from 12 May 1944 to 8 May 1945. Obversely, Harris devoted 36 percent of his efforts over the same time span to area bombing, while Doolittle employed his forces on area or area-like raids only 16 percent of the time throughout the last year of the war. Despite the fact that Bomber Command devoted more energy to oil bombing than the Eighth, could it have done more and, as the critics imply, was Harris deliberately disobeying his directives? In June and July 1944 the German night fighters were still a force to be reckoned with. In June, Harris sent only four main-force raids into Germany, all against oil targets in the Ruhr and suffered losses of 10 percent. In July he sent 10 more major raids into Germany, including five raids against oil targets in the Ruhr. Heavy bomber sorties against city areas doubled those against oil.

The Eighth surpassed these efforts by only 150 tons in June and 1,750 tons in July. By that time German synthetic oil production had fallen precipitously. The Eighth's initial bombing in May dropped production from 380,000 tons per month to 200,000 tons. In the next two months production dropped to approximately 70,000. In August, Harris dispatched 10 heavy bomber raids against oil, five of them to French storage facilities, and 10 area raids into Germany. He sent the first major RAF daylight heavy bomber raid of the war—220 bomber aircraft attacked oil targets in Homburg. At this stage of the war, Bomber Command was more accurate by day than the Americans.

In September, Bomber Command made nine more daylight raids of 300 or more tons on oil targets in Germany but devoted three times that effort, including three daytime raids, to area bombing. In August, Bomber Command dropped 1,400 more tons of bombs on oil targets than did the Eighth but lagged behind by 3,100 tons in September. In October, Harris sent six major daylight raids against oil, but devoted 12 times that effort, including eight major day raids, to area bombing. Of the 11 daylight area raids of September and October, at least five, comprising 1,650 sorties, employed visual sighting. One of those, on Kleve, was at the request of the Allied ground forces; the other four could probably have been sent against oil targets. On two of the days in question Bomber Command conducted separate day raids on both city-area and oil targets.

The RAF, using daylight precision techniques, landed a far higher percentage of bombs on or near the aiming point than it did on night raids—a key point. Not only did Harris dispatch day raids against oil, he sent missions usually numbering 150 or fewer bombers. This maximized accuracy in that if more than 150 aircraft attacked the same point, accuracy of the following "excess" aircraft would be severely degraded by smoke and damage from the preceding units' attacks, not to mention the extra time given German antiaircraft artillery to fix the range of the incoming planes. Harris bombed up to the point of diminishing returns and no further. In this he made the most efficient use of his resources, although he may not have obeyed the spirit of his directive. On 1 November the air staff emphatically ordered Harris to concentrate on oil. He openly disagreed with the orders but carried them out, sending 13 raids towards the system. The weather was so bad during the month that none of Harris' four night oil raids and only two of his nine daylight raids used visual sighting.

In November only five of the Eighth's 40 major oil raids used visual sighting. Bad weather made it necessary to employ area techniques. However, thousands of bombs saturating a target area probably did not ensure that as many bombs would actually hit the oil targets with the same accuracy as far fewer bombs aimed visually in daylight. Every month before November 1944 the Eighth's percentage of sorties devoted to oil exceeded that of Bomber Command by 25 to 50 percent. In November the two air forces devoted an equal percentage of resources. From December until the war's end, Bomber Command's percentage of effort more than doubled that of the Eighth's. It would appear that Harris fulfilled his directives, including the British city-area policy that remained in force, albeit at a lower priority, throughout the period. Harris justified his effort on the basis of weather conditions and tactical considerations. Overall, the evidence suggests that the American bombs ruined the oil industry and British and American bombs flattened it and kept it flattened.

The Combined Bomber Offensive database also supplies insight into one of the most complex and perplexing problems concerning Anglo-American operations—the question of city-area bombing. Even though Bomber Command had a series of directives approved by the War Cabinet authorizing the practice, the question revolves around the extent of its efforts and their necessity but does not address the moral aspects of the necessity. However, throughout the conflict, weather and technological limitations on accuracy made area bombing a tactical imperative for the British and the Americans. From January 1942 onwards, Bomber Command spent 56 percent of its sorties on city-area bombing. When one subtracts the harassing nighttime raids of Mosquitoes, Bomber Command expended one-half of all its heavy bomber sorties—almost 500,000 tons—on area bombing. This composite figure masked variations over time. For example, from April 1943 through March 1944, when Harris finished the Battle of the Ruhr and fought the Battles of Hamburg and Berlin, Bomber Command released 40 percent of all its city-area tonnage, which accounted for 87 percent of its total tonnage for the period. The percentage of city-area tonnage declined during the pre–D-day and Normandy campaigns, reaching an all-time low of 3 percent in June 1944; most of those area attacks were on French cities at the direct order of Eisenhower. From December 1944 until the end of the war, the command dropped 50 percent of its entire city-area tonnage. That effort amounted to 46 percent of its entire tonnage for the period. Those are the figures. They should serve as a baseline for any further discussion.

For the Americans the question is not only how much, but whether or not it occurred at all. As mentioned above at least one major report of the Eighth Air Force prepared immediately after the war eliminated all reference to "city" bombing. However, individual mission reports prepared shortly after execution of the operations present a somewhat different story. They state that the Eighth expended 12.5 percent of its total tonnage (85,100 tons) in city bombing. Of that total, 72,000 tons were in 117 command bombings of Germany, either expressly ordered or authorized by Eighth Air Force headquarters. The orders to the combat units either expressly designated the center of the city as the target or authorized the bombing of the center of the city by radar as a specified secondary target if the visual primary target, such as a tank plant, was clouded over. Another 10,100 tons went in 159 targets of opportunity over Germany. Small units separated from their main formations or unable to bomb their primary and secondary targets sought out, with the permission and encouragement of official policy, cities, towns, or villages of opportunity to bomb. A final 3,000 tons landed on 21 French villages and towns near the Normandy landings in a series of attacks expressly ordered by Eisenhower. The records of the Fifteenth Air Force acknowledged only 10,700 tons of city bombing, 3 percent of its total tonnage. Some 2,000 of those tons fell on Yugoslav towns designated and specifically requested by Marshal Tito's forces as containing "enemy" garrisons.

The Eighth began command city bombings on 27 September 1943 with a mission against the port of Emden. It was no coincidence that the raid was the first operational use of radar by American bombers. In the 103 previous missions, 20 of which were substantially interfered with by weather en route or over the target, the Eighth attempted to strike its targets with daylight precision techniques. Some criticize this as a Pavlovian adherence to outmoded doctrine. In part it was, but the Eighth had no alternative. Since it had to bomb with daylight precision methods, or not at all, it made little sense to resort to area bombing and promoted the selection of precision targets, even if the accuracy in practice may have left something to be desired.

The advent of radar changed the equation. The Eighth could strike targets through overcast, as long as its planes could take off and land at their home bases. This technological advance meant a great increase in its rate of operations and in bombs delivered to enemy territory. It came at a price. The most common American radar, the H2X, a variant of Bomber Command's H2S, could identify coastal cities or cities with a distinctive river running through them because of the prominent contrast in images presented by ground and water. However, over a large city the radar tended to fuzz up with the clutter of too many varied returns. An ordinary operator could identify a city or built-up area using H2X but could not usually identify specific targets, such as marshaling yards or arms plants, within a city. It was with the knowledge of these limitations that raids dispatched in expectation of encountering clouds over the target were authorized to do what they were going to do in any case, drop their bombs on the city even if they could not see the target. Because of the dangers associated with bringing bombs back to base, crews seldom did so. H2X could not locate small targets, such as synthetic oil plants, which meant that the few days of visual bombing available for the nine non-summer months of the year over Germany were reserved for them. After 26 September 1943 the Eighth flew 256,500 effective combat bomber sorties, 48 percent of them, 124,000, used some form of radar-assisted bombing. Twenty-three percent of those sorties were city-area strikes.

On 21 July 1944 six separate groups of the Eighth's bombers totaling 312 aircraft made visual attacks on cities as targets of opportunity. This same day Gen Fred Anderson, Spaatz's deputy for operations, sent a new bombing policy memo to Doolittle and Twining. Anderson pointed to Spaatz's oft reiterated and continuing intention to direct bombing toward precision targets and categorically denied any intention to area bomb. However, having denied the intention, he proceeded to authorize the practice, "We will conduct bombing attacks through the overcast where it is impossible to get precision targets. Such attacks will include German marshaling yards whether or not they are located in German cities."[7] This memo had a chilling effect on Eighth Air Force official reports citing city bombing. Of the Eighth's reports that acknowledge their target as a city area, three-quarters of them (all but one during the 10-month period between 27 September 1943, when the Eighth initiated radar bombing and began designating a "city" as a target, and 21 July 1944) were written before the issuance of Anderson's memo. While the Eighth continued to order "city-area-like" raids that had the same statistical profile as its heretofore openly acknowledged city raids (more than 100 heavy bombers, carrying at least 20 percent firebombs, and using radar bombing techniques), it did not designate city areas as targets but instead reported them as being directed against a military target.[8] Seventy (85 percent) of these "city-area-like" raids conducted by the Eighth occurred in the nine months after Anderson's memo.

In short, the Eighth continued to order city-area missions, but no longer acknowledged the bulk of them as such in its official records. In other words, the Eighth's response to Anderson's memo was not to discontinue city-area bombing, but to conceal much of its city bombing rather than record it. Since Anderson could hardly have failed to notice that the Eighth was continuing to dispatch an average of seven city-area-like missions a month, and he took no further action, perhaps his memo was written more for posterity than for immediate compliance. Adding "city-area-like raids" and their 61,394 tons of ordnance (34 percent incendiaries) to the totals of reported city-area missions raised the overall sum of the Eighth's city bombing to 21.5 percent of its entire effort. The Fifteenth flew only six "city-area-like" raids, which included the two largest tonnages of firebombs it ever delivered—against the Vienna area on 5 and 6 November 1944.

From July 1941 onward, Bomber Command's directives instructed it to bomb German city areas for the purpose of lowering the morale and productivity of the German labor force. At the Anglo-American summit conference at Casablanca, in January 1943, Churchill, Roosevelt, and their Combined Chiefs of Staff formally established the Combined Bomber Offensive and, as part of its charter, directed both the American and British strategic air forces to undermine "the morale of the German people to a point where their capacity for armed resistance" was fatally weakened.[9] In its pursuit of that goal, chiefly by means of city or area bombing, Allied strategic bombing raised questions of moral and ethical significance.

During the war, area bombing was questioned on the floor of Parliament, first by the bishop of Chichester in February 1944 and then by Member of Parliament Richard Stokes in March 1945. More than a third of a century ago, David Irving resurrected the ghosts of Dresden.[10] One critic has written of the "evil of American bombing," calling it a "sin of a peculiarly modern kind because it seemed too inadvertent, seemed to have involved so little choice."[11] Another has noted that "the most important factor moving the AAF toward Douhetian war was the attitude of the country's top civilian and military leaders," and specifically has blamed Arnold, Marshall, Eisenhower, Lovett, Stimson, and Roosevelt as responsible for the shift to area bombing.[12] These critics and many others have recoiled at a policy that resulted in the death of hundreds of thousands of persons.

The RAF conducted most of the area bombing and, like the AAF, resorted to it because weaknesses in its operational technique left it no choice. Bomber Command persisted in area bombing after it had developed an accuracy surpassing even visual bombing as practiced by USSTAF. To belabor the enemy with the only weapon available was one thing, but to continue to use it when better means were at hand delayed the end of the war and needlessly killed tens of thousands. If the RAF earned any blame for its conduct of the air war, it was for its area bombing conducted after June 1944. In the autumn of 1943, the AAF also turned to city-area bombing. In contrast to RAF bombing, AAF nonvisual bombing never became particularly accurate. Arnold, Lovett, Spaatz, Eisenhower, and Marshall knew that bombing through overcast produced wildly imprecise results. If Stimson and Roosevelt did not know it, it was because they did not ask.

The RAF killed its hundreds of thousands and the AAF its tens of thousands. No completely authoritative figure of the number of European civilians killed by Anglo-American strategic bombing exists. However, opprobrium cannot be added up like a ledger book and an exact amount entered in each account. To whom should one assign the guilt for the 125,000 German civilians killed during the Russian storming of Berlin?[13] How should one weigh the murder of 325,000 Jews by the SS (Schutzstafel [protection echelon]) at the Treblinka death camp between 28 July and 21 September 1942.[14] To those who accepted the truism that two wrongs never make a right, then nothing can excuse the area bombing of the Allied strategic bomber campaign no matter how evil the German state. At the other extreme, those who believed any means justified the end find nothing abhorrent in area bombing. Between those opinions lies a vast middle ground. Area bombing cannot be examined as a separate, unique phenomenon judged only by numbers of missions flown and bombs dropped versus people killed. A more valid yardstick would be the extent to which the action contributed to ending the war as quickly as possible with minimum loss of life.

Placed in the context of the entire war against the European Axis, city-area bombing caused more civilian casualties than any other type of warfare employed by the British and American Allies. (See table 2.) Before condemning such bombing as a valueless military action, however, one should at least consider the work of the *United States Strategic Bombing Survey.* Although its overall report on the European war is little more than a paean of praise for strategic bombing and something of an apologia for area bombing, the work of its assessment divisions, published in over 150 subsidiary reports, still represents the largest and most comprehensive study of the results of the bomber offensive ever undertaken.[15]

On the whole these reports are more objective and analytic than the overall report, although still subject to some doubt as to completeness and willingness to criticize bombing. Although Nazi officials kept a tight rein on the Reich's workforce, and citizens of frequently bombed urban areas became habituated to attacks, an immediate postwar survey of the German civil population conducted by *USSBS* hinted that city-area strikes may well have hastened the end of the war. Area bombing depressed civilian morale, engendering defeatism, fear, hopelessness, fatalism, and apathy. Dislocation of public transport and public utilities further lowered morale. Industrial activity may also have declined, not so much from failure to work but in reducing above average workers to average.

The inhabitants of bombed cities became more susceptible to subversion. Evacuation programs that separated children from parents and placed them in Nazi-controlled camps also provoked much anxiety.[16] Further *USSBS* analysis revealed that although a bombed city recovered its preraid productive capacity within six to 11 months, it did so at the cost of squeezing out much of its consumer goods production—a finite source that began to dry up in late 1944. Critics have often seized upon this observation to demonstrate the practical as

Table 2. The Bomber Offensive by Country

Air Force	Target Country	No. Attacking Planes	No. Lost	High Explosives (tons)	Incendiary Bombs (tons)	Fragmentation Bombs (tons)	Total
Eighth	Austria	166	0	334	65	0	399
	Belgium	3,211	26	7,257	397	262	7,916
	Czechoslovakia	1,812	28	4,297	381	0	4,678
	Denmark	129	0	121	30	0	151
	France	56,236	543	131,873	4,294	7,073	143,140
	Germany	200,587	3,496	419,526	91,160	9,820	520,506
	Hungary	163	0	364	0	0	364
	Luxembourg	195	0	481	15	0	496
	Netherlands	5,211	24	3,301	215	2,829	6,345
	Norway	701	18	1,497	0	0	1,497
	Poland	580	22	900	139	0	1,039
	Rumania	128	1	287	0	0	287
	Switzerland	54	0	55	79	0	134
Ninth	Austria	65	2	162	0	0	162
	Greece	51	1	603	0	0	603
	Italy	2,076	24	4,892	47	55	4,994
	Libya	211	0	498	0	0	498
	Rumania	189	57	213	0	0	213
	Sicily	1,025	10	2,706	17	0	2,723
	Tunisia	119	2	264	0	0	264
Twelfth	Austria	138	19	260	0	0	260
	France	218	2	108	0	256	364

577

Table 2. (Continued)

Air Force	Target Country	Attacking Planes (no.)	No. Lost	High Explosives (tons)	Incendiary Bombs (tons)	Fragmentation Bombs (tons)	Total
	Germany	16	1	40	0	0	40
	Greece	304	5	694	0	52	746
	Italy	5,915	45	14,490	45	855	15,390
	Libya	13	1	24	0	0	24
	Sardinia	593	0	1,121	0	294	1,415
	Sicily	2,504	20	4,789	28	1,103	5,920
	Tunisia	1,363	11	2,285	0	448	2,733
Fifteenth	Albania	141	5	371	0	0	371
	Austria	31,462	769	67,122	2,241	2,025	71,388
	Bulgaria	1,094	9	2,360	278	64	2,701
	Czechoslovakia	4,529	81	9,353	253	1,028	10,634
	France	7,830	73	18,480	0	381	18,861
	Germany	16,714	460	34,973	1,182	2,033	38,188
	Greece	1,458	15	2,315	0	883	3,198
	Hungary	9,041	103	20,281	740	922	21,943
	Italy	36,065	265	78,985	1,061	7,740	87,786
	Poland	483	22	1,146	0	0	1,146
	Rumania	10,881	319	25,351	1,110	85	26,546
	Yugoslavia	8,755	65	19,394	146	1,031	20,571
Bmbr Cmd	Belgium	4,276	100	17,477	332	0	17,809
	Czechoslovakia	668	48	2,088	180	0	2,268
	Denmark	23	2	15	6	0	21

Table 2. (Continued)

Air Force	Target Country	Attacking Planes (no.)	No. Lost	High Explosives (tons)	Incendiary Bombs (tons)	Fragmentation Bombs (tons)	Total
	France	64,936	898	255,313	8,017	0	263,330
	Germany	184,849	5,603	494,330	197,621	0	691,951
	Italy	3,931	82	5,674	4,179	0	9,853
	Netherlands	11,241	139	21,382	366	0	21,748
	Norway	1,215	35	3,530	68	0	3,598
	Poland	337	16	917	15	0	932
205 Grp	Albania	6	0	16	0	0	16
	Austria	799	34	2,182	142	0	2,324
	Bulgaria	354	11	652	17	0	669
	Czechoslovakia	110	6	243	12	0	255
	France	218	1	367	0	0	367
	Germany	62	4	120	0	0	120
	Greece	322	2	656	30	0	686
	Hungary	1,361	46	2,590	175	0	2,765
	Italy	13,545	112	28,437	670	0	28,107
	Rumania	878	44	1,287	81	0	1,368
	Sardinia	471	2	778	37	0	815
	Sicily	1,731	30	3,233	16	0	3,249
	Tunisia	191	4	345	19	0	364
	Yugoslavia	3,712	31	5,083	46	0	5,129
All Country	Albania	147	5	387	0	0	387

579

Table 2. (Continued)

Air Force	Target Country	Attacking Planes (no.)	No. Lost	High Explosives (tons)	Incendiary Bombs (tons)	Fragmentation Bombs (tons)	Total
	Austria	32,630	824	70,060	2,448	2,025	74,533
	Belgium	7,487	126	24,734	729	262	25,725
	Bulgaria	1,448	20	3012	295	64	3,371
	Czechoslovakia	7,119	163	15,981	826	1,028	17,835
	Denmark	142	2	136	36	0	172
	France	129,438	1,517	406,141	12,311	7,710	426,162
	Germany	402,228	9,564	948,988	289,963	11,853	1,250,804
	Greece	2,135	23	4,268	30	935	5,233
	Hungary	10,565	149	23,235	915	922	25,072
	Italy	61,532	528	132,479	6,002	8,650	147,131
	Libya	224	1	522	0	0	522
	Netherlands	16,452	163	24,683	581	2,829	28,093
	Norway	1,916	53	5,027	68	0	5,095
	Poland	1,400	60	2,963	154	0	3,177
	Rumania	12,076	421	27,138	1,191	95	28,414
	Sardinia	1,064	2	1,899	37	294	2,230
	Sicily	5,260	60	10,728	61	1,103	11,892
	Switzerland	54	0	55	79	0	134
	Tunisia	1,673	17	2,894	19	448	3,361
	Yugoslavia	12,461	96	24,477	192	1,031	25,700
Total		707,652	13,794	1,730,288	315,952	39,249	2,085,479

well as moral futility of area bombing. They ignore the production lost before the city completely recovered and fail to
credit the loss of the additional production accruing to the war
effort that would have occurred if the city had continuously increased its contributions to the war effort. Also cities with a
rising rate of production before being struck "did not continue
to expand after even moderately heavy attacks."[17] These findings undercut the argument that city-area bombing was
counterproductive and that industrial output in bombed cities
actually rose after bombing attacks as enraged workers increased their productivity to avenge themselves on their tor-
mentors. Strategic bombing in World War II was an attritional
form of warfare. City-area bombing was, perhaps, the lowest
common denominator of that attrition in that it fell most
heavily on the entire home front, rather than on those most
responsible for war making. Nonetheless, in a total war, flattened production curves, apathy, and lowered morale can
work in many indirect ways to detract from the war effort.

One may well argue that city-area bombing did not return
results commensurate with its cost in effort to the Allied air
forces or in loss of civilian lives. It consumed more than half
of Bomber Command's total effort and accounted for almost
70 percent of its aircraft losses. The US Eighth Air Force devoted at least 13 percent of its bomb tonnage to city-area attacks and lost far more bombers, both in percentage of loss (3
percent) and in actual numbers (1,048) than raids against any
other single target system.

The report of the British Strategic Survey Unit (BSSU), the
far smaller UK counterpart of the *USSBS*, categorically states:
"In so far as the offensive against German towns was designed
to break the morale of the German civilian population, it clearly
failed. Far from lowering essential war production, it also
failed to stem a remarkable increase in the output of armaments."[18] The BSSU suggests that area bombing at its most effective point—in 1944—cost the Germans only 17 percent of
total potential industrial production and perhaps only one-
third of that figure in directly related war production.[19] This
finding is in part because German industry was so widely distributed that only a little more than 40 percent of it was even

associated with cities bombed and, of course, area bombing landed a higher concentration of bombs in the center and built-up areas of the city than in the factory areas usually situated at a city's outskirts. The BSSU admits that, like USSBS, it found it impossible to gather statistics on the effects of area bombing for the last nine months of the war. This was precisely the time that Bomber Command devoted its heaviest tonnage to area bombing while at the same time devoting half its effort to other target systems.

As for the cost in civilian lives of strategic bombing, surely area bombing was the form of bombing most responsible for such deaths, but no completely authoritative figure exists. USSBS, in what one must take as the lowest estimate, stated a figure of 300,000 German civilian deaths (50,000 of which it attributed to Allied tactical air operations), 780,000 wounded, and 7,500,000 made homeless.[20] Official German figures varied. In 1958 the official statistical publication of the Federal Republic of Germany, Deutschland Heute, attributed 500,000 German civilian deaths to "hostile action."[21] Not all of those losses, perhaps no more than 50 percent, can be attributed to Allied air operations. The German Democratic Republic (GDR, East Germany), before its demise, attributed the following casualty figures directly to the actions of Bomber Command and the Eighth and Fifteenth Air Forces, 410,000 dead and 650,000 wounded.[22] The GDR had no incentive to minimize civilian casualties caused by the Anglo-Americans. Deaths of civilians in German-occupied countries, the product of collateral damage rather than deliberate area attacks, would add several tens of thousands more dead.[23] Given the official figures, at least one of which (USSBS) was the result of a systematic survey, figures of "between 750,000 and one million German" deaths, such as that given in a recent article by A. Noble Frankland, one of the official British historians of the strategic campaign, significantly overstate the number of deaths attributable to Anglo-American bombing.[24]

In all, the Anglo-Americans dropped between 600,000 and 675,000 tons of bombs in city-area or area-like attacks. It may have been an immoral practice, it may have been a disproportionate use of military force against a civilian population, and it may have absorbed an inordinate amount of resources better employed on more vulnerable target systems, but to argue that such bombing had no significant effect on the German war effort flies in the face of the evidence and logic. One must also understand that for much of the war, probably through March 1944, the operational limitations of Bomber Command made area bombing by far the most practical technique with which to employ the bombers. It was not a question of area bombing versus some other target system, but a question of area bombing or nothing. The same number of sorties and bombs expended on "precision" night targets would not, by any measure, have been more likely to produce decisive results for the simple reason that the vast majority of those sorties and bombs would have failed to strike within a mile or less of their targets. In the final analysis, given the intimate interconnections between city areas, the urban workforce, and the transportation nodes and industries in urban areas, it is virtually impossible to assess or even quantify one aspect of the damage inflicted by the bomber offensive in isolation from the others. However, the laying waste of Germany's urban areas, at the very minimum, lowered the productivity of the workforce and absorbed energy and goods in the process of wartime reconstruction and recovery that could have otherwise contributed to the war effort. However, unlike the transportation and synthetic oil campaigns, city-area bombing cannot be said to have made a decisive contribution in and of itself to the defeat of Germany.

The bomber offensive cost the Allied airmen, particularly the RAF, heavily. (See table 3.) At its peak strength in the Second World War, the RAF consisted of a little more than 1,000,000 men and women. The official history states that of that number 340,000 men served as aircrews.[25] However, Harris states that 125,000 aircrews entered into operations with Bomber Command.[26] Of that number, 55,573 died, 47,260 in combat and 8,090 in training. Two out of every five men did not live to complete their tours of duty; of those who lived, another one in five was either taken prisoner (9,800) or wounded (8,200). The figure of 40 percent killed during the course of the campaign far exceeded that of British infantry on the western front in World War I.

Table 3. Bomber Command Aircrew Casualties—3 September 1939–8 May 1945 (Derived from Webster and Frankland, *Strategic Air Offensive*, appendix 41: Bomber Command Casualties, 4:440.)

Operational casualties	Total
Killed	5,582
Presumed dead	41,548
Died (POW)	138
Missing now safe	2,868
P.O.W. now safe	9,784
Wounded	4,200
Total operational casualties	64,120
Non-operational casualties	
Killed	8,090
Wounded	4,203
Died other causes	215
Missing now safe	83
POW now safe	54
Non-operational total	12,645
Total dead	55,435
Total POW now safe	9,838
Total wounded	8,403
Total missing now safe	2,951
Total casualties	76,765
Total all RAF operational dead (9/3/39–8/14/45)[a]	70,253

[a]Saunders, *The Fight is Won*, 392.

As John Terraine pointed out, it is especially ironic that strategic bombing, a tactic marketed in part for inexpensiveness as compared to trench warfare, resulted in the deaths of so many first-class personnel. Bomber Command's dead aircrews, men in almost every way of a quality comparable to those who served as officers of British Empire forces in the First World War, exceeded the number of British Empire officers killed in World War I by 40 percent (38,000 to 55,000).[27] The great percentage of aircrews committed to Bomber Command further illustrated the large British and RAF commitment to the bomber offensive.

As odd as it may seem, the exact number of casualties of the US Eighth and Fifteenth Air Forces has never been satisfactorily separated from the thicket of official numbers. The official figures cited in table 4 include those suffered by the US Ninth and Twelfth Air Forces. Their casualties, in tactical operations, would comprise somewhere between 5 and 20 percent of the total for their respective theaters of operations. On 20 May 1945 the Fifteenth gave its combat casualty figures as 2,703 killed in action (KIA) and died of wounds, 2,553 wounded, and 17,918 missing in action (MIA), captured, and interned, for a total of 23,174.[28] Many of those listed as missing in action would later be determined to have been killed in combat or captured. The same records further indicate that no more than 95,000 men, throughout the Fifteenth's history, were available for service in bomber crews. At its peak strength in March 1945, the Fifteenth would probably have had no more than 15,000 men in bomber crews.[29] Comparable numbers for the Eighth in March 1945 are approximately 25,000 men in bomber crews.[30] By very rough extrapolation from the Fifteenth's figures and adding in crews serving from August 1942 through 1 November 1943, somewhere between 225,000 and 250,000 men in bomber crews saw operational service with the Eighth. The Eighth's casualties may have run as high as 58,000: 18,000 dead, 6,500 wounded, and 33,500 missing.[31] The AAF's official casualty figures, compiled by AAF headquarters for publication in December of 1945, differ from the final US Army statistics, substantially so, in the case of operations in the Mediterranean.[32]

Despite their inconsistencies, the above casualty figures permit some overall generalization. American bomber crews suffered overall casualties at a rate of only one-quarter to one-third that of Bomber Command (58,000 out of 250,000 for the Eighth Air Force versus 76,000 out of 125,000 for Bomber Command). This difference was in great part a simple function of the nature of the enemy opposition encountered. Bomber Command conducted 45 percent of its entire effort before 31 March 1944, the approximate date on which AAF long-range escort fighters established daylight air supremacy over Germany and the date on which the command scaled back its

Table 4. USAAF Casualties In European, North African, and Mediterranean Theaters of Operation, 1942–1946 (Derived from Department of the Army, "Army Battle Casualties and Nonbattle Deaths in World War II—Final Report" [Washington, DC: Dept of Army, GPO, June 1, 1953], pp. 84–88)

Killed in Action	
ETO	23,805
North Africa and MTO	9,997
Total KIA	33,802
Wounded and Injured in Action (Died of wounds)	
ETO	9,299 (510)
NATO and MTO	4,428 (276)
Total wounded	13,727 (786)
Captured and Interned (POWs dying in captivity)	
ETO[a]	26,064 (148)
NATO and MTO	7,350 (54)
Total captured	33,414 (202)
Missing in Action (returned to duty)	
ETO	2,853 (2,316)
North Africa and MTO	3,642 (3,125)
Total MIA	6,495 (5,441)
Total Casualties (ETO)	62,021
Total Casualties (North Africa) and MTO	25,417
Total AAF (All theaters) KIA	44,785
Total AAF (All theaters) Wounded or Injured in Action (Died in Captivity)	18,364 (1,004)
Total AAF (All theaters) Captured and Interned (Died in Captivity)	41,057 (2,783)
Total AAF (All theaters) MIA (returned to duty)	11,176 (7,556)
Total AAF (All theaters) Casualties	115,382
Total AAF Aircraft Accident Deaths (7 December 1941–31 Dec 1946)	25,844

[a]This figure apparently includes all AAF prisoners recovered from POW camps in Germany. It would, therefore, count a great many American aircrews captured by the Germans in the Mediterranean (belonging to the Ninth, Twelfth, and Fifteenth Air Forces) and thence transferred to Germany.

deep operations over Germany to concentrate on France and Belgium in support of the cross-channel invasion. In that early period it had a loss rate of 4.4 percent of its effective sorties (6,150 bomber aircraft in 137,000 sorties). The bulk of those aircraft fell to the fighter aircraft, the most efficient killer of other aircraft. Unlike antiaircraft artillery, by its nature fixed in place for the static defense of a single target, fighter interceptors can be massed from numerous locations to defend all targets within range of the air battle. From 1 April 1944 to 31 August 1944, with few operations flown into the German night fighter defenses, the command expended 20 percent of its total wartime effort and sustained a loss rate of 2 percent. The command expended 35 percent of its total sorties in the last phases of the bomber offensive (1 September 1944 to 8 May 1945). With the night fighters hamstrung from day attacks on their fields and lack of early warning and defensive depth, the Eighth suffered a loss rate of only 1 percent. The Eighth suffered bomber loss rates in each period of operations comparable to those of Bomber Command: 4.2 percent in operations before 31 March 1944, 1.5 percent during the summer 1944, and 0.8 percent after 1 September 1944. The Eighth's distribution of effort (the percentage of total sorties flown) differed significantly from Bomber Command's: 14 percent (1,684 bombers lost in 39,000 sorties) before 31 March 1944, 31 percent in the summer of 1944 (1,378 bombers lost in 85,000 sorties), and 55 percent (1,082 bombers lost in 148,500 sorties) after 1 September 1944. In each phase of the bomber offensive, individual American and British bomber crews underwent approximately the same or similar experiences at the same rate or intensity. However, as a whole the men of Bomber Command suffered more severely because they flew a higher percentage of the overall effort when German fighter defenses were at their strongest, namely, before 31 March 1944. Thus, RAF aircrews had to run the gantlet of intact German fighter defenses.

The figures show one important and stark difference in the experience of American and British bomber crews—the probability of living through a shoot down. A British bomber crewman had only a little better than one chance in five of surviving the loss of his aircraft. His American counterpart had three chances in five of surviving to live in a prisoner of war camp or of evading and escaping capture. The principal reason for this disparity was design differences between American and British bombers.[33] For example, in British heavy bombers the crew compartments had no access to the bomb bays, while the B-17 had open bomb bays that served as designated emergency parachute exits for four of the 10 aircrew members. The Lancaster bomber had only one emergency exit—at the front of the aircraft—as opposed to four (counting the bomb bays) for the B-17. Even within Bomber Command the Halifax's superior emergency exit arrangements gave its aircrew a survival rate far higher than their compatriots in the Lancaster (1:2.8 in a Halifax versus 1:5 in a Lancaster).[34]

Finally, the casualties suffered in the bomber offensive demonstrated the depth of the national and service commitments to strategic bombing. Bomber Command absorbed from one-third to one-half of all the RAF's trained aircrews and suffered two-thirds of its total dead. As for the Eighth and Fifteenth, they absorbed three-quarters of their service's casualties even after one counts the complete loss of all ground and most aircrews in the initial disastrous campaign in the Philippines.[35] After subtracting the casualties of the Ninth and Twelfth Air Forces (which during the entire course of their own operations lost 200 heavy bombers in combat), one still arrives at a figure of as many as 27,000 dead (virtually all aircrew) sustained by the two American strategic air forces. This number exceeds that of US Marine Corps (19,733) deaths in World War II.[36] Total AAF dead in the war against Germany 33,802 also exceeded those of the US Navy (31,485)—including naval air—in the war against Japan.[37]

To these inexpressibly sad figures of young men dead before their time must be added a figure that demonstrates once again that a measure of futility almost invariably accompanies the endeavors of mankind. In examining the bombing of Hitler's oil industry, American observers at synthetic oil plants and Ploesti discovered that not all the bombs that had been so laboriously produced, shipped, and then carried in the face of the enemy to their targets had exploded. *USSBS* determined that on average 16.4 percent of all the bombs that actually landed inside the fences of 13 synthetic oil plants failed to explode.[38] Taken as a whole, one of every six of the Allied bombers that attacked these targets in effect flew empty. A study of bombing at Ploesti found only 5.5 percent duds but determined that most of that figure, 3.8 percent, came from human error. The bombardier and crew had failed to pull the arming wires from the bombs. The bomb patterns revealed that this error was not random in each bomb load, but that it usually happened in an entire string of bombs—a sure indication that the crew had failed to arm their entire load. The report concluded that there was no reason to assume that the crew error figure of 3.8 percent did not occur in all bombing raids.[39] Under the stress of battle, or from lack of training and discipline, one in every 25 American bombers had accidentally disarmed themselves.

Some analysts have criticized the selection of targets. For example, Maj Gen Haywood S. Hansell Jr., one of the AAF's chief strategic and targeting planners, who participated in both AWPD-1 and AWPD-42 and led a B-29 bomber command against Japan, faulted the Allies' failure to bomb the eight grinding-wheel manufacturing plants and electric power generation network.[40] The loss of abrasive grinding wheels would have crippled the German armaments industry by denying it the ability to machine metal castings, such as gun barrels, shells, and crankshafts. Likewise loss of electrical power might have severely crippled German war production across a spectrum of manufacturing processes. Also, the *USSBS* suggested that an investment of 12,000 to 15,000 tons of bombs a month on German transportation targets beginning in February 1944 instead of September 1944 would have caused the German war economy to collapse months earlier and in time for the effect of that collapse to be fully felt by the troops at the front.[41] Although such arguments presuppose more detailed intelligence and more accurate intelligence evaluation than were available, their proponents were correct in their assessment that the strategic bombing effort could have been employed more efficiently but only if Spaatz and, to a lesser extent, Harris had been free to operate in a vacuum with no necessity to

589

respond to the bureaucratic, institutional, and operational forces surrounding them.

From March through July 1944 the German night fighter and needs of Overlord and the beachhead undermined the bomber offensive's ability to conduct unfettered strategic bombing. Once Spaatz and Doolittle had obtained a measure of air superiority through their aggressive use of long-range escort fighters, the all-consuming bureaucratic battle between the oil and transportation plans began. Having committed himself to oil, Spaatz could hardly shift gears by pointing to other target systems even more likely to bring the Nazis to heel without appearing fickle or foolish. Crossbow bombing, a requirement imposed on the strategic bombers by British domestic political considerations, was by far the biggest waste of blood, aircraft, and bombs of the entire strategic campaign.

In the summer of 1944, USSTAF crushed the German oil industry. By 14 September it was able to bomb where it willed. However, four months of bad weather did not allow enough days of visual bombing to strike and, if necessary, restrike the oil plants let alone other target systems requiring precise bombing. Bad weather forced Spaatz to sanction attacks on marshaling yards (transportation) in major cities. Those attacks, in conjunction with transportation and complementary city-area attacks by Bomber Command, razed the yards and the towns, strangled the Reichsbahn in its own rolling stock, and wrecked the German war economy. By the end of January 1945 adding a new industrial target system would have made little significant difference.

On the basis of performance (see table 5), the strategic bombing campaign fulfilled three-fourths of the Casablanca directive: it brought about "the progressive destruction and dislocation of the German military, industrial and economic system." It did not, however, break the morale of the German people, although it may well have made it more brittle and, to some extent, undermined it. The oil campaign of the summer of 1944 was the fulfillment of the prewar doctrines of precision bombardment. American strategic bombers selected an indispensable military target system (oil shortages had a far greater effect on the German armed forces than on German industry),

Table 5. The Bomber Offensive by Target System

Air Force	Target System	No. Aircraft Attacking	No. Aircraft Lost	Tons HE	Tons IB	Tons Frag	Total Tons
Eighth	Airfields	32,925	367	68,495	7,084	5,410	80,989
	Air Industry	15,520	617	27,379	10,600	843	38,822
	AFVs	3,827	43	7,961	2,139	151	10,251
	Armaments	6,047	93	12,598	3,123	326	16,047
	Bearings	1,966	168	2,886	1,683	0	4,569
	City*	57,711	1,243	97,620	47,750	959	146,329
	Industrial Areas	3,780	184	7,736	1,831	80	9,647
	Noball	11,498	76	32,636	226	0	32,862
	Oil	27,067	533	69,305	794	195	70,294
	Port Areas	2,456	51	6,216	155	28	6,399
	Tactical Targets	14,970	36	28,816	1,479	11,006	41,337
	Targets of Opportunity (T/O)	5,606	81	11,207	2,562	228	13,997
	Transportation	70,440	459	176,284	14,438	450	191,172
	U-boats	5,782	185	13,991	1,113	164	15,268
Fifteenth	Airfields	12,530	195	16,047	609	10,835	27,491
	Air Industry	5,966	268	13,299	674	505	14,478
	AFVs	2,357	79	5,448	347	0	5,795
	Armaments	865	25	1,817	244	0	2,061
	Bearings	704	23	1,609	321	0	1,930
	City*	5,623	116	11,778	1,332	120	13,230

*Includes command ordered and authorized city attacks, target of opportunity city attacks, and "area-like" attacks.

Table 5. (Continued)

Air Force	Target System	No. Attacking Aircraft	No. Aircraft Lost	Tons HE	Tons IB	Tons Frag	Total Tons
	Industrial Areas	1,160	12	2,571	0	0	2,571
	Noball	132	4	329	0	0	329
	Oil	24,820	688	56,459	745	82	57,286
	Port Areas	3,622	33	8,600	145	0	8,745
	Tactical Targets	8,766	46	14,974	2	4,506	19,482
	T/O	279	0	554	104	10	668
	Transportation	60,281	657	143,244	2,488	141	145,873
	U-boats	1,151	15	3,179	0	0	3,179
Bmr Cmd	Airfields	4,593	68	18,574	321	0	18,895
	Air Industry	1,215	39	4,039	556	0	4,595
	AFVs	21	0	107	0	0	107
	Armaments	1,900	65	4,258	1,581	0	5,839
	Bearings	77	0	216	15	0	231
	City	142,857	4,810	318,670	193,639	0	512,309
	Industrial Areas	24	0	25	0	0	25
	Mining	13,189	359	0	0	0	0
	Noball	15,406	132	70,416	594	0	71,010
	Oil	22,370	358	99,936	1,598	0	101,534
	Port Areas	3,238	70	10,400	125	0	10,525
	Tactical Targets	17,055	122	91,488	1210	0	92,698
	T/O	17	0	26	8	0	34
	Transportation	29,406	639	134,156	3,400	0	137,556
	U-boats	6,370	100	19,342	4,568	0	23,910

attacked it by visual means, and brought aviation gasoline production to a virtual halt by September 1944. That was what American heavy bombers were supposed to do.

The transportation campaign demonstrated the triumph of wartime necessity over prewar theory. The Americans had fielded an almost all-weather force of limited accuracy whilst Bomber Command had refined its marking techniques to a high level. The constant cloud cover during the autumn of 1944 negated any hope of consistent precision bombing—hence, the selection of the marshaling yards, a target system of more economic than military importance. Any significant breakdown of the German wartime economy would eventually have dramatic consequences at the front line. The strategic offensive, even though it frequently had to bomb through clouds with partial visual means, managed to bomb out the marshaling yards, wreck the coal transportation nexus, and bring German industry to its knees. The strategic bombing effort inflicted severe, if not fatal, damage to the German military and German war economy.

The slow buildup of Bomber Command and the Eighth, thanks in part to the bottleneck of Anglo-American shipping availability, the diversion of strength to the Pacific and the Mediterranean, operational difficulties, intelligence errors that led to overestimating damage inflicted, and debates concerning targeting delayed the buildup of the force and prevented its most efficient application to crucial sectors of the German war economy. However, what the bombing did accomplish was substantial in contributing to Germany's defeat. The Anglo-American bombing offensive brought the war to the German people long before their armies were forced back onto German soil. In a war in which the effort of civilian workers on the production lines was as essential to victory as the fighting of the soldiers on the front lines, the very existence of the strategic bombing offensive encouraged US and British civilians and inflicted pain and suffering on the enemy. The British may have devoted 40 to 50 percent of their total war production to the air forces; the United States expended up to 35 percent; and the Germans up to 40 percent. German war production increased throughout the war, reaching its peak in the third quarter of 1944. Strategic air bombardment undoubtedly kept that increase from going higher still. It forced the dispersion of factories and the building of underground facilities, made German production more vulnerable to transportation disruption, lowered production by forcing smaller, more labor-intensive, production units that denied the Germans the manufacturing economies of scale available to their enemies, disorganized workers' lives, and lowered their productivity. In ways great and small—and utterly incalculable—strategic bombing made German war production less efficient and effective than it would have been if the bombers had not flown night after night and day after day.

Strategic bombing also forced the Germans into an enormous defense and reconstruction effort, diverting German aircraft manufacture almost exclusively into fighter and interceptor production. The bombing of oil not only limited mobility, but as a side effect greatly reduced nitrogen production, hampering the manufacture of explosives and fertilizers. By 1944, Germany had two million soldiers, civilians, and prisoners of war engaged in ground antiaircraft defense, more than the total number of workers in its aircraft industry. And on any given day or night, most of this force, spread throughout the breadth of the land to defend all targets, stood idle, while the Allied bombers struck only a relatively few areas. An additional million workers were engaged in repair and rebuilding; the oil industry alone absorbed 250,000. Albert Speer estimated that 30 percent of total gun output and 20 percent of heavy ammunition output was intended for air defense, a significant loss to the ground forces of high-velocity weapons suitable for antitank defense. It took an average of 16,000 88 mm flak shells to bring down a single Allied heavy bomber.[42] Speer further estimated that 50 percent of electro-technical production and one-third of the optical industry was devoted to radar and signals equipment for the antiaircraft effort, further starving the front lines of essential communications equipment.[43]

Strategic bombing failed to meet the most ambitious goal set for it by the very airmen who practiced it. Strategic bombing did not, as an independent force, bring about the defeat of Germany. If one were forced to select a single military service most responsible for the destruction of Hitler's regime, the Red Army would have primacy of place. There is little evidence that the highest

Anglo-American leadership expected strategic bombing alone to drive Germany out of the war, although both Churchill and Roosevelt apparently regarded a large strategic bombing campaign as a necessary prerequisite for the decisive land campaign. The failure to reach its most extreme goal should not obscure strategic bombing's real accomplishments, as it has for many critics.[44]

The Allied strategic bombing campaign was a decisive factor in the defeat of Germany by the Allied coalition. The strategic bombing campaign distracted a significant amount of German resources from the ground fronts, reduced German war production, and hampered the conduct of the war by the German armed forces by denying them sufficient oil. Strategic bombing could not reasonably have been expected to do more. It vindicated the treasure expended on it. If in the final analysis it accomplished its ends more by brute force than by elegant precision, the fault lay in the unrealistic assumptions of prewar doctrine as to wartime accuracy, the vagaries of European weather, and the limitations of radar technology.

Notes

1. All statistics in this chapter, unless otherwise specifically attributed, are derived from the Bomber Offensive database on the CD accompanying this book.

2. This calculation is based on Table F-4: "USAF Weighted Inflation Indices Based on Inflation and Outlay Rates," USAF *Statistical Digest, FY 1993*, prepared by the deputy assistant secretary (cost and economics) and assistant secretary (financial management and comptroller of the Air Force), Washington, DC, 1 November 1994, F-127. The procurement cost of a B-2, (one billion in 1993 dollars adjusted to constant 1949 dollars (multiplied by 0.158) is $158,000,000.00. By comparison, a single B-17 cost $250,000.00 in constant 1949 dollars. The actual average cost of all B-17s procured from 1937 to 1945 in then-year dollars makes this comparison even more unfavorable to the B-2.

3. Werrell, *Eighth Air Force Bibliography*, lists 2,794 separate items.

4. See Davis, *Spaatz*, 262–66, for a discussion of creation of the Fifteenth Air Force and the reasoning behind it.

5. Defined as Germany, Austria, and Czechoslovakia for the purposes of this book.

6. Hastings, *Bomber Command*, 388–89.

7. Memo, Anderson to director of operations, 21 July 1944, Spaatz Papers, Subject File 1929–1945.

8. This consists of all Eighth Air Force raids of over 100 heavy bombers, sighting with H2X, and carrying over 20 percent firebombs.

9. CCS 166/1/D, memo by the Combined Chiefs of Staff, subject: The Bomber Offensive from the United Kingdom, 21 January 1943, published in Department of State, *FRUS: Conferences at Washington, 1941–1942, and Casablanca, 1943*, 781–82.

10. See Irving, *Destruction of Dresden*.

11. Sherry, *Rise of American Air Power*, 254.

12. Schaffer, *Wings of Judgment*, 106.

13. Keegan, "Berlin," 82–83.

14. Arad, *Belzec, Sobilor, Treblinka*, 392.

15. See *USSBS, Summary Report (European War)*, 1–42.

16. *USSBS*, Morale Division, *Effects of Strategic Bombing on German Morale*, vol. 64b, pt. 1, 1–2. *USSBS* based these conclusions on interviews with 3,711 civilians in the Allied occupation zones.

17. *USSBS*, Area Studies Division, *Economic Effects of the Air Offensive against German Cities*, vol. 31, 24.

18. BSSU, *The Strategic Air War against Germany, 1939–1945*, a confidential document published by His Majesty's Government, no date c.a. mid-1947, 79. The BSSU was established in June 1945, at the recommendation of the secretary of state for air, and absorbed and continued the work of the British Bombing Research Mission and the Bombing Analysis Unit of the Allied Expeditionary Air Forces, established, respectively, in September and October 1944. Although it cooperated closely with the *USSBS* and made no attempt to duplicate its work the BSSU's conclusions are its own. Like *USSBS* the BSSU is not unbiased in its analysis of the result of the strategic offensive. In particular, thanks to Prof. Solly Zuckerman, whose personality dominated the work of the BSSU and who authored the pre–D-day transportation plan, the BSSU's final report singles out the bombing of the German transportation system, especially the state railway system, as the most important and by far the most effective aspect of Anglo-American strategic bombing. In spite of this prejudice the final report contained much useful information and insight. The 20 pages of its 15th and 16th chapters: "Reasons Underlaying Failure of Primary Strategic Aim of Offensive against Cities" and "The Extent to Which Area Attacks Lowered Potential War Production," together form one of the best and most succinct explanations of the strength and resiliency of the German war economy available.

19. Ibid., 93.

20. *USSBS, Summary Report (European War)*, 6; *USSBS, Economic Effects of the Air Offensive*, 3. The Area Studies Division report makes the distinction between deaths from strategic and tactical bombing.

21. *Deutschland Heute* (1958), 156, cited in Parks "Air War and Law of War," 1, n. 1. He notes that the *Deutschland Heute* attributes a further 1,550,000 German civilian deaths to losses in the Eastern provinces.

22. Groehler, *Geschchte des Luftkriegs*, 509.

23. Other than attacks requested by Allied ground forces and Yugoslav partisans, Allied area attacks on cities in German-occupied territory were confined to Bomber Command's area attacks of French U-boat ports in 1943, Anglo-American attacks on French towns in support of the Normandy invasion, and

a few isolated incidents in the Mediterranean. Bomber Command also made several area attacks on northern Italian cities while that nation was at war with Great Britain between June 1940 and September 1943. For example, see AAF Evaluation Board in the ETO, "The Effectiveness of the Third Phase of Tactical Air Operations in the European Theater, 5 May 1944–8 May 1945," appendix G: Deaths Resulting from Air Attacks (Dayton, Ohio: February 1946, (164) cites the *Defense Passif*, "the French organization responsible for statistics regarding casualties from air attacks," as recording 36,000 French dead "as a result of all type of air attacks" for the year 1944.

24. Bear and Foot, *Oxford Companion to World War II*, s.v. "strategic bombing offensive."

25. Saunders, *Fight Is Won*, 370.

26. Harris, *Bomber Offensive*, 267. Harris gives no documentation for this figure of 125,000. Richards, *Hardest Victory* (305), cites Harris's figure but with the following caveat, "[He] has recorded the number of aircrew as who flew in Bomber Command as 125,000. Assuming that this figure is correct and relates to operations . . . ." In the same work, Richards states (297) the following, "at the peak in April 1944 over 30,000 of the 226,000 aircrew in Bomber Command—a total which includes those in administration and training—came from Canada, Australia, and New Zealand." Given the disparate figures cited by Richards, who did not remark upon their difference, Harris's figure must be treated with some caution, although it is the only number currently available. Examples from the RAF AHB monograph on Bomber Command lend further insight (AHB, RAF Narrative, *The R.A.F. in the Bombing Offensive against Germany*, vol. 4, *The Final Phase*, 262–67). In June 1944 Bomber Command's frontline units (71 and 1/2 heavy bomber squadrons and 6 and 1/2 Mosquito squadrons) had aircrews totaling approximately 15,000 officers and enlisted men. That force was supported by a large training force of no less than 700 four-engine bombers and 1,200 mediums. Not counting flying personnel in the command's operational training units, that force had 1,700 officers and 25,000 other ranks employed in the heavy bomber conversion units and Lancaster finishing schools. At peak strength in March 1945, the command had approximately 20,500 aircrews in its frontline units. Taking the above figures into consideration, Harris's number of 125,000 total aircrew members seeing operations throughout the war seems somewhat low, given the fact that the 47,000 dead crew members had to be replaced as well as those who completed their tours. Even accepting Harris's figure leads to a realization of the sheer number of trained aircrews required to sustain the bombing offensive. The frontline aircrews of the command would appear to have turned over perhaps as many as six or seven times.

27. Terraine, *Time for Courage*, 682.

28. Fifteenth Air Force Statistical Control Unit, "The Statistical Story of the Fifteenth Air Force," 22, AFHRA, microfilm reel A6432, starting frame 800.

29. Davis, *Spaatz*, Statistical Appendix No. 10. This appendix states that in March 1945 Headquarters AAF credited the Fifteenth with 1,660 heavy bombers on hand and in the first line. However, the records of both the Eighth

and the Fifteenth indicate that throughout the war bombers on hand in the tactical units and available for combat amounted on average to only 85 percent of bombers "assigned." (See, Eighth Air Force Statistical Control Unit, "Statistical Summary of Eighth Air Force Operations, 17 Aug 1942–8 May 1945," 10 June 1945, 14, AFHRA, microfilm reel A5875, starting fr. 826.) These same records note that crews "available" lagged behind the number of bombers in the tactical units by approximately 10 percent until August 1944 when "available" crews began to exceed combat aircraft in the tactical units by 10 or more percent. The "effective strength for combat," apparently those bombers and crews that could actually be employed in combat, was normally 5 percent less than the total of crews available. For example, in January 1945, the Eighth's peak strength in terms of bombers "assigned" (2,799), only 2,179 bombers were "on hand [in] operational tactical units." At the same time the Eighth had 2,295 bomber crews "available." Yet this resulted in only 1,651 bombers counted as that air force's "effective strength for combat." It would follow from these figures that the number of aircrew entering into combat was considerably less than the number of available aircraft and aircrews.

30. Eighth Air Force Statistical Control Unit, "Statistical Summary of Eighth Air Force Operations, 17 August 1942–8 May 1945," 10 June 1945, AFHRA, microfilm reel A5875, starting fr. 826, This lists 2,480 bomber crews "available," 14.

31. AAF Evaluation Board, ETO, "The Effectiveness of Third Phase Tactical Air Operations in the European Theater, 5 May 1944 to 8 May 1945," August 1945 (Dayton, OH: February 1946), 8, lists Ninth Air Force casualties from October 1943–May 1945 as 1,529 killed; 1,262 wounded; and 1,910 missing [not counting returned POWs] and First Tactical Air Force (Provisional) losses from 1 November 1944 to 8 May 1945 as 52 killed and 162 missing. Subtracting these tactical losses from the AAF's official theater figures and rounding yields the figures cited in the text. In 1947, in reply to one of the authors of the AAF official history, Alfred F. Simpson, the Office of the Air Surgeon General, memorandum to Dr. Colman from Lt Col Robert E. Lyons, chief, Biometrics Division, Office of the Air Surgeon, subject: Eighth and Ninth Air Force Dead, 2 April 1947, supplied the following figures for Ninth and Eighth Air Force Dead:

Air Force	Totals
Eighth	
Nonbattle	1,555
Known KIA	2,886
Presumed dead, reported dead from POW, etc.	14,030
WIA died	441
Total Eighth dead	18,912
Ninth	
Nonbattle	658
Known KIA	563
Presumed dead, reported dead from POW, etc.	1,130
WIA died	75
Total Ninth dead	2,426

Given that the ETO Evaluation Board's numbers did not reflect the final disposition of those missing (died, POW returned, and MIA) they and the Air Surgeon's numbers would seem comparable for "Battle Deaths."

32. *Army Air Forces Statistical Digest, World War II* (Washington: AAF Office of Statistical Control, December 1945). The appropriate casualty tables have been republished in Davis, *Spaatz*, statistical appendices 4, 5, and 6. The AAF official figures, which include the losses of the Ninth and Twelfth Air Forces are:

Died, ETO	19,876
Died, MTO (Including North African Operations)	10,223
Total Battle Deaths	30,099
Wounded, ETO	8,413
Wounded, MTO (inc. NA)	4,944
Total wounded in battle	13,357
Missing, interned and captured, ETO	35,121
Missing, interned and captured, MTO (inc. NA)	15,985
Total	51,106
Total Battle Casualties, ETO	63,410
Total Battle Casualties, MTO (inc. NA)	31,155
Total AAF Battle Casualties in war against European Axis	94,565

Many of the missing listed in this compilation would later be determined to have died in combat or to have been captured.

33. Arthur Williamson, "Expediency of War: RAF Bomber Aircrew Survival January–March 1944," paper submitted for part II tripos for the degree of B.A. (Hons) at the University of Cambridge, 1993, 46–56.

34. Williamson, 8.

35. Department of the Army, "Army Battle Casualties," gives AAF casualties in the loss and recapture of the Philippines as 3,996 dead, 737 wounded, 4,306 captured, 1,976 MIA—40 percent of all casualties incurred by the AAF in the war against Japan. Most of the casualties were ground personnel and occurred in the islands' fall. The vast majority of the AAF personnel combat losses in the ETO and MTO were aircrews.

36. Werrell, "Strategic Bombing of Germany in World War II" (708), cites a figure of 29,000 dead for the Eighth and Fifteenth. For Marine deaths, see Department of Defense, American Forces Information Service, *Defense 91: Almanac*, chart: "Service Casualties in Major Wars and Conflicts (as of 30 September 1990) (September/October 1991)," 47.

37. For US Navy casualties, see Clodfelter, *Warfare and Armed Conflicts*, 2:958.

38. *USSBS, Oil Division Final Report*, 130. The figures for duds was 12.9 percent American bombs, 18.9 percent RAF bombs, and 24 percent unidentified bombs. The bulk of the bombs failed to explode because they landed on their sides rather than on the nose fuses.

39. Report, Fifteenth Air Force, Operational Research Section, subject: Study of Unexploded Bombs on Ploesti, 19 April 1945, AFHSO, microfilm reel B5549, fr. 1637.

40. Hansell, 130–31. The loss of abrasive grinding wheels would have crippled the German armaments industry by denying it the ability to machine metal castings, such as gun barrels, shells, and crankshafts.

41. *USSBS*, The Effects of Strategic Bombing on German Transportation, vol. 200, 5.

42. Murray, *German Military Effectiveness*, 78.

43. Overy, *Air War*, 157.

44. For a recent criticism of strategic bombing on this ground see Pape, *Bombing to Win*. This work is a case study of strategic bombing campaigns to which Pape applies a controversial model of coercion, defined in such manner as to ignore almost any result of strategic bombing other than surrender of the enemy. His analysis of the European bombing campaign, whatever its merits, is flawed by a careless attention to detail, such as dating the Butt report to August 1942 (268, n. 35), which tends to bring Pape's conclusions into doubt.

Abbreviations and Code Names

Abbreviations

AAF	Army Air Forces
AAC	Army Air Corps
ABDA	American-British-Dutch-Australian
ACTS	Air Corps Tactical School
AEAF	Allied Expeditionary Air Force
AFHRA	Air Force Historical Research Agency (formerly Air Force Historical Research Center [AFHRC] and Alfred F. Simpson Historical Research Center), Maxwell AFB, AL
AFHSO	Air Force History Support Office
AFV	armored fighting vehicle
AHB	Air Historical Branch (RAF), Public Records Office, British Air Ministry
AOC	air officer commanding
ARP	air-raid precaution
AS	Air Service
ASV	air-to-surface vessel
AVM	air vice marshal
AWPD	Air War Plans Division
BBC	British Broadcasting Corporation
BBSU	British Bombing Survey Unit
BC	Bomber Command
BD	bombardment division
BDA	bomb damage assessment
BSSU	British Strategic Survey Unit
BW	bombardment wing
CBO	Combined Bomber Offensive

CCS	Combined Chiefs of Staff
CEP	circular error probable
CIGS	Chief of the Imperial General Staff
ETO	European theater of operations
flak	*flugobwehrkanonen*
frag	fragmentation
FRUS	foreign relations of the United States
GC and CS	Government Code and Cipher School (British)
GDR	German Democratic Republic
GEE	station-to-aircraft radio bombing device
GH	Gee-H
GHQ	General Headquarters
H2S	air-to-surface radar, British terminology
H2X	air-to-surface radar, American terminology
HCU	heavy conversion units
HE	high explosives
HMSO	His/Her Majesty's Stationery Office
IB	incendiary bomb
IFF	identification, friend or foe
JCS	Joint Chiefs of Staff
JIC	Joint Intelligence Committee (British)
JSM	Joint Staff Mission (British)
KIA	killed in action
LST	landing ship tank
MAAF	Mediterranean Allied Air Forces
MAC	Mediterranean Air Command
MAN	Maschinenfabrik Augsburg-Nürnberg
MASAF	Mediterranean Allied Strategic Air Force

MEW	Ministry of Economic Warfare (British)
MH	micro-X radar
MIA	missing in action
MP	member of Parliament
NAAF	Northwest African Air Forces
NARA	National Archives and Records Administration
NASAF	Northwest African Strategic Air Force
NATAF	Northwest African Tactical Air Force
NDRC	American National Defense Research Committee
NSDAP	Nationalsozialistische Deutsche Arbeiterpartei
Oboe	aircraft-to-station radio bombing devise
OCMH	Office of Chief of Military History (Army)
ORS	Operational Research Section
OSS	American Office of Strategic Services
OTU	operational training unit
PFF	Pathfinder force
POW	prisoner of war
PRO	Public Records Office, Kew, United Kingdom
PRO AIR	Public Records Office, Air Ministry
PRO FO	Public Records Office, Foreign Office
PRO PREM	Public Records Office, Prime Minister
PWE	Psychological Warfare Executive (British)
RAF	Royal Air Force
RG	Records Group
RUSI	Royal United Services Institute

SACAEF	Supreme Allied Commander Allied Expeditionary Force
SHAEF	Supreme Headquarters Allied Expeditionary Force
SOE	Special Operations Executive (British)
SOP	standard operating procedure
SS	Schutzstaffel
TCC	Troop Carrier Command
USAAF	United States Army Air Forces
USAMEAF	US Army Middle Eastern Air Forces
USSAFE	United States Strategic Air Forces in Europe
USSBS	United States Strategic Bombing Survey
USSTAF	US Strategic Air Forces
VHF	very high frequency
W. S. C.	Winston S. Churchill

Code Names

Big Boy	Winston Churchill before the Casablanca conference
Blunderbuss	Enigma machine code setting
Carbetbagger	Eighth Air Force Special Operations supply and personnel missions in support of European resistance groups
Circus	Combined Fighter and Bomber Command antiair operations over France
Clarion	Allied air plan for widespread, mid-level bombardment of lesser German transportation targets
Culverin	Enigma machine code setting

Enigma	Standard German code machine
Fish	High grade German code (*Geheim-schrieber* device not Enigma machine)
Fortitude	Pre–Normandy Invasion Air Deception Plan
Frantic	AAF shuttle bombing missions between US bases in Great Britain and Italy to and from the USSR
Noball	Allied bombing of V-1 and V-2 target systems
Overlord	Code name for Allied Normandy invasion
Thunderclap	Allied plan for aerial bombardment of German leadership
Ultra	Allied code-breaking of German Enigma code machine

Bibliography

Original Sources

US Air Force Historical Research Agency, Maxwell AFB, Alabama
Records of the Army Air Forces Air Staff, 1941–1945
Records of the Eighth Air Force, 1942–1945
Records of the Fifteenth Air Force, 1943–1945
Records of the Ninth Air Force, 1942–1943
Records of the Mediterranean Allied Air Force, 1944–1945
Records of the Northwest African Air Force, 1943
Records of the Royal Air Force, 1941–1945
Records of the Twelfth Air Force, 1942–1943
Records of the US Strategic Air Forces in Europe, 1944–1945
USAF Oral History Collection

USAF Academy Library, Colorado Springs, Colorado
Kuter, Lawrence S., Papers
McDonald, George C., Papers
Green, Murray, Collection on Henry H. Arnold

USAF Historical Support Office, Bolling AFB, Washington, D.C.
Dresden Subject File
Microfilm collection of the holdings of the USAF Historical Research Center

US Army Military History Institute, Carlisle, Pennsylvania
Bradley, Omar N., Papers

US Library of Congress, Manuscript Division, Washington, D.C.
Arnold, Henry H., Papers
Doolittle, James H., Papers
Eaker, Ira C., Papers
Spaatz, Carl A., Papers
Twining, Nathan F., Papers
Vandenberg, Hoyt S., Papers

US National Archives and Records Administration, College Park, Maryland
Record Group 18, Records of the Army Air Forces, 1941–1945
Record Group 165, Records of the War Department General Staff, 1941–1945

Record Group 218, Records of the Combined Chiefs of Staff, 1942–1945

War Department Classified Message Center File, 1942–1945

British Air Ministry, Air Historical Branch, London, England.
(See http://www.raf.mod.uk/history/narratives.html for a complete list of official narratives.)

AHB Narrative. *Anglo–American Collaboration in the War over North West Europe, 1940–1942.*

———. *The Liberation of North-Western Europe.* 5 vols.

Vol. 1. *The Planning and Preparation of the Allied Expeditionary Force for the Landings in Normandy, 1942–1944.*

Vol. 2. *The Administrative Preparations.*

Vol. 3. *The Landings in Normandy.*

Vol. 4. *The Break-Out and Advance to the Lower Rhine, June–Sept, 1944.*

Vol. 5. *From the Rhine to the Baltic, Oct 1944–May 1945.*

———. *The RAF in the Bombing Offensive against Germany.* 5 vols.

Vol. 1. *Pre-War Evolution of Bomber Command, 1917–1939.*

Vol. 2. *Restricted Bombing, September 1939–May 1941.*

Vol. 3. *Area Bombing and Makeshift Force, June 1941–Feb 1942.*

Vol. 4. *A Period of Expansion and Experiment, Mar 1942–Jan 1943.*

Vol. 5. *The Full Offensive, Feb 1943–May 1944.*

Public Records Office, Kew, England
Air Ministry/2
Air Ministry/8
Air Ministry/9
Air Ministry/23
Prime Minister/3

Royal Air Force Museum, Hendon, England

The Papers of James Robb

United States Strategic Bombing Survey

Works Cited

Books, Monographs, and Secondary Works

Ambrose, Stephen E. *The Supreme Commander: The War Years of General Dwight D. Eisenhower*. Garden City, N.Y.: Doubleday and Co., 1970.

Arad, Yitzak. *Belzec, Sobilor, Treblinka: The Operation Rheinhard Death Camps*. Bloomington, Ind.: Indiana University Press, 1987.

Arnold, Henry H. *Global Mission*. New York: Harper and Row, 1949.

Bennett, Ralph. *Ultra in the West: The Normandy Campaign 1944–45*. New York: Scribner, 1980.

Blumenson, Martin. *Breakout and Pursuit*. United States in World War II, European Theater of Operations. Washington, D.C.: OCMH, 1961.

———. *Salerno to Cassino*, vol. 11, pt. 3. The United States Army in World War II, The Mediterranean Theater of Operations. Washington, D.C.: OCMH, 1969.

Bond, Horatio, ed. *Fire and the Air War*. Boston: National Fire Protection Association, 1946.

Boylan, Bernard. *Development of the Long–Range Escort Fighter*. USAF Historical Study 136. Maxwell AFB, Ala.: USAF Historical Division, Air University, 1956.

Bradley, Omar N. *A Soldier's Story*. New York: Henry Holt, 1951.

Brereton, Lewis H. *The Brereton Diaries*. New York: William Morrow, 1946.

Butcher, Harry C. *My Three Years with Eisenhower, The Personal Diary of Captain Harry C. Butcher, USNR, Naval Aide to General Eisenhower, 1942–1945*. New York: Simon and Schuster, 1946.

Chandler, Alfred D. *The Papers of Dwight David Eisenhower: The War Years*. 4 vols. Baltimore: Johns Hopkins Press, 1970.

Churchill, Winston S. *The Second World War*. Vol. 4, *The Hinge of Fate*. Boston: Houghton Mifflin Co., 1950.

Copp, DeWitt S. *Forged in Fire: The Strategy and Decisions in the Air War Over Europe, 1940–1945.* Garden City, N.Y.: Doubleday and Co., 1982.

Crane, Conrad C. *Bombs, Cities, and Civilians: American Airpower Strategy in World War II.* Lawrence, Kans.: University Press of Kansas, 1993.

Craven, Wesley Frank, and James Lea Cate, eds. *The Army Air Forces in World War II.* Vol. 1, *Plans and Early Operations, January 1939 to August 1942.* 1948–1958. New imprint, Washington, D.C.: Office of Air Force History, 1983.

―――. Vol. 2, *Europe: Torch to Pointblank, August 1942 to December 1943.*

―――. Vol. 3, *Europe: Argument to V–E Day, January 1944 to May 1945.*

―――. Vol. 6, *Men and Planes.*

Davis, Richard G. *Carl A. Spaatz and the Air War in Europe.* Washington, D.C.: Center for Air Force History, 1993.

Dear, I. C. B. *The Oxford Companion to World War II.* New York: Oxford University Press, 1995.

D'Este, Carlo. *Decision in Normandy.* New York: E. P. Dutton, 1983.

Freeman, Roger. *Mighty Eighth War Diary.* London: Jane's, 1981.

Frisbee, John L., ed. *Makers of the United States Air Force.* Washington, D.C.: Office of Air Force History, 1987.

Futrell, Robert Frank. *Ideas, Concepts, Doctrine: Basic Thinking in the United States Air Force, 1907–1964.* Maxwell AFB, Ala.: Air University Press, 1971.

Galland, Adolph. *The First and the Last: The German Fighter Force in World War II.* Mesa, Ariz.: Champlin Museum Press, 1986.

Garland, Albert N., Howard McGraw Smyth, and Martin Blumenson. *Sicily and the Surrender of Italy.* The United States Army in World War II, The Mediterranean Theater of Operations, vol. 2. Washington, D.C.: OCMH, 1965.

Gilbert, Martin. *Auschwitz and the Allies.* New York: Holt, Rinehart, and Winston, 1981.

Glines, Carroll V. *Jimmy Doolittle, Daredevil Aviator and Scientist.* New York: Macmillan, 1972.

Grabmann, Walter. *German Air Force Air Defense Operations.* USAF Historical Study 164. Maxwell AFB, Ala.: USAF Historical Division, Air University, 1956.

Groehler, Olaf. *Geschchte des Luftkriegs 1910 bis 1980.* Berlin: Militarverlag der Deutschen Demokratischen Republik, 1981.

Groves, Leslie R. *Now It Can Be Told: The Story of the Manhattan Project.* New York: Harper and Brothers, 1962.

Haines, William W. *ULTRA and the History of the United States Strategic Air Force in Europe vs. the German Air Force.* Frederick, Md.: University Publications of America, 1980.

Hamilton, Nigel. *Master of the Battlefield: Monty's War Years, 1942–1944.* New York: McGraw–Hill, 1983.

Hansell, Haywood S., Jr. *The Air Plan that Defeated Hitler.* Atlanta: Higgins–McArthur/Longino and Porter, 1972.

———. *The Strategic Air War against Germany and Japan: A Memoir.* Washington, D.C.: Office of Air Force History, 1986.

Harris, Arthur. *The Bomber Offensive.* 1947. Reprint (with new introduction by Denis Richards, of 1947 edition published by Collins). Novato, Calif.: Presidio Press, 1990.

Hastings, Max. *Bomber Command.* New York: Dial, 1980.

Hinsley, F. H. *British Intelligence in the Second World War: Its Influence on Strategy and Operations.* 5 vols. London, HMSO, 1981.

Holley, Irving Brinton, Jr. *Buying Aircraft: Matériel Procurement for the Army Air Forces.* United States Army in World War II, Special Studies. Washington, D.C.: OCMH, 1964.

Holloway, David. *Stalin and the Bomb: The Soviet Union and Atomic Energy 1939–1956.* New Haven, Conn.: Yale University Press, 1994.

Irving, David. *The Destruction of Dresden.* New York: Holt, Rinehart and Winston, 1964.

———. *The Mare's Nest.* Boston: Little, Brown and Co., 1964.

Jones, Neville. *The Beginnings of Strategic Air Power: A History of the British Bomber Force, 1923–1939.* London: Frank Cass, 1987.

Jones, Vincent C. *Manhattan: The Army and the Atomic Bomb.* United States Army in World War II. Special Studies. Washington, D.C.: Center of Military History, 1985.

Kelsey, Benjamin S. *The Dragon's Teeth.* Washington, D.C.: Smithsonian Institution Press, 1982.

Kimball, Warren F., ed. *Churchill and Roosevelt: The Complete Correspondence.* 3 vols. Princeton, N.J.: Princeton University Press, 1983.

Kingston–McCloughry, E. J. *The Direction of War: A Critique of the Political Direction and High Command in War.* London: Jonathan Cape, 1956.

Kreis, John F., ed. *Piercing the Fog: Intelligence and Army Air Force Operations in World War II.* Washington, D.C.: Air Force History and Museums Program, 1996.

Leighton, Robert W., and Richard M. Coakley. *Global Logistics and Strategy 1940–1943.* United States Army in World War II, The War Department. Washington, D.C.: OCMH, GPO, 1955.

Mark, Eduard. *Aerial Interdiction: Air Power and the Land Battle in Three American Wars.* Washington, D.C.: Center for Air Force History, 1994.

Matloff, Maurice. *Strategic Planning for Coalition Warfare, 1943–1944.* Washington, D.C.: OCMH, GPO, 1959.

McArthur, Charles W. *Operations Analysis in the U.S. Army Eighth Air Force in World War II.* The History of Mathematics. Providence, R.I.: American Mathematical Society, 1990.

McFarland, Stephen L., and Wesley Phillips Newton. *To Command the Sky: The Battle for Air Superiority over Germany, 1942–1944.* Washington, D.C.: Smithsonian Institution Press, 1991.

McKee, Alexander. *Dresden 1945: The Devil's Tinder Box.* New York: E. P. Dutton, 1984.

Messenger, Charles. *"Bomber" Harris and the Strategic Bombing Offensive, 1939–1945.* New York: St. Martin's Press, 1984.

Mierzejewski, Alfred C. *The Collapse of the German War Economy, 1944–1945: Allied Air Power and the German National Railway.* Chapel Hill, N.C.: University of North Carolina Press, 1988.

Molony, C. J. C., F. C. Flynn, H. L. Davies, and T. P. Gleave. *The Campaign in Sicily 1943 and the Campaign in Italy 3rd September 1943 to 31st March 1944*. The Mediterranean and the Middle East, vol. 5. London: HMSO, 1973.

Morison, Samuel Eliot. *Sicily–Salerno–Anzio: January 1943–June 1944*. Vol. 9. History of United States Naval Operations in World War II. Boston: Little, Brown and Co., 1954.

Murray, Williamson. *German Military Effectiveness*. Baltimore: The Nautical and Aviation Publishing Corporation of America, 1992.

———. *Strategy for Defeat: The Luftwaffe, 1933–1945*. Maxwell AFB, Ala.: Air University Press, 1983.

Overy, R. J. *The Air War*. New York: Stein and Day, 1980.

Pape, Robert A. *Bombing to Win: Air Power Coercion in War*. Ithaca, N.Y.: Cornell University Press, 1996.

Parton, James. *"Air Force Spoken Here": General Ira Eaker and the Command of the Air*. Bethesda, Md.: Adler and Adler, 1986.

Pogue, Forrest C. *The Supreme Command*. United States Army in World War II. The European Theater of Operations. Washington, D.C.: OCMH, 1954.

Putney, Diane F., ed. *Ultra and the Army Air Forces in World War II*. Washington, D.C.: Office of Air Force History, 1987.

Reynolds, Quentin. *The Amazing Mr. Doolittle*. New York: Appleton–Century–Crofts, 1953.

Richards, Denis. *The Hardest Victory: RAF Bomber Command in the Second World War*. New York: W. W. Norton and Co., 1994.

———. *The Royal Air Force, 1939–1945*. Vol. 1, *The Fight at Odds*. London: HMSO, 1953.

Roskill, S. W. *The War at Sea, 1939–1945*. Vol. 3, part 1, *The Offensive 1st June 1943–31st May 1944*. London: HMSO, 1960.

Rostow, W. W. *Pre–Invasion Bombing Strategy: General Eisenhower's Decision of March 25, 1944*. Austin, Tex.: University of Texas Press, 1981.

Saunders, Hilary St. George. *The Royal Air Force 1939–1945.* Vol. 3, *The Fight is Won.* London: HMSO, 1975.

Saward, Dudley. *Bomber Harris: The Story of Sir Arthur Harris.* Garden City, N.Y.: Doubleday and Co., 1985.

Schaffer, Ronald. *Wings of Judgment American Bombing in World War II.* New York: Oxford University Press, 1985.

Schmid, Josef, and Walter Grabmann. *The German Air Force versus the Allies in the West.* Vol. 2, *The Struggle for Air Supremacy over the Reich: 1 January 1944–31 March 1944.* USAF Historical Study 158. Maxwell AFB, Ala.: USAF Historical Division, Air University, 1954.

Sherry, Michael S. *The Rise of American Air Power: The Creation of Armageddon.* New Haven, Conn.: Yale University Press, 1987.

Sherwood, Robert E. *Roosevelt and Hopkins: An Intimate History.* Rev. ed. New York: Harper and Brothers, 1950.

Smith, Walter Bedell. *Eisenhower's Six Great Decisions: Europe 1944–1945.* New York: Longmans, Green, and Co., 1956.

Speer, Albert. *Inside the Third Reich: Memoirs.* New York: Macmillan, 1970.

Stacey, C. P. *Official History of the Canadian Army in the Second World War.* Vol. 3, *The Victory Campaign: The Operations in North-West Europe 1944–1945.* Ottawa, Canada: Queen's Printer and Controller of Stationery, 1960.

Swanborough, F. G. *United States Military Aircraft since 1909.* New York: Putnam, 1963.

Tedder, Arthur. *With Prejudice: The War Memoirs of Marshal of the Royal Air Force, Lord Tedder GCB.* Boston: Little, Brown and Co., 1966.

Terraine, John. *A Time for Courage: The Royal Air Force in the European War, 1939–1945.* New York: Macmillan, 1985.

Thomas, Hugh. *The Spanish Civil War.* Rev. ed. New York: Harper and Brothers Publishers, 1977.

Thomas, Lowell, and Edward Jablonski. *Doolittle: A Biography.* Garden City, N.Y.: Doubleday and Co., 1976.

US Department of Defense, American Forces Information Service. *Defense 91: Almanac September/October 1991.*

United Kingdom, Air Ministry. *The Rise and Fall of the German Air Force, 1933–1945.* London: 1947.

United Kingdom, British Bombing Survey Unit. *The Strategic Air War against Germany, 1939–1945*. London: 1947.

United States. Department of State. *Foreign Relations of the United States: The Conferences at Washington, 1941–1942, and Casablanca, 1943*. Washington, D.C.: GPO, 1968.

———. *Foreign Relations of the United States Diplomatic Papers: The Conferences at Malta and Yalta, 1945*. Washington, D.C.: GPO, 1955.

———. *Foreign Relations of the United States: The Conferences at Cairo and Teheran 1943*. Washington, D.C.: GPO, 1961.

Watson, Mark S. *Chief of Staff; Pre–War Plans and Preparations*. United States Army in World War I. The War Department. Washington, D.C.: OCMH, 1950.

Webster, Charles, and Noble Frankland. *The Strategic Air Offensive against Germany, 1939–1945*. London: HMSO, 1961.

Weigley, Russell Frank. *Eisenhower's Lieutenants: The Campaign of France and Germany, 1944–1945*. Bloomington, Ind.: Indiana University Press, 1981.

Werrell, Kenneth P. *Eighth Air Force Bibliography: An Extended Essay and Listing of Published and Unpublished Materials*. Manhattan, Kans.: Aerospace Historian/Eighth Air Force Historical Society, 1981.

Zilbert, Edward R. *Albert Speer and the Nazi Ministry of Arms: Economic Institutions and Industrial Production in the German War Economy*. East Brunswick, N.J.: Associated University Presses, 1981.

Zuckerman, Solly. *From Apes to Warlords*. New York: Harper and Row, 1978.

Articles

Coningham, Arthur. "The Development of Tactical Air Forces," RUSI *Journal*, 91, May 1946.

Keegan, John. "Berlin." *MHQ: The Quarterly Journal of Military History*, no. 11 (Winter 1990).

Kindleberger, Charles F. "World War II Strategy," *Encounter*, November 1978.

Kirkland, Faris R. "French Air Strength in May 1940." *Air Power History*, Spring 1993.

Lytton, Henry D. "Bombing Policy in the Rome and Pre–Normandy Invasion Aerial Campaigns of World War II: Bridge–Bombing Strategy Vindicated and Railyard–Bombing Strategy Invalidated." *Military Affairs*, April 1983.

Middleton, Drew. "Boss of the Heavyweights," *Saturday Evening Post*, 20 May 1944.

Parks, W. Hays. "Air War and the Law of War." *The Air Force Law Review* 32, no. 1.

Rostow, W. W. "The Controversy over World War II Bombing." *Encounter*, August–September 1980.

Tedder, Arthur. "Air, Land, and Sea Warfare." RUSI *Journal*, 91, May 1946.

Werrell, Kenneth P. "The Strategic Bombing of Germany in World War II: Costs and Accomplishments." *Journal of American History* 72, December 1986.

Index

GPO ☆ U.S. GOVERNMENT PRINTING OFFICE: 2006–736-718/F5878